Using Clarion
Professional Develo

Y0-AGO-407

Mark S. Burgess

Addison-Wesley Publishing Company, Inc.

Reading, Massachusetts   Menlo Park, California   New York
Don Mills, Ontario   Wokingham, England   Amsterdam   Bonn
Sydney   Singapore   Tokyo   Madrid   San Juan
Paris   Seoul   Milan   Mexico City   Taipei

Many of the designations used by manufacturers and sellers to distinguish their products are claimed as trademarks. Where those designations appear in this book, and Addison-Wesley was aware of a trademark claim, the designations have been printed in initial caps or all caps.

Library of Congress Cataloging-in-Publication Data

Burgess, Mark, 1957–
    Using Clarion professional developer / Mark S. Burgess.
        p.   cm.
    Includes bibliographical references and index.
    ISBN 0-201-57054-8
    1. Data base management.   2. Clarion Professional developer
(Computer program)   I. Title.
    QA76.9.D3B87   1991
    005.75'65--dc20   91-14409
                                                                CIP

Cover design by Doliber Skeffington
Set in 11-point Times Roman by Context Publishing Services,
San Diego, CA

ISBN 0-201-57054-8
1 2 3 4 5 6 7 8 9-MW-9594939291
First printing February, 1991

Dedication

To Nila Barton and Milton Burgess,
Thanks for getting to know each other.

Contents

Foreword

I really didn't set out to design a computer language. I would rather have used
BASIC, or Pascal, or C, or even dBASE, for that matter. But I couldn't stand
the pain. Everybody was talking about "user friendly" computers, but nobody
seemed to care whether they were "programmer friendly." I did. In my notes
for the foreword of the first Clarion *Reference Manual*, I expressed my
feelings about the programming tools I had been using:

> Clarion has been on my mind since a FORTRAN compiler kicked me off for missing an
> "H" count in a FORMAT statement. The author of the compiler must have thought I
> could count better than the computer. FORTRAN has grown up since those days, but
> you still can't follow a large program. COBOL is wordy; "ENVIRONMENT DIVI-
> SION." It takes two pages of code just to get started, and the implementations are
> Teutonic: "STATEMENT 112 MISSING PERIOD-LEVEL E ERROR." A polite com-
> piler would supply a period if it knew where it belonged. PASCAL is all BEGINs,
> ENDs, and type declarations. Its syntax rules are always in the way. C is great, but
> where's the I/O? BASIC brings in the newcomers but doesn't take them anywhere. The
> database products aren't really languages, they are just batch files in disguise.
>
> A programming language ought to help the programmer, requiring the fewest state-
> ments needed to clearly define a process. Sequences that are always required should
> never be required. Some old notions are due for review: Why treat a memory-mapped
> display like a Teletype? Why call loop statements DO WHILE, FOR, PERFORM, or
> anything but LOOP? Why don't compilers generate data type conversions? Why have
> ENTRYs, EXTERNs, and link steps? Why so much punctuation? Why waste unused
> memory? And why are compilers so fussy?

A lot has happened in the six years since I wrote those paragraphs, but the
words still speak to me. We dropped that foreword from the *Language*

Reference in Version 2.0 of the Clarion Professional Developer, mostly because the new product included an optional link step. And with Clarion growing in popularity, the tone seemed a little strident for a mainstream product. But we never changed our mission to build "programmer friendly" development tools.

Mark Burgess was an early Clarion developer. He grew with us through that difficult period when the documentation was always a few versions behind. So last year, at COMDEX in Las Vegas, Mark told me he was writing a book about the Clarion Professional Developer, the kind of book he wanted when he first started with Clarion.

Using Clarion Professional Developer is a "programmer friendly" book that delivers the spirit of Clarion in a readable and informative way. Mark points out all the pitfalls and opportunities that he has uncovered in his research into Clarion. So let Mark Burgess be your Clarion pathfinder. He's a terrific guide.

Bruce D. Barrington
Chairman and Chief Engineer
Clarion Software Corporation

Acknowledgments

In writing this book, I've gotten support from a lot of quarters. It all starts with my parents and my family: the time, money, and effort they've put into helping me start and stay in business made it possible for me to be here to write this book in the first place. In fact, I used a loan from their credit card for the capital to buy my first copy of Clarion several years ago. I paid back that loan, but I cannot ever repay what they've done for me—I can only hope to pass on some of the benefits to others. To Yvonne, my gratitude goes for adjusting her life and schedule to allow me in, and for greeting yet another weekend spent on "The Book" with good cheer.

To Larry Lux, my thanks for the code he contributed, the testing time and the research he put in, plus sharing the continuous flow of bulletins he gathers about what's going on in other parts of the computer business. Thanks to Steve Greiner and Kevin Knoepp for their input on the relational database and language comparison chapters. And, thanks to all the folks on the Compu-Serve DBMS forum and the Clarion BBS for the questions and the answers that formed a daily part of my work on the book.

To Bob Zaunere, John Herron, Bruce Barrington, and Bob Shumate of Clarion, it might be trite to say I couldn't have done it without you, but I couldn't have and wouldn't have wanted to.

At Addison-Wesley, my thanks go to Julie Stillman: thanks for the chance; Debbie McKenna: thanks for those special envelopes; to Margaret Hill:

thanks for the English; to Lauralee Butler: who ought to get the purple heart for publishing for crunching schedule and text together; and most especially: my thanks and appreciation go to Elizabeth Grose, Editor-Diplomat, for working so hard via fax, multi-hour phone calls, express mail, and sometimes even rail, to make what I sent her (or didn't send) into a book.

Introduction

To pick up any tool and envision all of the clever and interesting ways to use it can be difficult. The rich and well integrated selection of tools in Clarion Professional Developer presents a great opportunity to be creative—if you know where to start. This book can serve as both a starting point and a source of advice along the way.

This book is for the serious practitioner—independent developers, contract programmers and corporate applications developers—who have discovered the Clarion environment and are eager to produce work. The Clarion environment promotes software development at many levels. You can go as deeply into controlling interrupts and switching bits as you want or you can write an application without ever entering a text editor. It is a true business programming language. I attempted to write the book I wished I had when I first got into Clarion. It is not a repeat of the information in the user manuals from Clarion—unless there is some useful addition to that data. This book can help you get the feel for the reach and depth of Clarion. Then you can attack the *Language Reference* to burrow into all the particulars of the language.

Serious practitioners live in corporate MIS departments or small businesses. At the higher end of the scale exist developers who create vertical market applications and contract programmers. This book can lead the latter group into the fastest, most bug-free application delivery environment they could wish for. With Clarion, the basics for screen handling, database definition and manipulation as well as customer support are so ingrained in the development environment itself that simply being known as a Clarion house will speak to your ability to deliver quality, advanced applications on time and under budget.

I went through a long testing and searching cycle looking for an application development environment before I chose Clarion. Program development on the PC has changed significantly since the days of the BASIC programming I did in 1982. Clarion looked to me like a language that would allow me to produce the applications I needed to produce on schedule, minimizing development risk.

I wanted an environment that was deep enough to write serious applications and had plenty of support to cover all those contingencies you never imagine up front. I didn't want a code generator that merely cranked out the interface and left me to hand code the database handler. I also did not want to get tied into a stack of third party tools such as those dBase III Plus required. Freedom from the cost of run times was important, also.

Clarion represents a new view of the programmer's task. Beginning with version 2.1, someone familiar with Clarion's abilities can sit down and develop a completed, compiled application in fifteen minutes with only a data dictionary to start. That's amazing to most people today . . . it would have been white magic to someone in 1982.

When Bruce Barrington, founder of Clarion, begat this language, he was looking for a way to make the program development process easier. He's done well as a programmer himself, but he wanted to take that knowledge and create a language that would pass on what he had learned to save others from repeating it. Now we all profit from his goal.

Still, with this new tool comes new problems. As we shift away from worrying about whether we've handled video memory properly, or from spending an eight hour day merely writing code, we can cover more ground. But that added reach means more attention needs to be paid to the planning process up front. It becomes imperative that you understand the impact of your actions today on the code you produce tomorrow because things happen very fast in an environment like Clarion. If you don't understand the impact of the file prefix on tracking memory, you could cause yourself hours of unnecessary labor, and negate the power of speedy, quality application generation available with Clarion.

This book emphasizes clean application development and takes maximum advantage of the work the folks at Clarion Software have already put into their product. This book places an emphasis on taking advantage of that environment and helps you bridge that last gap in your familiarity with a very powerful software tool.

You'll find sample code written both with Designer and by hand in the Editor. The example code demonstrates some, but by no means all, of Clarion's power. The remainder of your exploration will be up to you. Several complete applications appear, though improvements and refinements can be made to all of them. Where the code was written manually, I departed from the Clarion coding conventions in terminating statements with "END!(structure)" in place of the standard period "." that Clarion uses in the model files to terminate IF, CASE, and LOOP statements. Other members of the Clarion community have chosen more complex code notation. You can choose the style you like after you've gotten into the language.

And that raises another point. The support from the Clarion community is broad based. When I started the San Diego User's group several years ago, there were almost 100 other groups around the country. You'll find Clarion afficionados on various bulletin boards around the country including CompuServe, the PC Information Group, Clarion's own support BBS, and others. You'll also find a large group of Clarion users who are refugees from other language environments. Talking with them can be a lot of fun. Their excitement is tangible over Clarion's removal of the limitations they used to battle in those other environments.

I hope this book helps you enjoy your time with Clarion. And I hope that the programs you produce prove profitable for you in terms of happy users and successful projects. That has been my experience with Clarion and I hope it is yours, too.

Chapter 1

Programming in the Clarion Environment

The Clarion Call

If you are reading these words, you must have received the "clarion call" to a new age in software development. Clarion Professional Developer represents another step away from manipulating bits, bytes, and interrupts and toward creating effective applications with minimal trouble. Many programmers buy Clarion purely on the strength of the language itself. Today, you have additional tools that harness that language to take maximum advantage of the personal computer.

Personal computers are useful because software can be created to manipulate mathematical calculations, storage media, and output devices economically. Clarion encapsulates that power in a set of tools that constitute a complete development environment. Clarion is not merely a database language nor is it just a screen painter or report writer. With no more than a cursory knowledge of programming, a personal computer, and Clarion Professional Developer, you can create a functional, usable, useful application that will exist free from other software required at run time or from requirements to operate only inside the original working environment in interpretive mode.

In the past, computer users had two choices when it came time to get software for a task: 1) buy an off-the-shelf application and hope that it allowed the input, storage, and logical retrieval of the information requiring processing; or 2) pay a programmer to transfer your request for that information processing into a custom system. The first approach resulted in many dusty shelves of software that didn't fit the task and a lot of frustrated users.

The second option resulted in unfinished or bug-ridden software that never made it into daily use.

Of course, the exceptions to these two outcomes are what has fueled the personal computer revolution in business and at home. As the personal computer came into prominence, a few brave souls ventured into writing their own applications. Some took to the spreadsheet or word processing macro to do that processing. In contrast to a real programming language, these tools were pushed too hard, asked to do too much. The alternative, however, was to get down into manipulating the bits, the busses, and the interrupts that move information around a PC.

Imagine trying to build a house under these conditions: You must locate, harvest, and manufacture your own lumber; locate, mine, smelt, and then forge your own nails; sit down at a drawing table and invent such constructs as window, door, support beam, and so on—and then go build the house! At every step in the process, you risk not knowing enough about the lower level task and doing a job that causes the project to fail because you didn't mill the lumber straight or you made nails that snap off when hit with a hammer.

Traditional programming worked just like that. Nothing was done for you. You had to invent every concept, every movement the system made, from merely finding a spot on the screen to locating and retrieving a single bit of data from the storage medium.

Clarion is the next logical step in program development. Setting the value of individual bits by throwing switches on a board took more effort and time than coding in assembler language, which took more effort and time than writing in C, which takes more effort and time than writing with the Clarion language, which takes more effort and time than using the Quick Start function of Clarion 2.1. With Clarion, the effort and time can now be shifted away from spending several hours drawing a menu on the screen and, instead, focused on developing the best possible way to request, store, and communicate information.

Clarion's History

Clarion 1.0 was introduced at the COMDEX computer trade show in the spring of 1985. That version stood on the strength of the language and a few utilities—Designer (the source code generator) and Translator (the object module and linking step) did not exist yet.

The germinal idea for Clarion sprang from Bruce Barrington, founder of Clarion Software and chief architect for the programming environment.

Barrington's long-time experience in the world of computer languages helped him form the central ideas that gave birth to the Clarion language.

Working for McDonnell-Douglas in 1970, Barrington was one of the first to purchase a computer called the IV 70 made by IV Phase, Inc., a firm later acquired by Motorola. He left McDonnell-Douglas in 1973 to start the predecessor to what became a company called HBO, Inc., where he helped write the Real Operating System (ROS) for the IV 70 and then a macro language to run under ROS. HBO, Inc., created a hospital information system using that macro language, which they sold to large hospital management concerns like Humana, Inc. Part of Clarion's future began with HBO's relationship to Humana. That's where Barrington met John Herron who was to become Clarion's interface master and is now vice president of development.

With HBO on the rise and about to go public, Barrington resigned from the day-to-day operations in 1979 but retained a seat on HBO's board of directors. The public offering actually occurred in 1981. It was the success of Barrington's hospital information system that created the financial base that would later steer Clarion through difficult times.

At about this time, of course, the first evidence of the revolution in personal computers began to be apparent. Its portent was not lost on Barrington. Summoning the lessons from his experience in languages like COBOL and PL/I, he began to examine the market for business programming languages and to look at what the PC was capable of doing. He found two things. First, COBOL and PL/I, although competent environments, were too wordy and arcane, in Barrington's view. (Even today, those two languages don't appear widespread on the PC.) Second, no other language appeared to offer what Barrington had created with the higher level macro language for the ROS. There was IBM's BASIC, but it lacked file definitions and other features. The PC lowered the entry level for computing, but there was no good way to write programs.

Then dBASE II came along—it was messy, but at least you could write a program. Coming from a formal background in computer languages, Barrington couldn't accept having to "SET TALK OFF" to start a program. That sort of feature, the lack of type declarations and conversions, and other missing pieces led Barrington to view dBase as not much more than a batch language. The world, he believed, still lacked a true business application programming environment for the PC. Barrington Systems, the precursor to Clarion Software, was born in 1983 to take a shot at solving that problem.

Barrington pulled together a team of four programmers, giving each one a separate area to work. That method, allocating responsibility to one programmer for each functional part of Clarion, persists in Clarion's development department today. The first four subjects were the compiler, the processor, the database management, and the utilities. Barrington himself took the role of chief designer. They chose to write the system in Wizard C—a language later purchased by Borland and renamed Turbo C.

Working in Clarion

Choosing a Development Path

Clarion offers two avenues to development: **Designer** and **Direct Code**. If you like to work with bare code, Clarion eases the process somewhat by providing the same screen and report generator that appears in Designer, but it is accessible from inside Editor. Then you can easily drop back into the generated code and make whatever changes you need.

Designer is not an application manager—but if you're careful about it, you can use it as one. Designer encapsulates large portions of the Clarion language, allowing you to make references in object-oriented style. With Clarion 2.1, you can create an application in less than five minutes, defining nothing yourself except the Data Fields to be used. Granted, this sort of quickie application generator won't deliver complex applications, but it can be used to get a jump start on a development project.

Working in Designer provides a smoother transition from a dead start to producing usable work. You learn the language and generate useful applications at the same time. You still get exposure to the way the code works—in fact, you'll have to look at it to accomplish some objectives. Your access to the bare code in Designer appears as INCLUDE files, OTHER files, and Edit and Setup Procedures, which we'll explain in later chapters. Studying an application as it comes out of Designer can help you see where Designer inserts these statements in order to use them effectively.

The Language

One of the most important moves Bruce Barrington and the design team made was to get very friendly with a thesaurus as they designed the Clarion language. Clarion is a terse, clear, and concise language. It borrows standard terms like GET and PUT from other languages, but it overhauls expressions as required. For example, the term used to describe a loop is, amazingly, LOOP—*not* DO WHILE or FOR or PERFORM. Clarion gives you all the logical functions of most programming languages—statements like CASE;

IF, THEN, ELSE; and a new function called EXECUTE. (We'll get into the common terminology and naming conventions in a later chapter.)

Clarion's file definitions allow you to load a file structure just once on program startup if you want, and then call the variables within that file whenever you want. There is no need to change the database currently in use. In addition, Clarion's dynamically updated keys and indexes that require update on command allow your system to handle data quickly and to operate in batch mode efficiently.

Character-Based Graphics

In Clarion you can define Screen structures and file structures within the program. Now, instead of rebuilding a screen within your code, you just call the screen you want to open. If you decide you want to save the contents of the screen underneath, just declare the new screen as a window.

Clarion is a character-based application environment—although with the introduction of the Graphics LEM (Language Extension Module), it's possible to build applications with a much more graphical look. However, since the Graphics LEM was developed by a third party, it is wise to understand the limits it imposes before you begin integrating it into your applications. It requires a memory-resident program that controls video activity and cannot be opened as a window under normal Clarion operations—it requires the entire screen. However, the screen painting facility of the basic package provides a significant amount of graphic ability. You can draw smooth lines and use block characters to produce bar charts and draw boxes around areas of both the screen and the printer. Because Clarion supports the extended ASCII character set, there is no need to develop drivers to support printers that already support extended characters.

Because building screens is so easy, your ability to improve data entry speed and clarity is improved immensely. Within Designer or Editor, you can paint screens using the cursor keys and a few quick hot-key combinations. Each of these functions is addressed in a later chapter.

Network Ready

You can create a multiuser version of your applications in Clarion to run on a local area network quite easily. Clarion provides several utilities for ensuring the integrity of shareable files on the network. Simply by running Designer using the Network Model, you can have a program with all the built-in messaging and file locking required of a true multiuser application.

No Dead Ends

Clarion acknowledges that no one can anticipate all your needs and no language will do everything just as you need it done. Since Clarion was written in the C language, the object modules it produces can be linked together with other object modules you create in C. These are known in Clarion as language extension modules (LEMs). We'll cover the ins and outs of building and using language extension modules in later chapters.

General Practices You Should Follow

Clarion rewards planning. If you follow a few simple rules for planning and producing your application, you'll save yourself lots of work downstream and you'll take the most advantage of the Clarion environment. Some of these items are simply good database design practices. We'll touch on all of these in later parts of the book, but they bear mention now.

Write Out Your Database Definition

Clarion provides excellent memory management, if you set up your database dictionary carefully. That's not to say that forgiveness isn't in the system, but you might as well handle these issues at the beginning. We'll lead you through the ways to recover if you don't take this step seriously, but you'll be happier if that part of the book is, as they say, "interesting, but not fascinating."

Clarion uses a three-character file prefix for every file variable you will use. There are some circumstances when you can get away without using prefixes, but it's better not to interrupt a compile because you left the prefixes out or by not picking your names properly. Without prefixes, you must monitor your file names to ensure there are no duplicates used—and that hampers efficiency. You can't use just LAST_NAME to store someone's name in two different data files, for instance. In addition, as you'll read later on, there are ways to set up Memo Fields and other speed-enhancing structures to increase your overall speed. Although Clarion provides a nice set of restructuring tools, it makes things easier if you don't have to use them too much.

Review Your Entry Screens

Even before you draw your first entry screen, look at the kinds of information you'll be adding and editing on those screens. Because Clarion's screen-generating facility is so quick, it's easy to wind up with a bunch of entry screens that do not have a standard, easy-to-read look to them. Use the CTRL-G procedure in Designer and the copy functions in Editor to use the same screen declarations as much as possible. This will also help you to be consistent in the on-screen help tips you give for such things as the Help key or the keys for moving around the screen.

To Do Overlays or Not to Do Overlays

It doesn't really matter whether or not your applications will require overlays. It is a good idea to act as if they do, and then you won't have a lot of work to do later. In Designer, set the COMBINE WITH MODULE: option to a blank to ensure that each procedure appears in its own module under a separate DOS filename. Managing overlays with the Overlay Manager or even manually is a lot easier this way. If you are manually coding without Designer, rearranging your map will be less painful if you can simply grab the three lines that make a procedure reference and move them. Otherwise, you'll be forced to get into each file with Editor to keep track of where everything is.

Use Separate Application Subdirectories

Don't put all your applications into one subdirectory. In the first place, for a large application, by the time you finish generating code or creating separate module files, and compile and translate the code, you'll have a lot of files to track. If you don't use separate subdirectories, you'll get into lots of trouble doing maintenance and keeping your hard disk clean and uncluttered. If you put Clarion in your DOS path, you can get into each subdirectory, type "clarion", and access the environment. However, if you want to retain the default settings for each application, put a copy of CLARION.COM in that subdirectory. Do not mix your application files with your Clarion programming tools. All it takes to make a disaster is to clean your disk of .CLA files and, in the process, wipe out the standard key files or some other element.

Do Not Ignore the Warning in Designer

Automatically generating code is nice—right up to the point that it automatically generates hours of extra work. Until you learn to keep track of what you've done and how it affects your program, *always* regenerate your entire program when you see the message shown in Figure 1-1.

Do Not Request Listings with Each Compile

The listing mentioned in Tailor and on the Compiler screen means you'll generate a copy of the source file complete with page breaks, page numbers, and line numbering. Until you're ready to document your application, these

Figure 1-1   Take this Designer warning seriously. The selective source generation allows you to re-create the code only for the procedure you changed, saving hours over the life of a development project. Take care in performing partial source generation until you understand the impact it will have on your application.

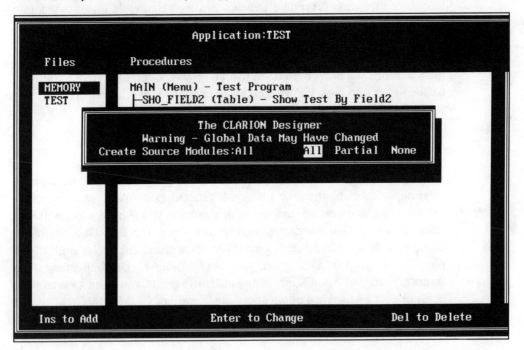

Figure 1-2   The Clarion Debugger Error Screen.

```
                    The CLARION Debugger

Stopped for:'RECORD NOT AVAILABLE'
Stopped at :TEST1/MAIN/58            (Ctrl-S for source)
Called from:TEST/TEST/45             (Ctrl-F for source)
Memory left:122K                     (Ctrl-X to execute)
```

listings only take up space on your hard disk. Unless you like working with the code in that fashion, it's better to leave the History option turned off until the point that you want to file away your source code.

Maintain Control of Your Source Files

With the ".CLA" files of source code themselves, if you use Designer and eliminate a procedure from your application *after* you've generated code for it, you'll have a collection of orphan files wandering around your source directory. However, be careful not to delete files you'll need. For instance, you might mistakenly delete a data file that your program does not automatically re-create. The top part of the error screen pops up with Debugger when an attempt to put a record in a file fails, as shown in Figure 1-2.

Summary

Clarion heralds a new role for the programmer and the programmer's relationship with a software-creating language. It is one of the first and most integrated business programming environments available today. Created by people familiar with the problems inherent in more traditional languages, Clarion takes full advantage of the video presentation and flexibility of the personal computer. After you absorb a few words of cautionary advice, you can launch into your first project with only this book, *Using Clarion Professional Developer*, and a quiet afternoon. In this chapter we focused on what you need to think about before you start working in Clarion and discussed the background of the language.

Chapter 2

The Clarion Environment

DOS File Extensions

Clarion uses nineteen DOS file extensions to identify files throughout the system. (See Table 2-1.) It's helpful to know what these are before you begin coding so you won't step on the ones you'll need for certain processes. For instance, to operate your program in runtime mode using either CPRO.EXE (the Processor) or CRUN.EXE (the Runtime), you need the .PRO file only; but to use the debugger in the Processor, you need the .SYM files as well.

By renaming some of these files, you can hang onto previous versions of your program. For instance, you can maintain different archives of your Designer .APP file by renaming the .BAP file sequentially. As soon as you save your Designer .APP file, the new .BAP file overwrites the old one.

The compiler files aren't worth much of your attention. Even though Clarion 2.1 has the ability to do partial compiles, you should rerun Translator to regenerate an all new set of .OBJs even if you only changed one procedure. More about this will be discussed in Chapter 12.

The Programming Tools

The Clarion environment consists of fourteen programs (Table 2-2) and one menu program, CLARION.COM. You can operate Clarion from that menu program or you can operate each individual program separately. Later on, we'll discuss the use of switches and hiding functions, like file conversions, from the user.

Table 2-1   Extensions for Files Used in the Clarion Environment

Extension	Source	Function
.DAT	Application data	Data file extension.
.K##	Application data	Key or index file extension (## = numbers).
.MEM	Application data	Memo file extension.
.PRO	Compiler	Intermediate runtime program.
.SYM	Compiler	Symbol file for debugging in Processor.
.SUM	Compiler	Holds last message of compiler run.
.ERR	Compiler	List of compile errors for last compile.
.CLA	Designer	Clarion source code for compiling and running.
.APP	Designer	Holds application design for editing.
.BAP	Designer	Archive copy of Designer .APP file.
.BAK	Editor	When configured in Tailor to do so, holds preedit version of a document.
.HLP	Helper	Contains logic and screens for user help.
.EXE	.RTLink	Executable program.
.MDL	Shipped w/ utilities	Template for generating code in Designer.
.OBJ	Translator	Converts .PRO, .SYM, .BIN files prior to linking into .EXE.
.ARF	Translator	Automatic response file for linker settings.
.MAP	.RTLink	Linker address map.
.RTL	.RTLink	Runtime library for multiple executable programs.
.BIN	DOS EXE2BIN	Binary file used with the LEMs.

When you work with Clarion, if you stay in Designer, the development process is similar to that shown in Figure 2-1. If you choose to skip using Designer, the flow goes more like the second branch of Figure 2-1, starting with Editor.

Table 2-2 The Programs that Make Up the Clarion Environment

Program	Title	Function
CCMP.EXE	Compiler	Generates processor files (.PRO) required to run the program or create executable file.
CCVT.EXE	Converter	Rebuilds database files in new format.
CXRF.EXE	Cross-reference	Builds procedure dictionary and checks logic tree for orphan procedures.
CDES.EXE	Designer	Design application and generate code.
CDIR.EXE	Director	DOS file manager.
CEDT.EXE	Editor	For writing or changing code directly.
CFIL.EXE	Filer	Rebuilds files and keys to new definition based on the source code file definition.
CHLP.EXE	Helper	Manages writing help for tagged procedures or fields.
CPRO.EXE	Processor	Runs intermediate processor (.PRO) files with debugging enabled.
CRUN.EXE	Runtime	Runs intermediate processor (.PRO) files with no debugging.
CSCN.EXE	Scanner	Allows viewing and editing of data files.
CSRT.EXE	Sorter	Allows packing, sorting, and key deletion on data files.
CTLR.EXE	Tailor	Configures the programming environment.
CTRN.EXE	Translator	Converts processor files to object modules and calls the linker to make an executable file (.EXE).

In most cases, you'll loop through the Designer ➜ Compiler ➜ Editor cycle until you get a program that Processor runs successfully. Then you'll switch to Editor ➜ Compiler ➜ Processor as you refine the functionality. With Clarion 2.1 you can make those edits to your code from inside Designer, if that's where you started. In either case, you can edit and compile individual modules to refine your program in chunks.

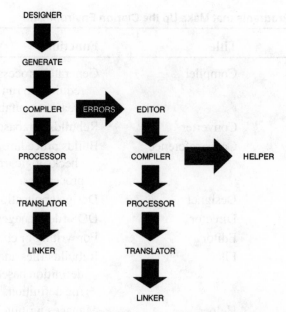

Figure 2-1   The development process using the tools of Clarion Professional Developer.

The other programs listed in Table 2-1 come into play as either debugging tools or, as in the case with Helper, additional development tools. You'll use Scanner when you want to check the data written to a file or to plant values to see how they react. You'll use Filer every time you redefine a key or a database file and need to reformat your test data.

Clarion Remembers: CLARION.COM

Operating Clarion from CLARION.COM (typing "clarion" at the DOS prompt) provides advantages you cannot get if you operate the programs separately. These advantages include the ability to hot key between programming tools and default starting points for each tool. Some information about the current application in development is stored elsewhere. For example, the HELP file and starting procedure for the Designer .APP file is stored in the .APP file itself. However, certain information stored in CLARION.COM tracks your application work. This information is kept in memory. Table 2-3 shows the information it stores.

In addition, CLARION.COM also remembers which procedures Designer regenerates when you do a partial code generation. Because of this, the

Table 2-3   Items Tracked by CLARION.COM

Program	Title	Function
CDES.EXE	Designer	Last .APP file saved with path.
CCMP.EXE	Compiler	Last .CLA file compiled with path.
CEDT.EXE	Editor	Last .CLA saved with path.
CFIL.EXE	Filer	Last .CLA file accessed with Editor.
CHLP.EXE	Helper	Last .HLP file and help window edited.
CPRO.EXE	Processor	Last .PRO file run with processor.
CSCN.EXE	Scanner	.DAT file for last successful .PRO run.
CSRT.EXE	Sorter	.DAT file for last successful .PRO run.
CTLR.EXE	Tailor	Development environment settings.
CTRN.EXE	Translator	.PRO file from last compiled .CLA and the location of the linker in the DOS path.
CXRF.EXE	Cross-reference	.PRO file from last compiled .CLA.

hot-key macros you can queue from inside Designer will handle only the newly generated code. For instance, if you finish altering a procedure inside Designer that does not change the global structures, you can press SHIFT-F7 and Clarion regenerates the code for the changed procedure only, recompiles that procedure, and then restarts the application with the Processor.

Some memory-resident programs (TSRs) interfere with CLARION.COM and cause it to forget the settings it would otherwise retain. This happens when memory is cleared or changed by the TSR or if you shut the PC off before Clarion has a chance to write the information to the CLARION.COM disk file. In most cases, if you have accessed the main Clarion menu before you lose power, for example, the data was transferred successfully from memory to disk.

In the multiuser environment, if you need to access your development programs from a different terminal, CLARION.COM is the only file that must be resident on the local terminal. Of course, this does not relieve you from the copyright protection you signed up for when you bought a single-user license. But if you are the only one accessing your copy of Clarion, this is an easy way to keep yourself mobile for debugging from multiple locations on your office network.

Defaults for Clarion Tools

The title you give the Designer file (.APP) becomes the default for loading information into the other tools for Clarion. The title gets loaded into CLARION.COM and comes up as the default in Editor as "(title).CLA" when you select Editor either through the menu or by pressing SHIFT-F5.

Designer: The name you use for the title of your Designer file (.APP) automatically appears as the title of the PROGRAM statement in the generated code. All the modules, or DOS files, used to hold separate procedures created during program generation use this name plus a number as in TEST01.CLA, TEST02.CLA, TEST03.CLA, and so on. In addition, inside each submodule, MEMBER is the first statement. It identifies which program this module belongs to, and MEMBER uses the title of the PROGRAM statement and the title you gave to your Designer file like this: MEMBER(title).

Compiler: When you select the Compiler function either through the main Clarion menu or by pressing SHIFT-F6, (title).CLA will be the file it attempts to compile. In addition, all the related files that the compiler creates (.SYM, .PRO, and .MAP) will have that name as their DOS filename.

Translator: When you start Translator, either directly from the menu or by selecting the SHIFT-F7 keystroke combination, the default for the resulting files uses the PROGRAM statement title for the .OBJ, .ARF, and .EXE files.

Setting Up to Program

The Clarion installation utility provides a quick and easy method for setting up the programming environment on your system. You are given several options when you install Clarion for the first time. Most experienced Clarioners transfer only what the installation program refers to as utilities. These are the Clarion tools given in Table 2-3. However, if you want the full benefit of the tutorial, the sample files, and the other programs accompanying Clarion, then choose the first selection, "All Programs." However, be certain you have at least 4 megabytes of space on the disk on which you plan to store the environment if you plan to install only the program files, and at least 7 megabytes if you select "All Programs."

You can let that utility modify your path to include the subdirectory containing the development environment, but you'll need to change the settings for the option to modify the CONFIG.SYS file. The default given in the installation utility is FILES=30 and BUFFERS=20. That is sufficient to get Clarion running, but not sufficient for a large program.

When Clarion runs an application made in Designer with either Processor or Runtime, it opens every program file (.PRO), every data file (.DAT), and every key file (.K##). If you programmed the application outside of Designer, you still have control over whether the data files stay open. Native Designer, however, opens them and leaves them all open. You can easily check the number of files your system has open once you successfully start it in the Processor by pressing CTRL-Break to get the Debugging screen. Then CTRL-F gives you the file data.

Remember to make the same environment changes when you move to another system. Using the Clarion Software Distribution Kit is a good method for transferring a developing application for testing. If you like the installation program Clarion uses, you can make the same utility for your applications by using the Distribution Kit.

It is best to set up separate subdirectories for maintaining your developing applications. If you use the standard model files (discussed in the Designer section), you may want to make modifications to the model to suit a particular application. Since you should always make a copy of the model files before you begin programming, moving a copy of the model to the subdirectory dedicated to your application will take care of any confusion.

Clarion 2.1 introduced a version of the .RTLink linker to ship with the development environment. It will be added by the installation utility. More will be covered about .RTLink in later chapters. For other linkers that you might use, be sure you have the path properly constructed to grab the current one when you use the Translator. Most installations of DOS include the DOS linker. Many times the path is set up to include the DOS subdirectory near the front of the path string. When you use the Translator, it automatically searches the path for the linker you specify in the order of subdirectories in that path. By setting up the path properly, you can ensure that the right linker is selected.

As you get deeper into the Clarion world, you will be using other resources with your Clarion applications: third-party developers' tools like Overlay Manager, and language extension modules like the Graphics LEM or the DataBase Three LEM. We'll discuss how to set up each of these environments on your system as we get into those special areas of Clarion.

Summary

The Clarion environment is based on a series of tools you can transport and operate independently, but which have links that allow you to use them together. A standard series of file extensions help you identify and keep separate the output from each of these tools, thereby reducing the confusion that can arise when every file has the same extension or no discipline exists at all. In this chapter we focused on the physical tool set Clarion provides to help you employ the right tool at the right time.

Chapter 3

The Clarion Language

The heart of the Clarion system is the robust programming language. The other tools constructed by Clarion and available in the Developer's kit are intended merely to support application development as supervised and built by the Clarion language. This chapter is not intended to replace the *Clarion Language Reference* shipped with the software development kit from Clarion. In this chapter, we attempt to give you a framework in which to place each aspect of the language for better use—whether you work in bare code or use the output of Designer. In fact, to use Designer most effectively, you must grasp the underlying language.

Logical Structures

Program Layout

Clarion programs are modular. That means more than you might think at first. That modularity applies at almost every level of the environment. A real benefit comes when you understand how to manipulate the larger chunks of your application. The amount of production coding you're forced to do is greatly reduced when you see that Clarion's modularity not only appears in terms of procedures but in terms of the code within the procedures. The right to declare structures in Clarion, some that can even be universal, makes the programming task much easier. Figure 3-1 is an outline of a sample Clarion application.

Figure 3-1   This is a sample skeleton of a Clarion program. This can't be compiled or run, but it shows the basic elements of Clarion program structure.

```
TEST PROGRAM                      ! Defines program name
INCLUDEs                          ! Ports in other files at
                                  !    compile time
GLOBAL_KEYS   EQUATEs             ! Sets variables for keystrokes

   MAP                            ! The map for procedure and
      PROCedures(NAME)            !    function location
      MODULEs(NAME)               ! The DOS file where this
         PROCedures(NAME)         !    procedure is located
      END!MODULE                  ! Terminates procedure definition
      MODULEs(NAME)               ! The DOS file where this
         PROCedure(NAME)          !    procedure is located
      END!MODULE                  ! Terminates procedure definition
   END!MAP                        ! Terminates map definition

FILENAME    file attributes       ! File header definition
KEYNAME     key definition        ! Key or index definitions
   RECORD                         
      FIELDS...   data type        ! List of fields defining record
   END!RECORD                     ! Terminates field list
END!FILE                          ! Terminates file definition

   CODE                           ! Start of procedural program
   OPENFILES procedure call       ! Opens data and key files
   FIRST_PROCedure                ! Call to the first procedure
   RETURN                         ! Returns to DOS
```

We will deal with each of the items listed in Figure 3-1 in various places in the rest of the book as well as in this chapter. The sample in Figure 3-1 does not illustrate some of the features of Clarion, like local routines, but it does provide a framework for us to begin the discussion. For now let's concentrate on how the thought process of a Clarion program runs.

Overall Structure

A Clarion program can have a variety of structures. If you work in Designer, you'll find it generates more complex procedures than you might write simply because Clarion had to allow for many variations in the way we all create applications. Later in this book we'll examine the program flow (see Figure 3-2) that Clarion uses in Designer-generated programs. However, to write any programs in Clarion, you must first know about certain fixed elements, which are discussed in this section.

The first section of a Clarion program can be viewed as the "internal organs" of the application. These include identifying the name of the application, the special keys to be used, any global items that require declaring, the layout of the different modules of the program and their locations, and finally the structure of each file. This area has cousins in each module you write, but only in the primary or main module can you declare system-wide characteristics like global file definitions and other global variables. The last segment, beginning with the CODE statement, is where the operational code for performing application functions appears.

The declarations you make in the global section of the program are valid throughout the program. That means that memory variables you wish to carry over from procedure to procedure must be set in the root program. In addition, at the head of each MEMBER module, you can set variables local to that one procedure that are dropped when that procedure is closed and control returns to the calling program.

Compiler Statements, Directives, and Structures

Statements, directives, and structures drive the Clarion compiler while it constructs the object code to be linked into the final executable program. These commands, embedded in your program, instruct the compiler on how to treat the lines of code you are about to send it. It is possible to get confused about certain terms. A procedure can appear in a Member Module, which is identified by a MODULE statement. Often a statement will signal the start of a structure—as in a CASE statement, which appears at the top of a Case structure.

Figure 3-2   Skeleton of the flow of a Clarion program.

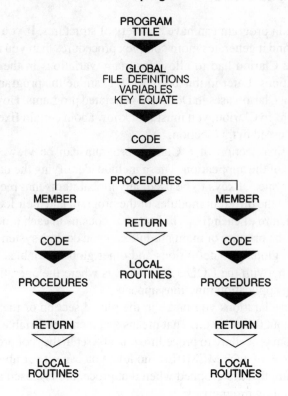

The *Clarion Language Reference* splits the compiler directives into two groups. The first group is called statements. The second set is called compiler directives. There is little difference between the statements and the directives, though. Except for the PROGRAM statement and all the Structures, you can use most statements and directives throughout your application. Table 3-1 is not meant to explain each element, but rather to help you organize your

Table 3-1 **Elements of the Clarion Language that Drive the Clarion Compiler and Provide the Infrastructure of a Clarion Application Program**

Statements	Directives	Structures
PROGRAM	TITLE	MAP
MEMBER	SUBTITLE	MODULE
PROC	EJECT	AREA
FUNC	OMIT	OVERLAY
PROCEDURE	SOURCE	
FUNCTION	INCLUDE	
CODE	EQUATE	
ROUTINE	SIZE	
END		

thinking about how the language is constructed. We'll discuss a few cogent points about each command in a logical order in this chapter, but, for the basics on each of these commands, refer to the *Clarion Language Reference*.

The PROGRAM Statement

The PROGRAM statement gives your application its identity. Whatever you call your application in Designer appears as the PROGRAM title in the main module of code. You must use this name in the MEMBER( ) statement for all the submodules you identify as PROCEDUREs in separate DOS files or that Designer generates as separate files. The executable program created at link time is called by this name.

Keep the name to eight characters (the limit of a DOS filename). If you create a program entirely in Editor, the first errors you get will warn you about two things: the length of the program name and the truncated module DOS filenames. If, for instance, you attempt to name a file "TEST12345," the error shown in Figure 3-3 results when you compile. There can be only one PROGRAM statement per executable file. That does not mean you can have only one per application. In "chained" programs—applications made of several executable files—there will be one PROGRAM statement for each executable file. The title you choose to give this statement affects several other places in your application and in the development process.

Figure 3-3 **Error message text from the ERROR file created by the compiler when a PROGRAM name is too long for DOS to create submodules with the same name.**

```
Compiled on   6/25/90   5:02 PM  {TEST1234}
                   2 MESSAGES FOUND IN TEST1234.CLA
W 155 @1/1:     'TEST12345' - LABEL TRUNCATED FOR FILENAME
E 204 @23/17:   ''TEST1234'' MODULE HAS ALREADY BEEN DECLARED
```

The Map Structure

Think of the Map as a guide for the compiler to find the elements of your program. The compiler does this by locating the DOS file that contains them and the particular functions or procedures within that file you want to perform. Even if every procedure in your program were contained in the root program, you'd still need a Map to identify them. The Map is what you divide up to create overlays. Some third-party software, like the Overlay Manager from Mitten Software, rewrites the Map to organize those overlays and then includes it as a separate DOS file itself. Unless named in the Map, Clarion won't include a module in the stream compilation. A sample Map structure is shown in Figure 3-4.

The PROC Statement: PROC statements appear only in the Map structure and nowhere else in a Clarion program. Their sole function is to identify the names of the procedures contained in the DOS file identified as a module. They can also appear without the module statement if the procedure is contained in the root program.

Figure 3-4   **Sample Map structure, complete with overlay and area structures.**

```
AREA
  OVERLAY
    MODULE('DOS_FILE')
      PROC(PROC_NAME)
  . . .
```

Figure 3-5 **This Designer screen depicts the options update form for a table. On this form you can specify with which module you wish to combine the procedure. If you leave that field blank, Designer uses the PROGRAM name appended with a number to specify the DOS filename that becomes the module name. When using third-party tools like Overlay Manager, it is better to put every procedure in its own module, as they may be divided up anyway.**

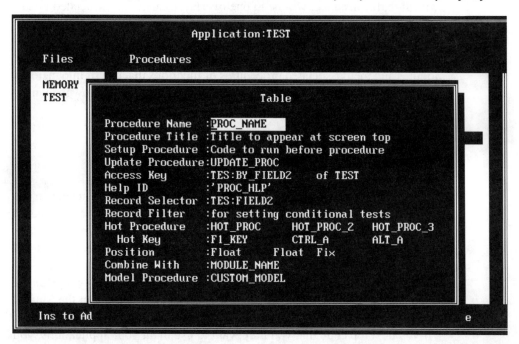

The FUNC Statement: The FUNC statement also appears in the same place as a PROC statement. However, FUNC identifies a separate module of code as a function and not a procedure. We'll discuss the difference between the two a little later on.

The MODULE Statement: The MODULE statement identifies the DOS file that contains the procedures and functions named in the file. In Designer, each procedure type has an options screen that contains a line "Combine With," as shown in Figure 3-5. It determines the name of the module as it appears in the Map.

The Area Structure: Think of an area as a meeting room where the chairs represent procedures. You must hold your meetings (overlays) one at a time in memory and everyone within the overlay (procedures and functions) must attend. Each person has to come to the meeting prepared—they can't call on someone who'll be in a later meeting in the same room (area).

An area marks a space in memory just big enough to hold the largest overlay in the group. Once the space is filled with one overlay, you cannot fit another one from the same area. The net result is that only the procedures needed for the operation at the moment get loaded into memory. A Table Procedure, for instance, will be in one overlay area and its associated update form will appear in another area.

The Overlay Structure: The Overlay structure contains the names of the modules and their associated procedures or functions that can fit into memory compatibly. We'll discuss more about the role of overlays and how to manage them in Chapter 12.

The MEMBER Statement

The MEMBER statement identifies the other DOS files that appear in the Map as modules. It is the first statement in each of those attached chunks of code. Don't place the MEMBER statement in column 1 of your program. (Column 1 is reserved for labels and variable definitions.) The PROGRAM name you selected must be the parameter of the MEMBER statement—although you can include a new module in a program if you simply replace the parameter and be sure the DOS file is mentioned as a module in the Map of the other program.

   If you develop code that you may want to use in all your applications, you leave out the parameter and make the module universal. It must still be mentioned in the Map according to the DOS file (module) that contains it. To make the term universal, type the parentheses next to each other with no space or other characters after the term, like this: MEMBER( ). The only concession you must make is to either place the file containing such a procedure in the same directory as the root program or specify its path in the Map.

   The one disadvantage of this construction is that you cannot change and then compile the universal module by itself, even after successfully compiling the rest of the application. It must be compiled in stream form with the root program.

The PROCEDURE Statement

Within a member module, you identify a procedure with steps that do not constitute a single function that returns a value that it declared in the Map. You can have any number of procedures within a module, but it is best to maintain a limit of only those that are related to the present function. When compiling, this will shorten the error correction routine because you can make a fix in one procedure without recompiling a lot of unrelated code.

Procedures can also accept parameters from elsewhere in the program. Designer does not directly support this method. Nowhere in the Designer setup are you given a chance to specify the variables to be passed to a procedure. However, in handwritten code, this is a handy function for user-specified parameters. You can ask the user for a filename and then pass the filename to the procedure to perform a process. A workaround in Designer is to call the procedure in the "Edit Procedure" line of the Field Options screen (discussed in Chapters 8, 9, 10, and 11).

The FUNCTION Statement

A FUNCTION statement (FUNC) is very much like a procedure except that it can pass information back through to the program. In addition, FUNCTION can be a binary program and need not be written in Clarion.

The ROUTINE Statement

A routine can only appear in a procedure outside of the main program (in other words, after the termination point of the program). It is a separate section of code, viewed as local by the procedure. However, when set off as a ROUTINE, it can be called several times. The Designer Table Procedure uses ROUTINES extensively to repeat responses to a change in the records displayed in a table. You call a ROUTINE with the DO statement.

INCLUDE Directive

You can place INCLUDE anywhere in your Clarion programs. The INCLUDE directive instructs the Compiler to break from its stream through the code in the DOS file currently under compilation and pull in code from another DOS file. This can be a handy tool for setting off chunks of code that you use in every application and that do not constitute procedures.

Used in the main program module prior to the CODE statement, INCLUDEs create code that is global to the application. Designer positions these statements just after the PROGRAM statement.

Since the Edit and Setup Procedures in Designer are limited to 255 characters, you can use INCLUDE to add in chunks of code that are larger than that. As a general rule, though, try not to make those bits of code too large. They do not have the same benefit as separate procedures because you cannot compile them separately. To compile and test an INCLUDEd set of code, you must compile the procedure in which it is included.

EQUATE Directive

You can set EQUATEs throughout the program in the definition area (in other words, above the CODE statement). This is a tool to condense phrases or to give a more understandable name to some element of your program. EQUATEs are commonly used in the "Keys" files (the included files Designer inserts in the main program module) to translate the numeric key codes to English for more readable source code. You can name a specific picture to be used in formatting a variable; you can even rename keywords in the Clarion language.

Program Control

In this section, we'll step through the basics of the Clarion control language. You'll want to have the *Clarion Language Reference* at your side while you read this section; we'll try not to repeat that manual, instead giving you some principles with which to organize your understanding of the language. Look to the *Clarion Language Reference* for more information on each command. In general, you'll want to keep it nearby to supplement your reading in this book.

Hello, World

Now that you have a nodding acquaintance with the basic structure of a Clarion program, we'll write the standard "Hello, World" program. Then, later in the book, we'll build on this program to demonstrate various concepts you'll need. Figure 3-6 shows the simplest program possible to write and compile in the Clarion language.

We should really say that this is the simplest program written in *good* Clarion. If you return to the DOS prompt after compiling it and clear the

Figure 3-6   The traditional "Hello, World" program in Clarion.

```
SAMPLE   PROGRAM                      ! Name of the program
         CODE                         ! Beginning of the program

         SHOW(12,35,'Hello, World')   ! Display at row 12 column 35
         ASK                          ! Wait for a keystroke
         RETURN                       ! Go back to DOS
```

screen, this program will run, paint "Hello, World" in the middle of your screen, and return to the prompt. It is possible to compile and run the program if you remove the last two lines, "ASK" and "RETURN." However, that's not very good programming for several reasons. First, if you run this program while still in the Clarion shell, the words will paint over the screen that Clarion provides. Second, the "ASK" is the only program control you've given the user of this little gem. Third, even though you can get away with leaving out the "RETURN," your code would never show an exit point, which is a bad practice.

Clarion provides, figuratively, a complete box of tools for logic, calculating, and output constructs for controlling your program logically: LOOP, IF, CASE structures, and more. The whole environment promotes modular programming. The code that Designer generates has four phases:

1. Screen structure definition (if any used in the procedure)
2. Local variable definition (if any used in the procedure)
3. Procedure setup (preliminary opening of screens and onetime preprocessing)
4. Event loop (waiting for a keystroke to perform the main tasks of the procedure)

The Main Event Loop

As with the rest of the book, we'll discuss the way Designer generates code as if it were a programmer. We'll illustrate ways in which to use the Clarion language through Designer alongside manually coded samples like "Hello,World." One of the more significant techniques that Designer uses, which is not something the language requires, but is a pretty nifty application of its constructs, is the Main Event Loop.

Once you enter a Designer-written procedure, you first set up the Screen structure, which is necessary because screens are local to the procedure. Then you go through some setup during which the screen is opened and other events take place, like saving variables from the last procedure. Next you enter a primary loop structure. Unlike other applications, it's not necessary to say DO WHILE or use some other complex construction when you want a procedure to loop over and over. You simply say LOOP and then terminate that structure. This is analogous to the event-based system that Microsoft Windows uses. Once into the loop, the system spins away, waiting either for certain conditions to be satisfied, as with a report, or for user input. Once you understand how the Designer code is designed, your debugging efforts will be much more effective.

Hint: Clarion uses a period (.) or END to signify the final line of code for all structures including screens, file definitions, and logic structures. In logic structures, it may not signify the termination point of the procedure because other commands like BREAK, EXIT, or CYCLE may cause the structure to terminate before reaching one of these two terminating symbols.

The EXECUTE Statement

Another unique Clarion statement is EXECUTE. EXECUTE works something like a CASE statement without the OF construction for the test. It executes the line of code at the number passed to the statement. You can use this statement to select a choice from a menu, process an expression, or call a procedure. Designer uses EXECUTE in only three ways:

1. To execute a procedure on a menu pick by the user;
2. To put, add, or delete a record in an update form; and
3. To initialize global messages.

As with other Clarion functions, you can get creative with this statement. Its primary purpose is to select a statement to process on a line directly beneath it according to the number (1 through whatever) passed to it. It is similar to a CASE statement, but it eliminates the need for the test line (OF in a CASE structure) before allowing the next statement to be processed.

A CASE statement would look like this:

```
CASE    MENU_ITEM()
        OF  1
            PERFORM PROCEDURE NUMBER ONE
        OF 2
            PERFORM PROCEDURE NUMBER TWO
        etc...
```

The same problem solved with an IF structure would look like this:

```
IF MENU_ITEM = 1
        PERFORM PROCEDURE NUMBER ONE
ELSIF MENU_ITEM = 2
        PERFORM PROCEDURE NUMBER TWO
etc...
```

That very same problem solved with EXECUTE would look like this:

```
EXECUTE MENU_ITEM*
        PERFORM PROCEDURE NUMBER ONE
        PERFORM PROCEDURE NUMBER TWO
```

*In Designer, the CHOICE( ) function returns the menu item selected by the order stipulated in the Screen structure.

Of the three methods, EXECUTE is the only one that has no trap for a condition when the condition being tested cannot be met—if, for instance, MENU_ITEM were 3. In both the Case and If structures, you can place an ELSE, which performs a default process.

Traffic Cops: DO, GOTO, EXIT, BREAK, CYCLE, and RETURN

Each of these "traffic cops" directs the flow of a Clarion application by pointing the program flow in a particular direction. Although you can use each of these commands almost anywhere in a program, some conditions apply to each one. For instance, you may BREAK out of a loop, but you actually make that call from inside an IF statement seated inside the loop.

- DO is the only instruction, other than calling a procedure by name, that branches to other instructions before returning to the next line to continue. All of the others permanently pass control to a specific point in the program—never to return. In all cases where you would use these expressions except DO, the program has satisfied the reason it entered that part of the application and must now go on to another segment of the program.
- GOTO, if you must use it, grabs your program flow and sends it to another *labeled* location within the same procedure. It cannot be used to exit from a local routine or transfer control out of a procedure. Good programming practices say to avoid using this statement. It's viewed as a heavy-handed method for controlling program flow because it does not knit your code together in an easily followed track.
- EXIT is used to leave a local routine called with DO to go back inside its calling procedure. You'll never need to use EXIT at the absolute end of a local routine, only if you need to terminate the routine before it ends naturally and returns to the next line after the DO call.
- BREAK terminates a loop and drops your program's attention to the next statement after the loop. This is often used to detect an "aborting" keystroke such as "If Keycode( )=ESC_KEY then Break."
- CYCLE causes a loop to terminate its current run prematurely and return to the top of the loop for another run. Designer uses this statement when it fills a table under the supervision of a filter. If the condition isn't met, no processing is done on the current record. The loop cycles back to read the next record.
- RETURN works at any point in any application to terminate processing by the current procedure to go back to the calling procedure and to DOS if you make the call from inside the very first procedure in the application.

In a parody of indecisiveness, the pseudocode shown in Figure 3-7 illustrates the function of each of the preceding statements.

We'll discuss several other Clarion language constructs for directing program flow later in the book. These include CALL, RUN, RUNSMALL, CHAIN, RESTART, and STOP. Each of these statements (except STOP and RESTART) involves the access of another executable file from within a Clarion application and not just a branching within the same application.

Figure 3-7   A very dumb procedure not meant to represent quality program code, but only to show you how the "traffic cops" direct program flow.

```
              MEMBER('S ONLY)
CLOWNING  PROCEDURE
          CODE
          IF MADE A MISTAKE TO COME HERE THEN RETURN;ENDIF
          DO SUMTHIN AND COME BACK TO THE NEXT LINE
          LOOP UNTIL WE GET DIZZY SOMEWHERE
            IF SUMTHIN DIDN'T GIVE A RESULT THEN DO SUMTHIN
            CASE OF RESULT
              OF RESULT NUMBER ONE
                IF DIZZY ALREADY
                  BREAK OUT OF THE LOOP
                ELSE
                  RUN BACK TO THE TOP OF THE LOOP
                END THE IF
              OF RESULT NUMBER TWO
                DO SUMTHIN THEN QUIT CLOWNING
            ENDCASE
          ENDLOOP
          RETURN (GO BACK TO THE PREVIOUS PROCEDURE)

SUMTHIN   LOCAL ROUTINE
          LOOP UNTIL ALMOST DIZZY OR 30 TIMES
              IF DIZZY THEN EXIT;ENDIF
              TURNAROUND(RESULT)
          ENDLOOP
```

STOP suspends processing, presents a message, and (depending on your choice) continues the program, or sends you back to the DOS prompt.

Decision Tools: CASE and IF

Clarion provides two methods for low-level decision making in the Case and If structures. You normally use the Case method when you want to find one particular value for a variable and then quickly fall out to the next command after the Case structure. It is generally faster for finding that value than an If structure. However, it is possible to build a Case structure that looks just like an If statement, and vice versa.

In Designer, If structures are used to test one condition, for example, *whether or not* an escape key was pressed. Case structures are used to test for *which* key was pressed while sampling several different candidates.

Getting Data: NEXT, PREVIOUS, and GET

These three statements are the primary tools for pulling data from a Clarion file. You use NEXT and PREVIOUS to look through a file in sequential order, reading the next available record in whichever direction you're going. Normally, you would use these after putting the file into some known order with SET. However, you can issue a NEXT or PREVIOUS at any time to read the record adjacent to the one you just read or set the file pointer to. (But a SET must have been issued, or NEXT and PREVIOUS will find nothing.) If your request to read a record makes no sense because you are at the end (EOF) or the beginning (BOF) of the file when you issue the NEXT or PREVIOUS (respectively), you'll get the error message "RECORD NOT AVAILABLE."

GET is like a long arm that you can use to reach into the file at any point and read a record. You put the intelligence for *where* you want to look right into the GET statement as in:

```
GET(TheFile,CurrentPointerPosition)
```

or

```
GET(TheFile,MatchingRecordInKey)
```

Looking Around Data Files: SET and SKIP

SET and SKIP by themselves do not read a record. Therefore, they are much faster methods for moving through files than methods (like NEXT and PREVIOUS) that read each record into memory. SET arranges the file according to a key and points to a record according to the second parameter given, or it merely points to the first record in the file in key order or record number order. SKIP, on the other hand, picks the file pointer up and moves it past whatever number of records you want to bypass (forward or backward in the file). SKIP is normally used when you want to quickly pop to another location in the file without reading every record you pass on the way. To read the record once you arrive with either SET or SKIP, you must issue a NEXT, PREVIOUS, or GET.

Storing and Unstoring Data: ADD, APPEND, PUT, and DELETE

All four of these statements take a record from memory and then add it to the data file (ADD or APPEND), change the record already in the file (PUT), or mark an existing record for deletion (DELETE). In addition, all four of these commands accept only one parameter: the filename. The command, then, refers to the record in memory for whatever file you referenced.

- ADD attaches a new record to a data file and updates the key files.
- APPEND attaches the new record, but *does not* update the keys.
- PUT requires that the record already exist in the data file, and then it overwrites whatever was there before and updates the keys like an ADD.
- DELETE marks as inactive the record in memory for the file referenced. *DELETE does not remove the data from the disk.* You can recover a deleted record by using the Scanner application, providing you don't use the RECLAIM attribute on the file specification. If you used that attribute and your user added more records to the database, then some, if not all, of the deleted records were written over by the new ones. If the RECLAIM attribute is included in the file definition and a record is added, Clarion will try to fill in blank spots left by deleted records. Otherwise, the record is added onto the end of the file.

Summary

Clarion is a highly structured, procedural language. If you view it as such, you can organize your programming effort to take efficient advantage of the internal structures built into the language and serviced by its tools. The modularity of a Clarion application provides functional clarity within each segment of source code, and there are plenty of devices for talking between the different types of structures. In this chapter we focused on the anatomy of a Clarion application and the "nervous system" you can provide to users in order for them to operate it.

Chapter 4

Screen Structures

The Screen structure is one of the most powerful facilities in Clarion. That might seem a little biased toward the appearance of things, but the net effect is easy screen construction and additional modularity inside a Clarion Procedure. In addition, the access you have to edit that structure through both Designer and Editor makes the whole facility very efficient for creating application programs with good-looking and practical user presentations.

The Anatomy of a Screen

Designer generates Screen structures and you can create them easily with the screen formatter in Editor. The primary procedures (Table, Menu, Form) each have distinctive Screen structures, but their characteristics can overlap to the point where a non-Designer-generated screen may not be distinguishable as any one of those mainstream types. Screen structures exist outside of the operational code like a file structure, but you operate them from inside the CODE statement nonetheless, through the variables enwrapped in functions like SCROLL and POINT. Though it can be done, it's not a good idea to make Screen structures global, because they eat memory.

The Components

Like all the major Clarion structures (File, Screen, and Report), the first line sets the identity of the structure. The first thing you learn is that it is a screen and not a file or report. Then other information appears regarding the prefix for screen variables, colors, and placement. The label to the far left will be the tag you use to call this screen from within the program code.

Hint: When creating several Screen structures from within the Editor using the screen formatter, be sure you return to the code it generates and give unique labels to each structure within the same procedure. Designer automatically ensures these errors do not occur.

The screen depicted in Figure 4-1 occupies the entire display area of the video monitor—or at least of a standard 25-row × 80-column monitor. If you type this program into your system using the Clarion Editor, you can see how the structure appears on the screen simply by placing your cursor in Figure 4-2 between the "Screen" label and the terminating period and pressing CTRL-F. Check your *Clarion Utilities Guide* for more information on operating the Clarion Editor.

The first line of the Screen structure sets the prefix for all screen-bound variables as well as the colors used as a default for the screen and the fixed location of the window (if there is one). All graphics are placed into a Clarion screen in the same manner that Clarion provides "picture" formats to place variables on both screens and reports. You pick the row and column where you want the graphic to start, and then you describe a string to be displayed. The extended ASCII character set used to draw lines as well as the alphabet and punctuation are considered graphics.

Figure 4-1   "Hello, World" screen.

Figure 4-2 **Sample "Hello, World" screen display without code is included to do more than simply open, pause, and close the display. We'll display the "Hello" with code.**

```
SAMPLE      PROGRAM

SCREEN      SCREEN   PRE(SCR),HUE(7,0)
                ROW(5,20)       STRING('<218,196{41},191>')
                ROW(6,20)       REPEAT(9);STRING('<179,0{41},179>')  .
                ROW(15,20)      STRING('<192,196{41},217>')
                ROW(8,35)       STRING('HELLO, WORLD')


                CODE            ! START OF PROGRAM
                OPEN(SCREEN)    ! DISPLAY THE SCREEN
                ASK             ! WAIT FOR KEYSTROKE
                CLOSE(SCREEN)   ! REMOVE THE SCREEN
                RETURN          ! RETURN TO DOS PROMPT
```

Locations in a screen are specified with the ROW and COL statements. ROW is more complex because it contains references to both columns and rows as well as the relative position instruction available in both structures. Once you place something with ROW, you can then set the next item with COL if you choose—the output will be to the same row.

Notice that the preceding Screen structure contains a Repeat structure. This structure can be used only in Screen and Report structures, and it makes your code more efficient by packing instructions for creating lots of graphics into a single statement. (This is the same method used by many archiving utilities for saving file space.) The string definition that follows the row and column placement (here set with ROW(6,20)) is repeated nine times. That replaces repeating the statement itself nine times.

That's all there is to drawing a screen in Clarion. The features that distinguish a menu from a table from an update form will be discussed in separate sections later in this chapter.

Saving the Screen Underneath

When you open a screen, it destroys the video memory for the screen before it. If you want to save that previous screen, you must open this new screen as a window. There are two ways to save the prior screens. You can use the screen formatters in both Editor and Designer to shrink the display from full screen to a partial (or window) display. Or you can add the WINDOW attribute to the screen definition.

If you work in Editor, you can merely add the WINDOW attribute to the first line or identity of the screen. If you use the screen formatter, the screen first appears, after you press CTRL-F, filling the whole screen. Then, the first time you press CTRL-W to change the size of the window, the code is automatically written to your source file (when you save it with CTRL-Enter) with WINDOW set as an attribute of the screen. After that, even if you return to the screen formatter and fill the whole monitor area, the WINDOW term stays as an attribute until you remove it manually.

In Designer, the default for the screen forms of all display related procedures comes up as a window. Even if you increase the size of the windowed screen to fill the monitor, the generated code will contain the WINDOW attribute.

You can move a window into a specific display location by pressing CONTROL and the M key twice, using the cursor keys to place the menu, and then pressing Enter to lock it into place. (Pressing the M key only once while holding the Control key down will only enable the moving of items within the window by letting you highlight the area to move.) However, if you want the window to appear in that location without exception, you must set the window to a "fixed" location and not allow it to float around the screen. In Designer, you must choose between FIXED and FLOAT in the options menu you reach by pressing CTRL-O. In Editor, you must start the screen formatter as described earlier and then press CTRL-S to view the source. Then you place the cursor on the SCREEN source code line and press ENTER to display the options menu. This is also where you select the option to print an image of the screen into your source code.

Hint: It is recommended that you set windows into a fixed location and not allow them to float around the screen in all cases except the update form for a table. This provides greater control over the display and does not add to processing time or memory load. It also prevents having instructions at the bottom of the menu appear in awkward forms—for instance, having the "<F1> Help" appear at the bottom of the latest window and just above the same instruction for the window beneath it. It also gives you greater ability to show the users where they've come from in the system. The update form pops to new locations in the screen over a table to give you the best view of your present location in the table, if it is allowed to float.

Graphics and Documentation

When you draw tracks or borders or paint an area of the screen, the instructions for these appear within the Screen structure. In addition, Editor provides the ability to plant the extended ASCII character picture of the screen into the code above the actual Screen structure itself. This does not cause a problem during compilation because you can use the Clarion compiler directive OMIT to set those lines off from the operational code.

To print that image of the screen into your source code, go to Editor and start the screen formatter by placing your cursor within the Screen structure (that is, between the "Screen" label and the terminating period for the structure) and pressing CTRL-F. Now press CTRL-S to access the source code in a window. Place the highlight bar on the top line of the structure—where it says "SCREEN"—and press Enter. That will pop up an options menu as shown in Figure 4-3.

Clarion recognizes two methods of commenting source code. Designer generates comments adjacent to each line of code set off with the exclamation mark (!). To be allowed to write comments without prefacing each line with !, use the OMIT directive. Starting somewhere other than column 1 of the code, type OMIT('NAME OF THE Omit SIGN'). Then type in your comments, taking advantage of word wrap and other Editor word processing features. Then, on a separate line, type in the sign you entered between the parentheses as the OMIT parameter.

Figure 4-3 **This is the characteristics window in Editor's screen formatter for configuring a Screen structure. You plant an image of the screen into the source code when you set "Comment" to "Yes." Notice the line of source described in this window at the bottom of the window.**

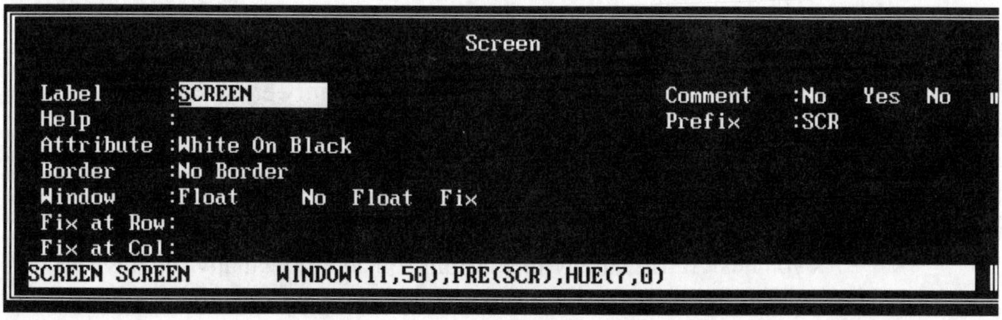

To represent the tracks, Clarion uses the Repeat structure and the escape sequences for the character you used when you drew on the background. Using the TAILOR program provided with Clarion, you can set the source code generation to create the actual extended ASCII symbols or you can show their escape sequences.

If you plan to print the source code on a printer that does not support the actual characters from the extended set themselves, you should not use Editor's ability to put the screen picture into your code and you should set TAILOR to convert the tracks to the escape sequences. You should test your printer's ability before the last time you use Designer to generate code or before you go to the trouble of setting the switch in Editor to put the screen picture into your source code.

Opening and Closing Screens and Memory

> **WARNING**
> **If you open a full screen without the WINDOW attribute, you will destroy the video memory for all the screens opened, but not closed prior to that. All currently opened windows will be closed and that memory released. That means, as you return to previous procedures, you will have to manually reopen each window.**

The Screen structures appearing in Clarion procedures must be opened before they display anything. Once opened, they occupy memory and must be closed to free that memory. As a general rule, a full screen in Clarion takes about 100 bytes of memory once it's opened. A window of the same size as the screen (25×80), however, takes over 4K. As you might expect, a window exactly half the size of the screen takes only 1.8K. These are minimum figures measured using Processor and lower than you will be using per screen. In practice, your screens will have different amounts of graphics, fields, and other contents that will boost the amount of memory each consumes.

Hint: If you have additional memory above 640K RAM, Clarion uses that space to store screens in memory when you open additional windows.

As you design software with Clarion, consider how many screens you will have open during any one section of your program. Each open screen takes away from the memory you have available for key caching and file buffers.

One advantage of the Overlay Manager from Mitten Software is the critical path calculation that shows the longest set of procedures that call each other in a series. You can use overlays and other methods for reducing memory.

When using Designer, be careful about manually closing screens. Designer depends on certain Screen structures being in place once it returns from hot procedures and other update calls. If a screen is closed, the screen variables it held are also wiped out.

Hint: When you open a screen, you also validate the variables in the screen. For instance, only after a screen is open will a change show in the screen message inserted into each update form by Designer.

More on Clarion's Warnings

In the *Clarion Language Reference*, Clarion warns you *against* two ways of handling screens: placing a screen in global memory and placing two Screen structures in the same procedure. The dangers that Clarion is concerned about are duplicate field equate labels and improper screen closings. However, these two techniques can be very useful, although neither one is supported in Designer. Remember, Designer was constructed to promote error-free programs, and these two techniques can cause problems if they are not handled properly.

Screens in Global Memory: As the reference manual states, if an application has only one screen, placing that screen in global memory will reduce the amount of space it would take up if it were replicated in all the procedures in an application. For instance, if you had a status screen with the same variables getting set by different procedures, say, on different hot keys, you don't need to place that Screen structure in each procedure. Another good application of a screen in global memory would be a window opened in various places around your application to provide messages to the user.

However, remember that global memory, once filled, cannot be reclaimed or released. Space is allocated based on what could be in the system. In addition, whatever label you give the screen and its field equates globally (discussed in Chapter 5) cannot be referenced by any other screen you might use.

Two Screens in the Same Procedure: Placing two screens in the same procedure can be useful for a number of reasons. This is another function you cannot do with Designer. Clarion also applies rules to what happens in memory when you open and close screens. For instance, the ACTION variable used in Designer gets reset whenever you open a full screen. We'll discuss more about the ACTION variable in Chapter 9.

You can place a second Screen structure in a procedure to call for displaying a special user message or even to update other variables in the record not displayed in the primary screen. The recommended procedure for that in Designer, however, is to use the next procedure of the options menu for an update form.

As the *Clarion Language Reference* points out, there is nothing inherently wrong with using two screens in the same procedure just as long as you close them both and do not open a full nonwindow screen over the top of either.

Freestyle Screen Access

Clarion does not require that you use Screen structures to access the screen. Many of the statements and functions discussed in this chapter apply only to such Screen structures as Entry and Repeat. However, you can place items on the screen without opening a Screen structure and even read them back with Clarion.

The SHOW Statement: A common debugging and user-notification tool is to use the SHOW statement to place characters on the screen. To use SHOW to send yourself messages during development, use Editor to place it into your code followed by an ASK statement, as follows:

```
Show(row, column,'notes to show variable = ' & variable)
ask
```

In this form, you can test the contents of variables and send other messages from inside your code without going through Processor's debugger. For some purposes, the Debugger can be disorienting and take too long to run through a series of commands—if you use STEP, the Debugger screen flashes back on the screen after each jump in the code. For instance, if you wanted to see the results of a transfer of value from one variable to the next, you could use SHOW to display both variables on screen adjacent to notes describing each one. If you placed that construction inside a loop, you need only press a key to allow the program to take the next step. In the revision to our "Hello, World" example shown in Figure 4-4, we want to see each increment of the implicit variable (COUNT#) displayed on the screen.

Figure 4-4 Hello, World program using the SHOW statement inside a loop structure to display to the screen and the BLANK statement to erase what was shown.

```
SAMPLE    PROGRAM

SCREEN    SCREEN   PRE(SCR),HUE(7,0)
             ROW(5,20)      STRING('<218,196{41},191>')
             ROW(6,20)      REPEAT(9);STRING('<179,0{41},179>')  .
             ROW(15,20)     STRING('<192,196{41},217>')
             ROW(8,35)      STRING('SAMPLE SCREEN')
                     .

             CODE                                 ! START OF PROGRAM
             OPEN(SCREEN)                         ! DISPLAY THE SCREEN
             LOOP 10 TIMES                        ! DO 10 LOOPS
                COUNT#  += 1                      ! ADD TO COUNTER
                SHOW(12,30,'The Count is: ' & COUNT#)
                                                  ! DISPLAY MESSAGE
                ASK                               ! KEYSTROKE WAIT
                BLANK(12,44,1,2)                  ! ERASE COUNTER
                     .                            ! END OF LOOP
             CLOSE(SCREEN)                        ! RETIRE SCREEN
             RETURN                               ! RETURN TO DOS
```

The LOOK, SCROLL, and TYPE Statements: The LOOK statement allows you to read information from the screen (video memory, that is), placing it into a variable according to a picture format. This is a handy function for times when there will be information on the screen not contained in a screen variable you can read directly. For instance, if you used the TYPE or SHOW statement to put something on the screen to display a warning, it won't be contained in a variable you can read directly. So, using LOOK, you can read what is there and place it in a variable for processing.

In addition, the SCROLL function, although used most often in the Table Procedure to move the items in the table up and down, can be used elsewhere. For instance, you could scroll the whole screen image off of the monitor as a showy transition between functions. Or you could scroll a portion of the screen in order to place something else there without losing from view what was already displayed—like the inside of a table, leaving the frame around it intact.

Menu Screens

The code that Designer creates for a menu is given in Figure 4-5. In each Clarion screen, the position, background coloring, and special characters are handled the same way in the top line of the structure. The next set of statements draw the lines and place the nonfunctional text onto the screen. The differences for a menu structure begin with the use of the MENU statement. The two ENTRY statements in Figure 4-5 establish fields for menu processing, but they are not selections and do not actually contain data.

In the Designer implementation of a menu (as shown in Figure 4-5), the USE variable for the menu structure uses an "implicit" variable—in this case, a string. That implicit variable remains valid for as long as the Screen structure remains in memory. So, if your application opens a menu that calls more procedures, your position in the menu is maintained when you return to it.

Hint: Implicit variables are temporary variables you can use inside a Clarion program that need not be declared before they are actually used. This makes them handy for holding elements needed only during one part of processing. You create an implicit variable by creating an alphanumeric string with no breaking spaces that has a last character of (") for a string, ($) for a real, and (#) for a short. (See Chapter 5 for variable descriptions.)

The Designer model does not include the "immediate," or IMM, attribute of the Menu structure. With that attribute set, if you press the first nonblank character of a menu selection, the USE variable is updated immediately.

Figure 4-5   A sample menu Screen structure without menu select.

```
MENUS    PROCEDURE
SCREEN   SCREEN        PRE(SCR),WINDOW(15,50),HUE(7,0)
         ROW(1,1)      STRING('<201,205{48},187>')
         ROW(2,1)      REPEAT(13);STRING('<186,0{48},186>')  .
         ROW(15,1)     STRING('<200,205{48},188>')
                       ENTRY,USE(?FIRST_FIELD)
                       ENTRY,USE(?PRE_MENU)
                       MENU,USE(MENU_FIELD"),REQ
         (menu items and their position go here)
             .                            .
```

Normally, Clarion automatically moves the highlight bar to each statement beginning with the character you press. If you set the IMM attribute, you get one press operation of a menu without the need to press ENTER when you reach the selection.

However, be sure you set each menu selection to start with a unique letter for that menu. If you have two items that begin with the same letter, pressing that letter always starts the selection that comes first alphabetically. Such a situation can be very frustrating for a user. One workaround for a menu where you cannot or do not want to change the beginning letter and you have duplicates can be found in the KEY attribute. This is not supported by Designer. You must edit the generated menu code to include KEY as an attribute for a particular menu selection. Then you can set it to read a character or a particular keycode. (See the list of key equates for what keycodes to use in the *Clarion Language Reference*.)

A feature Clarion's Designer does not support is the DESC attribute of the MENU statement. If you position the MENU statement with a row and column coordinate and add a picture to it (for example, ROW(14,6) MENU(@S40)), you can use Editor to add a description or instruction to each menu selection. So, as the user cursors through each menu selection, the Menu Field fills with those instructions. If you were to use the DESC and KEY attributes of the MENU statement in our sample Menu structure, the resulting code would appear as shown in Figure 4-6.

The Entry Fields using FIRST_FIELD and PRE_MENU are called "Dummy" Fields. These are fields with no parameters used to control processing in a Designer-generated procedure. Both Menu and Table Procedures use a "PRE_" Dummy Field. In Menus you'll see PRE_MENU; in Tables you'll see PRE_POINT. In Form Procedures you'll see the additional Dummy Field called LAST_FIELD. We'll cover more about using the fields in a Menu Procedure in Chapter 8.

Using the Menu structure in Figure 4-6, the screen would appear as shown in Figure 4-7.

Notice also in Figure 4-7 that the two menu selections start with the same character and yet we've included the IMM attribute on the MENU field setup. Since the IMM attribute means to complete the field as soon as MENU_FIELD" gets filled with something, striking the letter T would always start the first menu item. But, since we've also included the KEY attribute, we can assign a letter to respond to. In this case, we've selected other letters within the string. Good programming practice would be to place the letter in parentheses to tell the user which letter you've used as the KEY attribute.

Figure 4-6   The same Screen structure as in Figure 4-5 modified with Editor to include the IMM, DESC, and KEY attributes. The initialized code shows the additions made to the code.

```
MENU      PROCEDURE

SCREEN    SCREEN    WINDOW(15,50),PRE(SCR),HUE(7,0)
                    ROW(1,1)    STRING('<201,205{48},187>')
                    ROW(2,1)    STRING('<186,0{48},186>')
                    ROW(3,1)    STRING('<199,196{48},182>')
                    ROW(4,1)    REPEAT(11);STRING('<186,0{48},186>')  .
                    ROW(15,1)   STRING('<200,205{48},188>')
                     COL(50)    ENTRY,USE(?FIRST_FIELD)
                    ROW(2,7)    STRING('Message:')
                     COL(15)    ENTRY(@S30),USE(MEM:MESSAGE),HUE(0,7)
                    ROW(3,43)   ENTRY,USE(?PRE_MENU)
                    ROW(14,6)   MENU(@S40),USE(MENU_FIELD"),REQ,IMM
                    ROW(6,14)   STRING('The First Menu Selection'),KEY('F')    |
                                DESC('Instructions for the First Selection')
                    ROW(8,17)   STRING('The Second Selection'),KEY('S')        |
                                DESC(TEST")
                      .    .
```

Figure 4-7   The MENU_FIELD" string containing the string contents of the DESC attribute appears in this figure at "Instructions for the First Selection" while the highlight bar is on the first of the two menu selections.

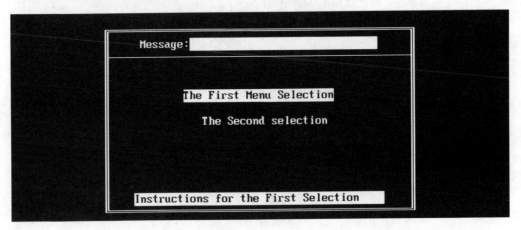

Hint: *Remember, whenever you make changes to Clarion's Designer-generated code, those changes will get wiped out if you regenerate the code. As a rule, try to include any code writing into one of Designer's facilities like the Setup Procedure in the Procedure Options Form or the Edit Procedure in a field display. As another workaround, you can generate the initial code, make the changes, and then rename the procedure as an Other Procedure in Designer.*

Table Screens

The primary difference between table screens and form or menu screens appears within the second Repeat structure in the Designer-generated sample in Figure 4-8. In this case, the repeated elements make up the scrolling portion of the table. As with all the Designer-generated code, the FIRST_FIELD and the PRE_POINT Entry Fields are used to control processing based on the location of the cursor on the screen. For instance, when you use a Locator Field in a table, it goes after the FIRST_FIELD Entry Field in the Screen structure.

The Repeat structure in concert with the POINT statement create the scrolling bar you'll see in Clarion tables. The variables set by the INDEX, USE, and ESC attributes control the responses of Designer-generated code during table processing.

If you were to read the code as English, starting at the line with the Repeat structure, it would read like this: repeat 1 row and do it every line. Use the

Figure 4-8 The Designer-generated code for a table Screen structure.

```
TABLES          PROCEDURE

SCREEN  SCREEN                  PRE(SCR),WINDOW(21,50),HUE(7,0)
                ROW(1,1)        STRING('<201,205{48},187>')
                ROW(2,1)        REPEAT(19);STRING('<186,0{48},186>')  .
                ROW(21,1)       STRING('<200,205{48},188>')
                                ENTRY,USE(?FIRST_FIELD)
                                ENTRY,USE(?PRE_POINT)
                                REPEAT(1),EVERY(0),INDEX(NDX)
                ROW(1,1)            POINT(0,0),USE(?POINT),ESC(?-1)
                   .                .
```

Figure 4-9   The Screen structure code generated by Designer.

```
FORMS     PROCEDURE

SCREEN    SCREEN                  PRE(SCR),WINDOW(9,44),HUE(7,0)
                 ROW(1,1)         STRING('<201,205{42},187>')
                 ROW(2,1)         REPEAT(7);STRING('<186,0{42},186>') .
                 ROW(9,1)         STRING('<200,205{42},188>')
                 ROW(4,4)         STRING('MESSAGE:')
                 ROW(5,4)         STRING('PAGE    :')
                 ROW(6,4)         STRING('LINE    :')
                 ROW(7,4)         STRING('DEVICE  :')
MESSAGE   ROW(3,8)                STRING(30),ENH
                                  ENTRY,USE(?FIRST_FIELD)
                 ROW(4,12)        ENTRY(@s30),USE(MEM:MESSAGE)
                 ROW(5,12)        ENTRY(@n3),USE(MEM:PAGE)
                 ROW(6,12)        ENTRY(@n3),USE(MEM:LINE)
                 ROW(7,12)        ENTRY(@s30),USE(MEM:DEVICE)
                                  ENTRY,USE(?LAST_FIELD)

                      .
```

NDX variable to store a number beginning with a 1 for each line in the table. Point to the first row of the displayed table and use the field equate label ?POINT to mark the location for field processing. Finally, the ESC attribute tells the program that pressing the Escape key will take you one field backward. The different strategies for handling tables and the different fields you can display in a table structure are covered in Chapter 9.

Form Screens

The Screen structure for a form uses the ENTRY statement more than the other structures. It is also the plainest of the Screen structures in Clarion. You manipulate the graphic elements such as boxes and text the same as you would in all screens: by setting the row and column location with the ROW statement and then specifying a string.

In a Designer-generated form Screen structure, the graphics all appear at the beginning of the structure and the Entry Fields appear last—just as the

Figure 4-10 The form Screen structure as it appears in both Designer and the screen formatter in Editor.

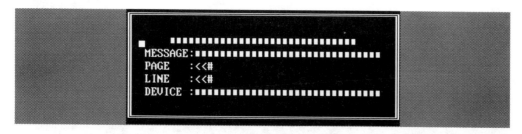

menu selections appear in menus and the scrolling portion of a table appears in those structures. The order of the Entry Fields also determines the number Clarion assigns to each field in the structure. You could control access to that field using the SELECT function, for instance, and that number.

Notice the FIRST_FIELD and LAST_FIELD Dummy Fields in the form structure in Figure 4-9. They do not have string pictures after their Entry Fields, so they are merely placeholders to assist in processing the screen for user input. The Screen structure is shown in Figure 4-10.

The fields appear in Figure 4-10 as a series of white blocks the same length as that given next to their entry equivalents in the program code in Figure 4-9. Note the numeric pictures as they appear on the screen for page and line number. Clarion automatically maintains two numbers.

Summary

Taking complete advantage of the exacting control that a PC programmer can exert over the video display, Clarion provides a handy, structured approach to addressing the screen. You can create screen layouts with Clarion's high-level tools and still manipulate absolute locations and functionality such as extended ASCII characters or a full range of color. In this chapter we discussed how you can manipulate the screen through the higher-level tools of the Clarion language to get a look that's pleasing and, above all, serviceable to the user.

Chapter 5

File Structures

Clarion creates two forms of DOS files: its own format and straight ASCII text. Both types can be read from inside the DOS environment and outside of Clarion. (To get the information you'll need to read the proprietary Clarion formatted files with a program written in a language other than Clarion, you'll need Clarion's *Technical Bulletins* 117, 118, 120, and 121.) The *Clarion Language Reference* distinguishes between these two file types by calling their own formatted files "Clarion" files (naturally enough) and the ASCII files DOS files. Clarion provides functions for handling both types from within Clarion. This chapter discusses the construction of files and their elements. More about accessing the data appears in other chapters.

The Anatomy of a Clarion Data File

A Clarion data file performs three functions:

1. Gives the data file an identity.
2. Defines the keys or indexes to be used to access the data in the file.
3. Defines the fields in the record including a separate group defining Memo Fields.

The elements of a Clarion data file are illustrated in Figure 5-1.

In effect, one file definition in the main program is responsible for the creation of three actual DOS files: .DAT is the database file; .K## are the key files, and .MEM is the memo file. Theoretically you can have up to 255 keys

Figure 5-1   The elements of a Clarion data file.

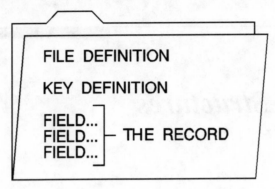

defined in the file, but only one data file and only one memo file. (We'll talk more about maximum number of keys later on in this chapter.) The file structure in Figure 5-2 shows all the variable types that Clarion supports with only one key and one index file as well as the one memo file allowed per data file.

The FILE Statement

The FILE statement in a file structure works just like the SCREEN statement in a Screen structure discussed in Chapter 4. First, you specify the label by which you'll call the file from within your program. Then it's identified as a Clarion file with the keyword FILE. The attributes given to this sample file include the three most commonly used:

- PRE gives the prefix for all the variables used in the file record, and that distinguishes them from screen variables (SCR) and memory table variables (TBL) discussed later.
- CREATE means if the system does not find the file on the disk, it will create an empty file.
- RECLAIM means the system will fit new records into the slots of deleted records when it can to save space.

There are other parameters you could set up in the file definition line that include a specific path name for the file. Especially when using Designer, it is

Figure 5-2   A sample Clarion data file using all of possible elements to include in a data file, including indexes, keys, memos, and all of the available variable types.

```
TEST   FILE,PRE(TES),CREATE,RECLAIM,PROTECT ! The file header
       OWNER('The Owner ID'),ENCRYPT
BY_FIRST_KEY KEY(TES:FIRST),DUP,NOCASE,OPT ! The key defined
BY_2ND_INDEX INDEX(TES:SECOND),NOCASE,OPT  ! The index defined
SEVENTH        MEMO(500)                   ! The memo reference
RECORD         RECORD                      ! Start of the record
GROUP_FIELD GROUP                          ! Start of a group
FIRST            STRING(10)                !  First record field
LAST             STRING(20)
SECOND           DECIMAL(4,2)              !  Second record field
                 .                         ! End of the group
THIRD          BYTE                        ! Third record field
FOURTH         SHORT                       ! Fourth record field
FIFTH          LONG                        ! Fifth record field
SIXTH          REAL                        ! Sixth record field
       .         .                         ! End of record
          GROUP,OVER(TES:SEVENTH)          ! The memo area
TES_MEMO_ROW STRING(10),DIM(50)
       .         .
```

better not to enter a specific path name in File options while developing a program. If you do so, and you move the application to another location on your disk or another computer, the application won't be able to find your test database files during test runs in Processor unless you go to the trouble of moving them, too. However, as a security device, the CREATE option can be used as a way to hinder the program from being moved around by users. To give a path name, all you need do is add the NAME attribute to that top line like this:

```
NAME(C:\subdirectory\subdirectory)
```

In Designer, you set this up on the Options screen in the file definition screen as depicted in Figure 5-3.

Figure 5-3 The File Options window for setting the header information that appears in the first line of the file definition in the Designer-generated code.

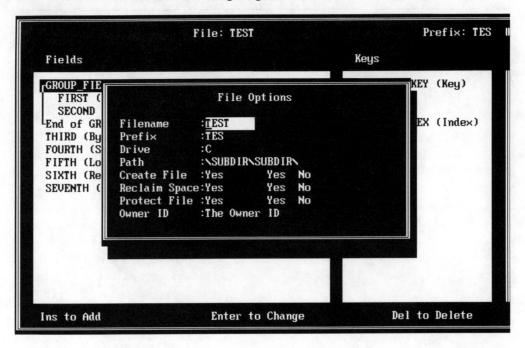

File Security

Two other items you can set in Designer regarding overall file specifications include the PROTECT and OWNER ID attributes. PROTECT prevents a data file from being changed by any of the Clarion utilities. You can only read or write to the file from within a Clarion application. That prevents anyone from making changes without the supervision of your application program.

The OWNER ID (created with the OWNER statement) changes the header information in the Clarion data file so that the file cannot be opened unless the correct OWNER ID is supplied. That allows you to control access to the data file from within your program. You can use a secure password function to set the OWNER ID somewhere else in the program before any attempt is made to open the file prior to processing.

To further hide the data in the file, you can encrypt the entire data file using the ENCRYPT attribute. This prevents access to the record information in the file. The file then becomes unreadable to anyone except those with authorized access through the Clarion application.

Keys and Indexes

The keys and indexes for a Clarion data file are described in the file definition beneath the structure configuration line. In the sample shown in Figure 5-2, we've defined both a key and an index. Keys are dynamically updated lists of fields from the records in a database that you use to quickly locate information in the database. Clarion uses a proprietary B-tree format for file access, which uses these keys. They are maintained in memory according to the space available and can contain multiple fields up to 245 bytes.

There are a few differences between a key and an index, but they are very much alike. With indexes you cannot use the OPT (suppress Null Fields) or NOCASE (to turn off consideration of letter case in comparing fields) attributes as you can with keys, and you must call for indexes to be updated explicitly. Clarion does not automatically rebuild indexes with calls to Copy, Rename, Remove, Create, Pack, and Empty as it will with keys. You will use indexes most often for batch processing, where you need a particularly large index that will only be processed one time or that will not interfere with the user operating the program.

Creating Keys with Designer

When you create keys inside Designer, each cluster of fields defined as a key constitutes a file required by your application to run. To create a key in Designer, you simply press INSERT while your cursor is in the File Maintenance screen for a file in the Keys column. (See Figure 5-4.)

Each of the parameters shown in the key definition options in Figure 5-4 appears in the file definition code detailing the key. Selecting "Exclude Nulls" places the OPT attribute in the key definition code. That attribute screens out the records in the file with empty fields contained in this key. Selecting "Case Sensitive" causes Clarion to sort the database, distinguishing between upper- and lowercase letters. In other words, "A" comes before all lowercase letters including "a."

Auto-Numbered Key Fields

Clarion constructs the code for auto-numbered Key Fields automatically in Designer. If you want to code it into a program yourself, it is the one feature in the file definition in Designer that does not appear in the file definition in

Figure 5-4 This is the Key Options window for creating a key or index in a Designer file definition. This is the screen that pops up when you insert a new key or place the cursor or highlight bar on the top line of a key definition.

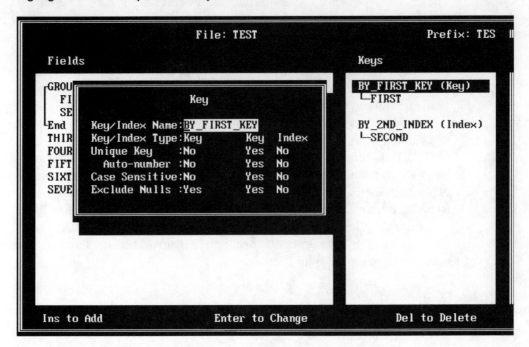

the global memory space in the main module of the program. Instead, this signals Designer to insert code to maintain the numbering sequence.

Selecting "Unique Key" in the Designer key file options means that no two records can have the same elements in this key. If you answer no to this option, Clarion places the DUP attribute in the key definition. You must use this feature to use the auto-numbering feature. You can have as many unique keys as you like, but only one key can be auto-numbered. The Auto-numbered Field must be the last field in the key. You won't see any code generated by Designer in the Form Procedure for updating the file. The Auto-numbered Field gets its new number in two places in the Table Procedure accessing the file: when the file tests out to be empty and when you insert a new record into the table.

It's easy to set your file up in Designer thinking you'll get auto-numbering and it doesn't appear. The two schemes for auto-numbering are described here and illustrated in Figure 5-5.

Figure 5-5   This diagram illustrates the two methods Clarion provides in Designer to auto-number a field in a database. Notice that you can restart the count for each subgroup with a multipart key. This is handy for invoices or student tracking.

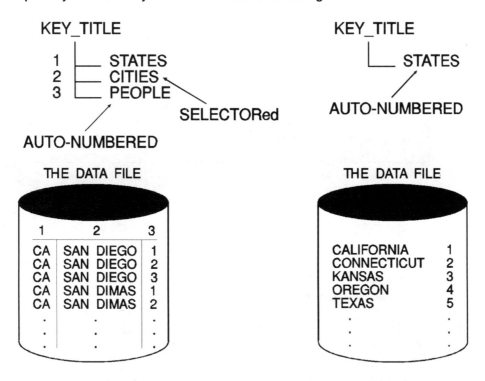

1. If you build a multipart key, you must use the Selector function in the table options screen when accessing a file with an Auto-numbered Field in it. If you *don't* use the Selector, the key remains unique, but no auto-numbering occurs. To set this up, place the next to last field as the field for use as the Selector. That causes the table to present only those records that match the value in the Selectored Field, with all of its auto-numbered companions. In this way, you can start the counter over *within the same file* for a new group of records headed by the Selectored Field, which, obviously, may have duplicates because other fields that are not the last field may have duplicates.

2. Your only other choice is a one-part key. The field in a one-part key will be numbered sequentially starting with 1.

> **Caution**
> If you deleted the record with the highest number in an auto-num-
> bered file under either a single or multipart key, you may cause a
> problem with any related files using that field. In that case, if you
> add a new record, you will be given the same number as the de-
> leted record. In which case, any records in related files will have a
> new relative. This occurs only if you delete the highest auto-num-
> bered value. You can avoid confusion by inserting your own test
> prior to the deletion to compensate for the increment, if it matters
> to your database structure.

You can, of course, build your own auto-numbering scheme. In that case, a
popular method is to put a field that holds a counter in the top relational file of
a sequence. In other words, to keep a count of the people in the preceding
database, you could add a field to the Cities database (not pictured) to
increment or decrement whenever you added or deleted a person from the
People database (pictured).

Where Do Keys Come From?

Once you've defined it in the record structure, the Key file is created at the
same time the data file is created. In standard Designer-generated code,
anytime you open a file, the key is checked and rebuilt as necessary. If the
attempt to open the file reveals that the file itself is missing, the CREATE
command constructs both the data file and its keys. If the file exists and is
successfully opened but returns an error code of 46 ("KEY FILE MUST BE
REBUILT"), the Build function is called to reconstruct the key.

The BUILD Statement: In most Clarion applications, expecting to rebuild
the key when you start the program may cause your application to run out of
memory. Rebuilding the keys for a series of files ties up memory and rapidly
causes your application to terminate with an error. If you plan to move large
data files and do not want to transport the keys as well, you have several
options.

You can use the SORTER utility (CSRT.EXE) to pack the data files,
removing any records marked for deletion and stripping out the key files.
Then, by passing a DOS batch file with command parameters, you can unpack

the file and rebuild the keys. (SORTER is distributable, and this process can be hidden from the user, if you choose.)

Another technique you can employ is to rebuild each key, one at a time. That is, instead of calling BUILD with the filename and rebuilding all the keys, you pass the name of each key to the Build function like this:

```
BUILD(FIL:KEY_NAME)
```

That leaves more memory free and helps you restart your application. If you rebuild keys from within a Clarion application, you can use the BUFFER and CACHE commands to manage extended memory for speed and key size more effectively. More about keys and memory appears in Chapter 20.

If you have modified the program in some way, you must have a copy of the source code for the file definitions available and use FILER (CFIL.EXE) to rebuild the keys. If you altered a record definition, FILER posts a message that says the fields will be converted. If only the keys themselves have changed, it says the record layout is the same. Nevertheless, you must still rebuild the file by pressing CTRL-ENTER to update the key files. FILER then posts a message that says the data file is being created. This does not mean that a *new* file is being created, only that the keys are being reconstructed. FILER is also freely distributable—you can give it or send it to your users without paying a royalty to Clarion. FILER can also be driven with a batch file command line that is hidden from the user.

 Hint: *If you plan to transport a source file containing the file definitions to use FILER for rebuilding keys, you must strip out any INCLUDEs that appear in it or FILER will return an error stating that it can't find them. You may not notice this on your development system because the INCLUDEd files are probably in the path and therefore are detectable by FILER. Removing the standard INCLUDEs inserted by Designer for the key equate files, for instance, will not affect your attempt to rebuild keys.*

Clarion's compiler actually lets you create up to 255 keys with one Key Field each, but the chances are pretty good that your program won't run with that many—there won't be any room left in the environment for the application once all those files are opened. Practically speaking, you probably will never exceed 100 keys—and even then you should examine the efficiency of your search techniques and look at creating a branch data file or using multipart keys to evaluate your data.

Multipart keys can be used to search through a database file in a more structured manner. To create a multipart key, you merely add more fields from the database record to the key definition. In evaluating the key, Clarion looks at the key definition as it reads from left to right: the left-most field is considered the primary key and the file is first sorted by that key. We'll discuss more about keys and file access using them later on in Chapters 9 and 10.

The Record

The record area of a Clarion data file contains the fields you'll use to store data. You can use seven different variable types (not counting the group function) with Clarion, and you can have up to 65K of information in each record. In Designer, you build that record in the left side of the file maintenance screen while you create the keys for the file on the right side of the screen. The Designer screen used to create the data structure in Figure 5-6 appears in Figure 5-7.

Figure 5-6   Designer-generated code for opening files on program startup. To save memory, you can move this function to a separate file and open files only as you need them.

```
G_OPENFILES  PROCEDURE                          !OPEN FILES
  CODE                                          ! & CHECK FOR ERROR
  SHOW(25,1,CENTER('OPENING FILE: ' & 'TEST',80))
                                                !DISPLAY FILE NAME
  OPEN(TEST)                                    !OPEN THE FILE
  IF ERROR()                                    !RETURNED AN ERROR
    CASE ERRORCODE()                            !CHECK FOR ERROR
    OF 46                                       ! REBUILD KEYS
      SETHUE(0,7)                               !  BLACK ON WHITE
      SHOW(25,1,CENTER('REBUILDING KEY FILES FOR TEST',80))
                                                !SHOW MSG
      BUILD(TEST)                               !REBUILD THE KEYS
      SETHUE(7,0)                               !  WHITE ON BLACK
      BLANK(25,1,1,80)                          !  BLANK THE MESSAGE
    OF 2                                        !IF NOT FOUND,
      CREATE(TEST)                              ! CREATE
    ELSE                                        ! ANY OTHER ERROR
      LOOP;STOP('TEST: ' & ERROR()).           !  STOP EXECUTION
  . .
```

Figure 5-7 This is the File Summary window in Clarion's Designer that you use to create the data files for a Clarion application. The fields in the record structure appear on the left-hand side with their variable types, and the keys and indexes appear on the right. Notice the use of the group that contains the First and Second Fields. These can now be referred to together as GROUP_FIELD. This is a handy tool for saving and for other variable handling you may need to optimize.

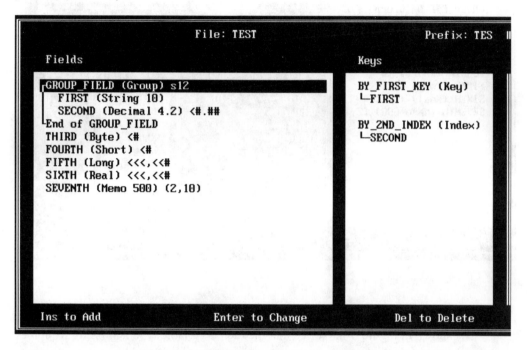

```
            File: TEST                          Prefix: TES

  Fields                                Keys

 ┌GROUP_FIELD (Group) s12              BY_FIRST_KEY (Key)
 │  FIRST (String 10)                  └FIRST
 │  SECOND (Decimal 4.2) <#.##
 └End of GROUP_FIELD                   BY_2ND_INDEX (Index)
   THIRD (Byte) <#                     └SECOND
   FOURTH (Short) <#
   FIFTH (Long) <<<,<<#
   SIXTH (Real) <<<,<<#
   SEVENTH (Memo 500) (2,10)




  Ins to Add          Enter to Change          Del to Delete
```

Where to Place File Structures

If you include the file definitions for your Clarion data files in the global area of the main program module, as Designer does, you must not attempt to redefine them later or you will get a conflict. In Designer-generated code, the application defines and opens (or creates) its data files on program startup and then leaves them open for the run of the application. It places all the file definitions in the same area for global information containing the MAP and the global memory file following the PROGRAM statement.

You can move a definition into another procedure, but you will not be able to access that file from any other procedure unless you have redefined the file in the calling procedure and closed it before leaving each procedure that opened it. If the file is still open when you redefine it, you will get an error.

Figure 5-8   The Field entry screen for creating a record structure.

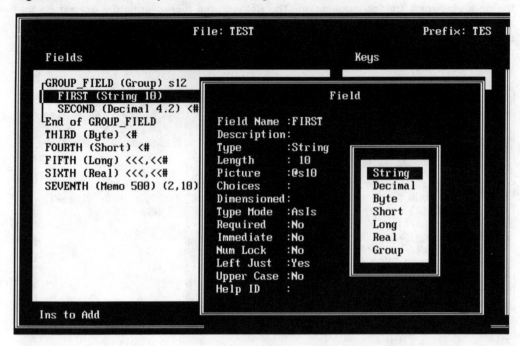

You can add a field to a record structure in Clarion using the entry screen shown in Figure 5-8. Notice that the memo variable type is missing from the list of selectable types in the pop-up window. There can be only one Memo Field per data file, and, as you can tell by inspecting the generated code and the display of records, the memo type is already in use in this file. Before a memo is assigned in a file, it appears in the pop-up window with the rest of the variable types.

The Clarion Memory File

In Designer, Clarion provides an area in which to add global memory variables. (See Figure 5-9.) These variables are not stored in any file, but they are available to temporarily hold values in any procedure in your program. Global variables entered into Clarion within a file structure allow you to access them through a form just as if they were a disk-based file. This can be useful for storing user defaults and letting the customer set temporary values. However, since there can be only one value for each variable, there is no need for a key

Figure 5-9 The file maintenance area for entering global memory variables in Clarion. The variables pictured are the defaults given to every Designer-generated program. You add fields just as you do in the fields of the regular database file maintenance area.

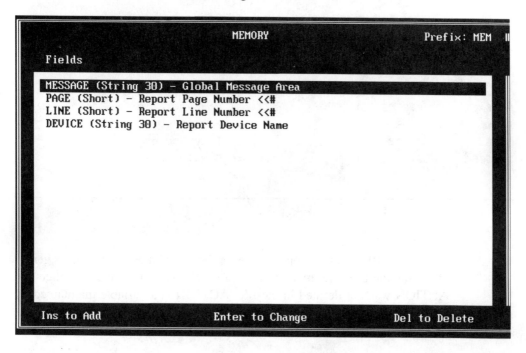

or the table structure. The Designer-generated global variables appear in Figure 5-10.

Relational Databases and Multiuser Files

A Short Note on Multiuser

Clarion provides both a relational and a multiuser file handling facility. However, at least in the case of the multiuser capabilities, there is nothing to do regarding file construction. You build the files exactly as if they were for a single user only. If you use Designer, the only switch you need to make to create a multiuser application is to change from the standard model file to the network model to generate the code. Well, it's not quite *that* simple, but we'll get into more detail on multiuser Clarion applications in Chapter 15.

Figure 5-10   The global variables most commonly used in Designer-generated code.

```
ACTION          SHORT               !0 = NO ACTION
                                    !1 = ADD RECORD
                                    !2 = CHANGE RECORD
                                    !3 = DELETE RECORD
                                    !4 = LOOKUP FIELD
                GROUP,PRE(MEM)
MESSAGE         STRING(30)          !Global Message Area
PAGE            SHORT               !Report Page Number
LINE            SHORT               !Report Line Number
DEVICE          STRING(30)          !Report Device Name
                .
```

Figure 5-10 shows the source code for the global memory variables generated from the Designer memory file screen shown in Figure 5-9. Notice that ACTION was not defined in the file. ACTION is a variable maintained by Clarion to supervise file interface. At least in Designer, you cannot remove it or change it unless you do so directly in the generated source code.

Relational Databases in Clarion

The relational scheme possible with Clarion is handled very simply: you must place a field in one database that is identical to a field in the related database file. It's that simple. Once you set that up, any information between files can be combined. The Designer facilities in Clarion merely automate the standard methods for looking up information in one file based on the related field in the current file. We'll get into greater detail on how to handle relational links when we discuss form and table techniques in Chapters 9 and 10.

Summary

With the same modularity found throughout the language, the Clarion data file structures provide interior coherence. The Clarion File structure contains variable types for flexible and efficient storage, as well as fast data retrieval through dynamically-maintained keys. In this chapter we focused on how data are organized both in memory and on disk, in variable form as well as how variables construct a record.

Chapter 6

Report Structures

As with screens and files, Clarion's Designer provides a method for automating the construction of reports. Later on, in Chapter 12, we'll discuss in greater detail how to manipulate a report in Clarion. This chapter focuses more on the *what* of a report. We'll discuss how that structure gets built both manually and in Designer and how it works.

The Clarion Report structure replaces many instructions you would otherwise be forced to write and send to the printer yourself. Automatic printing of headers and footers at the end of the page and positioning fields for printing are some examples. If you get to know the Report structures through Designer, you'll find a wealth of output talent for your applications.

Revisiting "Hello, World"—Report Minded

Clarion provides direct access to the printer with commands. The Report structure discussed in this chapter is a further step toward automatic report creation. But, before we discuss how the structure works, let's look at how Clarion "talks" to the printer using an old friend, "Hello, World." This time, however, we'll use the printer and not the screen.

Only one statement in Clarion applies exclusively to reports and does not appear in a Report structure: PRINT. Every other statement in the Clarion language can be used in a Report Procedure, even screen-related commands (for displaying report printing status, for instance).

The simplest program for printed output you can write in Clarion appears in Figure 6-1. Both the PRINT(@FF) or form feed and the RETURN state-

Figure 6-1   A simple report program.

```
PRINTER   PROGRAM                    ! IDENTIFIES PROGRAM TO COMPILER

          CODE                       ! STARTS THE PROGRAM
          PRINT('Hello, World')      ! SENDS STRING TO PRINTER
          PRINT(@FF)                 ! SENDS FORM FEED TO PRINTER
          RETURN                     ! GO BACK TO THE DOS PROMPT
```

ments could be left out and the program would still send "Hello, World" to your printer. A corner of the page it would produce is pictured in Figure 6-2.

The Anatomy of a Report Structure

The Report structure works just like a Screen structure. It must appear between the PROGRAM or the PROCEDURE statement and the CODE statement; that is, it must be declared before the program code that uses it begins to run. It can be edited with the report formatter in Editor. And it is a structure called from inside a program. A Report worksheet in Designer before the code is generated is shown in Figure 6-3, and the generated code appears in Figure 6-4.

The Clarion Report structure works like this: instead of working out a report layout every time you want to print a report inside your running code, you can create a template (the structure) into which you send information. The structure handles the printer, getting it set up correctly, inserting footers when the page feed comes, and so on. So, in the code section of the program, you

Figure 6-2   A corner of the page that the program in Figure 6-1 would produce.

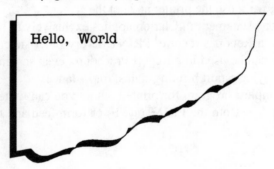

Hello, World

Figure 6-3   This is a Report worksheet in Designer or Editor.

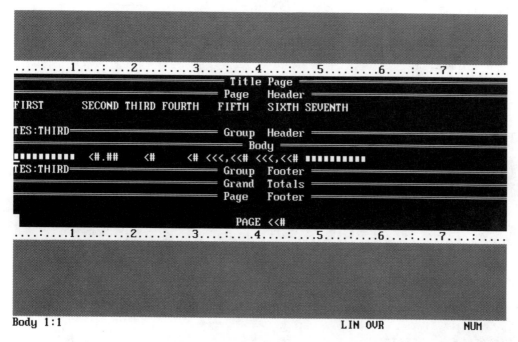

spend your time finding and preparing the data to print. When you're ready, you merely call a one-line statement (the selected structure) that prints that section of the report. It greatly simplifies the programming required to produce a report.

To create a report using a Clarion Report structure, you look through the database you want to report on, filling the current record in memory with information. When it's appropriate—based on the contents of the record and the physical parameters of the page—you call for a particular part of the Report structure to be printed.

The REPORT Statement

A Designer-generated report actually contains two separate Report structures. This method is not required, but it was placed there by Clarion to provide for complex title pages that require the tracking of line numbers and pages separately from the main body of the report. Opening a Report structure initializes the internally tracked variables for page number and line number. Although these are explicitly named memory variables in the memory file

Figure 6-4   The program code generated by either Designer or Editor's screen formatter in Figure 6-3.

```
TITLE       REPORT WIDTH(80),PRE(TTL)
RPT_HEAD        DETAIL
                .   .

REPORT      REPORT WIDTH(80),PAGE(MEM:PAGE),LINE(MEM:LINE),PRE(RPT)
PAGE_HEAD       HEADER
        COL(1)      STRING('FIRST {6}SECOND THIRD FOURTH    FIFTH    SIXTH '   |
                        & 'SEVENTH') CTL(@LF2)
                    .

DETAIL      DETAIL
        COL(1)      STRING(10),USE(TES:FIRST)
        COL(13)     STRING(@n5.2),USE(TES:SECOND)
        COL(22)     STRING(@n2),USE(TES:THIRD)
        COL(29)     STRING(@n2),USE(TES:FOURTH)
        COL(32)     STRING(@n7),USE(TES:FIFTH)
        COL(40)     STRING(@n7),USE(TES:SIXTH)
        COL(48)     STRING(10),USE(TES:SEVENTH) CTL(@LF)
                        .                              .

DETAILA     DETAIL
MEMO_1      COL(48)     STRING(10) CTL(@LF)
                    .

DETAILB     DETAIL
                    .

RPT_FOOT    DETAIL
                    .

PAGE_FOOT   FOOTER
    ROW(+1,37)      STRING('PAGE')
        COL(42)     STRING(@n3),USE(MEM:PAGE) CTL(@LF)
                CTL(@FF)
        .   .
```

created in Designer, they are not incremented with explicit code in the Report Procedure, but by Clarion itself. Keep this in mind as you place your printer control codes into a report. You'll get nonsensical results if you place them inappropriately. For instance, don't begin a line count in the title section that you plan to use in the main report.

Figure 6-5   The layout of a Report structure as created by Clarion's Designer. Each level holds specific layout and printer instructions required by the report.

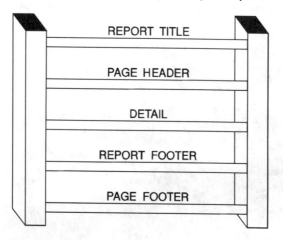

Hint: Within each item of the Report structure shown in Figure 6-5, each construct is terminated by a period or END until the report itself is terminated the same way.

The REPORT statement is tasked with setting the overall parameters for the report—like page size (width and length) as well as the temporary variable name given the items that will be printed on the page. The Designer tool for setting the parameters of the REPORT statement appear in Figure 6-6. If you'll recall in Screen structures, each variable that was sent to the screen had three components: the field from the file record, the USE variable in memory, and the screen variable (usually shown as SCR in Designer). In reports, that same setup exists with the standard Designer prefix of RPT before each variable is actually printed.

Hint: Refer to Chapter 9 to read about a fourth variable used in tables, which Designer tags with a prefix of TBL, that fits in between the SCR screen variable and the USE variable.

In addition, the REPORT statement establishes which DEVICE you'll send the report to. In Designer, all you can do is route the report to different DOS devices—including the disk by sending it to a DOS file on the disk. Those devices include the standard output ports that include the console or CON.

If Clarion does not recognize the device you've chosen as one of those listed in Table 6-1, it automatically assumes that what you've listed as the

Figure 6-6   This shows the Report Option window for setting the global information for a report in Designer. Here in the Setup Procedure is where you can declare what device you want to use for the report and the page length, both of which appear as attributes of the REPORT statement.

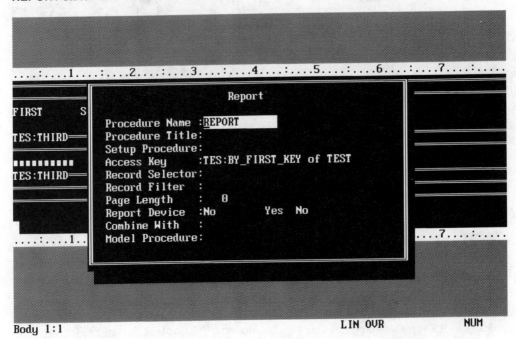

device is a DOS filename and it writes the report to that file on your disk. If you select the CON device to send the report to the screen, you won't get very good results for a long report without taking a couple of steps inside the code.

Sending Reports to the Screen: When you send a report to the CON device, you will probably want to achieve three changes. First, you will not want the system to overwrite whatever is on the screen and not restore it when finished. Even for a short report, that will leave your users with an active cursor on the screen where they chose to run the report, but little else to guide them. The underlying screen will have been erased by the output of the report. To solve that initial problem, you'll need to go into the Report Procedure and add a full-screen, window structure to the code. Then, you open that screen as the first step in the report and close it as the last step. Using a window like this saves the underlying screen while the report scrolls across the screen.

Table 6-1   The Report Devices Available for Receiving the Output of a Clarion Report Structure

Device	Description
CON	The monitor
PRN	Default
LPT1	Parallel port 1
LPT2	Parallel port 2
LPT3	Parallel port 3
AUX	Same as COM1
COM1	Serial port 1
COM2	Serial port 2
NUL	No device
"TEXT.TXT"	DOS file on disk

The second change is that of the actual setting of the device you said you wanted to use in the Report Options menu. All that answering "Yes" to that option does is place the phrase

```
DEVICE(MEM:DEVICE)
```

as an attribute in both the title and main body REPORT statements. The system, if you're using Designer, still doesn't know where you want to send the report. So, in the Setup Procedure in the Report Options screen, you must select the device you want to use. The following phrase routes the report to the monitor when the "Device" option in the Report Options screen is set to "Yes":

```
MEM:DEVICE = 'CON'
```

You'll need to use this procedure for all redirection of printing devices that you use while programming in Designer. You can also create a form to pop up when the report is selected to allow the user to set the report destination. In that case, MEM:DEVICE gets set by the user.

The third change you will want to make involves the control your user has over the report as it scrolls by. Remember, it is going to the screen as just another output device. There are no built-in controls to manage the data as it goes flying by. You must change the code that does the printing to effect that rapid scrolling. Chapter 11 has a discussion about how to make a change to the program to give your user control and a way to manually code sending reports to the screen.

The HEADER and FOOTER Statements

Headers and footers are handled differently in a Clarion Report structure. Clarion prints a header automatically after first starting the report. The footer gets printed after every page overflows with data requiring another page followed by a page break, and the header for the next page. You can, at any time, call for either the footer or header to be printed. When you set the page length, Clarion automatically prints headers and footers according to that page length—there is no explicit code causing them to be printed. In both cases, the position of the page and the lines following each item are determined by the page length specified in the Report structure and the size of the header or footer. Clarion automatically compensates for the size of each of the structures.

You can place whatever you want in both headers and footers from the record currently in memory, or you can add free text. If a header in Designer contains a field from the key used to access the file for the report, each time that field changes, the system performs a page break (that is, positions and prints the footer, sends a form feed to go to the next page, and prints the header) before continuing on with the detail lines.

 Hint: Printer control sequences do not increment the page or line counters; that is, they are nonprinting instructions to the printer that will not take up room on your report.

The Detail Lines

The detail lines in a Clarion report print as each record is read from the database. In most Designer-generated reports, you lay out those fields across the page, one field at a time. Then, as each detail structure is printed, Designer and the report formatter in Editor insert a line feed as it prints the last field to prepare for the next record to be printed. Normally, Clarion places the next field one column to the right of the last field, unless that line feed gets inserted. Good programming practice demands that limits be tested to place things properly.

The only irregularity that requires your attention in printing the detail lines appears with the memo field. Even though Designer shows the memo field as only one line, the width given in terms of columns in the file definition, the entire contents of the memo is printed as large as that field has been specified. The next record to be printed prints on the line after the last line of the memo.

Summary

Because output is not intelligible unless formatted before it is sent to a reproduction device, Clarion provides the same organizational flexibility on paper as it does on the screen without sacrificing ease of construction. In this chapter we focused on how the Report structure is put together and how that assembly affects the printed page according to both the printer's characteristics and the data files the report accesses.

Chapter 7

Application Design

Database Method

The Relational Model

Clarion's native database method is relational. It is not naturally a networked database. ("Network" in this sense refers to a particular data structure and not to whether Clarion supports multiuser systems.) In a networked database environment, the address of the data is maintained. You can have duplicate keys, but the keys are independent from the data to which they refer. Although you could create a network structure in Clarion using its file pointer facilities, none of the development tools provides much support for that. You would be going outside the realm of the Clarion system.

To get a better understanding of the theoretical underpinnings of Clarion's approach to database management, we'll turn to the two most prominent authorities on relational databases: E. F. Codd and C. J. Date. Employed by IBM since 1949, Codd was the originator of the relational model with his paper "Derivability, Redundancy, and Consistency of Relations Stored in Large Data Banks" (Codd, 1969). His most recent book, *The Relational Model for Database Management, Version 2*, published by Addison-Wesley in 1990, updates the model with new features. Date cofounded Codd and Date International as a consulting firm with Codd. Date's most recent book, *An Introduction to Database Systems*, Volume 1, Fifth Edition, also published by

Addison-Wesley in 1990, provides a more expansive and accessible introduction to the relational model, which is defined more abstractly by Codd.

There are twelve rules, according to Codd, that define a database management system as conforming to the relational model (the paraphrased rules are
from Date's book):

1. The information rule: information in a database must be represented
   only by values in column positions within rows of tables.
2. The guaranteed access rule: every individual scalar value in the
   database must be logically addressable by specifying the name of the
   containing table, the name of the containing column, and the primary
   key value of the containing row.
3. Systematic treatment of null values: missing and inapplicable information must be represented in a distinctly different manner than regular
   values, and independent of data type.
4. Active online catalog based on the relational model: an online, inline
   relational catalog must be accessible to users via query language.
5. The comprehensive data sublanguage rule: the sublanguage must
   a) have linear syntax; b) be useable both interactively and with applications; c) support data definition and manipulation, security and integrity constraints, and transaction management operations.
6. The view updating rule: all views that are theoretically updatable must
   be updatable by the system.
7. High-level insert, update, and delete.
8. Physical data independence.
9. Logical data independence.
10. Integrity independence.
11. Distribution independence.
12. The nonsubversion rule: the interface cannot allow "record-at-a-time"
    access to subvert the system by bypassing a relational security or
    integrity constraint.

Date defines a relational database in two separate areas of the fifth edition
of his book: first, as a database perceived by its users as a collection of tables
(and nothing but tables); and second, as a database perceived by the user as a
collection of time-varying, normalized relations of assorted degrees. (The
process of normalization will be discussed later in this chapter.)

I present this short list of the rules to give you an idea of the considerations
involved in relational database methodology. To truly understand these rules,
you may want to read the two books cited. The point of citing these references
to relational theory is to show that creating database applications can be a

disciplined endeavor. There are fundamental, proven concepts that might save you from needless complexity and later problems if you learn and adhere to them as you design systems. The Clarion language, though it does not contain *set* management language per se, contributes to creating theoretically solid applications.

Clarion's relational database language provides constructs for creating one-to-one, one-to-many, and, indirectly, many-to-many relationships. A one-to-one relationship exists, for example, when there is one social security number for each individual in the nation. The invoice is a classic example of a one-to-many relation: there is only one invoice number, but many items are listed in the invoice.

Figure 7-1 depicts a one-to-many relation. To match the illustration to the explanation in the caption, the arrows in the diagram point from the Primary Key Field to the Foreign Key Field in the subsidiary data file. In true relational modeling, they should be pointing the other way—from foreign key to primary key. (A primary key is the Key Field unique to each record in the data file. The foreign key is the Key Field in a data file that is the primary key for a related data file.) The many-to-many relation is the most difficult to construct and to track. An example of a database built on that scheme might be one to track a school's enrollment: there are many students and each one has registered for multiple seminars.

In Clarion, you can most easily construct a many-to-many relation with three files as demonstrated in Figure 7-2. A standard many-to-many relation means that a record in one of two data files can refer to multiple records in the other data file and vice versa. To handle that in Clarion, you place a file in the

Figure 7-1 The one-to-many relational database structure of Clarion using three files. Given the Customer Number from the first file, you can find out all the ordered items for that customer in the third file.

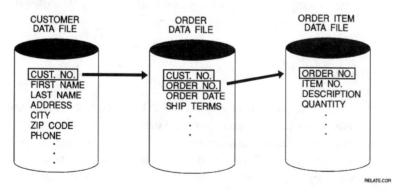

RELATE.COR

Figure 7-2   The Clarion solution to many-to-many database configuration using an interme-diate file to store the unique combinations between the two primary data files.

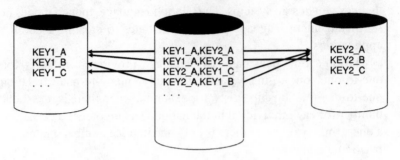

middle with a record that combines a key value from each data file with a uniquely keyed record for each connection between the original two data files.

Clarion's database implementation is relational because it relies on the specific contents of data fields, rather than on an internal database key or data storage addresses, to determine any connections between tables (called data files by Clarion). Think of it like this: it matters to Clarion who lives in the "house." In a network database, the address of the house is what establishes the relation.

Clarion is not, however, a strictly relational database according to doctrine because it does (optionally) allow duplicate primary key values to exist on the same table. That may offend the purists, but it makes life much easier when you want to build a database where the real world contains duplicates of a particular entity and it doesn't matter which of the duplicates is matched with a subordinate entity. The kitting function, that is, creating a tub of un-assembled parts in preparation for manufacturing, is a classic example. It doesn't matter which washers you combine with the bolts, and all the bolts are identical as long as they are the same part. Figure 7-3 shows the different schemes used for database configuration.

Data Design

The first job in designing an application in Clarion, as in all database develop-ment environments, is to determine the data entities, or classes of data, you'll need and the relations between them. That means finding out what persons, places, or things you'll have to organize in the data to automate the business functions designed to be covered by the application. An entity might be an Employee or a Mailing Address or an Inventory Item. Beside entities and their

Figure 7-3   The data structures for a relational database.

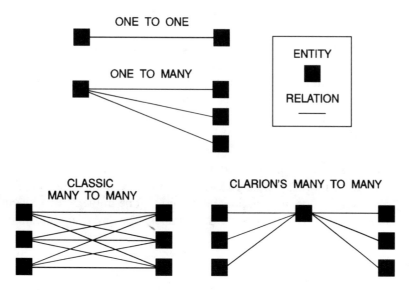

relations, the system will contain elements, called attributes, that modify the data, for example, a Currency Symbol Field in the record.

Relations depict interaction between elements of the data files that constitute a database. For example, an Order is the interaction between a Customer and an Item. Another sample relation is a membership: an Item holds membership as a Part in an Order. A third form of relation is referred to as "further definition," and an example would be a Customer Name that gives more detailed information about a Customer Number.

Some data structures can be difficult to classify as entities or relations. A data structure with information about a Department can be thought of as a relation between a Manager and her Employees, or it can be seen as an entity, as in Department of Transportation or Group 4. A data structure about Class can be the intersection of an Instructor, a particular Course, and a set of Students.

Normalization

Once you've pinned down the entities, you'll want to normalize the data to remove repeating groups and be sure that each Data Field in the table depends on the primary key and only the primary key. For instance, in constructing a database for video tapes, you might have included a catalog number in which the first four digits identify the studio that released the film. Thus every data file will contain duplications of the studio identification since each one has released a number of films. In this case, normalizing would remove the studio identifier to a new data file where each studio was listed only once, which makes the original data file smaller and more efficient.

Another step in the normalizing process is the removal of fields that can be derived from other data items and calculated either on the run or just before presenting the data. This would include totals of any kind, for example, an Extended Amount that was the product of Unit Price and Quantity Ordered. The goal of normalization is to make the database more efficient in terms of storage space occupied, speed of access, and ease of maintenance.

After trimming the stored data to just the necessary entities, associations between entities in a relational database can be implemented by embedding "foreign keys" or by creating other tables. For one-to-one relationships (an Employee has a Manager), you can embed the foreign key (for Manager) as a data element in the "owner" (Employee) table. For one-to-many relations, you can create a table that has a primary key consisting of the primary key of the "owner" plus the primary key of the "member" of the relation. (In the Assignments table, this would be: Employee with Project ID, or Project ID with Employee, depending on how you need to search through the data.)

Other Models (and Other Languages)

In a hierarchical model, the implementation of a one-to-many relationship would place the owner's primary key at the beginning of the member's data record. (In Figure 7-1, that would mean the primary key of the Customer data file (Customer Number) would appear at the beginning of the member's record (Order data file).) So, the Manager table may have a primary key (Manager), and the Employee table has the primary key (Manager, Employee). With this design, you'll repeat the Manager key value for each occurrence of a related Employee record. Because Manager is at the top of the primary key for the Employee table, you'll need that value first in order to search through the data. (In Chapter 9 we will discuss presetting that value in the Setup Procedure for a table.)

In a networked database, the address of the data, or its internal database key, is the means by which data are accessed and related to data in other tables. To establish a relationship between an Employee and a Project, the database key (an address pointer) for the particular Employee and the database key for the particular Project would be maintained in a separate table (say, Project-Employee). If you looked up all the Project-Employees (reading through the Project-Employee table), additional table reads issued to the Project and Employee tables would be required to determine which Employee and which Project are represented by the specific occurrence of Project-Employee.

This can also be done by setting aside a place on one of the tables to keep track of the occurrences of the other data with which this one participates. This is like having a list of Employees on the main Project Record. Processing this design can get quite involved, so it's better to split out this recurring group (Project-Employee) to another table.

Networked databases reduce data redundancy and storage requirements by using database keys or address pointers (which are generally shorter than the contents of a relational key) and they add some flexibility, but the input/output computational time costs of chasing down the real data once the address has been found are very high.

Clarion's Relational Model

Clarion provides a relational database access method. In a strictly defined relational database, each line of a Clarion data file is an element of the table where the first fields constitute the primary key. Consider an application that depicts Students, Courses, and their intersection, Enrollments. The relationship between Students and Classes is many-to-many because a student can take many courses and a course has many students. In a relational database structure, this model would be implemented with three files (or relational tables): Students with a primary key of Social Security Number; Courses with a primary key of Course Number, Year, Semester, Days Offered, and Instructor; and Enrollments. The Enrollments file (or relational table) would contain a record (or row in the table) for each valid Student/Course combination. In a relational database, these rows would include columns for the full primary keys of both tables in the relation.

Codd defines a properly constructed data file in a database as having one unique key as follows:

> Each base R-table has exactly one primary key. This key is a combination of columns (possibly just one column) such that: 1) the value of the primary key in each row of the pertinent R-table identifies that row uniquely (i.e., it distinguishes that row from every other row in that R-table); 2) if the primary key is a composite and if one of the columns is dropped from the primary key, the first property is no longer guaranteed.

In Clarion, you can designate a key to be unique and, for good database management practice, you should always define the primary key that way. Clarion provides lots of room to add more keys for performing specific functions. In opposition to the classical relational model as defined by Codd, C. J. Date, and others, Clarion allows you to create a data file with duplicate key values even if it is the primary or only key available. For instance, suppose the primary key for Courses cited in the preceding example was in use. Now, suppose you wanted to construct a report using the Selector function to allow only those courses held on Mondays to pass through the Selector into the report. If you used that key and preset the value for the Days Offered Field in the primary key, whatever values were contained in Course Number, Year, and Semester would also be used in the evaluation. Since you want *all* courses on Mondays, you don't need to include those other values in the filtering or selection process. So, in Clarion you can create a secondary key with only the Days Offered. Now, when you start that Table Procedure accessed via the secondary key, you'll get the results you sought.

Clarion's relational database structure duplicates the contents and type of field from one database to another. Using a common field to all the databases in a relational system, you can match a record in one database file with related records in another file. Clarion places those "keys" into separate files—both the data type and the contents. Because the key files are built from fewer fields, the searches through those files are much faster than a search that requires the system to examine *every* field in each data record. Designer naturally supports the keys and keyed lookup that gives Clarion its relational power.

The Impact of the Relational Model on Application Design

Clarion uses a one-to-many type of structure. That is, if you have *one* Customer Number (using the preceding ordering example) you can locate *many* of their orders and if you have *one* order number you can locate *many* related order items. That is the natural style for Designer. You can construct a second type of database with Clarion using the many-to-many structure as well. In that method, if you add a fourth file to the preceding example for multiple shipping addresses for each customer, you can relate a parts order through the invoice number to different shipping locations. That is, the many parts can be related to the many shipping addresses (where "many" means "more than one").

One of the hazards of working in a relational format is the possibility of filling your user's hard disk with unrelated information. That does not mean your software will be writing limericks out of the data that your users enter into the system. It does mean that you can easily delete the master record for a database, making "orphans" of related data throughout the system. Thus Clarion does not automatically provide complete means for maintaining relational integrity—you must create those procedures yourself. In fact, the only relational integrity Clarion can guarantee is to keep close watch on the creation of a record with a duplicate and warn you in those cases when you've designed a data file to have a unique key. The problem of orphans is one you'll have to iron out yourself. But don't despair. There are at least two solutions to this problem, which we'll look at in the next section.

Deleting the Children of a Master Record

The Problem: The goal of these procedures is to ensure that when a master or parent record is deleted, the related children are also deleted. If that doesn't happen, two problems ensue. First, and the least problematic, is the amount of unrecoverable storage that gets chewed up over time as you delete parent records who leave steadily growing numbers of orphans in the related file. To delete the orphans, you could ask the user to go to some sort of editing table and pull up the records individually, matching each one against the key information in the parent file. However, that requires you to directly view that related file when you could be adding those items behind the scenes. This would be an awfully cumbersome bookkeeping function as well as a sign of a poorly designed system.

The second problem that arises when you delete a parent and leave related records intact is that the parent key is no longer sensitive to the uniqueness of the deleted record. A new record—unrelated to the children of its predecessor—may be added to the system. If it's an accurate match to the deleted key value, that new record will have relatives popping out all over the place. Like someone who suddenly comes into a lot of money and develops close friends and relatives they didn't know they had, chances are those relationships aren't appropriate. Now the database is not only taking unnecessary space with orphans (children with no parents), it is corrupted. One way that corruption becomes evident is when a value gets inserted as a new primary key value that matches an older, deleted value with undeleted children in a related file. Suddenly, the new value has an instant family—unintentionally.

Two Solutions: You can use Designer to handle this child problem in two ways; the first method can be entered in a manually coded procedure, if you wish, and the second method involves a change to the model. In the Floppy

Disk Catalog System, the important maintenance task comes when you delete a Disk Label. You must ensure that the associated filenames are removed from the Files data file to keep the database clear of orphans.

The first method requires that you add something to the Setup Procedure to retain the ACTION setting and to the Next Procedure in the Update Form for the table from which you are deleting a parent record. Since the primary Update Form resets the global ACTION variable to indicate completion of editing the table that called it, we must retain that setting to perform a test on it in the Next Procedure. So, somewhere in the Setup Procedure, you should type: SAVEDACTION# = ACTION. Then, in the Setup Procedure, type the following:

```
IF ACTION = 3;FIL:NUMBER = DIS:NUMBER;DELCHILD.    !DELETE CHILDREN
```

Now, if you use Designer, you create an Other Procedure called DELCHILD so that the generated map in the main program file will contain that as a procedure. In a separate DOS file, you would enter the lines of code shown in Figure 7-4.

You could insert this code in your own manually coded Form Procedure to branch out to a related file, or you could use the INCLUDE statement to include the code in the Designer Form Procedure in the Next Procedure step. In either case, this executes only when the user is deleting a master record and only then if the procedure finds matches for the reference in the parent file.

Figure 7-4　The code for deleting potential orphans from a related file in the FLOPPY DISK CATALOG Program.

```
DELCHILD          PROCEDURE
NUMBER    STRING(4)                          !CREATE SAVED VARIABLE
  CODE                                       !START THE CODE
  NUMBER = FIL:NUMBER                        !RETAIN COMPARE FIELD
  SET(FIL:BY_NUMBER,FIL:BY_NUMBER)           !POSITION POINTER IN FILE
  LOOP UNTIL EOF(FILES)                      !LOOP UNTIL COMPLETE
    NEXT(FILES)                              ! READ THE NEXT  RECORD
    IF FIL:NUMBER <> NUMBER THEN BREAK.      ! LEAVE IF NO MORE VALID
    DELETE(FILES)                            ! DELETE RECORD
    .                                        !RECYCLE LOOP
```

A second method involves modifying the Form Procedure and the Table structure in the Standard Model. A similar method was derived by Ken Weiss of Watermark Consulting, author of the Watermark Models for Clarion and of an article in the *Clarion Technical Journal* on the subject of relational integrity. Though derived separately, both approaches were confined to the facilities available in Designer. This procedure is not a native Designer construction. The first step is to modify the model procedure for a FORM.

 Hint: Make a copy of the original model procedure and rename it within the model file whenever you want to create a new method. Never modify the original version.

The copy of the Form Procedure will be called RELFORM, and the change shown in Figure 7-5 should be made to the LAST_FIELD process in the Case structure within the FORM.

The Form Procedure provides for three positions to update three different secondary files. As discussed in Chapter 10, normally this procedure merely replaces the values related to the secondary files with a PUT. As you can see from the ELSE section of the area we are concerned with in Figure 7-5, this section of the Form Procedure code executes just after the primary file Edit Procedure takes place. We want to call the Delete Procedure for the related files only when the primary file has performed a deletion, which, as you can see from the Execute structure, is the result when ACTION is set to 3.

Designer uses the @FILENAME keyword to insert the secondary filenames you entered in the Form Procedure Options window. Notice that each file must have its own procedure. However, you can use the same model procedure for all three as we will soon discuss. The unique identifier for each procedure that you create *must* be preceded by an underscore. No other character will successfully compile, although several will actually perform the substitution during Designer's code generating.

The Form Procedure provides the only Options window (of the Designer procedures) involved in the exchange of TABLE to FORM in the course of deleting a record that will give us access to the filenames of the secondary files *and* the proper setting of the ACTION variable. Just as the Table Options window is the only one that will provide access to the file keys, we need this procedure to efficiently delete records from the related files.

Notice that ACTION is set to zero when the LAST_FIELD code is complete. That signals the TABLE that the editing action was successful. We can no longer track the kind of editing that was called without using an additional variable in the calling Table Procedure. We will actually manufacture a procedure name on the fly when Designer replaces the keyword with the real

Figure 7-5   The modification necessary in a copy of the Form Procedure called DELFORM to initiate the deletion of potential orphans in a related file.

```
OF ?LAST_FIELD                  !FROM THE LAST FIELD
  EXECUTE ACTION                ! UPDATE THE FILE
    ADD(@FILENAME)              !   ADD NEW RECORD
    PUT(@FILENAME)              !   CHANGE EXISTING RECORD
    DELETE(@FILENAME)           !   DELETE EXISTING RECORD
  .
  IF ERRORCODE( ) = 40          !  DUPLICATE KEY ERROR
    MEM:MESSAGE = ERROR( )      !  DISPLAY ERR MESSAGE
    SELECT(2)                   !  POSITION TO TOP OF FORM
    CYCLE                       !  GET OUT OF EDIT LOOP
  ELSIF ERROR( )                ! CHECK FOR UNEXPECTED ERROR
    STOP(ERROR( ))              !  HALT EXECUTION
  .                             !  TERMINATES IF STRUCTURE
  .                             !  TERMINATES CASE STRUCTURE
```

The decision point to initiate the child delete procedure.

```
IF ACTION = 3
  @FILENAME2_CHILD1             !  DELETE RELATED FILES
  @FILENAME3_CHILD2             !  DELETE RELATED FILES
  @FILENAME4_CHILD3             !  DELETE RELATED FILES
ELSE
  PUT(@FILENAME2)               !  UPDATE SECONDARY FILES
  PUT(@FILENAME3)               !  UPDATE SECONDARY FILES
  PUT(@FILENAME4)               !  UPDATE SECONDARY FILES
.
```

```
@NEXTFORM                       !  CALL NEXT FORM PROCEDURE
ACTION = 0                      !  SET ACTION TO COMPLETE
RETURN                          !  AND RETURN TO CALLER
```

filename. If this procedure was, indeed, an update, then the PUT takes place normally. However, if a record is being deleted from the parent file, this modification calls for up to three other files to be inspected for related records and purged also.

The next step is to create a special form of TABLE, with a status display screen for each record it finds and deletes in the related file. Copy the normal Table Procedure in the model and then begin whittling it down. Replace the calls to higher level keyword procedures with the keywords you actually need, as shown in Figure 7-6.

This model code is slightly different than the standard model procedures. First, the screen that displays is fixed and cannot be modified from within Designer. When you use this model procedure in an application, for your own bookkeeping, paint a screen inside Designer containing text describing the underlying process. The code generated for this procedure always shows the same status screen.

After you have created the model procedure as shown in Figure 7-6, execute the following steps to ensure that potential orphans are deleted from related files when you delete from the master or parent file.

1. Within Designer, go to the Form Procedure used as the Update Form of the table that displays the parent records. Place the correct names of the secondary files related to the records in that parent file into the Form Options window.
2. Place the name of the revised Form Procedure in the model procedure slot of the Form Options window (in this case, it's called RELFORM).
3. Create a new Table Procedure and give it the filename of the file related to the parent that it will be accessing, appended with the word CHILD1. If more than one related file is entered into the Form Options window of the parent file's update form, be sure you add the number (CHILD1, CHILD2, . . .) in the right order.
4. Place the parent variable in the Setup Procedure of the Table Options window that you just created. This is compared against the related records in the secondary file that this Table Procedure will be examining.
5. Do not include an Update Procedure.
6. Put the primary key variable that relates to the parent file into the Access Key slot of the Table Options window for the secondary file delete table.
7. Place the name of the key variable from this secondary file, which equates to the key variable from the parent file, in the Record Selector slot.
8. Type in the name of the special model procedure you created patterned after Figure 7-6.

Figure 7-6   The model procedure in the Standard Model for processing potential orphan deletes from files related to the primary file.

```
*CHILD*********************************************************  *
@PROCNAME      PROCEDURE

SCREEN    SCREEN       WINDOW(10,48),HUE(7,0)
          ROW(1,1)     STRING('<218,196{46},191>')
          ROW(2,1)     REPEAT(8);STRING('<179,0{46},179>') .
          ROW(10,1)    STRING('<192,196{46},217>')
          ROW(5,15)    STRING('Deleted Records:')
          ROW(9,14)    STRING('*'),HUE(30,0)
            COL(18)    STRING('DO NOT INTERRUPT'),HUE(30,0)
            COL(36)    STRING('*'),HUE(30,0)
MESSAGE       ROW(2,5) STRING(40)
COUNT         ROW(5,32) STRING(@N4)


  GROUP,PRE(SAV)
    @SELECTFIELDS                               !SELECT FIELDS
  .
CODE
OPEN(SCREEN)                                    !DISPLAY STATUS SCREEN
MESSAGE = CENTER('DELETING CHILDREN FROM: ' |
           & '@FILENAME'& '.DAT',SIZE(MESSAGE)) !POST PROCESSING MESSAGE
CACHE(@KEYNAME,.25)                             !CACHE KEY FILE
@SAVEFIELD = @FIELD                             !SAVE COMPARISON VALUE
SET(@KEYNAME,@KEYNAME)                          !  POSITION POINTER IN FILE
LOOP UNTIL EOF(@FILENAME)                       !LOOP UNTIL COMPLETE
  NEXT(@FILENAME)                               ! READ THE NEXT RECORD
  IF @FIELD <> @SAVEFIELD THEN BREAK.           ! LEAVE IF NO MORE VALID
  COUNT += 1                                    ! INCREMENT COUNTER
  DELETE(@FILENAME)                             ! OTHERWISE DELETE RECORD
  .                                             !RECYCLE LOOP
CLOSE(SCREEN)                                   !REMOVE THE SCREEN
RETURN                                          !GO TO CALLING PROC
```

9. Select the message you want to display to yourself while the code is generating. Type the message onto the screen where you would normally paint the fields and other items for the table. Whatever you do at this point will not show in the completed application. If you examine the special model code we created, the Screen structure shown in Figure 7-7 is hard coded and does not contain any of the normal keywords Designer uses to construct the screens you build.

The preceding steps should allow you to delete the related records from a file automatically. If no secondary files exist, these steps will not have any impact at all. (The concepts behind the modification to the model used in this example will be discussed in Chapter 15.)

Figure 7-7 The file delete display hard-coded into the model procedure for deleting potential orphans from data files related to deleted master file records.

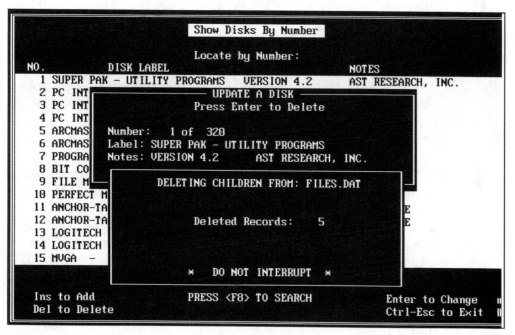

Manual Coding and Designer

If you visit the electronic mail channels like CompuServe and Clarion's BBS, where you see Clarion discussed, you'll probably also see a debate on using Designer versus manual coding. There are true believers on both sides of the issue. What matters most, though, is the method you choose for each circumstance. Throughout this book, we try to show both methods so that you come to a better overall understanding of Clarion. The trick is in knowing when to break out of Designer and when to stay in it.

Designer's Role

Applications Manager: In a departure from traditional programming styles, Designer provides an environment that will help you keep track of your work. In more traditional modes, you would maintain a text file or some other means to keep track of which modules were included in your program and which DOS files held those modules. That can get fairly messy, and you are in constant danger of losing an important "include" file or of copying over the top of your latest revision from an archive. There are products that will document the code for you, but they are usually not included with the development environment.

With Designer, you can manage your application a little more closely and with a little more assurance. In the first place, if you stay inside Designer, you will have, at the very least, some method for identifying the modules you need to include in the program. There are some precautions you should consider, however.

The Application Tree pictured in Figure 7-8 describes the dependencies of the procedures in the FLOPPY DISK CATALOG program. The Update Procedures appear below their associated Table Procedure and any other procedure called from inside a procedure (like lookup tables or Other Procedures) appear beneath the calling procedure. If you place a procedure in a line (like in a Setup Procedure for a table) and include additional code (like a conditional statement), the procedure you call will appear at the bottom of the Application Tree without any visible connections.

Hint: You can choose from more than one Update Procedure for editing a table. For instance, if you wanted to show different information depending on which key was pressed (<INS>, <ENTER> or <DEL>), you would insert the following code in the Update Procedure slot of the Table Options window:

```
IF ACTION = 1;ADD_FORM;ELSIF ACTION = 2;EDIT_FORM;ELSE DEL_FORM.
```

This code calls a different form depending on whether you are adding, editing, or deleting data from the table. However, none of these procedures will show their connections to the table on the Application Tree.

In each Options window, you are provided a means for entering a description for each procedure. This description appears to the right of the procedure name. For Other Procedures, the end of the description line includes the name of the DOS file that contains the procedure as it will be identified in the Map of the main program module. When you create a procedure in your application that Designer does not link with a line, it's a good idea to document that connection by typing the related procedure's name in the Description lines for both the called and the calling procedure. This works like quick shorthand to help you keep track of where your procedures link up in the Application Tree.

You cannot move the references to procedures within the Application Tree. Each item appears in the order in which it is called from the menu. You can

Figure 7-8   The Application Tree for the FLOPPY DISK CATALOG program. Notice the reference in the FILES_CHILD1 procedure up to the procedure in the top of the tree that calls it, UPD_DISKS.

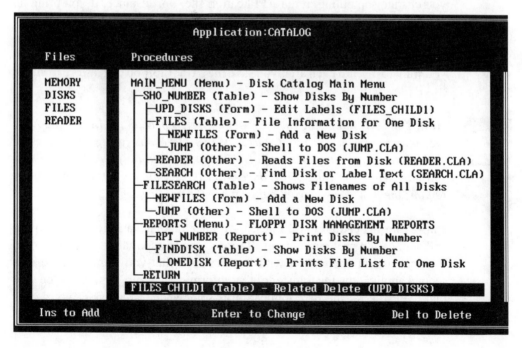

rename and reorder them, if you like, by changing their position in the menu. For unlinked procedures, they are shown in the order in which they were created. In addition, for both the Application Tree and the File list, you can get printed summaries of each side of the screen by placing the cursor on that side and pressing the CTRL-L combination. On the files side, you can get more detailed file and variable information by going into the file definition and pressing the same key combination.

The all-important file you need to track while using Designer is the .APP file. You can re-create your entire application (without the Other Procedures) from that file alone. If for some reason that file is damaged, you can replace it by copying the .BAP file and giving it the extension .APP.

WARNING
Always copy and never rename the .BAP file. If you do, and the same conditions exist that damaged your original application file (.APP), you will lose your application.

When you archive your development work, be sure to archive both the .APP and the .BAP files. The Backup APplication file is created whenever you change something in the APPlication file. For instance, if you bring an old application into a new version of Clarion, the old .APP file is converted and a new version of the .BAP file is created in the same form that the application was in when you got into it. That way, if you make changes that you want to discard even after you save the .APP file, you can restore from the .BAP file.

Hint: You can change the Base Procedure referenced in the Base window of the application when you first start Designer merely by typing in a new Base Procedure. It will appear as a ToDo in the Application Tree. Alternatively, you can delete the Base Procedure from the Application Tree and simply rename the new one you want called when the application first starts.

Importing Procedures and Files: Another major advantage of prototyping and application programming in Clarion is the transportability of your code. If you write an application with features in it that you want to reuse in a second application, the transfer of that information is very easy. First, be sure that .APP file for the first application is somewhere on a disk drive in your system. While in the newly created .APP file inside Designer, press the

CTRL-G key combination. That will create a screen as shown in Figure 7-9. With this function, you can retrieve a procedure—lock, stock, and barrel—from the first application to insert into the new application, and all you have to do is give it a name unique to the current application. If you can't remember the name of the procedure you want, or if you can't find it in the directory you first entered, use the wildcard character (*) to enter file specifications that will pop up a list of the candidates in each area: procedures, files, and subdirectories. Check the *Clarion Utilities Guide* for Getting File definitions with CTRL-G; you'll have to extrapolate from that description and from what you have read here for "getting" procedures.

However, be careful about what happens next. If you changed the variable definitions, or the variables used in the old procedure do not exist in the new application, the procedure will have blanks where the fields should appear in the screen definitions. You can solve this problem in two ways. First, you can insert the field definitions (which you have written down from the old application) into the data files referenced by the procedures you imported. Go to

Figure 7-9 Using the CTRL-G key combination to copy a procedure within the same application in Designer. You can use this function to transfer a procedure definition from any other .APP file in your system.

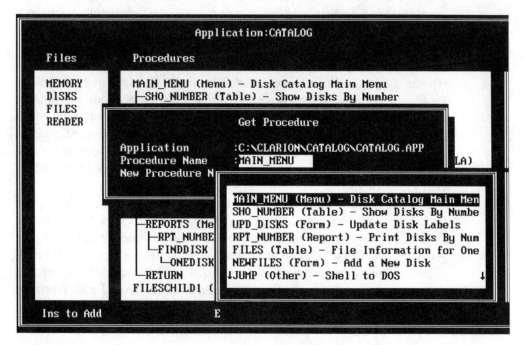

the appropriate file definition and place the variable there. Second, you can use the CTRL-G key combination in the *files* area to get the entire data file definition from the old application. Once you bring in the procedures, you can use the CTRL-O key combination to look at the Options window for the procedure to see exactly which of the files from the old application you were using. For Form Procedures, the filename will be given. The Table Procedures will show the key used to access the table. Menu Procedures, of course, don't usually reference a file.

Hint: *When you import a procedure from another application, don't bring its display screen up on your monitor immediately. Check to make sure the data file or the variables referenced by the procedure exist in the new application. If you view the procedure's display first and save the newly named imported procedure before its associated data file exists in the .APP, all the references to fields in the procedure that don't match both filename and field name will be lost, including any code you inserted into the Edit, Setup, or Next Procedures.*

The pop-up window in Figure 7-10 lists all the available procedures. You place the highlight bar on the procedure you want and press ENTER. Then you'll be asked to give the procedure a new name. If you are transferring the procedure from another application, you can keep the same name as long as it doesn't conflict with one already in the current application.

Fast Prototyping Using Quick Start: One terrifically fast way to prototype an application can be constructed from the Quick Start function and Designer's ability to import procedures from other applications. Start out by identifying the different modules of your program and single out the largest of these. Determine the data dictionary and decide on the file configuration you'll be using. Now go into Designer and create an application for that largest module. When the system asks if you want to Quick Start, answer yes (Y).

You'll only be able to create modules with one data file, so choose the largest one you'll be using in each module to enter into Quick Start. Add the Data Fields (up to ten) into the Quick Start form and let the .APP file generates code. Don't choose more than one field to be a Key Field for each of the ten fields you enter during this procedure. If you do, Designer will generate matching Table and Form Procedures for each Key Field. When the new .APP file finishes generating code, Clarion leaves you in the Application

Figure 7-10   The pop-up list of files in the current subdirectory eligible for importing into the .APP file list on the left of the Application Tree. It is possible to re-create a file definition even if all you have is the old data file.

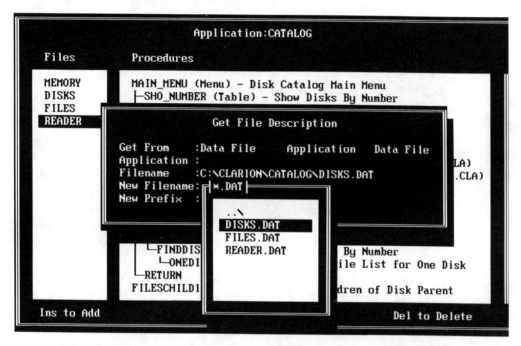

Tree. Repeat this step, creating separate .APP files for each major module of your program.

The next step is to return to the first .APP file and load it into Designer. Set this up as your main (and final) application, ensuring that the .APP filename is the one you want to use for your application, and so on. (Changing the name of the final executable program you create in Clarion will not affect its operation. You can choose a Designer .APP filename that is easier to work with or document and it won't necessarily be the starting name for your application when it's done.) You should already have the file structure written down (from when you first designed it). Keep it handy, and begin importing the file definitions from the other .APP files that you'll be needing. The amount of definition you can do with Quick Start is fairly limited, so you may want to spend some time later refining the variable definitions. However, don't actually do it yet or you'll foul up the procedure importing we're about to start.

Hint: If you import a Menu Procedure, all the procedure calls it makes will appear with the procedure name and ToDo where the description would be. If you plan to import a whole menu structure, get the Menu Procedure first and then you'll have its descendent procedure name for reference.

The last step is to use the CTRL-G function (as shown in Figure 7-10 for Data File importing) to bring in the procedures from the other .APP files into the Master file. You can't duplicate the names of any existing procedures, and the file definitions must match with a file in the current application. After you bring in all the procedures, you can insert your custom model procedures and custom code (with INCLUDEs, and Other, Edit, Setup, and Next Procedures) and then generate the application.

In just a few minutes, you can generate a complete application. With this approach, however, you are limited to the screen look that Clarion designed into Quick Start-generated code and, of course, you have to write in any relational hooks that you want. However, as a prototyping tool, it works very well.

The Source Code:　Even if you let Designer generate the source code, you still have a responsibility to maintain that code. Few serious application programmers will create applications in Designer that do not include some manual coding—in the setup for a Table or Form Procedure or in the Edit Procedure of a field. The nice part about Designer is that including those items in those spots lodged inside Designer helps retain the code if you retain good archives for the .APP file. However, if you add Other Procedures or make function calls to separate modules, you will need to keep track of them. A simple convention like a text file that travels with the .APP file can make all the difference. Another method you can use is to copy the Standard Model file and keep your documentation in the top of that file to be included in the .CLA files when they are generated.

Since the .CLA files for an application write over their previous versions, you don't want to make any notes you intend to be permanent in those files. However, many programmers create an application in pure Designer, develop it to a point, and then work with just the last generation of the code directly—never to return to Designer.

Still another and popular approach is to manually code everything outside of Designer. This approach relies on the power of the Clarion language and works very well. Many people, who began working with Clarion *before* Designer was introduced, bought the language—and many still do—for the power of the language itself. However, some of the productivity benefits that

Designer offers are not available under this approach. You can, though, use templates of code you have designed yourself and merely copy them into a new application. The modularity of the Clarion language supports this approach well.

One of the ways you can teach yourself the Clarion language is by writing a program with Designer and looking at how it creates the program in the language.

Hint: The Designer way of writing programs is not the only way to program in Clarion. It is limited by Clarion's intent to enable Designer to handle a wide variety of applications.

You can increase the readability of your programs in several ways.

- Comment the code you place into Setup, Edit, and Next Procedures by preceding the comment with an exclamation mark.
- Use the LIST compiler directive to add any code directly to the generated program when you have set some of the program off in an INCLUDE module. This will not appear in the code generated by Designer, but in the listing the compiler can optionally create during compile time.
- Follow the indentation practices of Designer, or adopt your own and stay consistent. Two useful modifications to Designer's output (and these can be placed in the model through global search and replace) include using the word END to terminate a structure instead of the period that Clarion uses. In addition, when manually coding, you can indicate the type of structure you are terminating as in END!IF and END!LOOP.
- Always document the changes to your source code. In Designer you can, using a hot-key combination hidden from the user, display a full-screen form with the information about a piece of code. Attaching that to your .APP file ensures you that the documentation will travel with the application and can be easily viewed. Use the modified model procedure for a form shown in Figure 7-11. For manually and Designer-coded programs (using the model procedure in Figure 7-11), the documentation should include enough information to tell a new programmer how to view the program or the module. Another useful method, though it forces you to keep track of more files, is to INCLUDE a document file in the setup of each procedure inside Designer (using the OMIT directive) that will become listed in the archived program files after compilation.

Figure 7-11   A model procedure for a form to display the modification history of a program from inside the Designer .APP file.

```
*DOCUFORM**********************************************************
 @PROCNAME     PROCEDURE

SCREEN        SCREEN        PRE(SCR),@SCREENOPT  ! SCREEN STRUCTURE
                           @PAINTS               ! FOREGROUND/BACKGROUND
                           .                     ! END OF SCREEN
STRUCTURE

CODE                                             ! START PROGRAM
OPEN(SCREEN)                                      ! DISPLAY DOCUMENT
ASK                                               ! WAIT FOR KEYSTROKE
CLOSE(SCREEN)                                     ! CLOSE DISPLAY
RETURN                                            ! GO BACK TO PROGRAM
```

Programming in Editor

Adherents to the manual coding approach to Clarion take maximum advantage of Clarion's efficient language and the robust tools it provides to develop an application. What are normally considered separate products in most of its competitors, Clarion wraps up into one bundle. The Editor provides a limited macro facility for creating your own automatic structures as well as the formatters for creating screens and reports by "painting" them on the screen.

There are many elements of the Clarion environment that just cannot be used in "pure Designer." For instance, you can use the Editor to list a whole bevy of special functions in one module file. You can refer to each function individually rather than include the whole file, or split each function into its own INCLUDE file. For instance, if you have a function for calculating the day of the week in the same file as other such utilities, you can ask the compiler to include only the one function by using the statement INCLUDE('UTILFILE.CLA',DAY_OF_WEEK).

The Debugger in the Processor provides a view of the internal workings of your program. However, the Debugger is not a full-screen, interactive debugging tool. You cannot set a value to monitor and have the system stop when it encounters that value. Although you can step through the program, the Debugger screen pops on and off the screen and makes it difficult to follow what is happening in the code. You can, however, stop and look at exactly where you are in the program when you are running in the processor, much like the stopping point depicted in Figure 7-12.

The examples of code throughout this book are mixed between manually coded procedures and those created with Designer. How you prefer to approach the programming task will help you decide which method to use. Facilities like the Debugger and Editor can be used in either mode. More important, though, you'll need to analyze the application you are about to create. You can use the Language Extension Module concept to augment the Clarion environment to fit the specific task you have.

However, Clarion's approach to relational databases via Designer or the language itself must factor heavily in your decision to apply the language to your task. It is best that you adopt standards for yourself and for others who may work on projects with you. Consider the programmer who created the application for the client with a multiuser system. Allowed to use a primary key with duplicates, the users of the system quickly got befuddled over whose record of a customer was accurate. That example may not be as far-fetched as

Figure 7-12 The Clarion Debugger displaying the source code below the line where program processing was suspended by the CTRL-BREAK key combination. From this point you could leave the processor by pressing the CTRL-BREAK key combination again or continue by pressing CTRL-ENTER. You cannot edit the code from here.

```
                         The CLARION Debugger

NO.       Stopped for:Ctrl-Break
  1 S     Stopped at :CATAL003/UPD_DISKS/36        (Ctrl-S for source)
  3 P     Called from:CATAL002/SHO_NUMBER/227      (Ctrl-F for source)
  4 P     Memory left:46K                          (Ctrl-X to execute)
  5 A
  6 A     36:   ACCEPT                                    !READ A F
  7 P     37:   IF KEYCODE() = REJECT_KEY THEN RETURN.    !RETURN O
  8 B     38:   EXECUTE ACTION                            !SET MESS
  9 F     39:     MEM:MESSAGE = 'Record will be Added'    !
 10 P     40:     MEM:MESSAGE = 'Record will be Changed'  !
 11 A     41:     MEM:MESSAGE = 'Press Enter to Delete'   !
 12 A     42:   .
 13 L     43:   IF KEYCODE() = ACCEPT_KEY                 !ON SCREE
 14 L     44:     UPDATE                                  !  MOVE A
 15 M     45:     SELECT(?)                               !  START
 16 M     46:     SELECT                                  !  EDIT A
          47:     CYCLE                                   !  GO TO
          48:   .
Ins    CATAL003.CLA 36:1                                        ge
Del                                                             xit
```

it sounds, but it illustrates the basic point that Clarion's power can easily lead to the construction of bad as well as good applications.

Much is handled inside the language, issues like memory consumption and port addressing that programmers struggling with lower level languages must face. Your task is a little easier. However, you may find that screens are so easy to generate that you get creative and adopt a different exiting method and a rotating selection of function keys to perform certain actions and window colors and painted tracks to the extent that your user would be less confused by a kaleidoscope!

Designer, by its all-around application-generating nature, creates a larger program than one hand-coded by an experienced Clarion programmer. It is also true that there is a growing market for third-party products and versions of the models that allow you to expand the language even further. The key is planning. The faster you can create an application custom fit to your specification, the more important it becomes to diagram the relations within the data you plan to manage in the application and to write out a standard for the screen methodology you'll use. Of course, the better you get to know Clarion, the easier this will be.

Summary

Clarion provides a rich environment for developing a wide variety of application software for the PC. It is not limited only to database work—though that is its strongest suit. Certain limitations exist when you use the Designer method to produce that software, but you can get as sophisticated as you like when you use the bare code—including inventing your own functions using the Language Extension Module (LEM) concept. In this chapter, we covered the methods of database design you need to know to take maximum advantage of the Clarion environment. We discussed different approaches you can take to solving common application development problems in bare Clarion and in Designer.

Chapter 8

Menu Techniques

The term "menu" intentionally conveys an image of a list of selections from which you pick what you want. With a menu-driven interface you don't have to remember how to operate the system from a command prompt. Clarion provides a rich environment for creating this kind of guide for the users of your program. You can get very creative and let Clarion do the underlying work for you.

A black box function performs tasks and causes reactions that you don't program directly. However, when you use a black box, you must be aware of those tasks and reactions to intelligently program the function. As a rule, because Clarion does take care of so much, you need to know what Clarion is doing so you can take full advantage of it in your applications.

There are two explicit references to menus in Clarion—the MENU statement itself and the screen form called a menu that is available in Designer. In both cases, the use of the MENU statement (the black box) creates the separate entity called a menu. Everything else associated with menus is just an application of the Clarion language's general capabilities.

So, what are the events and reactions that MENU causes inside of Clarion? They include maintaining a numeric index for each item in the menu and automatically interpreting the cursor key movements to move the highlight bar between those elements based on the ACCEPT statement. Once you make a selection, the CHOICE( ) function uses the numeric index to report on which item you selected, as shown in Figure 8-1.

Figure 8-1   The CHOICE( ) function detects which item a user selects when an ACCEPT statement processes the CHOICE( ) functon with the Enter key. The number of the item is determined by the number of the line it occupies beneath the MENU statement.

MENU STRUCTURE
  POSITION ONE
  POSITION TWO   CHOICE( )   2
  POSITION THREE

The Menu Command

The MENU command appears only in a Screen structure. You cannot use this command in the CODE segment of your program. In Chapter 4, you'll find the discussion of how to set up a menu inside a Screen structure. However, when you construct a Screen structure with a MENU structure, you now have access in the main CODE segment to control information supplied by the MENU.

The segment of code in Figure 8-2 is the simplest menu program possible within the limits Clarion imposes (an ACCEPT turns the menu on and any Clarion program must have at least one open screen).

Hint: A statement is a one-word command which performs some action. Statements often initiate a structure. A structure is a series of statements that perform together for a specific and often-used purpose. For instance, a CASE statement initiates the processing for a structure where subsidiary OF statements (not useable anywhere else) test the value of a condition established by the CASE statement.

The MENU statement looks at the lines of code beneath it as the menu selections. You cannot insert other lines of code in this structure. Editor knows this and, while in the screen formatter, will not allow you to choose any other screen field type after inserting a Menu Field. Using the MENU structure, the CHOICE( ) function can extract the number of the line below MENU you select by completing the ACCEPT (that is, when the highlight bar rests on a menu item and you press the Enter key). However, as long as you leave the row and column settings alone, you can reposition these string statements in your code and not affect the order in which they are processed. That number is determined by the order in which they appear on the screen.

Figure 8-2   This short program demonstrates a simple MENU structure. Enter and compile this short program to see the cursor and highlight control that the MENU statement provides separately from anything you write in your program. (The screen this program paints appears in Figure 8-3.)

```
MENUS           PROGRAM

SCREEN SCREEN          WINDOW(14,48),HUE(7,0)
          ROW(1,15)    PAINT(1,20),HUE(0,7)
          COL(1)       STRING('<201,205{13},0{20},205{13},187>')
          ROW(2,1)     REPEAT(12);STRING('<186,0{46},186>') .
          ROW(14,1)    STRING('<200,205{46},188>')
          ROW(1,16)    STRING('DEMONSTRATION MENU')
          ROW(4,3)     MENU,USE(MENU_HOLDER"),REQ,IMM
          ROW(5,15)         STRING('FIRST MENU SELECTION')
          ROW(7,15)         STRING('SECOND MENU SELECTION')
          ROW(9,15)         STRING('THIRD MENU SELECTION')
          .        .
          CODE
          OPEN(SCREEN)
          ACCEPT
          CLOSE(SCREEN)
          RETURN
```

Figure 8-3   The result of compiling and running the program in Figure 8-2.

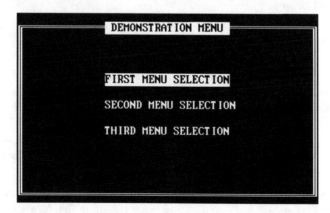

Hint: When you create a menu with Editor's screen formatter, the line of code with MENU in it will not display on the user's screen. You cannot write over the top of that statement with another field unknowingly. Unless you provide an on-screen parameter to the MENU statement for displaying the DESC attribute, it does not show up on the screen at all.

With the USE parameter of MENU, you can use other Clarion functions to track which menu item was selected and to control other functions. (The USE parameter of a MENU statement stipulates the name of the USE variable, as it is referred to in the *Clarion Language Reference*.) Normally the USE parameter, when displayed on the screen, shows the same text as the STRING parameter of the selected menu item. If you use the DESC attribute for the STRING, you can display that instead. In either case, there are a number of things you can do outside of the standard approach of launching another procedure.

The primary function of the USE parameter is to provide the memory variable. You can do this in two ways: with an implicit variable (as Designer does) or with a field equate label. With the implicit variable, the menu retains whichever item was selected to launch another procedure. When control returns to the menu, the highlight returns to that item instead of going to the top menu item, as is the Clarion default. For example,

```
ROW(4,3)    MENU,USE(MENU_HOLDER"),REQ,IMM
```

Hint: The local variables of a procedure retain their values as long as the procedure is invoked. That means if procedure A calls procedure B, procedure A's variables will stay set while procedure B runs. However, remember that if an overlay is reloaded, its variables are reinitialized to blank or to their default values.

The second method is to use a field equate label. For example,

```
ROW(4,3)    MENU,USE(?MENU_HOLDER),REQ,IMM


MENU_HOLDER           STRING(80)
```

In that case, however, you must define the variable somewhere. If you define it locally, it acts substantially the same as the implicit variable in the first method. However, you need to track menu selections even in closed Menu Procedures. In that case, you can define a tracking variable for each menu in your system in the global memory area. If you do that, you can restore a user's favorite menu picks from memory to speed entry. The preceding example of code shows how you would use the field equate label and how you would define the variable (as either local within the procedure or in global memory).

The Designer Menu Version

Designer creates the code for a Menu Procedure using generic structures that attempt to give you some flexibility in how you create Designer's menus. As with all the code that Designer generates, some of the code wouldn't be needed in a hand-coded procedure. Studying Clarion's method for one form of menu structure will help you understand how to use the language to create your own menus. In addition, by studying the way that Designer writes a menu, you can make small modifications—should they be needed—and remain within Designer. This is true especially since, like all Designer-created code, there are elements of the language Designer does not support that you might want to use.

The Designer-generated menus take advantage of the MENU statement, ACCEPT statement, color of the menu choice when selected, and the embedded function within MENU that allows you to start a menu choice by pressing the first letter. A Designer menu does not incorporate the MENU parameter, the DESC attribute, the KEY attribute to reassign which key will invoke the selection, the HLP attribute to assign help to each selection, or the IMM attribute to actuate the selection immediately after it is selected.

In using Designer to create a menu form, you have other functions available, including tying the selection to the procedure it will call, providing an Entry Field for setting a USE variable, and providing four different display variables to present items in the menu other than selections. These elements are all demonstrated later in this chapter.

A Sample Menu Procedure—Standard Designer

The code for the sample data entry menu shown in Figure 8-4 appears in Figure 8-5.

The Opening of the Menu Procedure: At the top of the procedure, of course, Designer always inserts the screen for the procedure. In Designer, it is not possible to create a procedure *without* a Screen structure. After the Screen structure is established, the CODE section of the program opens the actual processing.

Figure 8-4   Sample data entry menu.

Figure 8-5   This menu form choice appears exactly as Designer generated it.

```
          MEMBER('TEST')
MENU          PROCEDURE

SCREEN        SCREEN WINDOW(11,36),PRE(SCR),HUE(7,0)
              ROW(1,1)    STRING('<201,205{6},0{22},205{6},187>')
              ROW(2,1)    REPEAT(9);STRING('<186,0{34},186>') .
              ROW(11,1)   STRING('<200,205{8},0{19},205{7},188>')
              ROW(1,9)    STRING('DATA ENTRY MAIN MENU')
              ROW(11,10)  STRING('Press <<F1> for Help')
                COL(29)   ENTRY,USE(?FIRST_FIELD)
                COL(29)   ENTRY,USE(?PRE_MENU)
                COL(29)   MENU,USE(MENU_FIELD"),REQ
              ROW(3,6)    STRING('Editing Table by Last Name')
              ROW(5,3)    STRING('Editing Table by Customer Number')
              ROW(7,13)   STRING('Reports Menu')
              ROW(9,17)   STRING('QUIT')
                      .             .

  EJECT
  CODE
  OPEN(SCREEN)                             !OPEN THE MENU SCREEN
```

(continued)

Figure 8-5 *continued*

```
SETCURSOR                              !TURN OFF ANY CURSOR
MENU_FIELD" = ''                       !START MENU WITH FIRST ITEM
LOOP                                   !LOOP UNTIL USER EXITS
  ALERT                                !TURN OFF ALL ALERTED KEYS
  ALERT(REJECT_KEY)                    !ALERT SCREEN REJECT KEY
  ALERT(ACCEPT_KEY)                    !ALERT SCREEN ACCEPT KEY
  ACCEPT                               !READ A FIELD OR MENU CHOICE
  IF KEYCODE() = REJECT_KEY THEN RETURN.
                                       !RETURN ON SCREEN REJECT

  IF KEYCODE() = ACCEPT_KEY            !ON SCREEN ACCEPT KEY
    UPDATE                             !  MOVE ALL FIELDS FROM SCREEN
    SELECT(?)                          !  START WITH CURRENT FIELD
    SELECT                             !  EDIT ALL FIELDS
    CYCLE                              !  GO TO TOP OF LOOP
  .                                    !

  CASE FIELD()                         !JUMP TO FIELD EDIT ROUTINE
  OF ?FIRST_FIELD                      !FROM THE FIRST FIELD
    IF KEYCODE() = ESC_KEY THEN RETURN.
                                       !  RETURN ON ESC KEY

  OF ?PRE_MENU                         !PRE MENU FIELD CONDITION
    IF KEYCODE() = ESC_KEY             !  BACKING UP?
      SELECT(?-1)                      !    SELECT PREVIOUS FIELD
    ELSE                               !  GOING FORWARD
      SELECT(?+1)                      !    SELECT MENU FIELD
    .
  OF ?MENU_FIELD"                      !FROM THE MENU FIELD
    EXECUTE CHOICE()                   !  CALL THE SELECTED PROCEDURE
    NAME_TABLE                         !MENU SELECTION ONE
    CUST_TABLE                         !MENU SELECTION TWO
    REPORTS                            !MENU SELECTION THREE
    RETURN
  . . .
```

Figure 8-6   The setup code prior to the start of the main loop in a Designer-generated Menu Procedure.

```
CODE
OPEN(SCREEN)                 !OPEN THE MENU SCREEN
  SETCURSOR                  !TURN OFF ANY CURSOR
  MENU_FIELD" = ''           !START MENU WITH FIRST ITEM
```

If you had included any code in the Setup Procedure of the Options screen for the menu, it would appear in the segment shown in Figure 8-6. All Designer procedures have a section at the beginning of the program code that will run only once, when the procedure is opened. As you will hear throughout this book, Clarion's Designer takes advantage of an event-based processing architecture that places most of its procedural code after this initial setup. The application's "consciousness" then goes inside that repeating loop, waiting for the user to do something, that is, for an *event* to take place. Notice how the USE parameter of MENU is set to the first selection by being blanked as the procedure gets underway.

The Loop: The two major elements of the menu event loop include

1.   Setting the keyboard for responses
2.   Getting the response to
     a.   Leave the loop, or
     b.   Launch another procedure.

"Activate Keyboard" in Figure 8-7, sensitizes the keyboard to respond to special keys you specify or to standard keys like Enter. The Menu Procedure generated by Designer contains the processing tools used in the form as the menu can contain Entry Fields.

Bare Bones Menu Procedure: The entire Menu Procedure depicted in Figure 8-7 appears in the code in Figure 8-8.

As Figure 8-8 shows by omission, Designer inserts code from the model into its procedures to handle all the contingencies that every Designer user might employ. This stripped procedure opens the menu screen, turns the cursor off, and prepares the menu highlight bar to begin on the first item. Then, you can continue to poll the user for a keystroke. When ACCEPT returns the keystroke, the choice function extracts which position in the menu

Figure 8-7 The event processing loop inside a Clarion Designer-generated menu.

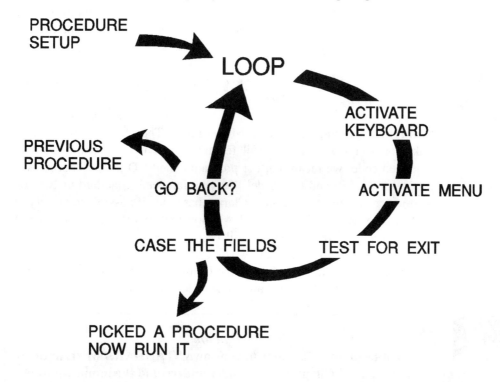

Figure 8-8 A pure menu procedure stripped of the extra code that Designer inserted to handle Entry Fields.

```
CODE
OPEN(SCREEN)                    !OPEN THE MENU SCREEN
SETCURSOR                       !TURN OFF ANY CURSOR
MENU_FIELD" = ''                !START MENU WITH FIRST ITEM
LOOP                            !LOOP UNTIL USER EXITS
   ACCEPT                       !READ A FIELD OR MENU CHOICE
   EXECUTE CHOICE()             !  CALL THE SELECTED PROCEDURE
     NAME_TABLE                 !MENU SELECTION ONE
     CUST_TABLE                 !MENU SELECTION TWO
     REPORTS                    !MENU SELECTION THREE
     RETURN
. .
```

was "accepted," and EXECUTE launches the procedure at whatever line number is below it in the code. When the processor's attention returns to this Menu Procedure from that called procedure, it jumps back into the cycle and waits for another keystroke.

Hint: Note that it is not necessary to explicitly close a screen opened inside a procedure when the procedure itself is terminated by RETURN.

Modifying Designer's Standard Model File: The model files in Clarion make for a unique and powerful feature. When we talk about Designer-generated code, we mean that the program called CDES.EXE accesses our design file (.APP) and the model file we referenced (Standard or Network) and then creates the source code. Clarion has made it possible to modify that model file to give you some control over how that source code gets generated. This concept and how it works will be discussed in detail in Chapter 15. However, in order to illustrate how you can edit the model file to create your own source code while leaning on the Clarion model paradigm, Figure 8-9 shows the model file for the "bare bones" Menu Procedure.

Caution
Do not begin modifications to your own STANDARD.MDL until you have read Chapter 15 and fully understand the implications of changing the model.

The Impact of a Hot Key: Now, let's examine what happens when you ask Designer to associate a hot key with this menu. Hot keys are a way to attach additional function selections to any screen. Their utility is that you need not be in any one place within a screen to use them—though you can restrict their use if you wish. All procedures in Designer, except for Other Procedures, provide a facility for hot keys. Once you name the Hot Procedure, you must assign a key sequence with which to call it.

You can enter up to three hot keys in Designer for access while a Menu Procedure is running. The screen in Figure 8-10 shows the first Hot Procedure and its associated hot key as well as the Entry Field for adding a second hot-keyed procedure. The hot keys can be any function key (F#) or any combination of ALT, SHIFT, or CTRL keys with any function key. Furthermore, ALT and CTRL can be paired with any letter of the alphabet, as in ALT-A, to launch a hot-keyed procedure.

Figure 8-9   The modified model procedure within the standard model for creating the bare bones menu. Note that the title of the procedure seated in the line of asterisks at the top has a different name than the Menu Procedure already in the model file. This is a copy of the original placed at the end of STANDARD.MDL.

```
*SHORTMENU***********************************************
@PROCNAME     PROCEDURE

SCREEN        SCREEN    PRE(SCR),@SCREENOPT
     @PAINTS
     @STRINGS
     @VARIABLES
     ENTRY,USE(?FIRST_FIELD)
     @FIELDS
     ENTRY,USE(?PRE_MENU)
     MENU,USE(MENU_FIELD"),REQ
       @CHOICES
    .    .
  CODE
  OPEN(SCREEN)                          !OPEN THE MENU SCREEN
  SETCURSOR                             !TURN OFF ANY CURSOR
  MENU_FIELD" = ''                      !START MENU WITH FIRST ITEM
  LOOP                                  !LOOP UNTIL USER EXITS
  ALERT                                 !TURN OFF ALL ALERTED KEYS
  ACCEPT                                !READ A FIELD OR MENU CHOICE
  EXECUTE CHOICE()                      !  CALL THE SELECTED PROCEDURE
  @MENU                                 !
   . .
```

The lines of code in the model file that pertain to calling and processing the hot keys relate directly to two tasks you must perform if you plan to use hot keys in your procedures. You must sensitize the particular key you wish to use and then call the Hot Procedure, as in Figure 8-11.

Of these three lines of code from the standard model, the two with the @ sign signify the keywords that Clarion uses to call two subroutines within the model. These will not be invoked unless the indication for a hot key exists in the .APP, or design, file. That's why you don't see any code in the standard sample Designer menu in Figure 8-11 relating to hot keys.

Figure 8-10   The first Hot Procedure and its hot key.

```
                              Menu

 Procedure Name :MENU
 Procedure Title:
 Setup Procedure:
 Help ID        :
 Hot Procedure  :HOT_KEY_PROC
    Hot Key     :F10_KEY
 Position       :Float      Float  Fix
 Combine With   :
 Model Procedure:SHORTMENU
```

Designer simply replaces the keyword @HOTKEY (as shown in Figure 8-12) with whatever hot key you selected in the Options menu, as in ALERT(F10_KEY). Once the hot key has been ALERTed, the Main Event Loop checks, in each revolution, whether the user has pressed that key. If so, it updates the current field in the current procedure, saves the current state of the ACTION variable, and runs the procedure called by the hot key. The keyword @HOTPROC (as shown in Figure 8-13) is the variable Clarion uses to identify the Hot Procedure. Then, when the Hot Procedure finishes, it returns to the next line, restores the ACTION variable, reselects the field the user was on when they pressed the hot key, and finally short circuits the Main Event Loop to start it at the top again.

Hint: The ACTION variable is a global variable that Clarion uses to make decisions about what type of process is taking place—an addition to the file, a deletion from the file, or a lookup.

Figure 8-11   The model file code which inserts the calls to a Hot Procedure.

```
@ALERT                                    !ALERT HOT KEYS
ACCEPT                                    !READ A FIELD OR
MENU CHOICE
@CHECKHOT                                 !ON HOT KEY, CALL
PROCEDURE
```

Figure 8-12   The subroutine called by @ALERT in the standard model file.

```
*ALERT*****************************************************************
  ALERT(@HOTKEY)                                   !ALERT HOT KEY
```

Remember, if the procedure called with a hot key opens a full screen, in non-window mode, it will scramble the video memory for the screen from which you called it. Be sure to make the Screen structures in most Hot Key Procedures create themselves as windows (with the WINDOW attribute in the top line of the Screen structure).

The most frequent uses for hot keys in menus are to call on a utility (like a pop-up calendar or calculator) or to quickly look up something before starting a Main Procedure. The Floppy Disk Catalog program in the appendices uses a hot key to leave the program temporarily and go to the DOS command line prompt. Now let's discuss each of the field types that Designer's Menu Procedure supports. The selections available appear in Figure 8-14.

The Impact of a Display Field: A Display Field is an area on the screen where data from the files can be shown, but it cannot be edited and it has no USE variable. It is set at the start of the Main Event Loop for the menu so that its contents display immediately after the screen is opened and are updated if there are any changes during the run of the Menu Procedure. This allows you

Figure 8-13   The model code for the subroutine that grabs the keystroke on the hot key and runs the Hot Procedure.

```
*CHECKHOT**************************************************************
  IF KEYCODE() = @HOTKEY            !ON HOT KEY
     UPDATE(?)                      !  RETRIEVE FIELD
     SAVACTN# = ACTION              !  SAVE ACTION
     @HOTPROC                       !  CALL HOT KEY PROCEDURE
     ACTION = SAVACTN#              !  RESTORE ACTION
     SELECT(?)                      !  DO SAME FIELD AGAIN
     CYCLE                          !  AND LOOP AGAIN
```

Figure 8-14   The selection of menu choices for adding fields to a menu form in Designer.

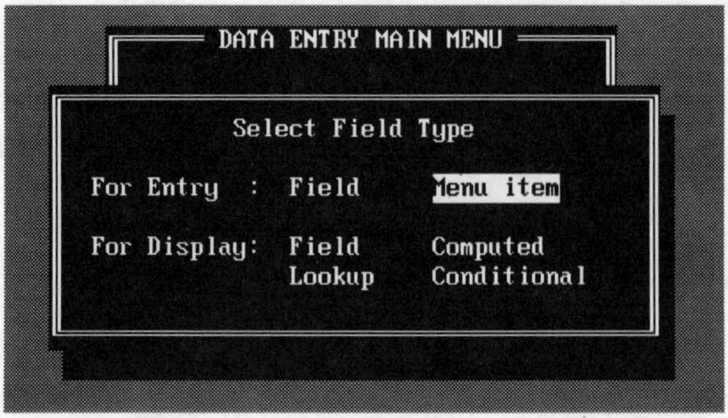

to edit the values by changing information in a file or in memory. The example shown in Figure 8-15 demonstrates the use of DISPLAY variables.

The sample code in Figure 8-15 contains the variable setting functions for the other field types that could appear on a menu. Notice that the Entry Fields are not displayed. The Case structure that follows this section of code processes the Entry Fields as they appear in the Screen structure.

The cursor never stops on a Display Field, and the user has no way to address it directly. You must provide the user some other field type to alter the information the Display Field contains. However, because Designer places them inside the Main Event Loop, Display Fields can be used to show real-time data coming into the system from another location. If the memory variable is updated, so is the Display Field.

The Impact of an Entry Field: An Entry Field in a menu can set header information for the screen, or check passwords, or set criteria for use in procedures called by menu items, or set values for other purposes—like altering the contents of a DISPLAY variable on the same screen. It can also be used to get information from a file. The form Designer uses to create an Entry Field in a menu is built exactly like, and works just like, the one used for placing Entry Fields into an input form. The code to create an Entry Field in a screen appears in Figure 8-16.

A popular use for Entry Fields is for password protection of certain menus. When you open a Menu Procedure created by Designer, the cursor always pauses on the Entry Fields before making the menu items active. The order in which the fields appear in the Screen structure determines the order the cursor uses to travel to the menu. So, you can use the Lookup facility in an Entry Field to look into a list of valid users in one Entry Field and then ask them to

Figure 8-15   Sample code demonstrating sections of the Event Loop.

```
LOOP                                    !LOOP UNTIL USER EXITS
```

The Look-Up Field Code

```
UPDATE                          .        !UPDATE RECORD KEYS
TES:THIRD = TES:FIRST                    !MOVE RELATED KEY FIELDS
GET(TEST,TES:BY_FIRST_KEY)               !READ THE RECORD
IF ERROR() THEN CLEAR(TES:RECORD).       !NOT FOUND? CLEAR RECORD
SCR:SECOND = TES:SECOND                  !DISPLAY LOOKUP FIELD
```

The Computed Field Code

```
SCR:MESSAGE = MEM:MESSAGE
SCR:COMPUTED = 'comp field'
```

The Conditional Field Code

```
IF action                                !EVALUATE CONDITION
  SCR:CONDIT = 'action = true'           !   CONDITION IS TRUE
ELSE                                     !OTHERWISE
  SCR:CONDIT = 'action  = false'         !   CONDITION IS FALSE
  .


MEM:DEVICE = SCR:COMPUTED
ALERT                                    !TURN OFF ALL ALERTED KEYS
ALERT(REJECT_KEY)                        !ALERT SCREEN REJECT KEY
ALERT(ACCEPT_KEY)                        !ALERT SCREEN ACCEPT KEY
ACCEPT
```

---

match a password with a second Entry Field when you read the user record they selected into memory. More about how you can popup a table with values from another file for selection into an Entry Field will appear in Chapter 10.

You can rearrange the order of the Entry Fields and the menu structure within the Screen structure to force the menu to be active immediately. However, Designer does not make it easy for you to access those fields again.

Figure 8-16 **The code from a Screen structure for placing an Entry Field on the screen in a menu. Note that the Entry Field specification is sandwiched between the two "Dummy" Fields that Clarion uses to control exit from and entry into the screen.**

```
           ENTRY,USE(?FIRST_FIELD)
ROW(3,32)  ENTRY(@s20),USE(MEM:NAME),LFT,OVR,HUE(0,7),SEL(0,7)
           ENTRY,USE(?PRE_MENU)
```

You must find another way to SELECT those fields for entry. One possible method is through the procedure called by a menu selection. You could, for instance, call an intermediate procedure that would perform a decision that could redirect you back into the menu with the Entry Fields selected or take you on into another procedure normally.

The Impact of a Lookup Field: A Lookup Field in a menu works exactly like a lookup from an entry form, except that there is no user interaction. It uses a key value to locate a value in another file and places that value on display. You should use this type of field when a value that you need to make the menu operational is not already in memory, and when you cannot ask the user to enter it. Popular uses for this field include grabbing the company name and address to display in the banner of a procedure when that information may change—as with multi-company accounting systems that use the same screens for each function but for different firms.

A Pull-Down Menu Sample

One of the more popular menu formats is called a pull-down. It is so named because you strike a key and the menu appears below the item used to call it, which is usually in a horizontal line of items at the top of the screen. (See Figure 8-17.) Designer does not support a full-function pull-down menu, but we'll discuss how close you can get and then we'll show you a full-blown pull-down system.

Designer's Pull-Down Menu

The primary action you take to create what looks like a pull-down menu in Designer is to create a main menu with the horizontal menu items and then create submenus that line up in the proper places on the screen. The Designer

Figure 8-17 The pull-down menu sample as it appears in both Designer and manually written code.

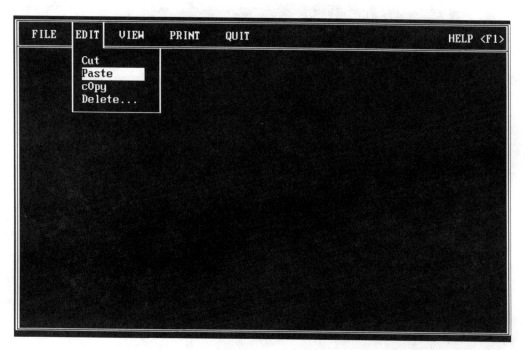

screen for creating the pull-down sample in Figure 8-18 shows five procedures branching from the Main Procedure—the last, of course, being a simple return to DOS. Then, carefully lining the submenus up, we can achieve the effect of a pull-down menu.

The menu-calling conventions in Designer do not change to accommodate a pull-down menu style. The menus appear just as they would normally and the main menu cursor travels up and down the horizontal main menu bar. You can also run as many menus deep as you like with this setup. Each submenu calls another submenu. However, that raises one of the big disadvantages of creating a pull-down menu in Designer. You can only return to the main menu by escaping back through the menu tree by the same route you took when you entered it. Most commonly, the Pull-Down Menu facility lets you access menus horizontally—at all levels.

A Manual Version of the Pull-Down Menu

The manual version of the pull-down menu allows additional flexibility to include all the features you would normally expect to find in a pull-down

Figure 8-18   The screen for the Designer-generated pull-down menu.

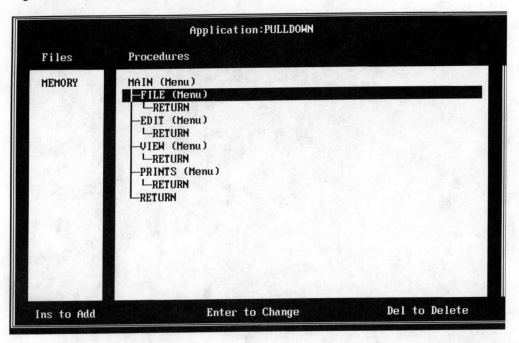

menu. However, this comes at the expense of some complexity. This version allows us to move between main menu settings, without putting the submenus away, by pressing either an ALT key combination or by using the left and right cursor keys to move laterally. We are also able, in this version, to change the sensitive key from the first letter to something else to ensure that each

Figure 8-19   The Edit submenu for the pull-down menu in Figure 8-18 as it appears in the screen formatter in both Designer and Editor. Notice that the sensitive key for each item in the submenu is unique. A different letter or number for each menu selection supports one-touch menu access. You cannot change the hot key in Designer, only through Editor's field editing in the screen formatter.

menu selection can be called with a unique letter within each submenu. (See Figure 8-19.) The segments of code displayed and discussed in this section are not intended to be standalone programs. The entire program code for this manually coded version of the pull-down menu appears at the end of the chapter.

In this case, Designer was used to generate the original Screen structures and then each of the submenu choices was incorporated into a Routine structure callable from within the Main Procedure. The SHORTMENU model procedure was used to reduce the amount of possible "equate duplication" that might occur when the Screen structures are combined. The local routines and the Screen structures were combined in the Main Procedure to allow the local routines to share the screen definitions and variable states of the Main Procedure.

Hint: *When you call a procedure from within another procedure, you do not have access to all the variables because you do not have access to the calling procedure's Screen structure. Use the local routine to set off a segment of code from your procedures without leaving the procedure. They are especially useful for segments of code that are called frequently during a single procedure.*

Unique Naming Conventions Required: Notice that the Screen structures were all included in one procedure. Normally you would avoid this setup. Designer never combines two Screen structures into one procedure. However, this method allows us to switch quickly between structures from within the same procedure. The two elements of the structures that had to be unique were 1) the name used to call the structure itself, and 2) any variable definitions or field equate labels.

Simple Main Program: The manual pull-down sample (beginning in Figure 8-20) appears as one DOS file in place of the six DOS files that Designer generated—one for each menu and submenu. However, notice that no files are opened—including a memory file group—to run this program. The sample demonstrates the menu concepts only. The file opening procedures, if there were files, would appear in the main program area as usual.

The map and the special key files used appear in the global section of the program. Then we simply call the Main Menu Procedure and let it do the rest of the work.

After the opening section of the program shown in Figure 8-20 come two procedures, Help and Notes, which are accessed throughout the program to pop up special messages. The Help Procedure is simply a window containing text. It was not created by Clarion's HELPER utility as we have not yet

Figure 8-20　The beginning of the hand-coded PULLDOWN program. This is the main module whose job it is to set the global values and call the Main Menu Procedure which, in turn, provides access to the submenus.

```
PULLDOWN     PROGRAM                    !IDENTIFIES THE PROGRAM
      INCLUDE('STD_KEYS.CLA')           !PUT THE STANDARD KEY CODES IN
      INCLUDE('ALT_KEYS.CLA')           !PUT THE ALT KEY CODES IN
      MAP                               !MAP THE MAIN PROCEDURES
        PROC(MAIN)                      !MAIN MENU
        PROC(NOTES)                     !INCOMPLETE PROCEDURE NOTICE
        PROC(HELPS)                     !HELP SCREEN
      .
      CODE                              !START OF MAIN PROGRAM
      MAIN                              !CALL MAIN MENU
      RETURN                            !GO BACK TO DOS
```

discussed the use of that tool. The Notes Procedure is called from the items in the submenus and demonstrates how you can pass a value from one procedure to the next. The EXECUTE statement in each subroutine passes its name to the Notes Procedure that displays it.

To pass a value in a procedure, no map changes are necessary as they are when defining a function within an Other Procedure. The variable carrying the passed material must be defined in both procedures. (In this case, we're using an implicit variable for that purpose.) Then, to pass the data, you set the following variable:

```
PROCEDURE_CALLED(PASS_VARIABLE)
```

Then, in the beginning of the called procedure, you must define that passing variable by giving it as a parameter for the procedure:

```
              MEMBER('MYPROG')
SPECIAL_PROC  PROCEDURE(PASS_VARIABLE)
```

Then comes the opening of the Main Menu Procedure followed by all the screen definitions for the main menu and the submenus. Each has a unique label and no field equates are used, so no conflicting variable definitions (meaning one variable defined in two places) exist. Then comes the main

Figure 8-21   The Main Menu Procedure for the manually coded PULLDOWN program.

```
CODE
  OPEN(SCREEN)                              !OPEN THE MENU SCREEN
  SETCURSOR                                 !TURN OFF ANY CURSOR
  MENU_FIELD" = ''                          !START MENU WITH FIRST ITEM
  LOOP                                      !LOOP UNTIL USER EXITS
    ALERT                                   !TURN OFF ALL ALERTED KEYS
    ALERT(F1_KEY)                           !ALERT HELP KEY
    ALERT(ESC_KEY)                          !ALERT SCREEN REJECT KEY
    ACCEPT                                  !READ A FIELD OR MENU CHOICE
    IF KEYCODE() = F1_KEY THEN HELPS.       !SHOW HELP
    IF KEYCODE() = ESC_KEY THEN RETURN.     !RETURN ON SCREEN REJECT
    EXECUTE CHOICE()                        !  CALL THE SELECTED PROCEDURE
         DO FILE                            !  FIRST MENU SELECTION
         DO EDIT                            !  SECOND MENU SELECTION
         DO VIEW                            !  THIRD MENU SELECTION
         DO PRINTS                          !  FOURTH MENU SELECTION
         RETURN                             !  GO BACK TO DOS
         .                                  !END OF MENU SELECTIONS
         .
```

body of the Main Menu Procedure. With a simplified menu-processing Event Loop, the Main Menu Procedure responds to each item selection by calling a subroutine. (See the Execute structure in Figure 8-21.)

The Subroutines: Each of the subroutines in this program contains its own Menu Procedure, which is almost a duplicate of the main menu program. The difference appears in the responses to the keystrokes it makes. (See Figure 8-22.)

To handle the special keys, we first must "sensitize" them by putting them on ALERT. That means we can test to see if they were pressed— otherwise the ACCEPT statement does not tell whether they were pressed or not. Since each subroutine uses the same set of keys, we've condensed the program by placing the ALERT instructions into one subroutine called from within each submenu subroutine. (See Figure 8-23.) To look for which key was pressed, we're using KEYSTROKE( ). The difference between that command and KEYBOARD( ) is the ACCEPT inside the

Figure 8-22   The Edit submenu subroutine.

```
EDIT       ROUTINE
  OPEN(EDITSCREEN)              !OPEN THE MENU SCREEN
  SETCURSOR                     !TURN OFF ANY CURSOR
  MENU_FIELD" = ''             !START MENU WITH FIRST ITEM
  LOOP                          !LOOP UNTIL USER EXITS
    DO ALERTS                   !ALERT SPECIAL KEYS
    ACCEPT                      !READ A FIELD OR MENU CHOICE
    CASE KEYCODE()              !GET KEYSTROKE
    OF ALT_F                    !ON THE HOT KEY
      CLOSE(EDITSCREEN)         !  CLOSE THE PRESENT SCREEN
      DO FILE                   !  CALL NEW MAIN MENU ITEM
      EXIT                      !  GO BACK TO LAST PROCEDURE
    OF ALT_V                    !ON THE HOT KEY
      CLOSE(EDITSCREEN)         !  CLOSE THE PRESENT SCREEN
      DO VIEW                   !  CALL NEW MAIN MENU ITEM
      EXIT                      !  GO BACK TO LAST PROCEDURE
    OF ALT_P                    !ON THE HOT KEY
      CLOSE(EDITSCREEN)         !  CLOSE THE PRESENT SCREEN
      DO PRINTS                 !  CALL NEW MAIN MENU ITEM
      EXIT                      !  GO BACK TO LAST PROCEDURE
    OF ALT_Q                    !ON THE HOT KEY
      RETURN                    !  GO BACK TO DOS
    OF F1_KEY                   !ON THE HOT KEY
      HELPS                     !   SHOW HELP SCREEN
    OF ESC_KEY                  !ON THE HOT KEY
      CLOSE(EDITSCREEN)         !   CLOSE THIS MENU
      EXIT                      !   GO TO MAIN PROCEDURE
    OF LEFT_KEY                 !ON THE HOT KEY
      CLOSE(EDITSCREEN)         !  CLOSE THIS SCREEN
      DO FILE                   !  GO TO NEW MENU
      RESTART                   !   GO TO MAIN IF NEW
    OF RIGHT_KEY                !ON THE HOT KEY
      CLOSE(EDITSCREEN)         !  CLOSE THIS SCREEN
      DO VIEW                   !   GO TO NEW MENU
      RESTART                   !   GO TO MAIN IF NEW
```

(continued)

Figure 8-22 *continued*

```
EXECUTE CHOICE()                !CALL THE SELECTED PROCEDURE
   NOTES('CUT')                 !  FIRST MENU SELECTION
   NOTES('PASTE')               !  SECOND MENU SELECTION
   NOTES('COPY')                !  THIRD MENU SELECTION
   NOTES('DELETE')              !  FOURTH MENU SELECTION
 . .
```

Main Event Loop. KEYBOARD( ) looks for keys that have been pressed but not yet processed. KEYSTROKE( ) looks for the last keystroke processed by an ACCEPT or an ASK. This explains why the ALERTs are performed before the ACCEPT statement and why the Case structure testing for the KEYCODE( ) follows the ACCEPT.

The Case structure looks for which key was pressed and responds accordingly. In the case of the ALT key combinations, the system calls the appropriate main menu item. Remember that, to use an ALT key, you must either set the EQUATE yourself or INCLUDE the ALT_KEYS.CLA file that Clarion provides. The cursor keys, on the other hand, call the next (or previous) submenu to provide the lateral menu references.

Figure 8-23   This is the sub-subroutine that sensitizes the special keys so that KEYCODE() can be used to launch a process. Notice that ALERT is called by itself at the beginning. This turns off all previous ALERTed keys. Since calling ALERT against the same key twice in a row results in turning it off, calling ALERT by itself ensures that you maintain control.

```
ALERTS       ROUTINE              !PREPARE WATCH ON SPECIAL KEYS
    ALERT                         !TURN OFF ALL ALERTED KEYS
    ALERT(F1_KEY)                 !ALERT HELP KEY
    ALERT(LEFT_KEY)               !ALERT CURSOR KEYS
    ALERT(RIGHT_KEY)
    ALERT(ESC_KEY)                !ALERT SCREEN REJECT KEY
    ALERT(ALT_F)                  !ALERT MENU HOT KEYS
    ALERT(ALT_E)
    ALERT(ALT_V)
    ALERT(ALT_P)
    ALERT(ALT_Q)
```

Notice how each segment of the Case structure closes the current screen before calling the next subroutine. The reason that the standard test for each subroutine is not, itself, a subroutine is because you cannot pass a parameter to the CLOSE command representing the screen. Notice also the use of the RESTART function when you return from a subroutine. RESTART called without parameters reruns the program from the first procedure, which, in this case, is the main menu.

Finally, notice the use of the parameter passing performed in the EXE-CUTE statement. The Notes Procedure is called and the parameter that gets passed is displayed in the Screen structure that Notes places on the screen. You could just as well pass other information—for example, accounting data, a record number, and the contents of a key variable—to a procedure in a similar fashion.

A Menu with a Working Screen

Clarion menu screens also allow you to let the user work right on the menu itself. This looks like a natural thing to do when you look at the generic screen structure capabilities in Clarion. However, Designer also offers these same capabilities with very little extra coding. You can preset variables, perform calculations, and set other defaults to be used later in the program—all using Designer and a few of the Expressions and Edit Procedures within the field setup screens.

The sample discussed in this section is a ragtag assembly of most of the field types Designer allows you to add to a menu. The Designer-generated source code for the main menu (pictured in Figure 8-24) appears at the end of the chapter.

Entry Fields and the Menu Structure in a Designer Menu

When this procedure starts, the entire screen displays with some defaults. All of the purely Calculated Fields fill at once and the cursor comes to rest on the Entry Field at the top of the screen. Designer does not allow you to place the menu selections (the strings within the Menu structure) prior to the Entry Fields no matter where you place them on the screen. So, it's no surprise that Designer does not allow you to exit from the Menu structure to go to an Entry Field without a special procedure. The order in which Entry Fields are

Figure 8-24 A utility screen built in a menu form entirely in Designer.

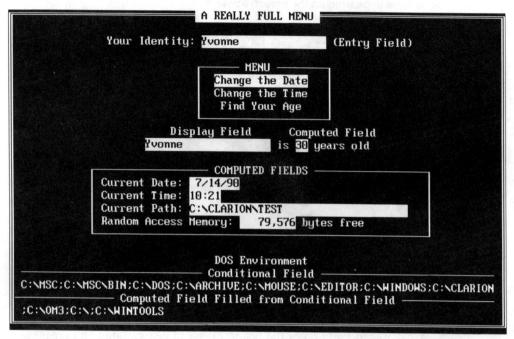

processed is not screen related, however, but related to which line in the Screen structure the Entry Field occupies.

Display Fields in a Designer Menu: Display Fields operate differently than Computed Fields. Display Fields show the contents of what must be a preexisting variable—in the memory file, in a disk file, or even an implicit variable. Designer attaches an "SCR" prefix to all variables shown on a Screen structure.

Hint: You cannot look at a screen variable ("SCR:" in Designer) using the Debugger. Therefore, if you want to see the contents of a Display or Computed Field, you must provide either a memory or implicit variable to view anything that should be displaying to the screen. It is best, also, to make that variable local to the procedure to ensure that you don't get a value that was placed globally.

As with Computed Fields in a menu, you can change the contents while still in the same screen. The logical comparisons for the contents of Display variables get refreshed with each turn of the menu Event Loop.

Figure 8-25 The Computed field screen form within Designer with the placement and picture of the variable appearing on the screen above it.

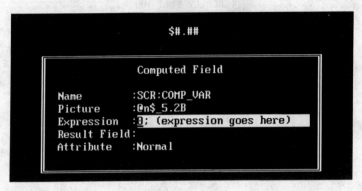

Computed Fields in a Designer Menu: Computed Fields are powerful tools in a Designer menu. You can access much of the Clarion language from a Computed Field to do everything from simply translating a variable into a different picture to complex equations—all within the Expression slot of the Computed Field screen. The Computed Field in Figure 8-25 displays its result dollars.

A Computed Field takes the Name of the screen variable you create and sets it equal to the Expression. The BIGMENU example uses this, for instance, to calculate someone's age. The Expression appears as the right side of the equation like this:

```
AGE(deformat(mem:birth,@d1))
```

However, this presents a problem if you want to execute a more complex operation. To put whatever you want into that Expression, simply set the field equal to zero, place a line separating semicolon, and then enter the Expression you want to use. The Computed Field form screen shot in Figure 8-25 is an example of that. You can loop through another file or set conditional statements or whatever you like, providing that you eventually set SCR:COMP_VAR equal to some value (unless you want the zero to display).

> ### *Caution*
> Do not fill in any Expression (for Computed Fields) or Edit Procedures (for Entry Fields) all the way out to their 255-character maximum. The generated source code will not compile. You'll get a message from the Compiler saying that you don't have "a valid source code file," and when you go into Editor to fix it, you'll find it says "Information may have been lost during program loading." The problem is, the Edit Procedure and the Expression will only pass these tests if they contain no more than 249 characters. It's a simple matter to fix. Just go into Editor and find the offending line of code. You'll see the extra code was merely wrapped to the next line. Reattach it to the end or make a logical break in the Expression and it will compile.

Conditional Display Fields in a Designer Menu: Again, Conditional Display Fields are updated the same way as any other Display Field. The conditional statements can be placed into the Designer screen form as is shown in Figure 8-26. The code generated from this screen form appears in Figure 8-27.

Figure 8-26   The screen input form Designer uses to enter a Conditional Display Field into a menu.

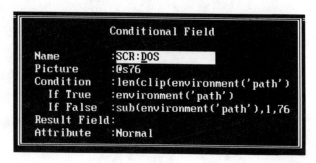

Figure 8-27   The result of the code for the Conditional Display Field that appears in the Environment area of the BIGMENU sample screen in Figure 8-26.

```
IF len(clip(environment('path'))) < 76      !EVALUATE CONDITION
   SCR:DOS = environment('path')            !  CONDITION IS TRUE
ELSE                                         !OTHERWISE
   SCR:DOS = sub(environment('path'),1,76)
   dos2" = sub(environment('path'),77,76)    !CONDITION IS FALSE
```

Summary

Since the first user forgot how to log on to a mainframe, menus have been our method for remembering how to use computer software. By combining elements of the Clarion language (including some created especially to support menus), you can create intelligent menus that will help users take advantage of the software you write. In this chapter we discussed the methods for creating simple menus that call different parts of the application, as well as menus that actually display information and perform other work.

The Pull-Down Menu Sample Source Code

PULLDOWN.CLA

```
PULLDOWN    PROGRAM
            INCLUDE('STD_KEYS.CLA')           !PUT THE STANDARD KEY CODES IN
            INCLUDE('ALT_KEYS.CLA')           !PUT THE ALT KEY CODES IN
            MAP                               !MAP THE MAIN PROCEDURES
              PROC(MAIN)                      !MAIN MENU
              PROC(NOTES)                     ! INCOMPLETE PROCEDURE NOTICE
              PROC(HELPS)
            END!MAP
CLOSER      STRING(20)
            CODE                              !START OF MAIN PROGRAM
            MAIN                              !CALL MAIN MENU
            RETURN                            !GO BACK TO DOS


NOTES       PROCEDURE(CHOOSE")                !FOR PROCEDURES NOT DEFINED

SCREEN SCREEN     WINDOW(7,49),AT(10,17),HUE(7,0)
        ROW(1,1)  STRING('<201,205{47},187>')
        ROW(2,1)  REPEAT(5);STRING('<186,0{47},186>') .
        ROW(7,1)  STRING('<200,205{10},0{27},205{10},188>')
        ROW(3,13) STRING('MENU SELECTION:')
        ROW(5,13) STRING('PRESS ANY KEY TO CONTINUE')
        ROW(7,12) STRING('Memory Available:')
CHOSEN  ROW(3,29) STRING(10)
RAM          ROW(7,30) STRING(@n9)
       END!SCREEN

  CODE
  OPEN(SCREEN)                                ! OPEN NOTES SCREEN
  RAM = MEMORY()                              ! GET AVAILABLE MEMORY
  CHOSEN = CHOOSE"                            ! MOVE NOTE INTO SCREEN
  ASK                                         ! WAIT FOR A KEYSTROKE
  CLOSE(SCREEN)                               ! PUT SCREEN AWAY
  RETURN                                      !RETURN TO CALLER

HELPS       PROCEDURE                         !FOR PROCEDURES NOT DEFINED

SCREEN      SCREEN WINDOW(11,49),AT(13,16),HUE(7,0)
        ROW(1,1)  STRING('<201,205{47},187>')
        ROW(2,1)  REPEAT(9);STRING('<186,0{47},186>') .
        ROW(11,1) STRING('<200,205{47},188>')
```

(continued)

```
         ROW(2,3)    STRING('Use the ALT key and first letter combination')
         ROW(3,3)    STRING('to start the main menu items anywhere in the')
         ROW(4,3)    STRING('menu system.')
         ROW(6,3)    STRING('Use the capitalized letter in each menu item')
         ROW(7,3)    STRING('in the sub menus to launch those procedures.')
         ROW(9,13)   STRING('PRESS ANY KEY TO CONTINUE')
       END!SCREEN


    CODE                          !PROGRAM START
    OPEN(SCREEN)                  !SHOW HELP SCREEN
    ASK                           !WAIT FOR KEYSTROKE
    CLOSE(SCREEN)                 !PUT HELP AWAY
    RETURN                        !RETURN TO CALLER


MAIN        PROCEDURE

SCREEN SCREEN       WINDOW(25,80),PRE(SCR),HUE(7,0)
         ROW(1,1)    STRING('<201,205{78},187>')
         ROW(2,1)    STRING('<186,0{78},186>')
         ROW(3,1)    STRING('<204,205{78},185>')
         ROW(4,1)    REPEAT(21);STRING('<186,0{78},186>') .
         ROW(25,1)   STRING('<200,205{78},188>')
         ROW(2,71)   STRING('HELP <<F1>')
         ROW(25,80)  MENU,USE(MENU_FIELD"),REQ,IMM
         ROW(2,4)     STRING('FILE'),KEY(ALT_F)
           COL(11)    STRING('EDIT'),KEY(ALT_E)
           COL(18)    STRING('VIEW'),KEY(ALT_V)
           COL(26)    STRING('PRINT'),KEY(ALT_P)
           COL(35)    STRING('QUIT'),KEY(ALT_Q)
                     END!MENU

       END!SCREEN

FILESCREEN SCREEN   WINDOW(8,15),AT(1,3),PRE(SCR),HUE(7,0)
         ROW(1,1)    STRING('<209,205{4},209,205{9}>')
         ROW(2,1)    STRING('<179,0{4},179>')
         ROW(3,1)    STRING('<181,0{4},212,205{8},209>')
         ROW(4,1)    REPEAT(4);STRING('<179,0{13},179>') .
         ROW(8,1)    STRING('<192,196{13},217>')
         ROW(2,2)    STRING('FILE'),ENH
           COL(9)    STRING('EDIT')
           COL(10)   MENU,USE(MENU_FIELD"),REQ,IMM
         ROW(4,3)     STRING('Save          ')
         ROW(5,3)     STRING('save As...    '),KEY('A')
         ROW(6,3)     STRING('Directory     ')
         ROW(7,3)     STRING('deleTe...     '),KEY('T')
                     END!MENU

       END!SCREEN
```

(continued)

```
EDITSCREEN SCREEN    WINDOW(8,15),AT(1,10),PRE(SCR),HUE(7,0)
        ROW(1,1)     STRING('<209,205{4},209,205{9}>')
        ROW(2,1)     STRING('<179,0{4},179>')
        ROW(3,1)     STRING('<181,0{4},212,205{8},209>')
        ROW(4,1)     REPEAT(4);STRING('<179,0{13},179>') .
        ROW(8,1)     STRING('<192,196{13},217>')
        ROW(2,2)     STRING('EDIT'),ENH
          COL(9)     STRING('VIEW')
          COL(12)    MENU,USE(MENU_FIELD"),REQ,IMM
        ROW(4,3)       STRING('Cut        ')
        ROW(5,3)       STRING('Paste      ')
        ROW(6,3)       STRING('cOpy       '),KEY('O') ! GIVE NEW HOT KEY
        ROW(7,3)       STRING('Delete... ')
                     END!MENU
      END!SCREEN


VIEWSCREEN SCREEN    WINDOW(8,15),AT(1,17),PRE(SCR),HUE(7,0)
        ROW(1,1)     STRING('<209,205{4},209,205{9}>')
        ROW(2,1)     STRING('<179,0{4},179>')
        ROW(3,1)     STRING('<181,0{4},212,205{8},209>')
        ROW(4,1)     REPEAT(4);STRING('<179,0{13},179>') .
        ROW(8,1)     STRING('<192,196{13},217>')
        ROW(2,2)     STRING('VIEW'),ENH
          COL(10)    STRING('PRINT')
          COL(14)    MENU,USE(MENU_FIELD"),REQ,IMM
        ROW(4,3)       STRING('Zoom in ')
        ROW(5,3)       STRING('zoom Out '),KEY('O')! GIVE NEW HOT KEY
        ROW(6,3)       STRING('Restore ')
        ROW(7,3)       STRING('Move      ')
                     END!MENU
      END!SCREEN


PRINTSCREEN SCREEN   WINDOW(8,17),AT(1,25),PRE(SCR),HUE(7,0)
        ROW(1,1)     STRING('<209,205{5},209,205{10}>')
        ROW(2,1)     STRING('<179,0{5},179>')
        ROW(3,1)     STRING('<181,0{5},212,205{9},209>')
        ROW(4,1)     REPEAT(4);STRING('<179,0{15},179>') .
        ROW(8,1)     STRING('<192,196{15},217>')
        ROW(2,2)     STRING('PRINT'),ENH
          COL(11)    STRING('QUIT')
          COL(14)    MENU,USE(MENU_FIELD"),REQ,IMM
        ROW(4,3)       STRING('Setup printer ')
        ROW(5,3)       STRING('seTup page    '),KEY('T')
          ROW(6,3)   STRING('Review        ')
          ROW(7,3)   STRING('GO!           ')
                     END!MENU
      END!SCREEN
```

(continued)

```
        EJECT
        CODE
        OPEN(SCREEN)                            !OPEN THE MENU SCREEN
        SETCURSOR                               !TURN OFF ANY CURSOR
        MENU_FIELD" = ''                        !START MENU WITH FIRST ITEM
        LOOP                                    !LOOP UNTIL USER EXITS
          ALERT                                 !TURN OFF ALL ALERTED KEYS
          ALERT(F1_KEY)                         !ALERT HELP KEY
          ALERT(ESC_KEY)                        !ALERT SCREEN REJECT KEY
          ACCEPT                                !READ A FIELD OR MENU CHOICE
          IF KEYCODE() = F1_KEY THEN HELPS.     !SHOW HELP
          IF KEYCODE() = ESC_KEY THEN RETURN.   !RETURN ON SCREEN REJECT
          EXECUTE CHOICE()                      !  CALL THE SELECTED PROCEDURE
             DO FILE                            !   FIRST MENU SELECTION
             DO EDIT                            !   SECOND MENU SELECTION
             DO VIEW                            !   THIRD MENU SELECTION
             DO PRINTS                          !   FOURTH MENU SELECTION
             RETURN                             !   GO BACK TO DOS
          END!EXECUTE                           !END OF MENU SELECTIONS
        END!LOOP                                !END OF LOOP


FILE            ROUTINE
        OPEN(FILESCREEN)                        !OPEN THE MENU SCREEN
        SETCURSOR                               !TURN OFF ANY CURSOR
        MENU_FIELD" = ''                        !START MENU WITH FIRST ITEM
        LOOP                                    !LOOP UNTIL USER EXITS
          DO ALERTS                             !ALERT SPECIAL KEYS
          ACCEPT                                !READ A FIELD OR MENU CHOICE
          CASE KEYCODE()                        !GET KEYSTROKE
          OF ALT_E                              !ON THE HOT KEY
             CLOSE(FILESCREEN)                  !  CLOSE THE PRESENT SCREEN
             DO EDIT                            !  CALL NEW MAIN MENU ITEM
             EXIT                               !  GO BACK TO LAST PROCEDURE
          OF ALT_V                              !ON THE HOT KEY
             CLOSE(FILESCREEN)                  !  CLOSE THE PRESENT SCREEN
             DO VIEW                            !  CALL NEW MAIN MENU ITEM
             EXIT                               !  GO BACK TO LAST PROCEDURE
          OF ALT_P                              !ON THE HOT KEY
             CLOSE(FILESCREEN)                  !  CLOSE THE PRESENT SCREEN
             DO PRINTS                          !  CALL NEW MAIN MENU ITEM
             EXIT                               !  GO BACK TO LAST PROCEDURE
          OF ALT_Q                              !ON THE HOTKEY
             RETURN                             !  GO BACK TO DOS
          OF F1_KEY                             !SHOW HELP SCREEN
             HELPS
          OF ESC_KEY                            !RETURN ON SCREEN REJECT
             CLOSE(FILESCREEN)                  !CLOSE THIS MENU
```

(continued)

```
        EXIT                        !RETURN TO MAIN PROCEDURE
    OF RIGHT_KEY                    !CHECK FOR CURSOR KEY
        CLOSE(FILESCREEN)           !CLOSE THIS SCREEN
        DO EDIT                     !GO TO NEW MENU
        RESTART                     !GO TO MAIN IF NEW
    END!CASE
    EXECUTE CHOICE()                !  CALL THE SELECTED PROCEDURE
        NOTES('SAVE')              !  FIRST MENU SELECTION
        NOTES('SAVE AS...')        !  SECOND MENU SELECTION
        NOTES('DIRECTORY')         !  THIRD MENU SELECTION
        NOTES('DELETE...')         !  FOURTH MENU SELECTION
    END!EXECUTE
  END!LOOP


EDIT            ROUTINE
  OPEN(EDITSCREEN)                  !OPEN THE MENU SCREEN
  SETCURSOR                         !TURN OFF ANY CURSOR
  MENU_FIELD" = ''                  !START MENU WITH FIRST ITEM
  LOOP                              !LOOP UNTIL USER EXITS
    DO ALERTS                       !ALERT SPECIAL KEYS
    ACCEPT                          !READ A FIELD OR MENU CHOICE
    CASE KEYCODE()                  !GET KEYSTROKE
    OF ALT_F                        !ON THE HOT KEY
        CLOSE(EDITSCREEN)           !  CLOSE THE PRESENT SCREEN
        DO FILE                     !  CALL NEW MAIN MENU ITEM
        EXIT                        !  GO BACK TO LAST PROCEDURE
    OF ALT_V                        !ON THE HOT KEY
        CLOSE(EDITSCREEN)           !  CLOSE THE PRESENT SCREEN
        DO VIEW                     !  CALL NEW MAIN MENU ITEM
        EXIT                        !  GO BACK TO LAST PROCEDURE
    OF ALT_P                        !ON THE HOT KEY
        CLOSE(EDITSCREEN)           !  CLOSE THE PRESENT SCREEN
        DO PRINTS                   !  CALL NEW MAIN MENU ITEM
        EXIT                        !  GO BACK TO LAST PROCEDURE
    OF ALT_Q                        !ON THE HOTKEY
        RETURN                      !  GO BACK TO DOS
    OF F1_KEY                       !ON HOT KEY
        HELPS                       !  SHOW HELP SCREEN
    OF ESC_KEY                      !ON HOT KEY
        CLOSE(EDITSCREEN)           !  CLOSE THIS MENU
        EXIT                        !  GO TO MAIN PROCEDURE
    OF LEFT_KEY                     !CHECK FOR CURSOR KEY
        CLOSE(EDITSCREEN)           !  CLOSE THIS SCREEN
        DO FILE                     !  GO TO NEW MENU
        RESTART                     !  GO TO MAIN IF NEW
    OF RIGHT_KEY                    !CHECK FOR CURSOR KEY
        CLOSE(EDITSCREEN)           !  CLOSE THIS SCREEN
```

(continued)

```
        DO VIEW                        !  GO TO NEW MENU
        RESTART                        !  GO TO MAIN IF NEW
      END!CASE
      EXECUTE CHOICE()                 !  CALL THE SELECTED PROCEDURE
          NOTES('CUT')                 !  FIRST MENU SELECTION
          NOTES('PASTE')               !  SECOND MENU SELECTION
          NOTES('COPY')                !  THIRD MENU SELECTION
          NOTES('DELETE')              !  FOURTH MENU SELECTION
      END!EXECUTE
    END!LOOP

VIEW          ROUTINE
  OPEN(VIEWSCREEN)                     !OPEN THE MENU SCREEN
  SETCURSOR                            !TURN OFF ANY CURSOR
  MENU_FIELD" = ''                     !START MENU WITH FIRST ITEM
  LOOP                                 !LOOP UNTIL USER EXITS
    DO ALERTS                          !ALERT SPECIAL KEYS
    ACCEPT                             !READ A FIELD OR MENU CHOICE
    CASE KEYCODE()                     !GET KEYSTROKE
    OF ALT_F                           !ON THE HOT KEY
       CLOSE(VIEWSCREEN)               !  CLOSE THE PRESENT SCREEN
       DO FILE                         !  CALL NEW MAIN MENU ITEM
       EXIT                            !  GO BACK TO LAST PROCEDURE
    OF ALT_E                           !ON THE HOT KEY
       CLOSE(VIEWSCREEN)               !  CLOSE THE PRESENT SCREEN
       DO EDIT                         !  CALL NEW MAIN MENU ITEM
       EXIT                            !  GO BACK TO LAST PROCEDURE
    OF ALT_P                           !ON THE HOT KEY
       CLOSE(VIEWSCREEN)               !  CLOSE THE PRESENT SCREEN
       DO PRINTS                       !  CALL NEW MAIN MENU ITEM
       EXIT                            !  GO BACK TO LAST PROCEDURE
    OF ALT_Q                           !ON THE HOTKEY
       RETURN                          !  GO BACK TO DOS
    OF F1_KEY                          !ON HOT KEY
       HELPS                           !  SHOW HELP SCREEN
    OF ESC_KEY                         !RETURN ON SCREEN REJECT
       CLOSE(VIEWSCREEN)               !  ALERT CURSOR KEYS
       EXIT                            !  GO TO MAIN MENU
    OF LEFT_KEY                        !CHECK FOR CURSOR KEY CHOICE
       CLOSE(VIEWSCREEN)               !  CLOSE THIS SCREEN
       DO EDIT                         !  GO TO NEW MENU
       RESTART                         !  GO TO MAIN IF NEW
    OF RIGHT_KEY                       !CHECK FOR CURSOR KEY
       CLOSE(VIEWSCREEN)               !  CLOSE THIS SCREEN
       DO PRINTS                       !  GO TO NEW MENU
       RESTART                         !  GO TO MAIN IF NEW
    END!CASE
```

(continued)

```
    EXECUTE CHOICE()                    !  CALL THE SELECTED PROCEDURE
        NOTES('ZOOM IN')                !  FIRST MENU SELECTION
        NOTES('ZOOM OUT')               !  SECOND MENU SELECTION
        NOTES('RESTORE')                !  THIRD MENU SELECTION
        NOTES('MOVE')                   !  FOURTH MENU SELECTION
    END!EXECUTE
  END!LOOP

PRINTS          ROUTINE
  OPEN(PRINTSCREEN)                     !OPEN THE MENU SCREEN
  SETCURSOR                             !TURN OFF ANY CURSOR
  MENU_FIELD" = ''                      !START MENU WITH FIRST ITEM
  LOOP                                  !LOOP UNTIL USER EXITS
    DO ALERTS                           !ALERT SPECIAL KEYS
    ACCEPT                              !READ A FIELD OR MENU CHOICE
    CASE KEYCODE()                      !GET KEYSTROKE
    OF ALT_F                            !ON THE HOT KEY
       CLOSE(PRINTSCREEN)               !  CLOSE THE PRESENT SCREEN
       DO FILE                          !  CALL NEW MAIN MENU ITEM
       EXIT                             !  GO BACK TO LAST PROCEDURE
    OF ALT_E                            !ON THE HOT KEY
       CLOSE(PRINTSCREEN)               !  CLOSE THE PRESENT SCREEN
       DO EDIT                          !  CALL NEW MAIN MENU ITEM
       EXIT                             !  GO BACK TO LAST PROCEDURE
    OF ALT_V                            !ON THE HOT KEY
       CLOSE(PRINTSCREEN)               !  CLOSE THE PRESENT SCREEN
       DO VIEW                          !  CALL NEW MAIN MENU ITEM
       EXIT                             !  GO BACK TO LAST PROCEDURE
    OF ALT_Q                            !ON THE HOTKEY
       RETURN                           !  GO BACK TO DOS
    OF F1_KEY                           !ON HIT KEY
       HELPS                            !  SHOW HELP SCREEN
    OF ESC_KEY                          !ON HOT KEY
       CLOSE(PRINTSCREEN)               !  CLOSE THIS SCREEN
       EXIT                             !  GO TO MAIN PROCEDURE
    OF LEFT_KEY                         !CHECK FOR CURSOR KEY
       CLOSE(PRINTSCREEN)               !  CLOSE THIS SCREEN
       DO VIEW                          !  GO TO NEW MENU
       RESTART                          !  GO TO MAIN IF NEW
    END!CASE
    EXECUTE CHOICE()                    !  CALL THE SELECTED PROCEDURE
        NOTES('SETUP PRINTER')          !  FIRST MENU SELECTION
        NOTES('SETUP PAGE')             !  SECOND MENU SELECTION
        NOTES('REVIEW')                 !  THIRD MENU SELECTION
        NOTES('PRINTING...')            !  FOURTH MENU SELECTION
    END!EXECUTE
  END!LOOP
```

(continued)

```
ALERTS     ROUTINE                       !PREPARE WATCH ON SPECIAL KEYS
           ALERT                         !TURN OFF ALL ALERTED KEYS
           ALERT(F1_KEY)                 !ALERT HELP KEY
           ALERT(LEFT_KEY)               !ALERT CURSOR KEYS
           ALERT(RIGHT_KEY)
           ALERT(ESC_KEY)                !ALERT SCREEN REJECT KEY
           ALERT(ALT_F)                  !ALERT MENU HOT KEYS
           ALERT(ALT_E)
           ALERT(ALT_V)
           ALERT(ALT_P)
           ALERT(ALT_Q)
```

The Bigmenu Sample Source Code

BIGMENU.CLA

```
BIGMENU  PROGRAM
           INCLUDE('STD_KEYS.CLA')
           INCLUDE('CTL_KEYS.CLA')
           INCLUDE('ALT_KEYS.CLA')
           INCLUDE('SHF_KEYS.CLA')

REJECT_KEY   EQUATE(CTRL_ESC)
ACCEPT_KEY   EQUATE(CTRL_ENTER)
TRUE         EQUATE(1)
FALSE        EQUATE(0)

           MAP
             PROC(G_OPENFILES)
             MODULE('BIGMENU1')
               PROC(MAIN_MENU)
               .
             MODULE('BIGMENU2')
               PROC(DATE)
               .
             MODULE('BIGMENU3')
               PROC(TIME)
               .
             MODULE('BIGMENU4')
               PROC(BIRTH)
               .
             INCLUDE('DOS1.CPY')
           .
```

(continued)

```
                EJECT('FILE LAYOUTS')
                EJECT('GLOBAL MEMORY VARIABLES')
ACTION          SHORT                                !0 = NO ACTION
                                                     !1 = ADD RECORD
                                                     !2 = CHANGE RECORD
                                                     !3 = DELETE RECORD
                                                     !4 = LOOKUP FIELD


                GROUP,PRE(MEM)
MESSAGE         STRING(30)                           !Global Message Area
PAGE            SHORT                                !Report Page Number
LINE            SHORT                                !Report Line Number
DEVICE          STRING(30)                           !Report Device Name
DATE            STRING(8)
TIME            STRING(5)
BIRTH           STRING(8)
NAME            STRING(20)
                   .

                EJECT('CODE SECTION')
  CODE
  SETHUE(7,0)                                        !SET WHITE ON BLACK
  BLANK                                              !  AND BLANK
  G_OPENFILES                                        !OPEN OR CREATE FILES
  SETHUE()                                           !    THE SCREEN
  MAIN_MENU
  RETURN                                             !EXIT TO DOS


G_OPENFILES   PROCEDURE                              !OPEN FILES & CHECK FOR ERROR
  CODE
  BLANK                                              !BLANK THE SCREEN
```

BIGMENU1.CLA

```
                MEMBER('BIGMENU')
MAIN_MENU       PROCEDURE

SCREEN          SCREEN        PRE(SCR),WINDOW(25,80),AT(1,1),HUE(15,1)
                ROW(1,31)   PAINT(1,20),HUE(0,7)
                ROW(21,3)   PAINT(4,76),HUE(15,0)
                ROW(23,18)  PAINT(1,47),HUE(15,1)
                ROW(21,32)  PAINT(1,20),HUE(15,1)
                ROW(20,33)  PAINT(1,17),HUE(15,0)
                ROW(13,33)  PAINT(1,17),HUE(15,0)
```

(continued)

```
ROW(5,38)    PAINT(1,6),HUE(15,0)
ROW(1,1)     STRING('<201,205{29},0{20},205{29},187>')
ROW(2,1)     REPEAT(4);STRING('<186,0{78},186>') .
ROW(6,1)     REPEAT(3);STRING('<186,0{29},179,0{20},179,0{27},186>') .
ROW(9,1)     STRING('<186,0{29},192,196{20},217,0{27},186>')
ROW(10,1)    REPEAT(3);STRING('<186,0{78},186>') .
ROW(13,1)    STRING('<186,0{12},218,196{18},0{17},196{18},191,0{11}>' |
             & '<186>')
ROW(14,1)    REPEAT(4);STRING('<186,0{12},179,0{53},179,0{11},186>') .
ROW(18,1)    STRING('<186,0{12},192,196{53},217,0{11},186>')
ROW(19,1)    REPEAT(6);STRING('<186,0{78},186>') .
ROW(25,1)    STRING('<200,205{78},188>')
ROW(5,31)    STRING('<218,196{6},0{6},196{8},191>')
ROW(21,3)    STRING('<196{29},0{19},196{28}>'),HUE(15,1)
ROW(23,2)    STRING('<196{16},0{46},196{15}>'),HUE(15,1)
ROW(1,32)    STRING('A REALLY FULL MENU')
ROW(3,17)    STRING('Your Identity:')
    COL(53)  STRING(' (Entry Field)')
ROW(5,39)    STRING('MENU')
ROW(10,27)   STRING('Display Field {6}Computed Field')
ROW(11,44)   STRING('is')
    COL(50)  STRING('years old')
ROW(13,34)   STRING('COMPUTED FIELDS')
ROW(14,16)   STRING('Current Date:')
ROW(15,16)   STRING('Current Time:')
ROW(16,16)   STRING('Current Path:')
ROW(17,16)   STRING('Random Access Memory:')
    COL(48)  STRING('bytes free')
ROW(20,34)   STRING('DOS Environment')
ROW(21,33)   STRING('Conditional Field')
ROW(23,19)   STRING('Computed Field Filled from Conditional Field')
NAME   ROW(11,23)   STRING(20),HUE(0,7)
BIRTH     COL(47)   STRING(@n2),HUE(0,7)
DATE   ROW(14,30)   STRING(@d1),HUE(0,7)
TIME   ROW(15,30)   STRING(@t1),HUE(0,7)
PATH   ROW(16,30)   STRING(@s35),HUE(0,7)
RAM    ROW(17,38)   STRING(@n9),HUE(0,7)
DOS    ROW(22,3)    STRING(@s76)
DOS2   ROW(24,3)    STRING(@s76)
                    ENTRY,USE(?FIRST_FIELD)
       ROW(3,32)    ENTRY(@s20),USE(MEM:NAME),LFT,OVR,HUE(0,7),SEL(0,7)
                    ENTRY,USE(?PRE_MENU)
                    MENU,USE(MENU_FIELD"),REQ
       ROW(6,34)       STRING('Change the Date')
       ROW(7,34)       STRING('Change the Time')
       ROW(8,35)       STRING('Find Your Age')
                 .                .
```

(continued)

```
EJECT
CODE
OPEN(SCREEN)                                   !OPEN THE MENU SCREEN
SETCURSOR                                      !TURN OFF ANY CURSOR
MENU_FIELD" = ''                               !START MENU WITH FIRST ITEM
LOOP                                           !LOOP UNTIL USER EXITS
  SCR:NAME = MEM:NAME
  SCR:BIRTH = AGE(deformat(mem:birth,@d1))
  SCR:DATE = today()
  SCR:TIME = clock()
  SCR:PATH = path()
  SCR:RAM = memory()
  IF len(clip(environment('path'))) < 76       !EVALUATE CONDITION
    SCR:DOS = environment('path')              !  CONDITION IS TRUE
  ELSE                                         !OTHERWISE
    SCR:DOS = sub(environment('path'),1,76);dos2" = sub(environment('path'),77,76)
                                               !CONDITION IS FALSE

  SCR:DOS2 = dos2"
  ALERT                                        !TURN OFF ALL ALERTED KEYS
  ALERT(REJECT_KEY)                            !ALERT SCREEN REJECT KEY
  ALERT(ACCEPT_KEY)                            !ALERT SCREEN ACCEPT KEY
  ACCEPT                                       !READ A FIELD OR MENU CHOICE
  IF KEYCODE() = REJECT_KEY THEN RETURN.       !RETURN ON SCREEN REJECT

  IF KEYCODE() = ACCEPT_KEY                    !ON SCREEN ACCEPT KEY
    UPDATE                                     !  MOVE ALL FIELDS FROM SCREEN
    SELECT(?)                                  !  START WITH CURRENT FIELD
    SELECT                                     !  EDIT ALL FIELDS
    CYCLE                                      !  GO TO TOP OF LOOP
  .                                            !

  CASE FIELD()                                 !JUMP TO FIELD EDIT ROUTINE
  OF ?FIRST_FIELD                              !FROM THE FIRST FIELD
    IF KEYCODE() = ESC_KEY THEN RETURN.        !  RETURN ON ESC KEY

  OF ?MEM:NAME

  OF ?PRE_MENU                                 !PRE MENU FIELD CONDITION
    IF KEYCODE() = ESC_KEY                     !  BACKING UP?
      SELECT(?-1)                              !    SELECT PREVIOUS FIELD
    ELSE                                       !  GOING FORWARD
      SELECT(?+1)                              !    SELECT MENU FIELD
    .
  OF ?MENU_FIELD"                              !FROM THE MENU FIELD
    EXECUTE CHOICE()                           !  CALL THE SELECTED PROCEDURE
      DATE                                     !
```

(continued)

```
              TIME                                        !
              BIRTH                                       !
    . . .
```

BIGMENU2.CLA

```
          MEMBER('BIGMENU')
DATE          PROCEDURE

SCREEN        SCREEN        PRE(SCR),WINDOW(5,28),HUE(15,0)
              ROW(1,1)    STRING('<218,196{26},191>')
              ROW(2,1)    REPEAT(3);STRING('<179,0{26},179>') .
              ROW(5,1)    STRING('<192,196{26},217>')
              ROW(3,6)    STRING('New Date:')
                          ENTRY,USE(?FIRST_FIELD)
              COL(16)     ENTRY(@d1),USE(MEM:DATE),LFT,OVR
              ROW(4,9)    PAUSE('Press <<ENTER>'),USE(?PAUSE_FIELD)
                          ENTRY,USE(?LAST_FIELD)

                  .

    EJECT
    CODE
    OPEN(SCREEN)                              !OPEN THE SCREEN
    SETCURSOR                                 !TURN OFF ANY CURSOR
    DISPLAY                                   !DISPLAY THE FIELDS
    LOOP                                      !LOOP THRU ALL THE FIELDS
      ALERT                                   !RESET ALERTED KEYS
      ALERT(ACCEPT_KEY)                       !ALERT SCREEN ACCEPT KEY
      ALERT(REJECT_KEY)                       !ALERT SCREEN REJECT KEY
      ACCEPT                                  !READ A FIELD
      IF KEYCODE() = REJECT_KEY THEN RETURN.  !RETURN ON SCREEN REJECT KEY

      IF KEYCODE() = ACCEPT_KEY               !ON SCREEN ACCEPT KEY
        UPDATE                                !  MOVE ALL FIELDS FROM SCREEN
        SELECT(?)                             !  START WITH CURRENT FIELD
        SELECT                                !  EDIT ALL FIELDS
        CYCLE                                 !  GO TO TOP OF LOOP
      .                                       !

      CASE FIELD()                            !JUMP TO FIELD EDIT ROUTINE
      OF ?FIRST_FIELD                         !FROM THE FIRST FIELD
        IF KEYCODE() = ESC_KEY THEN RETURN.   !  RETURN ON ESC KEY

      OF ?MEM:DATE
        SETTODAY(DEFORMAT(MEM:DATE,@d1));dates# = deformat(mem:date)
```

(continued)

```
        OF ?PAUSE_FIELD                           !ON PAUSE FIELD
          IF KEYCODE() <> ENTER_KEY|              !IF NOT ENTER KEY
          AND KEYCODE() <> ACCEPT_KEY|            !AND NOT CTRL-ENTER KEY
          AND KEYCODE() <> 0                      !AND NOT NONSTOP MODE
            BEEP                                  !  SOUND KEYBOARD ALARM
            SELECT(?PAUSE_FIELD)                  !  AND STAY ON PAUSE FIELD
                 .
      OF ?LAST_FIELD                              !FROM THE LAST FIELD
        ACTION = 0                                !  SET ACTION TO COMPLETE
        RETURN                                    !  AND RETURN TO CALLER
    . .
```

BIGMENU3.CLA

```
          MEMBER('BIGMENU')
TIME          PROCEDURE

SCREEN        SCREEN       PRE(SCR),WINDOW(5,28),HUE(15,0)
            ROW(1,1)     STRING('<218,196{26},191>')
            ROW(2,1)     REPEAT(3);STRING('<179,0{26},179>') .
            ROW(5,1)     STRING('<192,196{26},217>')
            ROW(3,8)     STRING('New Time:')
                         ENTRY,USE(?FIRST_FIELD)
              COL(18)    ENTRY(@t1),USE(MEM:TIME),LFT,OVR
            ROW(4,9)     PAUSE('Press <<ENTER>'),USE(?PAUSE_FIELD)
                         ENTRY,USE(?LAST_FIELD)
                .

    EJECT
    CODE
    OPEN(SCREEN)                                !OPEN THE SCREEN
    SETCURSOR                                   !TURN OFF ANY CURSOR
    DISPLAY                                     !DISPLAY THE FIELDS
    LOOP                                        !LOOP THRU ALL THE FIELDS
      ALERT                                     !RESET ALERTED KEYS
      ALERT(ACCEPT_KEY)                         !ALERT SCREEN ACCEPT KEY
      ALERT(REJECT_KEY)                         !ALERT SCREEN REJECT KEY
      ACCEPT                                    !READ A FIELD
      IF KEYCODE() = REJECT_KEY THEN RETURN.    !RETURN ON SCREEN REJECT KEY

      IF KEYCODE() = ACCEPT_KEY                 !ON SCREEN ACCEPT KEY
        UPDATE                                  !  MOVE ALL FIELDS FROM SCREEN
        SELECT(?)                               !  START WITH CURRENT FIELD
        SELECT                                  !  EDIT ALL FIELDS
```

(continued)

```
      CYCLE                                    !  GO TO TOP OF LOOP
    .                                          !

    CASE FIELD()                               !JUMP TO FIELD EDIT ROUTINE
    OF ?FIRST_FIELD                            !FROM THE FIRST FIELD
      IF KEYCODE() = ESC_KEY THEN RETURN.      !  RETURN ON ESC KEY

    OF ?MEM:TIME
      SETCLOCK(DEFORMAT(MEM:TIME,@t1));times# = deformat(mem:time)

      OF ?PAUSE_FIELD                          !ON PAUSE FIELD
        IF KEYCODE() <> ENTER_KEY|             !IF NOT ENTER KEY
        AND KEYCODE() <> ACCEPT_KEY|           !AND NOT CTRL-ENTER KEY
        AND KEYCODE() <> 0                     !AND NOT NONSTOP MODE
          BEEP                                 !  SOUND KEYBOARD ALARM
          SELECT(?PAUSE_FIELD)                 !  AND STAY ON PAUSE FIELD
          .
    OF ?LAST_FIELD                             !FROM THE LAST FIELD
      ACTION = 0                               !  SET ACTION TO COMPLETE
      RETURN                                   !  AND RETURN TO CALLER

  . .
```

BIGMENU4.CLA

```
          MEMBER('BIGMENU')
BIRTH         PROCEDURE

SCREEN        SCREEN        PRE(SCR),WINDOW(5,29),HUE(15,0)
              ROW(1,1)      STRING('<218,196{27},191>')
              ROW(2,1)      REPEAT(3);STRING('<179,0{27},179>')  .
              ROW(5,1)      STRING('<192,196{27},217>')
              ROW(3,3)      STRING('Your Birth Date:')
                            ENTRY,USE(?FIRST_FIELD)
              COL(20)       ENTRY(@d1),USE(MEM:BIRTH),LFT,OVR
                            ENTRY,USE(?LAST_FIELD)

            .

  EJECT
  CODE
  OPEN(SCREEN)                                 !OPEN THE SCREEN
  SETCURSOR                                    !TURN OFF ANY CURSOR
  DISPLAY                                      !DISPLAY THE FIELDS
  LOOP                                         !LOOP THRU ALL THE FIELDS
    ALERT                                      !RESET ALERTED KEYS
    ALERT(ACCEPT_KEY)                          !ALERT SCREEN ACCEPT KEY
```

(continued)

```
ALERT(REJECT_KEY)                            !ALERT SCREEN REJECT KEY
ACCEPT                                       !READ A FIELD
IF KEYCODE() = REJECT_KEY THEN RETURN.       !RETURN ON SCREEN REJECT KEY

IF KEYCODE() = ACCEPT_KEY                    !ON SCREEN ACCEPT KEY
  UPDATE                                     !  MOVE ALL FIELDS FROM SCREEN
  SELECT(?)                                  !  START WITH CURRENT FIELD
  SELECT                                     !  EDIT ALL FIELDS
  CYCLE                                      !  GO TO TOP OF LOOP
.                                            !

CASE FIELD()                                 !JUMP TO FIELD EDIT ROUTINE
OF ?FIRST_FIELD                              !FROM THE FIRST FIELD
  IF KEYCODE() = ESC_KEY THEN RETURN.        !  RETURN ON ESC KEY

OF ?LAST_FIELD                               !FROM THE LAST FIELD
  ACTION = 0                                 !  SET ACTION TO COMPLETE
  RETURN                                     !  AND RETURN TO CALLER
. .
```

Chapter 9

Table Techniques

Tables are one of the most powerful tools that Clarion provides. In fact, Designer is built around the Menu-Table-Form layout for its application style, with the table as the center of activity. However, it's important to remember that these tables are built from the Clarion language and do not exist as separate, callable entities. There is no TABLE command, although there is a Table structure that we'll discuss when we cover memory tables later on in this chapter.

You must use various elements of the language to create and manipulate the screen and the data to achieve the application look you desire. Language elements like POINT and SCROLL get you headed in the right direction, but they do not themselves constitute a complete table. By the way, the term "table" refers to a list of data elements or fields grouped by record with a window that allows those groups of records to scroll down the screen when there are too many to view. This is in contrast to Form, which is for displaying the contents of a single record for adding, editing, and deleting; and Menu, which is for moving around the application.

What Makes a Table

The first example we'll use to discuss the structure and function of a table is from a program for marking items in a table. A sample of such a table is shown in Figure 9-1, and its Screen structure is given in Figure 9-2. The entire MARKER program can be found at the end of this chapter. As we cover

Figure 9-1   A typical table for a Clarion program, with scrolling lines and a selection bar. This one demonstrates how you can mark items in a table without going to an Update Form.

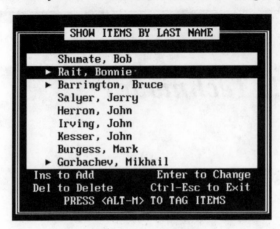

each aspect of the program, we'll discuss the elements of a table and how you can make them work inside your applications.

The Screen Structure

The three elements that create a table in Clarion are the Screen structure, the local "tracking" variables, and the program that manipulates it. That might sound terribly obvious, but those elements have standard components without which you cannot build a table. You need an area of the screen designated for scrolling the data. You need some way to point to a row of data as the current row. You need some method to interpret the keystrokes that move the data in the table up and down, to grab and edit the record for the current row, or to add a new record to the table.

In the Screen structure, the important components consist of defining the area that will be scrollable and establishing some structure for pointing to a line (or record) in that area. As discussed in Chapter 4, the two language elements that perform those tasks are POINT and REPEAT. As with all other Screen structures, you can include Entry Fields and Display Fields as well. The rest of the Screen structure for a table consists of whatever screen painting, drawing, and explanatory text you choose to include.

Figure 9-2 This is the Screen structure for the table shown in Figure 9-1. Notice how the Index for the Repeat structure is a variable. That allows the program to identify the rows in the table to perform actions by row like filling the table or scrolling up and down on a keystroke.

```
SCREEN    SCREEN        PRE(SCR),WINDOW(15,41),HUE(15,1)
```

The Graphics Area

```
          ROW(1,3)    PAINT(11,37),HUE(0,7)
          ROW(2,3)    PAINT(1,37),HUE(15,1)
          ROW(1,1)    STRING('<201,205{7},0{25},205{7},187>'),HUE(15,1)
          ROW(2,1)    REPEAT(13);STRING('<186,0{39},186>'),HUE(15,1)   .
          ROW(15,1)   STRING('<200,205{39},188>'),HUE(15,1)
          ROW(1,10)   STRING('SHOW ITEMS BY LAST NAME')
          ROW(12,4)   STRING('Ins to Add'),HUE(11,1)
            COL(24)   STRING('Enter to Change'),HUE(11,1)
          ROW(13,4)   STRING('Del to Delete'),HUE(11,1)
            COL(23)   STRING('Ctrl-Esc to Exit'),HUE(11,1)
          ROW(14,9)   STRING('PRESS <<ALT-M> TO TAG ITEMS')
```

The Field Entry Area

```
                      ENTRY,USE(?FIRST_FIELD)
                      ENTRY,USE(?PRE_POINT)
```

The Repeat and Point Structure

```
                      REPEAT(9),EVERY(1),INDEX(NDX)
          ROW(3,3)    POINT(1,37),USE(?POINT),ESC(?-1)
```

The Fields Definition Area

```
SPACE     COL(3)      STRING(@s1)
MARKED    COL(6)      STRING(1)
NAME      COL(8)      STRING(@s30)
SPACE2    COL(39)     STRING(@s1)
            .           .
```

The Repeat Structure in a Table

The Repeat structure in a table essentially describes what the scrollable area of a table will be. In Designer, it will be as wide as the number of fields across and extend to the first graphic character beneath that. If you are coding manually, you can cause this Repeat structure to go over those graphic characters, if you should want to for some reason. However, Designer limits the number of lines in a Repeat structure to the amount that will fit before the first ASCII character like a (prompt or a line), or it simply stops at the edge of the window or screen.

A Repeat structure in a table can be thought of as a single definition of the variables to be shown, with a way to repaint those variables with new values based on a count. Your only alternative to this method would be to continually blank the screen out and use a statement like SHOW to redisplay each line across the screen. Now, you've got a setup that disconnects the file variable from the screen display. There is no field equate for something merely painted on the screen with SHOW or TYPE. You'd have to keep track of what line you were on and relate that information to which record had been called for display so that you could maintain that position for scrolling the table and updating the records. What a mess!

When you create a Repeat structure with the following statement

```
REPEAT(9),EVERY(1),INDEX(NDX)
(field display definitions)
END!REPEAT
```

you will fill 9 rows in the table according to the color attributes you selected for the field displays themselves. You can change the color of the display by changing the Normal and Selected color selections you made in Designer or Editor, or by painting over an area of the scrollable part of the table. However, don't try to divide the columns by drawing a track in Designer as is pictured in the *Clarion Language Reference* manual. It will not appear when the Repeat structure fills its eligible area.

To avoid having your fields start on the very edge of the highlighted area, you can insert a Computed Field in Designer or use a Placeholder Field in the Repeat structure. If you refer to Figure 9-2, you'll see two variables called SPACE and SPACE2 in the Repeat structure. These are empty fields and do not display data, but they cause the highlight bar and the scrolling area to enlarge to encompass them. This makes the screen easier to read when you are using a different color for the scrolling area.

Figure 9-3   The local variables used by a Designer-generated table to locate rows in the table for scrolling and filling with data. These variables are hard-coded into the Table model procedure.

```
NDX        BYTE                    !REPEAT INDEX FOR  POINT AREA
ROW        BYTE                    !ACTUAL ROW OF SCROLL  AREA
COL        BYTE                    !ACTUAL COLUMN OF  SCROLL AREA
COUNT      BYTE(9)                 !NUMBER OF ITEMS TO SCROLL
ROWS       BYTE(9)                 !NUMBER OF ROWS TO  SCROLL
COLS       BYTE(37)                !NUMBER OF COLUMNS  TO SCROLL
FOUND      BYTE                    !RECORD FOUND FLAG
NEWPTR     LONG                    !POINTER TO NEW RECORD
```

To draw dividing lines, you can use either of these two methods:

1. Paint the space between the fields a different or darker color. This does not hurt the scrolling functions or interfere with speed.
2. Create a Computed Field in Designer or add a field in Editor (like the placeholder discussed earlier) and set it equal to the character for a straight line down in extended ASCII ('<179>'). This slows the table down a little, but it makes a nice dividing line.

Another method for dividing the screen appears in the annotated examples that come with the Developer's kit. You can use the Repeat structure to show columns or rows by giving a Repeat structure with cells that (in the case of the CHECKS program in the Examples) give you 4 columns across and 14 rows down. Note, however, that the Point Field only covers 16 characters across or one column's worth. This causes 4×14, or 56, records to be displayed, and the cursor travels down each column before going to the top of the next one. The local variables declared for tracking table movement appear in Figure 9-3.

The Scrolling Portion of a Table

The scrolling portion of the table is partly determined by the Repeat structure and partly by the SCROLL statement in the program itself. The Repeat

Figure 9-4   The leading screen for a simple program that demonstrates the control Clarion can exert over the speaker in a PC.

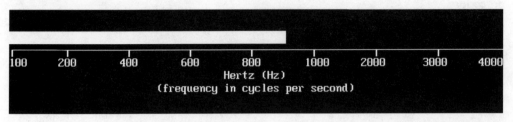

structure supplies the rows of records to be scrolled and identifies those rows for both reading and placing the records in the table. The SCROLL statement merely identifies that same area and instructs the compiler to move a specific number of lines either up or down. The local variables defined for the preceding Table Procedure (as they appeared in Figure 9-2) are used by the SCROLL statement to move the contents of the table. The Point Field is used to determine the number of rows to scroll in a Designer-generated table. The ROWS function returns the number of lines contained in the field labeled with the equate ?POINT. The sample program in Figure 9-4 is a playful use of the SCROLL statement to move one section of the screen. The code for the program is given in Figure 9-5.

At the completion of the run from 100 to 4000 Hz depicted in Figure 9-4, the program scrolls a message in one small section of the screen along the bottom to demonstrate a simple use of the SCROLL statement. The program leaves the graphic above the scrolling area untouched.

The POINT Statement in a Table

The POINT statement in a table is the method Clarion uses to locate record data in an environment where information is moving around on a screen and not stationary, as with a data entry form. A POINT statement simply points to a location on the screen that is determined by the number of rows down and columns across you specify. The repeat index set in the Repeat structure in a table (its most common use) locates the record data associated with that position in the table. That index variable must be related by your program to the file record from which it came. In a Designer-generated table, the index variable relates to a line in the memory table associated with the on-screen table, and that structure relates via a pointer to the file on the disk. (See Figure 9-6.)

Figure 9-5 The code for the simple sound program that demonstrates scrolling a portion of the screen to display a message.

```
BEEPER      PROGRAM

SCREEN    SCREEN       HUE(7,0)
          ROW(11,1)  STRING('<218,196{8},194,196{9},194,196{9},194,196{9}>'  |
                     & '<194,196{9},194,196{9},194,196{9},194,196{9},191>')
          ROW(12,1)  STRING('100 {5}200 {7}400 {7}600 {7}800 {7}1000 {5}2000' |
                     & ' {6}3000 {5}4000')
          ROW(13,36) STRING('Hertz (Hz)')
          ROW(14,25) STRING(' (frequency in cycles per second)')
          END!SCREEN
            CODE
            OPEN(SCREEN)                   !OPEN THE DISPLAY
            FREQ# = 100                    !SET THE LOWEST FREQ.
             LOOP 50 TIMES                 !GO TO 1000Hz
               COL# +=1                    ! MOVE ONE COLUMN
               LOOP 2 TIMES                ! JUMP TWO FREQS
                 FREQ# += 9                !   GO UP AN OCTAVE
               END!LOOP                    !END OF JUMP
                 BEEP(FREQ#,6)             !MAKE THE NOISE
                 SHOW(10,COL#,'_')         !DRAW THE BAR
             END!LOOP                      !REACHED 1000Hz
            SHOW(10,COL#+1,'_')            !DRAW FILL CHARACTER
            LOOP 15 TIMES                  !GO TO 4000Hz
                 COL# += 2                 ! MOVE 2 COLS AT A TIME
                 FREQ# += 200              ! RAISE THE FREQS
                 BEEP(FREQ#,12)            ! MAKE A NOISE
                   SHOW(10,COL#,'__')      ! DRAW THE BAR
            END!LOOP                       !REACHED 4000
            SHOW(6,1,CENTER('THA...THAT' & '<39>' & 'S ALL FOLKS!',80))
            BEEP(400,25);BEEP(50,30)    ! TA-DAH!
            BEEP(400,10);BEEP(50,6)
            BEEP(400,10);BEEP(50,20); BEEP(530,70)
            SHOW(21,1,CENTER('SOUND EFFECTS',80))    !BEGIN CREDITS
            BEEP(50,100)                             !SILENT PAUSE
            MESSAGE" = 'courtesy of'
            DO SCROLLER                              !SCROLL SCREEN
            MESSAGE" = 'CLARION PROFESSIONAL DEVELOPER'
            DO SCROLLER                              !SCROLL SCREEN
            MESSAGE" = 'PRESS ANY KEY TO EXIT'
            DO SCROLLER                    !SCROLL SCREEN
            ASK                            !WAIT FOR KEYSTROKE
            CLOSE(SCREEN)                  !CLOSE DISPLAY
            RETURN                         !GO BACK TO DOS
```

(continued)

Figure 9-5   *continued*

```
SCROLLER   ROUTINE                              !SCROLLING ROUTINE
           LOOP                                 !CYCLE TO BREAK
             COUNT# += 1                        ! ADD TO COUNTER
             SCROLL(17,1,9,80,1)                ! SCROLL SCREEN PATCH
             BEEP(50,14)                        !SILENT PAUSE
             IF COUNT# = 4 THEN BEEP(50,100).   !SILENT PAUSE
             IF COUNT# = 7
               SHOW(25,1,CENTER(MESSAGE",80))   !SHOW CREDIT
             END!IF
             IF COUNT# = 8 THEN BREAK.          !GET OUT WHEN DONE
           END!LOOP
           COUNT# = 0                           !RESET SCROLL COUNTER
```

The POINT statement is naturally a stationary vehicle—there is no mechanism within the statement itself to cause movement, as with the SCROLL statement. It points to the one place on the screen that you set in the initial Screen structure. It does not accept implicit or explicitly defined variables. It only moves when new parameters get passed to it via one of the subroutines you may write or that already appear in Designer to respond to keystrokes. The INDEX attribute of the Repeat structure sets the variable used to move the Point Field between records or locations around the screen. Each intersec-

Figure 9-6   The process by which a Designer-generated table retrieves a record for processing based on the location of the Point Field in the table.

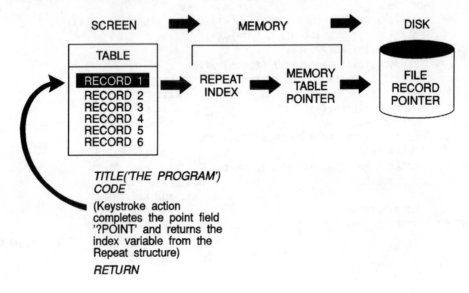

tion of the Repeat structure is numbered and the POINT highlight bar pops to that location whenever the INDEX variable is changed. The POINT and REPEAT statements working in tandem are shown in Figure 9-7.

Instead of filling the screen with records from a file, the program in Figure 9-7 works more like a menu. The items "UPPER," "LOWER," and

Figure 9-7   A simple program to demonstrate the POINT and REPEAT statements.

```
POINTER   PROGRAM
          INCLUDE('STD_KEYS.CLA')

SCREEN    SCREEN   WINDOW(11,35),AT(8,24),HUE(7,0)! SCREEN STRUCTURE
          ROW(1,1)   STRING('<218,196{33},191>')
          ROW(2,1)   REPEAT(9);STRING('<179,0{33},179>') .
          ROW(11,1)  STRING('<192,196{33},217>')
          ROW(5,16)  STRING('UPPER')
          ROW(7,16)  STRING('MIDDLE')
          ROW(9,16)  STRING('LOWER')
MESSAGE   ROW(2,3)   STRING(30)                    ! SCREEN MESSAGE
                     REPEAT(3),EVERY(2),INDEX(NDX) ! REPEAT STRUCTURE
          ROW(5,14)     POINT(1,10),USE(?POINTER)  !POINT STATEMENT
                     END!REPEAT
          END

NDX       BYTE                               ! REPEAT INDEX

          CODE
          OPEN(SCREEN)                       ! START THE DISPLAY
          ALERT                              ! TURN OFF ALERT KEYS
          ALERT(ESC_KEY)                     ! SENSITIZE THE ESCAPE KEY
          ALERT(ENTER_KEY)                   ! SENSITIZE THE ENTER KEY
          LOOP                               ! START PROCESSING LOOP
          LOOP                               ! START PROCESSING LOOP
            ACCEPT                           !   PROCESS KEYSTROKE
            IF KEYCODE( ) = ESC_KEY THEN BREAK. !   EXIT ON ESCAPE KEY
            IF KEYCODE( ) = ENTER_KEY          !   POST MESSAGE ON ENTER KEY
              MESSAGE = CENTER('INDEX = ' & NDX,30)
            END!IF
            IF NDX < 3                       ! TEST INDEX
              NDX += 1                       !   INCREMENT INDEX
            ELSE                             ! OTHERWISE
              NDX = 0                        !   RESET INDEX
            END!IF                           ! END LOOP AND END IF
          END!LOOP
          CLOSE(SCREEN)                      ! CLOSE UP DISPLAY
          RETURN                             ! GO BACK TO DOS
```

"MIDDLE" are entered directly onto the screen when the Screen structure is created. They are, however, placed in alignment with the first placement of the POINT statement at row 5, column 15.

The POINT statement then declares a highlight bar 1 row high by 10 columns long. That just happens to cover the word "UPPER." Now the Repeat structure runs three items deep, spaced two lines apart. In the code for this little program, the important part appears where the NDX variable gets incremented. Each keystroke completed registers a change in the INDEX that drives the POINT statement to a new location. The keystroke sensitivities used to operate the Point Field are given in Chapter 8.

Play around with this little program until you feel comfortable with the impact of the Repeat structure in concert with the Point Field. Try disabling the If structure to see what happens when the INDEX variable is not incremented. Try getting the value of the ?POINTER or field equate USE variable of the POINT statement and using the SHOW statement to display it on the screen. You can see how this simple structure could be used to construct a menu. With a simple EXECUTE statement to respond to whichever INDEX number was last selected, you could call a procedure—very much as the Menu structure does. (See Chapter 8.) For a table, you simply add the scrolling functions, read the file, and fill the Repeat structure with data from that file.

Designer's Way

If you create a table using Designer, you will be forced down certain paths. For instance, Designer does not support a menu structure within a table. Designer's paradigm for scrolling tables is to show a maximum of 80 characters across, with single or multiple rows of data from each record. The common keystrokes are:

- the Enter key, for editing table entries;
- the Insert key, for adding records;
- the Delete key, for deleting records.

We will focus on how Designer handles tables in order to cover all the basic techniques of Clarion tables that you would use in manually coding your programs.

Figure 9-8   The Options screen for creating a table in Designer.

```
                         Application:CHANGE

      Files          Procedures

      MEMORY
      INFO                                   Table

                 Procedure Name   :MAIN_TABLE
                 Procedure Title  :Show Data By Last
                 Setup Procedure  :
                 Update Procedure:UPD_DATA
                 Access Key       :INF:BY_LAST        of INFO
                 Help ID          :
                 Record Selector  :INF:LAST
                 Record Filter    :
                 Hot Procedure    :
                   Hot Key        :
                 Position         :Float      Float   Fix
                 Combine With     :
                 Model Procedure  :


      Ins to Ad                                                   e
```

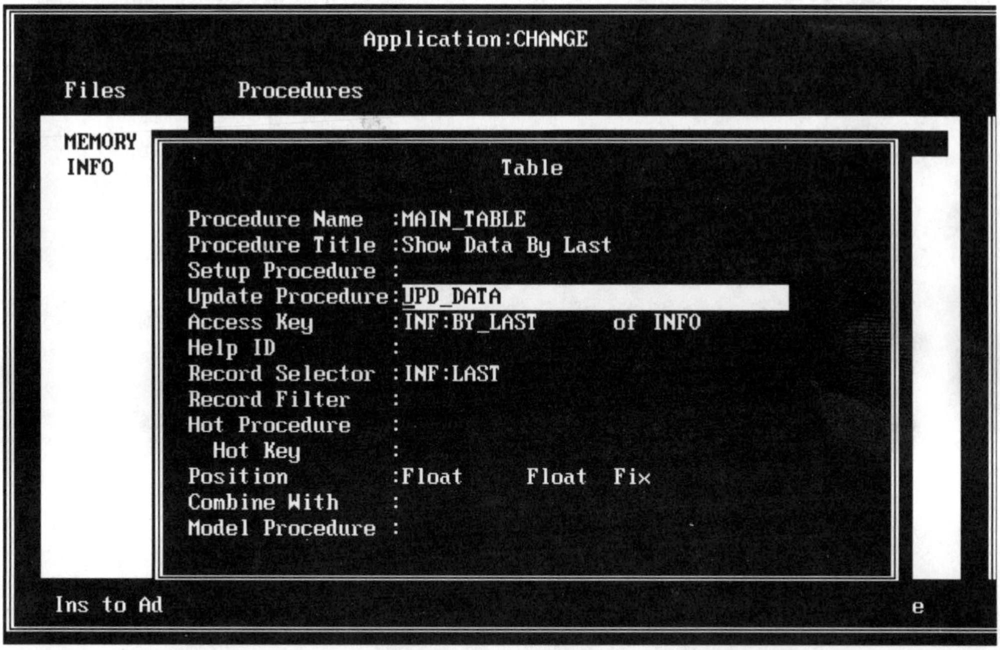

Creating a Table

"Table" is one of the four choices for procedure type when you work in Designer. The unique elements of the Options screen for creating a table in Designer include the Update Procedure, the Access Key, the Record Selector, and the Record Filter. (See Figure 9-8.) As with all Designer forms, you can insert code at the beginning of the procedure in the Setup Procedure to execute once as you start up the table.

The Update Procedure

Traditionally, the Update Procedure calls a form with the fields from the record displayed in the table. In the Designer "Application Tree" diagram, the name of the Update Procedure will appear as a child of the Table Procedure. However, you can use this option to take several powerful steps. For instance,

Figure 9-9   The code for the table shown in Figure 9-1 from the Main Event Loop that calls the Update Procedure for the first time when no records exist in the file. It is started based on what part of the nonscrolling part of the table the FIELD( ) statement returns as current.

```
OF ?POINT                            !PROCESS THE POINT FIELD
    IF RECORDS(TABLE) = 0            !IF THERE ARE NO RECORDS
       CLEAR(ITE:RECORD)            ! CLEAR RECORD AREA
       ACTION = 1                   !  SET ACTION TO ADD
       GET(ITEMS,0)                 !  CLEAR PENDING RECORD
       UPD_ITEMS                    !  CALL FORM FOR NEW RECORD
       NEWPTR = POINTER(ITEMS)      !   SET POINTER TO NEW RECORD
       DO FIRST_PAGE                !  DISPLAY THE FIRST PAGE
       IF RECORDS(TABLE) = 0        !  IF THERE AREN'T ANY RECORDS
         RECORDS# = FALSE           !    INDICATE NO RECORDS
         SELECT(?PRE_POINT-1)       !    SELECT THE PRIOR FIELD
       .
       CYCLE                        !    AND LOOP AGAIN
     .                              ! END OF LOOP
```

this procedure line can be used to write code before and after the actual Update Procedure itself is called, and you can perform procedures that update a file without ever branching to another file. The keystrokes that call this code are the Enter, Delete, and Insert keys. Each one is handled differently. The only other cause for the Update Procedure to be called in a Designer-generated table is when no records exist in the file when the table is started as shown in Figure 9-9. Figure 9-10 shows the code created by Designer to handle the editing keys made available to the user.

Depending on which key was pressed, you could update a file without ever calling a form. Let's walk through what happens when each of the keys is pressed inside the Main Event Loop for a Designer-generated table. Each press of the Insert key, the Enter key, and the Delete key calls the Update Procedure. The ↑ and ↓ cursor keys scroll the table one line, and the PgUp and PgDn keys (as well as combinations with the Control key) pop the windows to another complete set of records from the file.

Adding a Record: When you add a record, Designer builds the code to respond to the Insert key. The Main Event Loop is checking for that key to be pressed by using a Case structure to determine what KEYCODE( ) the AC-CEPT statement acknowledged. Remember, the combination of ACCEPT

Figure 9-10 The section of the code for the Figure 9-1 table that calls the Update Procedure based on the user's keystrokes. This also appears in the Main Event Loop. Notice how the setting for the ACTION variable changes according to what key is pressed. This is where the intelligence is transferred to the Update Procedure to tell it whether a record is being added, changed, or deleted.

```
CASE KEYCODE( )                             !PROCESS THE KEYSTROKE
```

For Adding a Record (ACTION = 1)

```
OF INS_KEY                                  !INS KEY
  CLEAR(ITE:RECORD)                         !  CLEAR RECORD AREA
  ACTION = 1                                !  SET ACTION TO ADD
  GET(ITEMS,0)                              !  CLEAR PENDING RECORD
  UPD_ITEMS                                 !  CALL FORM FOR NEW RECORD
  IF ~ACTION                                !  IF RECORD WAS ADDED
    NEWPTR = POINTER(ITEMS)                 !    SET POINTER TO NEW RECORD
    DO FIND_RECORD                          !    POSITION IN FILE
```

For Editing a Record (ACTION = 2)

```
OF ENTER_KEY                               !ENTER KEY
OROF ACCEPT_KEY                            !CTRL-ENTER KEY
  DO GET_RECORD                            !  GET THE SELECTED RECORD
  IF ACTION = 4 AND KEYCODE( ) = ENTER_KEY !  IF THIS IS A LOOKUP REQUEST
    ACTION = 0                             !    SET ACTION TO COMPLETE
    BREAK                                  !    AND RETURN TO CALLER
  .
  IF ~ERROR( )                             !  IF RECORD IS STILL THERE
    ACTION = 2                             !    SET ACTION TO CHANGE
    UPD_ITEMS                              !    CALL FORM TO CHANGE REC
    IF ACTION THEN CYCLE.                  !    IF SUCCESSFUL REDISPLAY
  .
  NEWPTR = POINTER(ITEMS)                  !    SET POINTER TO NEW RECORD
```

For Deleting a Record (ACTION = 3)

```
OF DEL_KEY                                 !DEL KEY
  DO GET_RECORD                            !  READ THE SELECTED RECORD
  IF ~ERROR( )                             !  IF RECORD IS STILL THERE
    ACTION = 3                             !    SET ACTION TO DELETE
    UPD_ITEMS                              !    CALL FORM TO DELETE
    IF ~ACTION                             !    IF SUCCESSFUL
      N# = NDX                             !      SAVE POINT INDEX
      DO SAME_PAGE                         !      RE-DISPLAY
      NDX = N#                             !      RESTORE POINT INDEX
  . .
```

and KEYCODE( ) removes the keystroke from the keyboard buffer. (You would use the KEYBOARD( ) function if you were not processing an AC-CEPT and wanted to leave the keystroke in the buffer for some reason.) Then, the Update Procedure is called with the global ACTION variable preset to prejudice the procedure toward a specific file function.

Hint: The global ACTION variable is not magically adjusted inside Clarion. It is maintained explicitly in the code. Its values, for reference only, are listed in the global section of the main program. Those values indicate how Designer will set ACTION depending on the process at hand. You can screen all sorts of actions in the Setup Procedure of each major procedure type by testing for the value of ACTION.

The primary steps for adding a record to the data file follow:

1. First the existing record in memory is cleared (if there was one)
2. The global ACTION variable is set to 1 to signify that the Update Procedure should treat this particular event as adding a record, which means the final step in the Form Procedure will be to execute an ADD. (This will be covered in Chapter 10.)
3. Call the Update Procedure or whatever code you wish to use to update the file.
4. After returning from the Update Procedure, check to see how that procedure left the global ACTION variable. If nothing changed, that is, if the ACTION variable is still set to Add (1), do nothing. If it was set to zero (also known as "FALSE"), find out what the file pointer is set to and go get the contents of the new record.
5. Go back to the top of the Main Event Loop.

Changing a Record: Designer builds the code in such a way that, to change a record, you must place the highlight bar created by the Point Field on the record you want to change and press the Enter key. Also, since the combination of the Control and Enter keys was equated to the ACCEPT_KEY phrase in the main program segment, Designer also recognizes it as a request to edit a record in a table.

To edit a record in a data file, Designer-generated code requires the following steps:

1. Immediately retrieve the record from the disk file.
2. Check to see if this Enter keystroke was to complete an Entry Field for a lookup in another table. If so, reset ACTION to no action and break

out of this procedure. If it wasn't that kind and there hasn't been any other error, set the ACTION to 2 (or edit/change) and call the Update Procedure.

3. If you come back from the Update Procedure and nothing happened (that is, ACTION = 0), simply recycle. If something did happen, reset the memory table pointer to the record where the pointer now exists in the primary file and perform the FIND_RECORD routine. (There will be more on this subroutine later in this chapter.)

4. Go back to the top of the Main Event Loop.

If you look in the model file, you might have trouble tracking down the places that ACTION gets set to 4, or Lookup. That's because the only model code to set a lookup explicitly is related to the keyword BUILDTABLE. The others—and that includes AUTOTABLE, HOTTABLE, and ENTER-TABLE—are all called implicitly whenever you create a Lookup Field in another procedure of any kind that might access this current table. Different code will be inserted from one of those keyword procedures whenever you set up the application that way. AUTOTABLE is called when you say the lookup hot key is "automatic"; ENTERTABLE is used when you set the lookup hot key to ENTER_KEY; and HOTTABLE is used for all the other keys you are allowed to use. (Keywords and the model are discussed in Chapter 15.)

If you were to change the Update Procedure from calling a whole separate procedure, you could perform other operations. For instance, suppose you wanted merely to date stamp records. The Update Procedure could read like this:

```
IF ACTION = 2 THEN FIL:DATE = TODAY( );PUT(FILE);ACTION = 0.
```

In this sequence, when someone pressed the Enter key, the variable for file date would get set to today's date. Then the file would be updated (PUT(FILE)), and the action would be set to tell the table that the record had been changed. Examine the code for Enter key processing to confirm how this statement might work.

Deleting a Record: In step with the two previous keystrokes, Designer builds code to respond to the Delete key for deleting a record. Again, it is not necessary to call a separate procedure. You might be accessing a database where the primary record was to remain, but all of its children (also known as related records in another database) were to be deleted. You could insert the name of an Other Procedure or even of an INCLUDE file (if you wanted to take advantage of the routine local to the current procedure) to perform those deletions.

The steps taken by the Designer-generated deletion procedure work like this:

1. Get the record indicated by the index of the Point Field.
2. If there is some sort of error with that, just cycle back to the top of the Main Event Loop.

   If there are no errors, ACTION is set to 3 (for delete) and the Update Procedure is called.
3. Upon returning from the Update Procedure, if ACTION indicates the process was performed as requested (i.e., a record was deleted), the present Repeat structure index variable is retained while the SAME_PAGE subroutine is called. After the page is redisplayed, this index variable is reset, which ensures that the cursor remains near where the deleted record had been.

Hint: ERROR( ) returns the actual error message, whereas ERRORCODE( ) returns the numeric code for that message. If no error is encountered, they both return empty-handed and test out FALSE.

The Positioning Keys—PgUp, PgDn, UP, and DOWN: The code for each of the keys that Designer deems valid for moving around a table performs two functions: finding the next record to display and adjusting the table of records around it to show as full a table as possible, given the number of records in the file. (See Figure 9-11.)

These keys are processed on the same pass through the Main Event Loop as the Update Procedure keys, except that they don't call any editing form. Notice how the ↑ and ↓ cursor keys are the only means for using the SCROLL function in a Table Procedure. That's because they are the only way to move the scroll area one record at a time in one direction.

The Memory Table

Before we get into the Option selections involving the key files, let's consider the memory table that Designer creates, the code for which is shown in Figure 9-12.

As a means of reducing memory requirements for a large table, a Designer-based table displays the values placed in an intermediate place called a memory table. It is made of the records from the data file, with the addition of

**Figure 9-11   The code used in a Designer-based table to move the cursor and refill the table
with data.**

```
OF DOWN_KEY                                    !DOWN ARROW KEY
  DO SET_NEXT                                  !  POINT TO NEXT RECORD
  DO FILL_NEXT                                 !  FILL A TABLE ENTRY
  IF FOUND                                     !  FOUND A NEW RECORD
    SCROLL(ROW,COL,ROWS,COLS,ROWS(?POINT))     !    SCROLL THE SCREEN UP
    GET(TABLE,RECORDS(TABLE))                  !  GET RECORD FROM TABLE
      DO FILL_SCREEN                           !  DISPLAY ON SCREEN
  .


OF PGDN_KEY                                    !PAGE DOWN KEY
  DO SET_NEXT                                  !  POINT TO NEXT RECORD
  DO NEXT_PAGE                                 !  DISPLAY THE NEXT PAGE

OF CTRL_PGDN                                   !CTRL-PAGE DOWN KEY
  DO LAST_PAGE                                 !  DISPLAY THE LAST PAGE
  NDX = RECORDS(TABLE)                         !  POSITION POINT BAR

OF UP_KEY                                      !UP ARROW KEY
  DO SET_PREV                                  !  POINT TO PREVIOUS RECORD
  DO FILL_PREV                                 !  FILL A TABLE ENTRY
  IF FOUND                                     !  FOUND A NEW RECORD
    SCROLL(ROW,COL,ROWS,COLS,-(ROWS(?POINT)))  ! SCROLL THE SCREEN DOWN
      GET(TABLE,1)                             !  GET RECORD FROM TABLE
        DO FILL_SCREEN                         !  DISPLAY ON SCREEN
  .


OF PGUP_KEY                                    !PAGE UP KEY
  DO SET_PREV                                  !  POINT TO PREVIOUS RECORD
  DO PREV_PAGE                                 !  DISPLAY THE PREVIOUS PAGE

OF CTRL_PGUP                                   !CTRL-PAGE UP
  DO FIRST_PAGE                                !  DISPLAY THE FIRST PAGE
  NDX = 1                                      !  POSITION POINT BAR
```

Figure 9-12 The memory table definition in the local variable defining area of a Table Procedure built with Designer.

```
TABLE           TABLE,PRE(TBL)                  !TABLE OF RECORD DATA
SPACE             STRING(@S1)
MARKED            STRING(1)
NAME              STRING(@s30)
SPACE2            STRING(@S1)
FIRST             STRING(10)
LAST              STRING(20)
PTR               LONG                          !  POINTER TO FILE RECORD
```

a field called PTR, which holds the pointer position of the record in the disk file. A Designer-based application fills a memory table with only the items that appear in the display window of a Table Procedure. Older versions of Clarion (prior to version 2.1) constructed a memory table of all the records that qualified from using a Selector or Filter. As you scroll up and down or move throughout the table, the application transfers the valid records in and out of the memory table. In Figure 9-13, the second step in memory is to reference the pointer maintained by the memory table.

This system of pointers is a powerful function for Clarion. It takes advantage of the construct of the C language called doubly linked lists. That is, any data record is linked via pointer to the record in front of it and (to make the double part) to the record behind it. Those related records need not be

Figure 9-13 The three structures (and their pointer types) that hold data when displaying a table in Designer-generated code. Designer assigns the prefix shown for the screen display and the memory table. The prefix for the data file is the one you give it when you create it.

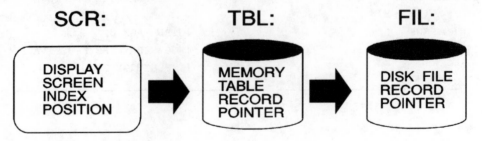

sequential in the file, which makes for fast, efficient searches through it. For example, when you create records in a data file, they enter that data file in record order, unless you turn on the RECLAIM attribute (see Chapter 5 for more details). If you access the file in key order, the system uses that forward and backward pointer scheme to jump from record to record to give you the order you requested. Fortunately, Clarion does all of this behind the scenes. The important concept here is that the memory table contains a record pointer that relates to the disk file. We'll discuss the impacts of this setup when we talk about Computed Fields in a table a little later on in this chapter.

The Access Key

The Access Key determines the order in which the Table Procedure will access the data file. In Designer, you must first define the Access Key while you are defining the data file. Designer does not allow you to add a nonexistent file to be the Access Key so you can add it later. The Access Key can be a single or multipart key. Figure 9-14 shows the first use of the Access Key in Designer-generated code.

Figure 9-14 This is the code from the MARKER table (contained in the MARKER Program) pictured in Figure 9-1 where the Access Key is first used.

```
CACHE(ITE:BY_LAST,.25)              !CACHE KEY FILE
IF ACTION = 4                       !  TABLE LOOKUP REQUEST
  NEWPTR = POINTER(ITEMS)           !  SET POINTER TO RECORD
  IF NOT NEWPTR                     !  RECORD NOT PASSED TO TABLE
    SET(ITE:BY_LAST,ITE:BY_LAST)    !    POSITION TO CLOSEST RECORD
    NEXT(ITEMS)                     !    READ RECORD
    NEWPTR = POINTER(ITEMS)         !  SET POINTER
  .
  DO FIND_RECORD                    !  POSITION FILER
ELSE
  NDX=1
  DO FIRST_PAGE
.
```

This is the point where you determine which variable you'll be able to use in the following two slots for Filters and Selectors as well as the Locate function inside the table. The first place this key gets referenced in standard Designer is the selection of a key to place in cache as the procedure is starting. After that, you'll see the impact of your selection of Access Key in the code when the table is first called and each time a SET is issued to the file to put it in order.

If you are calling this table as a look up to an Entry Field in another menu, table, or edit form, the FIND_RECORD routine tries to come as close as possible to the record preset in the Form Procedure. (We'll discuss more about lookups from a form in the next chapter.)

The key cache is first established using the Access Key you selected. In this case, the key is set to occupy 25% of available memory. Then the test for a lookup is performed. If there was no exact match to the key value from the other file, the cursor is placed as close as possible to the value of the fields in the ITE:BY_LAST key—the Access Key you selected on the Options screen. If there was an exact match or when the closest matching record is found, the FIND _RECORD routine is used to place the cursor in the proper place and display the contents of the record. (See Figure 9-15.)

The FIND_RECORD routine is the beginning of a chain of subroutines that Clarion's Designer generates to read the data file and display the table. It is a subroutine you call whenever you need to locate the cursor according to the contents of the Access Key and not merely according to a different page.

The flow diagram in Figure 9-16 shows the process that takes place whenever this subroutine is called from the main program by another subroutine.

Figure 9-15   The FIND_RECORD routine in the MARKER program. The Access Key used is ITE:BY_LAST with "last name" as the only field in the single-part key.

```
FIND_RECORD ROUTINE                       !POSITION TO SPECIFIC RECORD
  SET(ITE:BY_LAST,ITE:BY_LAST,NEWPTR)     !POSITION FILE
  IF NEWPTR = 0                           !NEWPTR NOT SET
    NEXT(ITEMS)                           !  READ NEXT RECORD
    NEWPTR = POINTER(ITEMS)               !  SET NEWPTR
    SKIP(ITEMS,-1)                        !  BACK UP TO DISPLAY RECORD

  .

  FREE(TABLE)                             !  CLEAR THE RECORD
  DO NEXT_PAGE                            !  DISPLAY A PAGE
```

Figure 9-16   The FIND_RECORD routine and the subroutines of a Designer-generated table that it uses.

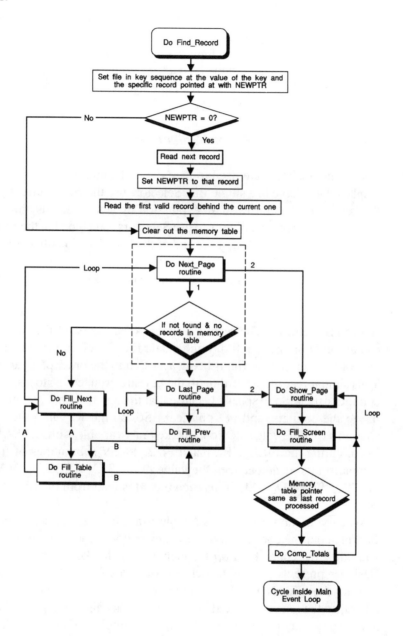

Remember, this is Designer's version of how to locate a record and display a table full of records around it.

We will not be diagramming each and every subroutine in a Designer-generated table. However, beginning with FIND_RECORD, we will focus on a few of the key processes, including what happens when you press a hot key and what happens when a table is first brought up and the field select lands on the equate label for the first field (a Dummy Field).

Record Filters and Record Selectors

Filters and Selectors are used to pare down the numbers or types of records displayed in a table in a single file. Selectors use the value currently stored in the key, and filters throw in an expression by which records are included or excluded. (An example of how to use Selectors is included in the SELECTOR CHANGING PROGRAM at the end of this chapter.) In both cases, these are not single-impact statements, but rather instructions to the Designer code generator to place certain constructs in the code to filter through the data file for display.

Record Selectors:　The record selector is the fastest of the two forms you can use in Designer to sift through a data file. A Selector Field takes advantage of the fact that the file is being accessed in the order of a particular key. Thus similar records, according to the key, are grouped (so to speak) together contiguously. ("So to speak" because that linkage is probably logical according to the pointers, and not physical.) So, on the way into the procedure, Clarion saves the value stored in the key in a variable with an "SAV" prefix. Then, during the FILL_NEXT and FILL_PREV subroutines of the table, a comparison is made between the value of the SAV:RECORD_VALUE and the FIL:RECORD_VALUE as each record is read from the file. (See Figure 9-17.)

When you choose to access a table using a Selector Field, you must be careful about the construction of the key that you use. You must ensure that you know the contents of *all* the elements of that key. For a multipart key, Designer presents you with a choice of fields to use for the Selector and presents those fields in order of importance to the key. If you choose any field other than the top or first field in the key, you are also saying that the Selector must evaluate more than one criteria. For example, let's work with a file that has a multipart key with fields in the order shown in Figure 9-18. The key itself is shown in Figure 9-19.

Figure 9-17 **The FILL_NEXT subroutine from the Table Procedure. This shows the comparison performed on the value in a key. If the values no longer match, the loop is broken and the FOUND flag returns still set to FALSE.**

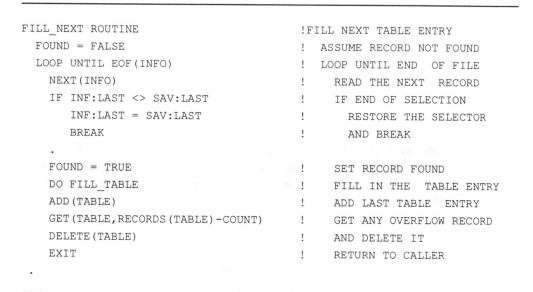

```
FILL_NEXT ROUTINE                          !FILL NEXT TABLE ENTRY
  FOUND = FALSE                            !  ASSUME RECORD NOT FOUND
  LOOP UNTIL EOF(INFO)                     !  LOOP UNTIL END  OF FILE
    NEXT(INFO)                             !    READ THE NEXT  RECORD
    IF INF:LAST <> SAV:LAST                !    IF END OF SELECTION
       INF:LAST = SAV:LAST                 !       RESTORE THE SELECTOR
       BREAK                               !       AND BREAK
     .
    FOUND = TRUE                           !    SET RECORD FOUND
    DO FILL_TABLE                          !    FILL IN THE  TABLE ENTRY
    ADD(TABLE)                             !    ADD LAST TABLE  ENTRY
    GET(TABLE,RECORDS(TABLE)-COUNT)        !    GET ANY OVERFLOW RECORD
    DELETE(TABLE)                          !    AND DELETE IT
    EXIT                                   !    RETURN TO CALLER
  .
```

All three of the fields in Figure 9-18 can be used as Selectors. However, if you use JOIN_YEAR, then LAST_NAME will also be included in the selection criteria, but MEMBER_NO will not. That is, whatever values Clarion saves into SAV:LAST_NAME and SAV:JOIN_YEAR will determine what is included in the display of the table. If you know that one of them is empty,

Figure 9-18 **A Designer key setup for use as Selector Fields.**

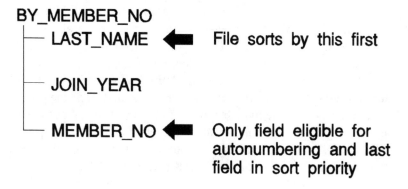

BY_MEMBER_NO
   — LAST_NAME ⬅ File sorts by this first

   — JOIN_YEAR

   — MEMBER_NO ⬅ Only field eligible for autonumbering and last field in sort priority

Figure 9-19   Sample multipart key.

```
BY_LASTNAME    KEY(FIL:LAST_NAME,FIL:JOIN_YEAR,FIL:MEMBER_NO),NOCASE,OPT
```

---

you will only be able to display the records in the file that have no value for that field. A common mistake is to select on a lower order field, forgetting that the fields above it will be included in the sifting process, and the table does not fill with the items you expected.

Selector Fields can be especially useful for table-to-table lookups. That is, you want to go from one table to another table, sorting the lookup file for a particular value you found in the first table. To do this, you must help Designer remember the variables you want to sift with by using the Setup Procedure. For instance, if you were in a generated directory of names (a file we'll call NAMES) and you wanted to press a hot key with the cursor on a name in order to look into the valid club member file (we'll call it MEMBERS) using the key in Figure 9-18, you would place the following code in the Setup Procedure for the table that accessed MEMBERS:

```
MEM:LAST_NAME = NAM:LAST_NAME
```

 Hint: The "MEM" prefix used here indicates that the variable being used to store the contents of NAM:LAST_NAME is part of the global memory allocation. Be sparing in your use of global variables like this. In this case, the program will transfer the value from MEM:LAST_NAME into a variable local to the table and there is no real need to maintain the value in global memory.

Then, when that Table Procedure started, you would ensure that the SAV:LAST_NAME value was the one you intended and the table would select for the proper values. This is shown in Figure 9-20 when "Adams" is placed in the field chosen as the Selector Field.

When the application reaches the INF:LAST field (within the Case structure testing for FIELD( )), it executes the code that starts the process of using a Selector. This code (which appears in Figure 9-21) takes the value entered into the top Entry Field in the table and sets up the selection process that the FILL_NEXT and FILL_PREV subroutines will use to display only the values that match the contents of that ENTRY variable. The data file is set in key

Figure 9-20 Table using an Entry Field at the top to set the value to be used as the Selector for the records to be displayed.

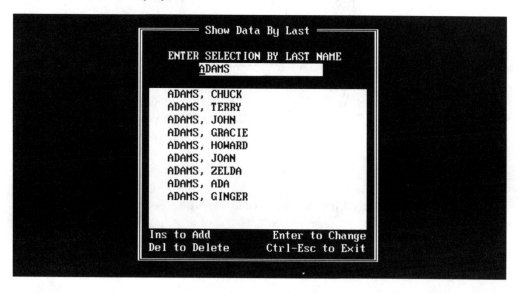

Figure 9-21 The code for starting the Selector process which restricts the display presented in the table in Figure 9-20 to the Entry Field at the top of the table.

```
OF ?INF:LAST                           !WHICH FIELD ARE WE IN?
  SAV:LAST = INF:LAST                  !  SAVE SELECTOR FIELD
  IF ACTION = 4                        !  TABLE LOOKUP REQUEST
    NEWPTR = POINTER(INFO)             !    SET POINTER TO RECORD
    IF NOT NEWPTR                      !    RECORD NOT PASSED  TO TABLE
      SET(INF:BY_LAST,INF:BY_LAST)     !      POSITION TO CLOSEST RECORD
      NEXT(INFO)                       !      READ RECORD
      NEWPTR = POINTER(INFO)           !      SET POINTER
      .
    DO FIND_RECORD                     !    POSITION FILE
  ELSE
    NDX = 1                            !    PUT SELECTOR BAR ON TOP ITEM
    DO FIRST_PAGE                      !    BUILD MEMORY TABLE OF KEYS
    .
  RECORDS# = TRUE                      !  ASSUME THERE ARE RECORDS
```

order with the pointer placed at the closest value to the contents of the INF:BY_LAST key, placed there through the Entry Field.

Record Filters: Record Filters are usually much slower than Selectors because they must look through every record in the file, matching the filter criteria to what they find in each record. To set up a filter, enter a valid Clarion expression that has something to do with the variables in the file you are reading with the Access Key. For instance, if you want to see all the people in the MEMBERS file we referenced in the preceding example who match two criteria for the same variable, you would use an expression like this:

```
MEM:LAST_NAME = 'Adams' and MEM:LAST_NAME = 'Goodwrench'
```

The table, filtered in this way, would list all the people with those two last names. A Selector can give you only one of these at a time since the Selector variable can have only one value.

In addition, you can make comparisons on ranges of values such as a range of invoice numbers, membership numbers, or dollar amounts. You can make whatever comparisons you want using the standard Boolean operators AND, OR, and NOT. Just remember to double check that your logic, reading from left to right, makes sense. (See Figure 9-22.)

The Filter code gets evaluated in the same place as the Selector code: the FILL_NEXT and FILL_PREV subroutines. Therefore, if you are filtering on only one variable for a single value and you can set the file in key order by that variable, you should use a Selector in place of a Filter. You can easily see why the Filter will be more inefficient. When it does not find its target, it simply cycles on to the next record rather than breaking out of the reading loop as the Selector does. That means your program must read a file that you've accessed with a Filter all the way through before it returns control.

It is sometimes useful to use both a Selector and a Filter. The Selector breaks out of the file when the value of its search variable no longer matches. However, within that subset, a Filter can be used to go another level deeper in selecting records. For instance, you might want to set a Selector to look at just the people in one particular city, but you only want to display this within a certain zip code range. You would set the Selector to the city variable and then give set the Filter with the range you wanted:

```
FIL:ZIPCODE > 92000 AND FIL:ZIPCODE < 93000
```

Figure 9-22 **The Filter expression looks at each record in the TABDAT file using the NEXT statement in a loop. If the evaluation returns FALSE, it cycles on to read the next record. If it evaluates TRUE, the rest of the subroutine executes. As with Selector, this same procedure is run with the FILL_PREV subroutine.**

```
FILL_NEXT ROUTINE                               !FILL NEXT TABLE ENTRY
  FOUND = FALSE                                 !  ASSUME RECORD NOT FOUND
  LOOP UNTIL EOF(TABDAT)                         !  LOOP UNTIL END OF FILE
    NEXT(TABDAT)                                 !     READ THE NEXT  RECORD
    IF ~(tab:last='Adams' and tab:last='Burgess') THEN CYCLE.!FILTER
    FOUND = TRUE                                 !     SET RECORD FOUND
    DO FILL_TABLE                               !     FILL IN THE TABLE ENTRY
    ADD(TABLE)                                   !     ADD LAST TABLE  ENTRY
    GET(TABLE,RECORDS(TABLE)-COUNT)             !     GET ANY OVERFLOW RECORD
    DELETE(TABLE)                               !     AND DELETE IT
    EXIT                                         !     RETURN TO CALLER
```

The Anatomy of a Table

In this section, let's walk through the code generated for the MARKER table pictured in Figure 9-1. We won't show the subroutine areas of the program except for what you've already seen, and we'll represent with just a note the main part of the Table Procedure you've already seen. Remember that this is just a procedure, part of a larger program, and is intended to demonstrate one method (Clarion's in this case) for processing a table.

First comes the part of the table that runs only the first time a Table Procedure starts up. The startup code is given in Figure 9-23.

Figure 9-24 shows the code that begins the Main Event Loop after table startup.

Running a Hot Key Procedure means turning control over to another procedure, which could look just like the present one. So, it is necessary to relocate the Point Field and reorient this table whenever you press a hot key. The flowchart in Figure 9-25 depicts the progress of control through processing a Hot Key Procedure.

Figures 9-26 and 9-27 show the next steps in the Main Event Loop.

Figure 9-23   The startup code for a table.

```
CODE
```

Save the value in the ACTION variable brought from the previous procedure to
perform the requested ADD, CHANGE, or DELETE later on in the procedure.

```
ACTION# = ACTION                          !SAVE ACTION
```

Prepare the screen.

```
OPEN(SCREEN)                              !OPEN THE SCREEN
SETCURSOR                                 !TURN OFF ANY CURSOR
```

Initialize the table operations' local variables, get the row and column of the
Point Field at startup, and set up the memory for filling up to 25% of free memory space with the ITE:BY_LAST key.

```
TBL:PTR = 1                               !START AT TABLE
ENTRY
  NDX = 1                                 !PUT SELECTOR BAR ON TOP ITEM
ROW = ROW(?POINT)                         !REMEMBER TOP ROW AND
COL = COL(?POINT)                         !LEFT COLUMN OF SCROLL AREA
RECORDS# = TRUE                           !INITIALIZE RECORDS FLAG
CACHE(ITE:BY_LAST,.25)                    !CACHE KEY FILE
```

If the value of the preceding ACTION variable indicates that this table was called
as part of a lookup in another part of the application, find out if anything was
sought in the file accessed by this table and try to make the closest match.
Otherwise, display the first records in the file in the order specified by the
Access Key given in the Options screen. Then begin the Main Event Loop.

```
IF ACTION = 4                             !  TABLE LOOKUP REQUEST
  NEWPTR = POINTER(ITEMS)                 !  SET POINTER TO  RECORD
  IF NOT NEWPTR                           !  RECORD NOT PASSED TO TABLE
    SET(ITE:BY_LAST,ITE:BY_LAST)          !    POSITION TO CLOSEST RECORD
    NEXT(ITEMS)                           !    READ RECORD
    NEWPTR = POINTER(ITEMS)               !    SET POINTER
```

(continued)

Figure 9-23 *continued*

```
  DO FIND_RECORD                  !  POSITION FILE
ELSE
  NDX = 1                         !  PUT SELECTOR BAR ON TOP ITEM
  DO FIRST_PAGE                   !  BUILD MEMORY TABLE  OF KEYS
  .
RECORDS# = TRUE                   !  ASSUME THERE ARE  RECORDS
```

Figure 9-24   The code viewed on every cycle of the Main Event Loop.

Begin the Main Event Loop.

```
LOOP                                     !LOOP UNTIL USER EXITS
```

Set the editing state back to what it was when the procedure started after a possible lookup.

```
ACTION = ACTION#                         !RESTORE ACTION
```

Turn off all previously ALERTed keys and then reset the keystroke according to their equate labels for saving data and sensitizing hot keys.

```
ALERT                                    !RESET ALERTED KEYS
ALERT(REJECT_KEY)                        !ALERT SCREEN REJECT KEY
ALERT(ACCEPT_KEY)                        !ALERT SCREEN ACCEPT KEY
ALERT(ALT_M)                             !ALERT HOT KEY
```

Process a keystroke and clear out the banner message of operations status.

```
ACCEPT                                   !READ A FIELD
MEM:MESSAGE = ''                         !CLEAR MESSAGE AREA
```

(continued)

Figure 9-24 *continued*

Call any Hot Key Procedures requested.

```
IF KEYCODE( ) = ALT_M                       !ON HOT KEY
   IF FIELD( ) = ?POINT THEN DO GET_RECORD.  !  READ RECORD IF NEEDED
   TAGGER                                    !  CALL HOT KEY PROCEDURE
   DO FIND_RECORD                            ! RESET TO SAME PAGE
   CYCLE                                     !  AND LOOP AGAIN
   .
```

Adding Fields to a Designer Table

The Table

A table can support the largest number of field types of any Designer procedure due to the additional scrolling portion combined with the fixed portion of
the display. It is a powerful display vehicle for that reason. In fact, the only
standard Screen structure a table *does not* support directly in Designer is
menu selections. However, you can add these manually, if you choose. The
code that Designer generates for a table is the most complex of all the work
that Designer accomplishes. To compensate for the myriad moves you might
put together in creating a table, Designer creates a long list of subroutines—
many of which we discussed previously. Figure 9-28 shows the Field Selection menu you will use to place Data Fields in a table.

Scrolling Fields

The Scrolling Display Field: The scrolling portion of the table is usually
responsible for the display of data from the file. The Scrolling Fields fill the
Repeat structure with data from the disk file via the memory table as discussed earlier. The standard workhorse for a table is the Scrolling Field. To
add a Scrolling Field to a table, the field must already exist in a data file and
there must be enough room from the current location of your cursor to the
edge of the window (or the screen, whichever is closer) for the field to fit
when its picture gets painted onto your display. That is true for adding fields

Figure 9-25   The flow of control that occurs when you select a hot key from a Table Procedure. Three hot keys are allowable from inside Designer, but you can add more by ensuring they remain unique and that the key you plan to use gets ALERTed at the top of the Main Event Loop.

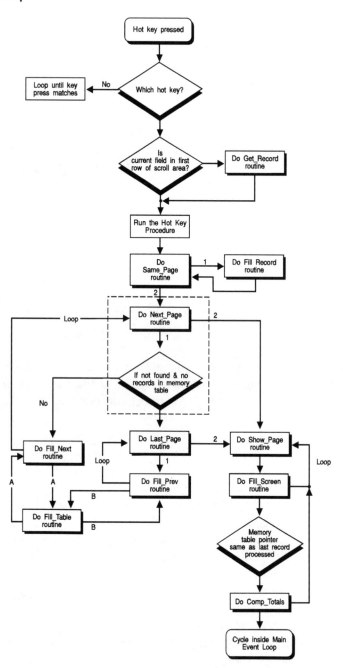

Figure 9-26   The opening sequence of the Main Event Loop.

Exit the whole procedure if the REJECT_KEY is pressed—as defined in the global memory section and ALERTed in the local processing section.

```
IF KEYCODE( ) = REJECT_KEY THEN BREAK.   !RETURN ON SCREEN REJECT KEY
```

Update any on-screen fields, even if the Point Field is not the Current Field.

```
IF  KEYCODE( ) = ACCEPT_KEY    |         !ON SCREEN ACCEPT KEY
    AND FIELD( ) <> ?POINT               !BUT NOT ON THE POINT FIELD
  UPDATE                                 !  MOVE ALL FIELDS FROM SCREEN
  SELECT(?)                              !  START WITH CURRENT FIELD
  SELECT                                 !  EDIT ALL FIELDS
  CYCLE                                  !  GO TO TOP OF LOOP
.
```

Start processing the Entry and Display Fields assigned to the table.

```
CASE FIELD( )                            !JUMP TO FIELD EDIT ROUTINE
```

---

to all screens in Designer and the screen formatter in Editor. The fields eligible for displaying as a standard Scrollable Field must be from the file accessed by the key you specified in the Options screen.

 Hint: In Editor, the error message will report the maximum size of the field picture that will fit while you are specifying the picture of a field.

The FIRST_PAGE subroutine is called from the OF ?POINT field in the Main Event Loop of the MARKER table program pictured in Figure 9-1. The actual code for the OF ?POINT condition appears in Figure 9-27. The OF ?POINT field executes whenever the field equate for ?POINT evaluates as TRUE—in other words, whenever the Point Field returns a position within the Repeat structure according to the Repeat structure INDEX attribute. Therefore, this section of code is run each time the program is focused on actions in the scrolling portion of the table. However, immediately upon entering the OF ?POINT segment of the CASE structure, a test is run to see if there are any records in the table. If not, the Update Procedure is called, and

Figure 9-27 The first elements of the Main Event Loop for processing on screen fields other than the scrolling portion.

```
OF ?FIRST_FIELD                     !FROM THE FIRST FIELD
  IF KEYCODE( ) = ESC_KEY    |      ! RETURN ON ESC KEY
  OR RECORDS# = FALSE               !  OR NO RECORDS
    BREAK                           !     EXIT PROGRAM
  .
```

The last Dummy Field for processing Entry Fields before passing control to the main scrolling function parts of the table.

```
OF ?PRE_POINT                       !PRE POINT FIELD CONDITION
  IF KEYCODE( ) = ESC_KEY           !  BACKING UP?
    SELECT(?-1)                     !    SELECT PREVIOUS FIELD
  ELSE                              !  GOING FORWARD
    SELECT(?POINT)                  !    SELECT MENU FIELD
  .
```

If the Point Field does not have a record to highlight (the file is empty), call the Update Form to put in the first record.

```
OF ?POINT                           !PROCESS THE POINT FIELD
  IF RECORDS(TABLE) = 0             !IF THERE ARE NO RECORDS
    CLEAR(ITE:RECORD)               ! CLEAR RECORD AREA
    ACTION = 1                      !  SET ACTION TO ADD
    GET(ITEMS,0)                    !  CLEAR PENDING RECORD
    UPD_ITEMS                       !  CALL FORM FOR NEW RECORD
    NEWPTR = POINTER(ITEMS)         !  SET POINTER TO NEW RECORD
    DO FIRST_PAGE                   !  DISPLAY THE FIRST PAGE
    IF RECORDS(TABLE) = 0           !  IF THERE AREN'T ANY RECORDS
      RECORDS# = FALSE              !     INDICATE NO RECORDS
      SELECT(?PRE_POINT-1)          !     SELECT THE PRIOR FIELD
    .
    CYCLE                           ! AND LOOP AGAIN
  .
```

Figure 9-28   The Field Selection menu for creating a Designer table.

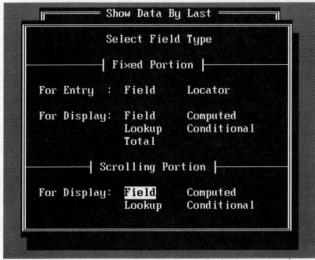

upon returning from that, if a record was added, the FIRST_PAGE subroutine is run.

As you can see from Figure 9-29, the SET issued to loop through the file to fill the table with data is set to a specific key, the key referenced in the Options screen when the table was first built in Designer. Therefore, if you reference any other data file, the Scrolling Fields will turn up empty. You must use one of the other methods to pull data from another file.

The Scrolling Lookup Field: One of the most efficient techniques for relating data between files is to use Designer's autonumbering function to maintain a numbered sequence of records in one file, while relating it to more complex and bulky fields in another. This way, you can track someone's name via their related record number and store information related to that person without having to store the entire name each time. These steps constitute some aspects of how to normalize your database. So, although you may be accessing the ORDERS data file, the order will contain the customer's number. Since that number appears in both the ORDERS file and the CUSTOMER file, you can use it in a Lookup Field to pull the Customer's name onto the screen to display it adjacent to the order displayed.

In Figure 9-30, Field to Display is the field that must already exist in a file. New Field Name creates the screen variable used to show the contents of that file variable. You call another key into play to access that second data file through File Access Key. Access Key Field and Related Field must be

Figure 9-29   This code is called when the table is first opened either immediately to display the data in the file or after the first record is added by the Update Procedure from the OF ?POINT spot in the first Case structure.

```
FIRST_PAGE ROUTINE                  !DISPLAY FIRST PAGE
  BLANK(ROW,COL,ROWS,COLS)
  FREE(TABLE)                       !  EMPTY THE TABLE
  CLEAR(ITE:RECORD,-1)              !  CLEAR RECORD TO LOW VALUES
  CLEAR(TBL:PTR)                    !  ZERO RECORD POINTER
  SET(ITE:BY_LAST)                  !  POINT TO FIRST RECORD
  LOOP NDX = 1 TO COUNT             !  FILL UP THE TABLE
    DO FILL_NEXT                    !     FILL A TABLE ENTRY
    IF NOT FOUND THEN BREAK.        !     GET OUT IF NO RECORD
    .
  NDX = 1                           !  SET TO TOP OF TABLE
  DO SHOW_PAGE                      !  DISPLAY THE PAGE
```

capable of exchanging the same data. That is, if the Related Field from the file currently accessed by the table is the order number, placing the customer number as Access Key Field causes the screen variable to turn up empty. Basically, with Access Key Field you tell Designer: "Here's how I want to access this other data file." Then you supply the value to be used in that Key Field by giving the matching Related Field, which contains the value for each particular record as the table is built.

Let's say we added a Lookup Field to the MARKER program shown in Figure 9-1 with a second line in each Scrolling Field for the company name where the name was kept in a secondary file called COMPANY. Then you

Figure 9-30   The entry form for a scrolling Lookup Field in a table.

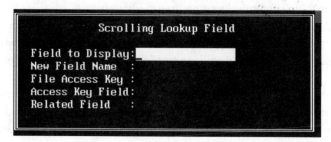

Figure 9-31　The subroutine called in various places in a Designer-generated table to place the records read from the file into the memory table for transfer to the screen variables for display in the table.

```
FILL_TABLE ROUTINE                          !MOVE FILE TO TABLE
  COM:LAST = ITE:LAST                       !MOVE RELATED KEY FIELDS
  GET(COMPANY,COM:BY_LAST)                  !READ THE RECORD
  IF ERROR( ) THEN CLEAR(COM:RECORD).       !IF NOT FOUND, CLEAR RECORD
  TBL:COMPANY = COM:COMPANY                 !DISPLAY LOOKUP FIELD
  TBL:MARKED = ITE:MARKED                   !FROM PRIMARY DATA FILE
  TBL:FIRST = ITE:FIRST                     !FROM PRIMARY DATA FILE
  TBL:LAST = ITE:LAST                       !FROM PRIMARY DATA FILE
  TBL:PTR = POINTER(ITEMS)                  !SAVE RECORD POINTER
  TBL:SPACE = ''                            !SPACER
  TBL:NAME = clip(ite:last)&', '&clip(ite:first) !COMPUTED FIELD
  TBL:SPACE2 = ''                           !SPACER
```

look up the person's company name by comparing the last name in the primary file with the last name match in the company file. This example could be dangerous if you allowed duplicate last names—this lookup would display the company name for only the first match of that last name. So, most probably, you would have a more complex key or use the autonumbering as described earlier to make the correct match. The code that performs the lookup occurs in the FILL_TABLE routine called (eventually) from the FIRST_PAGE subroutine, among others. (See Figure 9-31.)

The Scrolling Computed Field:　The Scrolling Computed Field is the flexible workhorse that allows you to tailor fields for display in a table without requiring the field to preexist in a data file definition. You can reformat a field from the data file into a different picture format. You can add spaces, draw lines, or create a quasi-Entry Field that will take input from a hot key directly to the table screen without an intermediate form.

One sophisticated use for Computed Fields in a table is to improve the readability of the screen. When you create a table with Designer, the background color for the scrolling portion will be whatever color you stipulated for the Scrolling Fields when you placed them on the screen. Thus, for left-justified text in a String Field or right-justified numbers in a Numeric Field, the characters in the field are right up against the edge of the color change and that can be hard on your eyes. So, to extend that scrolling portion, merely insert a Computed Field a character or two away from the end of each line and set the equation, or the Expression, to be a space by putting in two single quotes (''). That will appear in the source code as FIL:FIELD = ''. Nothing will print in those locations, but the repeating scroll will stand out from the data you do want to show.

In addition, you can use Scrolling Fields to perform calculations on the raw data displayed in the table. Keeping the calculated amounts out of the data file will make your file operations more efficient and reduce storage requirements. Anything you can put in Computed Fields, you should. Suppose you had a program that recorded your tasks and the hours you spent in a data file. You could construct a table showing the tasks and the hours and include a Computed Field that multiplied your labor rate against those hours and displayed the total price for that work. The calculations take place when the memory table variables are being set in the FILL_TABLE subroutine. (See Figure 9-32.) Again, as discussed in Chapter 8, you can put extended calculations into the Expression out to a maximum of 249 characters by first placing a zero or two single quotes and then a semicolon to signify a new line. In that scenario, the screen variable you set in the NAME slot will be set to a blank and you can assign it to the result you want to display at any time in the expression.

The one disadvantage of the Computed Field is the problem of totals or other analysis. Because its calculations are generated on the fly the effort to write the code and the time it takes to run the total can be inconvenient. For instance, if you have a file with a one-to-many relation to another file and you

Figure 9-32   The FILL_TABLE subroutine is where the result for Computed Fields is calculated. This occurs as each record is read from the file and placed in the memory table associated with the table display.

```
FILL_TABLE ROUTINE                               !MOVE FILE TO TABLE
  TBL:MARKED = ITE:MARKED                        !FROM PRIMARY DATA FILE
  TBL:FIRST = ITE:FIRST                          !FROM PRIMARY DATA FILE
  TBL:LAST = ITE:LAST                            !FROM PRIMARY DATA FILE
  TBL:PTR = POINTER(ITEMS)                       !SAVE RECORD POINTER
  TBL:SPACE = ''                                 !SPACER
  TBL:NAME = clip(ite:last)&', '&clip(ite:first) !COMPUTED FIELD
  TBL:SPACE2 = ''                                !SPACER
  TBL:HOLDER = 0;computation goes here;tbl:holder = comp_result
                                                 !COMPUTED FIELD
```

need totals for that secondary file, it is sometimes faster to create a storage variable in the primary file that retains the total of the secondary file. It will be calculated whenever the secondary file is accessed for editing. Then, for reports and table displays, those totals need not be recalculated.

Notice, also, that the result of a Computed Field is placed in the memory table variable which will then be placed in the actual display—transferred to a screen variable, that is, in the FILL_SCREEN subroutine. So, in your calculations for a Computed Field, be sure you plant the result of the Expression in the table variable. The Computed Field entry form makes it look like you can set the screen variable inside the Expression.

Don't forget you can use this same technique to call an INCLUDE file if the expression gets too large, or a whole separate procedure or function if there is some analysis you want to perform as the table is being generated.

The Scrolling Conditional Field: The Conditional Field works just like the Computed Field except that it allows your program to perform one of two different Expressions based on whether a statement is true or false. The code for this decision is processed as the table is filled by any of the ways you can disturb the contents: adding a new record, deleting an old one, or paging up and down. The code, once again, sets the values in the memory table during the FILL_TABLE subroutine in Designer-generated code and not directly to the screen variables. (See Figure 9-33.)

Display Fields

The Display Fields in a Table Procedure provide a wealth of flexibility. You can change the value of a key with an Entry Field. You can display the parent record at the top of the screen for the children shown in a table with a Lookup Field. You can insert code and perform operations inside Designer with a

Figure 9-33 The code that results from the Conditional Field processing in a Scrolling Conditional Field for a table. These table variables are transferred to the screen variables for display on the screen.

```
IF decision is true                               !EVALUATE CONDITION
  TBL:DECIDE = set the memory table value here    ! CONDITION IS TRUE
ELSE                                              !OTHERWISE
  TBL:DECIDE = otherwise set it here              ! CONDITION IS FALSE
.
```

Computed Field. You can total up or count records in a table. Designer divides the Display Fields between entry and display only. By calling the Entry Field and the Locator Field both Entry Fields, Clarion means these are the only two that can take keyboard input. The others take their contents from the data displayed or from preset variables as the procedure is started up.

The Locator Entry Field: The Locator Field provides a method for moving rapidly through the records in a table by entering the first few letters of a key variable used to access the data file. This method does not work with multipart keys (by itself), and you cannot have more than one Locator Field on any table generated by Designer. A big advantage of the Locator is that it does not suspend your access to the scrolling highlight bar for moving around the table as an Entry Field does.

The setup in Figure 9-34 would look the same if STU:FIRST were the Locator, which would work by itself. (We'll discuss later how to make this Locator successfully find records based on the second part of a two-part key.) This section of code appears in the OF ?POINT part of the Case structure, which means that it is processed when the focus is on the Point structure.

The Locator works by first filtering for the keystrokes that could be letters or numbers to allow them through. An implicit variable LEN# is maintained to check the length of the string entered into the Locator Field. The Backspace key erases characters. Then, when an appropriate keystroke is received, the trailing blanks of the variable are clipped away

```
CLIP(SCR:LOCATOR)
```

and the file is accessed according to those characters. Notice that the characters are appended to each other until the Backspace key or the Escape key is pressed. The Escape key test is performed separately and looks like this:

```
IF KEYCODE( ) = ESC_KEY      !  BACKING UP?
   SCR:LOCATOR = ''          !    CLEAR LOCATOR
   SETCURSOR                 !    AND TURN CURSOR OFF
ELSE                         !  GOING FORWARD
   LEN# = 0                  !    RESET TO START OF  LOCATOR
   SETCURSOR(ROW(SCR:LOCATOR),COL(SCR:LOCATOR)) !AND TURN CURSOR ON
 .
```

The only difficulty with the Locator function is that if the system finds the only matching target on the first few letters and the user types a long string into the Locator Field, the table will not return control to the user until after it

Figure 9-34 **The code from a program with a file called STUFF.DAT accessed for this table with a two-part key defined with STU:FIRST as the primary key and STU:SECOND as the secondary key. The Locator is performed on STU:SECOND.**

```
IF KEYCODE( ) > 31            |          !THE DISPLAYABLE CHARACTERS
      AND KEYCODE( ) < 255              !ARE USED TO LOCATE RECORDS
 IF LEN# < SIZE(SCR:LOCATOR)           ! IF THERE IS ROOM LEFT
   SCR:LOCATOR = SUB(SCR:LOCATOR,1,LEN#) & CHR(KEYCODE( ))
   LEN# += 1                           !   INCREMENT THE LENGTH
 .
     ELSIF KEYCODE( ) = BS_KEY         !BACKSPACE UNTYPES A CHARACTER
 IF LEN# > 0                           ! IF THERE ARE CHARACTERS LEFT
   LEN# -= 1                           !   DECREMENT THE LENGTH
   SCR:LOCATOR = SUB(SCR:LOCATOR,1,LEN#) !   ERASE THE LAST CHARACTER
 .
ELSE                                   !FOR ANY OTHER CHARACTER
 LEN# = 0                              !   ZERO THE LENGTH
 SCR:LOCATOR = ''                      !   ERASE THE LOCATOR FIELD
 .
SETCURSOR(ROW(SCR:LOCATOR),COL(SCR:LOCATOR)+LEN#) !AND RESET THE CURSOR
STU:SECOND = CLIP(SCR:LOCATOR)         !   UPDATE THE KEY FIELD
IF KEYBOARD( ) > 31          |         !THE DISPLAYABLE CHARACTERS
   AND KEYBOARD( ) < 255      |        !ARE USED TO LOCATE RECORDS
   OR KEYBOARD( ) = BS_KEY             !INCLUDE BACKSPACE
 CYCLE
 .
```

A keystroke was received; now set the file and the cursor at the nearest match.

```
IF LEN# > 0                           !ON A LOCATOR REQUEST
  STU:SECOND = CLIP(SCR:LOCATOR)       !UPDATE THE KEY FIELD
  SET(STU:BY_FIRST,STU:BY_FIRST)       !POINT TO NEW RECORD
  NEXT(STUFF)                          !READ A RECORD
  IF (EOF(STUFF) AND ERROR( ))         !IF EOF IS REACHED
    SET(STU:BY_FIRST)                  !  SET TO FIRST RECORD
    PREVIOUS(STUFF)                    !  READ THE LAST RECORD
  .
  NEWPTR = POINTER(STUFF)              !SET NEW RECORD POINTER
  SKIP(STUFF,-1)                       !BACK UP TO FIRST RECORD
  FREE(TABLE)                          !CLEAR THE TABLE
  DO NEXT_PAGE                         !AND DISPLAY A NEW PAGE
 .
```

has repeated the find process for each letter typed. There are two alternatives to this method.

First, you can place an Entry Field anywhere on the table except in the scrolling area (if you put it there, the scrolling part will stop on the line above where you put the Entry Field) to locate a record in the table. Simply place the Entry Field on the table and run a subroutine to locate the record you want by putting DO FIND_RECORD in the Edit Procedure. The user types in a value and presses Enter, and the existing FIND_RECORD subroutine in the Designer-generated table goes to the nearest match for what was entered. The disadvantage to this approach is that the cursor stops at that Entry Field when the table first starts and the user *must* press Enter to go to the scrolling portion.

The way around that limitation is to put the Entry Field in a separate window in an Other Procedure called with a hot key. This second method gives your users the chance to look for something in the file without hanging up on the Entry Field every time they got to the table.

If we were to modify the MARKER program in Figure 9-1, we would add a hot key to the Main Table Procedure to call an Other Procedure called Searcher. (See Figure 9-35.)

To make the code in Figure 9-35 work, you need to make one change in the Table Procedure that calls it. You must make a copy of the last two lines in the Enter key processing in the Table Procedure to replace DO SAME_PAGE that will be generated by Designer when you add the hot key for Searcher to the table. The Hot Key Procedure would then look like Figure 9-36.

The Table Entry Field: The primary use for Entry Fields in a table is to set the values for the key to access a file in order to sort or filter it. If you place the Entry Field at the top of a procedure, the cursor will stop at the Entry Field before it gives you the live scroll bar on the items in a table. Figure 9-20 shows that kind of Entry Field in action. But that is not the only use for Entry Fields in a table. As with all Designer Procedures, you can tailor tables to perform special functions. It is possible to enter data to a file through values that are placed in Entry Fields on a table. However, it requires hand-coding in the Edit Procedures to handle writing or reading the file you plan to use.

For instance, suppose you wanted to update a status date on a selected list of items for some reason, but then you wanted to inspect them. You could create a table, using a Selector Field, that would show only those records that met the Selector criterion. Then, you would add two Selector Fields, one for the special criterion and one for the date. The cursor automatically travels to the first of the Entry Fields before it goes on to the one for the date. The first Entry Field would provide the variable for use in the Edit Procedure of the

Figure 9-35 This is the Other Procedure for adding a pop-up search window for looking through last names in the MARKER program pictured in Figure 9-1. Notice that the IF statement is checking for the field number of the Search Text Input Field and not for its contents.

```
             MEMBER('MARKER')
SEARCHER     PROCEDURE
SFINDER      SCREEN      WINDOW(8,30),PRE(SCR),HUE(14,0,0)
             ROW(1,1)    STRING('<201,205{28},187>')
             ROW(2,1)    REPEAT(6);STRING('<186,0{28},186>') .
             ROW(8,1)    STRING('<200,205{28},188>')
             ROW(3,3)    STRING(' Enter a Last Name to Find '),HUE(14,0)
             ROW(4,3)    STRING('    and Touch (ENTER)'),HUE(14,0)
             ROW(6,7)    ENTRY(@s20),USE(finder),HUE(15,0),OVR
             END!SCREEN
FINDER               STRING(10)                   ! SEARCH STRING INPUT

      CODE
      FINDER = ''                          ! BLANK OUT INPUT
      ALERT                                ! TURN OFF HOT KEYS
      ALERT(ESC_KEY)                       ! SENSITIZE ESCAPE KEY
      ALERT(ENTER_KEY)                     ! SENSITIZE ENTER KEY
      OPEN(SFINDER)                        ! OPEN SEARCH SCREEN
      LOOP                                 ! PROCESS TO BREAK
         ACCEPT                            ! PROCESS KEYSTROKE
         IF KEYCODE( ) = ESC_KEY THEN BREAK.  ! EXIT ON ESCAPE KEY
         IF FIELD( )= ?Finder              ! TEST FOR FIELD NUMBER
           UPDATE;DISPLAY                  ! UPDATE USE VARIABLE
           ITE:LAST = CLIP(FINDER)         ! SET FILE VARIABLE
           UPDATE                          ! UPDATE FILE VARIABLE
           SET(ITE:BY_LAST,ITE:BY_LAST)    ! MOVE POINTER
           NEXT(ITEMS)                     ! READ THAT RECORD
           IF ERROR( ) THEN STOP(ERROR( )).  ! POST ERROR IF HAPPENS
           CLOSE(SFINDER)                  ! CLOSE THE SCREEN
           RETURN                          ! GO BACK TO TABLE
         END!IF                            ! END OF FIELD IF
      END!LOOP                             ! END OF PROCESS LOOP
      CLOSE(SFINDER)                       ! CLOSE SCREEN ON ESCAPE
      RETURN                               ! GO BACK TO TABLE
```

second Field. Then, in that Edit Procedure, you would access the file, select only those records that matched the first field's contents, and add the date to the record. When this loop had completed, it would display the edited records for your inspection. The loop required in the second field is shown in Figure 9-37.

Figure 9-36 The new Hot Key Procedure for calling the Other Procedure called Searcher. Notice that the existing locating of the pointer is stored in NEWPTR. That pointer location was established by the SET command in the Other Procedure.

```
IF KEYCODE( ) = F10_KEY                          !ON HOT KEY
  IF FIELD( ) = ?POINT THEN DO GET_RECORD. !  READ RECORD IF NEEDED
  SEARCHER                                 !  CALL HOT KEY PROCEDURE
  NEWPTR = POINTER(ITEMS)                  !  SET POINTER TO NEW RECORD
  DO FIND_RECORD                           !  POSITION IN FILE
  CYCLE                                    !  AND LOOP AGAIN
.
```

More commonly, you will set up an Entry Field to accept input from a user to tailor the contents of the table display according to a Selector or Filter. With a Filter, you could let the user set more than one criterion for what will be displayed by using Entry Fields and the criterion need not be part of the key, as is required by a Record Selector. In either case, you may want to use the Lookup function of an Entry Field to pop up a table to confirm that the user entered the right criterion from a related file to perform the selecting or filtering functions. This pop-up method will be discussed in more detail in Chapter 10.

Figure 9-37 This code could be inserted into the Edit Procedure of the second of two Entry Fields in a table. It assumes that you have set the table to access the file with a key called FIL:BY_KEY. That key has been set to use a Record Selector in the Options screen to select only those records that match the value of FIL:VARIABLE. This Edit Procedure will execute on the way into the Table Procedure before the records fill the table.

```
VARIABLE# = FIL:VARIABLE                 !SAVE 1ST ENTRY VARIABLE
DATE# = FIL:DATE                         !SAVE 2ND ENTRY VARIABLE
SET(FIL:BY_KEY,FIL:BY_KEY)               !SET THE POINTER TO KEY
LOOP UNTIL EOF(FILE)                      !LOOK THROUGH THE FILE
  NEXT(FILE)                             ! READ THE NEXT RECORD
  IF FIL:VARIABLE <> VARIABLE# THEN BREAK.   ! BREAK IF NO MATCH
  FIL:DATE = DATE#                       ! SET NEW DATE
  PUT(FILE)                              ! PUT CHANGED RECORD
END!LOOP                                  !END OF LOOP
FIL:VARIABLE = VARIABLE#                  !RESTORE SELECTOR
```

The Fixed Total Field: The Fixed Total Field can be used to sum up any Numeric Field in the scrolling section of the table. The total includes all the items shown, which means you can limit the total to only those items that passed through the Selector for display. You can also count the number of records and calculate an average on a Numeric Field (that is, add up all the records in the scrolling area and divide them by the count) so that the total will still do just the records that qualified for display. In standard Designer, the calculations are performed by a subroutine called COMP_FIELD, which appears as the last subroutine in the procedure. (See Figure 9-38.)

Notice how in a table (as shown in Figure 9-39) you can do sums, counts, and averages on values in temporary screen variables (SCR) as well as memory (MEM) and file variables (ITE, in this case). Be careful, though, you cannot view the contents of the screen variables in Clarion's Debugger to inspect the contents for troubleshooting.

The Fixed Display Field: The most common use for a Fixed Display Field is to put a message on the screen that you preset going into the procedure by setting the message memory variable in the Setup Procedure of the Table Options. If the value is not set when you first enter the table, it will be blank and stay that way until something in the program updates it and the screen variables are redisplayed. The Display Field appears in the very top of the Main Event Loop. Remember, there is nothing magical about a Display Field. It is a simple part of the Screen structure (an SCR: variable) to which Designer has assigned a specific task.

Figure 9-38 In Designer-generated code, the COMP_TOTAL procedure runs during a loop that sets up the table on procedure startup and then again when the table is rebuilt during the SHOW_PAGE subroutine. The variables used in the calculations are incremented and decremented during each of the major edits to the table items performed after the Enter, Delete, and Insert keys are set.

```
COMP_TOTALS  ROUTINE                          !CALCULATE TOTAL FIELDS
  IF NOT ACTN# THEN EXIT.                      !GET OUT IF ACTN NOT SET
  TOT:SUM += TBL:SPACE                         !TOTALS A FIELD
  TOT:COUNT += 1                               !COUNTS THE RECORDS
  TOT:AVERAGE += TBL:SPACE                     !AVERAGES THE TOTAL
  AVERAGE# += 1                                !THE AVERAGE COUNT
  ACTN# = 0                                    !CLEAR ACTION
```

Figure 9-39   The Total Field for a table.

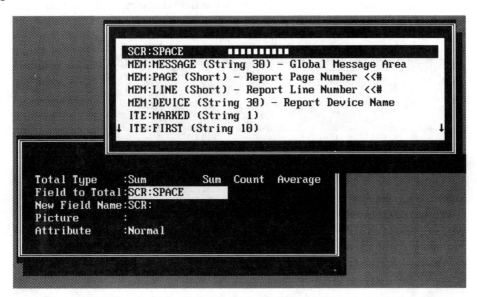

The Fixed Lookup Field: The Fixed Lookup Field works just like a combination of its scrolling cousin and a regular Fixed Display Field. It is used to show information from another record. One of the more common uses for this field type is to show the parent record for the child records that were chosen by setting a Record Selector in the Table Options. In this case, as soon as the first record that qualifies to be displayed is read, the key variable used to access the parent file is read and the information is extracted for display. (See Figure 9-40.)

The Fixed Computed Field: Figure 9-40 shows the application of the Fixed Computed Field, also. The total counts all the hours shown because it applies to all the records that qualified for display. To total a subset of the displayed records, we need to create a Filter (not the Record Filter in the Table Options) that will still allow the table to display both the records marked "BILLED" and the records not marked. The Fixed Computed Field can be used to display the output of a calculation performed in the Expression slot of the Fixed Computed Field display. The segment of code in Figure 9-41 can be placed into that slot to perform the task.

The Fixed Conditional Table Field: A Computed Field and a Conditional Field are very similar. The difference, as given in the explanation of the scrolling version, is that Designer provides a method for choosing between

Figure 9-40   The TIME SHEET program shows how a Display Field can be used to show information from related to the parent record for the field displayed in the scrolling portion of the table. The entire TIME SHEET program can be found at the end of this chapter.

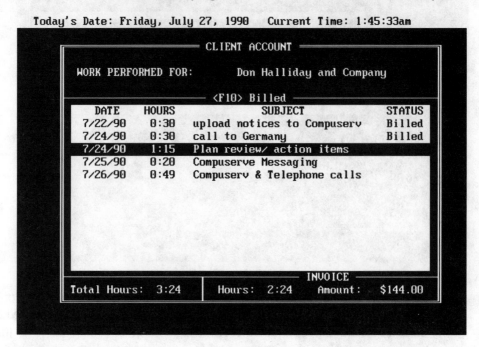

Figure 9-41   This code from the TIME SHEET program can be inserted into the Expression of a Fixed Computed Field to calculate and update a total of a partial number of the displayed records in a table.

```
SCR:INVOICE = 0                         !SET SCREEN TO ZERO
CLIENTNO# = HRS:CLIENTNO                 !SAVE CLIENT NUMBER
SET(HRS:BY_CLIENT,HRS:BY_CLIENT)         !ORGANIZE BY CLIENT NUMBER
LOOP UNTIL EOF(HOURS)                    !PROCESS TO END OFFILE
  NEXT(HOURS)                            !READ THE NEXT RECORD
  IF HRS:CLIENTNO <> CLIENTNO#           !DIFFERENT CLIENT ?
    BREAK                                !QUIT TOTALING
  END!IF
  IF HRS:BILLED = ''                     !BILLED YET ?
    SCR:INVOICE += ((HRS:COMPLETETIME - HRS:STARTTIME)+1) !ADD TO TOTAL
  END!IF                                 !END LOOP
END!LOOP
```

two different expressions based on a condition. The Fixed Conditional Field is calculated in the top of the Main Event Loop. So you have the opportunity to both preset the value for the comparison or to read it at some point during the operation of the table. It will only be updated and displayed on the screen, however, when that operation is performed as part of the Main Event Loop.

Other Special Table Techniques

Pop-Up Scan Using the INSTRING Function

In addition to the pop-search, by using the INSTRING function, you can look for partial bits of text within a field. Both the Locator and the Entry Field using the FIND_RECORD routine look only for the first characters in the field. The Floppy Disk Directory program pictured in Figure 9-42 uses both the pop-up Entry Field and the INSTRING function to locate text within a disk label file and a file containing filenames from each disk stored. (This program will be used later in this book for examples, too.)

Figure 9-42   The FLOPPY DISK DIRECTORY program.

```
                        Show Disks By Number

                     Locate by Number:
    NO.         DISK LABEL                          NOTES
      1 SUPER PAK - UTILITY PROGRAMS    VERSION 4.2  AST RESEARCH, INC.
      2 PC INTRO   -  1 OF
      3 PC INTRO   -  2 OF  ┌─────────────────────────────┐
      4 PC INTRO   -  3 OF  │ SEARCH THE LABELS & NOTES    │
      5 ARCMASTER            │  _____            │
      6 ARCMASTER            │ ───────── OR ─────────       │
      7 PROGRAMMING FAMILY   │ SEARCH FOR A FILENAME        │RAM
      8 BIT COM              └─────────────────────────────┘
      9 FILE MASTER                    BY GENESIS DATA SYSTEM
     10 PERFECT MENU                   DEMO DISK
     11 ANCHOR-TALK-VER. 1.0  1 OF 2   TELECOMMUNICATIONS SOFTWARE
     12 ANCHOR-TALK-VER. 1.13 2 OF 2   TELECOMMUNICATIONS SOFTWARE
     13 LOGITECH MOUSE   -  1 OF 2     DRIVER 3.2
     14 LOGITECH MOUSE   -  2 OF 2     PLUS PACKAGE 3.2
     15 MVGA   -   1 OF 2              UTILITIES DISK
                 PRESS <F9> TO READ DISK DIRECTORY
                 PRESS <F10> FOR FILES LIST
    Ins to Add          PRESS <F8> TO SEARCH        Enter to Change
    Del to Delete                                   Ctrl-Esc to Exit
```

Figure 9-43   The subroutine within the Other Procedure called for looking *anywhere* in the text strings stored for the file label and filename records. Notice that the If structure looks through two fields to locate the text stored in the temporary variable FIND.

```
LABELSEARCH   ROUTINE                              !LOOK FOR DISK
        SET(DISKS)                                 !START AT TOP OF FI
        LOOP UNTIL EOF(DISKS)                      !LOOK TO END OF FIL
          NEXT(DISKS)                              !READ NEXT RECORD
          IF INSTRING(CLIP(FIND),UPPER(DIS:LABEL),1) OR |
             INSTRING(CLIP(FIND),UPPER(DIS:NOTES),1) ! LOOK IN FIELD
          EXIT                                     !LEAVE PROCEDURE
          END!IF
        END!LOOP
```

First you must create an Other Procedure to build the pop-up Screen structure and perform the search through the file. Then, the same change is required in the Table Procedure to make that code work that you made to use the pop-up technique in the MARKER program. (See Figure 9-43.)

Figure 9-44   The code called by a hot key from the MARKER program to put an ASCII character into a Computed Field without leaving the table.

```
            MEMBER('MARKER')


TAGGER      PROCEDURE

            CODE
            IF ITE:MARKED  = ''      ! IF THE MARKER FIELD IS EMPTY
               ITE:MARKED = '<16>'   ! PUT A MARK THERE
            ELSE                     ! OTHERWISE
               ITE:MARKED = ''       ! BLANK OUT THE ONE ALREADY THERE
            END!IF
            PUT(ITEMS)               ! SAVE THE CHANGED RECORD
            SET(ITE:BY_LAST,ITE:BY_LAST)  ! KEEP THE POINTER IN PLACE
            RETURN                   ! GO BACK TO THE TABLE
```

Hot Key Processing as with the MARKER Program on the Table

Another use for Scrolling Computed Fields is for modifying a table without processing by a Form Procedure. The MARKER program focuses on that function. By setting up a hot key, you can permanently tag items in the table as you scroll through the table. (See Figure 9-44.)

Summary

In this chapter, we discussed how Clarion uses a powerful database display and manipulation tool: the table. Table, one of the four primary procedure types in Designer, employs few special language statements other than the one that scrolls the screen segment inside the table. Otherwise, as we've discussed in this chapter, the table is constructed entirely from standard statements used throughout the language. We traced the logical flow of the standard Designer table code as well as methods for hot key record access, special searching techniques, memory tables, and marking records.

The MARKER Program

MARKER.CLA—The Main Program Procedure

```
MARKER    PROGRAM
            INCLUDE('STD_KEYS.CLA')
            INCLUDE('CTL_KEYS.CLA')
            INCLUDE('ALT_KEYS.CLA')
            INCLUDE('SHF_KEYS.CLA')


REJECT_KEY    EQUATE(CTRL_ESC)
ACCEPT_KEY    EQUATE(CTRL_ENTER)
TRUE          EQUATE(1)
FALSE         EQUATE(0)

            MAP
              PROC(G_OPENFILES)
              MODULE('MARKER1')
                PROC(MAIN_TABLE)                !Show Items By Last
                .
              MODULE('MARKER2')
                PROC(UPD_ITEMS)                 !Update Items
                .
              MODULE('TAGGER')                  !Item Tagging Function
                PROC(TAGGER)
                .
              MODULE('SEARCHER')                !Search Utility
                PROC(SEARCHER)
                .
              .
              EJECT('FILE LAYOUTS')
ITEMS     FILE,PRE(ITE),CREATE,RECLAIM
BY_BOTH     KEY(ITE:FIRST,ITE:LAST),DUP,NOCASE,OPT
BY_LAST     KEY(ITE:LAST),DUP,NOCASE,OPT
RECORD      RECORD
MARKED        STRING(1)
FIRST         STRING(10)
LAST          STRING(20)
            . .


COMPANY   FILE,PRE(COM),CREATE,RECLAIM
BY_LAST     KEY(COM:LAST),DUP,NOCASE,OPT
RECORD      RECORD
LAST          STRING(20)
COMPANY       STRING(25)
            . .
```

(continued)

```
                EJECT('GLOBAL MEMORY VARIABLES')
ACTION          SHORT                               !0 = NO ACTION
                                                    !1 = ADD RECORD
                                                    !2 = CHANGE RECORD
                                                    !3 = DELETE RECORD
                                                    !4 = LOOKUP FIELD

          GROUP,PRE(MEM)
MESSAGE       STRING(30)                            !Global Message Area
PAGE          SHORT                                 !Report Page Number
LINE          SHORT                                 !Report Line Number
DEVICE        STRING(30)                            !Report Device Name
          .

            EJECT('CODE SECTION')
  CODE
  SETHUE(7,0)                                       !SET WHITE ON BLACK
  BLANK                                             !  AND BLANK
  G_OPENFILES                                       !OPEN OR CREATE FILES
  SETHUE()                                          !    THE SCREEN
  MAIN_TABLE                                        !Show Items By Last
  RETURN                                            !EXIT TO DOS

G_OPENFILES  PROCEDURE                              !OPEN FILES & CHECK FOR ERROR
  CODE
  SHOW(25,1,CENTER('OPENING FILE: ' & 'ITEMS',80)) !DISPLAY FILE NAME
  OPEN(ITEMS)                                       !OPEN THE FILE
  IF ERROR()                                        !OPEN RETURNED AN ERROR
    CASE ERRORCODE()                                ! CHECK FOR SPECIFIC ERROR
    OF 46                                           !   KEYS NEED TO BE REQUILT
      SETHUE(0,7)                                   !   BLACK ON WHITE
      SHOW(25,1,CENTER('REBUILDING KEY FILES FOR ITEMS',80)) !INDICATE MSG
      BUILD(ITEMS)                                  !   CALL THE BUILD PROCEDURE
      SETHUE(7,0)                                   !   WHITE ON BLACK
      BLANK(25,1,1,80)                              !   BLANK THE MESSAGE
    OF 2                                            !IF NOT FOUND,
      CREATE(ITEMS)                                 ! CREATE
    ELSE                                            ! ANY OTHER ERROR
      LOOP;STOP('ITEMS: ' & ERROR()).              !   STOP EXECUTION
  . .

  SHOW(25,1,CENTER('OPENING FILE: ' & 'COMPANY',80)) !DISPLAY FILE NAME
  OPEN(COMPANY)                                     !OPEN THE FILE
  IF ERROR()                                        !OPEN RETURNED AN ERROR
    CASE ERRORCODE()                                ! CHECK FOR SPECIFIC ERROR
    OF 46                                           !   KEYS NEED TO BE REQUILT
      SETHUE(0,7)                                   !   BLACK ON WHITE
      SHOW(25,1,CENTER('REBUILDING KEY FILES FOR COMPANY',80)) !INDICATE MSG
      BUILD(COMPANY)                                !   CALL THE BUILD PROCEDURE
```

(continued)

```
     SETHUE(7,0)                                !  WHITE ON BLACK
     BLANK(25,1,1,80)                           !  BLANK THE MESSAGE
   OF 2                                         !IF NOT FOUND,
     CREATE(COMPANY)                            !  CREATE
   ELSE                                         !  ANY OTHER ERROR
     LOOP;STOP('COMPANY: ' & ERROR()).          !  STOP EXECUTION
  . .


   BLANK                                        !BLANK THE SCREEN
```

MARKER1.CLA—The Table Procedure

```
          MEMBER('MARKER')
MAIN_TABLE    PROCEDURE


SCREEN        SCREEN       PRE(SCR),WINDOW(15,41),HUE(15,1)
              ROW(1,3)     PAINT(11,37),HUE(0,7)
              ROW(2,3)     PAINT(1,37),HUE(15,1)
              ROW(1,1)     STRING('<201,205{7},0{25},205{7},187>'),HUE(15,1)
              ROW(2,1)     REPEAT(13);STRING('<186,0{39},186>'),HUE(15,1)  .
              ROW(15,1)    STRING('<200,205{39},188>'),HUE(15,1)
              ROW(1,10)    STRING('SHOW ITEMS BY LAST NAME')
              ROW(2,5)     STRING('Press <<F10> to Search by Last Name')
              ROW(12,4)    STRING('Ins to Add'),HUE(11,1)
                COL(24)    STRING('Enter to Change'),HUE(11,1)
              ROW(13,4)    STRING('Del to Delete'),HUE(11,1)
                COL(23)    STRING('Ctrl-Esc to Exit'),HUE(11,1)
              ROW(14,9)    STRING('PRESS <<ALT-M> TO TAG ITEMS')
SUM           ROW(4,3)     STRING(@s10)
COUNT         ROW(5,3)     STRING(@s10)
AVERAGE       ROW(6,3)     STRING(@s10)
                           ENTRY,USE(?FIRST_FIELD)
                           ENTRY,USE(?PRE_POINT)
                           REPEAT(1),EVERY(1),INDEX(NDX)
              ROW(3,2)        POINT(1,39),USE(?POINT),ESC(?-1)
SPACE         COL(3)       STRING(@S1)
MARKED        COL(6)       STRING(1)
NAME          COL(8)       STRING(@s30)
SPACE2        COL(39)      STRING(@S1)
                  .             .


NDX           BYTE                             !REPEAT INDEX FOR POINT AREA
ROW           BYTE                             !ACTUAL ROW OF SCROLL AREA
COL           BYTE                             !ACTUAL COLUMN OF SCROLL AREA
COUNT         BYTE(1)                          !NUMBER OF ITEMS TO SCROLL
ROWS          BYTE(1)                          !NUMBER OF ROWS TO SCROLL
```

(continued)

```
COLS            BYTE(39)                              !NUMBER OF COLUMNS TO SCROLL
FOUND           BYTE                                  !RECORD FOUND FLAG
NEWPTR          LONG                                  !POINTER TO NEW RECORD

TABLE           TABLE,PRE(TBL)                        !TABLE OF RECORD DATA
SPACE           STRING(@S1)
MARKED          STRING(1)
NAME            STRING(@s30)
SPACE2          STRING(@S1)
LAST            STRING(20)
PTR             LONG                                  !  POINTER TO FILE RECORD
                  .
TOT_GROUP       GROUP,PRE(TOT)                        !TABLE TOTAL FIELDS
SUM             REAL
COUNT           REAL
AVERAGE         REAL
                  .

  EJECT
  CODE
  ACTION# = ACTION                                    !SAVE ACTION
  OPEN(SCREEN)                                        !OPEN THE SCREEN
  SETCURSOR                                           !TURN OFF ANY CURSOR
  CLEAR(TOT_GROUP)                                    !ZERO TOTALS
  AVERAGE# = 0
  TBL:PTR = 1                                         !START AT TABLE ENTRY
  NDX = 1                                             !PUT SELECTOR BAR ON TOP ITEM
  ROW = ROW(?POINT)                                   !REMEMBER TOP ROW AND
  COL = COL(?POINT)                                   !LEFT COLUMN OF SCROLL AREA
  RECORDS# = TRUE                                     !INITIALIZE RECORDS FLAG
  CACHE(ITE:BY_LAST,.25)                              !CACHE KEY FILE
  CLEAR(TOT_GROUP)                                    !ZERO TOTALS
  AVERAGE# = 0
  CLEAR(ITE:RECORD,-1)                                !CLEAR RECORD TO LOW VALUES
  CLEAR(TBL:PTR)                                      !SET POINTER TO ZERO
  SETHUE(BACKHUE(ROW,COL),BACKHUE(ROW,COL))           !TURN OFF DISPLAY
  BUFFER(ITEMS,.25)
  SET(ITEMS)                                          !  POINT TO FIRST RECORD
  LOOP UNTIL EOF(ITEMS)                               !LOOP UNTIL END OF FILE
    NEXT(ITEMS)                                       !  READ A RECORD
    ACTN# = 1                                         !SET ACTION FOR ADD
    DO FILL_TABLE                                     !  TOTAL SCREEN VARIABLES
    DO COMP_TOTALS                                    !  ADD TO TOTAL AMOUNT
      .
  SETHUE()                                            !TURN OFF SETHUE
  FREE(ITEMS)                                         !FREE MEMORY USED FOR BUFFERING
  FREE(TABLE)                                         !FREE MEMORY TABLE
  IF ACTION = 4                                       !  TABLE LOOKUP REQUEST
```

(continued)

```
  NEWPTR = POINTER(ITEMS)                   !  SET POINTER TO RECORD
  IF NOT NEWPTR                             !  RECORD NOT PASSED TO TABLE
    SET(ITE:BY_LAST,ITE:BY_LAST)            !    POSITION TO CLOSEST RECORD
    NEXT(ITEMS)                             !    READ RECORD
    NEWPTR = POINTER(ITEMS)                 !    SET POINTER
  .
  DO FIND_RECORD                            !  POSITION FILE
ELSE
  NDX = 1                                   !  PUT SELECTOR BAR ON TOP ITEM
  DO FIRST_PAGE                             !  BUILD MEMORY TABLE OF KEYS
.
RECORDS# = TRUE                             !  ASSUME THERE ARE RECORDS
LOOP                                        !LOOP UNTIL USER EXITS
  ACTION = ACTION#                          !RESTORE ACTION
  SCR:SUM = TOT:SUM
  SCR:COUNT = TOT:COUNT
  SCR:AVERAGE = TOT:AVERAGE/AVERAGE#
  ALERT                                     !RESET ALERTED KEYS
  ALERT(REJECT_KEY)                         !ALERT SCREEN REJECT KEY
  ALERT(ACCEPT_KEY)                         !ALERT SCREEN ACCEPT KEY
  ALERT(ALT_M)                              !ALERT HOT KEY
  ALERT(F10_KEY)                            !ALERT HOT KEY
  ACCEPT                                    !READ A FIELD
  IF KEYCODE() = ALT_M                      !ON HOT KEY
    IF FIELD() = ?POINT THEN DO GET_RECORD. !  READ RECORD IF NEEDED
    TAGGER                                  !  CALL HOT KEY PROCEDURE
    DO SAME_PAGE                            !  RESET TO SAME PAGE
    CYCLE                                   !  AND LOOP AGAIN
  .
  IF KEYCODE() = F10_KEY                    !ON HOT KEY
    IF FIELD() = ?POINT THEN DO GET_RECORD. !  READ RECORD IF NEEDED
    SEARCHER                                !  CALL HOT KEY PROCEDURE
    DO SAME_PAGE                            !  RESET TO SAME PAGE
    CYCLE                                   !  AND LOOP AGAIN
  .
  IF KEYCODE() = REJECT_KEY THEN BREAK.     !RETURN ON SCREEN REJECT KEY

  IF  KEYCODE() = ACCEPT_KEY     |          !ON SCREEN ACCEPT KEY
  AND FIELD() <> ?POINT                     !BUT NOT ON THE POINT FIELD
    UPDATE                                  !  MOVE ALL FIELDS FROM SCREEN
    SELECT(?)                               !  START WITH CURRENT FIELD
    SELECT                                  !  EDIT ALL FIELDS
    CYCLE                                   !  GO TO TOP OF LOOP
  .

  CASE FIELD()                              !JUMP TO FIELD EDIT ROUTINE

  OF ?FIRST_FIELD                           !FROM THE FIRST FIELD
```

(continued)

```
  IF KEYCODE() = ESC_KEY   |        ! RETURN ON ESC KEY
  OR RECORDS# = FALSE               ! OR NO RECORDS
    BREAK                           !   EXIT PROGRAM
  .

OF ?PRE_POINT                     !PRE POINT FIELD CONDITION
  IF KEYCODE() = ESC_KEY            ! BACKING UP?
    SELECT(?-1)                     !   SELECT PREVIOUS FIELD
  ELSE                              ! GOING FORWARD
    SELECT(?POINT)                  !   SELECT MENU FIELD
  .

OF ?POINT                         !PROCESS THE POINT FIELD
  IF RECORDS(TABLE) = 0           !IF THERE ARE NO RECORDS
    CLEAR(ITE:RECORD)             ! CLEAR RECORD AREA
    ACTION = 1                    ! SET ACTION TO ADD
    GET(ITEMS,0)                  ! CLEAR PENDING RECORD
    ACTN# = ACTION                !SAVE ACTION FOR COMP_TOTALS
    UPD_ITEMS                     ! CALL FORM FOR NEW RECORD
    NEWPTR = POINTER(ITEMS)       !   SET POINTER TO NEW RECORD
    DO FIRST_PAGE                 ! DISPLAY THE FIRST PAGE
    IF RECORDS(TABLE) = 0         ! IF THERE AREN'T ANY RECORDS
      RECORDS# = FALSE            !   INDICATE NO RECORDS
      SELECT(?PRE_POINT-1)        !   SELECT THE PRIOR FIELD
    .

    CYCLE                         !   AND LOOP AGAIN

  .

  CASE KEYCODE()                  !PROCESS THE KEYSTROKE

  OF INS_KEY                      !INS KEY
    CLEAR(ITE:RECORD)             ! CLEAR RECORD AREA
    ACTION = 1                    ! SET ACTION TO ADD
    GET(ITEMS,0)                  ! CLEAR PENDING RECORD
    ACTN# = ACTION                !SAVE ACTION FOR COMP_TOTALS
    UPD_ITEMS                     ! CALL FORM FOR NEW RECORD /
    IF ~ACTION                    ! IF RECORD WAS ADDED
      NEWPTR = POINTER(ITEMS)     !   SET POINTER TO NEW RECORD
      DO FIND_RECORD              !   POSITION IN FILE

  OF ENTER_KEY                    !ENTER KEY
  OROF ACCEPT_KEY                 !CTRL-ENTER KEY
    DO GET_RECORD                 ! GET THE SELECTED RECORD
    IF ACTION = 4 AND KEYCODE() = ENTER_KEY!  IF THIS IS A LOOKUP REQUEST
      ACTION = 0                  !   SET ACTION TO COMPLETE
      BREAK                       !   AND RETURN TO CALLER
    .

    IF ~ERROR()                   ! IF RECORD IS STILL THERE
      ACTION = 2                  !   SET ACTION TO CHANGE
      ACTN# = ACTION              !SAVE ACTION FOR COMP_TOTALS
      SUM$ = SCR:SPACE
```

(continued)

```
      AVERAGE$ = SCR:SPACE
      UPD_ITEMS                                   !     CALL FORM TO CHANGE REC
      IF ACTION THEN CYCLE.                       !     IF SUCCESSFUL RE-DISPLAY
      TOT:SUM -= SUM$
      TOT:COUNT -= 1
      TOT:AVERAGE -= AVERAGE$
      AVERAGE# -= 1
      .
    NEWPTR = POINTER(ITEMS)                        !     SET POINTER TO NEW RECORD
    DO FIND_RECORD                                 !     POSITION IN FILE
  OF DEL_KEY                                       !DEL KEY
    DO GET_RECORD                                  !  READ THE SELECTED RECORD
    IF ~ERROR()                                    !  IF RECORD IS STILL THERE
      ACTION = 3                                   !     SET ACTION TO DELETE
      ACTN# = ACTION                               !SAVE ACTION FOR COMP_TOTALS
      SUM$ = SCR:SPACE
      AVERAGE$ = SCR:SPACE
      UPD_ITEMS                                    !     CALL FORM TO DELETE
      IF ~ACTION                                   !     IF SUCCESSFUL
        TOT:SUM -= SUM$
        TOT:COUNT -= 1
        TOT:AVERAGE -= AVERAGE$
        AVERAGE# -= 1
        N# = NDX                                   !     SAVE POINT INDEX
        DO SAME_PAGE                               !     RE-DISPLAY
        NDX = N#                                   !     RESTORE POINT INDEX
  . .
  OF DOWN_KEY                                      !DOWN ARROW KEY
    DO SET_NEXT                                    !  POINT TO NEXT RECORD
    DO FILL_NEXT                                   !  FILL A TABLE ENTRY
    IF FOUND                                       !  FOUND A NEW RECORD
      SCROLL(ROW,COL,ROWS,COLS,ROWS(?POINT)) !     SCROLL THE SCREEN UP
      GET(TABLE,RECORDS(TABLE))                    !  GET RECORD FROM TABLE
      DO FILL_SCREEN                               !  DISPLAY ON SCREEN
      .

  OF PGDN_KEY                                      !PAGE DOWN KEY
    DO SET_NEXT                                    !  POINT TO NEXT RECORD
    DO NEXT_PAGE                                   !  DISPLAY THE NEXT PAGE

  OF CTRL_PGDN                                     !CTRL-PAGE DOWN KEY
    DO LAST_PAGE                                   !  DISPLAY THE LAST PAGE
    NDX = RECORDS(TABLE)                           !  POSITION POINT BAR

  OF UP_KEY                                        !UP ARROW KEY
    DO SET_PREV                                    !  POINT TO PREVIOUS RECORD
    DO FILL_PREV                                   !  FILL A TABLE ENTRY
    IF FOUND                                       !  FOUND A NEW RECORD
```

(continued)

```
        SCROLL(ROW,COL,ROWS,COLS,-(ROWS(?POINT)))! SCROLL THE SCREEN DOWN
        GET(TABLE,1)                      !  GET RECORD FROM TABLE
        DO FILL_SCREEN                    !  DISPLAY ON SCREEN
        .

      OF PGUP_KEY                         !PAGE UP KEY
        DO SET_PREV                       !  POINT TO PREVIOUS RECORD
        DO PREV_PAGE                      !  DISPLAY THE PREVIOUS PAGE

      OF CTRL_PGUP                        !CTRL-PAGE UP
        DO FIRST_PAGE                     !  DISPLAY THE FIRST PAGE
        NDX = 1                           !  POSITION POINT BAR
    . . .
    FREE(TABLE)                           !FREE MEMORY TABLE
    RETURN                                !AND RETURN TO CALLER

SAME_PAGE ROUTINE                         !DISPLAY THE SAME PAGE
  GET(TABLE,1)                            !  GET THE FIRST TABLE ENTRY
  DO FILL_RECORD                          !  FILL IN THE RECORD
  SET(ITE:BY_LAST,ITE:BY_LAST,TBL:PTR)    !  POSITION FILE
  FREE(TABLE)                             !  EMPTY THE TABLE
  DO NEXT_PAGE                            !  DISPLAY A FULL PAGE

FIRST_PAGE ROUTINE                        !DISPLAY FIRST PAGE
  BLANK(ROW,COL,ROWS,COLS)                !  EMPTY THE TABLE
  FREE(TABLE)                             !  EMPTY THE TABLE
  CLEAR(ITE:RECORD,-1)                    !  CLEAR RECORD TO LOW VALUES
  CLEAR(TBL:PTR)                          !  ZERO RECORD POINTER.
  SET(ITE:BY_LAST)                        !  POINT TO FIRST RECORD
  LOOP NDX = 1 TO COUNT                   !  FILL UP THE TABLE
    DO FILL_NEXT                          !    FILL A TABLE ENTRY
    IF NOT FOUND THEN BREAK.              !    GET OUT IF NO RECORD
    .
  NDX = 1                                 !  SET TO TOP OF TABLE
  DO SHOW_PAGE                            !  DISPLAY THE PAGE

LAST_PAGE ROUTINE                         !DISPLAY LAST PAGE
  NDX# = NDX                              !  SAVE SELECTOR POSITION
  BLANK(ROW,COL,ROWS,COLS)                !  CLEAR SCROLLING AREA
  FREE(TABLE)                             !  EMPTY THE TABLE
  CLEAR(ITE:RECORD,1)                     !  CLEAR RECORD TO HIGH VALUES
  CLEAR(TBL:PTR,1)                        !  CLEAR PTR TO HIGH VALUE
  SET(ITE:BY_LAST)                        !  POINT TO FIRST RECORD
  LOOP NDX = COUNT TO 1 BY -1             !  FILL UP THE TABLE
    DO FILL_PREV                          !    FILL A TABLE ENTRY
    IF NOT FOUND THEN BREAK.              !    GET OUT IF NO RECORD
    .                                     !  END OF LOOP
  NDX = NDX#                              !  RESTORE SELECTOR POSITION
```

(continued)

```
    DO SHOW_PAGE                          !  DISPLAY THE PAGE

FIND_RECORD ROUTINE                       !POSITION TO SPECIFIC RECORD
    SET(ITE:BY_LAST,ITE:BY_LAST,NEWPTR)   !POSITION FILE
    IF NEWPTR = 0                         !NEWPTR NOT SET
      NEXT(ITEMS)                         !  READ NEXT RECORD
      NEWPTR = POINTER(ITEMS)             !  SET NEWPTR
      SKIP(ITEMS,-1)                      !  BACK UP TO DISPLAY RECORD
    .
    FREE(TABLE)                           !  CLEAR THE RECORD
    DO NEXT_PAGE                          !  DISPLAY A PAGE

NEXT_PAGE ROUTINE                         !DISPLAY NEXT PAGE
    SAVECNT# = RECORDS(TABLE)             !  SAVE RECORD COUNT
    LOOP COUNT TIMES                      !  FILL UP THE TABLE
      DO FILL_NEXT                        !    FILL A TABLE ENTRY
      IF NOT FOUND                        !    IF NONE ARE LEFT
        IF NOT SAVECNT#                   !      IF REBUILDING TABLE
          DO LAST_PAGE                    !      FILL IN RECORDS
          EXIT                            !      EXIT OUT OF ROUTINE
        .
        BREAK                             !    EXIT LOOP
    . .
    DO SHOW_PAGE                          !  DISPLAY THE PAGE

SET_NEXT ROUTINE                          !POINT TO THE NEXT PAGE
    GET(TABLE,RECORDS(TABLE))             !  GET THE LAST TABLE ENTRY
    DO FILL_RECORD                        !  FILL IN THE RECORD
    SET(ITE:BY_LAST,ITE:BY_LAST,TBL:PTR)  !  POSITION FILE
    NEXT(ITEMS)                           !  READ THE CURRENT RECORD

FILL_NEXT ROUTINE                         !FILL NEXT TABLE ENTRY
    FOUND = FALSE                         !  ASSUME RECORD NOT FOUND
    LOOP UNTIL EOF(ITEMS)                 !  LOOP UNTIL END OF FILE
      NEXT(ITEMS)                         !    READ THE NEXT RECORD
      FOUND = TRUE                        !    SET RECORD FOUND
      DO FILL_TABLE                       !    FILL IN THE TABLE ENTRY
      ADD(TABLE)                          !    ADD LAST TABLE ENTRY
      GET(TABLE,RECORDS(TABLE)-COUNT)     !    GET ANY OVERFLOW RECORD
      DELETE(TABLE)                       !    AND DELETE IT
      EXIT                                !    RETURN TO CALLER
    .
PREV_PAGE ROUTINE                         !DISPLAY PREVIOUS PAGE
    LOOP COUNT TIMES                      !  FILL UP THE TABLE
      DO FILL_PREV                        !    FILL A TABLE ENTRY
      IF NOT FOUND THEN BREAK.            !    GET OUT IF NO RECORD
    .
    DO SHOW_PAGE                          !  DISPLAY THE PAGE
```

(continued)

```
SET_PREV ROUTINE                              !POINT TO PREVIOUS PAGE
  GET(TABLE,1)                                !  GET THE FIRST TABLE ENTRY
  DO FILL_RECORD                              !  FILL IN THE RECORD
  SET(ITE:BY_LAST,ITE:BY_LAST,TBL:PTR)        !  POSITION FILE
  PREVIOUS(ITEMS)                             !  READ THE CURRENT RECORD

FILL_PREV ROUTINE                             !FILL PREVIOUS TABLE ENTRY
  FOUND = FALSE                               !  ASSUME RECORD NOT FOUND
  LOOP UNTIL BOF(ITEMS)                        !  LOOP UNTIL BEGINNING OF FILE
    PREVIOUS(ITEMS)                           !     READ THE PREVIOUS RECORD
    FOUND = TRUE                              !     SET RECORD FOUND
    DO FILL_TABLE                             !     FILL IN THE TABLE ENTRY
    ADD(TABLE,1)                              !     ADD FIRST TABLE ENTRY
    GET(TABLE,COUNT+1)                        !     GET ANY OVERFLOW RECORD
    DELETE(TABLE)                             !     AND DELETE IT
    EXIT                                      !     RETURN TO CALLER
  .

SHOW_PAGE ROUTINE                             !DISPLAY THE PAGE
  NDX# = NDX                                  !  SAVE SCREEN INDEX
  LOOP NDX = 1 TO RECORDS(TABLE)              !  LOOP THRU THE TABLE
    GET(TABLE,NDX)                            !     GET A TABLE ENTRY
    DO FILL_SCREEN                            !     AND DISPLAY IT
    IF TBL:PTR = NEWPTR                        !     SET INDEX FOR NEW RECORD
      NDX# = NDX                              !     POINT TO CORRECT RECORD
      DO COMP_TOTALS                          !CALCULATE TABLE TOTALS
  . .
  NDX = NDX#                                  !  RESTORE SCREEN INDEX
  NEWPTR = 0                                  !  CLEAR NEW RECORD POINTER
  CLEAR(ITE:RECORD)                           !  CLEAR RECORD AREA

FILL_TABLE ROUTINE                            !MOVE FILE TO TABLE
  TBL:MARKED = ITE:MARKED
  TBL:LAST = ITE:LAST
  TBL:PTR = POINTER(ITEMS)                     !  SAVE RECORD POINTER
  TBL:SPACE = ''
  TBL:NAME = clip(ite:last)&', '&clip(ite:first)
  TBL:SPACE2 = ''

FILL_RECORD ROUTINE                           !MOVE TABLE TO FILE
  ITE:LAST = TBL:LAST

FILL_SCREEN ROUTINE                           !MOVE TABLE TO SCREEN
  SCR:SPACE = TBL:SPACE
  SCR:MARKED = TBL:MARKED
  SCR:NAME = TBL:NAME
  SCR:SPACE2 = TBL:SPACE2
```

(continued)

```
GET_RECORD ROUTINE                                    !GET SELECTED RECORD
  GET(TABLE,NDX)                                      !  GET TABLE ENTRY
  GET(ITEMS,TBL:PTR)                                  !  GET THE RECORD


COMP_TOTALS  ROUTINE                                  !CALCULATE TOTAL FIELDS
  IF NOT ACTN# THEN EXIT.                             !GET OUT IF ACTN NOT SET
  TOT:SUM += TBL:SPACE
  TOT:COUNT += 1
  TOT:AVERAGE += TBL:SPACE
  AVERAGE# += 1
  ACTN# = 0                                           !CLEAR ACTION
```

MARKER2.CLA—The Input Form Procedure

```
           MEMBER('MARKER')
UPD_ITEMS        PROCEDURE

SCREEN          SCREEN          PRE(SCR),WINDOW(9,36),HUE(15,4)
           ROW(1,12)    PAINT(1,14),HUE(0,7)
               COL(1)    STRING('<201,205{10},0{14},205{10},187>'),HUE(15,4)
           ROW(2,1)     REPEAT(7);STRING('<186,0{34},186>'),HUE(15,4) .
           ROW(9,1)     STRING('<200,205{34},188>'),HUE(15,4)
           ROW(1,13)    STRING('Update Items')
           ROW(4,4)     STRING('Marked:'),HUE(7,4)
           ROW(5,4)     STRING('First :'),HUE(7,4)
           ROW(6,4)     STRING('Last  :'),HUE(7,4)
MESSAGE    ROW(2,4)     STRING(30),HUE(15,4)
MARKED     ROW(4,11)    STRING(@S3),HUE(15,4)
                        ENTRY,USE(?FIRST_FIELD)
           ROW(5,11)    ENTRY(@s10),USE(ITE:FIRST),HUE(15,4),SEL(0,7)
           ROW(6,11)    ENTRY(@s20),USE(ITE:LAST),REQ,HUE(15,4),SEL(0,7)
           ROW(8,12)    PAUSE(' Press <<ENTER> '),USE(?PAUSE_FIELD),HUE(15,4)
                        ENTRY,USE(?LAST_FIELD)
                        PAUSE(''),USE(?DELETE_FIELD)


  EJECT
  CODE
  OPEN(SCREEN)                                        !OPEN THE SCREEN
  SETCURSOR                                           !TURN OFF ANY CURSOR
  DISPLAY                                             !DISPLAY THE FIELDS
  LOOP                                                !LOOP THRU ALL THE FIELDS
    MEM:MESSAGE = CENTER(MEM:MESSAGE,SIZE(MEM:MESSAGE))  !DISPLAY ACTION MESSAGE
    DO CALCFIELDS                                     !CALCULATE DISPLAY FIELDS
    ALERT                                             !RESET ALERTED KEYS
```

(continued)

```
ALERT(ACCEPT_KEY)                              !ALERT SCREEN ACCEPT KEY
ALERT(REJECT_KEY)                              !ALERT SCREEN REJECT KEY
ACCEPT                                         !READ A FIELD
IF KEYCODE() = REJECT_KEY THEN RETURN.         !RETURN ON SCREEN REJECT KEY
EXECUTE ACTION                                 !SET MESSAGE
  MEM:MESSAGE = 'Record will be Added'         !
  MEM:MESSAGE = 'Record will be Changed'       !
  MEM:MESSAGE = 'Press Enter to Delete'        !
  .
IF KEYCODE() = ACCEPT_KEY                       !ON SCREEN ACCEPT KEY
  UPDATE                                        !  MOVE ALL FIELDS FROM SCREEN
  SELECT(?)                                     !  START WITH CURRENT FIELD
  SELECT                                        !  EDIT ALL FIELDS
  CYCLE                                         !  GO TO TOP OF LOOP
  .
CASE FIELD()                                    !JUMP TO FIELD EDIT ROUTINE
OF ?FIRST_FIELD                                 !FROM THE FIRST FIELD
  IF KEYCODE() = ESC_KEY THEN RETURN.           !  RETURN ON ESC KEY
  IF ACTION = 3 THEN SELECT(?DELETE_FIELD).!    OR CONFIRM FOR DELETE

  OF ?PAUSE_FIELD                               !ON PAUSE FIELD
    IF KEYCODE() <> ENTER_KEY|                  !IF NOT ENTER KEY
    AND KEYCODE() <> ACCEPT_KEY|                !AND NOT CTRL-ENTER KEY
    AND KEYCODE() <> 0                          !AND NOT NONSTOP MODE
      BEEP                                      !  SOUND KEYBOARD ALARM
      SELECT(?PAUSE_FIELD)                      !  AND STAY ON PAUSE FIELD
      .
OF ?LAST_FIELD                                  !FROM THE LAST FIELD
  EXECUTE ACTION                                !  UPDATE THE FILE
    ADD(ITEMS)                                  !    ADD NEW RECORD
    PUT(ITEMS)                                  !    CHANGE EXISTING RECORD
    DELETE(ITEMS)                               !    DELETE EXISTING RECORD
    .
  IF ERRORCODE() = 40                           !  DUPLICATE KEY ERROR
    MEM:MESSAGE = ERROR()                       !    DISPLAY ERR MESSAGE
    SELECT(2)                                   !    POSITION TO TOP OF FORM
    CYCLE                                       !    GET OUT OF EDIT LOOP
  ELSIF ERROR()                                 !  CHECK FOR UNEXPECTED ERROR
    STOP(ERROR())                               !    HALT EXECUTION
    .
  ACTION = 0                                    !  SET ACTION TO COMPLETE
  RETURN                                        !  AND RETURN TO CALLER

OF ?DELETE_FIELD                                !FROM THE DELETE FIELD
  IF KEYCODE() = ENTER_KEY |                    !  ON ENTER KEY
  OR KEYCODE() = ACCEPT_KEY                     !  OR CTRL-ENTER KEY
    SELECT(?LAST_FIELD)                         !    DELETE THE RECORD
```

(continued)

```
            ELSE                                       !    OTHERWISE
               BEEP                                    !      BEEP AND ASK AGAIN
     . . .


CALCFIELDS   ROUTINE
  IF FIELD() > ?FIRST_FIELD                            !BEYOND FIRST_FIELD?
    IF KEYCODE() = 0 AND SELECTED() > FIELD() THEN EXIT. !GET OUT IF NOT NONSTOP
    .
  SCR:MESSAGE = MEM:MESSAGE
  IF ITE:MARKED = ''                                   !EVALUATE CONDITION
    SCR:MARKED = 'Yes'                                 !   CONDITION IS TRUE
  ELSE                                                 !OTHERWISE
    SCR:MARKED = 'No'                                  !   CONDITION IS FALSE
    .
```

TAGGER.CLA—The Marking Procedure

```
             MEMBER('MARKER')


TAGGER       PROCEDURE


             CODE
             IF ITE:MARKED  = ''                    ! If the record is not marked
                ITE:MARKED = '<16>'                 ! Mark it
             ELSE                                   ! Otherwise
                ITE:MARKED = ''                     ! Take the mark out
             END!IF
             PUT(ITEMS)                             ! Save the changed record
             SET(ITE:BY_LAST,ITE:BY_LAST)           ! Leave the pointer set
             RETURN                                 ! Go back to the table
```

The SELECTOR CHANGING Program

CHANGER.CLA—The Main Program Procedure

```
CHANGE     PROGRAM
             INCLUDE('STD_KEYS.CLA')
             INCLUDE('CTL_KEYS.CLA')
             INCLUDE('ALT_KEYS.CLA')
             INCLUDE('SHF_KEYS.CLA')


REJECT_KEY   EQUATE(CTRL_ESC)
ACCEPT_KEY   EQUATE(CTRL_ENTER)
```

(continued)

```
TRUE            EQUATE(1)
FALSE           EQUATE(0)

                MAP
                  PROC(G_OPENFILES)
                  MODULE('CHANGE1')
                    PROC(MAIN_TABLE)              !Show Data By Last
                      .
                  MODULE('CHANGE2')
                    PROC(UPD_DATA)                !Update Data
                      .
                  INCLUDE('DOS1.CPY')
                    .
                EJECT('FILE LAYOUTS')
INFO            FILE,PRE(INF),CREATE,RECLAIM
BY_LAST         KEY(INF:LAST),DUP,NOCASE,OPT
BY_FIRST        KEY(INF:FIRST),DUP,NOCASE,OPT
RECORD          RECORD
FIRST             STRING(10)
LAST              STRING(20)
        .  .

                EJECT('GLOBAL MEMORY VARIABLES')
ACTION          SHORT                         !0 = NO ACTION
                                              !1 = ADD RECORD
                                              !2 = CHANGE RECORD
                                              !3 = DELETE RECORD
                                              !4 = LOOKUP FIELD


                GROUP,PRE(MEM)
MESSAGE           STRING(30)                  !Global Message Area
PAGE              SHORT                       !Report Page Number
LINE              SHORT                       !Report Line Number
DEVICE            STRING(30)                  !Report Device Name
        .

                EJECT('CODE SECTION')
  CODE
  SETHUE(7,0)                                 !SET WHITE ON BLACK
  BLANK                                       !  AND BLANK
  G_OPENFILES                                 !OPEN OR CREATE FILES
  SETHUE()                                    !    THE SCREEN
  MAIN_TABLE                                  !Show Data By Last
  RETURN                                      !EXIT TO DOS

G_OPENFILES  PROCEDURE                        !OPEN FILES & CHECK FOR ERROR
```

(continued)

```
         CODE
         SHOW(25,1,CENTER('OPENING FILE: ' & 'INFO',80)) !DISPLAY FILE NAME
         OPEN(INFO)                                  !OPEN THE FILE
         IF ERROR()                                  !OPEN RETURNED AN ERROR
           CASE ERRORCODE()                          ! CHECK FOR SPECIFIC ERROR
           OF 46                                     !  KEYS NEED TO BE REQUILT
             SETHUE(0,7)                             !  BLACK ON WHITE
             SHOW(25,1,CENTER('REBUILDING KEY FILES FOR INFO',80)) !INDICATE MSG
             BUILD(INFO)                             !  CALL THE BUILD PROCEDURE
             SETHUE(7,0)                             !  WHITE ON BLACK
             BLANK(25,1,1,80)                        !  BLANK THE MESSAGE
           OF 2                                      !IF NOT FOUND,
             CREATE(INFO)                            ! CREATE
           ELSE                                      ! ANY OTHER ERROR
             LOOP;STOP('INFO: ' & ERROR()).         !  STOP EXECUTION
         . .


         BLANK                                       !BLANK THE SCREEN
```

CHANGER1.CLA—The Table Procedure

```
         MEMBER('CHANGE')
MAIN_TABLE    PROCEDURE


SCREEN        SCREEN       PRE(SCR),WINDOW(19,39),HUE(15,1)
              ROW(6,3)    PAINT(14,35),HUE(0,7)
              ROW(17,5)   PAINT(2,35),HUE(15,1)
              ROW(1,1)    STRING('<201,205{9},0{19},205{9},187>'),HUE(15,1)
              ROW(2,1)    REPEAT(17);STRING('<186,0{37},186>'),HUE(15,1) .
              ROW(19,1)   STRING('<200,205{37},188>'),HUE(15,1)
              ROW(1,12)   STRING('Show Data By Last')
              ROW(3,6)    STRING('ENTER SELECTION BY LAST NAME')
              ROW(17,3)   STRING('In'),HUE(11,1)
                COL(5)    STRING('s to Add'),HUE(11,1)
                COL(23)   STRING('Enter to Change'),HUE(11,1)
              ROW(18,3)   STRING('De'),HUE(11,1)
                COL(5)    STRING('l to Delete'),HUE(11,1)
                COL(22)   STRING('Ctrl-Esc to Exit'),HUE(11,1)
                            ENTRY,USE(?FIRST_FIELD)
              ROW(4,11)   ENTRY(@s20),USE(INF:LAST),REQ,SEL(0,7)
                            ENTRY,USE(?PRE_POINT)
                            REPEAT(11),EVERY(1),INDEX(NDX)
              ROW(6,5)       POINT(1,32),USE(?POINT),ESC(?-1)
NAME            COL(6)    STRING(@S30)
                .                    .
```

(continued)

```
NDX            BYTE                          !REPEAT INDEX FOR POINT AREA
ROW            BYTE                          !ACTUAL ROW OF SCROLL AREA
COL            BYTE                          !ACTUAL COLUMN OF SCROLL AREA
COUNT          BYTE(11)                      !NUMBER OF ITEMS TO SCROLL
ROWS           BYTE(11)                      !NUMBER OF ROWS TO SCROLL
COLS           BYTE(32)                      !NUMBER OF COLUMNS TO SCROLL
FOUND          BYTE                          !RECORD FOUND FLAG
NEWPTR         LONG                          !POINTER TO NEW RECORD

TABLE          TABLE,PRE(TBL)                !TABLE OF RECORD DATA
NAME           STRING(@S30)
LAST           STRING(20)
PTR            LONG                          !  POINTER TO FILE RECORD
               .

  EJECT
  CODE
  ACTION# = ACTION                           !SAVE ACTION
  OPEN(SCREEN)                               !OPEN THE SCREEN
  SETCURSOR                                  !TURN OFF ANY CURSOR
  TBL:PTR = 1                                !START AT TABLE ENTRY
  NDX = 1                                    !PUT SELECTOR BAR ON TOP ITEM
  ROW = ROW(?POINT)                          !REMEMBER TOP ROW AND
  COL = COL(?POINT)                          !LEFT COLUMN OF SCROLL AREA
  RECORDS# = TRUE                            !INITIALIZE RECORDS FLAG
  CACHE(INF:BY_LAST,.25)                     !CACHE KEY FILE
  IF ACTION = 4                             !  TABLE LOOKUP REQUEST
    NEWPTR = POINTER(INFO)                   !  SET POINTER TO RECORD
    IF NOT NEWPTR                            !  RECORD NOT PASSED TO TABLE
      SET(INF:BY_LAST,INF:BY_LAST)           !    POSITION TO CLOSEST· RECORD
      NEXT(INFO)                             !    READ RECORD
      NEWPTR = POINTER(INFO)                 !    SET POINTER
      .
    DO FIND_RECORD                           !  POSITION FILE
  ELSE
    NDX = 1                                  !  PUT SELECTOR BAR ON TOP ITEM
    DO FIRST_PAGE                            !  BUILD MEMORY TABLE OF KEYS
    .
  RECORDS# = TRUE                            !  ASSUME THERE ARE RECORDS
  LOOP                                       !LOOP UNTIL USER EXITS
    ACTION = ACTION#                         !RESTORE ACTION
    ALERT                                    !RESET ALERTED KEYS
    ALERT(REJECT_KEY)                        !ALERT SCREEN REJECT KEY
    ALERT(ACCEPT_KEY)                        !ALERT SCREEN ACCEPT KEY
    ACCEPT                                   !READ A FIELD
    IF KEYCODE() = REJECT_KEY THEN BREAK.    !RETURN ON SCREEN REJECT KEY

    IF  KEYCODE() = ACCEPT_KEY      |        !ON SCREEN ACCEPT KEY
```

(continued)

```
  AND FIELD() <> ?POINT            !BUT NOT ON THE POINT FIELD
    UPDATE                         !  MOVE ALL FIELDS FROM SCREEN
    SELECT(?)                      !  START WITH CURRENT FIELD
    SELECT                         !  EDIT ALL FIELDS
    CYCLE                          !  GO TO TOP OF LOOP
  .


  CASE FIELD()                     !JUMP TO FIELD EDIT ROUTINE

  OF ?FIRST_FIELD                  !FROM THE FIRST FIELD
    IF KEYCODE() = ESC_KEY    |    !  RETURN ON ESC KEY
    OR RECORDS# = FALSE            !  OR NO RECORDS
      BREAK                        !     EXIT PROGRAM
    .

  OF ?INF:LAST
    do find_record

  OF ?PRE_POINT                    !PRE POINT FIELD CONDITION
    IF KEYCODE() = ESC_KEY         !  BACKING UP?
      SELECT(?-1)                  !     SELECT PREVIOUS FIELD
    ELSE                           !  GOING FORWARD
      SELECT(?POINT)               !     SELECT MENU FIELD
    .

  OF ?POINT                        !PROCESS THE POINT FIELD
    IF RECORDS(TABLE) = 0          !IF THERE ARE NO RECORDS
      CLEAR(INF:RECORD)            !  CLEAR RECORD AREA
      ACTION = 1                   !  SET ACTION TO ADD
      GET(INFO,0)                  !  CLEAR PENDING RECORD
      UPD_DATA                     !  CALL FORM FOR NEW RECORD
      NEWPTR = POINTER(INFO)       !    SET POINTER TO NEW RECORD
      DO FIRST_PAGE                !  DISPLAY THE FIRST PAGE
      IF RECORDS(TABLE) = 0        !  IF THERE AREN'T ANY RECORDS
        RECORDS# = FALSE           !     INDICATE NO RECORDS
        SELECT(?PRE_POINT-1)       !     SELECT THE PRIOR FIELD
      .

    CYCLE                          !    AND LOOP AGAIN
    .

  CASE KEYCODE()                   !PROCESS THE KEYSTROKE

  OF INS_KEY                       !INS KEY
    CLEAR(INF:RECORD)              !  CLEAR RECORD AREA
    ACTION = 1                     !  SET ACTION TO ADD
    GET(INFO,0)                    !  CLEAR PENDING RECORD
    UPD_DATA                       !  CALL FORM FOR NEW RECORD
    IF ~ACTION                     !  IF RECORD WAS ADDED
      NEWPTR = POINTER(INFO)       !    SET POINTER TO NEW RECORD
      DO FIND_RECORD               !    POSITION IN FILE
    .
```

(continued)

```
OF ENTER_KEY                                    !ENTER KEY
OROF ACCEPT_KEY                                 !CTRL-ENTER KEY
  DO GET_RECORD                                 !   GET THE SELECTED RECORD
  IF ACTION = 4 AND KEYCODE() = ENTER_KEY!      IF THIS IS A LOOKUP REQUEST
    ACTION = 0                                  !      SET ACTION TO COMPLETE
    BREAK                                       !      AND RETURN TO CALLER
  .
  IF ~ERROR()                                   !   IF RECORD IS STILL THERE
    ACTION = 2                                  !      SET ACTION TO CHANGE
    UPD_DATA                                    !      CALL FORM TO CHANGE REC
    IF ACTION THEN CYCLE.                       !      IF SUCCESSFUL RE-DISPLAY
  .
  NEWPTR = POINTER(INFO)                        !      SET POINTER TO NEW RECORD
  DO FIND_RECORD                                !      POSITION IN FILE
OF DEL_KEY                                      !DEL KEY
  DO GET_RECORD                                 !   READ THE SELECTED RECORD
  IF ~ERROR()                                   !   IF RECORD IS STILL THERE
    ACTION = 3                                  !      SET ACTION TO DELETE
    UPD_DATA                                    !      CALL FORM TO DELETE
    IF ~ACTION                                  !      IF SUCCESSFUL
      N# = NDX                                  !         SAVE POINT INDEX
      DO SAME_PAGE                              !         RE-DISPLAY
      NDX = N#                                  !         RESTORE POINT INDEX
  . .
OF DOWN_KEY                                     !DOWN ARROW KEY
  DO SET_NEXT                                   !   POINT TO NEXT RECORD
  DO FILL_NEXT                                  !   FILL A TABLE ENTRY
  IF FOUND                                      !   FOUND A NEW RECORD
    SCROLL(ROW,COL,ROWS,COLS,ROWS(?POINT)) !      SCROLL THE SCREEN UP
    GET(TABLE,RECORDS(TABLE))                   !      GET RECORD FROM TABLE
    DO FILL_SCREEN                              !      DISPLAY ON SCREEN
  .

OF PGDN_KEY                                     !PAGE DOWN KEY
  DO SET_NEXT                                   !   POINT TO NEXT RECORD
  DO NEXT_PAGE                                  !   DISPLAY THE NEXT PAGE

OF CTRL_PGDN                                    !CTRL-PAGE DOWN KEY
  DO LAST_PAGE                                  !   DISPLAY THE LAST PAGE
  NDX = RECORDS(TABLE)                          !   POSITION POINT BAR

OF UP_KEY                                       !UP ARROW KEY
  DO SET_PREV                                   !   POINT TO PREVIOUS RECORD
  DO FILL_PREV                                  !   FILL A TABLE ENTRY
  IF FOUND                                      !   FOUND A NEW RECORD
    SCROLL(ROW,COL,ROWS,COLS,-(ROWS(?POINT)))!  SCROLL THE SCREEN DOWN
    GET(TABLE,1)                                !   GET RECORD FROM TABLE
```

(continued)

```
          DO FILL_SCREEN                    !   DISPLAY ON SCREEN
          .

      OF PGUP_KEY                           !PAGE UP KEY
        DO SET_PREV                         !   POINT TO PREVIOUS RECORD
        DO PREV_PAGE                        !   DISPLAY THE PREVIOUS PAGE

      OF CTRL_PGUP                          !CTRL-PAGE UP
        DO FIRST_PAGE                       !   DISPLAY THE FIRST PAGE
        NDX = 1                             !   POSITION POINT BAR
    . . .
    FREE(TABLE)                             !FREE MEMORY TABLE
    RETURN                                  !AND RETURN TO CALLER

SAME_PAGE ROUTINE                           !DISPLAY THE SAME PAGE
  GET(TABLE,1)                              !   GET THE FIRST TABLE ENTRY
  DO FILL_RECORD                            !   FILL IN THE RECORD
  SET(INF:BY_LAST,INF:BY_LAST,TBL:PTR)      !   POSITION FILE
  FREE(TABLE)                               !   EMPTY THE TABLE
  DO NEXT_PAGE                              !   DISPLAY A FULL PAGE

FIRST_PAGE ROUTINE                          !DISPLAY FIRST PAGE
  BLANK(ROW,COL,ROWS,COLS)
  FREE(TABLE)                               !   EMPTY THE TABLE
  CLEAR(INF:RECORD,-1)                      !   CLEAR RECORD TO LOW VALUES
  CLEAR(TBL:PTR)                            !   ZERO RECORD POINTER
  SET(INF:BY_LAST)                          !   POINT TO FIRST RECORD
  LOOP NDX = 1 TO COUNT                     !   FILL UP THE TABLE
    DO FILL_NEXT                            !     FILL A TABLE ENTRY
    IF NOT FOUND THEN BREAK.                !     GET OUT IF NO RECORD

    .
  NDX = 1                                   !   SET TO TOP OF TABLE
  DO SHOW_PAGE                              !   DISPLAY THE PAGE

LAST_PAGE ROUTINE                           !DISPLAY LAST PAGE
  NDX# = NDX                                !   SAVE SELECTOR POSITION
  BLANK(ROW,COL,ROWS,COLS)                  !   CLEAR SCROLLING AREA
  FREE(TABLE)                               !   EMPTY THE TABLE
  CLEAR(INF:RECORD,1)                       !   CLEAR RECORD TO HIGH VALUES
  CLEAR(TBL:PTR,1)                          !   CLEAR PTR TO HIGH VALUE
  SET(INF:BY_LAST)                          !   POINT TO FIRST RECORD
  LOOP NDX = COUNT TO 1 BY -1               !   FILL UP THE TABLE
    DO FILL_PREV                            !     FILL A TABLE ENTRY
    IF NOT FOUND THEN BREAK.                !     GET OUT IF NO RECORD
                                            !   END OF LOOP
    .
  NDX = NDX#                                !   RESTORE SELECTOR POSITION
  DO SHOW_PAGE                              !   DISPLAY THE PAGE
```

(continued)

```
FIND_RECORD ROUTINE                          !POSITION TO SPECIFIC RECORD
  SET(INF:BY_LAST,INF:BY_LAST,NEWPTR)        !POSITION FILE
  IF NEWPTR = 0                              !NEWPTR NOT SET
    NEXT(INFO)                               !   READ NEXT RECORD
    NEWPTR = POINTER(INFO)                   !   SET NEWPTR
    SKIP(INFO,-1)                            !   BACK UP TO DISPLAY RECORD
  .
  FREE(TABLE)                                !   CLEAR THE RECORD
  DO NEXT_PAGE                               !   DISPLAY A PAGE


NEXT_PAGE ROUTINE                            !DISPLAY NEXT PAGE
  SAVECNT# = RECORDS(TABLE)                  !   SAVE RECORD COUNT
  LOOP COUNT TIMES                           !   FILL UP THE TABLE
    DO FILL_NEXT                             !     FILL A TABLE ENTRY
    IF NOT FOUND                             !     IF NONE ARE LEFT
      IF NOT SAVECNT#                        !       IF REBUILDING TABLE
        DO LAST_PAGE                         !       FILL IN RECORDS
        EXIT                                 !       EXIT OUT OF ROUTINE
      .
      BREAK                                  !     EXIT LOOP
  . .
  DO SHOW_PAGE                               !   DISPLAY THE PAGE


SET_NEXT ROUTINE                             !POINT TO THE NEXT PAGE
  GET(TABLE,RECORDS(TABLE))                  !   GET THE LAST TABLE ENTRY
  DO FILL_RECORD                             !   FILL IN THE RECORD
  SET(INF:BY_LAST,INF:BY_LAST,TBL:PTR)       !   POSITION FILE
  NEXT(INFO)                                 !   READ THE CURRENT RECORD


FILL_NEXT ROUTINE                            !FILL NEXT TABLE ENTRY
  FOUND = FALSE                              !   ASSUME RECORD NOT FOUND
  LOOP UNTIL EOF(INFO)                       !   LOOP UNTIL END OF FILE
    NEXT(INFO)                               !     READ THE NEXT RECORD
    FOUND = TRUE                             !     SET RECORD FOUND
    DO FILL_TABLE                            !     FILL IN THE TABLE ENTRY
    ADD(TABLE)                               !     ADD LAST TABLE ENTRY
    GET(TABLE,RECORDS(TABLE)-COUNT)          !     GET ANY OVERFLOW RECORD
    DELETE(TABLE)                            !     AND DELETE IT
    EXIT                                     !     RETURN TO CALLER
  .
PREV_PAGE ROUTINE                            !DISPLAY PREVIOUS PAGE
  LOOP COUNT TIMES                           !   FILL UP THE TABLE
    DO FILL_PREV                             !     FILL A TABLE ENTRY
    IF NOT FOUND THEN BREAK.                 !     GET OUT IF NO RECORD
  .
  DO SHOW_PAGE                               !   DISPLAY THE PAGE
```

(continued)

```
SET_PREV ROUTINE                                      !POINT TO PREVIOUS PAGE
  GET(TABLE,1)                                        !  GET THE FIRST TABLE ENTRY
  DO FILL_RECORD                                      !  FILL IN THE RECORD
  SET(INF:BY_LAST,INF:BY_LAST,TBL:PTR)                !  POSITION FILE
  PREVIOUS(INFO)                                      !  READ THE CURRENT RECORD


FILL_PREV ROUTINE                                     !FILL PREVIOUS TABLE ENTRY
  FOUND = FALSE                                        !  ASSUME RECORD NOT FOUND
  LOOP UNTIL BOF(INFO)                                 !  LOOP UNTIL BEGINNING OF FILE
    PREVIOUS(INFO)                                     !    READ THE PREVIOUS RECORD
    FOUND = TRUE                                       !    SET RECORD FOUND
    DO FILL_TABLE                                      !    FILL IN THE TABLE ENTRY
    ADD(TABLE,1)                                       !    ADD FIRST TABLE ENTRY
    GET(TABLE,COUNT+1)                                 !    GET ANY OVERFLOW RECORD
    DELETE(TABLE)                                      !    AND DELETE IT
    EXIT                                               !    RETURN TO CALLER
  .

SHOW_PAGE ROUTINE                                     !DISPLAY THE PAGE
  NDX# = NDX                                          !  SAVE SCREEN INDEX
  LOOP NDX = 1 TO RECORDS(TABLE)                      !  LOOP THRU THE TABLE
    GET(TABLE,NDX)                                     !    GET A TABLE ENTRY
    DO FILL_SCREEN                                     !    AND DISPLAY IT
    IF TBL:PTR = NEWPTR                                !    SET INDEX FOR NEW RECORD
      NDX# = NDX                                       !    POINT TO CORRECT RECORD
  . .
  NDX = NDX#                                          !  RESTORE SCREEN INDEX
  NEWPTR = 0                                          !  CLEAR NEW RECORD POINTER
  CLEAR(INF:RECORD)                                   !  CLEAR RECORD AREA

FILL_TABLE ROUTINE                                   !MOVE FILE TO TABLE
  TBL:LAST = INF:LAST
  TBL:PTR = POINTER(INFO)                             !  SAVE RECORD POINTER
  TBL:NAME = CLIP(INF:LAST) & ', ' & CLIP(INF:FIRST)

FILL_RECORD ROUTINE                                  !MOVE TABLE TO FILE
  INF:LAST = TBL:LAST

FILL_SCREEN ROUTINE                                  !MOVE TABLE TO SCREEN
  SCR:NAME = TBL:NAME

GET_RECORD ROUTINE                                   !GET SELECTED RECORD
  GET(TABLE,NDX)                                       !  GET TABLE ENTRY
  GET(INFO,TBL:PTR)                                    !  GET THE RECORD
```

CHANGER2.CLA—The Input Form Procedure

```
            MEMBER('CHANGE')
UPD_DATA      PROCEDURE

SCREEN        SCREEN      PRE(SCR),WINDOW(7,36),HUE(15,4)
             ROW(1,1)    STRING('<201,205{34},187>'),HUE(15,4)
             ROW(2,1)    REPEAT(5);STRING('<186,0{34};186>'),HUE(15,4)   .
             ROW(7,1)    STRING('<200,205{34},188>'),HUE(15,4)
             ROW(2,14)   STRING('Update Data')
             ROW(4,4)    STRING('FIRST:'),HUE(7,4)
             ROW(5,4)    STRING('LAST :'),HUE(7,4)
MESSAGE       ROW(3,4)    STRING(30),HUE(15,4)
                         ENTRY,USE(?FIRST_FIELD)
             ROW(4,11)   ENTRY(@s10),USE(INF:FIRST),HUE(15,4)
             ROW(5,11)   ENTRY(@s20),USE(INF:LAST),REQ,HUE(15,4)
                         ENTRY,USE(?LAST_FIELD)
                         PAUSE(''),USE(?DELETE_FIELD)

                    .

  EJECT
  CODE
  OPEN(SCREEN)                                    !OPEN THE SCREEN
  SETCURSOR                                       !TURN OFF ANY CURSOR
  DISPLAY                                         !DISPLAY THE FIELDS
  LOOP                                            !LOOP THRU ALL THE FIELDS
    MEM:MESSAGE = CENTER(MEM:MESSAGE,SIZE(MEM:MESSAGE)) !DISPLAY ACTION MESSAGE
    DO CALCFIELDS                                 !CALCULATE DISPLAY FIELDS
    ALERT                                         !RESET ALERTED KEYS
    ALERT(ACCEPT_KEY)                             !ALERT SCREEN ACCEPT KEY
    ALERT(REJECT_KEY)                             !ALERT SCREEN REJECT KEY
    ACCEPT                                        !READ A FIELD
    IF KEYCODE() = REJECT_KEY THEN RETURN.        !RETURN ON SCREEN REJECT KEY
    EXECUTE ACTION                                !SET MESSAGE
      MEM:MESSAGE = 'Record will be Added'        !
      MEM:MESSAGE = 'Record will be Changed'      !
      MEM:MESSAGE = 'Press Enter to Delete'       !

    .
    IF KEYCODE() = ACCEPT_KEY                      !ON SCREEN ACCEPT KEY
      UPDATE                                      !   MOVE ALL FIELDS FROM SCREEN
      SELECT(?)                                   !   START WITH CURRENT FIELD
      SELECT                                      !   EDIT ALL FIELDS
      CYCLE                                       !   GO TO TOP OF LOOP

    .
    CASE FIELD()                                  !JUMP TO FIELD EDIT ROUTINE
    OF ?FIRST_FIELD                               !FROM THE FIRST FIELD
      IF KEYCODE() = ESC_KEY THEN RETURN.         !   RETURN ON ESC KEY
```

(continued)

```
        IF ACTION = 3 THEN SELECT(?DELETE_FIELD).!    OR CONFIRM FOR DELETE

    OF ?LAST_FIELD                              !FROM THE LAST FIELD
      EXECUTE ACTION                            !  UPDATE THE FILE
        ADD(INFO)                               !     ADD NEW RECORD
        PUT(INFO)                               !     CHANGE EXISTING RECORD
        DELETE(INFO)                            !     DELETE EXISTING RECORD
      .
      IF ERRORCODE() = 40                       !  DUPLICATE KEY ERROR
        MEM:MESSAGE = ERROR()                   !    DISPLAY ERR MESSAGE
        SELECT(2)                               !    POSITION TO TOP OF FORM
        CYCLE                                   !    GET OUT OF EDIT LOOP
      ELSIF ERROR()                             !  CHECK FOR UNEXPECTED ERROR
        STOP(ERROR())                           !    HALT EXECUTION
      .
      ACTION = 0                                !  SET ACTION TO COMPLETE
      RETURN                                    !  AND RETURN TO CALLER

    OF ?DELETE_FIELD                            !FROM THE DELETE FIELD
      IF KEYCODE() = ENTER_KEY |                !  ON ENTER KEY
      OR KEYCODE() = ACCEPT_KEY                 !  OR CTRL-ENTER KEY
        SELECT(?LAST_FIELD)                     !    DELETE THE RECORD
      ELSE                                      !  OTHERWISE
        BEEP                                    !    BEEP AND ASK AGAIN
  . . .

CALCFIELDS  ROUTINE
  IF FIELD() > ?FIRST_FIELD                              !BEYOND FIRST_FIELD?
    IF KEYCODE() = 0 AND SELECTED() > FIELD() THEN EXIT. !GET OUT IF NOT NONSTOP
  .
  SCR:MESSAGE = MEM:MESSAGE
```

The TIME SHEET Program

HOURS.CLA—Top Program and Files Procedure

```
HOURS     PROGRAM
              INCLUDE('STD_KEYS.CLA')
              INCLUDE('CTL_KEYS.CLA')
              INCLUDE('ALT_KEYS.CLA')
              INCLUDE('SHF_KEYS.CLA')

REJECT_KEY    EQUATE(CTRL_ESC)
ACCEPT_KEY    EQUATE(CTRL_ENTER)
```

(continued)

```
TRUE          EQUATE(1)
FALSE         EQUATE(0)

              MAP
                PROC(G_OPENFILES)
                MODULE('HOURS1')
                  PROC(MAIN)
                .
                MODULE('HOURS2')
                  PROC(CHRONOLOGY)                !COMPANY WIDE CLIENT WORK
                .
                MODULE('HOURS3')
                  PROC(LIST)                       !LIST OF CLIENTS
                .
                MODULE('HOURS4')
                  PROC(CLIENT)                     !ENTER CLIENT INFORMATION
                .
                MODULE('HOURS5')
                  PROC(WORK)                       !ENTER WORK AND HOURS
                .
                MODULE('HOURS6')
                  PROC(LISTLOOK)                   !LOOK UP CLIENT FOR SELECT TABL
                .
                MODULE('HOURS7')
                  PROC(BILLED)                     !LIST WORK FOR ONE CLIENT
                .
                MODULE('TIMER')
                  PROC(TIMER)                      !RUNNING CLOCK
                .
                MODULE('POPUP')
                  PROC(POPUP)                      !calendar
                .
                MODULE('BILL')
                  PROC(BILL)                       !MARK THE WORK AS INVOICED
                .
              .
              EJECT('FILE LAYOUTS')
HOURS     FILE,PRE(HRS),CREATE,RECLAIM
BY_DATE   KEY(HRS:DATE,HRS:STARTTIME,HRS:CLIENTNO),DUP,NOCASE,OPT
BY_CLIENT KEY(HRS:CLIENTNO,HRS:DATE),DUP,NOCASE,OPT
NOTES         MEMO(2000)                           !NOTES AND COMMENTS ON WORK
RECORD        RECORD
DATE          LONG                                 !DATE OF ACTIVITY
CLIENTNO      SHORT                                !CLIENT NUMBER FOR RELATION
SUBJECT       STRING(30)                           !SUBJECT OF WORK PERFORMED
STARTTIME     LONG                                 !TIME WORK STARTED
COMPLETETIME  LONG                                 !TIME WORK COMPLETED
BILLED        STRING(1)                            !BILLED OR NOT BILLED
```

(continued)

```
          . .
          GROUP,OVER(HRS:NOTES)
HRS_MEMO_ROW STRING(40),DIM(50)
          .


CLIENTS   FILE,PRE(CLI),CREATE,RECLAIM
BY_CLIENT  KEY(CLI:COMPANY,CLI:CLIENTNO),NOCASE,OPT
BY_CLIENTNO KEY(CLI:CLIENTNO),NOCASE,OPT
RECORD     RECORD
CLIENTNO     SHORT
RATE         DECIMAL(7,2)                     !HOURLY RATE
COMPANY      STRING(30)                       !COMPANY NAME OF CLIENT
PHONE        STRING(@P(###)###-####PB)
          . .


          EJECT('GLOBAL MEMORY VARIABLES')
ACTION       SHORT                            !0 = NO ACTION
                                              !1 = ADD RECORD
                                              !2 = CHANGE RECORD
                                              !3 = DELETE RECORD
                                              !4 = LOOKUP FIELD

          GROUP,PRE(MEM)
MESSAGE     STRING(30)                         !Global Message Area
PAGE        SHORT                              !Report Page Number
LINE        SHORT                              !Report Line Number
DEVICE      STRING(30)                         !Report Device Name
TO_BILL     STRING(5)                          !USED TO ADD UP ITEMS TO BILL
          .


          EJECT('CODE SECTION')
  CODE
  SETHUE(7,0)                                  !SET WHITE ON BLACK
  BLANK                                        !  AND BLANK
  G_OPENFILES                                  !OPEN OR CREATE FILES
  SETHUE()                                     !    THE SCREEN
  MAIN
  RETURN                                       !EXIT TO DOS

G_OPENFILES  PROCEDURE                         !OPEN FILES & CHECK FOR ERROR
  CODE
  SHOW(25,1,CENTER('OPENING FILE: ' & 'HOURS',80)) !DISPLAY FILE NAME
  OPEN(HOURS)                                  !OPEN THE FILE
  IF ERROR()                                   !OPEN RETURNED AN ERROR
    CASE ERRORCODE()                           ! CHECK FOR SPECIFIC ERROR
    OF 46                                      !  KEYS NEED TO BE REQUILT
      SETHUE(0,7)                              !  BLACK ON WHITE
      SHOW(25,1,CENTER('REBUILDING KEY FILES FOR HOURS',80)) !INDICATE MSG
      BUILD(HOURS)                             !  CALL THE BUILD PROCEDURE
```

(continued)

```
      SETHUE(7,0)                             !  WHITE ON BLACK
      BLANK(25,1,1,80)                        !  BLANK THE MESSAGE
  OF 2                                        !IF NOT FOUND,
    CREATE(HOURS)                             ! CREATE
  ELSE                                        ! ANY OTHER ERROR
    LOOP;STOP('HOURS: ' & ERROR()).           !  STOP EXECUTION
 . .


SHOW(25,1,CENTER('OPENING FILE: ' & 'CLIENTS',80)) !DISPLAY FILE NAME
OPEN(CLIENTS)                                 !OPEN THE FILE
IF ERROR()                                    !OPEN RETURNED AN ERROR
  CASE ERRORCODE()                            ! CHECK FOR SPECIFIC ERROR
  OF 46                                       !   KEYS NEED TO BE REQUILT
    SETHUE(0,7)                               !   BLACK ON WHITE
    SHOW(25,1,CENTER('REBUILDING KEY FILES FOR CLIENTS',80)) !INDICATE MSG
    BUILD(CLIENTS)                            !   CALL THE BUILD PROCEDURE
    SETHUE(7,0)                               !   WHITE ON BLACK
    BLANK(25,1,1,80)                          !   BLANK THE MESSAGE
  OF 2                                        !IF NOT FOUND,
    CREATE(CLIENTS)                           ! CREATE
  ELSE                                        ! ANY OTHER ERROR
    LOOP;STOP('CLIENTS: ' & ERROR()).         !  STOP EXECUTION
 . .


BLANK                                         !BLANK THE SCREEN
```

HOURS1.CLA—Main Menu Procedure

```
          MEMBER('HOURS')
MAIN          PROCEDURE

SCREEN        SCREEN      PRE(SCR),WINDOW(15,50),AT(6,16),HUE(15,1)
          ROW(1,1)    STRING('<201,205{48},187>'),HUE(15,1)
          ROW(2,1)    STRING('<186,0{48},186>'),HUE(15,1)
          ROW(3,1)    STRING('<204,205{48},185>'),HUE(15,1)
          ROW(4,1)    REPEAT(11);STRING('<186,0{48},186>'),HUE(15,1) .
          ROW(15,1)   STRING('<200,205{48},188>'),HUE(15,1)
          ROW(2,12)   STRING('KNOWLEDGE WORKS TIME TRACKING')
                      ENTRY,USE(?FIRST_FIELD)
                      ENTRY,USE(?PRE_MENU)
                      MENU,USE(MENU_FIELD"),REQ
          ROW(5,21)   STRING('CHRONOLOGY'),SEL(0,7)
          ROW(7,19)   STRING('HOURS BY CLIENT'),SEL(0,7)
          ROW(9,19)   STRING('LIST OF CLIENTS'),SEL(0,7)
          ROW(13,24)  STRING('QUIT'),SEL(0,7)
            .           .
```

(continued)

```
        EJECT
        CODE
        OPEN(SCREEN)                              !OPEN THE MENU SCREEN
        SETCURSOR                                 !TURN OFF ANY CURSOR
        MENU_FIELD" = ''                          !START MENU WITH FIRST ITEM
        IDLE(TIMER)                               !CALL SETUP PROCEDURE
        LOOP                                      !LOOP UNTIL USER EXITS
          ALERT                                   !TURN OFF ALL ALERTED KEYS
          ALERT(REJECT_KEY)                       !ALERT SCREEN REJECT KEY
          ALERT(ACCEPT_KEY)                       !ALERT SCREEN ACCEPT KEY
          ACCEPT                                  !READ A FIELD OR MENU CHOICE
          IF KEYCODE() = REJECT_KEY THEN RETURN.  !RETURN ON SCREEN REJECT

          IF KEYCODE() = ACCEPT_KEY               !ON SCREEN ACCEPT KEY
            UPDATE                                !  MOVE ALL FIELDS FROM SCREEN
            SELECT(?)                             !  START WITH CURRENT FIELD
            SELECT                                !  EDIT ALL FIELDS
            CYCLE                                 !  GO TO TOP OF LOOP
          .                                       !

          CASE FIELD()                            !JUMP TO FIELD EDIT ROUTINE
          OF ?FIRST_FIELD                         !FROM THE FIRST FIELD
            IF KEYCODE() = ESC_KEY THEN RETURN.   !  RETURN ON ESC KEY

          OF ?PRE_MENU                            !PRE MENU FIELD CONDITION
            IF KEYCODE() = ESC_KEY                !  BACKING UP?
              SELECT(?-1)                         !    SELECT PREVIOUS FIELD
            ELSE                                  !  GOING FORWARD
              SELECT(?+1)                         !    SELECT MENU FIELD
          .
          OF ?MENU_FIELD"                         !FROM THE MENU FIELD
            EXECUTE CHOICE()                      !  CALL THE SELECTED PROCEDURE
              CHRONOLOGY                          !  COMPANY WIDE CLIENT WORK
              BILLED                              !  LIST WORK FOR ONE CLIENT
              LIST                                !  LIST OF CLIENTS
              RETURN
        . . .
```

HOURS2.CLA—Chronology Procedure

```
            MEMBER('HOURS')
CHRONOLOGY    PROCEDURE

SCREEN        SCREEN        PRE(SCR),WINDOW(21,80),AT(4,1),HUE(15,0)
              ROW(4,45)   PAINT(16,34),HUE(0,7)
```

(continued)

```
              ROW(4,3)     PAINT(1,42),HUE(0,7)
              ROW(5,3)     PAINT(15,47),HUE(0,7)
              ROW(1,1)     STRING('<201,205{78},187>'),HUE(15,0)
              ROW(2,1)     STRING('<186,0{78},186>'),HUE(15,0)
              ROW(3,1)     STRING('<199,196{78},182>'),HUE(15,0)
              ROW(4,1)     REPEAT(17);STRING('<186,0{78},186>'),HUE(15,0)  .
              ROW(21,1)    STRING('<200,205{32},0{15},205{31},188>'),HUE(15,0)
              ROW(4,18)    STRING('<196{7},0{9},196{7},0{8},196{11},0{8},196{11}>')  |
                             HUE(0,7)
              ROW(2,34)    STRING('WORK PERFORMED')
              ROW(4,5)     STRING('DATE    HOURS')
                COL(26)    STRING('SUBJECT')
                COL(42)    STRING('BILLED'),HUE(0,7)
                COL(61)    STRING('CLIENT')
              ROW(20,4)    STRING('TOTAL:')
                COL(17)    STRING('hours')
              ROW(21,35)   STRING('<<F3> Calendar')
TOTAL         ROW(20,11)   STRING(@T1),HUE(14,0)
                           ENTRY,USE(?FIRST_FIELD)
                           ENTRY,USE(?PRE_POINT)
                           REPEAT(15),EVERY(1),INDEX(NDX)
              ROW(5,3)         POINT(1,76),USE(?POINT),ESC(?-1)
DATE            COL(3)     STRING(@D1)
SPENT           COL(12)    STRING(@T1)
SUBJECT         COL(18)    STRING(@S23)
BILLED          COL(42)    STRING(@S6)
COMPANY         COL(49)    STRING(30)
                  .              .


NDX           BYTE                             !REPEAT INDEX FOR POINT AREA
ROW           BYTE                             !ACTUAL ROW OF SCROLL AREA
COL           BYTE                             !ACTUAL COLUMN OF SCROLL AREA
COUNT         BYTE(15)                         !NUMBER OF ITEMS TO SCROLL
ROWS          BYTE(15)                         !NUMBER OF ROWS TO SCROLL
COLS          BYTE(76)                         !NUMBER OF COLUMNS TO SCROLL
FOUND         BYTE                             !RECORD FOUND FLAG
NEWPTR        LONG                             !POINTER TO NEW RECORD

TABLE         TABLE,PRE(TBL)                   !TABLE OF RECORD DATA
DATE          LONG                             !DATE OF ACTIVITY
SPENT         STRING(@T1)
SUBJECT       STRING(@S23)
BILLED        STRING(@S6)
COMPANY       STRING(30)                       !COMPANY NAME OF CLIENT
STARTTIME     LONG                             !TIME WORK STARTED
CLIENTNO      SHORT                            !CLIENT NUMBER FOR RELATION
PTR           LONG                             !  POINTER TO FILE RECORD
                  .
```

(continued)

```
TOT_GROUP    GROUP,PRE(TOT)                    !TABLE TOTAL FIELDS
TOTAL        REAL
             .

  EJECT
  CODE
  ACTION# = ACTION                             !SAVE ACTION
  OPEN(SCREEN)                                 !OPEN THE SCREEN
  SETCURSOR                                    !TURN OFF ANY CURSOR
  CLEAR(TOT_GROUP)                             !ZERO TOTALS
  TBL:PTR = 1                                  !START AT TABLE ENTRY
  NDX = 1                                      !PUT SELECTOR BAR ON TOP ITEM
  ROW = ROW(?POINT)                            !REMEMBER TOP ROW AND
  COL = COL(?POINT)                            !LEFT COLUMN OF SCROLL AREA
  RECORDS# = TRUE                              !INITIALIZE RECORDS FLAG
  CACHE(HRS:BY_DATE,.25)                       !CACHE KEY FILE
  CLEAR(TOT_GROUP)                             !ZERO TOTALS
  CLEAR(HRS:RECORD,-1)                         !CLEAR RECORD TO LOW VALUES
  CLEAR(TBL:PTR)                               !SET POINTER TO ZERO
  SETHUE(BACKHUE(ROW,COL),BACKHUE(ROW,COL))    !TURN OFF DISPLAY
  BUFFER(HOURS,.25)
  SET(HOURS)                                   !  POINT TO FIRST RECORD
  LOOP UNTIL EOF(HOURS)                        !LOOP UNTIL END OF FILE
    NEXT(HOURS)                                !  READ A RECORD
    ACTN# = 1                                  !SET ACTION FOR ADD
    DO FILL_TABLE                              !  TOTAL SCREEN VARIABLES
    DO COMP_TOTALS                             !  ADD TO TOTAL AMOUNT
  .
  SETHUE()                                     !TURN OFF SETHUE
  FREE(HOURS)                                  !FREE MEMORY USED FOR BUFFERING
  FREE(TABLE)                                  !FREE MEMORY TABLE
  IF ACTION = 4                                !  TABLE LOOKUP REQUEST
    NEWPTR = POINTER(HOURS)                    !  SET POINTER TO RECORD
    IF NOT NEWPTR                              !  RECORD NOT PASSED TO TABLE
      SET(HRS:BY_DATE,HRS:BY_DATE)             !    POSITION TO CLOSEST RECORD
      NEXT(HOURS)                              !    READ RECORD
      NEWPTR = POINTER(HOURS)                  !    SET POINTER
    .
    DO FIND_RECORD                             !  POSITION FILE
  ELSE
    NDX = 1                                    !  PUT SELECTOR BAR ON TOP ITEM
    DO FIRST_PAGE                              !  BUILD MEMORY TABLE OF KEYS
  .
  RECORDS# = TRUE                              !  ASSUME THERE ARE RECORDS
  LOOP                                         !LOOP UNTIL USER EXITS
    ACTION = ACTION#                           !RESTORE ACTION
    SCR:TOTAL = TOT:TOTAL
    ALERT                                      !RESET ALERTED KEYS
```

(continued)

```
ALERT(REJECT_KEY)                            !ALERT SCREEN REJECT KEY
ALERT(ACCEPT_KEY)                            !ALERT SCREEN ACCEPT KEY
ALERT(F3_KEY)                                !ALERT HOT KEY
ACCEPT                                       !READ A FIELD
IF KEYCODE() = F3_KEY                        !ON HOT KEY
   IF FIELD() = ?POINT THEN DO GET_RECORD.   !  READ RECORD IF NEEDED
  POPUP                                      !  CALL HOT KEY PROCEDURE
  DO SAME_PAGE                               !  RESET TO SAME PAGE
  CYCLE                                      !  AND LOOP AGAIN
  .

IF KEYCODE() = REJECT_KEY THEN BREAK.        !RETURN ON SCREEN REJECT KEY

IF  KEYCODE() = ACCEPT_KEY      |            !ON SCREEN ACCEPT KEY
AND FIELD() <> ?POINT                        !BUT NOT ON THE POINT FIELD
  UPDATE                                     !  MOVE ALL FIELDS FROM SCREEN
  SELECT(?)                                  !  START WITH CURRENT FIELD
  SELECT                                     !  EDIT ALL FIELDS
  CYCLE                                      !  GO TO TOP OF LOOP
  .


CASE FIELD()                                 !JUMP TO FIELD EDIT ROUTINE

OF ?FIRST_FIELD                              !FROM THE FIRST FIELD
  IF KEYCODE() = ESC_KEY      |              !  RETURN ON ESC KEY
  OR RECORDS# = FALSE                        !  OR NO RECORDS
    BREAK                                    !    EXIT PROGRAM
    .

OF ?PRE_POINT                                !PRE POINT FIELD CONDITION
  IF KEYCODE() = ESC_KEY                     !  BACKING UP?
    SELECT(?-1)                              !    SELECT PREVIOUS FIELD
  ELSE                                       !  GOING FORWARD
    SELECT(?POINT)                           !    SELECT MENU FIELD
    .

OF ?POINT                                    !PROCESS THE POINT FIELD
  IF RECORDS(TABLE) = 0                      !IF THERE ARE NO RECORDS
    CLEAR(HRS:RECORD)                        !  CLEAR RECORD AREA
    ACTION = 1                               !  SET ACTION TO ADD
    GET(HOURS,0)                             !  CLEAR PENDING RECORD
    ACTN# = ACTION                           !SAVE ACTION FOR COMP_TOTALS
    WORK                                     !  CALL FORM FOR NEW RECORD
    NEWPTR = POINTER(HOURS)                  !    SET POINTER TO NEW RECORD
    DO FIRST_PAGE                            !  DISPLAY THE FIRST PAGE
    IF RECORDS(TABLE) = 0                    !  IF THERE AREN'T ANY RECORDS
      RECORDS# = FALSE                       !    INDICATE NO RECORDS
      SELECT(?PRE_POINT-1)                   !    SELECT THE PRIOR FIELD

    CYCLE                                    !    AND LOOP AGAIN
    .
```

(continued)

```
CASE KEYCODE()                               !PROCESS THE KEYSTROKE

OF INS_KEY                                   !INS KEY
  CLEAR(HRS:RECORD)                          !  CLEAR RECORD AREA
  ACTION = 1                                 !  SET ACTION TO ADD
  GET(HOURS,0)                               !  CLEAR PENDING RECORD
  ACTN# = ACTION                             !SAVE ACTION FOR COMP_TOTALS
  WORK                                       !  CALL FORM FOR NEW RECORD
  IF ~ACTION                                 !  IF RECORD WAS ADDED
    NEWPTR = POINTER(HOURS)                  !    SET POINTER TO NEW RECORD
    DO FIND_RECORD                           !    POSITION IN FILE
  .
OF ENTER_KEY                                 !ENTER KEY
OROF ACCEPT_KEY                              !CTRL-ENTER KEY
  DO GET_RECORD                              !  GET THE SELECTED RECORD
  IF ACTION = 4 AND KEYCODE() = ENTER_KEY!   IF THIS IS A LOOKUP REQUEST
    ACTION = 0                               !    SET ACTION TO COMPLETE
    BREAK                                    !    AND RETURN TO CALLER
  .
  IF ~ERROR()                                !  IF RECORD IS STILL THERE
    ACTION = 2                               !    SET ACTION TO CHANGE
    ACTN# = ACTION                           !SAVE ACTION FOR COMP_TOTALS
    TOTAL$ = SCR:SPENT
    WORK                                     !    CALL FORM TO CHANGE REC
    IF ACTION THEN CYCLE.                    !    IF SUCCESSFUL RE-DISPLAY
    TOT:TOTAL -= TOTAL$
  .
  NEWPTR = POINTER(HOURS)                    !    SET POINTER TO NEW RECORD
  DO FIND_RECORD                             !    POSITION IN FILE
OF DEL_KEY                                   !DEL KEY
  DO GET_RECORD                              !  READ THE SELECTED RECORD
  IF ~ERROR()                                !  IF RECORD IS STILL THERE
    ACTION = 3                               !    SET ACTION TO DELETE
    ACTN# = ACTION                           !SAVE ACTION FOR COMP_TOTALS
    TOTAL$ = SCR:SPENT
    WORK                                     !    CALL FORM TO DELETE
    IF ~ACTION                               !    IF SUCCESSFUL
      TOT:TOTAL -= TOTAL$
      N# = NDX                               !      SAVE POINT INDEX
      DO SAME_PAGE                           !      RE-DISPLAY
      NDX = N#                               !      RESTORE POINT INDEX
  . .
OF DOWN_KEY                                  !DOWN ARROW KEY
  DO SET_NEXT                                !  POINT TO NEXT RECORD
  DO FILL_NEXT                               !  FILL A TABLE ENTRY
  IF FOUND                                   !  FOUND A NEW RECORD
    SCROLL(ROW,COL,ROWS,COLS,ROWS(?POINT)) ! SCROLL THE SCREEN UP
    GET(TABLE,RECORDS(TABLE))                !  GET RECORD FROM TABLE
```

(continued)

```
      DO FILL_SCREEN                      !  DISPLAY ON SCREEN
       .

   OF PGDN_KEY                            !PAGE DOWN KEY
      DO SET_NEXT                         !  POINT TO NEXT RECORD
      DO NEXT_PAGE                        !  DISPLAY THE NEXT PAGE

   OF CTRL_PGDN                           !CTRL-PAGE DOWN KEY
      DO LAST_PAGE                        !  DISPLAY THE LAST PAGE
      NDX = RECORDS(TABLE)                !  POSITION POINT BAR

   OF UP_KEY                              !UP ARROW KEY
      DO SET_PREV                         !  POINT TO PREVIOUS RECORD
      DO FILL_PREV                        !  FILL A TABLE ENTRY
      IF FOUND                            !  FOUND A NEW RECORD
         SCROLL(ROW,COL,ROWS,COLS,-(ROWS(?POINT)))! SCROLL THE SCREEN DOWN
         GET(TABLE,1)                     !  GET RECORD FROM TABLE
         DO FILL_SCREEN                   !  DISPLAY ON SCREEN
          .

   OF PGUP_KEY                            !PAGE UP KEY
      DO SET_PREV                         !  POINT TO PREVIOUS RECORD
      DO PREV_PAGE                        !  DISPLAY THE PREVIOUS PAGE

   OF CTRL_PGUP                           !CTRL-PAGE UP
      DO FIRST_PAGE                       !  DISPLAY THE FIRST PAGE
      NDX = 1                             !  POSITION POINT BAR
 . . .
 FREE(TABLE)                              !FREE MEMORY TABLE
 RETURN                                   !AND RETURN TO CALLER

SAME_PAGE ROUTINE                         !DISPLAY THE SAME PAGE
  GET(TABLE,1)                            !  GET THE FIRST TABLE ENTRY
  DO FILL_RECORD                          !  FILL IN THE RECORD
  SET(HRS:BY_DATE,HRS:BY_DATE,TBL:PTR)    !  POSITION FILE
  FREE(TABLE)                             !  EMPTY THE TABLE
  DO NEXT_PAGE                            !  DISPLAY A FULL PAGE

FIRST_PAGE ROUTINE                        !DISPLAY FIRST PAGE
  BLANK(ROW,COL,ROWS,COLS)
  FREE(TABLE)                             !  EMPTY THE TABLE
  CLEAR(HRS:RECORD,-1)                    !  CLEAR RECORD TO LOW VALUES
  CLEAR(TBL:PTR)                          !  ZERO RECORD POINTER
  SET(HRS:BY_DATE)                        !  POINT TO FIRST RECORD
  LOOP NDX = 1 TO COUNT                   !  FILL UP THE TABLE
    DO FILL_NEXT                          !     FILL A TABLE ENTRY
    IF NOT FOUND THEN BREAK.              !     GET OUT IF NO RECORD
     .
```

(continued)

```
      NDX = 1                                      !   SET TO TOP OF TABLE
      DO SHOW_PAGE                                 !   DISPLAY THE PAGE

LAST_PAGE ROUTINE                                  !DISPLAY LAST PAGE
      NDX# = NDX                                   !   SAVE SELECTOR POSITION
      BLANK(ROW,COL,ROWS,COLS)                     !   CLEAR SCROLLING AREA
      FREE(TABLE)                                  !   EMPTY THE TABLE
      CLEAR(HRS:RECORD,1)                          !   CLEAR RECORD TO HIGH VALUES
      CLEAR(TBL:PTR,1)                             !   CLEAR PTR TO HIGH VALUE
      SET(HRS:BY_DATE)                             !   POINT TO FIRST RECORD
      LOOP NDX = COUNT TO 1 BY -1                  !   FILL UP THE TABLE
        DO FILL_PREV                               !     FILL A TABLE ENTRY
        IF NOT FOUND THEN BREAK.                   !     GET OUT IF NO RECORD
      .                                            !   END OF LOOP
      NDX = NDX#                                   !   RESTORE SELECTOR POSITION
      DO SHOW_PAGE                                 !   DISPLAY THE PAGE


FIND_RECORD ROUTINE                                !POSITION TO SPECIFIC RECORD
      SET(HRS:BY_DATE,HRS:BY_DATE,NEWPTR)          !POSITION FILE
      IF NEWPTR = 0                                !NEWPTR NOT SET
        NEXT(HOURS)                                !   READ NEXT RECORD
        NEWPTR = POINTER(HOURS)                    !   SET NEWPTR
        SKIP(HOURS,-1)                             !   BACK UP TO DISPLAY RECORD
      .
      FREE(TABLE)                                  !   CLEAR THE RECORD
      DO NEXT_PAGE                                 !   DISPLAY A PAGE


NEXT_PAGE ROUTINE                                  !DISPLAY NEXT PAGE
      SAVECNT# = RECORDS(TABLE)                    !   SAVE RECORD COUNT
      LOOP COUNT TIMES                             !   FILL UP THE TABLE
        DO FILL_NEXT                               !     FILL A TABLE ENTRY
        IF NOT FOUND                               !     IF NONE ARE LEFT
          IF NOT SAVECNT#                          !       IF REBUILDING TABLE
            DO LAST_PAGE                           !       FILL IN RECORDS
            EXIT                                   !       EXIT OUT OF ROUTINE
          .
          BREAK                                    !     EXIT LOOP
      . .
      DO SHOW_PAGE                                 !   DISPLAY THE PAGE


SET_NEXT ROUTINE                                   !POINT TO THE NEXT PAGE
      GET(TABLE,RECORDS(TABLE))                    !   GET THE LAST TABLE ENTRY
      DO FILL_RECORD                               !   FILL IN THE RECORD
      SET(HRS:BY_DATE,HRS:BY_DATE,TBL:PTR)         !   POSITION FILE
      NEXT(HOURS)                                  !   READ THE CURRENT RECORD


FILL_NEXT ROUTINE                                  !FILL NEXT TABLE ENTRY
      FOUND = FALSE                                !   ASSUME RECORD NOT FOUND
```

(continued)

```
  LOOP UNTIL EOF(HOURS)                  !  LOOP UNTIL END OF FILE
    NEXT(HOURS)                          !     READ THE NEXT RECORD
    FOUND = TRUE                         !     SET RECORD FOUND
    DO FILL_TABLE                        !     FILL IN THE TABLE ENTRY
    ADD(TABLE)                           !     ADD LAST TABLE ENTRY
    GET(TABLE,RECORDS(TABLE)-COUNT)      !     GET ANY OVERFLOW RECORD
    DELETE(TABLE)                        !     AND DELETE IT
    EXIT                                 !     RETURN TO CALLER
  .

PREV_PAGE ROUTINE                        !DISPLAY PREVIOUS PAGE
  LOOP COUNT TIMES                       !  FILL UP THE TABLE
    DO FILL_PREV                         !     FILL A TABLE ENTRY
    IF NOT FOUND THEN BREAK.             !     GET OUT IF NO RECORD
  .

  DO SHOW_PAGE                           !  DISPLAY THE PAGE


SET_PREV ROUTINE                         !POINT TO PREVIOUS PAGE
  GET(TABLE,1)                           !  GET THE FIRST TABLE ENTRY
  DO FILL_RECORD                         !  FILL IN THE RECORD
  SET(HRS:BY_DATE,HRS:BY_DATE,TBL:PTR)   !  POSITION FILE
  PREVIOUS(HOURS)                        !  READ THE CURRENT RECORD


FILL_PREV ROUTINE                        !FILL PREVIOUS TABLE ENTRY
  FOUND = FALSE                          !  ASSUME RECORD NOT FOUND
  LOOP UNTIL BOF(HOURS)                  !  LOOP UNTIL BEGINNING OF FILE
    PREVIOUS(HOURS)                      !     READ THE PREVIOUS RECORD
    FOUND = TRUE                         !     SET RECORD FOUND
    DO FILL_TABLE                        !     FILL IN THE TABLE ENTRY
    ADD(TABLE,1)                         !     ADD FIRST TABLE ENTRY
    GET(TABLE,COUNT+1)                   !     GET ANY OVERFLOW RECORD
    DELETE(TABLE)                        !     AND DELETE IT
    EXIT                                 !     RETURN TO CALLER
  .

SHOW_PAGE ROUTINE                        !DISPLAY THE PAGE
  NDX# = NDX                             !  SAVE SCREEN INDEX
  LOOP NDX = 1 TO RECORDS(TABLE)         !  LOOP THRU THE TABLE
    GET(TABLE,NDX)                       !     GET A TABLE ENTRY
    DO FILL_SCREEN                       !     AND DISPLAY IT
    IF TBL:PTR = NEWPTR                  !     SET INDEX FOR NEW RECORD
      NDX# = NDX                         !     POINT TO CORRECT RECORD
      DO COMP_TOTALS                     !CALCULATE TABLE TOTALS
  . .
  NDX = NDX#                             !  RESTORE SCREEN INDEX
  NEWPTR = 0                             !  CLEAR NEW RECORD POINTER
  CLEAR(HRS:RECORD)                      !  CLEAR RECORD AREA

FILL_TABLE ROUTINE                       !MOVE FILE TO TABLE
  CLI:CLIENTNO = HRS:CLIENTNO            !MOVE RELATED KEY FIELDS
```

(continued)

```
        GET(CLIENTS,CLI:BY_CLIENTNO)             !READ THE RECORD
        IF ERROR() THEN CLEAR(CLI:RECORD).       !IF NOT FOUND, CLEAR RECORD
        TBL:COMPANY = CLI:COMPANY                !DISPLAY LOOKUP FIELD
        TBL:DATE = HRS:DATE
        TBL:STARTTIME = HRS:STARTTIME
        TBL:CLIENTNO = HRS:CLIENTNO
        TBL:PTR = POINTER(HOURS)                 !  SAVE RECORD POINTER
        TBL:SPENT = (HRS:COMPLETETIME - HRS:STARTTIME)+1
        TBL:SUBJECT = HRS:SUBJECT
        IF HRS:BILLED = 'B'                      !EVALUATE CONDITION
          TBL:BILLED = 'BILLED'                  !  CONDITION IS TRUE
        ELSE                                     !OTHERWISE
          TBL:BILLED = ''                        !  CONDITION IS FALSE
        .

FILL_RECORD ROUTINE                              !MOVE TABLE TO FILE
  HRS:DATE = TBL:DATE
  HRS:STARTTIME = TBL:STARTTIME
  HRS:CLIENTNO = TBL:CLIENTNO

FILL_SCREEN ROUTINE                              !MOVE TABLE TO SCREEN
  SCR:DATE = TBL:DATE
  SCR:SPENT = TBL:SPENT
  SCR:SUBJECT = TBL:SUBJECT
  SCR:BILLED = TBL:BILLED
  SCR:COMPANY = TBL:COMPANY

GET_RECORD ROUTINE                               !GET SELECTED RECORD
  GET(TABLE,NDX)                                 !  GET TABLE ENTRY
  GET(HOURS,TBL:PTR)                             !  GET THE RECORD

COMP_TOTALS  ROUTINE                             !CALCULATE TOTAL FIELDS
  IF NOT ACTN# THEN EXIT.                        !GET OUT IF ACTN NOT SET
  TOT:TOTAL += TBL:SPENT
  ACTN# = 0                                      !CLEAR ACTION
```

HOURS3.CLA—Client List Procedure

```
           MEMBER('HOURS')
LIST       PROCEDURE

SCREEN     SCREEN      PRE(SCR),WINDOW(20,50),AT(4,16),HUE(0,7)
           ROW(1,1)    STRING('<201,205{48},187>'),HUE(9,7)
           ROW(2,1)    STRING('<186,0{48},186>'),HUE(9,7)
           ROW(3,1)    STRING('<204,205{48},185>'),HUE(9,7)
           ROW(4,1)    REPEAT(16);STRING('<186,0{48},186>'),HUE(9,7)  .
```

(continued)

```
           ROW(20,1)   STRING('<200,205{48},188>'),HUE(9,7)
           ROW(2,21)   STRING('CLIENT LIST')
                           ENTRY,USE(?FIRST_FIELD)
                           ENTRY,USE(?PRE_POINT)
                           REPEAT(15),EVERY(1),INDEX(NDX)
           ROW(5,3)          POINT(1,46),USE(?POINT),ESC(?-1)
COMPANY    COL(4)      STRING(30)
PHONE      COL(35)     STRING(@P(###)###-####PB)
              .              .


NDX          BYTE                                  !REPEAT INDEX FOR POINT AREA
ROW          BYTE                                  !ACTUAL ROW OF SCROLL AREA
COL          BYTE                                  !ACTUAL COLUMN OF SCROLL AREA
COUNT        BYTE(15)                              !NUMBER OF ITEMS TO SCROLL
ROWS         BYTE(15)                              !NUMBER OF ROWS TO SCROLL
COLS         BYTE(46)                              !NUMBER OF COLUMNS TO SCROLL
FOUND        BYTE                                  !RECORD FOUND FLAG
NEWPTR       LONG                                  !POINTER TO NEW RECORD

TABLE        TABLE,PRE(TBL)                        !TABLE OF RECORD DATA
COMPANY      STRING(30)                            !COMPANY NAME OF CLIENT
PHONE        STRING(@P(###)###-####PB)
CLIENTNO     SHORT
PTR          LONG                                  !  POINTER TO FILE RECORD
              .

  EJECT
  CODE
  ACTION# = ACTION                                 !SAVE ACTION
  OPEN(SCREEN)                                     !OPEN THE SCREEN
  SETCURSOR                                        !TURN OFF ANY CURSOR
  TBL:PTR = 1                                      !START AT TABLE ENTRY
  NDX = 1                                          !PUT SELECTOR BAR ON TOP ITEM
  ROW = ROW(?POINT)                               !REMEMBER TOP ROW AND
  COL = COL(?POINT)                               !LEFT COLUMN OF SCROLL AREA
  RECORDS# = TRUE                                  !INITIALIZE RECORDS FLAG
  CACHE(CLI:BY_CLIENT,.25)                         !CACHE KEY FILE
  IF ACTION = 4                                    !  TABLE LOOKUP REQUEST
    NEWPTR = POINTER(CLIENTS)                      !  SET POINTER TO RECORD
    IF NOT NEWPTR                                  !  RECORD NOT PASSED TO TABLE
      SET(CLI:BY_CLIENT,CLI:BY_CLIENT)            !    POSITION TO CLOSEST RECORD
      NEXT(CLIENTS)                                !    READ RECORD
      NEWPTR = POINTER(CLIENTS)                    !    SET POINTER
       .
    DO FIND_RECORD                                 !  POSITION FILE
  ELSE
    NDX = 1                                        !  PUT SELECTOR BAR ON TOP ITEM
```

(continued)

```
   DO FIRST_PAGE                           !  BUILD MEMORY TABLE OF KEYS
.
RECORDS# = TRUE                            !  ASSUME THERE ARE RECORDS
LOOP                                       !LOOP UNTIL USER EXITS
  ACTION = ACTION#                         !RESTORE ACTION
  ALERT                                    !RESET ALERTED KEYS
  ALERT(REJECT_KEY)                        !ALERT SCREEN REJECT KEY
  ALERT(ACCEPT_KEY)                        !ALERT SCREEN ACCEPT KEY
  ACCEPT                                   !READ A FIELD
  IF KEYCODE() = REJECT_KEY THEN BREAK.    !RETURN ON SCREEN REJECT KEY

  IF  KEYCODE() = ACCEPT_KEY    |          !ON SCREEN ACCEPT KEY
  AND FIELD() <> ?POINT                    !BUT NOT ON THE POINT FIELD
    UPDATE                                 !  MOVE ALL FIELDS FROM SCREEN
    SELECT(?)                              !  START WITH CURRENT FIELD
    SELECT                                 !  EDIT ALL FIELDS
    CYCLE                                  !  GO TO TOP OF LOOP
  .

  CASE FIELD()                             !JUMP TO FIELD EDIT ROUTINE

  OF ?FIRST_FIELD                          !FROM THE FIRST FIELD
    IF KEYCODE() = ESC_KEY    |            !  RETURN ON ESC KEY
    OR RECORDS# = FALSE                    !  OR NO RECORDS
      BREAK                                !    EXIT PROGRAM
    .
  OF ?PRE_POINT                            !PRE POINT FIELD CONDITION
    IF KEYCODE() = ESC_KEY                 !  BACKING UP?
      SELECT(?-1)                          !    SELECT PREVIOUS FIELD
    ELSE                                   !  GOING FORWARD
      SELECT(?POINT)                       !    SELECT MENU FIELD
    .
  OF ?POINT                                !PROCESS THE POINT FIELD
    IF RECORDS(TABLE) = 0                  !IF THERE ARE NO RECORDS
      CLEAR(CLI:RECORD)                    !  CLEAR RECORD AREA
      ACTION = 1                           !  SET ACTION TO ADD
      GET(CLIENTS,0)                       !  CLEAR PENDING RECORD
      CLEAR(CLI:RECORD,1)                  !CLEAR RECORD TO HIGH VALUES
      SET(CLI:BY_CLIENTNO)                 !  POINT TO FIRST RECORD
      PREVIOUS(CLIENTS)                    !READ LAST KEY RECORD
      IF ERROR()                           !IF THERE WAS AN ERROR
        CLEAR(CLI:RECORD)                  !  CLEAR THE RECORD
        KEYFIELD# = 0                      !  INTITIALIZE THE FIELD
        IF KEYFIELD# = 0 THEN KEYFIELD# = 1. !  IF ITS 0 MAKE IT 1
      ELSE                                 !ELSE
        KEYFIELD# = CLI:CLIENTNO + 1       !  INCREMENT FIELD
      .
      CLEAR(CLI:RECORD)                    !CLEAR LAST KEY RECORD
```

(continued)

```
  CLI:CLIENTNO = KEYFIELD#                   !LOAD KEY FIELD
  CLIENT                                      !   CALL FORM FOR NEW RECORD
  NEWPTR = POINTER(CLIENTS)                   !     SET POINTER TO NEW RECORD
  DO FIRST_PAGE                               !   DISPLAY THE FIRST PAGE
  IF RECORDS(TABLE) = 0                       !   IF THERE AREN'T ANY RECORDS
    RECORDS# = FALSE                          !     INDICATE NO RECORDS
    SELECT(?PRE_POINT-1)                      !     SELECT THE PRIOR FIELD
    .
  CYCLE                                       !     AND LOOP AGAIN
  .
CASE KEYCODE()                                !PROCESS THE KEYSTROKE

OF INS_KEY                                    !INS KEY
  CLEAR(CLI:RECORD)                           !   CLEAR RECORD AREA
  ACTION = 1                                  !   SET ACTION TO ADD
  GET(CLIENTS,0)                              !   CLEAR PENDING RECORD
  CLEAR(CLI:RECORD,1)                         !CLEAR RECORD TO HIGH VALUES
  SET(CLI:BY_CLIENTNO)                        !   POINT TO FIRST RECORD
  PREVIOUS(CLIENTS)                           !READ LAST KEY RECORD
  IF ERROR()                                  !IF THERE WAS AN ERROR
     CLEAR(CLI:RECORD)                        !   CLEAR THE RECORD
     KEYFIELD# = 0                            !   INTITIALIZE THE FIELD
     IF KEYFIELD# = 0 THEN KEYFIELD# = 1.     !   IF ITS 0 MAKE IT 1
  ELSE                                        !ELSE
     KEYFIELD# = CLI:CLIENTNO + 1             !   INCREMENT FIELD
     .
  CLEAR(CLI:RECORD)                           !CLEAR LAST KEY RECORD
  CLI:CLIENTNO = KEYFIELD#                    !LOAD KEY FIELD
  CLIENT                                      !   CALL FORM FOR NEW RECORD
  IF ~ACTION                                  !   IF RECORD WAS ADDED
    NEWPTR = POINTER(CLIENTS)                 !     SET POINTER TO NEW RECORD
    DO FIND_RECORD                            !     POSITION IN FILE
    .
OF ENTER_KEY                                  !ENTER KEY
OROF ACCEPT_KEY                               !CTRL-ENTER KEY
  DO GET_RECORD                               !   GET THE SELECTED RECORD
  IF ACTION = 4 AND KEYCODE() = ENTER_KEY     !   IF THIS IS A LOOKUP REQUEST
    ACTION = 0                                !     SET ACTION TO COMPLETE
    BREAK                                     !     AND RETURN TO CALLER
    .
  IF ~ERROR()                                 !   IF RECORD IS STILL THERE
    ACTION = 2                                !     SET ACTION TO CHANGE
    CLIENT                                    !     CALL FORM TO CHANGE REC
    IF ACTION THEN CYCLE.                     !     IF SUCCESSFUL RE-DISPLAY
    .
  NEWPTR = POINTER(CLIENTS)                   !     SET POINTER TO NEW RECORD
  DO FIND_RECORD                              !     POSITION IN FILE
OF DEL_KEY                                    !DEL KEY
```

(continued)

```
        DO GET_RECORD                            !  READ THE SELECTED RECORD
        IF ~ERROR()                              !  IF RECORD IS STILL THERE
          ACTION = 3                             !    SET ACTION TO DELETE
          CLIENT                                 !    CALL FORM TO DELETE
          IF ~ACTION                             !    IF SUCCESSFUL
            N# = NDX                             !      SAVE POINT INDEX
            DO SAME_PAGE                         !      RE-DISPLAY
            NDX = N#                             !      RESTORE POINT INDEX
        . .
      OF DOWN_KEY                                !DOWN ARROW KEY
        DO SET_NEXT                              !  POINT TO NEXT RECORD
        DO FILL_NEXT                             !  FILL A TABLE ENTRY
        IF FOUND                                 !  FOUND A NEW RECORD
          SCROLL(ROW,COL,ROWS,COLS,ROWS(?POINT)) !    SCROLL THE SCREEN UP
          GET(TABLE,RECORDS(TABLE))              !  GET RECORD FROM TABLE
          DO FILL_SCREEN                         !  DISPLAY ON SCREEN
        .

      OF PGDN_KEY                                !PAGE DOWN KEY
        DO SET_NEXT                              !  POINT TO NEXT RECORD
        DO NEXT_PAGE                             !  DISPLAY THE NEXT PAGE

      OF CTRL_PGDN                               !CTRL-PAGE DOWN KEY
        DO LAST_PAGE                             !  DISPLAY THE LAST PAGE
        NDX = RECORDS(TABLE)                     !  POSITION POINT BAR

      OF UP_KEY                                  !UP ARROW KEY
        DO SET_PREV                              !  POINT TO PREVIOUS RECORD
        DO FILL_PREV                             !  FILL A TABLE ENTRY
        IF FOUND                                 !  FOUND A NEW RECORD
          SCROLL(ROW,COL,ROWS,COLS,-(ROWS(?POINT)))! SCROLL THE SCREEN DOWN
          GET(TABLE,1)                           !  GET RECORD FROM TABLE
          DO FILL_SCREEN                         !  DISPLAY ON SCREEN
        .

      OF PGUP_KEY                                !PAGE UP KEY
        DO SET_PREV                              !  POINT TO PREVIOUS RECORD
        DO PREV_PAGE                             !  DISPLAY THE PREVIOUS PAGE

      OF CTRL_PGUP                               !CTRL-PAGE UP
        DO FIRST_PAGE                            !  DISPLAY THE FIRST PAGE
        NDX = 1                                  !  POSITION POINT BAR
    . . .
    FREE(TABLE)                                  !FREE MEMORY TABLE
    RETURN                                       !AND RETURN TO CALLER

SAME_PAGE ROUTINE                                !DISPLAY THE SAME PAGE
  GET(TABLE,1)                                   !  GET THE FIRST TABLE ENTRY
```

(continued)

```
  DO FILL_RECORD                                      ! FILL IN THE RECORD
  SET(CLI:BY_CLIENT,CLI:BY_CLIENT,TBL:PTR)            ! POSITION FILE
  FREE(TABLE)                                         ! EMPTY THE TABLE
  DO NEXT_PAGE                                        ! DISPLAY A FULL PAGE

FIRST_PAGE ROUTINE                                   !DISPLAY FIRST PAGE
  BLANK(ROW,COL,ROWS,COLS)
  FREE(TABLE)                                         ! EMPTY THE TABLE
  CLEAR(CLI:RECORD,-1)                                ! CLEAR RECORD TO LOW VALUES
  CLEAR(TBL:PTR)                                      ! ZERO RECORD POINTER
  SET(CLI:BY_CLIENT)                                  ! POINT TO FIRST RECORD
  LOOP NDX = 1 TO COUNT                               ! FILL UP THE TABLE
    DO FILL_NEXT                                      !   FILL A TABLE ENTRY
    IF NOT FOUND THEN BREAK.                          !   GET OUT IF NO RECORD

  NDX = 1                                             ! SET TO TOP OF TABLE
  DO SHOW_PAGE                                        ! DISPLAY THE PAGE

LAST_PAGE ROUTINE                                    !DISPLAY LAST PAGE
  NDX# = NDX                                          ! SAVE SELECTOR POSITION
  BLANK(ROW,COL,ROWS,COLS)                            ! CLEAR SCROLLING AREA
  FREE(TABLE)                                         ! EMPTY THE TABLE
  CLEAR(CLI:RECORD,1)                                 ! CLEAR RECORD TO HIGH VALUES
  CLEAR(TBL:PTR,1)                                    ! CLEAR PTR TO HIGH VALUE
  SET(CLI:BY_CLIENT)                                  ! POINT TO FIRST RECORD
  LOOP NDX = COUNT TO 1 BY -1                         ! FILL UP THE TABLE
    DO FILL_PREV                                      !   FILL A TABLE ENTRY
    IF NOT FOUND THEN BREAK.                          !   GET OUT IF NO RECORD
  .                                                   ! END OF LOOP
  NDX = NDX#                                          ! RESTORE SELECTOR POSITION
  DO SHOW_PAGE                                        ! DISPLAY THE PAGE

FIND_RECORD ROUTINE                                  !POSITION TO SPECIFIC RECORD
  SET(CLI:BY_CLIENT,CLI:BY_CLIENT,NEWPTR)            !POSITION FILE
  IF NEWPTR = 0                                       !NEWPTR NOT SET
    NEXT(CLIENTS)                                     !   READ NEXT RECORD
    NEWPTR = POINTER(CLIENTS)                         !   SET NEWPTR
    SKIP(CLIENTS,-1)                                  !   BACK UP TO DISPLAY RECORD
  .
  FREE(TABLE)                                         ! CLEAR THE RECORD
  DO NEXT_PAGE                                        ! DISPLAY A PAGE

NEXT_PAGE ROUTINE                                    !DISPLAY NEXT PAGE
  SAVECNT# = RECORDS(TABLE)                           ! SAVE RECORD COUNT
  LOOP COUNT TIMES                                    ! FILL UP THE TABLE
    DO FILL_NEXT                                      !   FILL A TABLE ENTRY
    IF NOT FOUND                                      !   IF NONE ARE LEFT
      IF NOT SAVECNT#                                 !     IF REBUILDING TABLE
```

(continued)

```
          DO LAST_PAGE              !    FILL IN RECORDS
          EXIT                      !    EXIT OUT OF ROUTINE
        .
        BREAK                       !  EXIT LOOP
      . .
      DO SHOW_PAGE                  ! DISPLAY THE PAGE


SET_NEXT ROUTINE                    !POINT TO THE NEXT PAGE
  GET(TABLE,RECORDS(TABLE))         !  GET THE LAST TABLE ENTRY
  DO FILL_RECORD                    !  FILL IN THE RECORD
  SET(CLI:BY_CLIENT,CLI:BY_CLIENT,TBL:PTR)  !  POSITION FILE
  NEXT(CLIENTS)                     !  READ THE CURRENT RECORD


FILL_NEXT ROUTINE                   !FILL NEXT TABLE ENTRY
  FOUND = FALSE                     !  ASSUME RECORD NOT FOUND
  LOOP UNTIL EOF(CLIENTS)           !  LOOP UNTIL END OF FILE
    NEXT(CLIENTS)                   !    READ THE NEXT RECORD
    FOUND = TRUE                    !    SET RECORD FOUND
    DO FILL_TABLE                   !    FILL IN THE TABLE ENTRY
    ADD(TABLE)                      !    ADD LAST TABLE ENTRY
    GET(TABLE,RECORDS(TABLE)-COUNT) !    GET ANY OVERFLOW RECORD
    DELETE(TABLE)                   !    AND DELETE IT
    EXIT                            !    RETURN TO CALLER
  .

PREV_PAGE ROUTINE                   !DISPLAY PREVIOUS PAGE
  LOOP COUNT TIMES                  !  FILL UP THE TABLE
    DO FILL_PREV                    !    FILL A TABLE ENTRY
    IF NOT FOUND THEN BREAK.        !    GET OUT IF NO RECORD

  DO SHOW_PAGE                      !  DISPLAY THE PAGE


SET_PREV ROUTINE                    !POINT TO PREVIOUS PAGE
  GET(TABLE,1)                      !  GET THE FIRST TABLE ENTRY
  DO FILL_RECORD                    !  FILL IN THE RECORD
  SET(CLI:BY_CLIENT,CLI:BY_CLIENT,TBL:PTR)  !  POSITION FILE
  PREVIOUS(CLIENTS)                 !  READ THE CURRENT RECORD


FILL_PREV ROUTINE                   !FILL PREVIOUS TABLE ENTRY
  FOUND = FALSE                     !  ASSUME RECORD NOT FOUND
  LOOP UNTIL BOF(CLIENTS)           !  LOOP UNTIL BEGINNING OF FILE
    PREVIOUS(CLIENTS)               !    READ THE PREVIOUS RECORD
    FOUND = TRUE                    !    SET RECORD FOUND
    DO FILL_TABLE                   !    FILL IN THE TABLE ENTRY
    ADD(TABLE,1)                    !    ADD FIRST TABLE ENTRY
    GET(TABLE,COUNT+1)              !    GET ANY OVERFLOW RECORD
    DELETE(TABLE)                   !    AND DELETE IT
    EXIT                            !    RETURN TO CALLER
  .
```

(continued)

```
SHOW_PAGE ROUTINE                         !DISPLAY THE PAGE
  NDX# = NDX                              !  SAVE SCREEN INDEX
  LOOP NDX = 1 TO RECORDS(TABLE)          !  LOOP THRU THE TABLE
    GET(TABLE,NDX)                        !    GET A TABLE ENTRY
    DO FILL_SCREEN                        !    AND DISPLAY IT
    IF TBL:PTR = NEWPTR                   !    SET INDEX FOR NEW RECORD
      NDX# = NDX                          !    POINT TO CORRECT RECORD
  . .
  NDX = NDX#                              !  RESTORE SCREEN INDEX
  NEWPTR = 0                              !  CLEAR NEW RECORD POINTER
  CLEAR(CLI:RECORD)                       !  CLEAR RECORD AREA

FILL_TABLE ROUTINE                        !MOVE FILE TO TABLE
  TBL:COMPANY = CLI:COMPANY
  TBL:PHONE = CLI:PHONE
  TBL:CLIENTNO = CLI:CLIENTNO
  TBL:PTR = POINTER(CLIENTS)              !  SAVE RECORD POINTER

FILL_RECORD ROUTINE                       !MOVE TABLE TO FILE
  CLI:COMPANY = TBL:COMPANY
  CLI:CLIENTNO = TBL:CLIENTNO

FILL_SCREEN ROUTINE                       !MOVE TABLE TO SCREEN
  SCR:COMPANY = TBL:COMPANY
  SCR:PHONE = TBL:PHONE

GET_RECORD ROUTINE                        !GET SELECTED RECORD
  GET(TABLE,NDX)                          !  GET TABLE ENTRY
  GET(CLIENTS,TBL:PTR)                    !  GET THE RECORD
```

HOURS4.CLA—Client Entry Form Procedure

```
          MEMBER('HOURS')
CLIENT          PROCEDURE

SCREEN          SCREEN      PRE(SCR),WINDOW(7,80),HUE(15,0)
                ROW(1,1)    STRING('<218,196{78},191>'),HUE(9,0)
                ROW(2,1)    REPEAT(5);STRING('<179,0{78},179>'),HUE(9,0) .
                ROW(7,1)    STRING('<192,196{78},217>'),HUE(9,0)
                ROW(4,3)    STRING('COMPANY:'),HUE(14,0)
                  COL(44)   STRING('PHONE:'),HUE(14,0)
                  COL(65)   STRING('RATE:'),HUE(14,0)
                  COL(70)   STRING(' '),HUE(15,0)
MESSAGE         ROW(2,25)   STRING(30),ENH
CLIENTNO        ROW(3,9)    STRING(@N4),HUE(0,0)
                            ENTRY,USE(?FIRST_FIELD)
```

(continued)

```
          ROW(4,12)   ENTRY(@s30),USE(CLI:COMPANY),LFT
            COL(51)   ENTRY(@P(###)###-####PB),USE(CLI:PHONE),LFT,OVR
            COL(71)   ENTRY(@n$7.2),USE(CLI:RATE),INS,SEL(0,7)
          ROW(6,28)   PAUSE('Press <<ENTER> to Accept'),USE(?PAUSE_FIELD)
                      ENTRY,USE(?LAST_FIELD)
                      PAUSE(''),USE(?DELETE_FIELD)
                .


EJECT
CODE
OPEN(SCREEN)                                      !OPEN THE SCREEN
SETCURSOR                                         !TURN OFF ANY CURSOR
DISPLAY                                           !DISPLAY THE FIELDS
LOOP                                              !LOOP THRU ALL THE FIELDS
  MEM:MESSAGE = CENTER(MEM:MESSAGE,SIZE(MEM:MESSAGE))  !DISPLAY ACTION MESSAGE
  DO CALCFIELDS                                   !CALCULATE DISPLAY FIELDS
  ALERT                                           !RESET ALERTED KEYS
  ALERT(ACCEPT_KEY)                               !ALERT SCREEN ACCEPT KEY
  ALERT(REJECT_KEY)                               !ALERT SCREEN REJECT KEY
  ACCEPT                                          !READ A FIELD
  IF KEYCODE() = REJECT_KEY THEN RETURN.          !RETURN ON SCREEN REJECT KEY
  EXECUTE ACTION                                  !SET MESSAGE
    MEM:MESSAGE = 'Record will be Added'          !
    MEM:MESSAGE = 'Record will be Changed'        !
    MEM:MESSAGE = 'Press Enter to Delete'         !
  .
  IF KEYCODE() = ACCEPT_KEY                        !ON SCREEN ACCEPT KEY
    UPDATE                                        !  MOVE ALL FIELDS FROM SCREEN
    SELECT(?)                                     !  START WITH CURRENT FIELD
    SELECT                                        !  EDIT ALL FIELDS
    CYCLE                                         !  GO TO TOP OF LOOP
  .
  CASE FIELD()                                    !JUMP TO FIELD EDIT ROUTINE
  OF ?FIRST_FIELD                                 !FROM THE FIRST FIELD
    IF KEYCODE() = ESC_KEY THEN RETURN.           !  RETURN ON ESC KEY
    IF ACTION = 3 THEN SELECT(?DELETE_FIELD).!      OR CONFIRM FOR DELETE

  OF ?CLI:COMPANY                                 !COMPANY NAME OF CLIENT
    IF DUPLICATE(CLI:BY_CLIENT)                   !  CHECK FOR DUPLICATE KEY
      MEM:MESSAGE = 'CREATES DUPLICATE ENTRY'     !    MOVE AN ERROR MESSAGE
      SELECT(?CLI:COMPANY)                        !    STAY ON THE SAME FIELD
      BEEP                                        !    SOUND THE KEYBOARD ALARM
      CYCLE                                       !    AND LOOP AGAIN
    .

  OF ?PAUSE_FIELD                                 !ON PAUSE FIELD
    IF KEYCODE() <> ENTER_KEY|                    !IF NOT ENTER KEY
    AND KEYCODE() <> ACCEPT_KEY|                  !AND NOT CTRL-ENTER KEY
```

(continued)

```
        AND KEYCODE() <> 0                          !AND NOT NONSTOP MODE
          BEEP                                      !  SOUND KEYBOARD ALARM
          SELECT(?PAUSE_FIELD)                      !  AND STAY ON PAUSE FIELD

  OF ?LAST_FIELD                                    !FROM THE LAST FIELD
    EXECUTE ACTION                                  !  UPDATE THE FILE
      ADD(CLIENTS)                                  !    ADD NEW RECORD
      PUT(CLIENTS)                                  !    CHANGE EXISTING RECORD
      DELETE(CLIENTS)                               !    DELETE EXISTING RECORD
    .
    IF ERRORCODE() = 40                             !  DUPLICATE KEY ERROR
      MEM:MESSAGE = ERROR()                         !    DISPLAY ERR MESSAGE
      SELECT(2)                                     !    POSITION TO TOP OF FORM
      CYCLE                                         !    GET OUT OF EDIT LOOP
    ELSIF ERROR()                                   !  CHECK FOR UNEXPECTED ERROR
      STOP(ERROR())                                 !    HALT EXECUTION
    .
    ACTION = 0                                      !  SET ACTION TO COMPLETE
    RETURN                                          !  AND RETURN TO CALLER

  OF ?DELETE_FIELD                                  !FROM THE DELETE FIELD
    IF KEYCODE() = ENTER_KEY |                      !  ON ENTER KEY
    OR KEYCODE() = ACCEPT_KEY                        !  OR CTRL-ENTER KEY
      SELECT(?LAST_FIELD)                           !    DELETE THE RECORD
    ELSE                                            !  OTHERWISE
      BEEP                                          !    BEEP AND ASK AGAIN
  . . .

CALCFIELDS  ROUTINE
  IF FIELD() > ?FIRST_FIELD                         !BEYOND FIRST_FIELD?
    IF KEYCODE() = 0 AND SELECTED() > FIELD() THEN EXIT. !GET OUT IF NOT NONSTOP
  .
  SCR:MESSAGE = MEM:MESSAGE
  SCR:CLIENTNO = CLI:CLIENTNO
```

HOURS5.CLA—Work Recording Procedure

```
          MEMBER('HOURS')
WORK          PROCEDURE

SCREEN        SCREEN      PRE(SCR),WINDOW(15,59),HUE(15,1)
              ROW(1,1)    STRING('<218,196{57},191>'),HUE(14,1)
              ROW(2,1)    REPEAT(13);STRING('<179,0{57},179>'),HUE(14,1)  .
              ROW(15,1)   STRING('<192,196{21},0{15},196{21},217>'),HUE(14,1)
              ROW(4,4)    STRING('Date:')
              ROW(6,4)    STRING('Subject:')
```

(continued)

```
                 ROW(8,4)    STRING('Start Time:')
                    COL(23)  STRING('Complete Time:')
                    COL(45)  STRING('Hours:')
                 ROW(15,24)  STRING('<<F3> Calendar')
MESSAGE          ROW(2,16)   STRING(30),ENH
COMPANY          ROW(4,22)   STRING(30),HUE(15,1)
HOURS            ROW(8,52)   STRING(@t1)
                             ENTRY,USE(?FIRST_FIELD)
                 ROW(4,9)    ENTRY(@D1),USE(HRS:DATE),NUM,OVR
                    COL(18)  ENTRY,USE(HRS:CLIENTNO)
CLIENTNO            COL(18)  STRING(@N4),HUE(9,1)
                 ROW(6,17)   ENTRY(@s30),USE(HRS:SUBJECT),LFT,ESC(?-1)
                 ROW(8,16)   ENTRY(@T1),USE(HRS:STARTTIME),OVR
                    COL(38)  ENTRY(@T1),USE(HRS:COMPLETETIME),OVR
                 ROW(10,11)  TEXT(4,40),USE(HRS:NOTES),LFT
                             ENTRY,USE(?LAST_FIELD)
                             PAUSE(''),USE(?DELETE_FIELD)
          .

    EJECT
    CODE
    OPEN(SCREEN)                                    !OPEN THE SCREEN
    SETCURSOR                                       !TURN OFF ANY CURSOR
    IF HRS:DATE = 0;HRS:DATE  = TODAY().;IF ACTION = 2;
    SELECT(?HRS:SUBJECT);UPDATE;DISPLAY.;
    IF HRS:STARTTIME = '' THEN HRS:STARTTIME = CLOCK().!CALL SETUP PROCEDURE
    DISPLAY                                          !DISPLAY THE FIELDS
    LOOP                                             !LOOP THRU ALL THE FIELDS
      MEM:MESSAGE = CENTER(MEM:MESSAGE,SIZE(MEM:MESSAGE)) !DISPLAY ACTION MESSAGE
      DO CALCFIELDS                                  !CALCULATE DISPLAY FIELDS
      ALERT                                          !RESET ALERTED KEYS
      ALERT(ACCEPT_KEY)                              !ALERT SCREEN ACCEPT KEY
      ALERT(REJECT_KEY)                              !ALERT SCREEN REJECT KEY
      ALERT(F3_KEY)                                  !ALERT HOT KEY
      ACCEPT                                         !READ A FIELD
      IF KEYCODE() = F3_KEY                          !ON HOT KEY
         UPDATE(?)                                   !  RETRIEVE FIELD
         SAVACTN# = ACTION                           !  SAVE ACTION
         POPUP                                       !  CALL HOT KEY PROCEDURE
         ACTION = SAVACTN#                           !  RESTORE ACTION
         SELECT(?)                                   !  DO SAME FIELD AGAIN
         CYCLE                                       !  AND LOOP AGAIN
      .
      IF KEYCODE() = REJECT_KEY THEN RETURN.         !RETURN ON SCREEN REJECT KEY
      EXECUTE ACTION                                 !SET MESSAGE
        MEM:MESSAGE = 'Record will be Added'         !
        MEM:MESSAGE = 'Record will be Changed'       !
        MEM:MESSAGE = 'Press Enter to Delete'        !
      .
```

(continued)

```
IF KEYCODE() = ACCEPT_KEY              !ON SCREEN ACCEPT KEY
  UPDATE                               !  MOVE ALL FIELDS FROM SCREEN
  SELECT(?)                            !  START WITH CURRENT FIELD
  SELECT                               !  EDIT ALL FIELDS
  CYCLE                                !  GO TO TOP OF LOOP
.
CASE FIELD()                           !JUMP TO FIELD EDIT ROUTINE
OF ?FIRST_FIELD                        !FROM THE FIRST FIELD
  IF KEYCODE() = ESC_KEY THEN RETURN.  !  RETURN ON ESC KEY
  IF ACTION = 3 THEN SELECT(?DELETE_FIELD).!  OR CONFIRM FOR DELETE

OF ?HRS:CLIENTNO                       !CLIENT NUMBER FOR RELATION
  CLI:CLIENTNO = HRS:CLIENTNO          !MOVE RELATED FIELDS
  GET(CLIENTS,CLI:BY_CLIENT)           !READ THE RECORD
  ACTION# = ACTION                     !SAVE ACTION
  ACTION = 4                           !REQUEST TABLE LOOKUP
  LIST                                 !CALL LOOKUP PROCEDURE
  IF ACTION                            !NO SELECTION WAS MADE
    SELECT(?HRS:CLIENTNO-1)            !  BACK UP ONE FIELD
    ACTION = ACTION#                   !  RESTORE ACTION
    CYCLE                              !  GO TO TOP OF LOOP
  .
  SCR:CLIENTNO = CLI:CLIENTNO          !DISPLAY LOOKUP FIELD
  HRS:CLIENTNO = CLI:CLIENTNO          !MOVE LOOKUP FIELD
  DISPLAY(?HRS:CLIENTNO)              !AND DISPLAY IT
  ACTION = ACTION#                     !RESTORE ACTION

OF ?LAST_FIELD                         !FROM THE LAST FIELD
  EXECUTE ACTION                       !  UPDATE THE FILE
    ADD(HOURS)                         !    ADD NEW RECORD
    PUT(HOURS)                         !    CHANGE EXISTING RECORD
    DELETE(HOURS)                      !    DELETE EXISTING RECORD
  .
  IF ERRORCODE() = 40                  !  DUPLICATE KEY ERROR
    MEM:MESSAGE = ERROR()              !    DISPLAY ERR MESSAGE
    SELECT(2)                          !    POSITION TO TOP OF FORM
    CYCLE                              !    GET OUT OF EDIT LOOP
  ELSIF ERROR()                        !  CHECK FOR UNEXPECTED ERROR
    STOP(ERROR())                      !    HALT EXECUTION
  .
  ACTION = 0                           !  SET ACTION TO COMPLETE
  RETURN                               !  AND RETURN TO CALLER

OF ?DELETE_FIELD                       !FROM THE DELETE FIELD
  IF KEYCODE() = ENTER_KEY |           !  ON ENTER KEY
  OR KEYCODE() = ACCEPT_KEY            !  OR CTRL-ENTER KEY
    SELECT(?LAST_FIELD)                !    DELETE THE RECORD
```

(continued)

```
        ELSE                                    !  OTHERWISE
          BEEP                                  !    BEEP AND ASK AGAIN
   . . .


CALCFIELDS    ROUTINE
  IF FIELD() > ?FIRST_FIELD                     !BEYOND FIRST_FIELD?
    IF KEYCODE() = 0 AND SELECTED() > FIELD() THEN EXIT. !GET OUT IF NOT NONSTOP
    .
  UPDATE                                        !UPDATE RECORD KEYS
  CLI:CLIENTNO = HRS:CLIENTNO                   !MOVE RELATED KEY FIELDS
  GET(CLIENTS,CLI:BY_CLIENT)                    !READ THE RECORD
  IF ERROR() THEN CLEAR(CLI:RECORD).            !IF NOT FOUND, CLEAR RECORD
  SCR:COMPANY = CLI:COMPANY                     !DISPLAY LOOKUP FIELD
  SCR:MESSAGE = MEM:MESSAGE
  SCR:CLIENTNO = HRS:CLIENTNO
  SCR:HOURS = (HRS:COMPLETETIME - HRS:STARTTIME)+1
```

HOURS6.CLA—Popup Client Selection Procedure

```
          MEMBER('HOURS')
LISTLOOK      PROCEDURE

SCREEN        SCREEN      PRE(SCR),WINDOW(20,50),AT(4,16),HUE(0,7)
            ROW(1,1)    STRING('<201,205{48},187>'),HUE(9,7)
            ROW(2,1)    STRING('<186,0{48},186>'),HUE(9,7)
            ROW(3,1)    STRING('<204,205{48},185>'),HUE(9,7)
            ROW(4,1)    REPEAT(16);STRING('<186,0{48},186>'),HUE(9,7) .
            ROW(20,1)   STRING('<200,205{48},188>'),HUE(9,7)
            ROW(2,21)   STRING('CLIENT LIST')
                        ENTRY,USE(?FIRST_FIELD)
                        ENTRY,USE(?PRE_POINT)
                        REPEAT(15),EVERY(1),INDEX(NDX)
            ROW(5,3)      POINT(1,46),USE(?POINT),ESC(?-1)
COMPANY       COL(4)    STRING(30)
PHONE         COL(35)   STRING(@P(###)###-####PB)
                .                 .

NDX           BYTE                          !REPEAT INDEX FOR POINT AREA
ROW           BYTE                          !ACTUAL ROW OF SCROLL AREA
COL           BYTE                          !ACTUAL COLUMN OF SCROLL AREA
COUNT         BYTE(15)                      !NUMBER OF ITEMS TO SCROLL
ROWS          BYTE(15)                      !NUMBER OF ROWS TO SCROLL
COLS          BYTE(46)                      !NUMBER OF COLUMNS TO SCROLL
FOUND         BYTE                          !RECORD FOUND FLAG
NEWPTR        LONG                          !POINTER TO NEW RECORD
```

(continued)

```
TABLE          TABLE,PRE(TBL)                  !TABLE OF RECORD DATA
COMPANY        STRING(30)                      !COMPANY NAME OF CLIENT
PHONE          STRING(@P(###)###-####PB)
CLIENTNO       SHORT
PTR            LONG                            !  POINTER TO FILE RECORD
               .

  EJECT
  CODE
  ACTION# = ACTION                            !SAVE ACTION
  OPEN(SCREEN)                                !OPEN THE SCREEN
  SETCURSOR                                   !TURN OFF ANY CURSOR
  TBL:PTR = 1                                 !START AT TABLE ENTRY
  NDX = 1                                     !PUT SELECTOR BAR ON TOP ITEM
  ROW = ROW(?POINT)                           !REMEMBER TOP ROW AND
  COL = COL(?POINT)                           !LEFT COLUMN OF SCROLL AREA
  RECORDS# = TRUE                             !INITIALIZE RECORDS FLAG
  CACHE(CLI:BY_CLIENT,.25)                    !CACHE KEY FILE
  IF ACTION = 4                               !   TABLE LOOKUP REQUEST
    NEWPTR = POINTER(CLIENTS)                 !   SET POINTER TO RECORD
    IF NOT NEWPTR                             !   RECORD NOT PASSED TO TABLE
      SET(CLI:BY_CLIENT,CLI:BY_CLIENT)        !     POSITION TO CLOSEST RECORD
      NEXT(CLIENTS)                           !     READ RECORD
      NEWPTR = POINTER(CLIENTS)               !     SET POINTER
      .
    DO FIND_RECORD                            !   POSITION FILE
  ELSE
    NDX = 1                                   !   PUT SELECTOR BAR ON TOP ITEM
    DO FIRST_PAGE                             !   BUILD MEMORY TABLE OF KEYS
    .
  RECORDS# = TRUE                             !   ASSUME THERE ARE RECORDS
  LOOP                                        !LOOP UNTIL USER EXITS
    ACTION = ACTION#                          !RESTORE ACTION
    ALERT                                     !RESET ALERTED KEYS
    ALERT(REJECT_KEY)                         !ALERT SCREEN REJECT KEY
    ALERT(ACCEPT_KEY)                         !ALERT SCREEN ACCEPT KEY
    ACCEPT                                    !READ A FIELD
    IF KEYCODE() = REJECT_KEY THEN BREAK.     !RETURN ON SCREEN REJECT KEY

    IF  KEYCODE() = ACCEPT_KEY      |         !ON SCREEN ACCEPT KEY
    AND FIELD() <> ?POINT                     !BUT NOT ON THE POINT FIELD
      UPDATE                                  !   MOVE ALL FIELDS FROM SCREEN
      SELECT(?)                               !   START WITH CURRENT FIELD
      SELECT                                  !   EDIT ALL FIELDS
      CYCLE                                   !   GO TO TOP OF LOOP
      .
    CASE FIELD()                              !JUMP TO FIELD EDIT ROUTINE
```

(continued)

```
OF ?FIRST_FIELD                          !FROM THE FIRST FIELD
  IF KEYCODE() = ESC_KEY     |           !   RETURN ON ESC KEY
  OR RECORDS# = FALSE                    !   OR NO RECORDS
    BREAK                                !     EXIT PROGRAM
  .
OF ?PRE_POINT                            !PRE POINT FIELD CONDITION
  IF KEYCODE() = ESC_KEY                 !   BACKING UP?
    SELECT(?-1)                          !     SELECT PREVIOUS FIELD
  ELSE                                   !   GOING FORWARD
    SELECT(?POINT)                       !     SELECT MENU FIELD
  .
OF ?POINT                                !PROCESS THE POINT FIELD
  IF RECORDS(TABLE) = 0                  !IF THERE ARE NO RECORDS
    CLEAR(CLI:RECORD)                    !   CLEAR RECORD AREA
    ACTION = 1                           !   SET ACTION TO ADD
    GET(CLIENTS,0)                       !   CLEAR PENDING RECORD
    CLEAR(CLI:RECORD,1)                  !CLEAR RECORD TO HIGH VALUES
    SET(CLI:BY_CLIENTNO)                 !   POINT TO FIRST RECORD
    PREVIOUS(CLIENTS)                    !READ LAST KEY RECORD
    IF ERROR()                           !IF THERE WAS AN ERROR
      CLEAR(CLI:RECORD)                  !   CLEAR THE RECORD
      KEYFIELD# = 0                      !   INTITIALIZE THE FIELD
      IF KEYFIELD# = 0 THEN KEYFIELD# = 1. !  IF ITS 0 MAKE IT 1
    ELSE                                 !ELSE
      KEYFIELD# = CLI:CLIENTNO + 1       !   INCREMENT FIELD
    .
    CLEAR(CLI:RECORD)                    !CLEAR LAST KEY RECORD
    CLI:CLIENTNO = KEYFIELD#             !LOAD KEY FIELD
    0;RETURN                             !   CALL FORM FOR NEW RECORD
    NEWPTR = POINTER(CLIENTS)            !    SET POINTER TO NEW RECORD
    DO FIRST_PAGE                        !   DISPLAY THE FIRST PAGE
    IF RECORDS(TABLE) = 0                !   IF THERE AREN'T ANY RECORDS
      RECORDS# = FALSE                   !     INDICATE NO RECORDS
      SELECT(?PRE_POINT-1)              !     SELECT THE PRIOR FIELD
    .
    CYCLE                                !     AND LOOP AGAIN
  .
  CASE KEYCODE()                         !PROCESS THE KEYSTROKE

  OF INS_KEY                             !INS KEY
    CLEAR(CLI:RECORD)                    !   CLEAR RECORD AREA
    ACTION = 1                           !   SET ACTION TO ADD
    GET(CLIENTS,0)                       !   CLEAR PENDING RECORD
    CLEAR(CLI:RECORD,1)                  !CLEAR RECORD TO HIGH VALUES
    SET(CLI:BY_CLIENTNO)                 !   POINT TO FIRST RECORD
    PREVIOUS(CLIENTS)                    !READ LAST KEY RECORD
    IF ERROR()                           !IF THERE WAS AN ERROR
      CLEAR(CLI:RECORD)                  !   CLEAR THE RECORD
```

(continued)

```
    KEYFIELD# = 0                             !  INTITIALIZE THE FIELD
    IF KEYFIELD# = 0 THEN KEYFIELD# = 1.      !  IF ITS 0 MAKE IT 1
  ELSE                                        !ELSE
    KEYFIELD# = CLI:CLIENTNO + 1              !  INCREMENT FIELD
  .
  CLEAR(CLI:RECORD)                           !CLEAR LAST KEY RECORD
  CLI:CLIENTNO = KEYFIELD#                    !LOAD KEY FIELD
  0;RETURN                                    !  CALL FORM FOR NEW RECORD
  IF ~ACTION                                  !  IF RECORD WAS ADDED
    NEWPTR = POINTER(CLIENTS)                 !    SET POINTER TO NEW RECORD
    DO FIND_RECORD                            !    POSITION IN FILE
  .
OF ENTER_KEY                                  !ENTER KEY
OROF ACCEPT_KEY                               !CTRL-ENTER KEY
  DO GET_RECORD                               !  GET THE SELECTED RECORD
  IF ACTION = 4 AND KEYCODE() = ENTER_KEY     !  IF THIS IS A LOOKUP REQUEST
    ACTION = 0                                !    SET ACTION TO COMPLETE
    BREAK                                     !    AND RETURN TO CALLER
  .
  IF ~ERROR()                                 !  IF RECORD IS STILL THERE
    ACTION = 2                                !    SET ACTION TO CHANGE
    0;RETURN                                  !    CALL FORM TO CHANGE REC
    IF ACTION THEN CYCLE.                     !    IF SUCCESSFUL RE-DISPLAY
  .
  NEWPTR = POINTER(CLIENTS)                   !    SET POINTER TO NEW RECORD
  DO FIND_RECORD                              !    POSITION IN FILE
OF DEL_KEY                                    !DEL KEY
  DO GET_RECORD                               !  READ THE SELECTED RECORD
  IF ~ERROR()                                 !  IF RECORD IS STILL THERE
    ACTION = 3                                !    SET ACTION TO DELETE
    0;RETURN                                  !    CALL FORM TO DELETE
    IF ~ACTION                                !    IF SUCCESSFUL
      N# = NDX                                !      SAVE POINT INDEX
      DO SAME_PAGE                            !      RE-DISPLAY
      NDX = N#                                !      RESTORE POINT INDEX
  . .
OF DOWN_KEY                                   !DOWN ARROW KEY
  DO SET_NEXT                                 !  POINT TO NEXT RECORD
  DO FILL_NEXT                                !  FILL A TABLE ENTRY
  IF FOUND                                    !  FOUND A NEW RECORD
    SCROLL(ROW,COL,ROWS,COLS,ROWS(?POINT))    !   SCROLL THE SCREEN UP
    GET(TABLE,RECORDS(TABLE))                 !  GET RECORD FROM TABLE
    DO FILL_SCREEN                            !  DISPLAY ON SCREEN
  .
OF PGDN_KEY                                   !PAGE DOWN KEY
  DO SET_NEXT                                 !  POINT TO NEXT RECORD
  DO NEXT_PAGE                                !  DISPLAY THE NEXT PAGE
```

(continued)

```
        OF CTRL_PGDN                              !CTRL-PAGE DOWN KEY
          DO LAST_PAGE                            !  DISPLAY THE LAST PAGE
          NDX = RECORDS(TABLE)                    !  POSITION POINT BAR

        OF UP_KEY                                 !UP ARROW KEY
          DO SET_PREV                             !  POINT TO PREVIOUS RECORD
          DO FILL_PREV                            !  FILL A TABLE ENTRY
          IF FOUND                                !  FOUND A NEW RECORD
            SCROLL(ROW,COL,ROWS,COLS,-(ROWS(?POINT)))! SCROLL THE SCREEN DOWN
            GET(TABLE,1)                          !  GET RECORD FROM TABLE
            DO FILL_SCREEN                        !  DISPLAY ON SCREEN
          .

        OF PGUP_KEY                               !PAGE UP KEY
          DO SET_PREV                             !  POINT TO PREVIOUS RECORD
          DO PREV_PAGE                            !  DISPLAY THE PREVIOUS PAGE

        OF CTRL_PGUP                              !CTRL-PAGE UP
          DO FIRST_PAGE                           !  DISPLAY THE FIRST PAGE
          NDX = 1                                 !  POSITION POINT BAR
    . . .
    FREE(TABLE)                                   !FREE MEMORY TABLE
    RETURN                                        !AND RETURN TO CALLER

SAME_PAGE ROUTINE                                 !DISPLAY THE SAME PAGE
  GET(TABLE,1)                                    !  GET THE FIRST TABLE ENTRY
  DO FILL_RECORD                                  !  FILL IN THE RECORD
  SET(CLI:BY_CLIENT,CLI:BY_CLIENT,TBL:PTR)        !  POSITION FILE
  FREE(TABLE)                                     !  EMPTY THE TABLE
  DO NEXT_PAGE                                    !  DISPLAY A FULL PAGE

FIRST_PAGE ROUTINE                                !DISPLAY FIRST PAGE
  BLANK(ROW,COL,ROWS,COLS)
  FREE(TABLE)                                     !  EMPTY THE TABLE
  CLEAR(CLI:RECORD,-1)                            !  CLEAR RECORD TO LOW VALUES
  CLEAR(TBL:PTR)                                  !  ZERO RECORD POINTER
  SET(CLI:BY_CLIENT)                              !  POINT TO FIRST RECORD
  LOOP NDX = 1 TO COUNT                           !  FILL UP THE TABLE
    DO FILL_NEXT                                  !    FILL A TABLE ENTRY
    IF NOT FOUND THEN BREAK.                      !    GET OUT IF NO RECORD
    .
  NDX = 1                                         !  SET TO TOP OF TABLE
  DO SHOW_PAGE                                    !  DISPLAY THE PAGE

LAST_PAGE ROUTINE                                 !DISPLAY LAST PAGE
  NDX# = NDX                                      !  SAVE SELECTOR POSITION
  BLANK(ROW,COL,ROWS,COLS)                        !  CLEAR SCROLLING AREA
```

(continued)

```
  FREE(TABLE)                                    !   EMPTY THE TABLE
  CLEAR(CLI:RECORD,1)                            !   CLEAR RECORD TO HIGH VALUES
  CLEAR(TBL:PTR,1)                               !   CLEAR PTR TO HIGH VALUE
  SET(CLI:BY_CLIENT)                             !   POINT TO FIRST RECORD
  LOOP NDX = COUNT TO 1 BY -1                    !   FILL UP THE TABLE
    DO FILL_PREV                                 !     FILL A TABLE ENTRY
    IF NOT FOUND THEN BREAK.                     !     GET OUT IF NO RECORD
  .                                              !   END OF LOOP
  NDX = NDX#                                     !   RESTORE SELECTOR POSITION
  DO SHOW_PAGE                                   !   DISPLAY THE PAGE

FIND_RECORD ROUTINE                             !POSITION TO SPECIFIC RECORD
  SET(CLI:BY_CLIENT,CLI:BY_CLIENT,NEWPTR)       !POSITION FILE
  IF NEWPTR = 0                                 !NEWPTR NOT SET
    NEXT(CLIENTS)                               !   READ NEXT RECORD
    NEWPTR = POINTER(CLIENTS)                   !   SET NEWPTR
    SKIP(CLIENTS,-1)                            !   BACK UP TO DISPLAY RECORD
  .
  FREE(TABLE)                                    !   CLEAR THE RECORD
  DO NEXT_PAGE                                   !   DISPLAY A PAGE

NEXT_PAGE ROUTINE                               !DISPLAY NEXT PAGE
  SAVECNT# = RECORDS(TABLE)                      !   SAVE RECORD COUNT
  LOOP COUNT TIMES                               !   FILL UP THE TABLE
    DO FILL_NEXT                                 !     FILL A TABLE ENTRY
    IF NOT FOUND                                 !     IF NONE ARE LEFT
      IF NOT SAVECNT#                            !       IF REBUILDING TABLE
        DO LAST_PAGE                             !         FILL IN RECORDS
        EXIT                                     !         EXIT OUT OF ROUTINE
      .
      BREAK                                      !     EXIT LOOP
  . .
  DO SHOW_PAGE                                    !   DISPLAY THE PAGE

SET_NEXT ROUTINE                                !POINT TO THE NEXT PAGE
  GET(TABLE,RECORDS(TABLE))                       !   GET THE LAST TABLE ENTRY
  DO FILL_RECORD                                  !   FILL IN THE RECORD
  SET(CLI:BY_CLIENT,CLI:BY_CLIENT,TBL:PTR)        !   POSITION FILE
  NEXT(CLIENTS)                                   !   READ THE CURRENT RECORD

FILL_NEXT ROUTINE                               !FILL NEXT TABLE ENTRY
  FOUND = FALSE                                   !   ASSUME RECORD NOT FOUND
  LOOP UNTIL EOF(CLIENTS)                         !   LOOP UNTIL END OF FILE
    NEXT(CLIENTS)                                 !     READ THE NEXT RECORD
    FOUND = TRUE                                  !     SET RECORD FOUND
    DO FILL_TABLE                                 !     FILL IN THE TABLE ENTRY
    ADD(TABLE)                                    !     ADD LAST TABLE ENTRY
    GET(TABLE,RECORDS(TABLE)-COUNT)               !     GET ANY OVERFLOW RECORD
```

(continued)

```
      DELETE(TABLE)                          !      AND DELETE IT
      EXIT                                   !      RETURN TO CALLER
    .

PREV_PAGE ROUTINE                            !DISPLAY PREVIOUS PAGE
  LOOP COUNT TIMES                           !  FILL UP THE TABLE
    DO FILL_PREV                             !    FILL A TABLE ENTRY
    IF NOT FOUND THEN BREAK.                 !    GET OUT IF NO RECORD
    .
  DO SHOW_PAGE                               !  DISPLAY THE PAGE

SET_PREV ROUTINE                             !POINT TO PREVIOUS PAGE
  GET(TABLE,1)                               !  GET THE FIRST TABLE ENTRY
  DO FILL_RECORD                             !  FILL IN THE RECORD
  SET(CLI:BY_CLIENT,CLI:BY_CLIENT,TBL:PTR)   !  POSITION FILE
  PREVIOUS(CLIENTS)                          !  READ THE CURRENT RECORD

FILL_PREV ROUTINE                            !FILL PREVIOUS TABLE ENTRY
  FOUND = FALSE                              !  ASSUME RECORD NOT FOUND
  LOOP UNTIL BOF(CLIENTS)                    !  LOOP UNTIL BEGINNING OF FILE
    PREVIOUS(CLIENTS)                        !    READ THE PREVIOUS RECORD
    FOUND = TRUE                             !    SET RECORD FOUND
    DO FILL_TABLE                            !    FILL IN THE TABLE ENTRY
    ADD(TABLE,1)                             !    ADD FIRST TABLE ENTRY
    GET(TABLE,COUNT+1)                       !    GET ANY OVERFLOW RECORD
    DELETE(TABLE)                            !    AND DELETE IT
    EXIT                                     !    RETURN TO CALLER
    .

SHOW_PAGE ROUTINE                            !DISPLAY THE PAGE
  NDX# = NDX                                 !  SAVE SCREEN INDEX
  LOOP NDX = 1 TO RECORDS(TABLE)             !  LOOP THRU THE TABLE
    GET(TABLE,NDX)                           !    GET A TABLE ENTRY
    DO FILL_SCREEN                           !    AND DISPLAY IT
    IF TBL:PTR = NEWPTR                      !    SET INDEX FOR NEW RECORD
      NDX# = NDX                             !    POINT TO CORRECT RECORD
    . .
  NDX = NDX#                                 !  RESTORE SCREEN INDEX
  NEWPTR = 0                                 !  CLEAR NEW RECORD POINTER
  CLEAR(CLI:RECORD)                          !  CLEAR RECORD AREA

FILL_TABLE ROUTINE                           !MOVE FILE TO TABLE
  TBL:COMPANY = CLI:COMPANY
  TBL:PHONE = CLI:PHONE
  TBL:CLIENTNO = CLI:CLIENTNO
  TBL:PTR = POINTER(CLIENTS)                 !  SAVE RECORD POINTER

FILL_RECORD ROUTINE                          !MOVE TABLE TO FILE
  CLI:COMPANY = TBL:COMPANY
  CLI:CLIENTNO = TBL:CLIENTNO
```

(continued)

```
FILL_SCREEN ROUTINE                              !MOVE TABLE TO SCREEN
  SCR:COMPANY = TBL:COMPANY
  SCR:PHONE = TBL:PHONE


GET_RECORD ROUTINE                               !GET SELECTED RECORD
  GET(TABLE,NDX)                                 !  GET TABLE ENTRY
  GET(CLIENTS,TBL:PTR)                           !  GET THE RECORD
```

HOURS7.CLA

```
          MEMBER('HOURS')
BILLED        PROCEDURE

SCREEN        SCREEN        PRE(SCR),WINDOW(21,62),AT(3,15),HUE(15,0)
          ROW(5,4)    PAINT(2,49),HUE(0,7)
          ROW(6,53)   PAINT(1,8),HUE(0,7)
          ROW(6,3)    PAINT(1,2),HUE(0,7)
          ROW(7,3)    PAINT(12,58),HUE(0,7)
          ROW(5,25)   PAINT(1,15),HUE(15,0)
          ROW(1,1)    STRING('<201,205{22},0{16},205{22},187>'),HUE(15,0)
          ROW(2,1)    REPEAT(3);STRING('<186,0{60},186>'),HUE(15,0)  .
          ROW(5,1)    STRING('<199,196{23},0{14},196{23},182>'),HUE(15,0)
          ROW(6,1)    REPEAT(13);STRING('<186,0{60},186>'),HUE(15,0)  .
          ROW(19,1)   STRING('<199,196{22},194,196{15},0{9},196{13},182>')        |
                         HUE(15,0)
          ROW(20,1)   STRING('<186,0{22},179,0{37},186>'),HUE(15,0)
          ROW(21,1)   STRING('<200,205{22},207,205{37},188>'),HUE(15,0)
          ROW(1,25)   STRING('CLIENT ACCOUNT')
          ROW(3,4)    STRING('WORK PERFORMED FOR:')
          ROW(5,26)   STRING('<<F10> Billed')
          ROW(6,7)    STRING('DATE      HOURS {14}SUBJECT {13}STATUS')
          ROW(19,41)  STRING('INVOICE')
          ROW(20,3)   STRING('Total Hours:')
            COL(27)   STRING('Hours:')
            COL(43)   STRING('Amount:')
COMPANY   ROW(3,30)   STRING(30),HUE(14,0)
TEST      ROW(4,15)   STRING(@s10),HUE(14,0)
TOTAL     ROW(20,16)  STRING(@T1),HUE(14,0)
INVOICE     COL(34)   STRING(@t1),HUE(14,0)
AMOUNT      COL(51)   STRING(@N$9.2),HUE(14,0)
                        ENTRY,USE(?FIRST_FIELD)
                        ENTRY,USE(?PRE_POINT)
                        REPEAT(12),EVERY(1),INDEX(NDX)
          ROW(7,3)        POINT(1,58),USE(?POINT),ESC(?-1)
DATE        COL(4)    STRING(@D1)
```

(continued)

```
SPENT          COL(15)     STRING(@T1)
SUBJECT        COL(23)     STRING(30)
BILLED         COL(54)     STRING(@s6)
                 .              .

NDX            BYTE                              !REPEAT INDEX FOR POINT AREA
ROW            BYTE                              !ACTUAL ROW OF SCROLL AREA
COL            BYTE                              !ACTUAL COLUMN OF SCROLL AREA
COUNT          BYTE(12)                          !NUMBER OF ITEMS TO SCROLL
ROWS           BYTE(12)                          !NUMBER OF ROWS TO SCROLL
COLS           BYTE(58)                          !NUMBER OF COLUMNS TO SCROLL
FOUND          BYTE                              !RECORD FOUND FLAG
NEWPTR         LONG                              !POINTER TO NEW RECORD

TABLE          TABLE,PRE(TBL)                    !TABLE OF RECORD DATA
DATE           LONG                              !DATE OF ACTIVITY
SPENT          STRING(@T1)
SUBJECT        STRING(30)                        !SUBJECT OF WORK PERFORMED
BILLED         STRING(@s6)
CLIENTNO       SHORT                             !CLIENT NUMBER FOR RELATION
PTR               LONG                           !  POINTER TO FILE RECORD
                 .

               GROUP,PRE(SAV)
CLIENTNO       SHORT

                 .

TOT_GROUP      GROUP,PRE(TOT)                    !TABLE TOTAL FIELDS
TOTAL          REAL

                 .

  EJECT
  CODE
  ACTION# = ACTION                               !SAVE ACTION
  OPEN(SCREEN)                                   !OPEN THE SCREEN
  SETCURSOR                                      !TURN OFF ANY CURSOR
  LISTLOOK;HRS:CLIENTNO = CLI:CLIENTNO;MEM:TO_BILL = 0!CALL SETUP PROCEDURE
  SAV:CLIENTNO = HRS:CLIENTNO                    !SAVE SELECTOR FIELD
  CLEAR(TOT_GROUP)                               !ZERO TOTALS
  TBL:PTR = 1                                    !START AT TABLE ENTRY
  NDX = 1                                        !PUT SELECTOR BAR ON TOP ITEM
  ROW = ROW(?POINT)                              !REMEMBER TOP ROW AND
  COL = COL(?POINT)                              !LEFT COLUMN OF SCROLL AREA
  RECORDS# = TRUE                                !INITIALIZE RECORDS FLAG
  CACHE(HRS:BY_CLIENT,.25)                       !CACHE KEY FILE
  LOOP                                           !LOOP UNTIL USER EXITS
    ACTION = ACTION#                             !RESTORE ACTION
    HRS:CLIENTNO = SAV:CLIENTNO                  !RESTORE SELECTOR FIELD
    SCR:TOTAL = TOT:TOTAL
    UPDATE                                       !UPDATE RECORD KEYS
```

(continued)

```
CLI:CLIENTNO = HRS:CLIENTNO                      !MOVE RELATED KEY FIELDS
GET(CLIENTS,CLI:BY_CLIENTNO)                     !READ THE RECORD
IF ERROR() THEN CLEAR(CLI:RECORD).              !IF NOT FOUND, CLEAR RECORD
SCR:COMPANY = CLI:COMPANY                        !DISPLAY LOOKUP FIELD
IF if this is true                               !EVALUATE CONDITION
  SCR:TEST = do this                             !  CONDITION IS TRUE
ELSE                                             !OTHERWISE
  SCR:TEST = but do this otherwise               !  CONDITION IS FALSE
  .

SCR:INVOICE = 0;CLIENTNO# = HRS:CLIENTNO;SET(HRS:BY_CLIENT,HRS:BY_CLIENT);
LOOP UNTIL EOF(HOURS);NEXT(HOURS);IF HRS:CLIENTNO <> CLIENTNO#;BREAK.;
IF HRS:BILLED = '';SCR:INVOICE += ((HRS:COMPLETETIME - HRS:STARTTIME)+1)..
SCR:AMOUNT = 0;GET(CLIENTS,CLI:BY_CLIENTNO);
SCR:AMOUNT = (((SCR:INVOICE)/100)/60)/60 * CLI:RATE
SCR:COMPANY = SCR:TEST
ALERT                                            !RESET ALERTED KEYS
ALERT(REJECT_KEY)                                !ALERT SCREEN REJECT KEY
ALERT(ACCEPT_KEY)                                !ALERT SCREEN ACCEPT KEY
ALERT(F10_KEY)                                   !ALERT HOT KEY
ACCEPT                                           !READ A FIELD
IF KEYCODE() = F10_KEY                           !ON HOT KEY
  IF FIELD() = ?POINT THEN DO GET_RECORD.        !  READ RECORD IF NEEDED
  BILL                                           !  CALL HOT KEY PROCEDURE
  DO SAME_PAGE                                   !  RESET TO SAME PAGE
  CYCLE                                          !  AND LOOP AGAIN
  .

IF KEYCODE() = REJECT_KEY THEN BREAK.            !RETURN ON SCREEN REJECT KEY


IF  KEYCODE() = ACCEPT_KEY    |                  !ON SCREEN ACCEPT KEY
AND FIELD() <> ?POINT                            !BUT NOT ON THE POINT FIELD
  UPDATE                                         !  MOVE ALL FIELDS FROM SCREEN
  SELECT(?)                                      !  START WITH CURRENT FIELD
  SELECT                                         !  EDIT ALL FIELDS
  CYCLE                                          !  GO TO TOP OF LOOP
  .

CASE FIELD()                                     !JUMP TO FIELD EDIT ROUTINE

OF ?FIRST_FIELD                                  !FROM THE FIRST FIELD
  IF KEYCODE() = ESC_KEY   |                     !  RETURN ON ESC KEY
  OR RECORDS# = FALSE                            !  OR NO RECORDS
    BREAK                                        !    EXIT PROGRAM
    .
  CLEAR(TOT_GROUP)                               !ZERO TOTALS
  CLEAR(HRS:RECORD,-1)                           !CLEAR RECORD TO LOW VALUES
  CLEAR(TBL:PTR)                                 !SET POINTER TO ZERO
  SETHUE(BACKHUE(ROW,COL),BACKHUE(ROW,COL))      !TURN OFF DISPLAY
  HRS:CLIENTNO = SAV:CLIENTNO                     !RESTORE SELECTOR FIELD
```

(continued)

```
  SET(HRS:BY_CLIENT,HRS:BY_CLIENT,TBL:PTR)    !  POINT PAST LAST RECORD
  LOOP UNTIL EOF(HOURS)                       !LOOP UNTIL END OF FILE
    NEXT(HOURS)                               !  READ A RECORD
    IF HRS:CLIENTNO <> SAV:CLIENTNO           !IF END OF SELECTION
      HRS:CLIENTNO = SAV:CLIENTNO             !  RESTORE THE SELECTOR
      BREAK                                   !  AND BREAK
    .
    ACTN# = 1                                 !SET ACTION FOR ADD
    DO FILL_TABLE                             !  TOTAL SCREEN VARIABLES
    DO COMP_TOTALS                            !  ADD TO TOTAL AMOUNT
  .
  SETHUE()                                    !TURN OFF SETHUE
  FREE(HOURS)                                 !FREE MEMORY USED FOR BUFFERING
  FREE(TABLE)                                 !FREE MEMORY TABLE
  IF ACTION = 4                               !  TABLE LOOKUP REQUEST
    NEWPTR = POINTER(HOURS)                   !  SET POINTER TO RECORD
    IF NOT NEWPTR                             !  RECORD NOT PASSED TO TABLE
      SET(HRS:BY_CLIENT,HRS:BY_CLIENT)        !    POSITION TO CLOSEST RECORD
      NEXT(HOURS)                             !    READ RECORD
      NEWPTR = POINTER(HOURS)                 !    SET POINTER
    .
    DO FIND_RECORD                            !  POSITION FILE
  ELSE
    NDX = 1                                   !  PUT SELECTOR BAR ON TOP ITEM
    DO FIRST_PAGE                             !  BUILD MEMORY TABLE OF KEYS
  .
  RECORDS# = TRUE                             !  ASSUME THERE ARE RECORDS
OF ?PRE_POINT                                 !PRE POINT FIELD CONDITION
  IF KEYCODE() = ESC_KEY                      !  BACKING UP?
    SELECT(?-1)                               !    SELECT PREVIOUS FIELD
  ELSE                                        !  GOING FORWARD
    SELECT(?POINT)                            !    SELECT MENU FIELD
  .
OF ?POINT                                     !PROCESS THE POINT FIELD
  IF RECORDS(TABLE) = 0                       !IF THERE ARE NO RECORDS
    CLEAR(HRS:RECORD)                         !  CLEAR RECORD AREA
    ACTION = 1                                !  SET ACTION TO ADD
    GET(HOURS,0)                              !  CLEAR PENDING RECORD
    ACTN# = ACTION                            !SAVE ACTION FOR COMP_TOTALS
    HRS:CLIENTNO = SAV:CLIENTNO               !RESTORE SELECTOR FIELD
    NEWPTR = POINTER(HOURS)                   !    SET POINTER TO NEW RECORD
    DO FIRST_PAGE                             !  DISPLAY THE FIRST PAGE
    IF RECORDS(TABLE) = 0                     !  IF THERE AREN'T ANY RECORDS
      RECORDS# = FALSE                        !    INDICATE NO RECORDS
      SELECT(?PRE_POINT-1)                    !    SELECT THE PRIOR FIELD
    .
    CYCLE                                     !    AND LOOP AGAIN
```

(continued)

```
CASE KEYCODE()                                  !PROCESS THE KEYSTROKE

OF INS_KEY                                      !INS KEY
  CLEAR(HRS:RECORD)                             !   CLEAR RECORD AREA
  ACTION = 1                                    !   SET ACTION TO ADD
  GET(HOURS,0)                                  !   CLEAR PENDING RECORD
  ACTN# = ACTION                                !SAVE ACTION FOR COMP_TOTALS
  HRS:CLIENTNO = SAV:CLIENTNO                   !RESTORE SELECTOR FIELD
  IF ~ACTION                                    !   IF RECORD WAS ADDED
    NEWPTR = POINTER(HOURS)                     !     SET POINTER TO NEW RECORD
    DO FIND_RECORD                              !     POSITION IN FILE
  .

OF ENTER_KEY                                    !ENTER KEY
OROF ACCEPT_KEY                                 !CTRL-ENTER KEY
  DO GET_RECORD                                 !  GET THE SELECTED RECORD
  IF ACTION = 4 AND KEYCODE() = ENTER_KEY!   IF THIS IS A LOOKUP REQUEST
    ACTION = 0                                  !     SET ACTION TO COMPLETE
    BREAK                                       !     AND RETURN TO CALLER
  .

  IF ~ERROR()                                   !   IF RECORD IS STILL THERE
    ACTION = 2                                  !     SET ACTION TO CHANGE
    ACTN# = ACTION                              !SAVE ACTION FOR COMP_TOTALS
    TOTAL$ = SCR:SPENT
    IF ACTION THEN CYCLE.                       !     IF SUCCESSFUL RE-DISPLAY
    TOT:TOTAL -= TOTAL$
  .

  NEWPTR = POINTER(HOURS)                       !     SET POINTER TO NEW RECORD
  DO FIND_RECORD                                !     POSITION IN FILE
OF DEL_KEY                                      !DEL KEY
  DO GET_RECORD                                 !   READ THE SELECTED RECORD
  IF ~ERROR()                                   !   IF RECORD IS STILL THERE
    ACTION = 3                                  !     SET ACTION TO DELETE
    ACTN# = ACTION                              !SAVE ACTION FOR COMP_TOTALS
    TOTAL$ = SCR:SPENT
    IF ~ACTION                                  !     IF SUCCESSFUL
      TOT:TOTAL -= TOTAL$
      N# = NDX                                  !       SAVE POINT INDEX
      DO SAME_PAGE                              !       RE-DISPLAY
      NDX = N#                                  !       RESTORE POINT INDEX
  . .

OF DOWN_KEY                                     !DOWN ARROW KEY
  DO SET_NEXT                                   !   POINT TO NEXT RECORD
  DO FILL_NEXT                                  !   FILL A TABLE ENTRY
  IF FOUND                                      !   FOUND A NEW RECORD
    SCROLL(ROW,COL,ROWS,COLS,ROWS(?POINT))  !    SCROLL THE SCREEN UP
    GET(TABLE,RECORDS(TABLE))                  !   GET RECORD FROM TABLE
    DO FILL_SCREEN                             !   DISPLAY ON SCREEN
  .
```

(continued)

```
      OF PGDN_KEY                                    !PAGE DOWN KEY
        DO SET_NEXT                                  !  POINT TO NEXT RECORD
        DO NEXT_PAGE                                 !  DISPLAY THE NEXT PAGE

      OF CTRL_PGDN                                   !CTRL-PAGE DOWN KEY
        DO LAST_PAGE                                 !  DISPLAY THE LAST PAGE
        NDX = RECORDS(TABLE)                         !  POSITION POINT BAR

      OF UP_KEY                                      !UP ARROW KEY
        DO SET_PREV                                  !  POINT TO PREVIOUS RECORD
        DO FILL_PREV                                 !  FILL A TABLE ENTRY
        IF FOUND                                     !  FOUND A NEW RECORD
          SCROLL(ROW,COL,ROWS,COLS,-(ROWS(?POINT)))) !  SCROLL THE SCREEN DOWN
          GET(TABLE,1)                               !  GET RECORD FROM TABLE
          DO FILL_SCREEN                             !  DISPLAY ON SCREEN
          .

      OF PGUP_KEY                                    !PAGE UP KEY
        DO SET_PREV                                  !  POINT TO PREVIOUS RECORD
        DO PREV_PAGE                                 !  DISPLAY THE PREVIOUS PAGE

      OF CTRL_PGUP                                   !CTRL-PAGE UP
        DO FIRST_PAGE                                !  DISPLAY THE FIRST PAGE
        NDX = 1                                      !  POSITION POINT BAR
    . . .
  FREE(TABLE)                                        !FREE MEMORY TABLE
  RETURN                                             !AND RETURN TO CALLER

SAME_PAGE ROUTINE                                    !DISPLAY THE SAME PAGE
  GET(TABLE,1)                                       !  GET THE FIRST TABLE ENTRY
  DO FILL_RECORD                                     !  FILL IN THE RECORD
  SET(HRS:BY_CLIENT,HRS:BY_CLIENT,TBL:PTR)           !  POSITION FILE
  FREE(TABLE)                                        !  EMPTY THE TABLE
  DO NEXT_PAGE                                        !  DISPLAY A FULL PAGE

FIRST_PAGE ROUTINE                                   !DISPLAY FIRST PAGE
  BLANK(ROW,COL,ROWS,COLS)
  FREE(TABLE)                                        !  EMPTY THE TABLE
  CLEAR(HRS:RECORD,-1)                               !  CLEAR RECORD TO LOW VALUES
  CLEAR(TBL:PTR)                                     !  ZERO RECORD POINTER
  HRS:CLIENTNO = SAV:CLIENTNO                        !RESTORE SELECTOR FIELD
  SET(HRS:BY_CLIENT,HRS:BY_CLIENT,TBL:PTR)           !  POINT PAST LAST RECORD
  LOOP NDX = 1 TO COUNT                              !  FILL UP THE TABLE
    DO FILL_NEXT                                     !    FILL A TABLE ENTRY
    IF NOT FOUND THEN BREAK.                         !    GET OUT IF NO RECORD
    .
  NDX = 1                                            !  SET TO TOP OF TABLE
  DO SHOW_PAGE                                       !  DISPLAY THE PAGE
```

(continued)

```
LAST_PAGE ROUTINE                                  !DISPLAY LAST PAGE
  NDX# = NDX                                        !  SAVE SELECTOR POSITION
  BLANK(ROW,COL,ROWS,COLS)                          !  CLEAR SCROLLING AREA
  FREE(TABLE)                                       !  EMPTY THE TABLE
  CLEAR(HRS:RECORD,1)                               !  CLEAR RECORD TO HIGH VALUES
  CLEAR(TBL:PTR,1)                                  !  CLEAR PTR TO HIGH VALUE
  HRS:CLIENTNO = SAV:CLIENTNO                       !RESTORE SELECTOR FIELD
  SET(HRS:BY_CLIENT,HRS:BY_CLIENT,TBL:PTR)          !  POINT PAST LAST RECORD
  LOOP NDX = COUNT TO 1 BY -1                       !  FILL UP THE TABLE
    DO FILL_PREV                                    !    FILL A TABLE ENTRY
    IF NOT FOUND THEN BREAK.                        !    GET OUT IF NO RECORD
  .                                                 !  END OF LOOP
  NDX = NDX#                                        !  RESTORE SELECTOR POSITION
  DO SHOW_PAGE                                      !  DISPLAY THE PAGE


FIND_RECORD ROUTINE                                !POSITION TO SPECIFIC RECORD
  SET(HRS:BY_CLIENT,HRS:BY_CLIENT,NEWPTR)          !POSITION FILE
  IF NEWPTR = 0                                    !NEWPTR NOT SET
    NEXT(HOURS)                                    !  READ NEXT RECORD
    NEWPTR = POINTER(HOURS)                        !  SET NEWPTR
    SKIP(HOURS,-1)                                 !  BACK UP TO DISPLAY RECORD
  .
  FREE(TABLE)                                      !  CLEAR THE RECORD
  DO NEXT_PAGE                                     !  DISPLAY A PAGE


NEXT_PAGE ROUTINE                                  !DISPLAY NEXT PAGE
  SAVECNT# = RECORDS(TABLE)                         !  SAVE RECORD COUNT
  LOOP COUNT TIMES                                  !  FILL UP THE TABLE
    DO FILL_NEXT                                    !    FILL A TABLE ENTRY
    IF NOT FOUND                                    !    IF NONE ARE LEFT
      IF NOT SAVECNT#                               !      IF REBUILDING TABLE
        DO LAST_PAGE                                !      FILL IN RECORDS
        EXIT                                        !      EXIT OUT OF ROUTINE
      .                                             !
      BREAK                                         !    EXIT LOOP
  . .
  DO SHOW_PAGE                                      !  DISPLAY THE PAGE


SET_NEXT ROUTINE                                   !POINT TO THE NEXT PAGE
  GET(TABLE,RECORDS(TABLE))                         !  GET THE LAST TABLE ENTRY
  DO FILL_RECORD                                    !  FILL IN THE RECORD
  SET(HRS:BY_CLIENT,HRS:BY_CLIENT,TBL:PTR)          !  POSITION FILE
  NEXT(HOURS)                                       !  READ THE CURRENT RECORD


FILL_NEXT ROUTINE                                  !FILL NEXT TABLE ENTRY
  FOUND = FALSE                                     !  ASSUME RECORD NOT FOUND
  LOOP UNTIL EOF(HOURS)                             !  LOOP UNTIL END OF FILE
    NEXT(HOURS)                                     !    READ THE NEXT RECORD
```

(continued)

```
    IF HRS:CLIENTNO <> SAV:CLIENTNO        !IF END OF SELECTION
       HRS:CLIENTNO = SAV:CLIENTNO         !   RESTORE THE SELECTOR
       BREAK                               !    AND BREAK
      .
    FOUND = TRUE                           !     SET RECORD FOUND
    DO FILL_TABLE                          !      FILL IN THE TABLE ENTRY
    ADD(TABLE)                             !      ADD LAST TABLE ENTRY
    GET(TABLE,RECORDS(TABLE)-COUNT)        !      GET ANY OVERFLOW RECORD
    DELETE(TABLE)                          !      AND DELETE IT
    EXIT                                   !      RETURN TO CALLER
   .
PREV_PAGE ROUTINE                          !DISPLAY PREVIOUS PAGE
  LOOP COUNT TIMES                         !  FILL UP THE TABLE
    DO FILL_PREV                           !    FILL A TABLE ENTRY
    IF NOT FOUND THEN BREAK.               !    GET OUT IF NO RECORD
   .
  DO SHOW_PAGE                             !  DISPLAY THE PAGE

SET_PREV ROUTINE                           !POINT TO PREVIOUS PAGE
  GET(TABLE,1)                             !  GET THE FIRST TABLE ENTRY
  DO FILL_RECORD                           !  FILL IN THE RECORD
  SET(HRS:BY_CLIENT,HRS:BY_CLIENT,TBL:PTR) !  POSITION FILE
  PREVIOUS(HOURS)                          !  READ THE CURRENT RECORD

FILL_PREV ROUTINE                          !FILL PREVIOUS TABLE ENTRY
  FOUND = FALSE                            !  ASSUME RECORD NOT FOUND
  LOOP UNTIL BOF(HOURS)                    !  LOOP UNTIL BEGINNING OF FILE
    PREVIOUS(HOURS)                        !    READ THE PREVIOUS RECORD
    IF HRS:CLIENTNO <> SAV:CLIENTNO        !IF END OF SELECTION
       HRS:CLIENTNO = SAV:CLIENTNO         !  RESTORE THE SELECTOR
       BREAK                               !   AND BREAK
      .
    FOUND = TRUE                           !     SET RECORD FOUND
    DO FILL_TABLE                          !      FILL IN THE TABLE ENTRY
    ADD(TABLE,1)                           !      ADD FIRST TABLE ENTRY
    GET(TABLE,COUNT+1)                     !      GET ANY OVERFLOW RECORD
    DELETE(TABLE)                          !      AND DELETE IT
    EXIT                                   !      RETURN TO CALLER
   .
SHOW_PAGE ROUTINE                          !DISPLAY THE PAGE
  NDX# = NDX                               !  SAVE SCREEN INDEX
  LOOP NDX = 1 TO RECORDS(TABLE)           !  LOOP THRU THE TABLE
    GET(TABLE,NDX)                         !    GET A TABLE ENTRY
    DO FILL_SCREEN                         !    AND DISPLAY IT
    IF TBL:PTR = NEWPTR                    !    SET INDEX FOR NEW RECORD
      NDX# = NDX                           !    POINT TO CORRECT RECORD
      DO COMP_TOTALS                       !CALCULATE TABLE TOTALS
   . .
```

(continued)

```
        NDX = NDX#                                  !  RESTORE SCREEN INDEX
        NEWPTR = 0                                  !  CLEAR NEW RECORD POINTER
        CLEAR(HRS:RECORD)                           !  CLEAR RECORD AREA


FILL_TABLE ROUTINE                                  !MOVE FILE TO TABLE
   TBL:DATE = HRS:DATE
   TBL:SUBJECT = HRS:SUBJECT
   TBL:CLIENTNO = HRS:CLIENTNO
   TBL:PTR = POINTER(HOURS)                         !  SAVE RECORD POINTER
   TBL:SPENT = (HRS:COMPLETETIME - HRS:STARTTIME)+1
   IF hrs:billed = 'B'                              !EVALUATE CONDITION
     TBL:BILLED = 'Billed'                          !  CONDITION IS TRUE
   ELSE                                             !OTHERWISE
     TBL:BILLED = ''                                !  CONDITION IS FALSE
     .


FILL_RECORD ROUTINE                                 !MOVE TABLE TO FILE
   HRS:CLIENTNO = TBL:CLIENTNO
   HRS:DATE = TBL:DATE


FILL_SCREEN ROUTINE                                 !MOVE TABLE TO SCREEN
   SCR:DATE = TBL:DATE
   SCR:SPENT = TBL:SPENT
   SCR:SUBJECT = TBL:SUBJECT
   SCR:BILLED = TBL:BILLED


GET_RECORD ROUTINE                                  !GET SELECTED RECORD
   GET(TABLE,NDX)                                   !  GET TABLE ENTRY
   GET(HOURS,TBL:PTR)                               !  GET THE RECORD


COMP_TOTALS  ROUTINE                                !CALCULATE TOTAL FIELDS
   IF NOT ACTN# THEN EXIT.                          !GET OUT IF ACTN NOT SET
   TOT:TOTAL += TBL:SPENT
   ACTN# = 0                                        !CLEAR ACTION
```

BILL.CLA—*Status Change Procedure*

```
        MEMBER('HOURS')


BILL         PROCEDURE

        CODE
        IF HRS:BILLED  = ''
          HRS:BILLED = 'B'
```

(continued)

```
ELSE
  HRS:BILLED = ''
  .
PUT(HOURS)
SET(HRS:BY_CLIENT,HRS:BY_CLIENT)
RETURN
```

Chapter 10

Form Techniques

Database Entry via Forms

Data-based software applications work well only if they have some way to talk with the users to find out what to do. Utility programs can run unattended and without any direct user input; they usually perform some manner of automated data entry by reading the files on a disk or scanning a particular subdirectory. Menus transfer instructions to the software to perform certain steps, but, for the most part, those steps must be predetermined—no new information enters the system. You pick from a selection, and the program performs some preset operation. Data-based systems, however, were built to receive, process, store, and retrieve *data* in order to create *information* for their users.

Clarion can receive data by two means: keyboard data entry and serial communications. We won't discuss all of the methods by which a Clarion application *could* accept input. Those methods include parallel communications (except for printing) and the mouse. Serial communications will be discussed in detail in Chapter 19, so we'll focus on keyboard entry, which in a traditional Clarion application, means processing a Form Procedure.

A form requires more participation on the part of the operator and the software than other elements of the application. As the primary vehicle for transferring data from the real world into the computer, a form must promote clarity, speed, and data integrity. A form cannot be too difficult to read nor can it create an actual barrier between the user of the software by requiring entries where none is necessary or demanding specific formats that are not appropriate for the data.

Any software application is the distillation of someone else's idea of how to do something. Unless you bought Clarion to write applications only you will use, you will be deciding how things should be done and your users will be forced to follow your method. It is your responsibility as the developer to use the facilities in Clarion to help the user. Clarion's ability to nest procedures, its easy configuration of entry screens as pop-up windows, and its ability to control the format and even the content of Entry Fields makes it an extremely powerful tool.

What a Form Does

A form should move the user logically from field to field. You can use the SELECT and SELECTED functions to control the defaults in a Clarion entry form, and you can use ALIAS, ALERT, and KEYCODE to control the keys you provide the user to perform a function. The Edit and Setup Procedures in a Designer form provide you with means for field post-processing. Unfortunately Clarion does not provide as straightforward a means for field *pre*-processing. However, we'll discuss methods you can use with the Computed Fields and other means for handling pre-processing, such as the Edit Procedure of the prior field.

The second responsibility of the Form Procedure is to manage the file I/O (input/output). If you use Designer, you must grapple with certain conditions if you choose I/O methods other than those natural to Designer. The natural Designer method requires that you fill in the fields of a form until you've touched each field on the screen and then place the entered data into the file as either a new record or an altered one, depending on the keystroke you used to call the form.

You can also leave the form early by pressing a Control key combination (usually CTRL-ENTER), and the data entered so far will be saved. However, if you make changes to Designer's method of File I/O, you must be conscious of the conditions under which Designer PUTs (replaces) a record instead of ADDing it (creates). For instance, you can update secondary files by naming them in the Options window of the form. You *cannot* add records to those secondary files; you can only replace a record that already existed. If you count on it operating any differently, you cause a problem unless you make the changes to the model file (or elsewhere in the source code) to account for these conditions.

What a Form Is: Ask and Entry Field Methods

A form is a patch of screen (or even the whole screen) with or without activated receptacles for processing data. The receptacles can be filled with entries from the keyboard or data from the disk (previously entered into the system from a keyboard) or data from a communications port. The key difference between a Form and other types of Screen Procedures is that the form's screen has special fields that can accept and process data that will be transferred to and from a file for editing. The other screen types simply present data painted onto them. In Designer, you can use the Form Procedure for that purpose: merely to show uneditable data. However, unless you modify the model (as we will do in this chapter) to strip out the unnecessary code, your application will be larger than necessary.

The ASK Method

Let's start by examining the simplest form we can build by revisiting the "Hello, World!" application from Chapter 4. As usual, Clarion provides a wealth of ways to get input from the user. The most common method used in Designer is the combination of Entry Fields in the Screen structure together with a Case structure that processes the result of the ACCEPT statement. However, we can circumvent the ENTRY statements in the Screen structure by using the ASK statement directly in the code. The ENTRY statement is, by far, a more flexible and efficient method for producing user entry forms. The following discussion of the ASK statement is intended for those who are migrating from the Dbase language; you may feel more comfortable with a very rough equivalent of the SAY,GET combination found in dBASE III Plus.

ASK has other uses in its unformatted mode. In Chapter 4's version of the "Hello, World!" program, we used the ASK statement to pause the program and wait for a keystroke before continuing on and closing the application. In addition, the ASK statement can be given parameters and made into a standalone screen Entry Field.

"Hello, World!" Using the ASK Statement

In Figure 10-1, we use the ASK statement to create an input form without relying on the Screen structure for anything more than painting a few words

Figure 10-1   The "Hello, World!" program from Chapter 4, revisited for demonstrating an entry form using the ASK statement.

```
HELLO        PROGRAM

SCREEN       SCREEN WINDOW(25,80),AT(1,1),HUE(7,0)
             ROW(1,1)    STRING('<201,205{78},187>')
             ROW(2,1)    REPEAT(23);STRING('<186,0{78},186>')  .
             ROW(25,1)   STRING('<200,205{78},188>')
             ROW(2,28)   STRING('"HELLO, WORLD!"  RE-VISITED')
             ROW(5,21)   STRING('Your First Name:')
             ROW(6,21)   STRING('Your Last Name:')
             ROW(7,21)   STRING('Today''s Date:')
             END!SCREEN

ESC_KEY   EQUATE(256)                    ! USE WORDS FOR ESCAPE

ROW       BYTE                           ! CREATE COUNTER VARIABLE
MESSAGE   STRING(78)                     ! CREATE TEXT VARIABLE

RECORD    GROUP                          ! PUT VARIABLES IN A GROUP
FIRST       STRING(10)                   !    FIRST NAME VARIABLE
LAST        STRING(10)                   !    LAST NAME VARIABLE
DATE        LONG                         !    DATE VARIABLE
            END                          ! END OF GROUP

  CODE                                   ! START THE CODE
  ROW = 5                                ! INITIALIZE ROW COUNT
  ALERT(ESC_KEY)                         ! SENSITIZE ESC KEY
  OPEN(SCREEN)                           ! OPEN THE WINDOW
  LOOP                                   ! START CONTINUOUS RUN
   EXECUTE (ROW - 4)                     !  SET STEP TO 1 - 3
     ASK(ROW,38,FIRST,@S10)             !    ENTER FIRST FIELD
     ASK(ROW,38,LAST,@S10)              !    ENTER 2ND FIELD
     ASK(ROW,38,DATE,@D1)               !    ENTER LAST FIELD
   END!EXECUTE                           !   TERMINATE CASE STRUCTURE
   IF KEYCODE( ) = ESC_KEY THEN BREAK.   !  LEAVE ON ESCAPE PRESS
   ROW += 1                              !  INCREMENT ROW COUNT
   IF ROW = 8                            !  IF ON THE LAST ROW
```

(continued)

Figure 10-1 *continued*

```
    MESSAGE = CENTER('HELLO, ' & CLIP(FIRST) & |
    ' ' & CLIP(LAST) & '. It''s ' |
    & FORMAT(DATE,@D4),SIZE(MESSAGE))        !   PREPARE MESSAGE
    SHOW(17,2,MESSAGE)                  !  DISPLAY MESSAGE
    ROW = 5                            !  RESET THE ROW COUNTER
    CLEAR(RECORD)                      !  ERASE THE VARIABLES
    BLANK(5,38,3,10)                   !  ERASE SCREEN
  END!IF                              !  TERMINATE IF STRUCTURE
END!LOOP                              ! TERMINATE LOOP
```

and a border. In this listing we're also introducing the application of a few other constructs of the Clarion language.

The Execute structure was used in Figure 10-1 to select the correct ASK statement for the proper row on the screen. By subtracting 4 from the current row number, we get a result of 1, 2, or 3, and that is the order in which the fields occur in the Execute structure. As we discussed in Chapter 8, the Execute structure does not allow you to run more than one statement per line. The Loop structure continues to spin, stopping at each ASK statement to process it as the ROW counter is incremented. The presence of the loop merely ensures that you stay in the program, recycling to the first field when you have completed the last one. The program stops at each ASK statement, waiting for it to be completed rather than spinning around the loop, considering each statement inside the loop. This is exactly the opposite manner in which Designer processes Entry Fields in a Screen structure for a Form Procedure. In the case of Designer, the Main Event Loop cycles continuously and a Case structure is used to test conditions for processing fields.

 Hint: The KEYCODE statement is used in Figure 10-1 because it returns the last ALERTed keystroke completed (or a default like the Enter key) and KEYBOARD returns the keystroke that still waits in the buffer to be processed. ASK processes the keystroke so that KEYBOARD will not work.

Nothing additional needs to be done to track keystrokes. The ASK statement processes the cursor keys and the Enter key as completing each field. However, it always goes to the next field in order, just as if you had pressed the Enter key, unless you ALERT the cursor keys and intercept them in order to perform some other operation—like returning to a previous Entry Field. In the sample depicted in Figure 10-1, we ALERTed the Escape key to use as an exit point when it is pressed to complete each Entry Field. You can set other ALERTs if you want to use other special functions from each field.

The ASK statement accepts a variable like ROW to position the string, but not a variable for the picture. So, we have to create a procedure to allow us to change the picture for the string. (Notice, also, that Clarion can convert the date stored as a LONG into a string for display.) If these statements were all string variables and we did not need the date format in the third field, we could have used only one ASK statement, which would have set a temporary STRING variable. Then an Execute structure could fill in each field according to the contents of that temporary variable, as follows:

```
ASK(ROW,COL,TEMP_VAR,@S10)
EXECUTE (ROW - 4)
   FIRST = TEMP_VAR
   LAST = TEMP_VAR
   THIRD = TEMP_VAR
END
```

In a Screen structure, you can include a STRING variable with a label for displaying information. However, in this version of the entry form, we are trying to minimize the participation of the Screen structure. Instead, we'll use the SHOW statement to display the output from entering data in the fields. First, however, we have to format the string to display. The CENTER function makes it possible to arrange the contents of the 80-character string as defined just above the CODE statement. You place the string contents into the CENTER function and then tell the function how long a space is needed to center whatever shows up in that string. The string is joined together with the ampersand (&), and the trailing spaces are shaved off from the STRING variables. The DATE variable gets formatted into a DATE string, with a date picture that cannot be used for entry, only for display. (Otherwise, the DATE variable would appear as the standard date equivalent of the number of days from January 1, 1800, to August 4, 1990, or 69250.) Next comes the payoff for having used the GROUP structure to encase the variables in one unit. The CLEAR function, when run against the GROUP variable, clears out all the variables in the GROUP. Since the ASK statement paints the field output to the console, you can use the BLANK statement to erase just the area of the display where the fields are located.

File Access from an ASK-Based Form

The next step in form processing is to place the results of the completed fields into permanent storage. Right now, "Hello, World!" as revisited disposes of each set of entries after displaying them on the screen in the SHOW statement. One handy method for using the ASK statement in a form is to repeatedly add information to a file without leaving the form. Just a few modifications to Figure 10-1 will provide the means for adding records to a file.

The first step is to add a file definition to the program by placing the variables defined merely as individual, global fields into a File structure, like this:

```
DATAFILE      FILE,CREATE        ! FILE DEFINITION HEADER
RECORD          RECORD          !   THE RECORD STRUCTURE
FIRST             STRING(10)    !    FIRST NAME VARIABLE
LAST              STRING(10)    !    LAST NAME VARIABLE
DATE              LONG          !    DATE VARIABLE
                END!RECORD      !  END OF RECORD
              END!FILE          ! END OF FILE STRUCTURE
```

Notice how the Group structure has been replaced in the FILE definition with a Record structure. The file, thus far, does not contain any keys, but the CREATE attribute allows Clarion to construct the file if an attempt is made to open it. However, explicit code using the CREATE (File) statement must be used to actually create the file.

Next, we must insert the code into the program for opening the file. At the start of the program, an attempt is made to open the file with OPEN(DATA-FILE). If the file does not exist, or there is a problem in opening it, an error is returned. Most commonly the file does not yet exist when you first start a program so the ERRORCODE "2" is returned, which is the same as the ERROR "File Not Found." Probably the best general step is to test for whether the ERROR condition is TRUE (meaning it has returned a result) and not worry about what the specific error might be, which is the approach Designer takes in the G_OPENFILES procedure.

The CREATE attribute must be in the file definition for the CRE-ATE(DATAFILE) instruction to work. Though Designer opens every file in the application on program startup, it can be more efficient to ensure that the files are all right by attempting to open them, creating them if they do not exist, and then closing them back down. Many of the file operations commands automatically open the file they address. SET, GET, and ADD open the file if it is not yet open. By attempting to open the file at program startup, you ensure that one of these statements doesn't get addressed to a nonexistent file. If that did happen, an error would be returned and the program would halt.

Hint: All the file access statements other than SET, GET, and ADD return an error when they are issued against a file that is not open or does not exist.

At this step in modifying "Hello," we'll cause the program to merely add each set of fields as we complete them. To do that, we need only insert ADD(DATAFILE) after the start of the If structure that processes on completion of the last field. This procedure does not allow you to back up to edit a previously entered record—only to add an unlimited number of records until you run out of time, disk space, or patience. The records are added to the file in record number order.

The Revised "Hello" Program as a File Editor

Now, we'll perform some major surgery to the program to turn it into a file editor complete with the ability to look at, edit, add, and delete the records in the database. The final program will look like the code in Figure 10-2.

In the new "Hello" program in Figure 10-2, the Main Event Loop now contains a simple If structure for deciding which mode, add or review, you have selected and it branches to the appropriate subroutine. Notice the key equates at the top of the program in the definition area. In Designer-generated programs, these equate labels are part of the INCLUDE files added into the very top of the main program module.

Hint: Remember, if you ALERT the same key twice in a row, the net effect will be to turn the key off. If you place an ALERT to a key inside a loop, be certain you call ALERT by itself to turn off all the ALERTed keys. That way, you'll be in tighter control of which keys you have turned on and you'll avoid unexpected results when the user selects a key you'd forgotten was still ALERTed.

As the program starts, it attempts to open the data file and creates the file if it does not yet exist. Then it issues a SET to prepare the file to be read with NEXT and PREVIOUS. SET places the file pointer at the first record in the data file, but it does not read the record—NEXT and PREVIOUS will handle that. To distinguish between the two modes (add and review), we've set up a variable, ADDMODE, to set to either true (that is, in add mode) by setting it

Figure 10-2 The revised version of "Hello" for viewing, editing, and deleting as well as adding records in a data file.

```
HELLO   PROGRAM

SCREEN  SCREEN       WINDOW(25,80),AT(1,1),HUE(7,0)   ! SCREEN STRUCTURE
        ROW(1,1)     STRING('<201,205{78},187>')
        ROW(2,1)     REPEAT(20);STRING('<186,0{78},186>') .
        ROW(22,1)    STRING('<186,0{46},24,25,0{30},186>')
        ROW(23,1)    REPEAT(2);STRING('<186,0{78},186>') .
        ROW(25,1)    STRING('<200,205{78},188>')
        ROW(2,28)    STRING('"HELLO, WORLD!"  RE-VISITED')
        ROW(4,21)    STRING('Record Number:')
        ROW(5,21)    STRING('Your First Name:')
        ROW(6,21)    STRING('Your Last Name:')
        ROW(7,21)    STRING('Today''s Date:')
        ROW(21,30)   STRING('Touch <<F9> to Add More')
        ROW(22,21)   STRING('Touch <<F10> Key to Review (')
          COL(51)    STRING('to Scroll)')
        ROW(23,32)   STRING('Touch <<ESC> to Exit')
        ROW(24,31)   STRING('Touch <<DEL> to Delete')
        END!SCREEN


ESC_KEY   EQUATE(256)                ! USE WORDS FOR KEYCODES
UP_KEY    EQUATE(262)                ! THESE ARE SET IN
DOWN_KEY  EQUATE(269)                !   DESIGNER BY INCLUDING
F9_KEY    EQUATE(2057)               !   THE FILE 'STD_KEYS.CLA'
F10_KEY   EQUATE(2058)
DEL_KEY   EQUATE(272)


TEXT      STRING(10)                 ! TEMPORARY TEXT FILE
ROW       BYTE                       ! ROW COUNTER
MESSAGE   STRING(78)                 ! FOR MESSAGES ON SCREEN
ADDMODE   BYTE                       ! CURRENT OPERATING MODE

DATAFILE       FILE,CREATE           ! FILE DEFINITION HEADER
RECORD         RECORD                !   THE RECORD STRUCTURE
FIRST               STRING(10)       !    FIRST NAME ~VARIABLE
LAST                STRING(10)       !    LAST NAME VARIABLE
```

(continued)

Figure 10-2   *continued*

```
DATE              LONG              !   DATE VARIABLE
            END!RECORD              !   END OF RECORD STRUCTURE
            END!FILE                !   END OF FILE STRUCTURE

  CODE                              !  START THE CODE
  ALERT                             !  TURN ALL KEYS OFF
  ALERT(ESC_KEY)                    !  SENSITIZE SPECIAL KEYS
  ALERT(UP_KEY)
  ALERT(DOWN_KEY)
  ALERT(F9_KEY)
  ALERT(F10_KEY)
  ROW = 5                           !  INITIALIZE THE ROW COUNT
  OPEN(SCREEN)                      !  OPEN THE WINDOW
  OPEN(DATAFILE)                    !  ATTEMPT TO OPEN THE FILE
  IF ERROR( )                       !    IF CAN'T OPEN
     CREATE(DATAFILE)               !     CREATE DATA FILE
     SET(DATAFILE)                  !     CLOSE THE DATA FILE
     DO ADDMORE                     !      BRANCH TO ADD ROUTINE
  END!IF
  SET(DATAFILE)                     !  ESTABLISH POINTER
  ADDMODE = 0                       !  TURN OFF ADDMODE
  LOOP                              !  BEGIN EVENT LOOP
    IF ADDMODE                      !  IN ADD MODE?
       DO ADDMORE                   !   BRANCH TO ADD ROUTINE
    ELSE                            !  OTHERWISE
       DO INSPECT                   !   BRANCH TO REVIEW ROUTINE
    END!IF
  END!LOOP

INSPECT  ROUTINE
  BLANK(4,38,4,10)                  !  ERASE SCREEN
  SHOW(3,2,CENTER('REVIEW MODE',78))   !  POST MODE MESSAGE
  LOOP                              !  START CONTINUOUS RUN
  ASK                               !  WAIT FOR ACTION
  BLANK(12,2,1,78)                  !  ERASE LAST ERROR MESSAGE
   CASE KEYCODE( )                  !  WAIT FOR KEYSTROKE
   OF F9_KEY                        !  ON F9 KEY
     CLEAR(RECORD)                  !   ERASE RECORD
```

(continued)

Figure 10-2   *continued*

```
        ADDMODE = 1                      !   TURN ON ADD MODE
        EXIT                             !   GO TO MAIN LOOP
    OF DEL_KEY                           !  ON DELETE KEY
        DELETE(DATAFILE)                 !   DELETE CURRENT RECORD
        PACK(DATAFILE)                   !   STRIP DELETED RECORDS
    OF ESC_KEY                           !  ON ESCAPE KEY
        RETURN                           !   EXIT PROGRAM
    OF UP_KEY                            !  ON UP CURSOR KEY
        PREVIOUS(DATAFILE)               !   READ FILE BACKWARDS
        IF ERROR( )                      !   IF NO RECORDS FOUND
          SHOW(12,2,CENTER('RECORD NOT AVAILABLE',78))! POST ERROR MESSAGE
        ELSE                             !    OTHERWISE
          BLANK(4,38,3,10)               !    ERASE SCREEN
          SHOW(4,38,POINTER(DATAFILE))   !     SHOW CURRENT REC NO.
          SHOW(5,38,FIRST)               !     SHOW RECORD
          SHOW(6,38,LAST)
          SHOW(7,38,FORMAT(DATE,@D1))
        END!IF
    OF DOWN_KEY                          !  ON DOWN CURSOR KEY
        NEXT(DATAFILE)                   !   READ FILE FORWARDS
        IF ERROR( )                      !   IF NO RECORDS
          SHOW(12,2,CENTER('RECORD NOT AVAILABLE',78))! POST ERROR MESSAGE
        ELSE                             !    OTHERWISE
          BLANK(4,38,3,10)               !    ERASE SCREEN
          SHOW(4,38,POINTER(DATAFILE))   !     GET CURRENT POINTER
          SHOW(5,38,FIRST)               !     POST RECORD
          SHOW(6,38,LAST)
          SHOW(7,38,FORMAT(DATE,@D1))
        END!IF
    END!CASE
  END!LOOP

ADDMORE   ROUTINE
  BLANK(4,38,4,10)                       ! ERASE SCREEN
  SHOW(3,2,CENTER('  ADD MODE  ',78))    ! POST MODE MESSAGE
  LOOP                                   ! BEGIN EVENT LOOP
   EXECUTE (ROW - 4)                     !  SET STEP TO 1 - 3
    ASK(ROW,38,FIRST,@S10)               !   ENTER FIRST FIELD
```

(continued)

Figure 10-2 *continued*

```
    ASK(ROW,38,LAST,@S10)              !   ENTER 2ND FIELD
    ASK(ROW,38,DATE,@D1)               !   ENTER LAST FIELD
  END!EXECUTE                          !   TERMINATE CASE STRUCTURE
  IF KEYCODE( ) = ESC_KEY THEN BREAK.! LEAVE ON ESCAPE PRESS
  IF KEYCODE( ) = F10_KEY              ! ON F10 KEY PRESS
      ADDMODE = 0                      ! TURN OFF ADD MODE
      EXIT                             ! GO BACK TO MAIN LOOP
  END!IF
  ROW += 1                             ! INCREMENT ROW COUNTER
  IF ROW = 8                           ! IF ON THE LAST ROW
    ADD(DATAFILE)                      !   OPEN & ADD TO THE FILE
    MESSAGE = CENTER('HELLO, ' & CLIP(FIRST) & |
    ' ' & CLIP(LAST) & '. It''s ' |
    & FORMAT(DATE,@D4),SIZE(MESSAGE))      !   PREPARE MESSAGE
    SHOW(17,2,MESSAGE)                 !   DISPLAY MESSAGE
    ROW = 5                            !   RESET THE ROW COUNTER
    CLEAR(RECORD)                      !   ERASE THE VARIABLES
    BLANK(5,38,3,10)                   !   ERASE SCREEN
  END!IF
END!LOOP
```

equal to 1 or not true (that is, in review mode) by setting it equal to 0. This is very similar to the ACTION variable that Designer uses to keep track of the current editing mode. Review mode is shown in Figure 10-3.

Once inside the selected routine, the Main Event Loop processes the key strokes we set up for the hot keys listed at the bottom of the screen as show in Figure 10-3. The SHOW statement displays the records read by NEXT and PREVIOUS in inspect mode. The ADDMODE routine most closely resembles the old version of "Hello, World!" given in Figure 10-1. In the If structure, when the final field is processed, the ADD statement adds a record to the data file. In Inspect mode, when the Delete key is pressed, the current record—the one last read by NEXT or PREVIOUS—is deleted from the data file. Since the file was established without the RECLAIM attribute, it is wise to use the PACK function to strip out the deleted records. However, if you use this method, be careful because the relationship between the record number and the contents of the record will be lost.

Figure 10-3   The one and only screen demonstrating the "Hello" program as a file editing form. (The code for this program appears in Figure 10-4.)

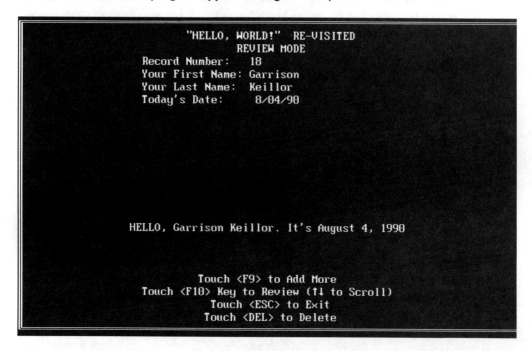

```
                         "HELLO, WORLD!"  RE-VISITED
                               REVIEW MODE
              Record Number:    18
              Your First Name: Garrison
              Your Last Name:  Keillor
              Today's Date:       8/04/90




              HELLO, Garrison Keillor. It's August 4, 1990



                     Touch <F9> to Add More
              Touch <F10> Key to Review (↑↓ to Scroll)
                      Touch <ESC> to Exit
                      Touch <DEL> to Delete
```

The Designer Method

The Form Procedure is one of the five horsemen of Designer's tools. Like Menu, Table, Report, and (though much less similar) Other Procedures, the Form Procedure represents less of a fixed tool than a particular configuration of the Clarion language as selected by Clarion's software engineers. The Form Procedure is the distillation of the language made to receive information and handle the file input/output operations in a way that is generic enough to cover many of the ways that Clarion users will attempt to apply it. The Form is the last step, so to speak, in the MENU-TABLE-FORM philosophy in Designer. You can call other forms or menus from inside a form, and the Entry Field is built to call a table as a reference.

Like its related procedures, the form has an Options screen and a selection of fields. The one field in the form that does not appear anywhere else is the Pause Field. The other fields may look similar in the selection screen that Designer presents, but the code they generate within a form is different. Therefore you should study how each is handled in order to better grasp how to use it. If you use the form for just a message window, you are including a very fat procedure—read as "code not in use." You should either hand-code such a message screen as an Other Procedure or create a custom model as we describe later on in this chapter.

The Options Window

So, you've selected Form from the list of Designer Procedures and now you're ready to begin implementing it. Like the other forms, the first screen you see is the Options window, as depicted in Figure 10-4.

Form Pre-Processing: The Setup Procedure: Like all Designer Procedures, the form has a Setup Procedure. Code inserted into this line of the Options window will run one time at the top of the procedure before the start of the Main Event Loop. This is handy for presetting variables that appear in the form when the form is called to add a record. Suppose that you wrote an application to keep track of your telephone numbers. Most of those numbers

Figure 10-4   The Form Options window for creating a Form Procedure in Designer.

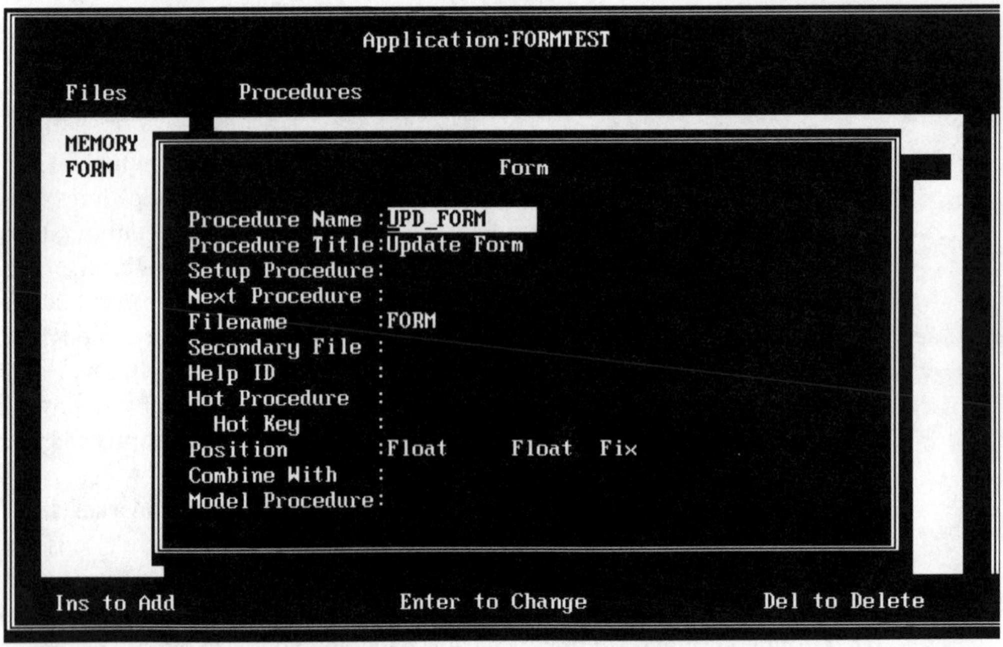

```
                        Application:FORMTEST

      Files           Procedures

    MEMORY
    FORM                                      Form
                Procedure Name :UPD_FORM
                Procedure Title:Update Form
                Setup Procedure:
                Next Procedure :
                Filename       :FORM
                Secondary File :
                Help ID        :
                Hot Procedure  :
                  Hot Key      :
                Position       :Float     Float  Fix
                Combine With   :
                Model Procedure:


     Ins to Add              Enter to Change           Del to Delete
```

probably would be in your same area code. So, in the Setup Procedure you would place the following line of code:

```
IF ACTION = 1 THEN FIL:AREA_CODE = '619'.
```

This code, loaded into the Setup Procedure, only sets the AREA_CODE variable to the default when a record is being added (that is, ACTION = 1).

The Setup Procedure can also be used to put the active cursor on a specific field, as when you are editing a form with fields you do not want to change once the record has been added. To do this, you would use the SELECT function. For example, suppose you wanted to skip over the Name Fields in the form depicted in Figure 10-5.

As you will see later in this section, this form actually contains, not the three Entry Fields you can see, but four more fields: the Message Field and three Dummy Fields. To place the cursor on the Date Field immediately, you must put the following code in the Setup Procedure:

```
SELECT(?+5)
```

Figure 10-5 A simple entry form created with Designer, shown here preparing to add a record to the table that called it.

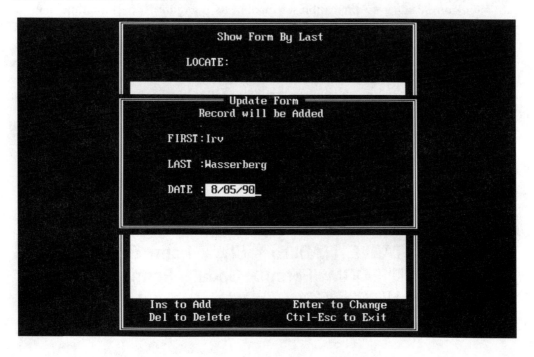

Or you can use the field equate label to identify the field by name with:

```
SELECT(?FIL:DATE)
```

This second method is preferable. It helps prevent you from leaving any fields set incorrectly should you change the order of the fields on the screen.

When you select a field by skipping over others, that field is designated as the first field in the form, and pressing the Escape key while the cursor sits on this field will cause you to exit from the form. You can see why this first field construct is in the code by referring to the form in Figure 10-5. However, the Up cursor key will take you to that field. To prevent the user from entering that field at all, you must either use the ALIAS function to remove the Up key from action or you must ALERT it and insert a test into the code or the model that will run when the user presses that key. A simple change in either of these ways placed into the FIRST_FIELD routine of the model procedure for a form will prevent the user from accessing that field.

Form Post-Processing: The Next Procedure and Secondary File: Following the completion of all the fields in the current Form Procedure, the Form Options window provides two slots for performing functions related to the current form. The impact of the Next Procedure as a single procedure call on Designer's Application screen appears in Figure 10-6. If multiple lines of code (separated by semicolons) are included in the Next Procedure, the graphic depiction as shown in Figure 10-6 does not appear. This is true for all of Designer's add-on procedures.

The Next Procedure slot in the Options window provides the first of three formal places at which you can insert a call to another procedure from within a Designer form. The *Clarion Language Reference* says that the Next Procedure is most often used to call a second or subsidiary entry form. That provides for multipart form processing so you can break up a big data entry

Figure 10-6   The section of the Designer Applications screen showing the layout for a form. The two procedures beneath the Update Form were set in the Options window for this form.

```
MAIN_TABLE [TABLE] - Show Form By Last
└─UPD_FORM [Form] - Update Form
    ├─ NEXT_PROC [ToDo]
    └─ HOT_KEY [ToDo]
```

job into more readable screens. However, with model or direct code modifications, you cannot back up through a series of forms that you chain together using the Next Procedure. To understand why, let's examine the code that Designer generated to create the form you see in Figure 10-5. The code is given in Figure 10-7.

The Next Procedure and the Secondary File slots in the Form Options window both affect LAST_FIELD processing. This is because they both are designed to take effect at the conclusion of the processing for the current form. Examine the code for the LAST_FIELD processing in Figure 10-7 and the code in Figure 10-8, which incorporates both a Next Procedure and a SECONDARY file.

As you can see from Figure 10-8, the Next Procedure executes after the record for the current procedure has been disposed of through the EXECUTE statement. Then, unless the action in the current form is to delete, the action for the second form is set to edit (that is, ACTION = 2) before calling the Next Procedure. That means you must not look for the second page of the form to be in add mode (ACTION = 1) even when this is the first time this record is being added with the multipage form.

Further, the addition of the record to the file prior to the completion of all the fields for the record could mean incomplete data. If you plan to change the key values for locating the record, be sure they are placed on the first page of the form or you may risk confusion. Also note that you can place more than just one procedure call in the Next Procedure slot. Now that the record has been added or edited by the main form, you can set other global values or perform other actions before the current form returns to the procedure that called it.

Notice in Figure 10-8 that the secondary file that you enter in the Form Options window (as it appears in Figure 10-1) is processed with a PUT and not by means of an optional ADD or DELETE. Thus any record you wish to add to the secondary data file must already exist when you run this procedure—even when you are adding a record for the very first time to the primary data file. Since the Designer-generated code does not perform any error checking on the PUT, you won't be notified if the PUT fails.

Hot-Key Processing in a Form Procedure: As with all of Designer's procedures, the addition of a hot key for the UPD_FORM appears in the Application screen as in Figure 10-6. The code for a Hot Key Procedure in a form is little different from that in a table. It occurs just after the ACCEPT in order to process the KEYCODE( ) return value and appears as in Figure 10-9. First, the contents of the Current Field or location of the cursor is updated. Then, the

Figure 10-7   This is the code generated by Designer for the form pictured in Figure 10-5.

```
              MEMBER('FORMTEST')
UPD_FORM      PROCEDURE

SCREEN        SCREEN      PRE(SCR),WINDOW(11,48),HUE(15,4)
              ROW(1,1)    STRING('<201,205{16},0{13},205{17},187>'),HUE(15,4)
              ROW(2,1)    REPEAT(9);STRING('<186,0{46},186>'),HUE(15,4)  .
              ROW(11,1)   STRING('<200,205{46},188>'),HUE(15,4)
              ROW(1,19)   STRING('Update Form')
              ROW(4,9)    STRING('FIRST:'),HUE(7,4)
              ROW(6,9)    STRING('LAST :'),HUE(7,4)
              ROW(8,9)    STRING('DATE :'),HUE(7,4)
MESSAGE       ROW(2,9)    STRING(30),HUE(15,4)
                          ENTRY,USE(?FIRST_FIELD)
              ROW(4,15)   ENTRY(@s10),USE(FOR:FIRST),HUE(15,4),SEL(0,7)
              ROW(6,15)   ENTRY(@s20),USE(FOR:LAST),REQ,HUE(15,4),SEL(0,7)
              ROW(8,15)   ENTRY(@D1),USE(FOR:DATE),HUE(15,4),SEL(0,7)
                          ENTRY,USE(?LAST_FIELD)
                          PAUSE(''),USE(?DELETE_FIELD)

              .

    EJECT
    CODE
    OPEN(SCREEN)                          !OPEN THE SCREEN
    SETCURSOR                             !TURN OFF ANY CURSOR
    DISPLAY                               !DISPLAY THE FIELDS
    LOOP                                  !LOOP THRU ALL THE FIELDS
      MEM:MESSAGE = CENTER(MEM:MESSAGE,SIZE(MEM:MESSAGE)) !DISPLAY ACTION MESSAGE
      DO CALCFIELDS                       !CALCULATE DISPLAY FIELDS
      ALERT                               !RESET ALERTED KEYS
      ALERT(ACCEPT_KEY)                   !ALERT SCREEN ACCEPT KEY
      ALERT(REJECT_KEY)                   !ALERT SCREEN REJECT  KEY
      ACCEPT                              !READ A FIELD
      IF KEYCODE( ) = REJECT_KEY THEN RETURN.  !RETURN ON SCREEN REJECT KEY
      EXECUTE ACTION                            !SET MESSAGE
        MEM:MESSAGE = 'Record will be Added'        !
        MEM:MESSAGE = 'Record will be Changed'  !
        MEM:MESSAGE = 'Press Enter to Delete'    !

      .
      IF KEYCODE( ) = ACCEPT_KEY          !ON SCREEN ACCEPT KEY
        UPDATE                            !  MOVE ALL FIELDS FROM SCREEN
        SELECT(?)                         !  START WITH CURRENT FIELD
        SELECT                            !  EDIT ALL FIELDS
        CYCLE                             !  GO TO TOP OF LOOP

      .
```

(continued)

Figure 10-7 *continued*

```
CASE FIELD( )                      !JUMP TO FIELD EDIT  ROUTINE
OF ?FIRST_FIELD                    !FROM THE FIRST FIELD
  IF KEYCODE( ) = ESC_KEY THEN RETURN.   ! RETURN ON ESC  KEY
  IF ACTION = 3 THEN SELECT(?DELETE_FIELD).!   OR CONFIRM FOR DELETE

OF ?LAST_FIELD                     !FROM THE LAST FIELD
  EXECUTE ACTION                   ! UPDATE THE FILE
    ADD(FORM)                      !     ADD NEW RECORD
    PUT(FORM)                      !     CHANGE EXISTING RECORD
    DELETE(FORM)                   !     DELETE EXISTING RECORD

  .
  IF ERRORCODE( ) = 40             !  DUPLICATE KEY ERROR
    MEM:MESSAGE = ERROR( )         !    DISPLAY ERR MESSAGE
    SELECT(2)                      !    POSITION TO TOP OF FORM
    CYCLE                          !    GET OUT OF EDIT LOOP
  ELSIF ERROR( )                   !  CHECK FOR UNEXPECTED ERROR
    STOP(ERROR( ))                 !    HALT EXECUTION
  .
  ACTION = 0                       !  SET ACTION TO COMPLETE
  RETURN                           !  AND RETURN TO CALLER

  OF ?DELETE_FIELD                 !FROM THE DELETE FIELD
    IF KEYCODE( ) = ENTER_KEY |    !  ON ENTER KEY
    OR KEYCODE( ) = ACCEPT_KEY     !  OR CTRL-ENTER KEY
      SELECT(?LAST_FIELD)          !    DELETE THE RECORD
    ELSE                           ! OTHERWISE
      BEEP                         !   BEEP AND ASK AGAIN
  . . .

CALCFIELDS   ROUTINE
  IF FIELD( ) > ?FIRST_FIELD       !BEYOND FIRST_FIELD?
    IF KEYCODE( ) = 0 AND SELECTED( ) > FIELD( ) THEN EXIT. !GET OUT IF NOT NON-
STOP
  .
  SCR:MESSAGE = MEM:MESSAGE
```

current editing ACTION that was set when the form was called is saved before launching the Hot Key Procedure and restored once that procedure is finished. Finally, the Original Field is reselected to be the current one. Don't try to reset the ACTION in the current Form Procedure within a Hot Key Procedure. As you can see, such a move would be wasted when the Hot Key Procedure returns.

Figure 10-8   The LAST_FIELD code from a Designer Form Procedure when the Next Procedure and SECONDARY File slots have items placed in them.

```
OF ?LAST_FIELD                          !FROM THE LAST FIELD
   EXECUTE ACTION                       !  UPDATE THE FILE
      ADD(FORM)                         !     ADD NEW RECORD
      PUT(FORM)                         !     CHANGE EXISTING RECORD
      DELETE(FORM)                      !     DELETE EXISTING RECORD
    .
   IF ERRORCODE( ) = 40                 !  DUPLICATE KEY ERROR
     MEM:MESSAGE = ERROR( )             !   DISPLAY ERR MESSAGE
     SELECT(2)                          !     POSITION TO TOP OF FORM
     CYCLE                              !     GET OUT OF EDIT LOOP
   ELSIF ERROR( )                       !  CHECK FOR UNEXPECTED ERROR
     STOP(ERROR( ))                     !     HALT EXECUTION
    .
```

The code for updating a SECONDARY File.

```
   PUT(SECOND)                          !   UPDATE SECONDARY FILES
```

```
   IF ACTION <> 3                       !IF THIS IS NOT A DELETE
     ACTION = 2                         !  SET ACTION TO CHANGE MODE
```

The code for calling a Next Procedure.

```
   NEXT_PROC                            !   CALL NEXT FORM PROCEDURE
```

```
   IF ACTION                           !   IF RECORD WAS NOT CHANGED
     SELECT(?LAST_FIELD - 1)           !     SELECT THE LAST ENTRY
     CYCLE                             !     AND LOOP AGAIN
 ..
 ACTION = 0                            !   SET ACTION TO COMPLETE
 RETURN                                !   AND RETURN TO CALLER
```

Figure 10-9   The code for a Hot Key Procedure in a Designer Form Procedure.

```
IF KEYCODE( ) = F10_KEY         !ON HOT KEY
   UPDATE(?)                     !  RETRIEVE FIELD
   SAVACTN# = ACTION             !  SAVE ACTION
   HOT_KEY                        !  CALL HOT KEY PROCEDURE
    ACTION = SAVACTN#            ! RESTORE ACTION
    SELECT(?)                    ! DO SAME FIELD AGAIN
    CYCLE                        !  AND LOOP AGAIN
   .
```

A Note About Procedure Color Selection in Designer: Once the Form Options menu is complete, you are asked to select the colors for the form background and the border tracks. Keep in mind that once you select a color for the background, you cannot change it. Actually, you can paint over it and make the screen look different, but the default color for the background will remain whatever you chose originally. On slower graphics monitors, a kind of rippling effect can take place as the underlying color paints first, followed by the color you used to paint over it. This is true for all of the Form Procedures you create in Designer. In fact, if you created a form and then decide to change its color, you could alter the Screen structure in Editor every time you regenerate the code. In the long run it's more efficient to redo the form.

Hint: The color you select for the background and foreground colors for a procedure determine the permanent default for that procedure's screen. You can change the color of the characters you type by pressing CTRL-V. One advantage of changing the character video mode over painting is that you can move the characters and their colors around the screen, whereas a painted area stays fixed in place and must be repainted to be removed.

Completing the Form Setup: After you select the colors and the frame style for the procedure, the Form Procedure setup asks if you want to populate the form. For short forms, this is very handy and reduces your form setup time. With one or two fields, you can almost allow Designer to populate the form and then simply save it with no further editing. However, for longer forms (that is, those with more fields), allowing Designer to populate the form will only create confusion. The "populating" tool places each field (from the file you referenced in the Form Options window as the primary data file) onto the screen as an Entry Field in order. You must delete the field and replace it if you want to change the field type.

Form Procedure Program Flow

Before we discuss the various field types in a Designer form, let's spend a few moments talking about the overall flow of the program code that Designer generates for a Form Procedure. The flow is diagrammed in Figure 10-10.

As with all Designer forms, the first step is to create the Screen structure and the Setup Procedures prior to the start of the Main Event Loop. The Main Event Loop first processes the ALERT keys, sets the edit message based on the ACTION variable set by the calling procedure, and calls the DO CALC_FIELDS subroutine for setting all the Calculated Fields. The Case structure processed in the Main Event Loop processes the Dummy Fields that act as placeholders at the beginning and end of the procedure's functionality.

The Screen Structure

The Screen structure in a Form Procedure contains the only references to the Entry Fields within the procedure unless you include code within the Edit Procedures for the fields themselves. When you do include code in that fashion, the Entry Field is referenced by its field equate label within the Case structure. We'll go into more detail on that later in this chapter.

The field equate labels used in the Case structure are tightly linked with the order of the fields in the Screen structure. The segment of code in Figure 10-11 represents the Entry Field section of the Screen structure for the form in Figure 10-5.

When you generate the Screen structure from Designer, the fields are placed inside the Screen structure in the order that you placed them on the screen, running from top left down to bottom right. That is the order the code assigns to the fields and that order determines the number you receive from the field equate label.

A field equate label does not contain the values of the variable—only the reference numbers for the field in the order in which they appear in the Screen structure. You create a field equate by taking the USE variable and placing a question mark in front of it. So, for the code in Figure 10-11, the field equate label for the variable FOR:FIRST would be ?FOR:FIRST and that construction would return the value of 2, that is, ?FOR:FIRST = 2. The values for the

Figure 10-10   The overall program flow for a Form Procedure in Designer.

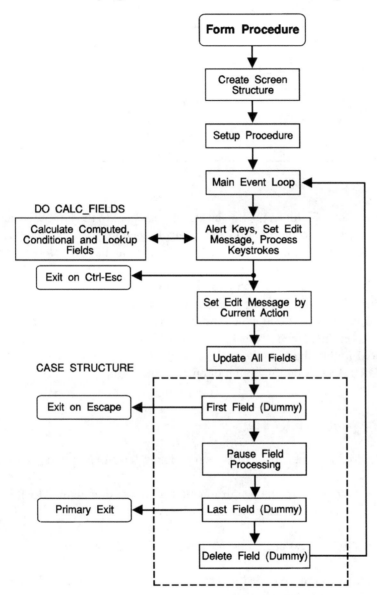

Figure 10-11   The Entry Field section of the Screen structure for the Form Procedure depicted in Figure 10-5.

```
1)                    ENTRY,USE(?FIRST_FIELD)
2)   ROW(4,15)  ENTRY(@s10),USE(FOR:FIRST),HUE(15,4),SEL(0,7)
3)   ROW(6,15)  ENTRY(@s20),USE(FOR:LAST),REQ,HUE(15,4),SEL(0,7)
4)   ROW(8,15)  ENTRY(@D1),USE(FOR:DATE),HUE(15,4),SEL(0,7)
5)                    ENTRY,USE(?LAST_FIELD)
6)                    PAUSE(''),USE(?DELETE_FIELD)
```

other Entry Fields in the Screen structure appear to the left of the actual code. If you were to put code in the Setup Procedure to start processing on the FOR:FIRST field, the SELECT statement would have to reference the second field in the Screen structure.

There are several strategies for controlling the flow of entry through a form. You can generate the Screen structure through Designer and then rearrange the order in which the fields process without disturbing their locations on the screen itself. For instance, if you shifted the FOR:LAST Entry Field line to the line above the FOR:FIRST line, the cursor would jump to FOR:LAST as the first point of entry in the form.

The Main Event Loop

The Main Event Loop in a Screen structure has three primary roles:

1. To prepare the environment for processing with ALERTs and the reading of user keystrokes with ACCEPT.
2. To update the USE variables from the fields on screen.
3. To process each field, including updating the file.

When you insert code into procedures for an Entry Field, a marker is set in the Case structure. The marker looks for the output of the FIELD function to select which field's functions to execute. The FIELD function returns the number of the field last processed or completed by ACCEPT.

The three "Dummy" Fields—FIRST_FIELD, LAST_FIELD, and DE-LETE_FIELD—are used to absorb the activity on the screen on the way into and out of the form. These fields do not accept the cursor unless you specifically select them (and that causes the cursor to go away), but they are placed into every Form Procedure within the Case structure. Each of these fields does not constitute a file variable, but merely the field equate number by which you can refer to their contents, which are valid only while the form is the current process.

Designer's construct for form processing with Dummy Fields include:

- FIRST_FIELD tests for an attempt to exit the procedure by backing out of it with the Escape key. Since this is the first potential process examined after the initial run of the CASE structure, the ACTION variable is tested to see the form was started in delete mode. If so, the processor immediately jumps to the processes underneath the DELETE_FIELD Dummy Field.
- LAST_FIELD is the next Logical Field after the last Entry Field on the form. As soon as this is the selected field (which occurs after the user accepts the last field visible on the screen), the file operations begin based on the setting of the ACTION variable by the procedure that called the form. It also tests to see if that file action resulted in a duplicate key error. After the completion of all the fields in the form, normal processing would perform the file action successfully, reset the ACTION variable to 0 to signal the Calling Procedure that everything went as planned, and then return control back to that Calling Procedure.
- DELETE_FIELD is the Dummy Field that is a stopping-off point in the process of deleting a record from the primary file. When the Calling Procedure has set the ACTION variable to 3 for deleting, a test is done in the FIRST_FIELD processing. The test directs a transfer of control to the DELETE_FIELD, which looks to see if the user performed the proper keystroke combination for deletion. In delete mode, you exit from this screen by pressing the Escape key, which is processed by the FIRST_FIELD code as well. Also, since both FIRST_FIELD and DE-LETE_FIELD are Dummy Fields, you don't see the cursor or highlight bar anywhere on the screen.

The Field Types

If you've read Chapters 8 and 9, you have seen all the field types except for the Pause Field, the one unique field type in a Form Procedure. However, as mentioned earlier, the *handling* of the field types you've seen in other proce-

Figure 10-12　The field type selection screen presented while creating a Form Procedure.

dures is different in a Form Procedure. We'll refer to Figure 10-12, the selection screen for field types, in the discussion of the various field types available in a Form Procedure.

Entry Types: Field and Pause:　Designer refers to only two kinds of fields as "Entry Fields." However, the distinction is not quite as clear as you might imagine. In fact, a Pause Field is much less like an Entry Field than a Lookup Field in terms of entering information into a data file.

The impact of selecting an Entry Field can be twofold. First, it places a line in the Screen structure, which, in itself, is enough to handle entry and edit of records in a file. The Entry Field and the ACCEPT processing of the user's keystrokes manage file maintenance. The ENTRY statement, as it appears in Figure 10-13, shows the picture for the screen variable and sets the file variable to be used to take the information from the screen variable when an UPDATE is issued.

A screen variable has no local definition because it is defined within the file structure in the global memory of the program. You can, for manually written procedures, put your own variable into that slot, but it must be defined either locally or in the global area. The only way around this is to use a field equate label to identify the variable. It works like an implicit variable that is only applicable to the current procedure and is not permanently stored anywhere.

Figure 10-13　An Entry Field in a Screen structure.

```
ROW(5,20)   ENTRY(@s10),USE(FOR:FIRST),HUE(15,4)
```

If you add code to the Setup Procedure or if you make this field into a Lookup Entry Field, then, between the FIRST_FIELD and LAST_FIELD processing, a field equate reference to the FOR:FIRST field gets inserted with the code to perform the lookup. The Entry Field in the Screen structure gets altered, depending on the type of lookup you requested.

The three choices for starting the lookup are by hot key, by Enter, and Automatic. When you get to the field setup with a hot key, you can press that key to go to the procedure you need to retrieve the data for the field. Otherwise, you can fill in the data as if it were a normal Entry Field. With Enter you can leave the field blank (unless you've tagged it as required) or you can type something in and press ENTER. If you have typed something, the code beneath the field equate (?FOR:FIRST) in the Case structure attempts to find a match for it in the referenced file. If a match can't be found, the code pops up the procedure, usually a table, for the user to make a selection.

Hint: Using the Enter key form of Entry Field Lookup is an excellent method for ensuring consistency in data entry without slowing down the user. If the user enters data correctly into the field the first time, no lookup is required.

For both the hot key and Enter selections, the field is completed by the key (the hot key gets added to the list of ALERTed keys), but with the Automatic selection, the Screen structure for the field is altered to make the Entry Field for the FOR:FIRST variable into a Dummy Field and replace the onscreen display with a screen variable that the CALC_FIELDS subroutine fills. The Dummy Field does not require a keystroke from the user to complete, so as soon as the program reaches that field according to the order of fields in the Screen structure, it completes automatically. The code beneath the field equate label then executes the lookup as shown in Figure 10-14.

Accompanying the insert of code in the Case structure for the lookup, the Entry Field is also changed in the Screen structure as depicted in Figure 10-15.

A Pause Field does not take input. It can be inserted into a Form Procedure to ask the user to complete it by pressing the Enter key before continuing on to other processing in the form. You can choose to display information, or simply to pause the screen at some point that will require the user to press a key before continuing on, as with DELETE_FIELD. You can also use it to give the user a chance to review a screen's worth of input after filling in the last field. That is the approach taken in Figure 10-16. Notice, however, that there are two angle brackets before the word "ENTER."

Figure 10-14   The field equate reference inserted into the program code for a Form Procedure that performs an Automatic lookup for a field.

```
OF ?FOR:FIRST
  SEC:STRINGS = FOR:FIRST                  !MOVE RELATED FIELDS
  GET(SECOND,SEC:BYSTRING)                 !READ THE RECORD
  ACTION# = ACTION                         !SAVE ACTION
  ACTION = 4                               !REQUEST TABLE LOOKUP
  TEST                                     !CALL LOOKUP PROCEDURE
  IF ACTION                                !NO SELECTION WAS MADE
    SELECT(?FOR:FIRST-1)                    ! BACK UP ONE FIELD
    ACTION = ACTION#                        ! RESTORE ACTION
    CYCLE                                   ! GO TO TOP OF LOOP
  .
  SCR:FIRST = SEC:STRINGS                  !DISPLAY LOOKUP FIELD
  FOR:FIRST = SEC:STRINGS                  !MOVE LOOKUP FIELD
  DISPLAY(?FOR:FIRST)                      !AND DISPLAY IT
  ACTION = ACTION#                         !RESTORE ACTION
```

 Hint: If you need to use a character that could confuse the Compiler into thinking you mean to speak to it, use two of the characters and the Compiler will know you mean simply to show the character. The angle bracket (as used in Figure 10-16) would normally cause the characters after it to be read as control codes. For instance, to send a character return/line feed sequence to the printer, you type <13,10>. This technique can also be used when you are concatenating strings and you want to show an apostrophe, as in the phrase:

```
FIL:VARIABLE = 'IT''S YOUR''S'
```

In a Designer-generated Form Procedure, the actual Pause Field is placed as the last field to complete no matter where you place it on the screen. The Standard Model provides for the PAUSE function only after all the EDITs have been listed in the Screen structure, as depicted in Figure 10-17.

The second Pause Field in the Screen structure model, which appears on the last line, is the delay used prior to completing a Delete Field. The Case structure, testing for the last field completed by the ACCEPT statement, processes the Pause Field in order to tell the FIELD( ) function which field equate to indicate.

Figure 10-15   This code replaces Figure 10-14 in the Screen structure when a field is designated as a Lookup Field that employs the Automatic keyboard interface.

```
            ROW(4,15)   ENTRY,USE(FOR:FIRST)
FIRST         COL(15)   STRING(@s10),HUE(15,4)
```

Display: Field, Computed, Conditional, and Lookup: The next set of fields you can add to a form can simply display data. They also can be used to extrapolate from other fields on screen or in a file to create a new piece of data for display or permanent storage. The simplest of these is the Field selection (refer to Figure 10-12). To use this field, the variable must already be in a file (either memory or a data file), and you have no control over the formatting of the display. Whichever picture or format you chose when you created the variable will be the formatted display. This is ideal for placing variables from the file you wish to display but which you do not want the user to edit, such as an Autonumbered Field or some other reference—like a key. This variable must either be in memory already or accessible as part of the primary file for this Form Procedure given in the Form Options window (depicted in Figure 10-2). As with other purely displayed information in a form, the screen variable for a display-only field is filled in by the variable it references in the CALC_FIELDS subroutine.

A Computed Field as appears in Figure 10-18 can be used to create information on the fly, based on values brought into memory via other means, including a home-grown lookup function using the lines of code (shown in Figure 10-19), typed as a single line in the expression and separated by semicolons.

The same principles we discussed in Chapter 9 on Computed, Conditional, and Lookup Fields can be applied to Form Procedures. In this case, however, the results must be only one value for display. Once the value is displayed

Figure 10-16   The Pause Field creation screen.

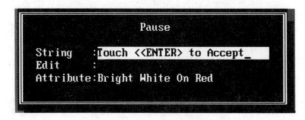

Figure 10-17   The code from the Standard Model and the generated code for a Pause Field.

```
@PROCNAME      PROCEDURE

SCREEN         SCREEN        PRE(SCR),@SCREENOPT
                             @PAINTS
                             @STRINGS
                             @VARIABLES
                             ENTRY,USE(?FIRST_FIELD)
                             @FIELDS
```

The insertion point for the Pause Field in the Standard Model.

```
                             @PAUSE
```

```
                             ENTRY,USE(?LAST_FIELD)
                             PAUSE(''),USE(?DELETE_FIELD)
                                         .
                                         .
                                         .
```

The resulting Screen structure code as generated.

```
   ROW(10,14) PAUSE('Press <<ENTER> to Accept'),USE(?PAUSE_FIELD)
                                         .
                                         .
                                         .
```

The Pause Field processing code in the Case structure.

```
OF ?PAUSE_FIELD                           !ON PAUSE FIELD
   IF KEYCODE( ) <> ENTER_KEY|            !IF NOT ENTER KEY
   AND KEYCODE( ) <> ACCEPT_KEY|          !AND NOT CTRL-ENTER KEY
   AND KEYCODE( ) <> 0                    !AND NOT NONSTOP MODE
     BEEP                                 !  SOUND KEYBOARD ALARM
     SELECT(?PAUSE_FIELD)                 !  AND STAY ON PAUSE FIELD
   .
```

Figure 10-18   A Computed Field used to display a count of the records in a file, as in the DISK CATALOG program. The "Number" is the display of an Autonumbered Field.

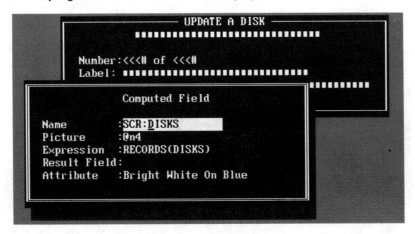

after being retrieved from a file with a lookup, or as the result of a calculation in a Computed Field, or as the result of a decision as in a Conditional Field, you can manipulate that value elsewhere in the form by calling the SCR version of the variable (that is, the one on display). In the case of a Lookup Field, the values from the record currently in memory can be used to retrieve information from another file. An example is shown in Figure 10-20.

Formatting Entry and Entry Validation: The Edit Procedure for a standard Entry Field can be used to format entry and to do entry validation. If you wanted be able to leave a field blank in some screens, but require entry in others, you can't set that variable up in Designer's file definition area as a required field, that is, with the REQ attribute in the Screen structure for that Entry Field. Instead, include the following code in the Edit Procedure:

```
IF FIL:VARIABLE = '' THEN SELECT(?).
```

Figure 10-19   Finding a record in another file using the expression of a Computed Field.

```
FIL:VAR1 = FIL:VAR2
SET(FIL:BY_VAR1,FIL:BY_VAR1)
NEXT(FILE)
(perform a calculation)
SCR:COMPUTED_FIELD = FIL:VAR1_FIELD
```

Figure 10-20   A Lookup Field that takes the current value for the FIL:NUMBER variable from the FILES data file and retrieves the disk label from the DISKS file in the CATALOG Program.

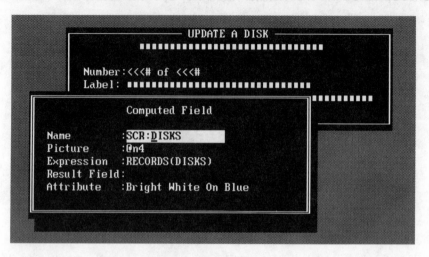

General Form Processing Information

The Variables

When you process data entry with a Form Procedure, it is important to understand where the information resides as your application takes in data from the user. One of the more common errors made by those new to Clarion is to misunderstand the relationship between the data displayed on the screen and data staged for access to a data file. The contents of a variable may not be what you see on the screen. It is also important that you understand how a Designer Form Procedure supervises the movement of variables between the screen and the file.

The three statements most concerned with this activity are ACCEPT, UPDATE, and DISPLAY. Of these three, ACCEPT is the most complex because it performs two functions, whereas the other two perform only one action.

- ACCEPT—Activates the selected Entry Field; and updates the USE variable on user completion of the field just activated.
- UPDATE—Places the Screen Field(s) contents into the USE variable(s).
- DISPLAY—Formats the USE variable(s) to display in the Screen Field(s).

Figure 10-21 To process an Entry Field in a Form Procedure, there are three paths to moving information to the file.

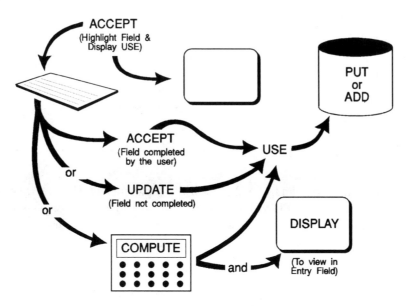

The UPDATE function is the reverse of the DISPLAY function. If the user completes each field as it is selected, nothing else is needed but the ACCEPT statement. However, it is possible to change a USE variable through a Computed Field or access to another procedure and the screen will not display what will actually be written to the file. Likewise, it is possible to change or add to the contents of an Entry Field and not alter the USE variable. Unless the user completes the field, the Main Event Loop that repeats the ACCEPT statement with each revolution does not update that USE variable—that is what the UPDATE statement is for. The ways in which ACCEPT, UPDATE, and DISPLAY function are summarized in Figure 10-21.

The important thing to remember, in terms of updating the file on the disk, is that whatever the contents of the USE variable turns out to be for each field in the record, that is what will be saved when the record is PUT or ADDed to the file.

Clarion provides several other functions important in the process of the variable management in Form Procedures. SELECT(?field) can be used to move the cursor from field to field around the entry form. Each time a SELECT(?field) is issued, the ACCEPT statement (in the next turn through the Main Event Loop) activates the new field. To complete all the fields at the

Figure 10-22   The code Designer inserts into a Form Procedure to save what is on the screen and exit the procedure.

```
IF KEYCODE( ) = ACCEPT_KEY          !ON SCREEN ACCEPT KEY
   UPDATE                           ! MOVE ALL FIELDS FROM SCREEN
   SELECT(?)                        !  START WITH CURRENT FIELD
   SELECT                           !  EDIT ALL FIELDS
   CYCLE                            !  GO TO TOP OF LOOP
   .
```

same time, you can use SELECT without parameters. However, be sure you have issued the UPDATE command to ensure that any changes you made to a field on the screen were transferred to the corresponding USE variable. You'll notice that Designer provides a way to exit the screen on completion of an EQUATEd keystroke called ACCEPT_KEY. The code for this appears in Figure 10-22.

From the code in Figure 10-22, you can see that the first step is to test for the ACCEPT_KEY combination that completed the Current Field as reported by the ACCEPT statement. Then the contents of all the fields on the screen are transferred to the corresponding USE variables by the UPDATE statement. The Current Field is reselected with the first form of SELECT, and then all the fields (including the Dummy Fields) are completed with the second form of the SELECT statement. The last step is to send the process back to the top of the Main Event Loop where the system exits. The Case structure stops the process on LAST_FIELD since that was completed by SELECT.

If you have questions about which field is current, you can at least find out which was the last field that ACCEPT processed by using the SELECTED( ) function. This function reports the field equate number for the last field completed by the SELECT function. It does not tell you when you completed a field by any other means than ACCEPT, however.

There are three functions—DISPLAY, UPDATE, and ERASE—that you can use to perform actions against particular sets of the fields on the screen. DISPLAY allows you to move the contents of the USE variable to a particular range of fields on the current screen (and it must be a contiguous range). UPDATE allows you to go in exactly the opposite direction over a chosen range. ERASE lets you set the field contents to empty and wipe out the USE variables all at once—just as if you'd cleared out each field with the cursor and then issued an UPDATE—or, conversely, if you'd set all the USE variables within a range to blank and then issued a DISPLAY.

The Minimum Form Model

Many times while working in Designer you'll want some method for popping up a short form to take a simple input for directing a printer or reset a memory variable. The existing Standard Model code for Designer was built to handle a great many more circumstances, and so, for this use, it will be a fat piece of code. However, with a few simple changes to the model, you can create a Form Procedure for this purpose that is much more efficient.

Hint: Remember, before making any changes to your standard or network models, make a copy of the existing model file. Also, never modify the existing procedure directly. Copy that portion of the model to the bottom of the file and make your changes there.

The default model to modify for this step is called FORM, and you can find it by loading the Standard Model file into Clarion's Editor and pressing the CTRL-S key combination to bring up the search window. Then enter 'PAUSE' as the search string—remember, that is a construct unique to the Form Procedure. Now, copy everything down to the end of the CALC_FIELDS subroutine and paste it into the model at the bottom of the file. The minimum form you need looks like the code in Figure 10-23.

The model code for the SHORTFORM Form Procedure can be fairly dangerous if you don't keep good notes in your model file about what a modified procedure like this will do. Many Clarion programmers create some sort of satellite documentation for every modification to the model they make—very much like the text file MODEL.DOC that Clarion ships along with the Professional Developer. For instance, SHORTFORM will not process hot keys, nor will it allow for Computed Fields (of any kind).

Most of the changes made to the Standard Model file for this modified Form Procedure involve deletions from the existing code. However, in one instance, to use this procedure to call reports, you must make one keyword change. The @NEXTFORM model code appears in Figure 10-24.

The @NEXTFORM keyword processes the Next Procedure entry you can make to the Form Options window. And that mini-procedure, in turn, calls the @NEXTPAGE keyword, which is what causes the actual procedure name you provided in the Next Procedure to be listed in the Designer-generated code. @NEXTPAGE is not explicitly listed in the model code because it is a protected keyword. Clarion does not yet allow access to those types of words. However, by changing @NEXTFORM to @NEXTPAGE, you can eliminate the extra code that @NEXTFORM surrounded the Next Procedure with. That code was designed to respond to another Entry Form Procedure and not a

Figure 10-23 The minimum Form Procedure for creating an Entry Field for procedure pre-processing or report destination redirection.

```
*SHORTFORM*************************************************************
@PROCNAME     PROCEDURE

SCREEN        SCREEN     PRE(SCR),@SCREENOPT
                         @PAINTS
                         @STRINGS
                         @FIELDS
                         @PAUSE
                         ENTRY,USE(?LAST_FIELD)

  EJECT
  CODE
  OPEN(SCREEN)                           !OPEN THE SCREEN
  SETCURSOR                              !TURN OFF ANY CURSOR
  DISPLAY                                !DISPLAY THE FIELDS
  LOOP                                   !LOOP THRU ALL THE FIELDS
    MEM:MESSAGE = CENTER(MEM:MESSAGE,SIZE(MEM:MESSAGE)) !DISPLAY ACTION MESSAGE
    ALERT                                !RESET ALERTED KEYS
    ALERT(REJECT_KEY)                    !ALERT SCREEN REJECT KEY
    ACCEPT                               !READ A FIELD
    IF KEYCODE( ) = REJECT_KEY THEN RETURN. !RETURN ON SCREEN REJECT KEY
    CASE FIELD( )                        !JUMP TO FIELD EDIT ROUTINE
    @EDITS
    OF ?LAST_FIELD                       !FROM THE LAST FIELD
    @NEXTPAGE                            !  CALL NEXT FORM PROCEDURE
    ACTION = 0                           !  SET ACTION TO COMPLETE
    RETURN                               !  AND RETURN TO CALLER
  . .
```

Figure 10-24 The @NEXTFORM model code from the Standard Model.

```
*NEXTFORM*************************************************************
  IF ACTION <> 3                         !IF THIS IS NOT A DELETE
    ACTION = 2                           !  SET ACTION TO CHANGE MODE
    @NEXTPAGE                            !  CALL NEXT FORM PROCEDURE
    IF ACTION                            !  IF RECORD WAS NOT CHANGED
      SELECT(?LAST_FIELD - 1)            !    SELECT THE LAST ENTRY
      CYCLE                              !    AND LOOP AGAIN
  ..
```

report. @NEXTFORM expects the ACTION variable to be changed by the called procedures. Since a report is not an Editing Procedure and therefore does not affect the ACTION variable, leaving the @NEXTFORM keyword in SHORTFORM would not allow this procedure to be retired back to its Calling Procedure. So, by changing the keyword to @NEXTPAGE, the report is run, the ACTION variable is set to 0, and the SHORTFORM procedure completes itself and retires.

Summary

Every software application needs some way to enter and store information so it can be retrieved and processed later. Clarion's data entry approach is called the Form Procedure. In Designer, the form has a specific set of procedural code to operate the keyboard interface and the variable handling for storing and retrieving information. Since the concept of the form is so tightly wrapped with data-handling techniques, this chapter illustrated many of the methods available for adding, editing, and deleting data. We discussed the Form Procedure created by Designer, as well as the other methods you can use, including a manually coded form.

Chapter 11

Report Techniques

Reporting Alternatives

There are actually four means by which you can create reports from Clarion data files:

1. Use Designer to knit the data file and Report Structure together.
2. Create the Report Structure in Editor and then write your own code to access it.
3. Use the Report Writer.
4. Export the data to a text file for translation to some other utility for importing, formatting, and output.

Both the Editor-based and Designer-based reports are hard-coded into the application. If the user does not like them or wants to make a change, the only response can be to recode them or to move that particular report into one of the other two reporting types. Between the two, Editor and Designer, the manually-coded version from Editor may prohibit sweeping changes the most. However, reports created inside the application require the least amount of user participation and can support the highest amount of data file and report structure manipulation.

The flexibility of Report Writer makes it a very useful tool for extending the life of an application, up to the point when the user needs a report that requires modifying the application. However, that requires training the user and causes a loss of control over the files that you'll need to re-create the report later. That is, with hard-coded reports, the information required to re-create the report is locked inside the application. With Report Writer it is possible for the user to lose either the database file or the report file created to produce the report in Report Writer. Without those files, you may find it difficult to re-create a report that the user constructed. However, this problem is nothing more complicated than the issue faced by users of most word processors. Just be careful that the user has not assumed that, since the application was launched from inside Clarion, backing up the .DAT files is sufficient protection for the system.

If you use an archiving method that saves only data files, be sure that the files with the .DEF file extensions get archived and stored in your back-ups. These are the files that Report Writer uses to construct reports. You'll find at least one for the actual report definition (more if you have more reports defined) and a minimum of one for the database definition.

 Hint: A "database" is not simply a data file. In a Clarion application, all of the data files together create the database. In Report Writer, the database can be fields pulled from one data file or fields collected together from a number of data files.

A user may need a custom presentation kit, or graphing tool, or some reporting method deriving information from the Clarion application. In such cases, you can set up an export of the data that will create an ASCII file in several formats for users to import into their graphics or spreadsheet package. If you care to take the time, the following Clarion *Technical Bulletins* will tell you everything you need to know about reading the file formats of the native Clarion files to access them directly: 117, Clarion Data Files; 118, Clarion Index and Key Files; and 121, Clarion Memos.

The Designer Way

As with most of Clarion, Designer provides a method for creating reports within the .APP, or application, file. This method provides the most complex reporting within a speed and flexibility factor. You can rearrange the face of a Designer report in a just a few minutes, performing relational lookups and computations very quickly. The down side is the labyrinthine procedure that results from the code generated by Designer. However, once you create a standard report, it is easy to use the Get facility (CTRL-G key combination) to grab a report from another application.

Report Setup

As with all Designer procedures, the first screen you see is the Options window, as pictured in Figure 11-1. This window looks very much like the one for a Table Procedure. Notice the availability of the Record Selector and Record Filter Procedure lines. The most outstanding and unique differences, however, involve the slots to specify the number of lines per page (Page Length) and the use of the Report Device.

The Report Options window can be placed on the screen in three ways:

1. By selecting a report to create in the Applications Tree.
2. By pressing CTRL-O while on a Report Procedure in the Applications Tree.
3. By pressing the same key combination while inside the Report worksheet.

Figure 11-1   The Report Options window.

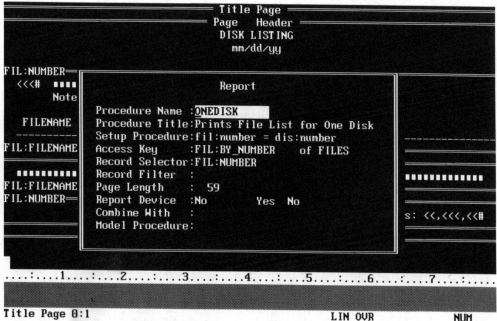

As we discussed in Chapter 9, the Setup Procedure can be used in conjunction with the Record Selector and Filter to control the contents of the report. This function can even be manipulated on the fly.

When you have completed the report setup, Designer asks if you want to populate the report automatically. If you answer yes to this question, all the fields in the file you indicated when you selected the Access Key are inserted into the Body Detail section of the report in order from left to right on the first line. Their associated filenames appear on the first line of the Page Header section of the Report worksheet. However, this can be quite inconvenient when the file record has many fields and you are trying to rearrange them into a sensible report format. If you plan to allow this report to print in portrait mode on 8.5" x 11" paper, the field lengths cannot exceed 80 characters (allowing for a space in between each field), presuming you make no changes to the font or the character spacing and use regular ASCII characters. Also, if you fill the report automatically and the fields extend beyond the 80 characters of one screen, the centering functions will use the established width to accommodate the fields that would fit. You cannot restore the original width in order to center headings at the top of the page within 80 characters, for instance, with the ALT-6 keystroke combination that you use to center text and fields on Report and Screen worksheets.

Changing the Contents of a Designer Report with a Form: To take control of the data that prints in Designer, you can choose several methods. One of the most convenient means is to use the modified Form Procedure from Chapter 10 shown in Figure 10-13. In that instance, you can call a Form Procedure that uses that modified procedure from a menu or a hot key and then place the Report Procedure in the Next Procedure slot of the Form Options window. From inside the form, you can set the variable for sifting the contents of the report by putting an Entry Field into the form that requests user input. Whatever the user types into that field can then be used in the Setup Procedure of the Report Procedure to set the filter (or record selector) of the file accessed in the report. The process is diagrammed in Figure 11-2.

Changing the Contents of a Report with a Table: Still another method involves the use of a modified Table Procedure as in the CATALOG Program. It is not necessary to make all of the changes to the Table Procedure we are about to recommend, but it will be less confusing if you remove the responses to some keystrokes. First, we'll remove the record-creating logic from this version of the Table Procedure. In the standard model, at the ?OF POINT condition in the Case structure (which tests for which field is completed), all the code that follows up to the next OF condition executes only

Figure 11-2 The process for changing the contents of a report based on a selector variable by calling the report from a Form Procedure.

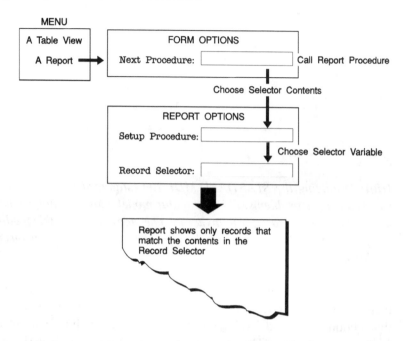

when the table is started with no records in the file. It then calls the Update form to enter the first record. You can allow the user to add records normally if you like, but this obscures the use of the specialized Table Procedure, that is, selecting a master record to print a report of the related records in another file. The modification (appearing in Figure 11-3) merely sounds a tone and returns to the menu that called it.

The next change we'll make to the model procedure removes any unnecessary responses to keystrokes irrelevant to the process of selecting a value to use to filter or select from the candidate data file. The change is to remove the OF INS_KEY and the OF DEL_KEY conditions from the Case structure. Removing these two sections of code eliminates any function of the Insert key or the Delete key when this Table Procedure is active. The next step is to set up the response of the ENTER_KEY to be consistent with its use elsewhere in Clarion. In most Designer applications, the Enter key is used to select a record from a table to edit. In this modified table, we'll set up the Enter key to select the record with the value to filter or select from the secondary file involved in the Report Structure.

Figure 11-3   The modified OF ?POINT condition in the Case structure of the Table Procedure that processes when no records exist in the file.

```
IF RECORDS(TABLE) = 0                !IF THERE ARE NO RECORDS
   BEEP(400,50)                      !SOUND ALARM
   RETURN                            !GO BACK TO CALLING PROCEDURE
 .                                   !END OF THE LOOP
@LOCATE                              !PERFORM LOCATOR LOGIC
```

 Hint: *Modifying the STANDARD.MDL file (standard model) for Designer work can cause problems. This particular model change is not extensive and may prove unnecessary for many users. The steps shown in this modification are presented to illustrate the workings of the model and the various types of modification you could make.*

Instead of processing the record for editing, we still grab the record into memory using the GET statement, but things change from there. Normally this section of the model Table Procedure checks to see if the current action is to look up something. That is, it checks the global ACTION variable. If that variable is set to 4 in this Table Procedure by the previous procedure, then it is in lookup mode. The previous procedure might have required the lookup to get a value to place in an Entry Field. Since we know that is not the case for this application of the model, the lookup verification can be removed. Further, there is no need to set the ACTION variable while processing a report (and it could conceivably cause a problem depending on how you use this custom Table Procedure). As the resulting ENTER_KEY processing indicates in Figure 11-4, the Update Procedure for the modified table can be used to enter the name of the report to be called.

In this modified Enter key processing, as soon as the ACCEPT statement in the top of the Main Event Loop processes a KEYSTROKE( ), the GET_REC-ORD subroutine is processed. Recall from the discussion in Chapter 9 that subroutine uses the present index position in the memory table to find the record in the file on disk and read it into memory. In case there is an error, the program jumps over the Update Procedure call and locates the record in the file where the pointer is set—regardless of the memory table positioning.

The logic goes something like this: If there is an error in the GET, set the local variable NEWPTR equal to the present pointer position in the file and run the FIND_RECORD subroutine. (The FIND_RECORD subroutine was

Figure 11-4 The modified Enter key processing for using the Update Procedure in the Table Options window to call a report instead of a form (when the modified model containing this procedure is used.)

```
OF ENTER_KEY    |                    !ENTER KEY
OROF ACCEPT_KEY                      !CTRL-ENTER KEY
   DO GET_RECORD                     !  GET THE SELECTED RECORD
   IF ~ERROR( )                      !  IF RECORD IS STILL THERE
      @TOTCHECK                      !     SAVE TOTALS
      @UPDATE                        !     CALL FORM TO CHANGE REC
      @TOTMINUS                      !     SUBTRACT CURRENT AMOUNTS
      .
   NEWPTR = POINTER(@FILENAME)       !     SET POINTER TO NEW RECORD
   DO FIND_RECORD                    !     POSITION IN FILE
```

explained in detail in Chapter 9.) However, if the GET was successful, the current totals displayed in the table are saved for redisplay and the Update Procedure is called. In our adaptation of the Table Procedure, this can now be the name of the Report Procedure.

The report is run and, when it returns control to the table, the process of repositioning in the table with the FIND_RECORD subroutine takes place just as if there had been an ERROR( ) in the earlier GET statement processing. The Table Procedure then recycles and the user can select yet another value with which to print the report.

Report Field Types

The types of fields available in a Report Procedure closely match those for a Table Procedure. The Control Field and the lack of "scrolling" fields clearly distinguish the Report Procedure setup in Designer from that of a Table Procedure. You shouldn't have any trouble remembering which worksheet is which since, as you can see from Figure 11-5, the Report worksheet clearly differs from the worksheets of the other procedures.

The Display Field: Each of the Report Field types shown in Figure 11-6, except for the Conditional Field, are used in the Report Procedure worksheet. The Display Field works just like a Scrolling Display Field in a Table Procedure. You simply select one of the fields from the data files defined for

Figure 11-5   The Report Procedure worksheet for the disk listing report in the FLOPPY DISK CATALOG program. (The complete listing for the Report Procedure generated by this worksheet appears at the end of this chapter.)

```
════════════════════════════════ Title Page ════════════════
──────────────────────────────── Page   Header ─────────────
                             DISK LISTING
                               mm/dd/yy

FIL:NUMBER═══════════════════════ Group  Header ═════════════
  <<<# ■■■■■■■■■■■■■■■■■■■■■■■■■■■■■■■
       Notes: ■■■■■■■■■■■■■■■■■■■■■■■■■■■■■■■■■■■■■■■

   FILENAME          SIZE       DATE       TIME      NOTES
  ───────────      ──────────  ─────────  ───────   ──────────
FIL:FILENAME═════════════════════ Group  Header ════════════
                                ══════════ Body ═════════════
  ■■■■■■■■■■■■■   <,<<<,<<#   mm/dd/yy   hh:mmXM   ■■■■■■■■■■■■■■■■■■■■■■■■■■■■■
FIL:FILENAME═════════════════════ Group  Footer ════════════
FIL:NUMBER═══════════════════════ Group  Footer ════════════
                                           Total Bytes: <<,<<<,<<#
──────────────────────────────── Grand  Totals ─────────────
──────────────────────────────── Page   Footer ─────────────

                               PAGE <<#
...:....1....:....2....:....3....:....4....:....5....:....6....:....7....:.....
```

Title Page 0:1   LIN OVR   NUM

the application and it appears in the report. If you include it in the Body Detail structure, it prints its contents repeatedly for each time the record is changed and the PRINT statement is used to print that structure. You cannot change the original picture of the field as defined for the data file—for that you need the Computed Field.

The only Display Field that merits much comment is the Memo Field. As with a table, when you select the Memo Field to place into your reports, the Report worksheet only displays the first line of the memo, taking up space just as wide as the number of columns you specified in the data dictionary when you defined it. This causes the Memo Field to be printed for as many lines as are stored in the memo. No page break occurs.

The Computed Field: The Computed Field, again, functions just like a Computed Field in a Table Procedure. You can insert a field for display, but you can change the picture used to display, clip several fields together to shorten the display area, or perform other calculations. You can use the Computed Field to display the date at the top of a report or to enforce an

Figure 11-6 The possible selections for field types in a Designer Report Procedure.

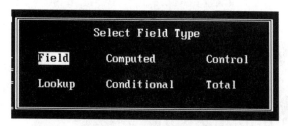

artificial line count on the items you select to print. (The LINE variable included in the default memory variables for a Designer application counts every single line on the page. Therefore, in the case of special line spacing and page headings, you cannot use the unmodified standard report to count the number of items printed on a page.)

The Lookup Field: The Lookup Field in a Designer Report Procedure relates records in the primary file to those in files not related to the report in any other way. In the case of printing an invoice, you would set the line items file as the primary access file (meaning you would specify a key from that file in the Report Options window) and then get the company name and address from a related file. In the case of the FLOPPY DISK CATALOG program, the description for the label of the disk is pulled from the related file for the list of files on that disk by means of the disk number common to both files, as shown in Figure 11-7.

The Total Field: The Total Field works just like the Fixed Display Total Field in a Table Procedure, except that you can total several different groups of items in a Report Procedure. If you wish to create subtotals, place the Total Field in the Group Footer structure for a variable used to separate the groups. In the sample Report Procedure of Figure 11-5, the variable for breaking up the groups is shown as the disk number. In addition, you can insert a count of line items within an invoice or, as in this case, the number of files in a floppy disk. By combining both the total figure and the count, you can arrive at an average for each group or for the entire report.

If you want to total the items from another file without listing each item, use the Computed Field to perform your own "lookup" with the following instruction in the Expression Field: 0;NEW:VAR = OLD:VAR;SET(NEW:BY_VAR,NEW:BY_VAR); LOOP UNTIL EOF(NEWFILE);NEXT(NEWFILE);TOTAL# += NEW:NUMBER.; RPT:TOTAL = TOTAL#.

**Figure 11-7   The Lookup Field used to print the description of a disk in the Report Proce-
dure for the disk listing in the CATALOG program. The description appears next to the disk
number (pictured as <<<#) in the Group Header structure of the report.**

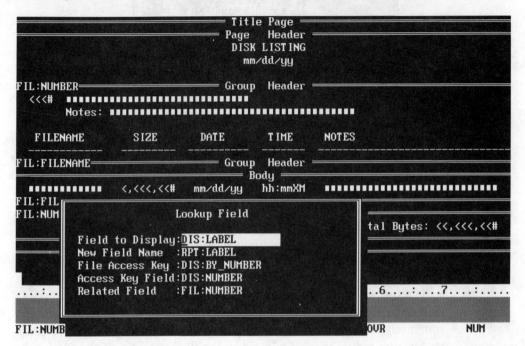

*Hint: The "O;" appearing at the beginning of this Expression satisfies the
requirements of the equation that Designer will build for the Report Field:
RPT:TOTAL. The line in the Designer-generated code will be: RPT:FIELD =
0. . .and then the rest of the Expression will follow. Without "O;" the equation
would be constructed incorrectly as RPT:TOTAL = NEW:VAR = OLD:VAR.*

Of course there are many variations on this code for performing other
activities. You must understand where in the generated code the Expression
falls before you can stretch the function to do too much.

The Control Field: The one field in a Designer Report that is unique to the
Report worksheet is the Control Field. This field, as pictured in Figure 11-8,
is to be used exclusively to talk to the printer with characters meant to control
the printer, not print on the page.

Five important concepts surround the Control Field: different printers, the
CTL attribute, the CONTROL statement, printer tokens, and printer escape

Figure 11-8   The Control Field from the Report worksheet.

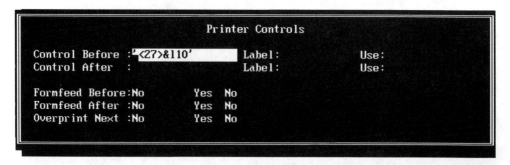

sequences. The first concept has little to do with Clarion and much to do with the printers your application will use. Each printer receives commands a little differently, depending on the manufacturer and the type of printer. There are (at least) two standards for general application of text control: those based on an Epson printer, and those that use the Hewlett-Packard Graphics Language, or HPGL. The examples discussed in this chapter apply to an HP LaserJet Series II.

The CONTROL statement and the CTL attribute work inside of the Screen structure. The CONTROL statement allows you to change the contents of a variable for controlling the printer, and the CTL attribute performs that function with a fixed value. The example in Figure 11-8 shows the escape sequence (so named because the first character is ESCAPE, or ASCII 027) for turning the text sideways to print in landscape mode. If you generate the report with the Control Field set up that way, the resulting code for the Screen structure will appear as shown in Figure 11-9.

There are two ways to enter this information into the Control Field for the escape sequence instruction for the printer. The HP LaserJet documentation gives the escape codes for many of the capabilities of the LaserJet printer. Most printer manufacturers publish a manual with similar instructions for their printers. The Landscape orientation can be represented in two ways. It can be shown as a string like this:

```
'<027,038,108,049,079>'
```

where the sequence to turn it off varies only in the second-to-the-last set of numbers as:

```
'<027,038,108,048,079>'
```

Figure 11-9   The Disk Listing report from the FLOPPY DISK CATALOG program showing the use of the CTL attribute for setting the printer.

```
RPT_NUMBER     PROCEDURE

TITLE       REPORT      LENGTH(59),WIDTH(80),PRE(TTL)
RPT_HEAD                DETAIL
            .             .
REPORT      REPORT      LENGTH(59),WIDTH(80),PAGE(MEM:PAGE),LINE(MEM:LINE)
                        PRE(RPT)
PAGE_HEAD              HEADER
```

The control sequence in CTL gets sent to the printer here with each page header printed:

```
            COL(1)     CTL('<27>&l10') STRING(' {30}Print Disks By Number')


            ROW(+2,1)   STRING('NUMBER LABEL {26}NOTES') CTL(@LF2)
                           .
DETAIL                 DETAIL
            COL(1)      STRING(@N_4),USE(DIS:NUMBER)
            COL(8)      STRING(30),USE(DIS:LABEL)
            COL(39)     STRING(40),USE(DIS:NOTES) CTL(@LF)
                           .
RPT_FOOT               DETAIL
                           .
PAGE_FOOT             FOOTER
            ROW(+1,37)  STRING('PAGE')
            COL(42)     STRING(@n3),USE(MEM:PAGE)
```

This sequence cancels the first one sent after each page is printed to ensure that the printer is left in the state your report found it.

```
            COL(45)     CTL('<27>&l00') CTL(@LF)

                        CTL(@FF)
      .             .
```

When you type this sequence into the Control Before or Control After Field and press the Enter key, Designer converts the sequence to the real escape sequence. Thus the sequence to turn on landscape mode would appear as it does in Figure 11-9.

If you choose to type it in that way, the system places the sequence into the CTL attribute as shown in Figure 11-9. The sequence, then, talks directly with the printer and does not print on the page. If it *does* print on the page, the printer accepted the sequence as characters and part of the report and will not respond to your intended command.

Hint: The escape sequence for underlining characters in a report on a LaserJet is '<027,038,100,068>' and will appear as "<27>&dD' and the sequence to turn it off will be '<027,038,100,064>' and appears as '<27>&d@'. Refer to the LaserJet manual for other control sequences you can use to customize your Clarion reports.

The CONTROL statement appears in the structure when you choose to use the label and the USE variable. To make this work, you must use a variable that already exists in either a memory file or disk file in your data dictionary. In that case, the Control Before and Control After Fields contain the picture for the variable as it is defined in the file. In Figure 11-10, the SINGLE DISK FILE LISTING program, the MESSAGE variable was used from the memory file. Generally speaking, you would want to create a separate variable to handle the control sequence job, and you will probably want to create a configuration file with a single record to hold this information. If you perform a GET on that first record, the necessary information would be in memory to set this sequence.

Now, you can place code into your application that sets the MEM:MESSAGE variable to a different escape sequence. In this way you can write a module of your program (as appears in the CATALOG Program) for setting the printer control with a utility function. The variable local to the Report Procedure is UNDERLINE and it must be set in the program. If you need a method to test various sequences before you incorporate them into a full

Figure 11-10   The page header from the File Listing report in the FLOPPY DISK CATALOG program using a variable and the CONTROL statement to send a control code sequence to the printer.

```
PAGE_HEAD               HEADER
UNDERLINE     COL(1)    CONTROL(30),USE(MEM:MESSAGE)
                        STRING(' {35}DISK LISTING')
DATE          ROW(+1,38) STRING(@D1) CTL(@LF2)
                        .
```

Figure 11-11   This code, placed into the Setup Procedure of a Report Procedure would display an Entry Field in the upper left-hand corner of the screen to get a value for sending a sequence to the printer.

```
SHOW(1,1,'ENTER CONTROL CODE: ')        !DISPLAY INSTRUCTION
ASK(1,21,MEM:MESSAGE,@S10)              !REQUEST INPUT
UNDERLINE = CLIP(MEM:MESSAGE)           !SET THE CONTROL VARIABLE
```

program, you can use the ASK statement to get input in real time when the report runs.

For instance, if you set up the report page header as shown in Figure 11-9, you could place the code into the Setup Procedure of the report as shown in Figure 11-11.

To enter an escape sequence into a string in this fashion, however, you cannot enter it as you did while in Designer. The intelligence for converting the string is contained in Designer. The *Clarion Utilities Manual* refers briefly to this function in the section on Designer. You must enter the escape sequence, complete with the non-ASCII version of the escape character itself, (←), along with the rest of the characters in the escape sequence as they would normally be converted by Designer.

The remaining choices in the Control Field selection window involve passing additional parameters to the Screen structure using the CTL attribute. In the case of formfeeds, the CTL Field contains the printer token for a formfeed (@FF). You could also pass the other printer tokens (@LF for line feed and @CR for carriage return) as well as the formfeed with the CONTROL statement variable. The last selection, Overprint Next, is a construction you could use with a report that was to fill in a form so that the order of the fields printed on the form was out of sequence with the way they could be called from the files or calculated. Using Overprint Next, you can print something on the right-hand side of the page and, instead of continuing naturally onto the next line, you could select "Yes" for this choice so that the print head would return to the left side of the page to print on the same line.

The Conditional Field: The Conditional Field, again, works like the Scrolling Conditional Field in the Table Procedure. You can choose to print different items depending on the state of another variable. If, for instance, a printer configuration value resided in memory that instructed the printer to turn landscape on or off, you could use the Conditional Field to make that decision.

The Flow

A Designer report is a complex piece of code because it must allow for the many variations you might create in the Report worksheet. The flowchart in Figure 11-12 shows the logic used to print a report according to the Designer Standard Model.

The first step constructs the report structure sections, which will be tapped later on in the procedure. The file is set according to the key that was specified in the Report Options window. The first record is read, the first page header is printed, and the Main Event Loop for the report begins. Notice how the NEXT_RECORD and PTR_BRK_HDR subroutines call the CHECK_PAGE subroutine. (This is part of the modularity of the procedure.) Some provision must be made at the beginning of the report to print the page header with any record information that might be called for in the report at that time. Since this process only takes place once, at the beginning of the report, it would be tempting to make this a separate and unique procedure. The Designer model is not always efficient in saving your programs from carrying extraneous code—it can't be and still accommodate all the things you might do. You might view this procedure as overly complex, but it takes care of the myriad of special circumstances you may introduce into the report, including the placement of formfeeds and a title page that cause the first page of records to actually print out on the second page of the report.

Once inside the Main Event Loop, the Body Detail of the first record read at the very beginning of the procedure is printed, the end of page is checked, and the next record is read. However, before that next record is printed, the procedure checks to see if the values that should trigger the group headers and footers to print have changed. If you examine the Report worksheet in Figure 11-5, the group header prints the disk label and the group footer prints a sum of the file sizes of files logged to that disk. The Main Event Loop looks at each of these values as it reads each record. When all the data have been read (and, in this case, no Selectors or Filters are used, so it reads to the end of the file), a flag is set to say the report is done. The last group footer is printed, the page is checked again for paging, and the report is closed out.

Figure 11-12   The logical flow of a standard Report Procedure created by Designer.

```
                        ┌─────────────┐
                        │ Print Title │
                        └─────────────┘
                               │
                        ┌─────────────┐
                        │  Set by key │
                        └─────────────┘
                               │
                        ┌─────────────┐      ┌─────────────┐
                        │ Next_Record │─────▶│ Check_Page  │
                        └─────────────┘◀─────└─────────────┘
                               │
                        ┌─────────────┐      ┌─────────────┐
                        │ Prt_Brk_Hdr │─────▶│ Check_Page  │
                        └─────────────┘◀─────└─────────────┘
                               │
                           ╱────────╲   DONE
                          ╱ Loop Until ╲──────────┐
                          ╲   Done    ╱           │
                           ╲────────╱             │
                               │                  │
                        ┌─────────────┐           │
                        │ Print Detail│           │
                        └─────────────┘           │
                               │                  │
                        ┌─────────────┐           │
                        │ Check_Page  │           │
                        └─────────────┘           │
                               │                  │
                        ┌─────────────┐           │
                        │ Next_record │           │
                        └─────────────┘           │
                               │                  │
                        ┌─────────────┐           │
                        │ Check_Break │           │
                        └─────────────┘           │
```

┌─────────────┐   ┌─────────────┐   ┌─────────────┐   ┌─────────────┐
│ Check_Page │◀────│ Prt_Brk_Ftr │   │ Prt_Brk_Ftr │────▶│ Check_Page │
└─────────────┘────▶└─────────────┘   └─────────────┘◀────└─────────────┘
                           │   │
┌─────────────┐   ┌─────────────┐   ┌─────────────┐
│ Check_Page │◀────│ Prt_Brk_Hdr │   │ Check_Page │
└─────────────┘────▶└─────────────┘   └─────────────┘
                                                 │
                                          ┌─────────────┐
                                          │ Close report│
                                          └─────────────┘

Structure Types Response to the PRINT Statement

The fundamental process of printing a report hinges on the handling of four structure types: Report, Header, Footer, and Detail. As you can tell from a quick glance at a printout of a Report Procedure, Designer creates labeled versions of these structures to be called from within the program. You can do the same thing in manually coded reports. The only restriction you must observe is this: you can have as many Detail structures as you like (and you can see that Designer creates several of these structures for the group breaks), but you can have only one per Report Procedure of the other types of structures.

The reason for using only one of these types of structures per report is because of the way each one is handled within a Report structure. The ability to declare the structure separately, as with screens, is a major advantage. In doing so, though, Clarion has imbued each type with certain traits that the compiler recognizes. For instance, when the overflow calls upon a Footer structure to print at the bottom of a page (signaled from the printer or set in the Report Options window), the structure automatically allocates the number of lines that the header occupies. The Body Detail merely prints its information and returns control back to read another record. No decisions are made by the Detail structure—not even a page break in the middle of a record.

Using the structures is very simple, once they are built. You simply fill the variables contained in the structure in some way and then call for the structure to be sent to the printer using the PRINT statement and the label for the structure. The only other task you must shoulder is to keep track of how many lines have been printed on the page to ensure appropriate page breaks. A very simple report (which, by the way, is one whole program) appears in Figure 11-13. It accesses the CATALOG data file called FILES and prints all the disk labels in that file. First, it prints a Header, which you'll notice is not explicitly called. Then it cycles through and prints each record. At the end, it calls for the Footer to be printed if the page maximum was not yet realized. The Footer prints automatically otherwise.

Retrieving data from the disk files is not complicated either. The trick is to grab the information in record-sized chunks from the disk as you need it and then call for the proper structure to be printed to plant that information on the page. The order of events should go something like this:

1. Create the reporting structure.
2. Open the report and open the data files to be printed.
3. Print the titles and page headings. (Notice how the Title structure created by a Designer report is merely another Report structure with only a Detail structure inside it.)
4. Grab the first record and perform whatever calculations, concatenations, or lookups you need to prepare the data for printing.
5. Print a detail line.
6. Check for page breaks and start over at step 4 again.

Figure 11-13   A simple printing program.

```
PRINTER         PROGRAM
REPORT     REPORT        WIDTH(80)
HEAD                     HEADER,PRE(HEA)
           COL(32)     STRING('THIS IS THE HEADER')
           ROW(+3,37)    STRING('The Body') CTL(@LF)
                         END!HEADER
BODY                     DETAIL,PRE(BOD)
LABEL      COL(26)     STRING(30),USE(DIS:LABEL) CTL(@LF)
                         END!DETAIL
FOOT                     FOOTER
           ROW(+2,32)    STRING('THIS IS THE FOOTER') CTL(@LF)
                         END!FOOTER
             END!REPORT

DISKS      FILE,PRE(DIS),CREATE,RECLAIM
BY_NUMBER  KEY(DIS:NUMBER),NOCASE,OPT
RECORD     RECORD
NUMBER        STRING(@N_4)
LABEL         STRING(30)
NOTES         STRING(40)
             END!RECORD
           END!FILE DEF

           CODE
           OPEN(REPORT)              !START THE REPORT
           SET(DISKS)                !ESTABLISH THE POINTER IN THE FILE   (OPEN IT)
           LOOP UNTIL EOF(DISKS)     !LOOK THROUGH ALL RECORDS IN THE FILE
            NEXT(DISKS)              !READ THE NEXT RECORD
            COUNT# += 1              !ADD TO LINE COUNT
            IF COUNT# = 5            !TEST FOR PAGE LIMIT
               PRINT(FOOT & @FF)     !PRINT THE FOOTER AND FEED PAGE
               PRINT(HEAD)           !PRINT NEXT PAGE HEADER
               COUNT# = 0            !RESET THE LINE COUNTER
            END!IF                   !END OF LINE COUNT TEST
            PRINT(BODY)              !PRINT THE BODY DETAIL LINES
           END!LOOP                  !TERMINATE THE PROCESSING LOOP
           IF COUNT# <= 5            !WHEN A LESS THAN WHOLE PAGE PRINTED LAST
             PRINT(FOOT)             !PRINT THE FOOTER
           END!IF                    !TERMINATE TEST OF SHORT PAGE
           PRINT(@FF)                !KICK OUT THE LAST PAGE
           CLOSE(REPORT)             !COMPLETE THE REPORT AND RETURN
           RETURN
```

The Report Writer

With Version 2.1 of the Professional Developer, Clarion introduced the Report Writer, which allowed developers to give users access to Clarion reporting methods without resorting to hard-coded reports. Yet, it is possible for applications developers to integrate the Report Writer into their applications so that it does not have to be started separately. With Report Writer you can achieve most of the same results of a native Clarion report, and you can allow for the user to change the report format without recoding. It is highly recommended that you, the applications developer, set up the database definitions to be used in creating reports if you install the full Report Writer with your application. If you merely install the runtime program RRUN.EXE, you will be forced to create both Database and Report definitions.

There are some differences in the command language, and it is important to understand how Report Writer's Join Fields work. The *Report Writer Manual* adequately describes most of its operation, so this discussion will focus on a few of the key concepts you will be using.

How the Data Files Get Linked

The task of using Report Writer can be divided into two areas: creating the eligible data and creating the report look. Setting up the data aspect has two important parts: the method for importing the file definition and the method for tying two file and field definitions together. It is possible, in these areas, to make Report Writer do a lot of extra work that will slow the reporting process down considerably.

You can bring the file definitions into Report Writer by tapping the data file directly or by reaching into the applications file (.APP). If you choose the latter, Report Writer attempts to add all the data files involved in that application, but it does not establish any of the links to interconnect information. You must do that manually.

You can interrelate fields from two files in two ways: you can indicate that they overlap and you can cause them to be joined. In both cases, you help Report Writer figure out how to manage the data. Once you bring the field definitions into Report Writer, they are all eligible to be included in a report. However, simply by the way you construct the overlapping and joined fields, you can make it impossible for Report Writer to find any data to display.

The best approach is to look at the keys already defined in the files within the application. Do what you can to specify the Joins you create with over-lapped fields *to exactly match these keys*. If you do not, Report Writer tries to build Index files on the fly while creating the view into the data that you might have requested from a particular report. That slows the reporting operation down considerably. When you have two files with identical fields, you do not necessarily have to show them as overlapping. When you do, Clarion assumes it will find the same information in both of them to relate two records.

You won't see the index files still sitting on the disk after you run such a report, and indexes don't reside in memory as do the dynamic keys found in regular Clarion. Report Writer creates them in response to your request for a nonexistent sort or key sequence. You can avoid this impact if you overlap the fields but do not join them. In that case, Report Writer is able to avoid duplicating field descriptions by storing them twice.

Calling from Inside an Application

As a developer, you may want to link Report Writer into applications seam-lessly. You can do this in two ways: by calling REPORTER.EXE directly or by running RRUN.EXE with parameters for the report definitions you have created. (Remember that RRUN is freely distributable and REPORTER is not—you must buy a copy of the Report Writer for each site.)

The RUN command provides a smooth way to call Report Writer-created reports. In fact, you can even create a separate database to allow your user to start different reports from inside your application. The example in Figure 11-14 shows the entry form for a file that maintains the location and the description of reports created by Report Writer.

The Table Procedure, which the form in Figure 11-14 feeds, can be used to start the listed report by simply pressing a hot key. The Hot Key Procedure within the Standard Model takes care of reading the record to place the information about the report into memory. Then, an Other Procedure, as appears in Figure 11-16, can be called with replaceable parameters for the RRUN command that substitutes the name of the report you want to run. This method is substantially like the Report Writer itself, in that it organizes a pick list of reports as you create them.

The next step is to establish a Hot Key Procedure called with the F10 key. After the F10 key is pressed, and before calling the Hot Key Procedure, Designer code generated from the Standard Model inserts code that will read the record underneath the highlight bar in the table, as shown in Figure 11-15.

Figure 11-14 This is the entry form to place a new report created by Report Writer into a file to allow it to run using the RRUN runtime package. The menu that started the selection appears at the bottom where you see "Runtime Report"; the Table Procedure entitled "Selection of Eligible Reports" appears underneath the form.

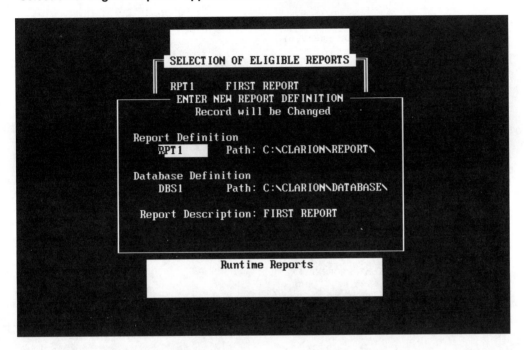

Figure 11-15 The Hot Key Procedure to call an Other Procedure from which to run the Report Writer runtime.

```
IF KEYCODE( ) = F10_KEY                          !ON HOT KEY
  IF FIELD( ) = ?POINT THEN DO GET_RECORD.       !  READ RECORD IF NEEDED
  RUNTIME                                        !  CALL HOT KEY PROCEDURE
  DO SAME_PAGE                                   !  RESET TO SAME PAGE
  CYCLE                                          !  AND LOOP AGAIN
```

Figure 11-16   The Other Procedure to run Report Writer.

```
        MEMBER('CATALOG')

RUNTIME  PROCEDURE
SCREEN   SCREEN        WINDOW,HUE(7,0)
         END!SCREEN
         CODE
         OPEN(SCREEN)
         RUN('c:\clarion\RRUN R=' & CLIP(REP:REPORT_PATH) & |
             CLIP(REP:REPORT_DEF) & '.DEF D=' & |
             CLIP(REP:DATABASE_PTH) & CLIP(REP:DATABASE_DEF) & '.DEF  O=S')
         CLOSE(SCREEN)
         RETURN


WRITER   PROCEDURE

SCREEN   SCREEN        WINDOW,HUE(7,0)
         END!SCREEN
         CODE
         OPEN(SCREEN)
         RUN('c:\clarion\REPORTER.EXE')
         CLOSE(SCREEN)
         RETURN
```

Now that the record is in memory, we have access to the values that will be needed to start the correct report from the runtime version of the Report Writer. We can set up an Other Procedure with variables in place of the replaceable parameters for RRUN.EXE as shown in Figure 11-16.

Both the Runtime and Writer Procedures open a Screen structure as a window before calling either Report Writer or the runtime version, RRUN.EXE. This saves the graphics underneath until after the reports are run and they can be restored. The RUN command starts both programs. This takes a temporary copy of the memory image of Clarion and saves it on the disk while the Report Writer is in operation. The replaceable parameters are "clipped" together to remove the trailing spaces from each of the variables. The syntax following RRUN.EXE, then, is the same as it would be if you were entering the parameters from a DOS batch file or at the DOS command prompt.

Unique Statement Types

In creating reports within Report Writer, many of its operations repeat functionality that is already in the Designer Report worksheet and the Editor Report formatter. The additional features consist mostly of providing menu-driven interfaces for many functions, including the construction of sort and filter entry. The Report Writer does provide a quick way to present tables in reverse sort order, something you must code on your own otherwise since Designer does not support it.

However, there are a few changes in the language for performing special computed functions that differ from the regular programming language. As you create reports, you should be aware of the following differences so that you can reduce the amount of confusion you'll experience in debugging the more intricate reports you build with Report Writer:

- INSTR is the command to perform what the regular Clarion refers to as INSTRING for searching for a substring inside another string. The syntax for the command parameters is the same, except that the Report Writer version does not include the fourth parameter for starting the search somewhere other than in the first position.
- NUMBER is a function not included in regular Clarion. It extracts a number from a string that contains both letters and numbers.
- HOUR is another function not included with regular Clarion. It returns the integer for the time of day.
- MINUS is the third and final function that does not appear in the regular Clarion language. MINUS reverses the sign of whatever number it was run against.
- SUBSTR is the Report Writer equivalent of SUBSTRING. They both perform exactly the same function.

Exporting Data

There are several reasons to extract information from a Clarion database. A standard printed report is the most common; the next most common function is to export information. In this section we'll discuss two methods for exporting information. We'll prepare an ASCII file for importing into another database program or spreadsheet, and we'll prepare a file for database publishing with Ventura Publisher.

The ASCII Export

The formats for ASCII exports vary from the SDF (or standard data file) format to DIF (or data interface format) and ASCII comma delimited or BASIC format. The BASIC format is probably the most common one used for text transfer, whereas the DIF format, originally designed for VisiCalc spreadsheet users, is most often used for numeric. The program that appears in this section exports a BASIC file.

You can go about creating a BASIC file in Clarion in two ways: through a regular report using Report Writer or by using the Clarion DOS file commands. The process for creating a BASIC file using the Report Writer is well documented in the *Report Writer Manual*.

The export of a data file to a BASIC file using Clarion statements requires the use of a DOS file definition. You may have noticed that you can create a DOS file by changing the DEVICE used in a standard Clarion report. However, that file is not organized in terms of DOS records that can be reread into a data file easily. To take control over the DOS record format, you must define a file as shown in Figure 11-17.

The DOS file must be defined ahead of time. A handy method for setting up the DOS record structure is to use the Control–W key combination from within Editor to split the screen and view the main program module where the Clarion file definitions reside. Then you can copy the lines of code from the Clarion file and place them inside the record structure for the DOS file. This ensures that you take the variable definitions with you so that both files match in your export procedure. In this case, since the target file is in BASIC format, the COMMA attribute is part of the file definition. This ensures all the qualities of a file using only the ASCII attribute plus it places commas and quotation marks between the fields.

When you begin the procedure, then, you must first open and/or create that DOS file to prepare it to receive the data. The next step in the procedure in Figure 11-17 is for the file to be emptied. This ensures that you aren't merely adding new records on top of the previously exported ones.

The next step in the procedure handles a feature available in the Clarion Converter utility. When Converter imports an ASCII file using delimiters, as in this case, it converts the first row of records into the variable names for the fields in the data file. By adding the first row of labels as a record, we can import this group of records into a new data file using these labels. Converter also uses the length of the fields in the first DOS record to establish the size of the fields in the new database. By padding each of the fields in the first record

Figure 11-17 The Export1 Procedure from the CATALOG program for sending data to a DOS file.

```
                MEMBER('CATALOG')
EXPORT1         PROCEDURE
SCREEN    SCREEN        WINDOW(3,42),AT(15,18),HUE(7,0)
          ROW(1,1)    STRING('<201,205{40},187>')
          ROW(2,1)    STRING('<186,0{40},186>')
          ROW(3,1)    STRING('<200,205{40},188>')
          ROW(2,7)    STRING('RECORDS EXPORTED:')
          COL(30)    STRING('of')
COUNT         COL(25)    STRING(@N4)
TOTAL         COL(33)    STRING(@N4)
        END!SCREEN
DOSFILE       DOS,COMMA,NAME('BASIC.TXT')     ! SET DOS FILE DEFINITION
RECORD          RECORD
NUMBER           STRING(20)
LABEL            STRING(20)
NOTES            STRING(20)
               END!RECORD
             END!FILE
             CODE
             OPEN(SCREEN)
             TOTAL = RECORDS(DISKS)
             OPEN(DOSFILE)                  ! OPEN DESTINATION FILE
             IF ERROR( ) THEN CREATE(DOSFILE).    ! CREATE IF NOT THERE
             EMPTY(DOSFILE)                 ! DUMP OLD CONTENTS
             NUMBER = 'NUMBER'              ! SET COLUMN TITLES
             LABEL = 'LABEL'
             NOTES = 'NOTES'
             ADD(DOSFILE)                   ! ADD COLUMN TITLES
             SET(DISKS)                     ! SET POINTER
             LOOP UNTIL EOF(DISKS)          ! LOOP THRU SOURCE  FILE
               NEXT(DISKS)                  ! READ NEXT FILES
                 COUNT += 1
                 NUMBER = LEFT(DIS:NUMBER)  ! SET DOS RECORDS
                 LABEL =  DIS:LABEL
                 NOTES =  DIS:NOTES
```

(continued)

Figure 11-17 *continued*

```
    ADD(DOSFILE)          ! ADD NEW RECORD
    END!LOOP              ! END OF LOOP
    CLOSE(DOSFILE)        ! CLOSE THE DOS FILE
    CLOSE(SCREEN)
    RETURN
```

with extra spaces, you can ensure that incoming data is not chopped off and that you won't need to enlarge these fields later.

After that, the next step is to loop through the source file and grab the records you want to export. Here is where you would place any tests for filters or other measures that would select from the data. You could preset a memory variable to check the values of a range of records to meet some criteria that would allow you to export only one section of the data file. You can also run this same process against several files from within the same procedure, tacking together data from several different files. As the values of each Clarion data file record are transferred to the DOS file record, the ADD command places them after the previous record written into the file. This is different from some other languages that force you to create the empty record and place the contents there.

Processing alongside the Export Procedure is a screen display that shows the number of records being processed and the total records in the data file. It is generally a good practice to show the user what is going on inside a hidden process like a file export. For large data files, it helps measure how long the process will take and also helps guarantee that the user will know if the system was suspended by some unknown error.

Finally, the DOS file has to be closed. It is not an absolute requirement that you close either the DOS file or the screen, or that you post the RETURN message, since all of this will occur when the procedure is complete and returns to its calling procedure. However, good programming practice regards these statements as documentation of operation as well as clean up.

To speed up the process of an export, you have several options. You could access the source file with a key and cache all the levels of that key in memory—if your system has enough expanded or extended memory. However, if you want to export the whole file and will not be filtering it, accessing the file in record order, as this procedure does, is the fastest method you can use.

Database Publishing with Ventura

A handy use for the export function just discussed is for database publishing. It is possible to export a data file formatted with regard to a style sheet in Xerox's Ventura Publisher. Only a few different steps are required to make your ASCII file compatible. The goal of the following procedure is to pull the names and addresses of individuals from a data file; prepare them to be printed in three-column pages with the individuals' names in bold and index entries seated between each name. That format allows Ventura to build an index automatically from the data entries with no additional user input.

Don't use the COMMA attribute in the DOS file definition; use only the DOS designation for the file. In this case, we want complete control over where the carriage return/line feed (CR/LF) characters are inserted into the process. Ventura considers any CR/LF occurrences as a delineation of a paragraph break. Since we want to be sparing with the paragraph tagging for simplicity and efficiency, we want to use the "soft-break" in Ventura to separate lines of the printout. In a regular Clarion report, the last field on a line initiates a CR/LF to start the next line in the Screen structure. Both the ASCII attribute and the COMMA attribute for a DOS file definition place a CR/LF at the end of a record when it is ADDed to a DOS file. In this procedure, we'll insert our own CR/LF (or '<13,10>') when we need it.

The first step is to build the status screen that will give the user an indication of how the processing of the procedure is percolating (pretty pithy, eh!). Your users will appreciate not being forced to look at a blank screen while they guess what is happening.

The next step is to create the DOS file definition. In this case, in place of a series of records transferred from the Clarion file to the DOS file, we will construct a character string according to a predetermined set of parameters and then add the string as a record in the DOS file. Since 250 characters is the largest character string possible in Clarion, that is how large we make this single record field.

The procedure in Figure 11-18 was created to export the membership of a professional society for publication in a directory. It begins by setting the members' names in alphabetical order by the last name with the key BY_LASTNAME and begins the process of looping through the source file. Nonmembers are excluded from this printout with a simple test on the Membership Field. When it hits a nonmember, the test short cuts the rest of the procedure by cycling back to the top of the loop.

Then the process begins of evaluating the length of the Name Field to take into account the width of the columns to be printed. In the formatting for WHOLENAME, the index variable for the Ventura is placed into the string

Figure 11-18   A procedure to port a Clarion data file of names and addresses into a DOS file for import to Ventura Publisher.

```
!---------------------------- EXPORT TO VENTURA PUBLISHER FOR MEMBER   DIRETORY
VENTURA    PROCEDURE
SCREEN          SCREEN         WINDOW(10,41),HUE(15,2)
                ROW(1,1)     STRING('É{39}»'),HUE(0,2)
                ROW(2,1)     REPEAT(8);STRING('<0{39}>'),HUE(0,2) .
                ROW(10,1)    STRING('{39}'),HUE(0,2)
                ROW(2,11)    STRING('PRINTS MEMBERSHIP ONLY'),HUE(0,2)
                ROW(8,9)     STRING(' (Creates "ALPHA.TXT" file)'),HUE(0,2)
                ROW(9,3)     STRING(' (Uses the "DIRECTRY.STY" Style
Sheet)'),HUE(0,2)
MESSAGE         ROW(4,2)     STRING(39)
COUNTER         ROW(6,17)    STRING(10)
                END!SCREEN
VPREADY   DOS,NAME('ALPHA.TXT')
          RECORD
HOLDER     STRING(250)
          END!RECORD
        END!FILE
WHOLENAME      STRING(250)
 CODE
 OPEN(SCREEN)
 COUNT# = 1
 MESSAGE = CENTER('CREATING ALPHA FILE',SIZE(MESSAGE))
 DISPLAY
 CREATE(VPREADY)
 OPEN(VPREADY)
 SET(NAM:BY_LASTNAME)
 LOOP UNTIL EOF(NAMES)
   COUNTER = CENTER(FORMAT(COUNT#,@N4),SIZE(COUNTER))
   NEXT(NAMES)
  IF NAM:MEMBERSHIP <> '2' THEN CYCLE.         ! CYCLE IF NONMEMBER
  ! CONFIGURE AND WRITE OUT THE MEMBER FIRST AND LAST NAME WITH PHONE
        LONGNAME# = LEN(CLIP(NAM:LAST)&', '&CLIP(NAM:FIRST))
        WHOLENAME = CLIP(NAM:LAST)&', '&CLIP(NAM:FIRST) & |
                '<<$I' & CLIP(NAM:COMPANY) & ';' & |
                CLIP(NAM:LAST) & ', ' & CLIP(NAM:FIRST) & '>'
    ! NO PHONE NUMBER
        IF SUB(NAM:PHONE,6,8) = '000-0000'
            HOLDER = '@MEMBER = ' & |              ! PLACE PARAGRAPH TAG
              CLIP(WHOLENAME) & '<13,10>'          ! WITH CONTACT NAME
            ADD(VPREADY,LEN(CLIP(HOLDER)))
        END!IF
    ! LONG CONTACT WITH PHONE
```

(continued)

Figure 11-18 *continued*

```
    IF LONGNAME# > 19 AND |                   ! CHECK NAME SIZE
       SUB(NAM:PHONE,6,8) <> '000-0000'
       HOLDER = '@MEMBER = ' & |              ! PLACE PARAGRAPH TAG
          CLIP(WHOLENAME) & '<<R>' & |        ! WITH CONTACT NAME
                 '<<T>' & NAM:PHONE & '<13,10>'
       ADD(VPREADY,LEN(CLIP(HOLDER)))
    ELSIF LONGNAME# <= 19 AND |
       SUB(NAM:PHONE,6,8) <> '000-0000'
       HOLDER = '@MEMBER = ' & |              ! PLACE PARAGRAPH TAG
          CLIP(WHOLENAME) & |                 ! WITH CONTACT NAME
                 '<<T>' & NAM:PHONE & '<13,10>'
       ADD(VPREADY,LEN(CLIP(HOLDER)))
    END!IF
  ! PHONE ONLY
    IF LONGNAME# = 0 AND |                     ! CHECK NAME SIZE
       SUB(NAM:PHONE,6,8) <> '000-0000'
       HOLDER = '@MEMBER = ' & |              ! PLACE PARAGRAPH TAG
                 '<<T>' & NAM:PHONE & '<13,10>'
       ADD(VPREADY,LEN(CLIP(HOLDER)))
    END!IF
! CONFIGURE AND WRITE OUT THE COMPANY NAME
    IF LEN(CLIP(NAM:COMPANY)) <> 0           ! CHECK COMPANY SIZE
       HOLDER = '@COMPANY = ' & |
          '<<~>' & CLIP(NAM:COMPANY) & '<13,10>' ! SET COMPANY  NAME
       ADD(VPREADY,LEN(CLIP(HOLDER)))        ! AND SECOND LINE
    END!IF
! IF MAILTO IS OFFICE OR OTHER THEN WRITE OUT STREET, CITY, STATE,  ZIP
  IF NAM:MAILTO <> 'home'
    IF NAM:STREET1 <> '' AND NAM:STREET2 = ''
       HOLDER = '@ADDRESS = ' & |
             '<<~>' & NAM:STREET1 & '<<R>'   ! SET STREET ADDRESS
       ADD(VPREADY,LEN(CLIP(HOLDER)))
    ELSIF NAM:STREET1 <> '' AND NAM:STREET2 <> ''
       HOLDER = '@ADDRESS = ' & |
             '<<~>' & NAM:STREET1 & '<<R>' & | ! SET STREET  ADDRESS
             '<<~>' & NAM:STREET2 & '<<R>'
       ADD(VPREADY,LEN(CLIP(HOLDER)))
    END!IF
    ADDRESS" = CLIP(NAM:CITY)&', '& NAM:STATE & '  ' & NAM:ZIP
    IF ADDRESS" <> '' AND NAM:STREET1 <> ''
       HOLDER = '<<~>' & ADDRESS" & '<13,10>'   ! SET CITY,STATE,ZIP
       ADD(VPREADY,LEN(CLIP(HOLDER)))
    ELSIF ADDRESS" <> ''
       HOLDER = '@ADDRESS = ' & |
             '<<~>' & ADDRESS" & '<13,10>'    ! SET CITY,STATE,ZIP
```

(continued)

Figure 11-18   *continued*

```
            ADD(VPREADY,LEN(CLIP(HOLDER)))
        END!IF
!  IF MAILTO IS HOME, WRITE OUT STREET ADDRESS
    ELSE
        IF NAM:HOME_STREET1 <> '' AND NAM:HOME_STREET2 = ''
            HOLDER = '@ADDRESS = ' & |
                    '<<~>' & NAM:HOME_STREET1 & '<<R>' ! SET STREET  ADDRESS
            ADD(VPREADY,LEN(CLIP(HOLDER)))
        ELSIF NAM:HOME_STREET1 <> '' AND NAM:HOME_STREET2 <> ''
            HOLDER = '@ADDRESS = ' & |
                    '<<~>' & NAM:HOME_STREET1 & '<<R>' & | ! SET STREET  ADDRESS
                    '<<~>' & NAM:HOME_STREET2 & '<<R>'
            ADD(VPREADY,LEN(CLIP(HOLDER)))
        END!IF
        ADDRESS" = CLIP(NAM:HOME_CITY)&', '& NAM:HOME_STATE & ' ' & NAM:HOME_ZIP
        IF ADDRESS" <> '' AND NAM:HOME_STREET1 <> ''
            HOLDER = '<<~>' & ADDRESS" & '<13,10>'   ! SET CITY,STATE,ZIP
               ADD(VPREADY,LEN(CLIP(HOLDER)))
        ELSIF ADDRESS" <> ''
            HOLDER = '@ADDRESS = ' & |
                    '<<~>' & ADDRESS" & '<13,10>'   ! SET CITY,STATE,ZIP
               ADD(VPREADY,LEN(CLIP(HOLDER)))
        END!IF
    END!IF
    COUNT# +=1
END!LOOP
CLOSE(VPREADY)
FLUSH(VPREADY)
MESSAGE = CENTER('VPREADY.TXT FILE CREATED - TOUCH A KEY',SIZE(MESSAGE))
ASK
CLOSE(SCREEN)
RETURN
```

for later retrieval by Ventura for creating the automatic index. Since the file must contain a construction of

```
<$Ivariable;index1,index2>
```

the right and left angle brackets (or chevrons) must be repeated twice so the program writing the file out to the disk understands that you want those symbols actually to print. This creates the proper format for an index entry in a Ventura file. Notice also that no CR/LF have yet been added to the string.

In this particular directory layout, the phone number is next to, or beneath (depending on length of the name), the name of the person being listed and it uses a separate paragraph tag from the rest of this person's listing. So, the HOLDER variable that constitutes the entire record for the DOS file is first filled with the format for a Ventura paragraph tag ("@MEMBER = '), and then the result of assembling the person's name into WHOLENAME is added along with the CR/LF in ASCII characters as '<13,10>'. In the case of the CR/LF, since we *do* want the compiler to interpret the angle brackets as commands, they are not given twice. (When the DOS file is typed out on the screen using the DOS command TYPE, these CR/LFs will not be visible.) Then the DOS file record is added using the ADD command and calculating the length to add it by measuring the contents of the only field in the record, HOLDER, using the LEN statement. This first ADD statement appears in case no phone number appears with the person's name. After that, If structures examine the length of the person's name to decide whether the phone number and the name will fit on the same line. If not, since we want to keep the same paragraph tag current for both lines when we put the phone number on a second line, we must insert the "soft" paragraph break character from Ventura. Again, this must be interpreted by the compiler as a character, so we use two angle brackets to set off the characters ('<<R>'), after the name resting in WHOLENAME is added to the DOS file record. The record written out to the DOS file should look like:

```
@MEMBER = WHOLENAME<R><T>NAM:PHONE<13,10>
```

where <T> stands for a tab and the CR/LF is not visible. (Later the <~> sign is used to represent a space.) This results in a listing in the finished directory that looks like this:

Public, John Q.

. . . . **(619)466-7266**

The width of the columns this procedure adheres to, the placement of the tabs, and the font styles and sizes are all determined by the style sheet in Ventura and can be changed without altering the program code. In fact, if the style sheet does not contain any paragraph tags, it will when this file is imported into what Ventura calls a Chapter.

This process is repeated as the entire data file of names and addresses is written out with these formatting characters placed around them. Each time the text must change paragraph tags, the current contents of the HOLDER record are ADDed to the DOS file. To find out what changes will be required for other configurations, simply type some sample data into Ventura, save the chapter, and then go look at the text file it created. All the symbols, except for CR/LF, will be visible. Your program must emulate, exactly, the text file that Ventura produced.

At the end of the loop, the tracking counter displayed in the status screen is incremented and the loop cycles around to read another record. When all the eligible records have been written out and the loop has reached the end of the source file, the DOS file is closed, memory is flushed, and a closing message is posted for the user to see that the process is complete.

All that remains is to load the DOS file into Ventura, matching it with the appropriate style sheet or setting the values for the paragraph tags. The best format to use to import this type of file is the import procedure that Ventura provides for Wordstar 4.0/5.0 files.

Summary

Clarion constructs reports in the same fashion as it does screens—with a structure. Both Designer and Editor can create those structures. The Report structure, as does the Screen structure, interacts with the program flow to extract data from the files and display it on the screen, printer, or other output device. In this chapter, we discussed the operations of a Report structure, how to manipulate a Report structure with your programs, and how Designer creates reports.

The CATALOG Program

CATALOG.CLA

```
CATALOG   PROGRAM
                INCLUDE('STD_KEYS.CLA')
                INCLUDE('CTL_KEYS.CLA')
                INCLUDE('ALT_KEYS.CLA')
                INCLUDE('SHF_KEYS.CLA')

REJECT_KEY      EQUATE(CTRL_ESC)
ACCEPT_KEY      EQUATE(CTRL_ENTER)
TRUE            EQUATE(1)
FALSE           EQUATE(0)

                MAP
                  PROC(G_OPENFILES)
                  MODULE('CATALO01')
                    PROC(MAIN_MENU)                 !Disk Catalog Main Menu
                    .
                  MODULE('CATALO02')
                    PROC(SHO_NUMBER)                !Show Disks By Number
                    .
                  MODULE('CATALO03')
                    PROC(UPD_DISKS)                 !Edit Labels (FILES_CHILD1)
                    .
                  MODULE('CATALO04')
                    PROC(RPT_NUMBER)                !Print Disks By Number
                    .
                  MODULE('CATALO05')
                    PROC(FILES)                     !File Information for One Disk
                    .
                  MODULE('CATALO06')
                    PROC(NEWFILES)                  !Add a New Disk
                    .
                  MODULE('CATALO07')
                    PROC(FILESEARCH)                !Shows Filenames of All Disks
                    .
                  MODULE('CATALO08')
                    PROC(REPORTS)                   !FLOPPY DISK MANAGEMENT REPORTS
                    .
                  MODULE('CATALO09')
                    PROC(ONEDISK)                   !Prints File List for One Disk
                    .
```

(continued)

```
            MODULE('CATALO10')
              PROC(FINDDISK)                    !Show Disks By Number
              .
            MODULE('CATALO11')
              PROC(FILES_CHILD1)                !Related Delete (UPD_DISKS)
              .
            MODULE('CATALO12')
              PROC(RUNTIME_MENU)                !SELECTION OF ELIGIBLE REPORTS
              .
            MODULE('CATALO13')
              PROC(NEW_REP)                     !ENTER NEW REPORT DEFINITION
              .
            MODULE('CATALO14')
              PROC(EXPORT1)

              .
            MODULE('JUMP')
              PROC(JUMP)                        !Shell to DOS
              .
            MODULE('READER')
              PROC(READER)                      !Reads Files from Disk
              .
            MODULE('SEARCH')
              PROC(SEARCH)                      !Find Disk or Label Text
              .
            MODULE('SPECIAL')
              PROC(WRITER)                      !Calls Report Writer
              PROC(RUNTIME)                     !Calls Report Writer Reports

              .
            INCLUDE('DOS1.CPY')

              .
            EJECT('FILE LAYOUTS')
DISKS     FILE,PRE(DIS),CREATE,RECLAIM
BY_NUMBER KEY(DIS:NUMBER),NOCASE,OPT
RECORD      RECORD
NUMBER        STRING(@N_4)
LABEL         STRING(30)
NOTES         STRING(40)

  . .

FILES     FILE,PRE(FIL),CREATE,RECLAIM
BY_NUMBER KEY(FIL:NUMBER,FIL:FILENAME),DUP,NOCASE,OPT
BY_FILENAME KEY(FIL:FILENAME),DUP,NOCASE,OPT
RECORD      RECORD
NUMBER        STRING(@N_4)
TIME          STRING(@T1)
DATE          STRING(@d1)
```

(continued)

```
SIZEBYTES      LONG
FILENAME       STRING(12)
NOTES          STRING(28)
          . .


READER     FILE,PRE(REA),CREATE,RECLAIM
RECORD        RECORD
LABEL            GROUP
BLANK              BYTE,DIM(21)
ATTRIB             BYTE
TIME               SHORT
DATE               SHORT
SIZEBYTES          LONG
FILENAME           STRING(13)
               .
          . .


REPORTER FILE,PRE(REP),CREATE,RECLAIM
BY_REPORT   KEY(REP:REPORT_PATH,REP:REPORT_NO),NOCASE,OPT
RECORD        RECORD
REPORT_NO     STRING(@N3)                    !TRACKING NUMBER FOR REPORTS
NOTES         STRING(20)                     !DESCRIPTION OF REPORT
REPORT_PATH   STRING(40)                     !PATH TO REPORT FILES
DATABASE_PTH  STRING(40)                     !PATH TO DATABASE DEFINITION
REPORT_DEF    STRING(8)                      !REPORT DEFINITION FILE
DATABASE_DEF  STRING(8)                      !DATABASE DEFINITION FILE
          . .


              EJECT('GLOBAL MEMORY VARIABLES')
ACTION        SHORT                          !0 = NO ACTION
                                             !1 = ADD RECORD
                                             !2 = CHANGE RECORD
                                             !3 = DELETE RECORD
                                             !4 = LOOKUP FIELD




              GROUP,PRE(MEM)
MESSAGE       STRING(30)                     !Global Message Area
PAGE          SHORT                          !Report Page Number
LINE          SHORT                          !Report Line Number
DEVICE        STRING(30)                     !Report Device Name
NUMBER        STRING(4)
          .


              EJECT('CODE SECTION')
```

(continued)

```
  CODE
  SETHUE(7,0)                                    !SET WHITE ON BLACK
  BLANK                                          !  AND BLANK
  HELP('CATALOG.HLP')                            !OPEN THE HELP FILE
  G_OPENFILES                                    !OPEN OR CREATE FILES
  SETHUE()                                       !   THE SCREEN
  MAIN_MENU                                      !Disk Catalog Main Menu
  RETURN                                         !EXIT TO DOS


G_OPENFILES  PROCEDURE                           !OPEN FILES & CHECK FOR ERROR
  CODE
  SHOW(25,1,CENTER('OPENING FILE: ' & 'DISKS',80)) !DISPLAY FILE NAME
  OPEN(DISKS)                                    !OPEN THE FILE
  IF ERROR()                                     !OPEN RETURNED AN ERROR
    CASE ERRORCODE()                             ! CHECK FOR SPECIFIC ERROR
    OF 46                                        !  KEYS NEED TO BE REQUILT
      SETHUE(0,7)                                !  BLACK ON WHITE
      SHOW(25,1,CENTER('REBUILDING KEY FILES FOR DISKS',80)) !INDICATE MSG
      BUILD(DISKS)                               !  CALL THE BUILD PROCEDURE
      SETHUE(7,0)                                !  WHITE ON BLACK
      BLANK(25,1,1,80)                           !  BLANK THE MESSAGE
    OF 2                                         !IF NOT FOUND,
      CREATE(DISKS)                              ! CREATE
    ELSE                                         ! ANY OTHER ERROR
      LOOP;STOP('DISKS: ' & ERROR()).            !  STOP EXECUTION
  . .


  SHOW(25,1,CENTER('OPENING FILE: ' & 'FILES',80)) !DISPLAY FILE NAME
  OPEN(FILES)                                    !OPEN THE FILE
  IF ERROR()                                     !OPEN RETURNED AN ERROR
    CASE ERRORCODE()                             ! CHECK FOR SPECIFIC ERROR
    OF 46                                        !  KEYS NEED TO BE REQUILT
      SETHUE(0,7)                                !  BLACK ON WHITE
      SHOW(25,1,CENTER('REBUILDING KEY FILES FOR FILES',80)) !INDICATE MSG
      BUILD(FILES)                               !  CALL THE BUILD PROCEDURE
      SETHUE(7,0)                                !  WHITE ON BLACK
      BLANK(25,1,1,80)                           !  BLANK THE MESSAGE
    OF 2                                         !IF NOT FOUND,
      CREATE(FILES)                              ! CREATE
    ELSE                                         ! ANY OTHER ERROR
      LOOP;STOP('FILES: ' & ERROR()).            !  STOP EXECUTION
  . .


  SHOW(25,1,CENTER('OPENING FILE: ' & 'READER',80)) !DISPLAY FILE NAME
  OPEN(READER)                                   !OPEN THE FILE
  IF ERROR()                                     !OPEN RETURNED AN ERROR
    CASE ERRORCODE()                             ! CHECK FOR SPECIFIC ERROR
```

(continued)

```
OF 46                                            !  KEYS NEED TO BE REQUILT
  SETHUE(0,7)                                     !  BLACK ON WHITE
  SHOW(25,1,CENTER('REBUILDING KEY FILES FOR READER',80)) !INDICATE MSG
  BUILD(READER)                                   !  CALL THE BUILD PROCEDURE
  SETHUE(7,0)                                     !  WHITE ON BLACK
  BLANK(25,1,1,80)                                !  BLANK THE MESSAGE
OF 2                                              !IF NOT FOUND,
  CREATE(READER)                                  ! CREATE
ELSE                                              ! ANY OTHER ERROR
  LOOP;STOP('READER: ' & ERROR()).               !  STOP EXECUTION
. .


SHOW(25,1,CENTER('OPENING FILE: ' & 'REPORTER',80)) !DISPLAY FILE NAME
OPEN(REPORTER)                                    !OPEN THE FILE
IF ERROR()                                        !OPEN RETURNED AN ERROR
  CASE ERRORCODE()                                ! CHECK FOR SPECIFIC ERROR
  OF 46                                           !  KEYS NEED TO BE REQUILT
    SETHUE(0,7)                                   !  BLACK ON WHITE
    SHOW(25,1,CENTER('REBUILDING KEY FILES FOR REPORTER',80)) !INDICATE MSG
    BUILD(REPORTER)                               !  CALL THE BUILD PROCEDURE
    SETHUE(7,0)                                   !  WHITE ON BLACK
    BLANK(25,1,1,80)                              !  BLANK THE MESSAGE
  OF 2                                            !IF NOT FOUND,
    CREATE(REPORTER)                              ! CREATE
  ELSE                                            ! ANY OTHER ERROR
    LOOP;STOP('REPORTER: ' & ERROR()).           !  STOP EXECUTION
. .


BLANK                                             !BLANK THE SCREEN
```

CATALO01.CLA

```
            MEMBER('CATALOG')
MAIN_MENU   PROCEDURE

SCREEN      SCREEN      PRE(SCR),WINDOW(17,29),AT(4,26),HUE(15,3)
            ROW(1,1)    STRING('<201,205{27},187>'),HUE(15,3)
            ROW(2,1)    REPEAT(2),EVERY(12);STRING('<186,0{27},186>'),HUE(15,3) .
            ROW(3,1)    STRING('<199,196{27},182>'),HUE(15,3)
            ROW(4,1)    REPEAT(9);STRING('<186,0{27},186>'),HUE(15,3) .
            ROW(13,1)   STRING('<204,205{27},185>'),HUE(15,3)
            ROW(15,1)   REPEAT(2);STRING('<186,0{27},186>'),HUE(15,3) .
            ROW(17,1)   STRING('<200,205{27},188>'),HUE(15,3)
            ROW(2,5)    STRING('THE KWI DISK DIRECTORY')
            ROW(14,3)   STRING('Conventional:')
```

(continued)

```
             ROW(15,3)   STRING('Virtual Disk:')
             ROW(16,3)   STRING('Total Virtual:')
DATE         ROW(4,12)   STRING(@D1),HUE(15,3)
CONVENT      ROW(14,18)  STRING(@n9),HUE(15,3)
DISK         ROW(15,18)  STRING(@n9),HUE(15,3)
BOTH         ROW(16,18)  STRING(@n9),HUE(15,3)
                         ENTRY,USE(?FIRST_FIELD)
                         ENTRY,USE(?PRE_MENU)
                         MENU,USE(MENU_FIELD"),REQ
             ROW(6,8)    STRING('DISKS BY NUMBER'),HUE(0,3),SEL(0,7)
             ROW(8,7)    STRING('FILE NAME SEARCH'),HUE(0,3),SEL(0,7)
             ROW(10,12)  STRING('REPORTS'),HUE(0,3),SEL(0,7)
             ROW(12,14)  STRING('Quit'),HUE(0,3),SEL(0,7)
         .                    .
```

```
EJECT
CODE
OPEN(SCREEN)                              !OPEN THE MENU SCREEN
SETCURSOR                                 !TURN OFF ANY CURSOR
MENU_FIELD" = ''                          !START MENU WITH FIRST ITEM
LOOP                                      !LOOP UNTIL USER EXITS
  SCR:DATE = TODAY()
  SCR:CONVENT = MEMORY(1)
  SCR:DISK = memory(2)
  SCR:BOTH = memory(3)
  ALERT                                   !TURN OFF ALL ALERTED KEYS
  ALERT(REJECT_KEY)                       !ALERT SCREEN REJECT KEY
  ALERT(ACCEPT_KEY)                       !ALERT SCREEN ACCEPT KEY
  ACCEPT                                  !READ A FIELD OR MENU CHOICE
  IF KEYCODE() = REJECT_KEY THEN RETURN.  !RETURN ON SCREEN REJECT

  IF KEYCODE() = ACCEPT_KEY               !ON SCREEN ACCEPT KEY
    UPDATE                                !  MOVE ALL FIELDS FROM SCREEN
    SELECT(?)                             !  START WITH CURRENT FIELD
    SELECT                                !  EDIT ALL FIELDS
    CYCLE                                 !  GO TO TOP OF LOOP
    .                                     !

  CASE FIELD()                            !JUMP TO FIELD EDIT ROUTINE
  OF ?FIRST_FIELD                         !FROM THE FIRST FIELD
    IF KEYCODE() = ESC_KEY THEN RETURN.   !  RETURN ON ESC KEY

  OF ?PRE_MENU                            !PRE MENU FIELD CONDITION
    IF KEYCODE() = ESC_KEY                !  BACKING UP?
      SELECT(?-1)                         !    SELECT PREVIOUS FIELD
    ELSE                                  !  GOING FORWARD
      SELECT(?+1)                         !    SELECT MENU FIELD
    .
```

(continued)

```
        OF ?MENU_FIELD"                      !FROM THE MENU FIELD
          EXECUTE CHOICE()                   !  CALL THE SELECTED PROCEDURE
            SHO_NUMBER                        !  Show Disks By Number
            FILESEARCH                        !  Shows Filenames of All Disks
            REPORTS                           !  FLOPPY DISK MANAGEMENT RE-
PORTS
          RETURN

   . . .
```

CATALO02.CLA

```
              MEMBER('CATALOG')
SHO_NUMBER     PROCEDURE


SCREEN         SCREEN         PRE(SCR),WINDOW(25,80),HLP('DISKLIST'),HUE(15,1)
               ROW(6,1)    PAINT(17,80),HUE(0,7)
               ROW(2,30)   PAINT(1,22),HUE(0,7)
               ROW(22,2)   PAINT(1,79),HUE(15,1)
               ROW(21,2)   PAINT(1,78),HUE(15,1)
               ROW(1,1)    STRING('<201,205{78},187>'),HUE(15,1)
               ROW(2,1)    REPEAT(23);STRING('<186,0{78},186>'),HUE(15,1)  .
               ROW(25,1)   STRING('<200,205{78},188>'),HUE(15,1)
               ROW(2,31)   STRING('Show Disks By Number')
               ROW(4,31)   STRING('Locate'),HUE(11,1)
                 COL(38)   STRING('by Number'),HUE(11,1)
                 COL(47)   STRING(':'),HUE(11,1)
               ROW(5,4)    STRING('NO. {10}DISK LABEL {29}NOTES')
               ROW(21,23)  STRING('PRESS <<F9> TO READ DISK DIRECTORY'),HUE(15,1)
               ROW(22,24)  STRING('   '),HUE(15,1)
                 COL(27)   STRING('PRESS <<F10> FOR FILES')
                 COL(49)   STRING('LIST'),HUE(15,1)
               ROW(23,5)   STRING('Ins to Add'),HUE(11,1)
                 COL(30)   STRING('PRESS <<F8> TO SEARCH'),HUE(15,1)
                 COL(62)   STRING('Enter to Change'),HUE(11,1)
               ROW(24,2)   STRING('.'),HUE(9,1)
                 COL(5)    STRING('Del to Delete'),HUE(11,1)
                 COL(59)   STRING('   '),HUE(15,1)
                 COL(62)   STRING('Ctrl-Esc to Exit'),HUE(11,1)
LOCATOR        ROW(4,48)   STRING(@N_4),HUE(11,1)
TEST           ROW(22,3)   STRING(@PXXXXXXP)
                           ENTRY,USE(?FIRST_FIELD)
                           ENTRY,USE(?PRE_POINT)
                           REPEAT(15),EVERY(1),INDEX(NDX)
               ROW(6,2)       POINT(1,78),USE(?POINT),ESC(?-1)
NUMBER         COL(3)   STRING(@N_4)
LABEL          COL(8)   STRING(30)
```

(continued)

```
NOTES           COL(39)     STRING(40)
                  .              .


NDX             BYTE                          !REPEAT INDEX FOR POINT AREA
ROW             BYTE                          !ACTUAL ROW OF SCROLL AREA
COL             BYTE                          !ACTUAL COLUMN OF SCROLL AREA
COUNT           BYTE(15)                      !NUMBER OF ITEMS TO SCROLL
ROWS            BYTE(15)                      !NUMBER OF ROWS TO SCROLL
COLS            BYTE(78)                      !NUMBER OF COLUMNS TO SCROLL
FOUND           BYTE                          !RECORD FOUND FLAG
NEWPTR          LONG                          !POINTER TO NEW RECORD


TABLE           TABLE,PRE(TBL)                !TABLE OF RECORD DATA
NUMBER          STRING(@N_4)
LABEL           STRING(30)
NOTES           STRING(40)
PTR             LONG                          !  POINTER TO FILE RECORD
                  .

  EJECT
  CODE
  ACTION# = ACTION                            !SAVE ACTION
  OPEN(SCREEN)                                !OPEN THE SCREEN
  SETCURSOR                                   !TURN OFF ANY CURSOR
  TBL:PTR = 1                                 !START AT TABLE ENTRY
  NDX = 1                                     !PUT SELECTOR BAR ON TOP ITEM
  ROW = ROW(?POINT)                           !REMEMBER TOP ROW AND
  COL = COL(?POINT)                           !LEFT COLUMN OF SCROLL AREA
  RECORDS# = TRUE                             !INITIALIZE RECORDS FLAG
  CACHE(DIS:BY_NUMBER,.25)                    !CACHE KEY FILE
  IF ACTION = 4                               !  TABLE LOOKUP REQUEST
    NEWPTR = POINTER(DISKS)                   !  SET POINTER TO RECORD
    IF NOT NEWPTR                             !  RECORD NOT PASSED TO TABLE
      SET(DIS:BY_NUMBER,DIS:BY_NUMBER)        !    POSITION TO CLOSEST RECORD
      NEXT(DISKS)                             !    READ RECORD
      NEWPTR = POINTER(DISKS)                 !    SET POINTER
      .
    DO FIND_RECORD                            !  POSITION FILE
  ELSE
    NDX = 1                                   !  PUT SELECTOR BAR ON TOP ITEM
    DO FIRST_PAGE                             !  BUILD MEMORY TABLE OF KEYS
    .
  RECORDS# = TRUE                             !  ASSUME THERE ARE RECORDS
  LOOP                                        !LOOP UNTIL USER EXITS
    ACTION = ACTION#                          !RESTORE ACTION
    SCR:TEST = 0
    MEM:MESSAGE = SCR:TEST
```

(continued)

```
ALERT                                            !RESET ALERTED KEYS
ALERT(REJECT_KEY)                                !ALERT SCREEN REJECT KEY
ALERT(ACCEPT_KEY)                                !ALERT SCREEN ACCEPT KEY
ALERT(F10_KEY)                                   !ALERT HOT KEY
ALERT(F9_KEY)                                    !ALERT HOT KEY
ALERT(F8_KEY)                                    !ALERT HOT KEY
ACCEPT                                           !READ A FIELD
IF KEYCODE() = F10_KEY                           !ON HOT KEY
  IF FIELD() = ?POINT THEN DO GET_RECORD.        !  READ RECORD IF NEEDED
  FILES                                          !  CALL HOT KEY PROCEDURE
  DO SAME_PAGE                                   !  RESET TO SAME PAGE
  CYCLE                                          !  AND LOOP AGAIN
.

IF KEYCODE() = F9_KEY                            !ON HOT KEY
  IF FIELD() = ?POINT THEN DO GET_RECORD.        !  READ RECORD IF NEEDED
  READER                                         !  CALL HOT KEY PROCEDURE
  DO SAME_PAGE                                   !  RESET TO SAME PAGE
  CYCLE                                          !  AND LOOP AGAIN
.

IF KEYCODE() = F8_KEY                            !ON HOT KEY
  IF FIELD() = ?POINT THEN DO GET_RECORD.        !  READ RECORD IF NEEDED
  SEARCH                                         !  CALL HOT KEY PROCEDURE
  DO SAME_PAGE                                   !  RESET TO SAME PAGE
  CYCLE                                          !  AND LOOP AGAIN
.

IF KEYCODE() = REJECT_KEY THEN BREAK.            !RETURN ON SCREEN REJECT KEY

IF  KEYCODE() = ACCEPT_KEY     |                 !ON SCREEN ACCEPT KEY
AND FIELD() <> ?POINT                            !BUT NOT ON THE POINT FIELD
  UPDATE                                         !  MOVE ALL FIELDS FROM SCREEN
  SELECT(?)                                      !  START WITH CURRENT FIELD
  SELECT                                         !  EDIT ALL FIELDS
  CYCLE                                          !  GO TO TOP OF LOOP
.


CASE FIELD()                                     !JUMP TO FIELD EDIT ROUTINE

OF ?FIRST_FIELD                                  !FROM THE FIRST FIELD
  IF KEYCODE() = ESC_KEY     |                   !  RETURN ON ESC KEY
  OR RECORDS# = FALSE                            !  OR NO RECORDS
    BREAK                                        !     EXIT PROGRAM
  .

OF ?PRE_POINT                                    !PRE POINT FIELD CONDITION
  IF KEYCODE() = ESC_KEY                         !  BACKING UP?
    SELECT(?-1)                                  !     SELECT PREVIOUS FIELD
  ELSE                                           !  GOING FORWARD
    SELECT(?POINT)                               !     SELECT MENU FIELD
  .
```

(continued)

```
    IF KEYCODE() = ESC_KEY                       !  BACKING UP?
      SCR:LOCATOR = ''                           !    CLEAR LOCATOR
      SETCURSOR                                  !    AND TURN CURSOR OFF
    ELSE                                         !  GOING FORWARD
      LEN# = 0                                   !    RESET TO START OF LOCATOR
      SETCURSOR(ROW(SCR:LOCATOR),COL(SCR:LOCATOR)) !AND TURN CURSOR ON
    .

  OF ?POINT                                      !PROCESS THE POINT FIELD
    IF RECORDS(TABLE) = 0                        !IF THERE ARE NO RECORDS
      CLEAR(DIS:RECORD)                          !  CLEAR RECORD AREA
      ACTION = 1                                 !  SET ACTION TO ADD
      GET(DISKS,0)                               !  CLEAR PENDING RECORD
      CLEAR(DIS:RECORD,1)                        !CLEAR RECORD TO HIGH VALUES
      SET(DIS:BY_NUMBER)                         !  POINT TO FIRST RECORD
      PREVIOUS(DISKS)                            !READ LAST KEY RECORD
      IF ERROR()                                 !IF THERE WAS AN ERROR
         CLEAR(DIS:RECORD)                       !  CLEAR THE RECORD
         KEYFIELD# = 0                           !  INTITIALIZE THE FIELD
         IF KEYFIELD# = 0 THEN KEYFIELD# = 1.    !  IF ITS 0 MAKE IT 1
      ELSE                                       !ELSE
         KEYFIELD# = DIS:NUMBER + 1              !  INCREMENT FIELD
      .
      CLEAR(DIS:RECORD)                          !CLEAR LAST KEY RECORD
      DIS:NUMBER = KEYFIELD#                     !LOAD KEY FIELD
      UPD_DISKS                                  !  CALL FORM FOR NEW RECORD
      NEWPTR = POINTER(DISKS)                    !    SET POINTER TO NEW RECORD
      DO FIRST_PAGE                              !  DISPLAY THE FIRST PAGE
      IF RECORDS(TABLE) = 0                      !  IF THERE AREN'T ANY RECORDS
        RECORDS# = FALSE                         !    INDICATE NO RECORDS
        SELECT(?PRE_POINT-1)                     !    SELECT THE PRIOR FIELD
      .
      CYCLE                                      !    AND LOOP AGAIN
    .
    IF KEYCODE() > 31                 |          !THE DISPLAYABLE CHARACTERS
    AND KEYCODE() < 255                          !ARE USED TO LOCATE RECORDS
      IF LEN# < SIZE(SCR:LOCATOR)                !  IF THERE IS ROOM LEFT
        SCR:LOCATOR = SUB(SCR:LOCATOR,1,LEN#) & CHR(KEYCODE())
        LEN# += 1                                !      INCREMENT THE LENGTH
      .
    ELSIF KEYCODE() = BS_KEY                     !BACKSPACE UNTYPES A CHARACTER
      IF LEN# > 0                                !  IF THERE ARE CHARACTERS LEFT
        LEN# -= 1                                !    DECREMENT THE LENGTH
        SCR:LOCATOR = SUB(SCR:LOCATOR,1,LEN#)    !    ERASE THE LAST CHARACTER
      .
    ELSE                                         !FOR ANY OTHER CHARACTER
      LEN# = 0                                   !  ZERO THE LENGTH
      SCR:LOCATOR = ''                           !  ERASE THE LOCATOR FIELD
    .
```

(continued)

```
SETCURSOR(ROW(SCR:LOCATOR),COL(SCR:LOCATOR)+LEN#) !AND RESET THE CURSOR
DIS:NUMBER = CLIP(SCR:LOCATOR)                     !    UPDATE THE KEY FIELD
IF KEYBOARD() > 31                      |          !THE DISPLAYABLE CHARACTERS
AND KEYBOARD() < 255                     |         !ARE USED TO LOCATE RECORDS
OR KEYBOARD() = BS_KEY                             !INCLUDE BACKSPACE
  CYCLE
.

IF LEN# > 0                                        !ON A LOCATOR REQUEST
  DIS:NUMBER = CLIP(SCR:LOCATOR)                   !    UPDATE THE KEY FIELD
  SET(DIS:BY_NUMBER,DIS:BY_NUMBER)                 !    POINT TO NEW RECORD
  NEXT(DISKS)                                      !    READ A RECORD
  IF (EOF(DISKS) AND ERROR())                      !    IF EOF IS REACHED
    SET(DIS:BY_NUMBER)                             !      SET TO FIRST RECORD
    PREVIOUS(DISKS)                                !      READ THE LAST RECORD
  .

  NEWPTR = POINTER(DISKS)                          !    SET NEW RECORD POINTER
  SKIP(DISKS,-1)                                   !    BACK UP TO FIRST RECORD
  FREE(TABLE)                                      !    CLEAR THE TABLE
  DO NEXT_PAGE                                     !    AND DISPLAY A NEW PAGE
.

CASE KEYCODE()                                     !PROCESS THE KEYSTROKE

OF INS_KEY                                         !INS KEY
  CLEAR(DIS:RECORD)                                !  CLEAR RECORD AREA
  ACTION = 1                                       !  SET ACTION TO ADD
  GET(DISKS,0)                                     !  CLEAR PENDING RECORD
  CLEAR(DIS:RECORD,1)                              !CLEAR RECORD TO HIGH VALUES
  SET(DIS:BY_NUMBER)                               !  POINT TO FIRST RECORD
  PREVIOUS(DISKS)                                  !READ LAST KEY RECORD
  IF ERROR()                                       !IF THERE WAS AN ERROR
    CLEAR(DIS:RECORD)                              !  CLEAR THE RECORD
    KEYFIELD# = 0                                  !  INTITIALIZE THE FIELD
    IF KEYFIELD# = 0 THEN KEYFIELD# = 1.           !  IF ITS 0 MAKE IT 1
  ELSE                                             !ELSE
    KEYFIELD# = DIS:NUMBER + 1                     !  INCREMENT FIELD
  .

  CLEAR(DIS:RECORD)                                !CLEAR LAST KEY RECORD
  DIS:NUMBER = KEYFIELD#                           !LOAD KEY FIELD
  UPD_DISKS                                        !  CALL FORM FOR NEW RECORD
  IF ~ACTION                                       !  IF RECORD WAS ADDED
    NEWPTR = POINTER(DISKS)                        !    SET POINTER TO NEW RECORD
    DO FIND_RECORD                                 !    POSITION IN FILE
  .

OF ENTER_KEY                                       !ENTER KEY
OROF ACCEPT_KEY                                    !CTRL-ENTER KEY
  DO GET_RECORD                                    !  GET THE SELECTED RECORD
  IF ACTION = 4 AND KEYCODE() = ENTER_KEY          !  IF THIS IS A LOOKUP REQUEST
    ACTION = 0                                     !    SET ACTION TO COMPLETE
```

(continued)

```
      BREAK                                    !        AND RETURN TO CALLER
    .
  IF ~ERROR()                                  !     IF RECORD IS STILL THERE
    ACTION = 2                                 !        SET ACTION TO CHANGE
    UPD_DISKS                                  !        CALL FORM TO CHANGE REC
    IF ACTION THEN CYCLE.                      !        IF SUCCESSFUL RE-DISPLAY
    .
  NEWPTR = POINTER(DISKS)                      !        SET POINTER TO NEW RECORD
  DO FIND_RECORD                               !     POSITION IN FILE
OF DEL_KEY                                     !DEL KEY
  DO GET_RECORD                                !     READ THE SELECTED RECORD
  IF ~ERROR()                                  !     IF RECORD IS STILL THERE
    ACTION = 3                                 !        SET ACTION TO DELETE
    UPD_DISKS                                  !        CALL FORM TO DELETE
    IF ~ACTION                                 !        IF SUCCESSFUL
      N# = NDX                                 !           SAVE POINT INDEX
      DO SAME_PAGE                             !           RE-DISPLAY
      NDX = N#                                 !           RESTORE POINT INDEX
  . .
OF DOWN_KEY                                    !DOWN ARROW KEY
  DO SET_NEXT                                  !     POINT TO NEXT RECORD
  DO FILL_NEXT                                 !     FILL A TABLE ENTRY
  IF FOUND                                     !     FOUND A NEW RECORD
    SCROLL(ROW,COL,ROWS,COLS,ROWS(?POINT))     !        SCROLL THE SCREEN UP
    GET(TABLE,RECORDS(TABLE))                  !        GET RECORD FROM TABLE
    DO FILL_SCREEN                             !        DISPLAY ON SCREEN
  .

OF PGDN_KEY                                    !PAGE DOWN KEY
  DO SET_NEXT                                  !     POINT TO NEXT RECORD
  DO NEXT_PAGE                                 !     DISPLAY THE NEXT PAGE

OF CTRL_PGDN                                   !CTRL-PAGE DOWN KEY
  DO LAST_PAGE                                 !     DISPLAY THE LAST PAGE
  NDX = RECORDS(TABLE)                         !     POSITION POINT BAR

OF UP_KEY                                      !UP ARROW KEY
  DO SET_PREV                                  !     POINT TO PREVIOUS RECORD
  DO FILL_PREV                                 !     FILL A TABLE ENTRY
  IF FOUND                                     !     FOUND A NEW RECORD
    SCROLL(ROW,COL,ROWS,COLS,-(ROWS(?POINT)))  ! SCROLL THE SCREEN DOWN
    GET(TABLE,1)                               !     GET RECORD FROM TABLE
    DO FILL_SCREEN                             !     DISPLAY ON SCREEN
  .

OF PGUP_KEY                                    !PAGE UP KEY
```

(continued)

```
        DO SET_PREV                              !  POINT TO PREVIOUS RECORD
        DO PREV_PAGE                             !  DISPLAY THE PREVIOUS PAGE

      OF CTRL_PGUP                               !CTRL-PAGE UP
        DO FIRST_PAGE                            !  DISPLAY THE FIRST PAGE
        NDX = 1                                  !  POSITION POINT BAR
    . . .
    FREE(TABLE)                                  !FREE MEMORY TABLE
    RETURN                                       !AND RETURN TO CALLER


SAME_PAGE ROUTINE                                !DISPLAY THE SAME PAGE
  GET(TABLE,1)                                   !  GET THE FIRST TABLE ENTRY
  DO FILL_RECORD                                 !  FILL IN THE RECORD
  SET(DIS:BY_NUMBER,DIS:BY_NUMBER,TBL:PTR)       !  POSITION FILE
  FREE(TABLE)                                    !  EMPTY THE TABLE
  DO NEXT_PAGE                                   !  DISPLAY A FULL PAGE


FIRST_PAGE ROUTINE                               !DISPLAY FIRST PAGE
  BLANK(ROW,COL,ROWS,COLS)
  FREE(TABLE)                                    !  EMPTY THE TABLE
  CLEAR(DIS:RECORD,-1)                           !  CLEAR RECORD TO LOW VALUES
  CLEAR(TBL:PTR)                                 !  ZERO RECORD POINTER
  SET(DIS:BY_NUMBER)                             !  POINT TO FIRST RECORD
  LOOP NDX = 1 TO COUNT                          !  FILL UP THE TABLE
    DO FILL_NEXT                                 !    FILL A TABLE ENTRY
    IF NOT FOUND THEN BREAK.                     !    GET OUT IF NO RECORD
    .
  NDX = 1                                        !  SET TO TOP OF TABLE
  DO SHOW_PAGE                                   !  DISPLAY THE PAGE


LAST_PAGE ROUTINE                                !DISPLAY LAST PAGE
  NDX# = NDX                                     !  SAVE SELECTOR POSITION
  BLANK(ROW,COL,ROWS,COLS)                       !  CLEAR SCROLLING AREA
  FREE(TABLE)                                    !  EMPTY THE TABLE
  CLEAR(DIS:RECORD,1)                            !  CLEAR RECORD TO HIGH VALUES
  CLEAR(TBL:PTR,1)                               !  CLEAR PTR TO HIGH VALUE
  SET(DIS:BY_NUMBER)                             !  POINT TO FIRST RECORD
  LOOP NDX = COUNT TO 1 BY -1                    !  FILL UP THE TABLE
    DO FILL_PREV                                 !    FILL A TABLE ENTRY
    IF NOT FOUND THEN BREAK.                     !    GET OUT IF NO RECORD
    .                                            !  END OF LOOP
  NDX = NDX#                                     !  RESTORE SELECTOR POSITION
  DO SHOW_PAGE                                   !  DISPLAY THE PAGE


FIND_RECORD ROUTINE                              !POSITION TO SPECIFIC RECORD
  SET(DIS:BY_NUMBER,DIS:BY_NUMBER,NEWPTR)        !POSITION FILE
  IF NEWPTR = 0                                  !NEWPTR NOT SET
```

(continued)

```
     NEXT(DISKS)                                  !  READ NEXT RECORD
     NEWPTR = POINTER(DISKS)                      !  SET NEWPTR
     SKIP(DISKS,-1)                               !  BACK UP TO DISPLAY RECORD
   .
   FREE(TABLE)                                    !  CLEAR THE RECORD
   DO NEXT_PAGE                                   !  DISPLAY A PAGE

NEXT_PAGE ROUTINE                                 !DISPLAY NEXT PAGE
   SAVECNT# = RECORDS(TABLE)                      !  SAVE RECORD COUNT
   LOOP COUNT TIMES                               !  FILL UP THE TABLE
     DO FILL_NEXT                                 !    FILL A TABLE ENTRY
     IF NOT FOUND                                 !    IF NONE ARE LEFT
       IF NOT SAVECNT#                            !      IF REBUILDING TABLE
         DO LAST_PAGE                             !        FILL IN RECORDS
         EXIT                                     !        EXIT OUT OF ROUTINE
       .
       BREAK                                      !      EXIT LOOP
   . .
   DO SHOW_PAGE                                   !  DISPLAY THE PAGE

SET_NEXT ROUTINE                                  !POINT TO THE NEXT PAGE
   GET(TABLE,RECORDS(TABLE))                      !  GET THE LAST TABLE ENTRY
   DO FILL_RECORD                                 !  FILL IN THE RECORD
   SET(DIS:BY_NUMBER,DIS:BY_NUMBER,TBL:PTR)       !  POSITION FILE
   NEXT(DISKS)                                    !  READ THE CURRENT RECORD

FILL_NEXT ROUTINE                                 !FILL NEXT TABLE ENTRY
   FOUND = FALSE                                  !  ASSUME RECORD NOT FOUND
   LOOP UNTIL EOF(DISKS)                          !  LOOP UNTIL END OF FILE
     NEXT(DISKS)                                  !    READ THE NEXT RECORD
     FOUND = TRUE                                 !    SET RECORD FOUND
     DO FILL_TABLE                                !    FILL IN THE TABLE ENTRY
     ADD(TABLE)                                   !    ADD LAST TABLE ENTRY
     GET(TABLE,RECORDS(TABLE)-COUNT)              !    GET ANY OVERFLOW RECORD
     DELETE(TABLE)                                !    AND DELETE IT
     EXIT                                         !    RETURN TO CALLER
   .

PREV_PAGE ROUTINE                                 !DISPLAY PREVIOUS PAGE
   LOOP COUNT TIMES                               !  FILL UP THE TABLE
     DO FILL_PREV                                 !    FILL A TABLE ENTRY
     IF NOT FOUND THEN BREAK.                     !    GET OUT IF NO RECORD
   .
   DO SHOW_PAGE                                   !  DISPLAY THE PAGE

SET_PREV ROUTINE                                  !POINT TO PREVIOUS PAGE
   GET(TABLE,1)                                   !  GET THE FIRST TABLE ENTRY
   DO FILL_RECORD                                 !  FILL IN THE RECORD
```

(continued)

```
      SET(DIS:BY_NUMBER,DIS:BY_NUMBER,TBL:PTR)        !   POSITION FILE
      PREVIOUS(DISKS)                                 !   READ THE CURRENT RECORD


FILL_PREV ROUTINE                                     !FILL PREVIOUS TABLE ENTRY
   FOUND = FALSE                                       !   ASSUME RECORD NOT FOUND
   LOOP UNTIL BOF(DISKS)                               !   LOOP UNTIL BEGINNING OF FILE
      PREVIOUS(DISKS)                                  !      READ THE PREVIOUS RECORD
      FOUND = TRUE                                     !      SET RECORD FOUND
      DO FILL_TABLE                                    !      FILL IN THE TABLE ENTRY
      ADD(TABLE,1)                                     !      ADD FIRST TABLE ENTRY
      GET(TABLE,COUNT+1)                               !      GET ANY OVERFLOW RECORD
      DELETE(TABLE)                                    !      AND DELETE IT
      EXIT                                             !      RETURN TO CALLER
    .

SHOW_PAGE ROUTINE                                     !DISPLAY THE PAGE
   NDX# = NDX                                          !   SAVE SCREEN INDEX
   LOOP NDX = 1 TO RECORDS(TABLE)                      !   LOOP THRU THE TABLE
      GET(TABLE,NDX)                                   !      GET A TABLE ENTRY
      DO FILL_SCREEN                                   !      AND DISPLAY IT
      IF TBL:PTR = NEWPTR                              !      SET INDEX FOR NEW RECORD
         NDX# = NDX                                    !      POINT TO CORRECT RECORD
    . .
   NDX = NDX#                                          !   RESTORE SCREEN INDEX
   NEWPTR = 0                                          !   CLEAR NEW RECORD POINTER
   CLEAR(DIS:RECORD)                                   !   CLEAR RECORD AREA

FILL_TABLE ROUTINE                                    !MOVE FILE TO TABLE
   TBL:NUMBER = DIS:NUMBER
   TBL:LABEL = DIS:LABEL
   TBL:NOTES = DIS:NOTES
   TBL:PTR = POINTER(DISKS)                            !   SAVE RECORD POINTER

FILL_RECORD ROUTINE                                   !MOVE TABLE TO FILE
   DIS:NUMBER = TBL:NUMBER

FILL_SCREEN ROUTINE                                   !MOVE TABLE TO SCREEN
   SCR:NUMBER = TBL:NUMBER
   SCR:LABEL = TBL:LABEL
   SCR:NOTES = TBL:NOTES

GET_RECORD ROUTINE                                    !GET SELECTED RECORD
   GET(TABLE,NDX)                                      !   GET TABLE ENTRY
   GET(DISKS,TBL:PTR)                                  !   GET THE RECORD
```

CATALO03.CLA

```
            MEMBER('CATALOG')
UPD_DISKS       PROCEDURE

SCREEN          SCREEN        PRE(SCR),WINDOW(8,53),HLP('UPDATE'),HUE(15,1)
              ROW(1,20)   PAINT(1,17),HUE(14,0)
                COL(1)    STRING('<218,196{18},0{15},196{18},191>'),HUE(14,1)
              ROW(2,1)    REPEAT(6);STRING('<179,0{51},179>'),HUE(14,1)  .
              ROW(8,1)    STRING('<192,196{51},217>'),HUE(14,1)
              ROW(1,21)   STRING('UPDATE A DISK'),HUE(14,0)
              ROW(4,4)    STRING('Number:'),HUE(14,1)
                COL(16)   STRING('of '),HUE(14,1)
              ROW(5,4)    STRING('Label: '),HUE(14,1)
              ROW(6,4)    STRING('Notes: '),HUE(14,1)
MESSAGE       ROW(2,13)   STRING(30),HUE(14,1)
NUMBER        ROW(4,11)   STRING(@N_4),HUE(15,1)
DISKS           COL(19)   STRING(@n4),HUE(15,1)
                          ENTRY,USE(?FIRST_FIELD)
              ROW(5,11)   ENTRY(@s30),USE(DIS:LABEL),HUE(15,1),SEL(0,7)
              ROW(6,11)   ENTRY(@s40),USE(DIS:NOTES),HUE(15,1),SEL(0,7)
                          ENTRY,USE(?LAST_FIELD)
                          PAUSE(''),USE(?DELETE_FIELD)
                .

  EJECT
  CODE
  OPEN(SCREEN)                                    !OPEN THE SCREEN
  SETCURSOR                                       !TURN OFF ANY CURSOR
  select(?dis:label)                              !CALL SETUP PROCEDURE
  DISPLAY                                         !DISPLAY THE FIELDS
  LOOP                                            !LOOP THRU ALL THE FIELDS
    MEM:MESSAGE = CENTER(MEM:MESSAGE,SIZE(MEM:MESSAGE)) !DISPLAY ACTION MESSAGE
    DO CALCFIELDS                                 !CALCULATE DISPLAY FIELDS
    ALERT                                         !RESET ALERTED KEYS
    ALERT(ACCEPT_KEY)                             !ALERT SCREEN ACCEPT KEY
    ALERT(REJECT_KEY)                             !ALERT SCREEN REJECT KEY
    ACCEPT                                        !READ A FIELD
    IF KEYCODE() = REJECT_KEY THEN RETURN.        !RETURN ON SCREEN REJECT KEY
    EXECUTE ACTION                                !SET MESSAGE
      MEM:MESSAGE = 'Record will be Added'        !
      MEM:MESSAGE = 'Record will be Changed'      !
      MEM:MESSAGE = 'Press Enter to Delete'       !
      .
    IF KEYCODE() = ACCEPT_KEY                     !ON SCREEN ACCEPT KEY
      UPDATE                                      !  MOVE ALL FIELDS FROM SCREEN
```

(continued)

```
      SELECT(?)                                  !  START WITH CURRENT FIELD
      SELECT                                     !  EDIT ALL FIELDS
      CYCLE                                      !  GO TO TOP OF LOOP
     .

   CASE FIELD()                                  !JUMP TO FIELD EDIT ROUTINE
   OF ?FIRST_FIELD                               !FROM THE FIRST FIELD
     IF KEYCODE() = ESC_KEY THEN RETURN.         !  RETURN ON ESC KEY
     IF ACTION = 3 THEN SELECT(?DELETE_FIELD).   !  OR CONFIRM FOR DELETE

   OF ?LAST_FIELD                                !FROM THE LAST FIELD
     EXECUTE ACTION                              !  UPDATE THE FILE
       ADD(DISKS)                                !    ADD NEW RECORD
       PUT(DISKS)                                !    CHANGE EXISTING RECORD
       DELETE(DISKS)                             !    DELETE EXISTING RECORD
      .
     IF ERRORCODE() = 40                         !  DUPLICATE KEY ERROR
       MEM:MESSAGE = ERROR()                     !    DISPLAY ERR MESSAGE
       SELECT(2)                                 !    POSITION TO TOP OF FORM
       CYCLE                                     !    GET OUT OF EDIT LOOP
     ELSIF ERROR()                               !  CHECK FOR UNEXPECTED ERROR
       STOP(ERROR())                             !    HALT EXECUTION
      .
     IF ACTION = 3
       FILES_CHILD1                              !  DELETE RELATED DATA
     ELSE
       PUT(FILES)                                !  UPDATE SECONDARY FILES
      .
     ACTION = 0                                  !  SET ACTION TO COMPLETE
     RETURN                                      !  AND RETURN TO CALLER

   OF ?DELETE_FIELD                              !FROM THE DELETE FIELD
     IF KEYCODE() = ENTER_KEY |                  !  ON ENTER KEY
     OR KEYCODE() = ACCEPT_KEY                    !  OR CTRL-ENTER KEY
       SELECT(?LAST_FIELD)                       !    DELETE THE RECORD
     ELSE                                        !  OTHERWISE
       BEEP                                      !    BEEP AND ASK AGAIN
  . . .

CALCFIELDS   ROUTINE
  IF FIELD() > ?FIRST_FIELD                             !BEYOND FIRST_FIELD?
    IF KEYCODE() = 0 AND SELECTED() > FIELD() THEN EXIT. !GET OUT IF NOT NONSTOP
   .
  SCR:MESSAGE = MEM:MESSAGE
  SCR:NUMBER = DIS:NUMBER
  SCR:DISKS = RECORDS(DISKS)
```

CATALO04.CLA

```
          MEMBER('CATALOG')

RPT_NUMBER    PROCEDURE

TITLE     REPORT        LENGTH(59),WIDTH(80),PRE(TTL)
RPT_HEAD                DETAIL
          .                  .
REPORT    REPORT        LENGTH(59),WIDTH(80),PAGE(MEM:PAGE),LINE(MEM:LINE)    |
                        PRE(RPT)
PAGE_HEAD               HEADER
              COL(1)    CTL('<27>&11O') STRING(' {30}Print Disks By Number')
              ROW(+2,1)     STRING('NUMBER LABEL {26}NOTES') CTL(@LF2)
                             .
DETAIL                  DETAIL
              COL(1)    STRING(@N_4),USE(DIS:NUMBER)
              COL(8)    STRING(30),USE(DIS:LABEL)
              COL(39)   STRING(40),USE(DIS:NOTES) CTL(@LF)
                             .
RPT_FOOT                DETAIL
                             .
PAGE_FOOT               FOOTER
              ROW(+1,37)    STRING('PAGE')
              COL(42)   STRING(@n3),USE(MEM:PAGE)
              COL(45)   CTL('<27>&10O') CTL(@LF)
                        CTL(@FF)
          .                  .


  CODE
  DONE# = 0                                 !TURN OFF DONE FLAG
  CLEAR(DIS:RECORD,-1)                      !MAKE SURE RECORD CLEARED
  PRINT(TTL:RPT_HEAD)                       !PRINT TITLE PAGE
  CLOSE(TITLE)                              !CLOSE TITLE REPORT
  SET(DIS:BY_NUMBER)                        !  POINT TO FIRST RECORD
  DO NEXT_RECORD                            !READ FIRST RECORD
  OPEN(REPORT)                              !OPEN THE REPORT
  LOOP UNTIL DONE#                          !READ ALL RECORDS IN FILE
    SAVE_LINE# = MEM:LINE                   !  SAVE LINE NUMBER
    LAST_REC# = POINTER(DISKS)
    PRINT(RPT:DETAIL)                       !  PRINT DETAIL LINES
    DO CHECK_PAGE                           !  DO PAGE BREAK IF NEEDED
    DO NEXT_RECORD                          !  GET NEXT RECORD
  .                                         !
  PRINT(RPT:RPT_FOOT)                       !PRINT GRAND TOTALS
```

(continued)

```
     DO CHECK_PAGE                              !  DO PAGE BREAK IF NEEDED
     CLOSE(REPORT)                              !CLOSE REPORT
     RETURN                                     !RETURN TO CALLER


NEXT_RECORD ROUTINE                            !GET NEXT RECORD
   LOOP UNTIL EOF(DISKS)                        !   READ UNTIL END OF FILE
     NEXT(DISKS)                                !      READ NEXT RECORD
     EXIT                                       !      EXIT THE ROUTINE
   .                                            !
   DONE# = 1                                    !  ON EOF, SET DONE FLAG


CHECK_PAGE ROUTINE                             !CHECK FOR NEW PAGE
   IF MEM:LINE <= SAVE_LINE#                    !  ON PAGE OVERFLOW
     SAVE_LINE# = MEM:LINE                      !     RESET LINE NUMBER
   .
   LOOP UNTIL NOT KEYBOARD()                    !LOOK FOR KEYSTROKE
     ASK                                        !GET KEYCODE
     IF KEYCODE() = REJECT_KEY                  !ON CTRL-ESC
       CLOSE(REPORT)                            !   CLOSE REPORT
       RETURN                                   !   ABORT PRINT
   . .
```

CATALO05.CLA

```
          MEMBER('CATALOG')
FILES          PROCEDURE

SCREEN         SCREEN        PRE(SCR),WINDOW(23,80),HUE(15,1)
               ROW(1,25)  PAINT(1,34),HUE(0,7)
               ROW(8,2)   PAINT(12,13),HUE(0,7)
               ROW(8,17)  PAINT(12,9),HUE(0,7)
               ROW(8,29)  PAINT(12,8),HUE(0,7)
               ROW(8,40)  PAINT(12,7),HUE(0,7)
               ROW(8,50)  PAINT(12,29),HUE(0,7)
               ROW(1,1)   STRING('<201,205{23},0{32},205{23},187>'),HUE(15,1)
               ROW(2,1)   REPEAT(4);STRING('<186,0{78},186>'),HUE(15,1)  .
               ROW(6,1)   REPEAT(2),EVERY(14)
                             STRING('<199,196{78},182>'),HUE(15,1)  .
               ROW(7,1)   REPEAT(13);STRING('<186,0{78},186>'),HUE(15,1)  .
               ROW(21,1)  REPEAT(2);STRING('<186,0{78},186>'),HUE(15,1)  .
               ROW(23,1)  STRING('<200,205{78},188>'),HUE(15,1)
               ROW(3,25)  STRING('Locate by Filename:'),HUE(14,1)
               ROW(5,7)   STRING('Total Disk Space Used: '),HUE(14,1)
                  COL(40) STRING('bytes'),HUE(14,1)
```

(continued)

```
                   COL(51)   STRING('Total Files Listed: '),HUE(14,1)
                  ROW(7,4)   STRING('FILE NAMES'),HUE(15,1)
                   COL(17)   STRING('FILE')
                   COL(22)   STRING('SI'),HUE(15,1)
                   COL(24)   STRING('ZE')
                   COL(29)   STRING('  DATE'),HUE(15,1)
                   COL(40)   STRING('TIME'),HUE(15,1)
                   COL(50)   STRING('NOTES'),HUE(15,1)
                  ROW(8,39)  STRING(' '),HUE(15,1)
                  ROW(21,14) STRING('Press <<INS> to Add'),HUE(11,1)
                   COL(48)   STRING('Press ALT-D to go to DOS'),HUE(15,1)
                  ROW(22,14) STRING('Press <<ESC> to Exit'),HUE(11,1)
                   COL(48)   STRING('Press <<ENTER> to Edit'),HUE(11,1)
LABEL             ROW(1,26)  STRING(30)
LOCATOR           ROW(3,45)  STRING(12)
SPACE             ROW(5,30)  STRING(@n9),HUE(14,1)
NUMBER             COL(71)   STRING(@n4),HUE(14,1)
                             ENTRY,USE(?FIRST_FIELD)
                             ENTRY,USE(?PRE_POINT)
                             REPEAT(12),EVERY(1),INDEX(NDX)
                  ROW(8,2)      POINT(1,77),USE(?POINT),ESC(?-1)
BLANK              COL(2)    STRING(@s1)
FILENAME           COL(3)    STRING(12)
SIZEBYTES          COL(17)   STRING(@n9)
DATE               COL(29)   STRING(@d1)
TIME               COL(40)   STRING(@T3)
NOTES              COL(50)   STRING(28)
BLANK2             COL(78)   STRING(@s1)
                      .          .


NDX        BYTE                              !REPEAT INDEX FOR POINT AREA
ROW        BYTE                              !ACTUAL ROW OF SCROLL AREA
COL        BYTE                              !ACTUAL COLUMN OF SCROLL AREA
COUNT      BYTE(12)                          !NUMBER OF ITEMS TO SCROLL
ROWS       BYTE(12)                          !NUMBER OF ROWS TO SCROLL
COLS       BYTE(77)                          !NUMBER OF COLUMNS TO SCROLL
FOUND      BYTE                              !RECORD FOUND FLAG
NEWPTR     LONG                              !POINTER TO NEW RECORD

TABLE      TABLE,PRE(TBL)                    !TABLE OF RECORD DATA
NUMBER         STRING(@n4)
BLANK          STRING(@s1)
FILENAME       STRING(12)
SIZEBYTES      LONG
DATE           STRING(@d1)
TIME           STRING(@T3)
NOTES          STRING(28)
```

(continued)

```
BLANK2          STRING(@s1)
NUMBER1         STRING(@N_4)
PTR             LONG                            !  POINTER TO FILE RECORD

                .
                GROUP,PRE(SAV)
NUMBER          STRING(@N_4)

                .
TOT_GROUP       GROUP,PRE(TOT)                  !TABLE TOTAL FIELDS
SPACE           REAL
NUMBER          REAL

                .

  EJECT
  CODE
  ACTION# = ACTION                              !SAVE ACTION
  OPEN(SCREEN)                                  !OPEN THE SCREEN
  SETCURSOR                                     !TURN OFF ANY CURSOR
  FIL:NUMBER = DIS:NUMBER                       !CALL SETUP PROCEDURE
  SAV:NUMBER = FIL:NUMBER                       !SAVE SELECTOR FIELD
  CLEAR(TOT_GROUP)                              !ZERO TOTALS
  TBL:PTR = 1                                   !START AT TABLE ENTRY
  NDX = 1                                       !PUT SELECTOR BAR ON TOP ITEM
  ROW = ROW(?POINT)                             !REMEMBER TOP ROW AND
  COL = COL(?POINT)                             !LEFT COLUMN OF SCROLL AREA
  RECORDS# = TRUE                               !INITIALIZE RECORDS FLAG
  CACHE(FIL:BY_NUMBER,.25)                      !CACHE KEY FILE
  LOOP                                          !LOOP UNTIL USER EXITS
    ACTION = ACTION#                            !RESTORE ACTION
    FIL:NUMBER = SAV:NUMBER                     !RESTORE SELECTOR FIELD
    SCR:SPACE = TOT:SPACE
    SCR:NUMBER = TOT:NUMBER
    UPDATE                                      !UPDATE RECORD KEYS
    DIS:NUMBER = FIL:NUMBER                     !MOVE RELATED KEY FIELDS
    GET(DISKS,DIS:BY_NUMBER)                    !READ THE RECORD
    IF ERROR() THEN CLEAR(DIS:RECORD).          !IF NOT FOUND, CLEAR RECORD
    SCR:LABEL = DIS:LABEL                       !DISPLAY LOOKUP FIELD
    ALERT                                       !RESET ALERTED KEYS
    ALERT(REJECT_KEY)                           !ALERT SCREEN REJECT KEY
    ALERT(ACCEPT_KEY)                           !ALERT SCREEN ACCEPT KEY
    ALERT(ALT_D)                                !ALERT HOT KEY
    ACCEPT                                      !READ A FIELD
    IF KEYCODE() = ALT_D                        !ON HOT KEY
      IF FIELD() = ?POINT THEN DO GET_RECORD.   !  READ RECORD IF NEEDED
      JUMP                                      !  CALL HOT KEY PROCEDURE
      DO SAME_PAGE                              !  RESET TO SAME PAGE
      CYCLE                                     !  AND LOOP AGAIN
```

(continued)

```
    IF KEYCODE() = REJECT_KEY THEN BREAK.              !RETURN ON SCREEN REJECT KEY

    IF  KEYCODE() = ACCEPT_KEY    |                    !ON SCREEN ACCEPT KEY
    AND FIELD() <> ?POINT                              !BUT NOT ON THE POINT FIELD
      UPDATE                                           !  MOVE ALL FIELDS FROM SCREEN
      SELECT(?)                                        !  START WITH CURRENT FIELD
      SELECT                                           !  EDIT ALL FIELDS
      CYCLE                                            !  GO TO TOP OF LOOP
    .

    CASE FIELD()                                       !JUMP TO FIELD EDIT ROUTINE

    OF ?FIRST_FIELD                                    !FROM THE FIRST FIELD
      IF KEYCODE() = ESC_KEY   |                       !  RETURN ON ESC KEY
      OR RECORDS# = FALSE                              !  OR NO RECORDS
        BREAK                                          !    EXIT PROGRAM
      .
      CLEAR(TOT_GROUP)                                 !ZERO TOTALS
      CLEAR(FIL:RECORD,-1)                             !CLEAR RECORD TO LOW VALUES
      CLEAR(TBL:PTR)                                   !SET POINTER TO ZERO
      SETHUE(BACKHUE(ROW,COL),BACKHUE(ROW,COL))        !TURN OFF DISPLAY
      FIL:NUMBER = SAV:NUMBER                          !RESTORE SELECTOR FIELD
      SET(FIL:BY_NUMBER,FIL:BY_NUMBER,TBL:PTR)         !  POINT PAST LAST RECORD
      LOOP UNTIL EOF(FILES)                            !LOOP UNTIL END OF FILE
        NEXT(FILES)                                    !  READ A RECORD
        IF FIL:NUMBER <> SAV:NUMBER                    !IF END OF SELECTION
           FIL:NUMBER = SAV:NUMBER                     !  RESTORE THE SELECTOR
           BREAK                                       !  AND BREAK
        .
        ACTN# = 1                                      !SET ACTION FOR ADD
        DO FILL_TABLE                                  !  TOTAL SCREEN VARIABLES
        DO COMP_TOTALS                                 !  ADD TO TOTAL AMOUNT
      .
      SETHUE()                                         !TURN OFF SETHUE
      FREE(FILES)                                      !FREE MEMORY USED FOR BUFFERING
      FREE(TABLE)                                      !FREE MEMORY TABLE
      IF ACTION = 4                                    !  TABLE LOOKUP REQUEST
        NEWPTR = POINTER(FILES)                        !  SET POINTER TO RECORD
        IF NOT NEWPTR                                  !  RECORD NOT PASSED TO TABLE
          SET(FIL:BY_NUMBER,FIL:BY_NUMBER)             !    POSITION TO CLOSEST RECORD
          NEXT(FILES)                                  !    READ RECORD
          NEWPTR = POINTER(FILES)                      !    SET POINTER
        .
        DO FIND_RECORD                                 !  POSITION FILE
      ELSE
        NDX = 1                                        !  PUT SELECTOR BAR ON TOP ITEM
        DO FIRST_PAGE                                  !  BUILD MEMORY TABLE OF KEYS
      .
```

(continued)

```
    RECORDS# = TRUE                             !  ASSUME THERE ARE RECORDS
OF ?PRE_POINT                                   !PRE POINT FIELD CONDITION
  IF KEYCODE() = ESC_KEY                        !  BACKING UP?
    SELECT(?-1)                                 !    SELECT PREVIOUS FIELD
  ELSE                                          !  GOING FORWARD
    SELECT(?POINT)                              !    SELECT MENU FIELD
  .
  IF KEYCODE() = ESC_KEY                        !  BACKING UP?
    SCR:LOCATOR = ''                            !    CLEAR LOCATOR
    SETCURSOR                                   !    AND TURN CURSOR OFF
  ELSE                                          !  GOING FORWARD
    LEN# = 0                                    !    RESET TO START OF LOCATOR
    SETCURSOR(ROW(SCR:LOCATOR),COL(SCR:LOCATOR)) !AND TURN CURSOR ON
  .
OF ?POINT                                       !PROCESS THE POINT FIELD
  IF RECORDS(TABLE) = 0                         !IF THERE ARE NO RECORDS
    CLEAR(FIL:RECORD)                           !  CLEAR RECORD AREA
    ACTION = 1                                  !  SET ACTION TO ADD
    GET(FILES,0)                                !  CLEAR PENDING RECORD
    ACTN# = ACTION                              !SAVE ACTION FOR COMP_TOTALS
    FIL:NUMBER = SAV:NUMBER                      !RESTORE SELECTOR FIELD
    NEWFILES                                    !  CALL FORM FOR NEW RECORD
    NEWPTR = POINTER(FILES)                      !    SET POINTER TO NEW RECORD
    DO FIRST_PAGE                               !  DISPLAY THE FIRST PAGE
    IF RECORDS(TABLE) = 0                       !  IF THERE AREN'T ANY RECORDS
      RECORDS# = FALSE                          !    INDICATE NO RECORDS
      SELECT(?PRE_POINT-1)                      !    SELECT THE PRIOR FIELD
    .
    CYCLE                                       !    AND LOOP AGAIN
  .
  IF KEYCODE() > 31            |                 !THE DISPLAYABLE CHARACTERS
  AND KEYCODE() < 255                           !ARE USED TO LOCATE RECORDS
    IF LEN# < SIZE(SCR:LOCATOR)                 !  IF THERE IS ROOM LEFT
      SCR:LOCATOR = SUB(SCR:LOCATOR,1,LEN#) & CHR(KEYCODE())
      LEN# += 1                                 !    INCREMENT THE LENGTH
    .
  ELSIF KEYCODE() = BS_KEY                      !BACKSPACE UNTYPES A CHARACTER
    IF LEN# > 0                                 !  IF THERE ARE CHARACTERS LEFT
      LEN# -= 1                                 !    DECREMENT THE LENGTH
      SCR:LOCATOR = SUB(SCR:LOCATOR,1,LEN#)     !    ERASE THE LAST CHARACTER
    .
  ELSE                                          !FOR ANY OTHER CHARACTER
    LEN# = 0                                    !  ZERO THE LENGTH
    SCR:LOCATOR = ''                            !  ERASE THE LOCATOR FIELD
  .
  SETCURSOR(ROW(SCR:LOCATOR),COL(SCR:LOCATOR)+LEN#) !AND RESET THE CURSOR
  FIL:FILENAME = CLIP(SCR:LOCATOR)              !    UPDATE THE KEY FIELD
  IF KEYBOARD() > 31           |                 !THE DISPLAYABLE CHARACTERS
```

(continued)

```
AND KEYBOARD() < 255            |     !ARE USED TO LOCATE RECORDS
OR KEYBOARD() = BS_KEY                !INCLUDE BACKSPACE
  CYCLE
.
IF LEN# > 0                          !ON A LOCATOR REQUEST
  FIL:NUMBER = SAV:NUMBER            !RESTORE SELECTOR FIELD
  FIL:FILENAME = CLIP(SCR:LOCATOR)   !   UPDATE THE KEY FIELD
  SET(FIL:BY_NUMBER,FIL:BY_NUMBER)   !   POINT TO NEW RECORD
  NEXT(FILES)                        !   READ A RECORD
  IF (EOF(FILES) AND ERROR())        !   IF EOF IS REACHED
    SET(FIL:BY_NUMBER)               !     SET TO FIRST RECORD
    PREVIOUS(FILES)                  !     READ THE LAST RECORD
  .
  NEWPTR = POINTER(FILES)            !   SET NEW RECORD POINTER
  SKIP(FILES,-1)                     !   BACK UP TO FIRST RECORD
  FREE(TABLE)                        !   CLEAR THE TABLE
  DO NEXT_PAGE                       !   AND DISPLAY A NEW PAGE
.
CASE KEYCODE()                       !PROCESS THE KEYSTROKE

OF INS_KEY                           !INS KEY
  CLEAR(FIL:RECORD)                  !   CLEAR RECORD AREA
  ACTION = 1                         !   SET ACTION TO ADD
  GET(FILES,0)                       !   CLEAR PENDING RECORD
  ACTN# = ACTION                     !SAVE ACTION FOR COMP_TOTALS
  FIL:NUMBER = SAV:NUMBER            !RESTORE SELECTOR FIELD
  NEWFILES                           !   CALL FORM FOR NEW RECORD
  IF ~ACTION                         !   IF RECORD WAS ADDED
    NEWPTR = POINTER(FILES)          !     SET POINTER TO NEW RECORD
    DO FIND_RECORD                   !     POSITION IN FILE
  .
OF ENTER_KEY                         !ENTER KEY
OROF ACCEPT_KEY                      !CTRL-ENTER KEY
  DO GET_RECORD                      !   GET THE SELECTED RECORD
  IF ACTION = 4 AND KEYCODE() = ENTER_KEY! IF THIS IS A LOOKUP REQUEST
    ACTION = 0                       !     SET ACTION TO COMPLETE
    BREAK                            !     AND RETURN TO CALLER
  .
  IF ~ERROR()                        !   IF RECORD IS STILL THERE
    ACTION = 2                       !     SET ACTION TO CHANGE
    ACTN# = ACTION                   !SAVE ACTION FOR COMP_TOTALS
    SPACE$ = FIL:SIZEBYTES
    NEWFILES                         !     CALL FORM TO CHANGE REC
    IF ACTION THEN CYCLE.            !     IF SUCCESSFUL RE-DISPLAY
    TOT:SPACE -= SPACE$
    TOT:NUMBER -= 1
  .
```

(continued)

```
      NEWPTR = POINTER(FILES)              !    SET POINTER TO NEW RECORD
    DO FIND_RECORD                         !    POSITION IN FILE
OF DEL_KEY                                 !DEL KEY
  DO GET_RECORD                            !  READ THE SELECTED RECORD
  IF ~ERROR()                              !  IF RECORD IS STILL THERE
    ACTION = 3                             !    SET ACTION TO DELETE
    ACTN# = ACTION                         !SAVE ACTION FOR COMP_TOTALS
    SPACE$ = FIL:SIZEBYTES
    NEWFILES                               !    CALL FORM TO DELETE
    IF ~ACTION                             !    IF SUCCESSFUL
      TOT:SPACE -= SPACE$
      TOT:NUMBER -= 1
      N# = NDX                             !      SAVE POINT INDEX
      DO SAME_PAGE                         !      RE-DISPLAY
      NDX = N#                             !      RESTORE POINT INDEX
    . .
OF DOWN_KEY                                !DOWN ARROW KEY
  DO SET_NEXT                              !  POINT TO NEXT RECORD
  DO FILL_NEXT                             !  FILL A TABLE ENTRY
  IF FOUND                                 !  FOUND A NEW RECORD
    SCROLL(ROW,COL,ROWS,COLS,ROWS(?POINT)) !    SCROLL THE SCREEN UP
    GET(TABLE,RECORDS(TABLE))              !  GET RECORD FROM TABLE
    DO FILL_SCREEN                         !  DISPLAY ON SCREEN
    .

OF PGDN_KEY                                !PAGE DOWN KEY
  DO SET_NEXT                              !  POINT TO NEXT RECORD
  DO NEXT_PAGE                             !  DISPLAY THE NEXT PAGE

OF CTRL_PGDN                               !CTRL-PAGE DOWN KEY
  DO LAST_PAGE                             !  DISPLAY THE LAST PAGE
  NDX = RECORDS(TABLE)                     !  POSITION POINT BAR

OF UP_KEY                                  !UP ARROW KEY
  DO SET_PREV                              !  POINT TO PREVIOUS RECORD
  DO FILL_PREV                             !  FILL A TABLE ENTRY
  IF FOUND                                 !  FOUND A NEW RECORD
    SCROLL(ROW,COL,ROWS,COLS,-(ROWS(?POINT)))! SCROLL THE SCREEN DOWN
    GET(TABLE,1)                           !  GET RECORD FROM TABLE
    DO FILL_SCREEN                         !  DISPLAY ON SCREEN
    .

OF PGUP_KEY                                !PAGE UP KEY
  DO SET_PREV                              !  POINT TO PREVIOUS RECORD
  DO PREV_PAGE                             !  DISPLAY THE PREVIOUS PAGE

OF CTRL_PGUP                               !CTRL-PAGE UP
```

(continued)

```
        DO FIRST_PAGE                                   !  DISPLAY THE FIRST PAGE
        NDX = 1                                         !  POSITION POINT BAR

  . . .
  FREE(TABLE)                                           !FREE MEMORY TABLE
  RETURN                                                !AND RETURN TO CALLER

SAME_PAGE ROUTINE                                       !DISPLAY THE SAME PAGE
  GET(TABLE,1)                                          !  GET THE FIRST TABLE ENTRY
  DO FILL_RECORD                                        !  FILL IN THE RECORD
  SET(FIL:BY_NUMBER,FIL:BY_NUMBER,TBL:PTR)              !  POSITION FILE
  FREE(TABLE)                                           !  EMPTY THE TABLE
  DO NEXT_PAGE                                          !  DISPLAY A FULL PAGE

FIRST_PAGE ROUTINE                                      !DISPLAY FIRST PAGE
  BLANK(ROW,COL,ROWS,COLS)
  FREE(TABLE)                                           !  EMPTY THE TABLE
  CLEAR(FIL:RECORD,-1)                                  !  CLEAR RECORD TO LOW VALUES
  CLEAR(TBL:PTR)                                        !  ZERO RECORD POINTER
  FIL:NUMBER = SAV:NUMBER                               !RESTORE SELECTOR FIELD
  SET(FIL:BY_NUMBER,FIL:BY_NUMBER,TBL:PTR)              !  POINT PAST LAST RECORD
  LOOP NDX = 1 TO COUNT                                 !  FILL UP THE TABLE
    DO FILL_NEXT                                        !    FILL A TABLE ENTRY
    IF NOT FOUND THEN BREAK.                            !    GET OUT IF NO RECORD
    .
  NDX = 1                                               !  SET TO TOP OF TABLE
  DO SHOW_PAGE                                          !  DISPLAY THE PAGE

LAST_PAGE ROUTINE                                       !DISPLAY LAST PAGE
  NDX# = NDX                                            !  SAVE SELECTOR POSITION
  BLANK(ROW,COL,ROWS,COLS)                              !  CLEAR SCROLLING AREA
  FREE(TABLE)                                           !  EMPTY THE TABLE
  CLEAR(FIL:RECORD,1)                                   !  CLEAR RECORD TO HIGH VALUES
  CLEAR(TBL:PTR,1)                                      !  CLEAR PTR TO HIGH VALUE
  FIL:NUMBER = SAV:NUMBER                               !RESTORE SELECTOR FIELD
  SET(FIL:BY_NUMBER,FIL:BY_NUMBER,TBL:PTR)              !  POINT PAST LAST RECORD
  LOOP NDX = COUNT TO 1 BY -1                           !  FILL UP THE TABLE
    DO FILL_PREV                                        !    FILL A TABLE ENTRY
    IF NOT FOUND THEN BREAK.                            !    GET OUT IF NO RECORD
    .                                                   !  END OF LOOP
  NDX = NDX#                                            !  RESTORE SELECTOR POSITION
  DO SHOW_PAGE                                          !  DISPLAY THE PAGE

FIND_RECORD ROUTINE                                     !POSITION TO SPECIFIC RECORD
  SET(FIL:BY_NUMBER,FIL:BY_NUMBER,NEWPTR)               !POSITION FILE
  IF NEWPTR = 0                                         !NEWPTR NOT SET
    NEXT(FILES)                                         !  READ NEXT RECORD
    NEWPTR = POINTER(FILES)      .                      !  SET NEWPTR
```

(continued)

```
        SKIP(FILES,-1)                   !  BACK UP TO DISPLAY RECORD
     .
     FREE(TABLE)                         !  CLEAR THE RECORD
     DO NEXT_PAGE                        !  DISPLAY A PAGE

 NEXT_PAGE ROUTINE                       !DISPLAY NEXT PAGE
    SAVECNT# = RECORDS(TABLE)            !  SAVE RECORD COUNT
    LOOP COUNT TIMES                     !  FILL UP THE TABLE
      DO FILL_NEXT                       !    FILL A TABLE ENTRY
      IF NOT FOUND                       !    IF NONE ARE LEFT
        IF NOT SAVECNT#                  !      IF REBUILDING TABLE
          DO LAST_PAGE                   !        FILL IN RECORDS
        EXIT                             !        EXIT OUT OF ROUTINE
          .
        BREAK                            !    EXIT LOOP
     . .
    DO SHOW_PAGE                         !  DISPLAY THE PAGE

 SET_NEXT ROUTINE                        !POINT TO THE NEXT PAGE
    GET(TABLE,RECORDS(TABLE))            !  GET THE LAST TABLE ENTRY
    DO FILL_RECORD                       !  FILL IN THE RECORD
    SET(FIL:BY_NUMBER,FIL:BY_NUMBER,TBL:PTR)  !  POSITION FILE
    NEXT(FILES)                          !  READ THE CURRENT RECORD

 FILL_NEXT ROUTINE                       !FILL NEXT TABLE ENTRY
    FOUND = FALSE                        !  ASSUME RECORD NOT FOUND
    LOOP UNTIL EOF(FILES)                !  LOOP UNTIL END OF FILE
      NEXT(FILES)                        !    READ THE NEXT RECORD
      IF FIL:NUMBER <> SAV:NUMBER        !IF END OF SELECTION
        FIL:NUMBER = SAV:NUMBER          !  RESTORE THE SELECTOR
        BREAK                            !  AND BREAK
          .
      FOUND = TRUE                       !    SET RECORD FOUND
      DO FILL_TABLE                      !    FILL IN THE TABLE ENTRY
      ADD(TABLE)                         !    ADD LAST TABLE ENTRY
      GET(TABLE,RECORDS(TABLE)-COUNT)    !    GET ANY OVERFLOW RECORD
      DELETE(TABLE)                      !    AND DELETE IT
      EXIT                               !    RETURN TO CALLER
        .
 PREV_PAGE ROUTINE                       !DISPLAY PREVIOUS PAGE
    LOOP COUNT TIMES                     !  FILL UP THE TABLE
      DO FILL_PREV                       !    FILL A TABLE ENTRY
      IF NOT FOUND THEN BREAK.           !    GET OUT IF NO RECORD
        .
    DO SHOW_PAGE                         !  DISPLAY THE PAGE

 SET_PREV ROUTINE                        !POINT TO PREVIOUS PAGE
```

(continued)

```
    GET(TABLE,1)                                ! GET THE FIRST TABLE ENTRY
    DO FILL_RECORD                              ! FILL IN THE RECORD
    SET(FIL:BY_NUMBER,FIL:BY_NUMBER,TBL:PTR)    ! POSITION FILE
    PREVIOUS(FILES)                             ! READ THE CURRENT RECORD


  FILL_PREV ROUTINE                             !FILL PREVIOUS TABLE ENTRY
    FOUND = FALSE                               ! ASSUME RECORD NOT FOUND
    LOOP UNTIL BOF(FILES)                       ! LOOP UNTIL BEGINNING OF FILE
      PREVIOUS(FILES)                           !   READ THE PREVIOUS RECORD
      IF FIL:NUMBER <> SAV:NUMBER               !IF END OF SELECTION
        FIL:NUMBER = SAV:NUMBER                 !   RESTORE THE SELECTOR
        BREAK                                   !   AND BREAK
      .
      FOUND = TRUE                              !   SET RECORD FOUND
      DO FILL_TABLE                             !   FILL IN THE TABLE ENTRY
      ADD(TABLE,1)                              !   ADD FIRST TABLE ENTRY
      GET(TABLE,COUNT+1)                        !   GET ANY OVERFLOW RECORD
      DELETE(TABLE)                             !   AND DELETE IT
      EXIT                                      !   RETURN TO CALLER
    .

  SHOW_PAGE ROUTINE                             !DISPLAY THE PAGE
    NDX# = NDX                                  ! SAVE SCREEN INDEX
    LOOP NDX = 1 TO RECORDS(TABLE)              ! LOOP THRU THE TABLE
      GET(TABLE,NDX)                            !   GET A TABLE ENTRY
      DO FILL_SCREEN                            !   AND DISPLAY IT
      IF TBL:PTR = NEWPTR                       !   SET INDEX FOR NEW RECORD
        NDX# = NDX                              !   POINT TO CORRECT RECORD
        DO COMP_TOTALS                          !CALCULATE TABLE TOTALS
    . .
    NDX = NDX#                                  ! RESTORE SCREEN INDEX
    NEWPTR = 0                                  ! CLEAR NEW RECORD POINTER
    CLEAR(FIL:RECORD)                           ! CLEAR RECORD AREA


  FILL_TABLE ROUTINE                            !MOVE FILE TO TABLE
    TBL:NUMBER = DIS:NUMBER
    TBL:FILENAME = FIL:FILENAME
    TBL:SIZEBYTES = FIL:SIZEBYTES
    TBL:DATE = FIL:DATE
    TBL:NOTES = FIL:NOTES
    TBL:NUMBER1 = FIL:NUMBER
    TBL:PTR = POINTER(FILES)                    ! SAVE RECORD POINTER
    TBL:BLANK = ''
    TBL:TIME = FIL:TIME
    TBL:BLANK2 = ''


  FILL_RECORD ROUTINE                           !MOVE TABLE TO FILE
    FIL:NUMBER = TBL:NUMBER1
```

(continued)

```
        FIL:FILENAME = TBL:FILENAME

FILL_SCREEN ROUTINE                                !MOVE TABLE TO SCREEN
    SCR:NUMBER = TBL:NUMBER
    SCR:BLANK = TBL:BLANK
    SCR:FILENAME = TBL:FILENAME
    SCR:SIZEBYTES = TBL:SIZEBYTES
    SCR:DATE = TBL:DATE
    SCR:TIME = TBL:TIME
    SCR:NOTES = TBL:NOTES
    SCR:BLANK2 = TBL:BLANK2

GET_RECORD ROUTINE                                 !GET SELECTED RECORD
    GET(TABLE,NDX)                                 !  GET TABLE ENTRY
    GET(FILES,TBL:PTR)                             !  GET THE RECORD

COMP_TOTALS  ROUTINE                               !CALCULATE TOTAL FIELDS
    IF NOT ACTN# THEN EXIT.                        !GET OUT IF ACTN NOT SET
    TOT:SPACE += TBL:SIZEBYTES
    TOT:NUMBER += 1
    ACTN# = 0                                      !CLEAR ACTION
```

CATALO06.CLA

```
              MEMBER('CATALOG')
NEWFILES      PROCEDURE

SCREEN        SCREEN        PRE(SCR),WINDOW(15,64),HUE(15,0)
              ROW(1,1)      STRING('<218,196{17},0{30},196{15},191>'),HUE(14,0)
              ROW(2,1)      STRING('<179,0{62},179>'),HUE(14,0)
              ROW(3,1)      STRING('<195,196{62},180>'),HUE(14,0)
              ROW(4,1)      REPEAT(11);STRING('<179,0{62},179>'),HUE(14,0) .
              ROW(15,1)     STRING('<192,196{62},217>'),HUE(14,0)
              ROW(2,5)      STRING('Disk No.:'),HUE(14,0)
                COL(19)     STRING(' Disk Label: '),HUE(14,0)
              ROW(4,16)     STRING('Enter a Filename:'),HUE(14,0)
              ROW(6,16)     STRING('Notes:'),HUE(14,0)
                COL(22)     STRING(' '),HUE(15,0)
              ROW(8,16)     STRING('File Size:'),HUE(14,0)
                COL(37)     STRING('bytes'),HUE(14,0)
              ROW(10,16)    STRING('Creation Date: '),HUE(14,0)
              ROW(12,16)    STRING('Creation Time: '),HUE(14,0)
MESSAGE       ROW(1,19)     STRING(30),HUE(14,0)
NUMBER        ROW(2,14)     STRING(@N_4)
LABEL           COL(32)     STRING(30)
```

(continued)

```
TIME        ROW(12,31)  STRING(@t3)
                        ENTRY,USE(?FIRST_FIELD)
            ROW(4,33)   ENTRY(@s12),USE(FIL:FILENAME)
            ROW(6,23)   ENTRY(@s28),USE(FIL:NOTES),LFT
            ROW(8,27)   ENTRY(@n9),USE(FIL:SIZEBYTES),NUM,INS
            ROW(10,31)  ENTRY(@d1),USE(FIL:DATE),LFT
            ROW(14,23)  PAUSE('Press <<ENTER> to Accept'),USE(?PAUSE_FIELD)
                        ENTRY,USE(?LAST_FIELD)
                        PAUSE(''),USE(?DELETE_FIELD)


EJECT
CODE
OPEN(SCREEN)                                !OPEN THE SCREEN
SETCURSOR                                   !TURN OFF ANY CURSOR
DISPLAY                                     !DISPLAY THE FIELDS
LOOP                                        !LOOP THRU ALL THE FIELDS
  MEM:MESSAGE = CENTER(MEM:MESSAGE,SIZE(MEM:MESSAGE)) !DISPLAY ACTION MESSAGE
  DO CALCFIELDS                             !CALCULATE DISPLAY FIELDS
  ALERT                                     !RESET ALERTED KEYS
  ALERT(ACCEPT_KEY)                         !ALERT SCREEN ACCEPT KEY
  ALERT(REJECT_KEY)                         !ALERT SCREEN REJECT KEY
  ACCEPT                                    !READ A FIELD
  IF KEYCODE() = REJECT_KEY THEN RETURN.    !RETURN ON SCREEN REJECT KEY
  EXECUTE ACTION                            !SET MESSAGE
    MEM:MESSAGE = 'Record will be Added'    !
    MEM:MESSAGE = 'Record will be Changed'  !
    MEM:MESSAGE = 'Press Enter to Delete'   !
  .

  IF KEYCODE() = ACCEPT_KEY                 !ON SCREEN ACCEPT KEY
    UPDATE                                  !  MOVE ALL FIELDS FROM SCREEN
    SELECT(?)                               !  START WITH CURRENT FIELD
    SELECT                                  !  EDIT ALL FIELDS
    CYCLE                                   !  GO TO TOP OF LOOP
  .

  CASE FIELD()                              !JUMP TO FIELD EDIT ROUTINE
  OF ?FIRST_FIELD                           !FROM THE FIRST FIELD
    IF KEYCODE() = ESC_KEY THEN RETURN.     !  RETURN ON ESC KEY
    IF ACTION = 3 THEN SELECT(?DELETE_FIELD). !  OR CONFIRM FOR DELETE

  OF ?PAUSE_FIELD                           !ON PAUSE FIELD
    IF KEYCODE() <> ENTER_KEY|              !IF NOT ENTER KEY
    AND KEYCODE() <> ACCEPT_KEY|            !AND NOT CTRL-ENTER KEY
    AND KEYCODE() <> 0                      !AND NOT NONSTOP MODE
      BEEP                                  !  SOUND KEYBOARD ALARM
      SELECT(?PAUSE_FIELD)                  !  AND STAY ON PAUSE FIELD
    .
```

(continued)

```
        OF ?LAST_FIELD                    !FROM THE LAST FIELD
          EXECUTE ACTION                  !  UPDATE THE FILE
            ADD(FILES)                    !    ADD NEW RECORD
            PUT(FILES)                    !    CHANGE EXISTING RECORD
            DELETE(FILES)                 !    DELETE EXISTING RECORD
            .
          IF ERRORCODE() = 40             !  DUPLICATE KEY ERROR
            MEM:MESSAGE = ERROR()         !    DISPLAY ERR MESSAGE
            SELECT(2)                     !    POSITION TO TOP OF FORM
            CYCLE                         !    GET OUT OF EDIT LOOP
          ELSIF ERROR()                   !  CHECK FOR UNEXPECTED ERROR
            STOP(ERROR())                ⸍!    HALT EXECUTION
            .
          ACTION = 0                      !  SET ACTION TO COMPLETE
          RETURN                          !  AND RETURN TO CALLER

        OF ?DELETE_FIELD                  !FROM THE DELETE FIELD
          IF KEYCODE() = ENTER_KEY |      !  ON ENTER KEY
          OR KEYCODE() = ACCEPT_KEY       !  OR CTRL-ENTER KEY
            SELECT(?LAST_FIELD)           !    DELETE THE RECORD
          ELSE                            !  OTHERWISE
            BEEP                          !    BEEP AND ASK AGAIN
      . . .

CALCFIELDS   ROUTINE
  IF FIELD() > ?FIRST_FIELD                      !BEYOND FIRST_FIELD?
    IF KEYCODE() = 0 AND SELECTED() > FIELD() THEN EXIT. !GET OUT IF NOT NONSTOP
    .
  UPDATE                                 !UPDATE RECORD KEYS
  DIS:NUMBER = FIL:NUMBER                 !MOVE RELATED KEY FIELDS
  GET(DISKS,DIS:BY_NUMBER)               !READ THE RECORD
  IF ERROR() THEN CLEAR(DIS:RECORD).     !IF NOT FOUND, CLEAR RECORD
  SCR:LABEL = DIS:LABEL                  !DISPLAY LOOKUP FIELD
  SCR:MESSAGE = MEM:MESSAGE
  SCR:NUMBER = FIL:NUMBER
  SCR:TIME = fil:time
```

CATALO07.CLA

```
        MEMBER('CATALOG')
FILESEARCH   PROCEDURE

SCREEN       SCREEN      PRE(SCR),WINDOW(25,80),HUE(15,1)
             ROW(5,1)    STRING('<201,205{30},0{19},205{28},187>'),HUE(15,1)
             ROW(6,1)    REPEAT(2);STRING('<186,0{77},186>'),HUE(15,1) .
```

(continued)

```
                ROW(8,1)    REPEAT(2),EVERY(14)
                               STRING('<199,196{77},182>'),HUE(15,1) .
                ROW(9,1)    REPEAT(13);STRING('<186,0{77},186>'),HUE(15,1) .
                ROW(23,1)   REPEAT(2);STRING('<186,0{77},186>'),HUE(15,1) .
                ROW(25,1)   STRING('<200,205{77},188>'),HUE(15,1)
                ROW(5,33)   STRING('SEARCH FOR A FILE'),HUE(14,1)
                ROW(7,25)   STRING('Locate by Filename:'),HUE(14,1)
                ROW(9,4)    STRING('No.'),HUE(14,1)
                  COL(8)    STRING('Disk Label'),HUE(14,1)
                  COL(39)   STRING(' File Name'),HUE(14,1)
                  COL(54)   STRING('Size'),HUE(14,1)
                  COL(63)   STRING('Date'),HUE(14,1)
                  COL(72)   STRING('Time'),HUE(14,1)
                ROW(10,38)  STRING(' '),HUE(14,1)
                  COL(70)   STRING(' '),HUE(15,1)
                ROW(23,14)  STRING('Press <<INS> to Add'),HUE(11,1)
                  COL(48)   STRING('Press ALT-D to go to DOS'),HUE(15,1)
                ROW(24,14)  STRING('Press <<ESC> to Exit'),HUE(11,1)
                  COL(48)   STRING('Press <<ENTER> to Edit'),HUE(11,1)
LOCATOR         ROW(7,45)   STRING(12)
                               ENTRY,USE(?FIRST_FIELD)
                               ENTRY,USE(?PRE_POINT)
                               REPEAT(12),EVERY(1),INDEX(NDX)
                ROW(10,2)       POINT(1,77),USE(?POINT),ESC(?-1)
SPACE           COL(2)      STRING(@s1)
NUMBER          COL(3)      STRING(@N_4)
LABEL           COL(8)      STRING(30)
FILENAME        COL(39)     STRING(12)
SIZEBYTES       COL(52)     STRING(@n9)
DATE            COL(62)     STRING(@d1)
TIME            COL(71)     STRING(@T3)
SPACE2          COL(78)     STRING(@s1)
                   .                  .

NDX             BYTE                           !REPEAT INDEX FOR POINT AREA
ROW             BYTE                           !ACTUAL ROW OF SCROLL AREA
COL             BYTE                           !ACTUAL COLUMN OF SCROLL AREA
COUNT           BYTE(12)                       !NUMBER OF ITEMS TO SCROLL
ROWS            BYTE(12)                       !NUMBER OF ROWS TO SCROLL
COLS            BYTE(77)                       !NUMBER OF COLUMNS TO SCROLL
FOUND           BYTE                           !RECORD FOUND FLAG
NEWPTR          LONG                           !POINTER TO NEW RECORD

TABLE           TABLE,PRE(TBL)                 !TABLE OF RECORD DATA
SPACE           STRING(@s1)
NUMBER          STRING(@N_4)
LABEL           STRING(30)
```

(continued)

```
FILENAME    STRING(12)
SIZEBYTES   LONG
DATE        STRING(@d1)
TIME        STRING(@T3)
SPACE2      STRING(@s1)
PTR             LONG                                !  POINTER TO FILE RECORD
              .                                          .

  EJECT
  CODE
  ACTION# = ACTION                                 !SAVE ACTION
  OPEN(SCREEN)                                      !OPEN THE SCREEN
  SETCURSOR                                         !TURN OFF ANY CURSOR
  TBL:PTR = 1                                       !START AT TABLE ENTRY
  NDX = 1                                           !PUT SELECTOR BAR ON TOP ITEM
  ROW = ROW(?POINT)                                 !REMEMBER TOP ROW AND
  COL = COL(?POINT)                                 !LEFT COLUMN OF SCROLL AREA
  RECORDS# = TRUE                                   !INITIALIZE RECORDS FLAG
  CACHE(FIL:BY_FILENAME,.25)                        !CACHE KEY FILE
  IF ACTION = 4                                     !  TABLE LOOKUP REQUEST
    NEWPTR = POINTER(FILES)                         !  SET POINTER TO RECORD
    IF NOT NEWPTR                                   !  RECORD NOT PASSED TO TABLE
      SET(FIL:BY_FILENAME,FIL:BY_FILENAME)          !    POSITION TO CLOSEST RECORD
      NEXT(FILES)                                   !    READ RECORD
      NEWPTR = POINTER(FILES)                       !    SET POINTER
             .
    DO FIND_RECORD                                  !  POSITION FILE
  ELSE
    NDX = 1                                         !  PUT SELECTOR BAR ON TOP ITEM
    DO FIRST_PAGE                                   !  BUILD MEMORY TABLE OF KEYS
         .
  RECORDS# = TRUE                                   !  ASSUME THERE ARE RECORDS
  LOOP                                              !LOOP UNTIL USER EXITS
    ACTION = ACTION#                                !RESTORE ACTION
    ALERT                                           !RESET ALERTED KEYS
    ALERT(REJECT_KEY)                               !ALERT SCREEN REJECT KEY
    ALERT(ACCEPT_KEY)                               !ALERT SCREEN ACCEPT KEY
    ALERT(ALT_D)                                    !ALERT HOT KEY
    ACCEPT                                          !READ A FIELD
    IF KEYCODE() = ALT_D                            !ON HOT KEY
      IF FIELD() = ?POINT THEN DO GET_RECORD.       !  READ RECORD IF NEEDED
      JUMP                                          !  CALL HOT KEY PROCEDURE
      DO SAME_PAGE                                  !  RESET TO SAME PAGE
      CYCLE                                         !  AND LOOP AGAIN
           .
    IF KEYCODE() = REJECT_KEY THEN BREAK.           !RETURN ON SCREEN REJECT KEY
```

(continued)

```
IF  KEYCODE() = ACCEPT_KEY    |            !ON SCREEN ACCEPT KEY
AND FIELD() <> ?POINT                      !BUT NOT ON THE POINT FIELD
  UPDATE                                   !  MOVE ALL FIELDS FROM SCREEN
  SELECT(?)                                !  START WITH CURRENT FIELD
  SELECT                                   !  EDIT ALL FIELDS
  CYCLE                                    !  GO TO TOP OF LOOP
.


CASE FIELD()                               !JUMP TO FIELD EDIT ROUTINE

OF ?FIRST_FIELD                            !FROM THE FIRST FIELD
  IF KEYCODE() = ESC_KEY    |              !  RETURN ON ESC KEY
  OR RECORDS# = FALSE                      !  OR NO RECORDS
    BREAK                                  !    EXIT PROGRAM
  .

OF ?PRE_POINT                              !PRE POINT FIELD CONDITION
  IF KEYCODE() = ESC_KEY                   !  BACKING UP?
    SELECT(?-1)                            !    SELECT PREVIOUS FIELD
  ELSE                                     !  GOING FORWARD
    SELECT(?POINT)                         !    SELECT MENU FIELD
  .

  IF KEYCODE() = ESC_KEY                   !  BACKING UP?
    SCR:LOCATOR = ''                       !    CLEAR LOCATOR
    SETCURSOR                              !    AND TURN CURSOR OFF
  ELSE                                     !  GOING FORWARD
    LEN# = 0                               !    RESET TO START OF LOCATOR
    SETCURSOR(ROW(SCR:LOCATOR),COL(SCR:LOCATOR)) !AND TURN CURSOR ON
  .

OF ?POINT                                  !PROCESS THE POINT FIELD
  IF RECORDS(TABLE) = 0                    !IF THERE ARE NO RECORDS
    CLEAR(FIL:RECORD)                      !  CLEAR RECORD AREA
    ACTION = 1                             !  SET ACTION TO ADD
    GET(FILES,0)                           !  CLEAR PENDING RECORD
    NEWFILES                               !  CALL FORM FOR NEW RECORD
    NEWPTR = POINTER(FILES)                !    SET POINTER TO NEW RECORD
    DO FIRST_PAGE                          !  DISPLAY THE FIRST PAGE
    IF RECORDS(TABLE) = 0                  !  IF THERE AREN'T ANY RECORDS
      RECORDS# = FALSE                     !    INDICATE NO RECORDS
      SELECT(?PRE_POINT-1)                 !    SELECT THE PRIOR FIELD
    .

    CYCLE                                  !    AND LOOP AGAIN
  .

  IF KEYCODE() > 31               |        !THE DISPLAYABLE CHARACTERS
  AND KEYCODE() < 255                      !ARE USED TO LOCATE RECORDS
    IF LEN# < SIZE(SCR:LOCATOR)            !  IF THERE IS ROOM LEFT
      SCR:LOCATOR = SUB(SCR:LOCATOR,1,LEN#) & CHR(KEYCODE())
      LEN# += 1                            !    INCREMENT THE LENGTH
    .
```

(continued)

```
ELSIF KEYCODE() = BS_KEY                            !BACKSPACE UNTYPES A CHARACTER
  IF LEN# > 0                                       !  IF THERE ARE CHARACTERS LEFT
    LEN# -= 1                                        !     DECREMENT THE LENGTH
    SCR:LOCATOR = SUB(SCR:LOCATOR,1,LEN#)           !     ERASE THE LAST CHARACTER
  .
ELSE                                                !FOR ANY OTHER CHARACTER
  LEN# = 0                                           !  ZERO THE LENGTH
  SCR:LOCATOR = ''                                   !  ERASE THE LOCATOR FIELD
.
SETCURSOR(ROW(SCR:LOCATOR),COL(SCR:LOCATOR)+LEN#)   !AND RESET THE CURSOR
FIL:FILENAME = CLIP(SCR:LOCATOR)                    !     UPDATE THE KEY FIELD
IF KEYBOARD() > 31              |                    !THE DISPLAYABLE CHARACTERS
AND KEYBOARD() < 255            |                    !ARE USED TO LOCATE RECORDS
OR KEYBOARD() = BS_KEY                              !INCLUDE BACKSPACE
  CYCLE
.
IF LEN# > 0                                         !ON A LOCATOR REQUEST
  FIL:FILENAME = CLIP(SCR:LOCATOR)                  !     UPDATE THE KEY FIELD
  SET(FIL:BY_FILENAME,FIL:BY_FILENAME)             !  POINT TO NEW RECORD
  NEXT(FILES)                                       !  READ A RECORD
  IF (EOF(FILES) AND ERROR())                       !  IF EOF IS REACHED
    SET(FIL:BY_FILENAME)                            !     SET TO FIRST RECORD
    PREVIOUS(FILES)                                 !     READ THE LAST RECORD
  .
  NEWPTR = POINTER(FILES)                            !  SET NEW RECORD POINTER
  SKIP(FILES,-1)                                     !  BACK UP TO FIRST RECORD
  FREE(TABLE)                                        !  CLEAR THE TABLE
  DO NEXT_PAGE                                       !  AND DISPLAY A NEW PAGE
.
CASE KEYCODE()                                       !PROCESS THE KEYSTROKE

OF INS_KEY                                           !INS KEY
  CLEAR(FIL:RECORD)                                 !  CLEAR RECORD AREA
  ACTION = 1                                         !  SET ACTION TO ADD
  GET(FILES,0)                                       !  CLEAR PENDING RECORD
  NEWFILES                                           !  CALL FORM FOR NEW RECORD
  IF ~ACTION                                         !  IF RECORD WAS ADDED
    NEWPTR = POINTER(FILES)                          !     SET POINTER TO NEW RECORD
    DO FIND_RECORD                                   !     POSITION IN FILE
  .
OF ENTER_KEY                                         !ENTER KEY
OROF ACCEPT_KEY                                      !CTRL-ENTER KEY
  DO GET_RECORD                                      !  GET THE SELECTED RECORD
  IF ACTION = 4 AND KEYCODE() = ENTER_KEY!          !  IF THIS IS A LOOKUP REQUEST
    ACTION = 0                                       !     SET ACTION TO COMPLETE
    BREAK                                            !     AND RETURN TO CALLER
  .
```

(continued)

```
      IF ~ERROR()                                   !   IF RECORD IS STILL THERE
        ACTION = 2                                  !     SET ACTION TO CHANGE
        NEWFILES                                    !     CALL FORM TO CHANGE REC
        IF ACTION THEN CYCLE.                       !     IF SUCCESSFUL RE-DISPLAY
      .
      NEWPTR = POINTER(FILES)                       !     SET POINTER TO NEW RECORD
      DO FIND_RECORD                                !     POSITION IN FILE
    OF DEL_KEY                                      !DEL KEY
      DO GET_RECORD                                 !   READ THE SELECTED RECORD
      IF ~ERROR()                                   !   IF RECORD IS STILL THERE
        ACTION = 3                                  !     SET ACTION TO DELETE
        NEWFILES                                    !     CALL FORM TO DELETE
        IF ~ACTION                                  !     IF SUCCESSFUL
          N# = NDX                                  !       SAVE POINT INDEX
          DO SAME_PAGE                              !       RE-DISPLAY
          NDX = N#                                  !       RESTORE POINT INDEX
      . .
    OF DOWN_KEY                                     !DOWN ARROW KEY
      DO SET_NEXT                                   ! POINT TO NEXT RECORD
      DO FILL_NEXT                                  ! FILL A TABLE ENTRY
      IF FOUND                                      ! FOUND A NEW RECORD
        SCROLL(ROW,COL,ROWS,COLS,ROWS(?POINT))  !   SCROLL THE SCREEN UP
        GET(TABLE,RECORDS(TABLE))                   !   GET RECORD FROM TABLE
        DO FILL_SCREEN                              ! DISPLAY ON SCREEN
      .
    OF PGDN_KEY                                     !PAGE DOWN KEY
      DO SET_NEXT                                   !   POINT TO NEXT RECORD
      DO NEXT_PAGE                                  !   DISPLAY THE NEXT PAGE

    OF CTRL_PGDN                                    !CTRL-PAGE DOWN KEY
      DO LAST_PAGE                                  !   DISPLAY THE LAST PAGE
      NDX = RECORDS(TABLE)                          !   POSITION POINT BAR

    OF UP_KEY                                       !UP ARROW KEY
      DO SET_PREV                                   !   POINT TO PREVIOUS RECORD
      DO FILL_PREV                                  !   FILL A TABLE ENTRY
      IF FOUND                                      !   FOUND A NEW RECORD
        SCROLL(ROW,COL,ROWS,COLS,-(ROWS(?POINT)))!  SCROLL THE SCREEN DOWN
        GET(TABLE,1)                                !   GET RECORD FROM TABLE
        DO FILL_SCREEN                              !   DISPLAY ON SCREEN
      .
    OF PGUP_KEY                                     !PAGE UP KEY
      DO SET_PREV                                   !   POINT TO PREVIOUS RECORD
      DO PREV_PAGE                                  !   DISPLAY THE PREVIOUS PAGE
```

(continued)

```
        OF CTRL_PGUP                                    !CTRL-PAGE UP
          DO FIRST_PAGE                                 !  DISPLAY THE FIRST PAGE
          NDX = 1                                       !  POSITION POINT BAR
    . . .
    FREE(TABLE)                                         !FREE MEMORY TABLE
    RETURN                                              !AND RETURN TO CALLER


SAME_PAGE ROUTINE                                       !DISPLAY THE SAME PAGE
  GET(TABLE,1)                                          !  GET THE FIRST TABLE ENTRY
  DO FILL_RECORD                                        !  FILL IN THE RECORD
  SET(FIL:BY_FILENAME,FIL:BY_FILENAME,TBL:PTR)          !  POSITION FILE
  FREE(TABLE)                                           !  EMPTY THE TABLE
  DO NEXT_PAGE                                          !  DISPLAY A FULL PAGE


FIRST_PAGE ROUTINE                                      !DISPLAY FIRST PAGE
  BLANK(ROW,COL,ROWS,COLS)
  FREE(TABLE)                                           !  EMPTY THE TABLE
  CLEAR(FIL:RECORD,-1)                                  !  CLEAR RECORD TO LOW VALUES
  CLEAR(TBL:PTR)                                        !  ZERO RECORD POINTER
  SET(FIL:BY_FILENAME)                                  !  POINT TO FIRST RECORD
  LOOP NDX = 1 TO COUNT                                 !  FILL UP THE TABLE
    DO FILL_NEXT                                        !    FILL A TABLE ENTRY
    IF NOT FOUND THEN BREAK.                            !    GET OUT IF NO RECORD
    .
  NDX = 1                                               !  SET TO TOP OF TABLE
  DO SHOW_PAGE                                          !  DISPLAY THE PAGE


LAST_PAGE ROUTINE                                       !DISPLAY LAST PAGE
  NDX# = NDX                                            !  SAVE SELECTOR POSITION
  BLANK(ROW,COL,ROWS,COLS)                              !  CLEAR SCROLLING AREA
  FREE(TABLE)                                           !  EMPTY THE TABLE
  CLEAR(FIL:RECORD,1)                                   !  CLEAR RECORD TO HIGH VALUES
  CLEAR(TBL:PTR,1)                                      !  CLEAR PTR TO HIGH VALUE
  SET(FIL:BY_FILENAME)                                  !  POINT TO FIRST RECORD
  LOOP NDX = COUNT TO 1 BY -1                           !  FILL UP THE TABLE
    DO FILL_PREV                                        !    FILL A TABLE ENTRY
    IF NOT FOUND THEN BREAK.                            !    GET OUT IF NO RECORD
    .                                                   !  END OF LOOP
  NDX = NDX#                                            !  RESTORE SELECTOR POSITION
  DO SHOW_PAGE                                          !  DISPLAY THE PAGE


FIND_RECORD ROUTINE                                     !POSITION TO SPECIFIC RECORD
  SET(FIL:BY_FILENAME,FIL:BY_FILENAME,NEWPTR)           !POSITION FILE
  IF NEWPTR = 0                                         !NEWPTR NOT SET
    NEXT(FILES)                                         !  READ NEXT RECORD
    NEWPTR = POINTER(FILES)                             !  SET NEWPTR
    SKIP(FILES,-1)                                      !  BACK UP TO DISPLAY RECORD
  .
```

(continued)

```
     FREE(TABLE)                                     !  CLEAR THE RECORD
     DO NEXT_PAGE                                    !  DISPLAY A PAGE


NEXT_PAGE ROUTINE                                    !DISPLAY NEXT PAGE
   SAVECNT# = RECORDS(TABLE)                         !  SAVE RECORD COUNT
   LOOP COUNT TIMES                                  !  FILL UP THE TABLE
     DO FILL_NEXT                                    !     FILL A TABLE ENTRY
     IF NOT FOUND                                    !     IF NONE ARE LEFT
       IF NOT SAVECNT#                               !       IF REBUILDING TABLE
         DO LAST_PAGE                                !         FILL IN RECORDS
         EXIT                                        !         EXIT OUT OF ROUTINE
         .
       BREAK                                         !       EXIT LOOP
     . .
   DO SHOW_PAGE                                      !  DISPLAY THE PAGE


SET_NEXT ROUTINE                                     !POINT TO THE NEXT PAGE
   GET(TABLE,RECORDS(TABLE))                         !  GET THE LAST TABLE ENTRY
   DO FILL_RECORD                                    !  FILL IN THE RECORD
   SET(FIL:BY_FILENAME,FIL:BY_FILENAME,TBL:PTR)      !  POSITION FILE
   NEXT(FILES)                                       !  READ THE CURRENT RECORD


FILL_NEXT ROUTINE                                    !FILL NEXT TABLE ENTRY
   FOUND = FALSE                                     !  ASSUME RECORD NOT FOUND
   LOOP UNTIL EOF(FILES)                             !  LOOP UNTIL END OF FILE
     NEXT(FILES)                                     !     READ THE NEXT RECORD
     FOUND = TRUE                                    !     SET RECORD FOUND
     DO FILL_TABLE                                   !     FILL IN THE TABLE ENTRY
     ADD(TABLE)                                      !     ADD LAST TABLE ENTRY
     GET(TABLE,RECORDS(TABLE)-COUNT)                 !     GET ANY OVERFLOW RECORD
     DELETE(TABLE)                                   !     AND DELETE IT
     EXIT                                            !     RETURN TO CALLER
     .
PREV_PAGE ROUTINE                                    !DISPLAY PREVIOUS PAGE
   LOOP COUNT TIMES                                  !  FILL UP THE TABLE
     DO FILL_PREV                                    !     FILL A TABLE ENTRY
     IF NOT FOUND THEN BREAK.                        !     GET OUT IF NO RECORD
     .
   DO SHOW_PAGE                                      !  DISPLAY THE PAGE


SET_PREV ROUTINE                                     !POINT TO PREVIOUS PAGE
   GET(TABLE,1)                                      !  GET THE FIRST TABLE ENTRY
   DO FILL_RECORD                                    !  FILL IN THE RECORD
   SET(FIL:BY_FILENAME,FIL:BY_FILENAME,TBL:PTR)      !  POSITION FILE
   PREVIOUS(FILES)                                   !  READ THE CURRENT RECORD


FILL_PREV ROUTINE                                    !FILL PREVIOUS TABLE ENTRY
```

(continued)

```
  FOUND = FALSE                          ! ASSUME RECORD NOT FOUND
  LOOP UNTIL BOF(FILES)                  ! LOOP UNTIL BEGINNING OF FILE
    PREVIOUS(FILES)                      !   READ THE PREVIOUS RECORD
    FOUND = TRUE                         !   SET RECORD FOUND
    DO FILL_TABLE                        !   FILL IN THE TABLE ENTRY
    ADD(TABLE,1)                         !   ADD FIRST TABLE ENTRY
    GET(TABLE,COUNT+1)                   !   GET ANY OVERFLOW RECORD
    DELETE(TABLE)                        !   AND DELETE IT
    EXIT                                 !   RETURN TO CALLER
  .

SHOW_PAGE ROUTINE                        !DISPLAY THE PAGE
  NDX# = NDX                             ! SAVE SCREEN INDEX
  LOOP NDX = 1 TO RECORDS(TABLE)         ! LOOP THRU THE TABLE
    GET(TABLE,NDX)                       !   GET A TABLE ENTRY
    DO FILL_SCREEN                       !   AND DISPLAY IT
    IF TBL:PTR = NEWPTR                  !   SET INDEX FOR NEW RECORD
      NDX# = NDX                         !   POINT TO CORRECT RECORD
  . .
  NDX = NDX#                             ! RESTORE SCREEN INDEX
  NEWPTR = 0                             ! CLEAR NEW RECORD POINTER
  CLEAR(FIL:RECORD)                      !   CLEAR RECORD AREA

FILL_TABLE ROUTINE                       !MOVE FILE TO TABLE
  DIS:NUMBER = FIL:NUMBER                !MOVE RELATED KEY FIELDS
  GET(DISKS,DIS:BY_NUMBER)               !READ THE RECORD
  IF ERROR() THEN CLEAR(DIS:RECORD).     !IF NOT FOUND, CLEAR RECORD
  TBL:NUMBER = DIS:NUMBER                !DISPLAY LOOKUP FIELD
  DIS:NUMBER = FIL:NUMBER                !MOVE RELATED KEY FIELDS
  GET(DISKS,DIS:BY_NUMBER)               !READ THE RECORD
  IF ERROR() THEN CLEAR(DIS:RECORD).     !IF NOT FOUND, CLEAR RECORD
  TBL:LABEL = DIS:LABEL                  !DISPLAY LOOKUP FIELD
  TBL:FILENAME = FIL:FILENAME
  TBL:SIZEBYTES = FIL:SIZEBYTES
  TBL:DATE = FIL:DATE
  TBL:PTR = POINTER(FILES)               ! SAVE RECORD POINTER
  TBL:SPACE = ''
  TBL:TIME = FIL:TIME
  TBL:SPACE2 = ''

FILL_RECORD ROUTINE                      !MOVE TABLE TO FILE
  FIL:FILENAME = TBL:FILENAME

FILL_SCREEN ROUTINE                      !MOVE TABLE TO SCREEN
  SCR:SPACE = TBL:SPACE
  SCR:NUMBER = TBL:NUMBER
  SCR:LABEL = TBL:LABEL
  SCR:FILENAME = TBL:FILENAME
```

(continued)

```
    SCR:SIZEBYTES = TBL:SIZEBYTES
    SCR:DATE = TBL:DATE
    SCR:TIME = TBL:TIME
    SCR:SPACE2 = TBL:SPACE2


GET_RECORD ROUTINE                              !GET SELECTED RECORD
  GET(TABLE,NDX)                                !  GET TABLE ENTRY
  GET(FILES,TBL:PTR)                            !  GET THE RECORD
```

CATALO08.CLA

```
          MEMBER('CATALOG')
REPORTS         PROCEDURE

SCREEN          SCREEN      PRE(SCR),WINDOW(13,38),HUE(0,7)
          ROW(1,1)   STRING('<218,196{2},0{32},196{2},191>'),HUE(14,7)
          ROW(2,1)   REPEAT(11);STRING('<179,0{36},179>'),HUE(14,7)  .
          ROW(13,1)  STRING('<192,196{36},217>'),HUE(14,7)
          ROW(1,5)   STRING('FLOPPY DISK MANAGEMENT REPORTS')
                     ENTRY,USE(?FIRST_FIELD)
                     ENTRY,USE(?PRE_MENU)
                     MENU,USE(MENU_FIELD"),REQ
          ROW(3,8)     STRING('Print a List of All Disks'),HUE(0,7)
          ROW(5,8)     STRING('Print a List for One Disk'),HUE(0,7)
          ROW(7,14)    STRING('Report Writer'),HUE(0,7)
          ROW(9,13)    STRING('Runtime Reports'),HUE(0,7)
          ROW(11,12)   STRING('Export BASIC File'),HUE(0,7)
                    .               .

    EJECT
    CODE
    OPEN(SCREEN)                                !OPEN THE MENU SCREEN
    SETCURSOR                                   !TURN OFF ANY CURSOR
    MENU_FIELD" = ''                            !START MENU WITH FIRST ITEM
    LOOP                                        !LOOP UNTIL USER EXITS
      ALERT                                     !TURN OFF ALL ALERTED KEYS
      ALERT(REJECT_KEY)                         !ALERT SCREEN REJECT KEY
      ALERT(ACCEPT_KEY)                         !ALERT SCREEN ACCEPT KEY
      ACCEPT                                    !READ A FIELD OR MENU CHOICE
      IF KEYCODE() = REJECT_KEY THEN RETURN.    !RETURN ON SCREEN REJECT

      IF KEYCODE() = ACCEPT_KEY                 !ON SCREEN ACCEPT KEY
        UPDATE                                  !  MOVE ALL FIELDS FROM SCREEN
        SELECT(?)                               !  START WITH CURRENT FIELD
        SELECT                                  !  EDIT ALL FIELDS
```

(continued)

```
        CYCLE                              !  GO TO TOP OF LOOP
        .                                  !

    CASE FIELD()                           !JUMP TO FIELD EDIT ROUTINE
    OF ?FIRST_FIELD                        !FROM THE FIRST FIELD
      IF KEYCODE() = ESC_KEY THEN RETURN.  !  RETURN ON ESC KEY

    OF ?PRE_MENU                           !PRE MENU FIELD CONDITION
      IF KEYCODE() = ESC_KEY               !  BACKING UP?
        SELECT(?-1)                        !    SELECT PREVIOUS FIELD
      ELSE                                 !  GOING FORWARD
        SELECT(?+1)                        !    SELECT MENU FIELD
        .
    OF ?MENU_FIELD"                        !FROM THE MENU FIELD
      EXECUTE CHOICE()                     !  CALL THE SELECTED PROCEDURE
        RPT_NUMBER                         !  Print Disks By Number
        FINDDISK                           !  Show Disks By Number
        WRITER                             !  Calls Report Writer
        RUNTIME_MENU                       !  SELECTION OF ELIGIBLE REPORTS
        EXPORT1                            !
    . . .
```

CATALO09.CLA

```
          MEMBER('CATALOG')

ONEDISK        PROCEDURE

TITLE     REPORT        LENGTH(59),WIDTH(80),PRE(TTL)
RPT_HEAD                DETAIL
          .                  .
REPORT    REPORT        LENGTH(59),WIDTH(80),PAGE(MEM:PAGE),LINE(MEM:LINE)      |
                        PRE(RPT)
PAGE_HEAD               HEADER
UNDERLINE COL(1)        CONTROL(30),USE(MEM:MESSAGE)
                        STRING(' {35}DISK LISTING')
DATE      ROW(+1,38) STRING(@D1) CTL(@LF2)
                    .
GRP_HEAD1               DETAIL
          COL(3)        STRING(@N_4),USE(FIL:NUMBER)
LABEL     COL(9)        STRING(30)
          ROW(+1,9)     STRING('Notes:')
NOTES     COL(16)       STRING(40)
          ROW(+2,4)     STRING('FILENAME {8}SIZE {7}DATE {7}TIME {5}NOTES')
```

(continued)

```
           ROW(+1,3)    STRING('-{12}   -{9}  -{10}  -{7}  -{30}') CTL(@LF)
                          .
DETAIL                  DETAIL
           COL(3)       STRING(12),USE(FIL:FILENAME)
           COL(18)      STRING(@n9),USE(FIL:SIZEBYTES)
           COL(30)      STRING(@d1),USE(FIL:DATE)
TIME       COL(41)      STRING(@t3)
           COL(51)      STRING(28),USE(FIL:NOTES) CTL(@LF)
                          .
GRP_FOOT1               DETAIL
           COL(56)      STRING('Total Bytes:')
TOTALBYTES COL(69)      STRING(@n10) CTL(@LF)
                          .
RPT_FOOT                DETAIL
                          .
PAGE_FOOT               FOOTER
           ROW(+1,37)   STRING('PAGE')
           COL(42)      STRING(@n3),USE(MEM:PAGE) CTL(@LF)
                        CTL(@FF)
           .              .


           GROUP,PRE(SAV)
NUMBER     STRING(@N_4)
             .

   CODE
   DONE# = 0                                    !TURN OFF DONE FLAG
   fil:number = dis:number                      !CALL SETUP PROCEDURE
   SAV:NUMBER = FIL:NUMBER                       !SAVE SELECTOR FIELD
   CLEAR(FIL:RECORD,-1)                          !MAKE SURE RECORD CLEARED
   FIL:NUMBER = SAV:NUMBER                       !RESTORE SELECTOR FIELD
   PRINT(TTL:RPT_HEAD)                           !PRINT TITLE PAGE
   CLOSE(TITLE)                                  !CLOSE TITLE REPORT
   SET(FIL:BY_NUMBER,FIL:BY_NUMBER)             !SET TO FIRST SELECTED RECORD
   DO NEXT_RECORD                                !READ FIRST RECORD
   RPT:DATE = TODAY()
   OPEN(REPORT)                                  !OPEN THE REPORT
   BRK_FLAG# = 0                                 !CLEAR BREAK LEVEL FLAG
   DO PRT_BRK_HDRS                               !PRINT GROUP HEADER(S)
   LOOP UNTIL DONE#                              !READ ALL RECORDS IN FILE
     SAVE_LINE# = MEM:LINE                       !  SAVE LINE NUMBER
     LAST_REC# = POINTER(FILES)
     PRINT(RPT:DETAIL)                           !  PRINT DETAIL LINES
     DO CHECK_PAGE                               !  DO PAGE BREAK IF NEEDED
     RPT:TOTALBYTES += FIL:SIZEBYTES
     DO NEXT_RECORD                              !  GET NEXT RECORD
     RPT:DATE = TODAY()
```

(continued)

```
      IF NOT DONE# THEN DO CHECK_BREAK.        !  CHECK FOR GROUP BREAK
    .                                          !
    BRK_FLAG# = 0                              !CLEAR BREAK LEVEL FLAG
    DO PRT_BRK_FTRS                            !PRINT GROUP FOOTER(S)
    PRINT(RPT:RPT_FOOT)                        !PRINT GRAND TOTALS
    DO CHECK_PAGE                              !  DO PAGE BREAK IF NEEDED
    CLOSE(REPORT)                              !CLOSE REPORT
    RETURN                                     !RETURN TO CALLER


NEXT_RECORD ROUTINE                            !GET NEXT RECORD
  LOOP UNTIL EOF(FILES)                        !  READ UNTIL END OF FILE
    NEXT(FILES)                                !    READ NEXT RECORD
    IF FIL:NUMBER <> SAV:NUMBER                !IF END OF SELECTION
      FIL:NUMBER = SAV:NUMBER                  !  RESTORE THE SELECTOR
      BREAK                                    !  AND BREAK
    .
    RPT:TIME = fil:time
    EXIT                                       !    EXIT THE ROUTINE
  .                                            !
  DONE# = 1                                    !  ON EOF, SET DONE FLAG

CHECK_PAGE ROUTINE                             !CHECK FOR NEW PAGE
  IF MEM:LINE <= SAVE_LINE#                    !  ON PAGE OVERFLOW
    SAVE_LINE# = MEM:LINE                      !    RESET LINE NUMBER
  .
  LOOP UNTIL NOT KEYBOARD()                    !LOOK FOR KEYSTROKE
    ASK                                        !GET KEYCODE
    IF KEYCODE() = REJECT_KEY                  !ON CTRL-ESC
      CLOSE(REPORT)                            !  CLOSE REPORT
      RETURN                                   !  ABORT PRINT
  . .


CHECK_BREAK  ROUTINE                           !CHECK FOR GROUP BREAK
  IF FIL:NUMBER <> SAV:NUMBER                  !BREAK ON NEW GROUP
    BRK_FLAG# = 1                              !SET BREAK LEVEL
    DO PRT_BRK_FTRS                            !PRINT FOOTERS FOR THIS LEVEL
    DO PRT_BRK_HDRS                            !PRINT HEADERS FOR THIS LEVEL
    EXIT                                       !RETURN TO REPORT
  .

PRT_BRK_HDRS ROUTINE                           !DO GROUP HEADERS
  IF BRK_FLAG# <= 1                            !CHECK BREAK LEVEL
    RPT:TOTALBYTES = 0
    DIS:NUMBER = FIL:NUMBER                    !MOVE RELATED KEY FIELDS
    GET(DISKS,DIS:BY_NUMBER)                   !READ THE RECORD
    IF ERROR() THEN CLEAR(DIS:RECORD).         !IF NOT FOUND, CLEAR RECORD
```

(continued)

```
        RPT:LABEL = DIS:LABEL                !DISPLAY LOOKUP FIELD
        DIS:NUMBER = FIL:NUMBER              !MOVE RELATED KEY FIELDS
        GET(DISKS,DIS:BY_NUMBER)             !READ THE RECORD
        IF ERROR() THEN CLEAR(DIS:RECORD).   !IF NOT FOUND, CLEAR RECORD
        RPT:NOTES = DIS:NOTES                !DISPLAY LOOKUP FIELD
        PRINT(GRP_HEAD1)                     ! PRINT GROUP HEADER
        DO CHECK_PAGE                        ! DO PAGE BREAK IF NEEDED
      .
    SAV:NUMBER = FIL:NUMBER                  !SAVE BREAK FIELD

PRT_BRK_FTRS ROUTINE                         !DO GROUP FOOTERS
  GET(FILES,LAST_REC#)                       !REREAD PREVIOUS RECORD
  IF BRK_FLAG# <= 1                          !CHECK BREAK LEVEL
    PRINT(GRP_FOOT1)                         ! PRINT GROUP FOOTER
    DO CHECK_PAGE                            ! DO PAGE BREAK IF NEEDED
  .
  SKIP(FILES,-1)                             !BACKUP ONE RECORD
  NEXT(FILES)                                !AND REREAD IT
```

CATALO10.CLA

```
          MEMBER('CATALOG')
FINDDISK     PROCEDURE

SCREEN       SCREEN       PRE(SCR),WINDOW(21,80),HUE(15,1)
             ROW(6,1)    PAINT(16,80),HUE(0,7)
             ROW(2,30)   PAINT(1,22),HUE(0,7)
             ROW(21,2)   PAINT(1,78),HUE(15,1)
             ROW(1,1)    STRING('<201,205{78},187>'),HUE(15,1)
             ROW(2,1)    REPEAT(19);STRING('<186,0{78},186>'),HUE(15,1) .
             ROW(21,1)   STRING('<200,205{78},188>'),HUE(15,1)
             ROW(2,27)   STRING(' SE'),HUE(14,0)
               COL(30)   STRING('LECT A DISK FOR PRINTI'),HUE(14,0)
               COL(52)   STRING('NG '),HUE(14,0)
             ROW(4,31)   STRING('Locate'),HUE(11,1)
               COL(38)   STRING('by Number'),HUE(11,1)
               COL(47)   STRING(':'),HUE(11,1)
             ROW(5,4)    STRING('NO. {10}DISK LABEL {29}NOTES')
LOCATOR      ROW(4,48)   STRING(@N_4),HUE(11,1)
                         ENTRY,USE(?FIRST_FIELD)
                         ENTRY,USE(?PRE_POINT)
                         REPEAT(15),EVERY(1),INDEX(NDX)
             ROW(6,2)       POINT(1,78),USE(?POINT),ESC(?-1)
NUMBER       COL(3)      STRING(@N_4)
LABEL        COL(8)      STRING(30)
```

(continued)

```
NOTES         COL(39)     STRING(40)
                 .             .


NDX           BYTE                              !REPEAT INDEX FOR POINT AREA
ROW           BYTE                              !ACTUAL ROW OF SCROLL AREA
COL           BYTE                              !ACTUAL COLUMN OF SCROLL AREA
COUNT         BYTE(15)                          !NUMBER OF ITEMS TO SCROLL
ROWS          BYTE(15)                          !NUMBER OF ROWS TO SCROLL
COLS          BYTE(78)                          !NUMBER OF COLUMNS TO SCROLL
FOUND         BYTE                              !RECORD FOUND FLAG
NEWPTR        LONG                              !POINTER TO NEW RECORD

TABLE         TABLE,PRE(TBL)                    !TABLE OF RECORD DATA
NUMBER          STRING(@N_4)
LABEL           STRING(30)
NOTES           STRING(40)
PTR             LONG                            !  POINTER TO FILE RECORD
                 .

  EJECT
  CODE
  ACTION# = ACTION                              !SAVE ACTION
  OPEN(SCREEN)                                  !OPEN THE SCREEN
  SETCURSOR                                     !TURN OFF ANY CURSOR
  TBL:PTR = 1                                   !START AT TABLE ENTRY
  NDX = 1                                       !PUT SELECTOR BAR ON TOP ITEM
  ROW = ROW(?POINT)                             !REMEMBER TOP ROW AND
  COL = COL(?POINT)                             !LEFT COLUMN OF SCROLL AREA
  RECORDS# = TRUE                               !INITIALIZE RECORDS FLAG
  CACHE(DIS:BY_NUMBER,.25)                      !CACHE KEY FILE
  IF ACTION = 4                                 !  TABLE LOOKUP REQUEST
    NEWPTR = POINTER(DISKS)                     !  SET POINTER TO RECORD
    IF NOT NEWPTR                               !  RECORD NOT PASSED TO TABLE
      SET(DIS:BY_NUMBER,DIS:BY_NUMBER)          !    POSITION TO CLOSEST RECORD
      NEXT(DISKS)                               !    READ RECORD
      NEWPTR = POINTER(DISKS)                   !    SET POINTER
      .
    DO FIND_RECORD                              !  POSITION FILE
  ELSE
    NDX = 1                                     !  PUT SELECTOR BAR ON TOP ITEM
    DO FIRST_PAGE                               !  BUILD MEMORY TABLE OF KEYS
    .
  RECORDS# = TRUE                               !  ASSUME THERE ARE RECORDS
  LOOP                                          !LOOP UNTIL USER EXITS
    ACTION = ACTION#                            !RESTORE ACTION
    ALERT                                       !RESET ALERTED KEYS
    ALERT(REJECT_KEY)                           !ALERT SCREEN REJECT KEY
```

(continued)

```
ALERT(ACCEPT_KEY)                               !ALERT SCREEN ACCEPT KEY
ACCEPT                                          !READ A FIELD
IF KEYCODE() = REJECT_KEY THEN BREAK.           !RETURN ON SCREEN REJECT KEY


IF  KEYCODE() = ACCEPT_KEY      |               !ON SCREEN ACCEPT KEY
AND FIELD() <> ?POINT                           !BUT NOT ON THE POINT FIELD
  UPDATE                                        !  MOVE ALL FIELDS FROM SCREEN
  SELECT(?)                                     !  START WITH CURRENT FIELD
  SELECT                                        !  EDIT ALL FIELDS
  CYCLE                                         !  GO TO TOP OF LOOP
  .


CASE FIELD()                                    !JUMP TO FIELD EDIT ROUTINE
OF ?FIRST_FIELD                                 !FROM THE FIRST FIELD
  IF KEYCODE() = ESC_KEY    |                   !  RETURN ON ESC KEY
  OR RECORDS# = FALSE                           !  OR NO RECORDS
    BREAK                                       !    EXIT PROGRAM
    .


OF ?PRE_POINT                                   !PRE POINT FIELD CONDITION
  IF KEYCODE() = ESC_KEY                        ! BACKING UP?
    SELECT(?-1)                                 !    SELECT PREVIOUS FIELD
  ELSE                                          ! GOING FORWARD
    SELECT(?POINT)                              !    SELECT MENU FIELD
    .

  IF KEYCODE() = ESC_KEY                        ! BACKING UP?
    SCR:LOCATOR = ''                            !    CLEAR LOCATOR
    SETCURSOR                                   !    AND TURN CURSOR OFF
  ELSE                                          ! GOING FORWARD
    LEN# = 0                                    !    RESET TO START OF LOCATOR
    SETCURSOR(ROW(SCR:LOCATOR),COL(SCR:LOCATOR)) !AND TURN CURSOR ON
    .
OF ?POINT                                       !PROCESS THE POINT FIELD
  IF RECORDS(TABLE) = 0                         !IF THERE ARE NO RECORDS
    BEEP(400,50)                                !SOUND ALARM
    RETURN                                      !GO BACK TO CALLING PROCEDURE
    .
  IF KEYCODE() > 31              |              !THE DISPLAYABLE CHARACTERS
  AND KEYCODE() < 255                           !ARE USED TO LOCATE RECORDS
    IF LEN# < SIZE(SCR:LOCATOR)                 !  IF THERE IS ROOM LEFT
      SCR:LOCATOR = SUB(SCR:LOCATOR,1,LEN#) & CHR(KEYCODE())
      LEN# += 1                                 !    INCREMENT THE LENGTH
      .

  ELSIF KEYCODE() = BS_KEY                      !BACKSPACE UNTYPES A CHARACTER
    IF LEN# > 0                                 !  IF THERE ARE CHARACTERS LEFT
      LEN# -= 1                                 !    DECREMENT THE LENGTH
      SCR:LOCATOR = SUB(SCR:LOCATOR,1,LEN#)     !    ERASE THE LAST CHARACTER
      .
```

(continued)

```
ELSE                                            !FOR ANY OTHER CHARACTER
  LEN# = 0                                      !  ZERO THE LENGTH
  SCR:LOCATOR = ''                              !  ERASE THE LOCATOR FIELD
.
SETCURSOR(ROW(SCR:LOCATOR),COL(SCR:LOCATOR)+LEN#) !AND RESET THE CURSOR
DIS:NUMBER = CLIP(SCR:LOCATOR)                  !   UPDATE THE KEY FIELD
IF KEYBOARD() > 31                    |         !THE DISPLAYABLE CHARACTERS
AND KEYBOARD() < 255                  |         !ARE USED TO LOCATE RECORDS
OR KEYBOARD() = BS_KEY                          !INCLUDE BACKSPACE
  CYCLE
.
IF LEN# > 0                                     !ON A LOCATOR REQUEST
  DIS:NUMBER = CLIP(SCR:LOCATOR)                !   UPDATE THE KEY FIELD
  SET(DIS:BY_NUMBER,DIS:BY_NUMBER)              !   POINT TO NEW RECORD
  NEXT(DISKS)                                   !   READ A RECORD
  IF (EOF(DISKS) AND ERROR())                   !   IF EOF IS REACHED
    SET(DIS:BY_NUMBER)                          !     SET TO FIRST RECORD
    PREVIOUS(DISKS)                             !     READ THE LAST RECORD
  .
  NEWPTR = POINTER(DISKS)                       !   SET NEW RECORD POINTER
  SKIP(DISKS,-1)                                !   BACK UP TO FIRST RECORD
  FREE(TABLE)                                   !   CLEAR THE TABLE
  DO NEXT_PAGE                                  !   AND DISPLAY A NEW PAGE
.
CASE KEYCODE()                                  !PROCESS THE KEYSTROKE

OF ENTER_KEY                                    !ENTER KEY
OROF ACCEPT_KEY                                 !CTRL-ENTER KEY
  DO GET_RECORD                                 !  GET THE SELECTED RECORD
  IF ~ERROR()                                   !  IF RECORD IS STILL THERE
    ONEDISK                                     !    CALL FORM TO CHANGE REC
  .
  NEWPTR = POINTER(DISKS)                       !    SET POINTER TO NEW RECORD
  DO FIND_RECORD                                !    POSITION IN FILE

OF DOWN_KEY                                     !DOWN ARROW KEY
  DO SET_NEXT                                   !  POINT TO NEXT RECORD
  DO FILL_NEXT                                  !  FILL A TABLE ENTRY
  IF FOUND                                      !  FOUND A NEW RECORD
    SCROLL(ROW,COL,ROWS,COLS,ROWS(?POINT)) !   SCROLL THE SCREEN UP
    GET(TABLE,RECORDS(TABLE))                   !  GET RECORD FROM TABLE
    DO FILL_SCREEN                              !  DISPLAY ON SCREEN
  .
OF PGDN_KEY                                     !PAGE DOWN KEY
  DO SET_NEXT                                   !  POINT TO NEXT RECORD
  DO NEXT_PAGE                                  !  DISPLAY THE NEXT PAGE
```

(continued)

```
      OF CTRL_PGDN                                !CTRL-PAGE DOWN KEY
        DO LAST_PAGE                              !  DISPLAY THE LAST PAGE
        NDX = RECORDS(TABLE)                      !  POSITION POINT BAR

      OF UP_KEY                                   !UP ARROW KEY
        DO SET_PREV                               !  POINT TO PREVIOUS RECORD
        DO FILL_PREV                              !  FILL A TABLE ENTRY
        IF FOUND                                  !  FOUND A NEW RECORD
          SCROLL(ROW,COL,ROWS,COLS,-(ROWS(?POINT)))! SCROLL THE SCREEN DOWN
          GET(TABLE,1)                            !  GET RECORD FROM TABLE
          DO FILL_SCREEN                          !  DISPLAY ON SCREEN
          .

      OF PGUP_KEY                                 !PAGE UP KEY
        DO SET_PREV                               !  POINT TO PREVIOUS RECORD
        DO PREV_PAGE                              !  DISPLAY THE PREVIOUS PAGE

      OF CTRL_PGUP                                !CTRL-PAGE UP
        DO FIRST_PAGE                             !  DISPLAY THE FIRST PAGE
        NDX = 1                                   !  POSITION POINT BAR
     . . .
    FREE(TABLE)                                   !FREE MEMORY TABLE
    RETURN                                        !AND RETURN TO CALLER

SAME_PAGE ROUTINE                                 !DISPLAY THE SAME PAGE
  GET(TABLE,1)                                    !  GET THE FIRST TABLE ENTRY
  DO FILL_RECORD                                  !  FILL IN THE RECORD
  SET(DIS:BY_NUMBER,DIS:BY_NUMBER,TBL:PTR)        !  POSITION FILE
  FREE(TABLE)                                     !  EMPTY THE TABLE
  DO NEXT_PAGE                                    !  DISPLAY A FULL PAGE

FIRST_PAGE ROUTINE                                !DISPLAY FIRST PAGE
  BLANK(ROW,COL,ROWS,COLS)
  FREE(TABLE)                                     !  EMPTY THE TABLE
  CLEAR(DIS:RECORD,-1)                            !  CLEAR RECORD TO LOW VALUES
  CLEAR(TBL:PTR)                                  !  ZERO RECORD POINTER
  SET(DIS:BY_NUMBER)                              !  POINT TO FIRST RECORD
  LOOP NDX = 1 TO COUNT                           !  FILL UP THE TABLE
    DO FILL_NEXT                                  !    FILL A TABLE ENTRY
    IF NOT FOUND THEN BREAK.                      !    GET OUT IF NO RECORD
    .
  NDX = 1                                         !  SET TO TOP OF TABLE
  DO SHOW_PAGE                                    !  DISPLAY THE PAGE

LAST_PAGE ROUTINE                                 !DISPLAY LAST PAGE
  NDX# = NDX                                      !  SAVE SELECTOR POSITION
  BLANK(ROW,COL,ROWS,COLS)                        !  CLEAR SCROLLING AREA
```

(continued)

```
  FREE(TABLE)                                  !   EMPTY THE TABLE
  CLEAR(DIS:RECORD,1)                          !   CLEAR RECORD TO HIGH VALUES
  CLEAR(TBL:PTR,1)                             !   CLEAR PTR TO HIGH VALUE
  SET(DIS:BY_NUMBER)                           !   POINT TO FIRST RECORD
  LOOP NDX = COUNT TO 1 BY -1                  !   FILL UP THE TABLE
    DO FILL_PREV                               !     FILL A TABLE ENTRY
    IF NOT FOUND THEN BREAK.                   !     GET OUT IF NO RECORD
  .                                            !   END OF LOOP
  NDX = NDX#                                   !   RESTORE SELECTOR POSITION
  DO SHOW_PAGE                                 !   DISPLAY THE PAGE


FIND_RECORD ROUTINE                            !POSITION TO SPECIFIC RECORD
  SET(DIS:BY_NUMBER,DIS:BY_NUMBER,NEWPTR)      !POSITION FILE
  IF NEWPTR = 0                                !NEWPTR NOT SET
    NEXT(DISKS)                                !   READ NEXT RECORD
    NEWPTR = POINTER(DISKS)                    !   SET NEWPTR
    SKIP(DISKS,-1)                             !   BACK UP TO DISPLAY RECORD
  .
  FREE(TABLE)                                  !   CLEAR THE RECORD
  DO NEXT_PAGE                                 !   DISPLAY A PAGE


NEXT_PAGE ROUTINE                              !DISPLAY NEXT PAGE
  SAVECNT# = RECORDS(TABLE)                    !   SAVE RECORD COUNT
  LOOP COUNT TIMES                             !   FILL UP THE TABLE
    DO FILL_NEXT                               !     FILL A TABLE ENTRY
    IF NOT FOUND                               !     IF NONE ARE LEFT
      IF NOT SAVECNT#                          !       IF REBUILDING TABLE
        DO LAST_PAGE                           !         FILL IN RECORDS
        EXIT                                   !         EXIT OUT OF ROUTINE

      BREAK                                    !     EXIT LOOP
  . .
  DO SHOW_PAGE                                 !   DISPLAY THE PAGE


SET_NEXT ROUTINE                               !POINT TO THE NEXT PAGE
  GET(TABLE,RECORDS(TABLE))                    !   GET THE LAST TABLE ENTRY
  DO FILL_RECORD                               !   FILL IN THE RECORD
  SET(DIS:BY_NUMBER,DIS:BY_NUMBER,TBL:PTR)     !   POSITION FILE
  NEXT(DISKS)                                  !   READ THE CURRENT RECORD


FILL_NEXT ROUTINE                              !FILL NEXT TABLE ENTRY
  FOUND = FALSE                                !   ASSUME RECORD NOT FOUND
  LOOP UNTIL EOF(DISKS)                        !   LOOP UNTIL END OF FILE
    NEXT(DISKS)                                !     READ THE NEXT RECORD
    FOUND = TRUE                               !     SET RECORD FOUND
    DO FILL_TABLE                              !     FILL IN THE TABLE ENTRY
    ADD(TABLE)                                 !     ADD LAST TABLE ENTRY
```

(continued)

```
     GET(TABLE,RECORDS(TABLE)-COUNT)        !   GET ANY OVERFLOW RECORD
     DELETE(TABLE)                          !   AND DELETE IT
     EXIT                                   !   RETURN TO CALLER
   .
PREV_PAGE ROUTINE                           !DISPLAY PREVIOUS PAGE
   LOOP COUNT TIMES                         !   FILL UP THE TABLE
     DO FILL_PREV                           !     FILL A TABLE ENTRY
     IF NOT FOUND THEN BREAK.               !     GET OUT IF NO RECORD
     .
   DO SHOW_PAGE                             !   DISPLAY THE PAGE

SET_PREV ROUTINE                            !POINT TO PREVIOUS PAGE
   GET(TABLE,1)                             !   GET THE FIRST TABLE ENTRY
   DO FILL_RECORD                           !   FILL IN THE RECORD
   SET(DIS:BY_NUMBER,DIS:BY_NUMBER,TBL:PTR) !   POSITION FILE
   PREVIOUS(DISKS)                          !   READ THE CURRENT RECORD

FILL_PREV ROUTINE                           !FILL PREVIOUS TABLE ENTRY
   FOUND = FALSE                            !   ASSUME RECORD NOT FOUND
   LOOP UNTIL BOF(DISKS)                    !   LOOP UNTIL BEGINNING OF FILE
     PREVIOUS(DISKS)                        !     READ THE PREVIOUS RECORD
     FOUND = TRUE                           !     SET RECORD FOUND
     DO FILL_TABLE                          !     FILL IN THE TABLE ENTRY
     ADD(TABLE,1)                           !     ADD FIRST TABLE ENTRY
     GET(TABLE,COUNT+1)                     !     GET ANY OVERFLOW RECORD
     DELETE(TABLE)                          !     AND DELETE IT
     EXIT                                   !     RETURN TO CALLER
   .
SHOW_PAGE ROUTINE                           !DISPLAY THE PAGE
   NDX# = NDX                               !   SAVE SCREEN INDEX
   LOOP NDX = 1 TO RECORDS(TABLE)           !   LOOP THRU THE TABLE
     GET(TABLE,NDX)                         !     GET A TABLE ENTRY
     DO FILL_SCREEN                         !     AND DISPLAY IT
     IF TBL:PTR = NEWPTR                    !     SET INDEX FOR NEW RECORD
       NDX# = NDX                           !     POINT TO CORRECT RECORD
   . .
   NDX = NDX#                               !   RESTORE SCREEN INDEX
   NEWPTR = 0                               !   CLEAR NEW RECORD POINTER
   CLEAR(DIS:RECORD)                        !   CLEAR RECORD AREA

FILL_TABLE ROUTINE                          !MOVE FILE TO TABLE
   TBL:NUMBER = DIS:NUMBER
   TBL:LABEL = DIS:LABEL
   TBL:NOTES = DIS:NOTES
   TBL:PTR = POINTER(DISKS)                 !   SAVE RECORD POINTER

FILL_RECORD ROUTINE                         !MOVE TABLE TO FILE
   DIS:NUMBER = TBL:NUMBER
```

(continued)

```
FILL_SCREEN ROUTINE                              !MOVE TABLE TO SCREEN
  SCR:NUMBER = TBL:NUMBER
  SCR:LABEL = TBL:LABEL
  SCR:NOTES = TBL:NOTES


GET_RECORD ROUTINE                               !GET SELECTED RECORD
  GET(TABLE,NDX)                                 !   GET TABLE ENTRY
  GET(DISKS,TBL:PTR)                             !   GET THE RECORD
```

CATALO11.CLA

```
          MEMBER('CATALOG')
FILES_CHILD1 PROCEDURE

SCREEN    SCREEN      WINDOW(10,48),HUE(7,0)
            ROW(1,1)  STRING('<218,196{46},191>')
            ROW(2,1)  REPEAT(8);STRING('<179,0{46},179>') .
            ROW(10,1) STRING('<192,196{46},217>')
            ROW(5,15) STRING('Deleted Records:')
            ROW(9,14) STRING('*'),HUE(30,0)
              COL(18) STRING('DO NOT INTERRUPT'),HUE(30,0)
              COL(36) STRING('*'),HUE(30,0)
MESSAGE     ROW(2,5) STRING(40)
COUNT       ROW(5,32) STRING(@N4)

          .

  GROUP,PRE(SAV)
NUMBER        STRING(@N_4)
   .
  CODE
  OPEN(SCREEN)                                   !DISPLAY STATUS SCREEN
  MESSAGE = CENTER('DELETING CHILDREN FROM: ' |
            & 'FILES'& '.DAT',SIZE(MESSAGE))     !POST PROCESSING MESSAGE
  CACHE(FIL:BY_NUMBER,.25)                        !CACHE KEY FILE
  SAV:NUMBER = FIL:NUMBER                         !SAVE COMPARISON VALUE
  SET(FIL:BY_NUMBER,FIL:BY_NUMBER)                !   POSITION POINTER IN FILE
  LOOP UNTIL EOF(FILES)                           !LOOP UNTIL COMPLETE
    NEXT(FILES)                                   ! READ THE NEXT RECORD
    IF FIL:NUMBER <> SAV:NUMBER THEN BREAK.       ! LEAVE IF NO MORE VALID
    COUNT += 1                                    ! INCREMENT COUNTER
    DELETE(FILES)                                 ! OTHERWISE DELETE RECORD
  .                                               !RECYCLE LOOP
  CLOSE(SCREEN)
  RETURN
```

CATALO12.CLA

```
          MEMBER('CATALOG')
RUNTIME_MENU PROCEDURE

SCREEN        SCREEN     PRE(SCR),WINDOW(16,35),HUE(15,1)
          ROW(1,3)   PAINT(1,32),HUE(0,7)
            COL(1)   STRING('<201,205,0{31},205,187>'),HUE(14,1)
          ROW(2,1)   REPEAT(14);STRING('<186,0{33},186>'),HUE(14,1)  .
          ROW(16,1)  STRING('<200,205{6},0{22},205{5},188>'),HUE(14,1)
          ROW(1,4)   STRING('SELECTION OF ELIGIBLE REPORTS')
          ROW(16,9)  STRING('Press <<F10> to Print')
                 ENTRY,USE(?FIRST_FIELD)
                 ENTRY,USE(?PRE_POINT)
                 REPEAT(13),EVERY(1),INDEX(NDX)
          ROW(3,3)     POINT(1,31),USE(?POINT),ESC(?-1)
REPORT_DEF  COL(4)   STRING(8)
NOTES       COL(13)  STRING(20)
              .            .


NDX         BYTE                         !REPEAT INDEX FOR POINT AREA
ROW         BYTE                         !ACTUAL ROW OF SCROLL AREA
COL         BYTE                         !ACTUAL COLUMN OF SCROLL AREA
COUNT       BYTE(13)                     !NUMBER OF ITEMS TO SCROLL
ROWS        BYTE(13)                     !NUMBER OF ROWS TO SCROLL
COLS        BYTE(31)                     !NUMBER OF COLUMNS TO SCROLL
FOUND       BYTE                         !RECORD FOUND FLAG   .
NEWPTR      LONG                         !POINTER TO NEW RECORD

TABLE       TABLE,PRE(TBL)               !TABLE OF RECORD DATA
REPORT_DEF STRING(8)                     !REPORT DEFINITION FILE
NOTES       STRING(20)                   !DESCRIPTION OF REPORT
REPORT_PATH STRING(40)                   !PATH TO REPORT FILES
REPORT_NO   STRING(@N3)                  !TRACKING NUMBER FOR REPORTS
PTR             LONG                     !  POINTER TO FILE RECORD
                .

  EJECT
  CODE
  ACTION# = ACTION                       !SAVE ACTION
  OPEN(SCREEN)                           !OPEN THE SCREEN
  SETCURSOR                              !TURN OFF ANY CURSOR
  TBL:PTR = 1                            !START AT TABLE ENTRY
  NDX = 1                                !PUT SELECTOR BAR ON TOP ITEM
  ROW = ROW(?POINT)                      !REMEMBER TOP ROW AND
  COL = COL(?POINT)                      !LEFT COLUMN OF SCROLL AREA
```

(continued)

```
RECORDS# = TRUE                          !INITIALIZE RECORDS FLAG
CACHE(REP:BY_REPORT,.25)                 !CACHE KEY FILE
IF ACTION = 4                            !  TABLE LOOKUP REQUEST
  NEWPTR = POINTER(REPORTER)             !  SET POINTER TO RECORD
  IF NOT NEWPTR                          !  RECORD NOT PASSED TO TABLE
    SET(REP:BY_REPORT,REP:BY_REPORT)     !    POSITION TO CLOSEST RECORD
    NEXT(REPORTER)                       !    READ RECORD
    NEWPTR = POINTER(REPORTER)           !    SET POINTER
  .
  DO FIND_RECORD                         !  POSITION FILE
ELSE
  NDX = 1                                !  PUT SELECTOR BAR ON TOP ITEM
  DO FIRST_PAGE                          !  BUILD MEMORY TABLE OF KEYS
.
RECORDS# = TRUE                          !  ASSUME THERE ARE RECORDS
LOOP                                     !LOOP UNTIL USER EXITS
  ACTION = ACTION#                       !RESTORE ACTION
  ALERT                                  !RESET ALERTED KEYS
  ALERT(REJECT_KEY)                      !ALERT SCREEN REJECT KEY
  ALERT(ACCEPT_KEY)                      !ALERT SCREEN ACCEPT KEY
  ALERT(F10_KEY)                         !ALERT HOT KEY
  ACCEPT                                 !READ A FIELD
  IF KEYCODE() = F10_KEY                 !ON HOT KEY
    IF FIELD() = ?POINT THEN DO GET_RECORD.  !  READ RECORD IF NEEDED
    RUNTIME                              !  CALL HOT KEY PROCEDURE
    DO SAME_PAGE                         !  RESET TO SAME PAGE
    CYCLE                                !  AND LOOP AGAIN
  .
  IF KEYCODE() = REJECT_KEY THEN BREAK.  !RETURN ON SCREEN REJECT KEY

  IF  KEYCODE() = ACCEPT_KEY      |      !ON SCREEN ACCEPT KEY
  AND FIELD() <> ?POINT                  !BUT NOT ON THE POINT FIELD
    UPDATE                               !  MOVE ALL FIELDS FROM SCREEN
    SELECT(?)                            !  START WITH CURRENT FIELD
    SELECT                               !  EDIT ALL FIELDS
    CYCLE                                !  GO TO TOP OF LOOP
  .

  CASE FIELD()                           !JUMP TO FIELD EDIT ROUTINE

  OF ?FIRST_FIELD                        !FROM THE FIRST FIELD
    IF KEYCODE() = ESC_KEY      |        !  RETURN ON ESC KEY
    OR RECORDS# = FALSE                  !  OR NO RECORDS
      BREAK                              !    EXIT PROGRAM
    .
  OF ?PRE_POINT                          !PRE POINT FIELD CONDITION
    IF KEYCODE() = ESC_KEY              !  BACKING UP?
```

(continued)

```
        SELECT(?-1)                          !    SELECT PREVIOUS FIELD
    ELSE                                      !    GOING FORWARD
        SELECT(?POINT)                        !    SELECT MENU FIELD
    .
  OF ?POINT                                   !PROCESS THE POINT FIELD
    IF RECORDS(TABLE) = 0                     !IF THERE ARE NO RECORDS
      CLEAR(REP:RECORD)                       !   CLEAR RECORD AREA
      ACTION = 1                              !   SET ACTION TO ADD
      GET(REPORTER,0)                         !   CLEAR PENDING RECORD
      NEW_REP                                 !   CALL FORM FOR NEW RECORD
      NEWPTR = POINTER(REPORTER)              !    SET POINTER TO NEW RECORD
      DO FIRST_PAGE                           !   DISPLAY THE FIRST PAGE
      IF RECORDS(TABLE) = 0                   !   IF THERE AREN'T ANY RECORDS
        RECORDS# = FALSE                      !      INDICATE NO RECORDS
        SELECT(?PRE_POINT-1)                  !      SELECT THE PRIOR FIELD
      .
      CYCLE                                   !    AND LOOP AGAIN
  .
  CASE KEYCODE()                              !PROCESS THE KEYSTROKE

  OF INS_KEY                                  !INS KEY
    CLEAR(REP:RECORD)                         !   CLEAR RECORD AREA
    ACTION = 1                                !   SET ACTION TO ADD
    GET(REPORTER,0)                           !   CLEAR PENDING RECORD
    NEW_REP                                   !   CALL FORM FOR NEW RECORD
    IF ~ACTION                                !   IF RECORD WAS ADDED
      NEWPTR = POINTER(REPORTER)              !      SET POINTER TO NEW RECORD
      DO FIND_RECORD                          !      POSITION IN FILE
    .
  OF ENTER_KEY                                !ENTER KEY
  OROF ACCEPT_KEY                             !CTRL-ENTER KEY
    DO GET_RECORD                             !   GET THE SELECTED RECORD
    IF ACTION = 4 AND KEYCODE() = ENTER_KEY   !   IF THIS IS A LOOKUP REQUEST
      ACTION = 0                              !      SET ACTION TO COMPLETE
      BREAK                                   !      AND RETURN TO CALLER
    .
    IF ~ERROR()                               !   IF RECORD IS STILL THERE
      ACTION = 2                              !      SET ACTION TO CHANGE
      NEW_REP                                 !      CALL FORM TO CHANGE REC
      IF ACTION THEN CYCLE.                   !      IF SUCCESSFUL RE-DISPLAY
    .
    NEWPTR = POINTER(REPORTER)                !      SET POINTER TO NEW RECORD
    DO FIND_RECORD                            !      POSITION IN FILE
  OF DEL_KEY                                  !DEL KEY
    DO GET_RECORD                             !   READ THE SELECTED RECORD
    IF ~ERROR()                               !   IF RECORD IS STILL THERE
      ACTION = 3                              !      SET ACTION TO DELETE
```

(continued)

```
        NEW_REP                                      !     CALL FORM TO DELETE
        IF ~ACTION                                   !     IF SUCCESSFUL
          N# = NDX                                   !        SAVE POINT INDEX
          DO SAME_PAGE                               !        RE-DISPLAY
          NDX = N#                                   !        RESTORE POINT INDEX
      . .
      OF DOWN_KEY                                     !DOWN ARROW KEY
        DO SET_NEXT                                  !  POINT TO NEXT RECORD
        DO FILL_NEXT                                 !  FILL A TABLE ENTRY
        IF FOUND                                     !  FOUND A NEW RECORD
          SCROLL(ROW,COL,ROWS,COLS,ROWS(?POINT)) !    SCROLL THE SCREEN UP
          GET(TABLE,RECORDS(TABLE))                  !  GET RECORD FROM TABLE
          DO FILL_SCREEN                             !  DISPLAY ON SCREEN

        .

      OF PGDN_KEY                                     !PAGE DOWN KEY
        DO SET_NEXT                                  !  POINT TO NEXT RECORD
        DO NEXT_PAGE                                 !  DISPLAY THE NEXT PAGE

      OF CTRL_PGDN                                    !CTRL-PAGE DOWN KEY
        DO LAST_PAGE                                 !  DISPLAY THE LAST PAGE
        NDX = RECORDS(TABLE)                         !  POSITION POINT BAR

      OF UP_KEY                                       !UP ARROW KEY
        DO SET_PREV                                  !  POINT TO PREVIOUS RECORD
        DO FILL_PREV                                 !  FILL A TABLE ENTRY
        IF FOUND                                     !  FOUND A NEW RECORD
          SCROLL(ROW,COL,ROWS,COLS,-(ROWS(?POINT)))! SCROLL THE SCREEN DOWN
          GET(TABLE,1)                               !  GET RECORD FROM TABLE
          DO FILL_SCREEN                             !  DISPLAY ON SCREEN

        .

      OF PGUP_KEY                                     !PAGE UP KEY
        DO SET_PREV                                  !  POINT TO PREVIOUS RECORD
        DO PREV_PAGE                                 !  DISPLAY THE PREVIOUS PAGE

      OF CTRL_PGUP                                    !CTRL-PAGE UP
        DO FIRST_PAGE                                !  DISPLAY THE FIRST PAGE
        NDX = 1                                      !  POSITION POINT BAR
    . . .
    FREE(TABLE)                                       !FREE MEMORY TABLE
    RETURN                                            !AND RETURN TO CALLER

SAME_PAGE ROUTINE                                     !DISPLAY THE SAME PAGE
  GET(TABLE,1)                                        !  GET THE FIRST TABLE ENTRY
  DO FILL_RECORD                                      !  FILL IN THE RECORD
  SET(REP:BY_REPORT,REP:BY_REPORT,TBL:PTR)            !  POSITION FILE
```

(continued)

```
   FREE(TABLE)                                ! EMPTY THE TABLE
   DO NEXT_PAGE                               ! DISPLAY A FULL PAGE


FIRST_PAGE ROUTINE                          !DISPLAY FIRST PAGE
   BLANK(ROW,COL,ROWS,COLS)
   FREE(TABLE)                                ! EMPTY THE TABLE
   CLEAR(REP:RECORD,-1)                       ! CLEAR RECORD TO LOW VALUES
   CLEAR(TBL:PTR)                             ! ZERO RECORD POINTER
   SET(REP:BY_REPORT)                         ! POINT TO FIRST RECORD
   LOOP NDX = 1 TO COUNT                      ! FILL UP THE TABLE
     DO FILL_NEXT                             !   FILL A TABLE ENTRY
     IF NOT FOUND THEN BREAK.                 !   GET OUT IF NO RECORD
   .
   NDX = 1                                    ! SET TO TOP OF TABLE
   DO SHOW_PAGE                               ! DISPLAY THE PAGE


LAST_PAGE ROUTINE                           !DISPLAY LAST PAGE
   NDX# = NDX                                 ! SAVE SELECTOR POSITION
   BLANK(ROW,COL,ROWS,COLS)                   ! CLEAR SCROLLING AREA
   FREE(TABLE)                                ! EMPTY THE TABLE
   CLEAR(REP:RECORD,1)                        ! CLEAR RECORD TO HIGH VALUES
   CLEAR(TBL:PTR,1)                           ! CLEAR PTR TO HIGH VALUE
   SET(REP:BY_REPORT)                         ! POINT TO FIRST RECORD
   LOOP NDX = COUNT TO 1 BY -1                ! FILL UP THE TABLE
     DO FILL_PREV                             !   FILL A TABLE ENTRY
     IF NOT FOUND THEN BREAK.                 !   GET OUT IF NO RECORD
   .                                          ! END OF LOOP
   NDX = NDX#                                 ! RESTORE SELECTOR POSITION
   DO SHOW_PAGE                               ! DISPLAY THE PAGE


FIND_RECORD ROUTINE                         !POSITION TO SPECIFIC RECORD
   SET(REP:BY_REPORT,REP:BY_REPORT,NEWPTR)  !POSITION FILE
   IF NEWPTR = 0                             !NEWPTR NOT SET
     NEXT(REPORTER)                          ! READ NEXT RECORD
     NEWPTR = POINTER(REPORTER)              ! SET NEWPTR
     SKIP(REPORTER,-1)                       ! BACK UP TO DISPLAY RECORD
   .
   FREE(TABLE)                                ! CLEAR THE RECORD
   DO NEXT_PAGE                               ! DISPLAY A PAGE


NEXT_PAGE ROUTINE                           !DISPLAY NEXT PAGE
   SAVECNT# = RECORDS(TABLE)                  ! SAVE RECORD COUNT
   LOOP COUNT TIMES                           ! FILL UP THE TABLE
     DO FILL_NEXT                             !   FILL A TABLE ENTRY
     IF NOT FOUND                             !   IF NONE ARE LEFT
       IF NOT SAVECNT#                        !     IF REBUILDING TABLE
         DO LAST_PAGE                         !       FILL IN RECORDS
```

(continued)

```
        EXIT                                           !      EXIT OUT OF ROUTINE
        .
      BREAK                                            !   EXIT LOOP
    . .
    DO SHOW_PAGE                                       !  DISPLAY THE PAGE

SET_NEXT ROUTINE                                       !POINT TO THE NEXT PAGE
  GET(TABLE,RECORDS(TABLE))                            !  GET THE LAST TABLE ENTRY
  DO FILL_RECORD                                       !  FILL IN THE RECORD
  SET(REP:BY_REPORT,REP:BY_REPORT,TBL:PTR)             !  POSITION FILE
  NEXT(REPORTER)                                       !  READ THE CURRENT RECORD

FILL_NEXT ROUTINE                                      !FILL NEXT TABLE ENTRY
  FOUND = FALSE                                        !  ASSUME RECORD NOT FOUND
  LOOP UNTIL EOF(REPORTER)                             !  LOOP UNTIL END OF FILE
    NEXT(REPORTER)                                     !    READ.THE NEXT RECORD
    FOUND = TRUE                                       !    SET RECORD FOUND
    DO FILL_TABLE                                      !    FILL IN THE TABLE ENTRY
    ADD(TABLE)                                         !    ADD LAST TABLE ENTRY
    GET(TABLE,RECORDS(TABLE)-COUNT)                    !    GET ANY OVERFLOW RECORD
    DELETE(TABLE)                                      !    AND DELETE IT
    EXIT                                               !    RETURN TO CALLER
    .

PREV_PAGE ROUTINE                                      !DISPLAY PREVIOUS PAGE
  LOOP COUNT TIMES                                     !  FILL UP THE TABLE
    DO FILL_PREV                                       !    FILL A TABLE ENTRY
    IF NOT FOUND THEN BREAK.                           !    GET OUT IF NO RECORD
    .
  DO SHOW_PAGE                                         !  DISPLAY THE PAGE

SET_PREV ROUTINE                                       !POINT TO PREVIOUS PAGE
  GET(TABLE,1)                                         !  GET THE FIRST TABLE ENTRY
  DO FILL_RECORD                                       !  FILL IN THE RECORD
  SET(REP:BY_REPORT,REP:BY_REPORT,TBL:PTR)             !  POSITION FILE
  PREVIOUS(REPORTER)                                   !  READ THE CURRENT RECORD

FILL_PREV ROUTINE                                      !FILL PREVIOUS TABLE ENTRY
  FOUND = FALSE                                        !  ASSUME RECORD NOT FOUND
  LOOP UNTIL BOF(REPORTER)                             !  LOOP UNTIL BEGINNING OF FILE
    PREVIOUS(REPORTER)                                 !    READ THE PREVIOUS RECORD
    FOUND = TRUE                                       !    SET RECORD FOUND
    DO FILL_TABLE                                      !    FILL IN THE TABLE ENTRY
    ADD(TABLE,1)                                       !    ADD FIRST TABLE ENTRY
    GET(TABLE,COUNT+1)                                 !    GET ANY OVERFLOW RECORD
    DELETE(TABLE)                                      !    AND DELETE IT
    EXIT                                               !    RETURN TO CALLER
    .
```

(continued)

```
SHOW_PAGE ROUTINE                           !DISPLAY THE PAGE
  NDX# = NDX                                !  SAVE SCREEN INDEX
  LOOP NDX = 1 TO RECORDS(TABLE)            !  LOOP THRU THE TABLE
    GET(TABLE,NDX)                          !    GET A TABLE ENTRY
    DO FILL_SCREEN                          !    AND DISPLAY IT
    IF TBL:PTR = NEWPTR                     !    SET INDEX FOR NEW RECORD
      NDX# = NDX                            !    POINT TO CORRECT RECORD
  . .
  NDX = NDX#                                !  RESTORE SCREEN INDEX
  NEWPTR = 0                                !  CLEAR NEW RECORD POINTER
  CLEAR(REP:RECORD)                         !  CLEAR RECORD AREA

FILL_TABLE ROUTINE                          !MOVE FILE TO TABLE
  TBL:REPORT_DEF = REP:REPORT_DEF
  TBL:NOTES = REP:NOTES
  TBL:REPORT_PATH = REP:REPORT_PATH
  TBL:REPORT_NO = REP:REPORT_NO
  TBL:PTR = POINTER(REPORTER)               !  SAVE RECORD POINTER

FILL_RECORD ROUTINE                         !MOVE TABLE TO FILE
  REP:REPORT_PATH = TBL:REPORT_PATH
  REP:REPORT_NO = TBL:REPORT_NO

FILL_SCREEN ROUTINE                         !MOVE TABLE TO SCREEN
  SCR:REPORT_DEF = TBL:REPORT_DEF
  SCR:NOTES = TBL:NOTES

GET_RECORD ROUTINE                          !GET SELECTED RECORD
  GET(TABLE,NDX)                            !  GET TABLE ENTRY
  GET(REPORTER,TBL:PTR)                     !  GET THE RECORD
```

CATALO13.CLA

```
          MEMBER('CATALOG')
NEW_REP        PROCEDURE

SCREEN         SCREEN      PRE(SCR),WINDOW(13,47),HUE(15,0)
          ROW(1,1)    STRING('<218,196{8},0{29},196{8},191>'),HUE(14,0)
          ROW(2,1)    REPEAT(11);STRING('<179,0{45},179>'),HUE(14,0)  .
          ROW(13,1)   STRING('<192,196{45},217>'),HUE(14,0)
          ROW(1,11)   STRING('ENTER NEW REPORT DEFINITION')
          ROW(4,4)    STRING('Report Definition')
          ROW(5,19)   STRING('Path:')
          ROW(7,4)    STRING('Database Definition')
          ROW(8,19)   STRING('Path:')
```

(continued)

```
             ROW(10,5)   STRING('Report Description:')
MESSAGE      ROW(2,10)   STRING(30),ENH
                             ENTRY,USE(?FIRST_FIELD)
             ROW(5,8)    ENTRY(@s8),USE(REP:REPORT_DEF),LFT
               COL(25)   ENTRY(@s20),USE(REP:REPORT_PATH),LFT
             ROW(8,8)    ENTRY(@s8),USE(REP:DATABASE_DEF),LFT
               COL(25)   ENTRY(@s20),USE(REP:DATABASE_PTH),LFT
             ROW(10,25)  ENTRY(@s20),USE(REP:NOTES),LFT
             ROW(12,13)  PAUSE('Press <<ENTER> to Accept'),USE(?PAUSE_FIELD)
                             ENTRY,USE(?LAST_FIELD)
                             PAUSE(''),USE(?DELETE_FIELD)

               .


EJECT
CODE
OPEN(SCREEN)                                 !OPEN THE SCREEN
SETCURSOR                                    !TURN OFF ANY CURSOR
DISPLAY                                      !DISPLAY THE FIELDS
LOOP                                         !LOOP THRU ALL THE FIELDS
  MEM:MESSAGE = CENTER(MEM:MESSAGE,SIZE(MEM:MESSAGE)) !DISPLAY ACTION MESSAGE
  DO CALCFIELDS                              !CALCULATE DISPLAY FIELDS
  ALERT                                      !RESET ALERTED KEYS
  ALERT(ACCEPT_KEY)                          !ALERT SCREEN ACCEPT KEY
  ALERT(REJECT_KEY)                          !ALERT SCREEN REJECT KEY
  ACCEPT                                     !READ A FIELD
  IF KEYCODE() = REJECT_KEY THEN RETURN.     !RETURN ON SCREEN REJECT KEY
  EXECUTE ACTION                             !SET MESSAGE
    MEM:MESSAGE = 'Record will be Added'     !
    MEM:MESSAGE = 'Record will be Changed'   !
    MEM:MESSAGE = 'Press Enter to Delete'    !

    .
  IF KEYCODE() = ACCEPT_KEY                   !ON SCREEN ACCEPT KEY
    UPDATE                                    !  MOVE ALL FIELDS FROM SCREEN
    SELECT(?)                                 !  START WITH CURRENT FIELD
    SELECT                                    !  EDIT ALL FIELDS
    CYCLE                                     !  GO TO TOP OF LOOP

    .
  CASE FIELD()                                !JUMP TO FIELD EDIT ROUTINE
  OF ?FIRST_FIELD                             !FROM THE FIRST FIELD
    IF KEYCODE() = ESC_KEY THEN RETURN.       !  RETURN ON ESC KEY
    IF ACTION = 3 THEN SELECT(?DELETE_FIELD).!   OR CONFIRM FOR DELETE

  OF ?REP:REPORT_PATH                         !PATH TO REPORT FILES
    IF DUPLICATE(REP:BY_REPORT)               !  CHECK FOR DUPLICATE KEY
      MEM:MESSAGE = 'CREATES DUPLICATE ENTRY' !    MOVE AN ERROR MESSAGE
      SELECT(?REP:REPORT_PATH)                !    STAY ON THE SAME FIELD
      BEEP                                    !    SOUND THE KEYBOARD ALARM
```

(continued)

```
        CYCLE                            !    AND LOOP AGAIN
  .

    OF ?PAUSE_FIELD                      !ON PAUSE FIELD
      IF KEYCODE() <> ENTER_KEY|         !IF NOT ENTER KEY
      AND KEYCODE() <> ACCEPT_KEY|       !AND NOT CTRL-ENTER KEY
      AND KEYCODE() <> 0                 !AND NOT NONSTOP MODE
        BEEP                             !  SOUND KEYBOARD ALARM
        SELECT(?PAUSE_FIELD)             !  AND STAY ON PAUSE FIELD
      .

    OF ?LAST_FIELD                       !FROM THE LAST FIELD
      EXECUTE ACTION                     !  UPDATE THE FILE
        ADD(REPORTER)                    !    ADD NEW RECORD
        PUT(REPORTER)                    !    CHANGE EXISTING RECORD
        DELETE(REPORTER)                 !    DELETE EXISTING RECORD
      .

      IF ERRORCODE() = 40                !  DUPLICATE KEY ERROR
        MEM:MESSAGE = ERROR()            !    DISPLAY ERR MESSAGE
        SELECT(2)                        !    POSITION TO TOP OF FORM
        CYCLE                            !    GET OUT OF EDIT LOOP
      ELSIF ERROR()                      !  CHECK FOR UNEXPECTED ERROR
        STOP(ERROR())                    !    HALT EXECUTION
      .

      ACTION = 0                         !  SET ACTION TO COMPLETE
      RETURN                             !  AND RETURN TO CALLER

    OF ?DELETE_FIELD                     !FROM THE DELETE FIELD
      IF KEYCODE() = ENTER_KEY |         !  ON ENTER KEY
      OR KEYCODE() = ACCEPT_KEY          !  OR CTRL-ENTER KEY
        SELECT(?LAST_FIELD)              !    DELETE THE RECORD
      ELSE                               !  OTHERWISE
        BEEP                             !    BEEP AND ASK AGAIN
  . . .

CALCFIELDS   ROUTINE
  IF FIELD() > ?FIRST_FIELD                      !BEYOND FIRST_FIELD?
    IF KEYCODE() = 0 AND SELECTED() > FIELD() THEN EXIT. !GET OUT IF NOT NONSTOP
  .

  SCR:MESSAGE = MEM:MESSAGE
```

CATALO14.CLA

```
            MEMBER('CATALOG')

EXPORT1        PROCEDURE

TITLE      REPORT        WIDTH(80),PRE(TTL),DEVICE(MEM:DEVICE)
RPT_HEAD                 DETAIL
             .             .
REPORT     REPORT        WIDTH(80),PAGE(MEM:PAGE),LINE(MEM:LINE),PRE(RPT)        |
                         DEVICE(MEM:DEVICE)
PAGE_HEAD                HEADER
                           .
DETAIL                   DETAIL
FIELD        COL(1)        STRING(79) CTL(@LF)

RPT_FOOT                 DETAIL

PAGE_FOOT                FOOTER
             .             .


 CODE
 DONE# = 0                              !TURN OFF DONE FLAG
 MEM:DEVICE = 'BASIC.TXT'               !CALL SETUP PROCEDURE
 CLEAR(DIS:RECORD,-1)                   !MAKE SURE RECORD CLEARED
 PRINT(TTL:RPT_HEAD)                    !PRINT TITLE PAGE
 CLOSE(TITLE)                           !CLOSE TITLE REPORT
 SET(DIS:BY_NUMBER)                     !  POINT TO FIRST RECORD
 DO NEXT_RECORD                         !READ FIRST RECORD
 APPEND# = FALSE                        !TURN OFF APPEND FLAG
 IF SUB(MEM:DEVICE,1,1) <> '+'          !NOT ALREADY APPENDING REPORTS
   MEM:DEVICE = '+' & MEM:DEVICE        !  APPEND DISK RPT TO TITLE
   APPEND# = TRUE                       !  SET FLAG TO TURN OFF APPEND
   .          .
 OPEN(REPORT)                           !OPEN THE REPORT
 LOOP UNTIL DONE#                       !READ ALL RECORDS IN FILE
   SAVE_LINE# = MEM:LINE                !  SAVE LINE NUMBER
   LAST_REC# = POINTER(DISKS)
   PRINT(RPT:DETAIL)                    !  PRINT DETAIL LINES
   DO CHECK_PAGE                        !  DO PAGE BREAK IF NEEDED
   DO NEXT_RECORD                       !  GET NEXT RECORD
   .                                    !
 PRINT(RPT:RPT_FOOT)                    !PRINT GRAND TOTALS
 DO CHECK_PAGE                          !  DO PAGE BREAK IF NEEDED
 CLOSE(REPORT)                          !CLOSE REPORT
```

(continued)

```
   IF APPEND#                                    !IF REPORT WAS APPENDED
     MEM:DEVICE = SUB(MEM:DEVICE,2,LEN(MEM:DEVICE)-1)!TURN OFF APPEND REPORT
   .
   RETURN                                        !RETURN TO CALLER


NEXT_RECORD ROUTINE                              !GET NEXT RECORD
  LOOP UNTIL EOF(DISKS)                          !   READ UNTIL END OF FILE
    NEXT(DISKS)                                  !     READ NEXT RECORD
    RPT:FIELD = '""' & CLIP(LEFT(dis:number)) & '","' & |
    clip(dis:label) & '","' & clip(dis:notes) & '"'
    EXIT                                         !     EXIT THE ROUTINE
  .                                              !
  DONE# = 1                                      !   ON EOF, SET DONE FLAG

CHECK_PAGE ROUTINE                               !CHECK FOR NEW PAGE
  IF MEM:LINE <= SAVE_LINE#                      !  ON PAGE OVERFLOW
    SAVE_LINE# = MEM:LINE                        !     RESET LINE NUMBER
  .
  LOOP UNTIL NOT KEYBOARD()                      !LOOK FOR KEYSTROKE
    ASK                                          !GET KEYCODE
    IF KEYCODE() = REJECT_KEY                    !ON CTRL-ESC
      IF APPEND#                                 !IF REPORT WAS APPENDED
        MEM:DEVICE = SUB(MEM:DEVICE,2,LEN(MEM:DEVICE)-1)!TURN OFF APPEND REPORT
      .
      CLOSE(REPORT)                              !  CLOSE REPORT
      RETURN                                     !  ABORT PRINT
  . .
```

Chapter 12

The Deliverable Product

Compiler, Translator, and Linker

If you install Clarion on a computer and immediately begin to use Designer, you can create an application with the Quick Start function and compile it without making a single adjustment to the development environment. That is quite an accomplishment for a PC-based database application. It's that last step, though, where you can still affect the quality of your application and your whole experience with Clarion.

The compilation process is the conversion of mixed English and Clarion languages into binary instructions (machine language) that the computer can understand and follow. The English part consists of the comments and notes that you've put into the program so that you and other humans can follow what is meant to happen inside the program. The compiler doesn't care—it doesn't even read these words. It finds the two methods for commenting (the !, or "bang" as COBOL programmers refer to it, and the OMIT statement) and ignores everything after that.

 Hint: *The comments that you add to your source code add very little to the overall size of your application. Those words do not pull in functionality from the libraries of C language–based functions that Clarion words do. So, comment as much as you need to make your source understandable to another programmer who was not involved in the creation of your program.*

The Clarion parts consist of the words that Clarion Software designed the compiler to recognize and respond to. Those words and the compiler's ability to understand what they mean when you, the programmer, string them together are what make a Clarion application. During the compilation process, you create the intermediate files called "pseudocode," which will be turned into the object modules that the Translator utility will create on the way to creating an executable file.

The pseudocode (.PRO files), together with the symbol files (.SYM) that the compiler also creates, constitute the environment for debugging the application. The symbol files are required to access the program with the Debugger facility, to stop the program on specific line numbers, and to test for the contents of variables used in the program. In fact, if you try to access the debugging facility and the compiler cannot locate the related .SYM files, instead of getting the Debugger, you'll get an error screen as depicted in Figure 12-1.

During the debugging routine, you cannot look at the values placed directly into the screen variables within the screen structures of your program. If you are not getting the onscreen results you want, try creating a temporary variable locally within the procedure that you want to test. Then use that variable to place the information originally slated for only the screen variable. Remember, though, that a local implicit variable cannot carry information between procedures. The Debugger does not allow you to put a local variable from another procedure into the Debugger screen until control transfers to that procedure. Then, any local variables that you entered from a previous procedure will appear with parentheses around them and will not be active.

Figure 12-1   The error screen that appears when you try to access the Debugger when no symbol files exist.

```
                        Processor Halt
CPRO Version 2.1 Release 2105  8/14/90  5:42 PM
Ctrl-Break
ERROR CODE:48  .SYM FILE NOT FOUND
DOS ERROR :2 FILE NOT FOUND
PROGRAM   :C:\CLARION\CATALOG\CATALOG.PRO
MODULE    :CATALO03.PRO
HALTED AT :UPD_DISKS
CALL FROM :CATALO02/SHO_NUMBER
                Press any key to continue
```

Investigating Your Application

There are several ways to find out what is happening inside your application. Simply pressing the Control–Break key combination while the processor is running brings up the Debugger as shown in Figure 12-2. The processor suspends work at the line of code that was just about to execute when your intervening keystrokes were received. At this point, you can enter and view the contents of or set the variables local to the current procedure or those global to the whole application.

You can monitor the steps (or jumps of the processor) that your program takes. You can:

- Set STEP on and cause the Debugger screen to pop up after each jump.
- Enter specific line numbers that, if that line is a jump, cause the Debugger screen to pop up.
- Set DISPLAY or DUMP on and get a report of each line number that constituted a jump. DISPLAY sends the result to the screen as shown in Figure 12-3, whereas DUMP sends it to a file.
- Put a STOP statement inside the code to cause the Debugger screen to pop up and display the message you put as a parameter to the STOP statement, for example,

```
STOP('JUST SAVED THE VARIABLE: ' & FIL:VARIABLE)
```

Hint: *Remember to place your STOP statements, and other debugging devices, in such a way that you can find them easily and remove them from the code before you deliver the application to the user. You can do this by placing a comment on that line using some simple phrase or word (the same one throughout) that you can then search for using Editor and replace with a blank line. In this way, for a development project in progress, you can leave your debugging code inside Designer, but strip it out of the generated code just before delivery.*

Other methods for watching variable content and monitoring program flow exist (some, including the placement of the SHOW statement, have been discussed in other locations around this book). Be sure, when you use SHOW to display variables, that you use a BLANK statement or a SHOW statement with an empty string for a parameter following each execution of the first SHOW statement. Otherwise, the display area for the variable you want to watch will dissolve into a scrambled mess. A sample of this application of the SHOW statement appears in Figure 12-4.

Figure 12-2   The Debugger screen with local variables still displayable while processing a different procedure.

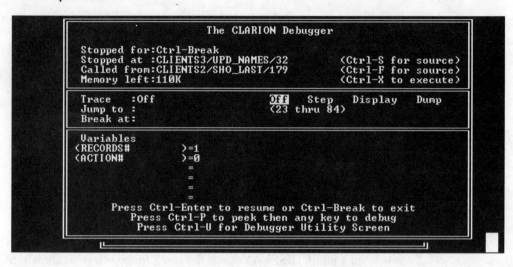

```
                    The CLARION Debugger

Stopped for:Ctrl-Break
Stopped at :CLIENTS3/UPD_NAMES/32            <Ctrl-S for source>
Called from:CLIENTS2/SHO_LAST/179           <Ctrl-F for source>
Memory left:110K                            <Ctrl-X to execute>

Trace   :Off                    Off   Step   Display   Dump
Jump to :                       <23 thru 84>
Break at:

Variables
<RECORDS#        >=1
<ACTION#         >=0
                 =
                 =
                 =
                 =
         Press Ctrl-Enter to resume or Ctrl-Break to exit
           Press Ctrl-P to peek then any key to debug
             Press Ctrl-U for Debugger Utility Screen
```

Figure 12-3   The display mode in the processor's Debugger for a program that begins by displaying a main menu, calls a table (SHO_LAST), and then, when the user presses Enter on an item in the table, calls the Update Procedure (UPD_NAMES).

```
┌══════════════════Show Names By Last═══════════════════┐
│                                                        │
│             The Debugger Trace Table                   │
│   72 - 42      251 - 252    90 - 92      36            │
│   44           333 - 336    100          39            │
│   51 - 52      354 - 359    113 - 114    45 - 47       │
│   55           337          128          48            │
│   61 - 62      334          133          27 - 28       │
│   66           340 - 345    139 - 146    81            │
│   63           254 - 255    149          84            │
│   SHO_LAST     70 - 80      162 - 164    29 - 33       │
│   49 - 58      83           173 - 174    38            │
│   67 - 68      90 - 94      175          36            │
│   242 - 248    98 - 100     359          39            │
│   298 - 302    72 - 80      176          45 - 46       │
│   345 - 351    83           180 - 182    50 - 51       │
│   303 - 307    90 - 92      UPD_NAMES    CAPS          │
│   249          100 - 101    23 - 28      12 - 26       │
│   247 - 248    104 - 106    81           UPD_NAMES     │
│   298 - 299    110 - 113    84           51 - 53       │
│   308 - 309    72 - 80      29 - 33      27 - 28       │
│   249          83           38           81 - 82       │
│   Press Enter to Resume      Press Esc for Debugger    │
```

Figure 12-4   Sample debugging code using the SHOW statement.

```
SHOW(1,1,'Variable = ' & FIL:VARIABLE)
ASK
BLANK(1,1,1,20)
```

In Figure 12-4, the ASK statement suspends processing to wait for you to see the results and press a key before it blanks out those results in preparation, for instance, for the next loop through the Main Event Loop and a new instance of the SHOW statement. As mentioned in Chapter 10, you can also use the ASK statement to set a variable on the fly.

 Hint: A jump in processing means that a line of code successfully executed and then jumped to the next line. The processor does not pop up the Debugger for each line of code it passes over. In other words, unless the jump lands on a call to a procedure, a function, or a control statement, the processor does not pop up the line of code in step trace mode. Try an experiment: Place a STOP statement in your code in several places in one procedure where you think the processor will travel. (A table is a good place to test the functioning of a loop.) Compile the procedure and run the processor. Now, set break lines at various places throughout the procedure in the "Break at" slot, and then watch the application. You'll see how the processor cycles through the loop without executing every statement. This becomes important when you are trying to track down why a particular piece of code is not working.

Executable Size

When you construct a Clarion application, the intermediate pseudocode you create with the compiler still requires the processor to run. In other words, the intelligence to interpret the statements in the program still resides in a separate place from the program itself. When you create the object code (with the .OBJ file extension), you prepare the processor pseudocode to marry with the standard object code in the Clarion Link Libraries with which you never have any direct contact.

When you load the Clarion environment onto your system, you install several files that you never deal with directly. They contain the heart of Clarion's ability to understand what you've written using the language. Those files are:

- CLARION1.LIB—the first of two files containing the C library functions required to be added to the .OBJ files you create with the translator to build an executable program.
- CLARION2.LIB—the second file as described in the first entry.
- CLARION.OBJ—the first of two files that are the "germ" of Clarion and contain the header information for all Clarion applications.
- CLARION0.OBJ—the second file as described in the previous entry.

Files that are used only with .RTLink Runtime Libraries include:

- CLARION.RTL—the runtime library of common Clarion functions when you divide one large executable program to operate separate, smaller executable programs using .RTLink. This file combines the functions in the two .LIB files.
- CLARION.RTT—the transfer file associated with CLARION.RTL; required only during linking.

There are several ways to reduce the size of your executable program. The first of three approaches we'll discuss involves removing expensive functions (that is, functionality with a lot of overhead), and the second approach involves splitting the program into separate, smaller files.

When you remove functions from your application, you prevent Clarion from linking in functionality from its libraries. For instance, the code that Clarion requires to create a Clarion file when your program tries to open one and doesn't find it takes up a considerable amount of space. You can trim between 15K and 25K, depending on the size of the application in the first place, by not placing the CREATE attribute in the file definition.

The second method breaks an application up into smaller executable programs with the common Clarion code residing in separate .RTL files. This reduces the size of an application in memory because it only loads the current executable programs, but it may increase the overall space you'll require to ship the program.

A last approach you can take toward reducing your application's executable size is to use stripped down model procedures (if you work in Designer). Many times you'll find yourself using several Menu Procedures that don't do anything more than present a selection of choices—no hot keys, no Entry

Fields, maybe not even any Display Fields. In that case, you could use a stripped down Menu Procedure as we discuss in Chapter 8.

Generating Lists

The compiler gives you the opportunity to generate separate source listings during each compile. While you create your application, it is best *not* to create listings. This burns disk space and has little benefit. The chances are pretty good that you will not use these listings in your programming. Until you are ready to document a deliverable product, all you can do with the listings is to print them out and look over your code. You'll find, however, that the actual source code itself serves this purpose just as well during the intermediate development stages. You'll spend most of your time bouncing over into the Editor to look at problem spots on the screen, anyway. That way, when you find what you want to fix, you can make the change, press the Shift-F6 key combination, and do a conditional compile right from within Editor—a function you could not perform if you were looking at the listing.

However, for documenting the final product, the Listing function is invaluable. You can set the source code to print out with page breaks, page numbers, and line numbering for easy reference during the maintenance phase of your project. Whenever you prepare your final documentation for a project, you should take the final .PRO files and compile them to create the final listing of source code to archive away with the relevant development files needed to re-create the system. The final document looks like the one shown in Figure 12-5, which is the code from the PRINTER.CLA program from Chapter 11.

Normally, this listing is built to center the title on 11" x 17" computer paper. However, you can reduce the space it takes by using the Tailor utility to embed control codes within the listing file to cause your printer to print the file in condensed mode.

Handling Errors

As you compile your programs and errors result—for whatever reason—Clarion prepares a file with the name of the module with the error and the file extension .ERR. These can be handy documentation tools. They do not get destroyed until the module successfully compiles. Clarion uses them to respond to the Control–E search for errors within Editor. If you lose track of where your problems were or even as a method for tracking your own hours, you can use the Control–X key combination from within Editor to make a

Figure 12-5   A sample of the output to the .LST file when the Listing option is selected when compiling a program.

```
PRINTER.CLA            CLARION COMPILER v2.1
                       8/14/90  9:20 PM PAGE 1
    1       PRINTER       PROGRAM
    2    1  REPORT   REPORT       WIDTH(80)
    3    2  HEAD                  HEADER,PRE(HEA)
    4    3            COL(32)     STRING('THIS IS THE HEADER')
    5    3            ROW(+3,37)  STRING('The Body') CTL(@LF)
    6    3                        END!HEADER
    7    2  BODY                  DETAIL,PRE(BOD)
    8    3  LABEL       COL(26)   STRING(30),USE(DIS:LABEL) CTL(@LF)
    9    3                        END!DETAIL
   10    2  FOOT                  FOOTER
   11    3            ROW(+2,32)  STRING('THIS IS THE FOOTER') CTL(@LF)
   12    3                        END!FOOTER
   13    2  END!REPORT
   14
   15    1  DISKS    FILE,PRE(DIS),CREATE,RECLAIM
   16    2  BY_NUMBER  KEY(DIS:NUMBER),NOCASE,OPT
   17    2  RECORD     RECORD
   18    3  NUMBER       STRING(@N_4)
   19    3  LABEL        STRING(30)
   20    3  NOTES        STRING(40)
   21    3             END!RECORD
   22    2           END!FILE DEF
   23
   24    1          CODE
   25    1          OPEN(REPORT)          !START THE REPORT
   26    1          SET(DISKS)         !ESTABLISH THE POINTER IN THE FILE (OPEN IT)
   27    1          LOOP UNTIL EOF(DISKS) !LOOK THROUGH ALL RECORDS IN THE FILE
   28    2            NEXT(DISKS)         !READ THE NEXT RECORD
   29    2            COUNT# += 1         !ADD TO LINE COUNT
   30    2            IF COUNT# = 5       !TEST FOR PAGE LIMIT
   31    3              PRINT(FOOT & @FF) !PRINT THE FOOTER AND FEED PAGE
   32    3              PRINT(HEAD)       !PRINT NEXT PAGE HEADER
   33    3              COUNT# = 0        !RESET THE LINE COUNTER
   34    3            END!IF              !END OF LINE COUNT TEST
   35    2            PRINT(BODY)         !PRINT THE BODY DETAIL LINES
   36    2          END!LOOP              !TERMINATE THE PROCESSING LOOP
   37    1          IF COUNT# <= 5   !WHEN A LESS THAN WHOLE PAGE PRINTED LAST
   38    2            PRINT(FOOT)         !PRINT THE FOOTER
   39    2          END!IF               !TERMINATE TEST OF SHORT PAGE
```

(continued)

Figure 12-5 *continued*

```
40   1              PRINT(@FF)            !KICK OUT THE LAST PAGE
41   1              CLOSE(REPORT)         !COMPLETE THE REPORT AND RETURN
42   1              RETURN
43
NO MESSAGES THIS COMPILE
```

---

copy of that .ERR file. As you collect these files, you get a date, time, and module for everything you've done that involved compiling. It can also be used as a way to backtrack through a problem when you have made several changes to the modules in a program.

When you compile a program and it has errors in several modules and you use the Control–E key combination to locate each error, Editor will tell you when you've finished viewing the errors in the first module that you accessed after the compile (when you pressed Esc and it automatically jumped to the first module with a problem). It presents a screen asking if you want to load the next file with errors. If you make that jump, using the Shift-F6 key combination with Editor only compiles the current module. You'll have to keep track of the others to recompile them yourself. If you attempt to start the application, it hangs on the modules that have not been fixed. You can always inventory the remaining .ERR files, which will tell you which modules have not yet been repaired.

If you have problems when you run the Translator utility (for example, you're out of disk space when the system tries to create the final executable program), it is not necessary to rerun Translator and remanufacture all the .OBJ files. Simply restart the linking process from the DOS command line using the Automatic Response File (.ARF) that Translator created. The command you type at the prompt is:

```
RTLINK @PROGRAM.ARF
```

where "PROGRAM" is the main module of your program. If you have the linker stored in another location that is not in your environment, you must type in the full path name for it, as well. This method works with all the linkers that work with Clarion.

Universal Modules and Other Procedures

You can create procedures that are universal to your applications. They will be compiled into the program without being explicitly defined inside Designer or added each time using Editor. For example, suppose that you have a time function that you want to present with a hot key in every application you create. In the model, you would add the procedure as a permanent part of the map as shown in Figure 12-6.

In TIMER.CLA, the program MEMBER statement would appear without the name of a parent program in it as in MEMBER( ). The second method requires less work since it always knows where the universal Timer Procedure resides. In the first method, TIMER.CLA would always have to appear in the same directory as the one that held the application being compiled. Though, with the second method, you must still put a "Timer" Other Procedure in the Application Tree.

Since they don't have any internal guidance about which application they belong to, universal modules cannot be compiled separately. Thus they must always be compiled as part of the stream compilation process for the main program module.

Memory Management

Memory Use

Clarion can really burn up memory space—that is, if you don't pay attention to the construction of your program with an eye toward memory. Almost everyone who works in Designer for any length of time has reached the point where an application got so complex that it wouldn't run Debugger while using Processor or wouldn't load into Processor at all. When you hit that point, it's time to start considering the use of overlays and Clarion's expanded memory support. Using the overlays should be your first move since you cannot be sure that all machines that will operate your program have either enough random access memory (RAM) to support virtual memory in RAM or available disk space to support virtual memory on the disk.

 Hint: Remember, if you plan to distribute your Clarion application to a wide range of computers, don't program in restrictions like a requirement for expanded memory. If you do add the requirement for virtual memory, be sure you include that setup or the instructions for that setup with your installation procedures.

Figure 12-6   Two methods for changing the Standard Model map with a permanently added procedure.

VERSION ONE

```
MAP
    PROC(G_OPENFILES)
    @RUNMAP
    @MODULES
    MODULE('TIMER')
        PROC(TIMER)
    END
END
```

VERSION TWO

```
MAP
    PROC(G_OPENFILES)
    @RUNMAP
    @MODULES
END
    INCLUDE(C:\CLARION\TEST\TIMER.CLA')
```

Memory Notes

Clarion provides a way to find out how much memory your system has available. The MEMORY function can tell you how much conventional memory the system has left for data after the application is loaded. Conventional memory is that memory under 640K in which your application will run. The MEMORY function can also tell you how much of the virtual memory is free. Virtual memory is established by a special setup you must place in the CONFIG.SYS file (discussed later in this chapter). Using the MEMORY function with 0, 1, or no parameters "( )", you can display the conventional memory, which appears as about 86K in Figure 12-7. The virtual memory is displayed the same way: by setting up a Computed Field with the same function—passing 2 in the MEMORY statement —the last number in Figure 12-7 is the combined value of both available to your program for data.

Figure 12-7   The main menu of the CATALOG program with the available dynamic memory displayed by the MEMORY function.

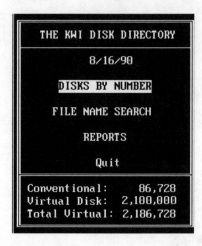

The program must still fit into the conventional memory slot, however. Only buffers, caches, the video images underneath a window, and some other "behind the scenes" elements of the program are placed into virtual memory.

The value displayed in MEMORY( ) will not change in the Menu Procedure shown in Figure 12-7 unless you cause the screen itself to be updated. Since moving the cursor among the menu choices does not update the screen, most Designer-created menus are not updated until after a procedure is launched and then the focus falls back onto the menu when that procedure is complete.

Cache versus Buffer

The CACHE statement works with keys and files and the BUFFER statement works only with sequential records in a file. As the *Clarion Language Reference* points out, using BUFFER while accessing a file by key is inefficient because the records stored in sequence in a key will probably not be stored in that same sequence in the file. Neither CACHE nor BUFFER work when files are opened with SHARE in a multiuser setting. The purpose of CACHE and BUFFER is to reduce the number of times a program must read data from the physical disk drive. If your program allocates a cache for a small lookup file to fill in one column of a table, for instance, and all the records in that file fit into the cache, then for all the time that the Table Procedure is operating, only one trip to the disk is necessary. Without the CACHE statement, each time

Figure 12-8   The schemes for allocating memory to the CACHE and BUFFER statements, using the second parameter in both.

SCHEME	PARAMETER
Percent of total available virtual memory	Greater than 0.0 or less than/equal to 1.0
Number of key levels	2 through 999
Bytes to allocate	1000 or more

you caused the additional records from the primary file to be read, the procedure would also be forced to perform the lookup disk reads to that secondary file.

In both cases, all the space allocated within the statement via the schemes in Figure 12-8 is filled according to the second parameter of the statement and the number of records in the file or the key. New records and changed records are replaced in the buffer and the cache.

From Figure 12-8, you can see that you cannot allocate less than 1K for a cache or it will be mistaken for a key level. In each case, for both the CACHE and BUFFER statements, the amount of memory occupied will only be that required to store the records from the file itself (BUFFER) or the key file and the associated records (CACHE) and no more than that.

In the Standard Model, the BUFFER and CACHE statements appear only twice. CACHE is automatically inserted before the Main Event Loop to cache 25% of available memory for the key used to build a table. BUFFER is used by the SETRECORD model procedure to buffer the records in a file when a Selector is *not* being used during the totaling calculations in a table. Both BUFFER and CACHE lose part of their space in memory if a new record is added to a memory table and there is no room. In the Standard Model, the CACHE statement called at the opening of a Table Procedure places into memory the key file used to access the file to build the table. That segment of the model procedure for a table appears in Figure 12-9.

This configuration will read as much of the key file as will fit into 25% of available memory—for all the fields in the key. If you have a large file with, for instance, a three-part key and you want to restrict the read to two levels of the key into the cache, you would specify the cache with a parameter of 2 instead of .25. In that case, only one disk hit would be necessary (to fill the third field in the key) to retrieve a record. Since a cache will not be updated with new records, this placement only adds efficiency when the Table Procedure is first started. After that, you must issue the FREE statement to release

Figure 12-9   The opening segment of the model file where the key file for the table is placed into a cache in memory.

```
CODE
ACTION# = ACTION                      !SAVE ACTION
OPEN(SCREEN)                          !OPEN THE SCREEN
SETCURSOR                             !TURN OFF ANY CURSOR
@SETUP                                !CALL SETUP PROCEDURE
@INITSELECTS                          !SAVE SELECTOR FIELDS
@TOTCLEAR                             !ZERO TOTAL ACCUMULATORS
TBL:PTR = 1                           !START AT TABLE ENTRY
NDX = 1                               !PUT SELECTOR BAR ON TOP ITEM
ROW = ROW(?POINT)                     !REMEMBER TOP ROW AND
COL = COL(?POINT)                     !LEFT COLUMN OF SCROLL AREA
RECORDS# = TRUE                       !INITIALIZE RECORDS FLAG
```

```
    CACHE(@KEYNAME,.25)               !CACHE KEY FILE
```

```
@BUILDTABLE                           !BUILD SCROLLING TABLE
LOOP                                  !LOOP UNTIL USER EXITS
```

the memory and then reissue the CACHE statement to rebuild the key in memory.

 Hint: Do not create key caches in memory for one-part keys. Keys with one Key Field are always in memory whether you explicitly call for the cache or not. This is part of Clarion's dynamically allocated key scheme.

Virtual Memory

Think of Clarion's virtual memory implementation as a prioritized roadmap through a series of disk drives (logical and physical) for memory usage. As in version 2.1 of Clarion, the concept of virtual memory was launched for Clarion applications. Virtual memory is a combination of conventional memory (that which exists below 640K in RAM) and expanded or extended memory (that which exists above the 1-megabyte line). Only the memory that is not used by your application or by any other RAM resident program is available for use as virtual memory. The application itself will not use any of the memory above 640K except to store some video memory and the caches and buffers mentioned in the previous section. None of Clarion (files or program) uses the 384K directly above the conventional 640K.

When you write an application for general use, be sure you check the environment of your development system to ensure you *are not* using more memory than the machines possess that you believe will be running your application. If you develop your application with the model files unmodified from what was shipped by Clarion, you will have some caches and buffers set up. Your customers will be in for difficulties if you have your development system set up to take advantage of memory above 640K and they do not. The large files those users create simply load much slower than on your machine. If you need that additional memory and you are careful to inform the users, you can ensure that the environment is properly configured through an installation process such as can be created with Clarion's Software Distribution Kit. The parameters for a sample system with 1 megabyte of *additional* RAM (above an initial 1 megabyte of conventional) and some room on the hard drive to take spill over appear in the AUTOEXEC.BAT file as shown in Figure 12-10.

There are five possible steps for virtual memory, zero through four, and the first one should never be a physical drive and the last one should probably be a location on a physical drive. You must create a logical drive in dynamic memory, not on a physical drive, to use virtual memory at all. In Figure 12-10, the first drive uses the RAM disk created in the CONFIG.SYS file by RAMDRIVE.SYS to hold 1 megabyte of caches, buffers, and other Clarion virtual memory residents. The second slot identifies the subdirectory named VIRTUAL on the physical C fixed disk drive for other virtual memory tasks.

The additional area on the physical hard drive is allocated for spillover. Normally, this spillover area will not be configured to store caches and buffers; to do so would eliminate their advantage because it would require disk reads. The reason for doing caches and buffers in the first place is to avoid reading the disk.

Figure 12-10   The lines from an AUTOEXEC.BAT file that configure virtual memory, Clarion style.

```
SET CLAVMO=Memory,10K
SET CLAVM1=D:\,1024,M
SET CLAVM2=C:\VIRTUAL,512
```

> ### *WARNING*
> **When you construct your virtual memory configuration, don't place an "M" after a physical disk drive. In that case, Clarion will treat that disk drive as a RAM disk and allow cache and buffer spillover to be stored there, which will create a redundancy with the keys.**

The spillover space can hold the temporary files created to operate the RUN command and some of the other memory image items that deal with program code.

Overlays

As mentioned in the discussion of executable size earlier in this chapter, most Clarion programmers will reach a point in the creation of an application where the program is too large to fit into memory. It may initially load, but then, as the user gets deeper into the program through a series of tables and pop-up forms, memory could fill up and throw them out of the program with a message like the one shown in Figure 12-11.

In many cases, there would have been sufficient memory to run the application if the programmer had used overlays. Overlays divide your application into chunks by dividing up the map in the main program module so that each chunk will fit into memory. Each chunk (or area) contains procedures that will not be in conflict if they occupy the same section of memory. As in Figure 12-12, you can see the MAIN_MENU and G_OPENFILES procedures occupy a different AREA than the primary table SHO_NUMBER. That is because only one overlay at a time can occupy an area. The two procedures

Figure 12-11   The error produced when a Clarion application cannot find enough conventional memory to run all of its parts.

```
                    Run Time Halt
CRUN Version 2.1 Release 2105  8/20/90  7:22 AM

ERROR CODE:8 INSUFFICIENT MEMORY
DOS ERROR  :0
PROGRAM    :C:\CLARION\CATALOG\CATALOG.PRO
MODULE     :CATALO02.PRO
HALTED AT  :SHO_NUMBER/56
CALL FROM  :CATALO01/MAIN_MENU/64
            Press any key to continue
```

Figure 12-12   A section of the overlay map for the CATALOG program.

```
!* * * * * * * * * * * * * * * * * * * * * * * * * * * * * * * *  *

    AREA ! Number  1
      OVERLAY
        MODULE('CATALO01')
          PROC(MAIN_MENU)
      . .
      OVERLAY
        MODULE('CATALOG1')
          PROC(G_OPENFILES)
      . .
    END !Area Number  1
!* * * * * * * * * * * * * * * * * * * * * * * * * * * * * * * *

    AREA ! Number  2
      OVERLAY
        MODULE('CATALO07')
          PROC(FILESEARCH)
      . .
      OVERLAY
        MODULE('CATALO02')
          PROC(SHO_NUMBER)
      . .
      OVERLAY
        MODULE('CATALO08')
          PROC(REPORTS)
      . .
    END !Area Number  2
!* * * * * * * * * * * * * * * * * * * * * * * * * * * * * * * *
```

can be loaded into the same area because they are not linked together. Notice, however, that the Update Procedure for the Table Procedure SHO_NUMBER (UPD_DISKS) is not in the same overlay area as the table. That is because the Table Procedure cannot call its Update Procedure if the Update Procedure is within the same area. An overlay area represents one specific chunk of memory. During application operation, two overlays cannot work in the same area simultaneously. When an overlay is loaded, all of the procedures in that overlay are loaded, too.

Third-party products like the Overlay Manager from Mitten Software analyze the memory requirements of your application automatically and create the overlay structure. As you would, Overlay Manager scans each procedure to look for links and memory size. Then, it organizes the application into overlays and groups the overlays by areas. You must determine the longest series of linked procedures to determine how much memory you will need. Each of the procedures in that long chain, then, must reside in a different area because no procedure within one overlay can call a procedure in another overlay within that same area. Figure 12-13 shows the "critical path" or largest amount of memory required by the CATALOG program.

Notice in Figure 12-13 that the DOS1 procedures are included in the "critical path." Binary modules like DOS1 cannot be placed in overlays. Notice also that the primary module for the program that contains all the global information is also contained in this path and takes the largest individual piece of memory.

You should experiment with your application until you can arrive at the optimal overlay configuration. To create your own overlay structure, you must follow a few simple rules:

- No procedure in one overlay can call another procedure in another overlay if both overlays exist in the same area.
- Each contiguous series of procedures (meaning each was either a predecessor or a successor to a procedure currently called) as in:

```
MENU-->TABLE -->FORM--->LOOKUP TABLE-->FORM
```

  must be held in memory at the same time, which means there cannot be procedures in different overlays in the same area.
- The sum of all the largest overlays in each area must not exceed available memory.
- Procedures contained in binary modules, Idle Procedures, and global constructs cannot be contained in an overlay.

After you construct your overlay map and test it by recompiling the source modules and running your program, you will need to use a linker that supports overlays. Clarion 2.1 comes bundled with .RTLink from Pocketsoft for that purpose. Everything you need to successfully operate .RTLink as an overlay-supporting linker will unpack onto your system when you install Clarion. The LINK.EXE that comes with DOS does not allow you to link object modules

Figure 12-13   The critical path calculated by Mitten's Overlay Manager for the CATALOG program.

```
============================= Largest Overlay in New Map =============================
                          High  Low  Memory                      Old  New  Calls Calls
   Procedure    Module    Code  Code Size    Entity Type         Area Area From  To
 NEXTDIR        DOS1       0    0     147    PROCEDURE             0    0    0    1
 SETDIR         DOS1       0    0     162    PROCEDURE             0    0    0    1
 CATALOG        CATALOG    0    0    4,253   PROCEDURE             0    0    3    1
 MAIN_MENU      CATALO01   1    1     909    PROCEDURE             0    1    3    1
 FILESEARCH     CATALO07   2    3    3,070   PROCEDURE             0    2    2    1
 FILES          CATALO05   3    3    3,606   PROCEDURE             0    3    2    1
 ONEDISK        CATALO09   4    4    1,416   PROCEDURE             0    4    0    1




                  Total Size    13,563
 == 8/20/90 ================= Free Memory 140.2K ================= 2:01PM ==
 F1-Help    F2-Switch View Forward    F3-Switch View Backward    Enter-View Detail
```

constructed with overlays. However, for applications that do not contain overlays, DOS link will work well. The ability to break a program into separate executable files with one runtime library of common Clarion elements is another advantage to the .RTLink that comes with Clarion.

When a Clarion application gets linked into an executable program, it grabs certain elements from the Clarion environment. If you use multiple executable programs within your application, those elements will be duplicated in each separate program. Using a runtime library (the file CLARION.RTL shipped with Professional Developer) places those common elements into the runtime library to be used by all of the executable programs, which are now much smaller since they don't contain those common Clarion elements. When you run Translator, you can select an option to use the .RTL and your executable file will be smaller and link much faster.

The Final Package

You must consider several important design considerations when creating an application. These considerations are separate from the internal operating design for such things as file structure and final overlay configuration. You must ensure, of course, that your application will run on the target machines. If you plan to operate your application from one floppy drive, you must conserve space. If you plan to create very large databases, configure your application to take advantage of extended or expanded memory. However, when creating a Clarion application, you must consider certain elements that have more direct contact with the user.

Keyboard and Screen Style

The user interface for Clarion is quite hospitable if you adopt the Designer conventions for MENU-TABLE-FORM. However, that is just the beginning of the interface considerations. The items in Figure 12-14 depict the keyboard conventions you will automatically program into your application if you accept the Designer models unaltered.

Figure 12-14   The keyboard conventions from Designer.

Keystroke	Function
<F1>	Calls the help screens.
<CTRL><ESC>	Aborts entry in a form without saving.
<CTRL><ENTER>	Completes entry in a form and saves everything entered so far.
<ESC>	Aborts field edit and retires all procedures if the focus is on the first item available in the form when it is first started.
<Backspace>	Deletes characters backwards one character at a time in Entry fields.
The cursor directional keys	Moves the cursor and highlight bars around depending on the procedure type.
<INS>	Calls the Update Procedure in a Table Procedure to enter a new record.
<DEL>	Calls the Update Procedure to delete a record by pressing ENTER.
<ENTER>	1) Accepts data entered into a field. 2) Calls the Update Procedure in a table to change an existing record. 3) Launches a procedure from a menu item.
<CTRL><Break>	Suspends program execution at any point and allows the user to exit the application or continue on.

Figure 12-15 The color palette for painting a window's "normal" color in Designer and Editor.

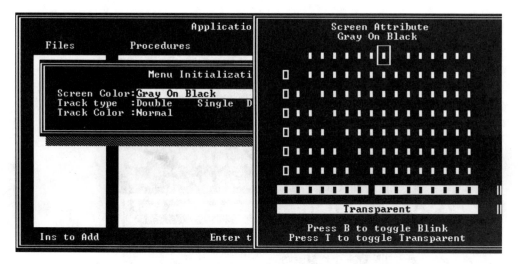

The screen colors that you choose should complement the action they portray. You should make an effort to make the current procedure screen stand out from prior windows still visible on the display. The speed and ease with which you can create windows in Clarion allow you to customize your application's look to best accommodate your users. In addition, you should know whether your program will be running on color or monochrome monitors. Some of the color schemes you create can be difficult to see in monochrome mode, even though they look fine in color.

The three chances you have to select colors are:

1. Selecting the underlying color and foreground for the whole window.
2. The foreground and background for the track or border.
3. The foreground and background video for the characters you type.

The color palette as shown in Figure 12-15 is the same for all of these, and it reacts the same when switching from monochrome to color and back.

Now the task is to choose the colors you will use in your application so they will play as well together on color as on monochrome monitors. It is best not to use those selections in the shaded areas on the right-hand side of the bottom color row in Figure 12-16 unless you want to underemphasize some characters on the screen.

Figure 12-16 The effect of switching from color to monochrome on the color palette in Designer and Editor's screen formatter.

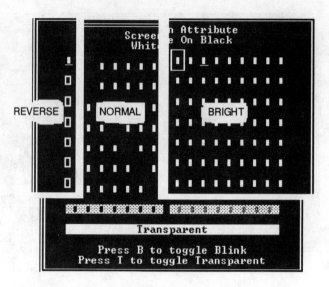

In addition to color, the screen should contain some form of user prompt for standard keys. Decide how you would like to show information about Help, hot keys, and other standard editing keys. There is no way to put standard script into a screen and still use Designer—although you can develop template screens and place them into procedures when you are using Editor's screen formatter.

Another helpful feature you can put into your programs is to line up the windows as they pop up on the screen and not allow them to float. That way, when you are several levels deep in a program, you can still see where you came from. This is especially handy for pop-up forms that use tiered tables for lookups to fill in the form as pictured in Figure 12-17.

Error Handling and Printer Setup

A Clarion program right out of Designer does not handle error conditions very gracefully. If your application should write to a full disk or the wrong device or to a printer that's not plugged in, you get an error response as shown in Figure 12-18 (for a full disk) and in Figure 12-19 (for an offline printer).

During any error condition involving non–Clarion aspects, there is a bit of a delay while the system figures out the problem. Usually you are forced to

Figure 12-17   An example of tiered pop-up windows.

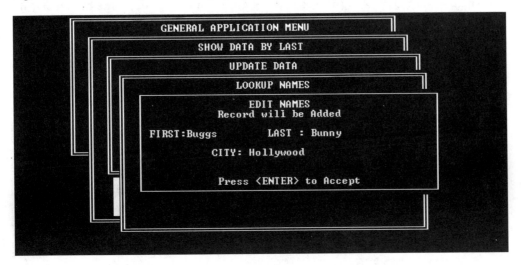

abort (as with Figure 12-18) or the only safe exit is to abort (as in Figure 12-19). To trap those errors sooner, you can write your own LEM (Language Extension Module; see Chapters 1 and 17) or purchase the CritErr LEM from Clarion. Several Clarion users have written similar routines, and they are available in the public domain on various Clarion-oriented bulletin board

Figure 12-18   The error screen that results when you try to save a new record when the disk is full.

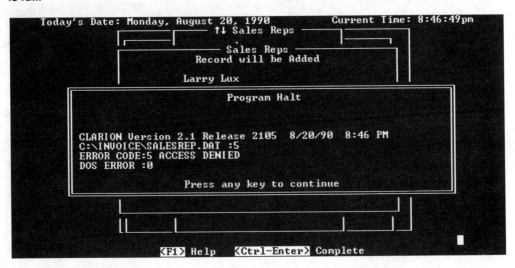

Figure 12-19   The error screen that results when a print request is sent to an offline printer. You can change the result error messages and the hot key for each one by running the OPTIONS program (shipped with Clarion) through CRUN.EXE.

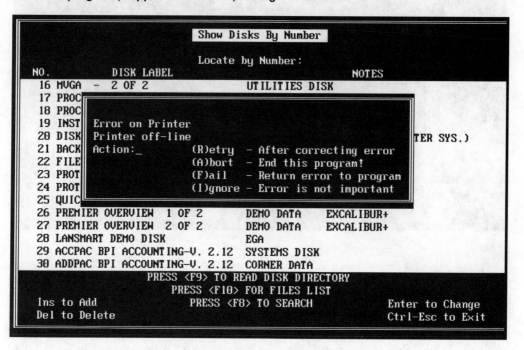

systems around the country. One effective way to help reduce the number of times users encounter a system error is to place a simple prompt form in the Setup Procedure for a Report Procedure. Post a reminder to prepare the printer and then wait for a keystroke to proceed. This does not prevent the user from sending data to an offline printer, but it can reduce the number of accidents.

Help

Helper is another useful tool for creating a usable and well-documented program. Where other application languages leave you to code your own help functions, Clarion not only provides a handy tool, but allows you to author the help text and construct what is really a satellite application while your main application is running. You can create menus in Clarion's Helper that call every Help screen associated with the application. You can create a Standard Keystrokes screen that you can then chain to each Help screen in your application so the user can access it with the PgDn key. You could even place a menu to call other sections of Help from that screen, also.

To use Helper effectively, the only real requirement you have to meet while the program is still in development is to decide where you want Help screens to be available and then to place the names for each screen within the application. Each Procedure Options window contains a slot for a Help screen name as does each variable you define for the application—even memory variables.

If you enter a Help screen name for a field variable, you cannot get help for the general form directly even when the focus of the form is on that field. The field-level Help screen overrides the form-level help and yields a message that no help exists if the field has a Help ID but no Help screen exists in the Help file associated with the application.

Hint: When you begin creating your Help screens, start off by creating one called TEMP or some other easy to remember name. Then build it with the standard look you want to give your Help screens—track color, background, foreground, special prompts. Then, as you access each assigned name from your Help screens you can use the Control–G key combination to get a copy of that template Help screen to use as the basis for the new help screen.

To access Helper from inside your application while running it in the processor as shown in Figure 12-20, press F1 to request the Help screen for wherever you are. If you assigned a name inside Designer or at some point when you edited the procedure in Editor, a red screen will pop up that says, "No Help for this topic can be found," and the name that was assigned to either the form or the field will appear at the top of the error screen. You can then call Helper by pressing SHIFT-F1. The name of the Help-screen-to-be will be assigned, and you can create it anew or begin by using the Control–G key combination to bring in a template as the preceding note suggests. If you access Helper alone, outside of the processor, you will be forced to write down or remember all the names for the Help IDs you assigned.

If you use Helper's ability to paint a section of a Help screen transparently so you can lay it over the top of the application screen to highlight certain areas, be sure you fix the Help screen in place. Otherwise, it will float around and the transparent area may not line up where you intended.

Figure 12-20   Building a Help screen in Processor.

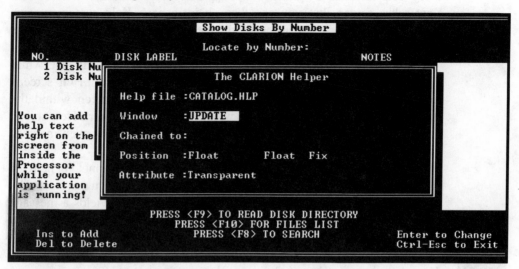

Installation Package

It is highly recommended that you create an installation procedure for any application that will be installed by someone other than yourself. Since a Clarion application can be constructed to create its own data files and you can distill the application down to the executable program and its associated help file, there is not a lot to install. However, most Clarion applications require at least 40 or 50 DOS FILES and BUFFERS to be opened so the CONFIG.SYS file must be set. That is reason alone for a general market package to contain an installation package to modify that DOS configuration file.

Further, many applications contain preentered information—like zip codes for the Zip Code LEM available from Clarion—and so there may be additional data files to install as well as special subdirectories to create. In addition, if you have a particularly large application with multiple executable files and a runtime library file (.RTL), you may find an installation utility convenient for yourself as well. Using the DOS LEM or another environment (even DOS batch files), you can write your own installation system. You can also use the Clarion Software Distribution Kit to create not only an install program, but a program to prepare the disks for installation (as pictured in Figure 12-21). The code for creating the installation files using the Software Distribution Kit from inside a Clarion application appears in Figure 12-22. The code for the complete application appears at the end of this chapter.

Figure 12-21 **The primary screen for a special program written in Clarion to create the installation files using Clarion's Software Distribution Kit.**

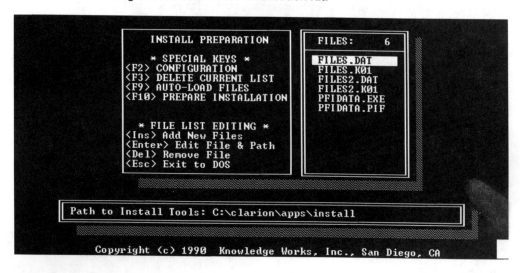

```
         INSTALL PREPARATION        FILES:     6

          * SPECIAL KEYS *          FILES.DAT
      <F2> CONFIGURATION            FILES.K01
      <F3> DELETE CURRENT LIST      FILES2.DAT
      <F9> AUTO-LOAD FILES          FILES2.K01
      <F10> PREPARE INSTALLATION    PFIDATA.EXE
                                    PFIDATA.PIF

          * FILE LIST EDITING *
      <Ins> Add New Files
      <Enter> Edit File & Path
      <Del> Remove File
      <Esc> Exit to DOS


    Path to Install Tools: C:\clarion\apps\install


        Copyright (c) 1990  Knowledge Works, Inc., San Diego, CA
```

Figure 12-22 **The program code for the Other Procedure. This Code is used in preparing and running the batch file process for creating the installation files used by Clarion's Software Distribution Kit.**

```
          MEMBER('MAKER')
WRITER         PROCEDURE
SCREEN     SCREEN       WINDOW(5,62),HUE(0,7)
             ROW(1,1)   STRING('<201,205{60},187>')
             ROW(2,1)   REPEAT(3);STRING('<186,0{60},186>') .
             ROW(5,1)   STRING('<200,205{60},188>')
MESSAGE      ROW(3,7)   STRING(50),HUE(20,7)
             END!SCREEN
BLANKER    SCREEN       HUE(7,0)
             END!SCREEN
DOSFILE    DOS,ASCII,NAME('COMPRESS.DAT')  ! DOS FILE STRUCTURE
           RECORD                          ! FILE TO SEND/RECEIVE
TEXT         STRING(150)                   ! GROUP NAME
           END!RECORD                      ! END OF GROUP, RECORD, FILE
         END!FILE
  CODE
  OPEN(SCREEN)
  GET(CONFIG,1)
```

(continued)

Figure 12-22 *continued*

```
MESSAGE = CENTER('CREATING CONFIGURATION FILE',SIZE(MESSAGE))
OPEN(DOSFILE)
IF ERROR( ) THEN CREATE(DOSFILE).
EMPTY(DOSFILE)
TEXT = 'ERASE DISKS = YES' & '<13,10>'
ADD(DOSFILE)
TEXT = '! LOCATION OF INSTALLATION PROGRAMS'
ADD(DOSFILE)
TEXT = 'COPY FILE = ' & CLIP(CON:SOURCEDISK) |
       & CLIP(CON:SOURCEPATH) & '\' & 'INSTALL.EXE'
ADD(DOSFILE)
TEXT = 'COPY FILE = ' & CLIP(CON:SOURCEDISK) |
       & CLIP(CON:SOURCEPATH) & '\' & 'READ.ME'
ADD(DOSFILE)
TEXT = 'TYPE FILE = ' & CLIP(CON:SOURCEDISK) |
       & CLIP(CON:SOURCEPATH) & '\' & 'READ.ME'
ADD(DOSFILE)
TEXT = '! PATH TO INSTALL PROGRAMS WHEN USING COMPLETED INSTALLATION'
ADD(DOSFILE)
TEXT = 'PATH TO INSTALL INTO = ' & CLIP(CON:DESTPATH) & '<13,10>'
ADD(DOSFILE)
TEXT = '! DO NOT CHANGE THESE SETTINGS'
ADD(DOSFILE)
TEXT = 'BUFFERS (CONFIG.SYS) = 35'
ADD(DOSFILE)
TEXT = 'FILES (CONFIG.SYS) = 35'
ADD(DOSFILE)
TEXT = 'REBOOT (YES/NO/ASK) = ASK'
ADD(DOSFILE)
TEXT = 'NONSTOP (YES/NO) = NO'
ADD(DOSFILE)
TEXT = 'AUTOEXEC (YES/NO) = YES'
ADD(DOSFILE)
TEXT = 'CONFIG (YES/NO) = YES'
ADD(DOSFILE)
TEXT = 'BATCH INSTALL = NO'
ADD(DOSFILE)
TEXT = 'COLOR = 07h,02h,1Fh,0Fh,70h,07h,7h,71h,0Fh,0Eh,0Eh,70h,7h,4Fh,4Fh'
ADD(DOSFILE)
TEXT = '<13,10>' & '! CHANGE THE TEXT TO CHANGE THE WINDOW TITLE'
ADD(DOSFILE)
TEXT = 'TITLE = ' & '''' & PLEION COMMUNICATIONS SYSTEM' & '''' & '
ADD(DOSFILE)
TEXT = 'LABEL FOR DISK #1 = ''TRANSFER DISK'''
```

(continued)

Figure 12-22 *continued*

```
ADD(DOSFILE)
TEXT = 'VOLUME NAME DISK #1 = ''TRANSFER .1'''
ADD(DOSFILE)
TEXT = '<13,10>' & '!--Maximum size of group prompt is 16'
ADD(DOSFILE)
TEXT = 'GROUP #1 PROMPT = ''TRANSFER FILES'''
ADD(DOSFILE)
TEXT = '   DEST. SUBDIRECTORY ='
ADD(DOSFILE)
SET(FILES)
LOOP UNTIL EOF(FILES)
  NEXT(FILES)
  TEXT = '   FILE    = ' & CLIP(FIL:PATH) & '\' & CLIP(FIL:FILENAME)
  POS# = INSTRING('\\',TEXT,1)
  IF POS# > 0
    TEXT = SUB(TEXT,1,POS#) & |
      SUB(TEXT,POS#+1,LEN(CLIP(TEXT)-POS#))
  END!IF
  ADD(DOSFILE)
END!LOOP
CLOSE(DOSFILE)
CLOSE(SCREEN)
OPEN(BLANKER)
SETCURSOR(1,1)
RUN('COMPRESS I=COMPRESS.DAT F=A:')
BLANK
SHOW(12,20,'INSTALLATION PACKAGE COMPLETE - TOUCH ANY KEY')
ASK
BLANK
OPEN(FILES)
RESTART(MAIN_TABLE)
RETURN
```

Summary

Clarion provides a rich set of integrated tools to create application programs. However, there are design issues that even a well-integrated system like this will not handle automatically. In fact, some of the things it *will* do automatically may not be what you want. Although it is possible to sit down at the keyboard and create a simple application in a few minutes with Clarion, creating a successful product requires that you deal with the issues of memory consumption, executable program size, screen design, and final installation. In this chapter, we focused on the issues under the surface of a Clarion application. We discussed compiling and debugging applications under development, the ins and outs of memory management, and the final, user-centered issues involving the day-to-day setup and operation of a Clarion application.

The INSTALLATION Program

MAKER.CLA

```
MAKER      PROGRAM
             INCLUDE('STD_KEYS.CLA')
             INCLUDE('CTL_KEYS.CLA')
             INCLUDE('ALT_KEYS.CLA')
             INCLUDE('SHF_KEYS.CLA')

REJECT_KEY  EQUATE(CTRL_ESC)
ACCEPT_KEY  EQUATE(CTRL_ENTER)
TRUE        EQUATE(1)
FALSE       EQUATE(0)

             MAP
               PROC(G_OPENFILES)
               MODULE('MAKER1')
                 PROC(MAIN_TABLE)                    !FILENAMES FOR INSTALLATION
                   .
               MODULE('MAKER2')
                 PROC(NEW_FILE)                      !ENTER FILE NAME FOR INSTALL
                   .
               MODULE('MAKER3')
                 PROC(CONFIG)                        !STORES CONFIGURATION
                   .
               MODULE('WRITER')
                 PROC(WRITER)                        !CREATES BATCH FILE
                   .
               MODULE('AUTO')
                 PROC(AUTO)                          !AUTOMATICALLY READS FILES
                   .
                 INCLUDE('DOS1.CPY')
                   .
             EJECT('FILE LAYOUTS')
FILES      FILE,PRE(FIL),CREATE,RECLAIM
BY_FILENAME KEY(FIL:FILENAME),DUP,NOCASE,OPT
RECORD       RECORD
FILENAME     STRING(12)                              !FILE NAME FOR INSTALLATION
PATH         STRING(40)                              !PATH LOCATION OF THE FILE
       .  .

CONFIG     FILE,PRE(CON),CREATE,RECLAIM
RECORD       RECORD
SOURCEDISK   STRING(2)                               !DISK WHERE INSTALL FILES KEPT
```

(continued)

```
SOURCEPATH    STRING(40)                        !PATH FOR INSTALL FILES
DESTPATH      STRING(40)                        !PATH TO INSTALL FILES INTO
APPLICATION   STRING(30)                        !NAME OF THE APPLICATION
              . .

SUBDIRS   FILE,PRE(SUB),CREATE,RECLAIM
RECORD        RECORD
PATH          STRING(80)                        !PATH LOCATION OF THE FILE
              . .

SUBDIRS2 FILE,PRE(SB2),CREATE,RECLAIM
RECORD        RECORD
PATH          STRING(80)                        !PATH LOCATION OF THE FILE
              . .

              EJECT('GLOBAL MEMORY VARIABLES')
ACTION        SHORT                             !0 = NO ACTION
                                                !1 = ADD RECORD
                                                !2 = CHANGE RECORD
                                                !3 = DELETE RECORD
                                                !4 = LOOKUP FIELD


              GROUP,PRE(MEM)
MESSAGE       STRING(30)                        !Global Message Area
PAGE          SHORT                             !Report Page Number
LINE          SHORT                             !Report Line Number
DEVICE        STRING(30)                        !Report Device Name
PATH          STRING(40)                        !STORED PATH NAME
              .

              EJECT('CODE SECTION')
  CODE
  SETHUE(7,0)                                   !SET WHITE ON BLACK
  BLANK                                         !   AND BLANK
  G_OPENFILES                                   !OPEN OR CREATE FILES
  SETHUE()                                      !   THE SCREEN
  MAIN_TABLE                                    !FILENAMES FOR INSTALLATION
  RETURN                                        !EXIT TO DOS

G_OPENFILES   PROCEDURE                         !OPEN FILES & CHECK FOR ERROR
  CODE
  SHOW(25,1,CENTER('OPENING FILE: ' & 'FILES',80)) !DISPLAY FILE NAME
  OPEN(FILES)                                   !OPEN THE FILE
  IF ERROR()                                    !OPEN RETURNED AN ERROR
    CASE ERRORCODE()                            ! CHECK FOR SPECIFIC ERROR
    OF 46                                       !  KEYS NEED TO BE REQUILT
```

(continued)

```
      SETHUE(0,7)                              !  BLACK ON WHITE
      SHOW(25,1,CENTER('REBUILDING KEY FILES FOR FILES',80)) !INDICATE MSG
      BUILD(FILES)                             !  CALL THE BUILD PROCEDURE
      SETHUE(7,0)                              !  WHITE ON BLACK
      BLANK(25,1,1,80)                         !  BLANK THE MESSAGE
    OF 2                                      !IF NOT FOUND,
      CREATE(FILES)                            ! CREATE
    ELSE                                       ! ANY OTHER ERROR
      LOOP;STOP('FILES: ' & ERROR()).          !  STOP EXECUTION
  . .


SHOW(25,1,CENTER('OPENING FILE: ' & 'CONFIG',80)) !DISPLAY FILE NAME
OPEN(CONFIG)                                  !OPEN THE FILE
IF ERROR()                                    !OPEN RETURNED AN ERROR
  CASE ERRORCODE()                            ! CHECK FOR SPECIFIC ERROR
  OF 46                                       !  KEYS NEED TO BE REQUILT
    SETHUE(0,7)                               !  BLACK ON WHITE
    SHOW(25,1,CENTER('REBUILDING KEY FILES FOR CONFIG',80)) !INDICATE MSG
    BUILD(CONFIG)                             !  CALL THE BUILD PROCEDURE
    SETHUE(7,0)                               !  WHITE ON BLACK
    BLANK(25,1,1,80)                          !  BLANK THE MESSAGE
  OF 2                                        !IF NOT FOUND,
    CREATE(CONFIG)                            ! CREATE
  ELSE                                        ! ANY OTHER ERROR
    LOOP;STOP('CONFIG: ' & ERROR()).          !  STOP EXECUTION
  . .


SHOW(25,1,CENTER('OPENING FILE: ' & 'SUBDIRS',80)) !DISPLAY FILE NAME
OPEN(SUBDIRS)                                 !OPEN THE FILE
IF ERROR()                                    !OPEN RETURNED AN ERROR
  CASE ERRORCODE()                            ! CHECK FOR SPECIFIC ERROR
  OF 46                                       !  KEYS NEED TO BE REQUILT
    SETHUE(0,7)                               !  BLACK ON WHITE
    SHOW(25,1,CENTER('REBUILDING KEY FILES FOR SUBDIRS',80)) !INDICATE MSG
    BUILD(SUBDIRS)                            !  CALL THE BUILD PROCEDURE
    SETHUE(7,0)                               !  WHITE ON BLACK
    BLANK(25,1,1,80)                          !  BLANK THE MESSAGE
  OF 2                                        !IF NOT FOUND,
    CREATE(SUBDIRS)                           ! CREATE
  ELSE                                        ! ANY OTHER ERROR
    LOOP;STOP('SUBDIRS: ' & ERROR()).         !  STOP EXECUTION
  . .


SHOW(25,1,CENTER('OPENING FILE: ' & 'SUBDIRS2',80)) !DISPLAY FILE NAME
OPEN(SUBDIRS2)                                !OPEN THE FILE
IF ERROR()                                    !OPEN RETURNED AN ERROR
  CASE ERRORCODE()                            ! CHECK FOR SPECIFIC ERROR
```

(continued)

```
      OF 46                                  !  KEYS NEED TO BE REQUILT
        SETHUE(0,7)                          !  BLACK ON WHITE
        SHOW(25,1,CENTER('REBUILDING KEY FILES FOR SUBDIRS2',80)) !INDICATE MSG
        BUILD(SUBDIRS2)                      !  CALL THE BUILD PROCEDURE
        SETHUE(7,0)                          !  WHITE ON BLACK
        BLANK(25,1,1,80)                     !  BLANK THE MESSAGE
      OF 2                                   !IF NOT FOUND,
        CREATE(SUBDIRS2)                     !  CREATE
      ELSE                                   !  ANY OTHER ERROR
        LOOP;STOP('SUBDIRS2: ' & ERROR()).   !  STOP EXECUTION
    . .

      BLANK                                  !BLANK THE SCREEN
```

MAKER1.CLA

```
        MEMBER('MAKER')
MAIN_TABLE     PROCEDURE

SCREEN    SCREEN     WINDOW(24,69),AT(2,7),PRE(SCR),HUE(15,1)
          ROW(21,3)  PAINT(1,65),HUE(7,0),TRN
          ROW(1,52)  PAINT(1,1),TRN
          ROW(1,53)  PAINT(16,6),TRN
          ROW(2,52)  PAINT(15,6),HUE(15,1)
          ROW(1,60)  PAINT(16,10),HUE(15,0)
          ROW(17,1)  PAINT(2,69),HUE(15,0)
          ROW(1,1)   PAINT(17,11),HUE(15,0)
          ROW(19,1)  PAINT(3,1),HUE(15,0)
          ROW(22,1)  PAINT(2,69),HUE(15,0)
          ROW(24,48) PAINT(1,22),HUE(15,0)
          ROW(24,1)  PAINT(1,22),HUE(15,0)
          ROW(19,69) PAINT(3,1),HUE(15,0)
          ROW(1,12)  STRING('<218,196{26},191,0,201,205{16},187>'),HUE(14,1)
          ROW(2,12)  STRING('<179,0{26},179,0,186,0{16},186>'),HUE(14,1)
          ROW(3,12)  STRING('<179,0{26},179,0,199,196{16},182>'),HUE(14,1)
          ROW(4,12)  REPEAT(12)
                       STRING('<179,0{26},179,0,186,0{16},186>'),HUE(14,1)  .
          ROW(16,12) STRING('<192,196{26},217,0,200,205{16},188>'),HUE(14,1)
          ROW(19,2)  STRING('<201,205{64},187>'),HUE(14,1)
          ROW(20,2)  STRING('<186,0{64},186>'),HUE(14,1)
          ROW(21,2)  STRING('<200,205{64},188>'),HUE(14,1)
          ROW(2,60)  REPEAT(15);STRING('<176>'),HUE(7,0)  .
          ROW(17,15) STRING('<176{46}>'),HUE(7,0)
          ROW(20,69) REPEAT(2);STRING('<176>'),HUE(7,0)  .
          ROW(22,5)  STRING('<176{65}>'),HUE(7,0)
```

(continued)

```
                 ROW(2,17)   STRING('INSTALL PREPARATION'),HUE(14,1)
                   COL(43)   STRING(' '),HUE(14,1)
                   COL(44)   STRING('FILE')
                   COL(48)   STRING('S'),HUE(15,1)
                   COL(49)   STRING(': '),HUE(14,1)
                 ROW(4,13)   STRING('    *'),HUE(14,1)
                   COL(18)   STRING(' '),HUE(15,1)
                   COL(19)   STRING('SPECIAL KEYS *'),HUE(14,1)
                 ROW(5,13)   STRING('<<F2> CONFIGURATION')
                 ROW(6,13)   STRING('<<F3> DELETE CURRENT LIST')
                 ROW(7,13)   STRING('<<F9> AUTO-LOAD FILES')
                 ROW(8,13)   STRING('<<F10> PREPARE')
                   COL(26)   STRING(' '),HUE(15,1)
                   COL(27)   STRING('INSTALLATION')
                 ROW(11,15)  STRING('* FILE LIST EDITING *'),HUE(14,1)
                 ROW(12,13)  STRING('<<Ins> Add New Files'),HUE(15,1)
                 ROW(13,13)  STRING('<<Enter> Edit File & Path'),HUE(15,1)
                 ROW(14,13)  STRING('<<Del> Remove File'),HUE(15,1)
                 ROW(15,13)  STRING('<<Esc> Exit to DOS'),HUE(15,1)
                 ROW(20,4)   STRING('Path to Install Tools: '),HUE(14,1)
                 ROW(24,6)   STRING('  Copyright (c) 1'),HUE(14,1)
                   COL(23)   STRING('990  Knowledge Works, Inc'),HUE(14,1)
                   COL(48)   STRING('., San Diego, CA  '),HUE(14,1)
COUNTER          ROW(2,51)   STRING(@N5)
PATH             ROW(20,27)  STRING(40)
                   COL(63)   ENTRY,USE(?FIRST_FIELD)
                   COL(63)   ENTRY,USE(?PRE_POINT)
                             REPEAT(12),INDEX(NDX)
                 ROW(4,43)     POINT(1,14),USE(?POINT),ESC(?-1)
FILENAME           COL(44)   STRING(12)

            .          .


NDX          BYTE                              !REPEAT INDEX FOR POINT AREA
ROW          BYTE                              !ACTUAL ROW OF SCROLL AREA
COL          BYTE                              !ACTUAL COLUMN OF SCROLL AREA
COUNT        BYTE(12)                          !NUMBER OF ITEMS TO SCROLL
ROWS         BYTE(12)                          !NUMBER OF ROWS TO SCROLL
COLS         BYTE(14)                          !NUMBER OF COLUMNS TO SCROLL
FOUND        BYTE                              !RECORD FOUND FLAG
NEWPTR       LONG                              !POINTER TO NEW RECORD

TABLE        TABLE,PRE(TBL)                    !TABLE OF RECORD DATA
FILENAME     STRING(12)                        !FILE NAME FOR INSTALLATION
PTR          LONG                              !  POINTER TO FILE RECORD

            .


        EJECT
```

(continued)

```
CODE
ACTION# = ACTION                            !SAVE ACTION
OPEN(SCREEN)                                !OPEN THE SCREEN
SETCURSOR                                   !TURN OFF ANY CURSOR
TBL:PTR = 1                                 !START AT TABLE ENTRY
NDX = 1                                     !PUT SELECTOR BAR ON TOP ITEM
ROW = ROW(?POINT)                           !REMEMBER TOP ROW AND
COL = COL(?POINT)                           !LEFT COLUMN OF SCROLL AREA
RECORDS# = TRUE                             !INITIALIZE RECORDS FLAG
CACHE(FIL:BY_FILENAME,.25)                  !CACHE KEY FILE
IF ACTION = 4                               !  TABLE LOOKUP REQUEST
  NEWPTR = POINTER(FILES)                   !  SET POINTER TO RECORD
  IF NOT NEWPTR                             !  RECORD NOT PASSED TO TABLE
    SET(FIL:BY_FILENAME,FIL:BY_FILENAME)    !    POSITION TO CLOSEST RECORD
    NEXT(FILES)                             !    READ RECORD
    NEWPTR = POINTER(FILES)                 !    SET POINTER
  .
  DO FIND_RECORD                            !  POSITION FILE
ELSE
  NDX = 1                                   !  PUT SELECTOR BAR ON TOP ITEM
  DO FIRST_PAGE                             !  BUILD MEMORY TABLE OF KEYS
 .
RECORDS# = TRUE                             !  ASSUME THERE ARE RECORDS
LOOP                                        !LOOP UNTIL USER EXITS
  ACTION = ACTION#                          !RESTORE ACTION
  SCR:PATH = MEM:PATH
  SCR:COUNTER = RECORDS(FILES)
  ALERT                                     !RESET ALERTED KEYS
  ALERT(REJECT_KEY)                         !ALERT SCREEN REJECT KEY
  ALERT(ACCEPT_KEY)                         !ALERT SCREEN ACCEPT KEY
  ALERT(F10_KEY)                            !ALERT HOT KEY
  ALERT(F2_KEY)                             !ALERT HOT KEY
  ALERT(F9_KEY)                             !ALERT HOT KEY
  ALERT(F3_KEY)
  ACCEPT                                    !READ A FIELD
  IF KEYCODE() = F10_KEY                    !ON HOT KEY
    IF FIELD() = ?POINT THEN DO GET_RECORD. !  READ RECORD IF NEEDED
    WRITER                                  !  CALL HOT KEY PROCEDURE
    DO SAME_PAGE                            !  RESET TO SAME PAGE
    CYCLE                                   !  AND LOOP AGAIN
  .
  IF KEYCODE() = F2_KEY                     !ON HOT KEY
    IF FIELD() = ?POINT THEN DO GET_RECORD. !  READ RECORD IF NEEDED
    CONFIG                                  !  CALL HOT KEY PROCEDURE
    DO SAME_PAGE                            !  RESET TO SAME PAGE
    CYCLE                                   !  AND LOOP AGAIN
  .
```

(continued)

```
IF KEYCODE() = F9_KEY                        !ON HOT KEY
  IF FIELD() = ?POINT THEN DO GET_RECORD.    !  READ RECORD IF NEEDED
  AUTO                                       !  CALL HOT KEY PROCEDURE
  DO SAME_PAGE                               !  RESET TO SAME PAGE
  CYCLE                                      !  AND LOOP AGAIN
  .
IF KEYCODE() = F3_KEY                        !ON HOT KEY
  EMPTY(FILES)
  BLANK(ROW,COL,ROWS,COLS)
  FREE(TABLE)                                !  EMPTY THE TABLE
  AUTO
  DO FIRST_PAGE
  CYCLE                                      !  AND LOOP AGAIN
  .
IF KEYCODE() = REJECT_KEY THEN BREAK.        !RETURN ON SCREEN REJECT KEY

IF  KEYCODE() = ACCEPT_KEY     |             !ON SCREEN ACCEPT KEY
AND FIELD() <> ?POINT                        !BUT NOT ON THE POINT FIELD
  UPDATE                                     !  MOVE ALL FIELDS FROM SCREEN
  SELECT(?)                                  !  START WITH CURRENT FIELD
  SELECT                                     !  EDIT ALL FIELDS
  CYCLE                                      !  GO TO TOP OF LOOP
  .

CASE FIELD()                                 !JUMP TO FIELD EDIT ROUTINE

OF ?FIRST_FIELD                              !FROM THE FIRST FIELD
  IF KEYCODE() = ESC_KEY     |               !  RETURN ON ESC KEY
  OR RECORDS# = FALSE                        !  OR NO RECORDS
    BREAK                                    !     EXIT PROGRAM
  .
OF ?PRE_POINT                                !PRE POINT FIELD CONDITION
  IF KEYCODE() = ESC_KEY                     !  BACKING UP?
    SELECT(?-1)                              !    SELECT PREVIOUS FIELD
  ELSE                                       !  GOING FORWARD
    SELECT(?POINT)                           !    SELECT MENU FIELD
  .
OF ?POINT                                    !PROCESS THE POINT FIELD
  IF RECORDS(TABLE) = 0                      !IF THERE ARE NO RECORDS
    IF EMPTIED# = 1
      EMPTIED# = 0
      CYCLE
    .
    AUTO                                     !  CALL HOT KEY PROCEDURE
    DO SAME_PAGE                             !  RESET TO SAME PAGE
    CYCLE                                    !    AND LOOP AGAIN
  .
```

(continued)

```
CASE KEYCODE()                                !PROCESS THE KEYSTROKE

OF INS_KEY                                    !INS KEY
  CLEAR(FIL:RECORD)                           !  CLEAR RECORD AREA
  ACTION = 1                                  !  SET ACTION TO ADD
  GET(FILES,0)                                !  CLEAR PENDING RECORD
  NEW_FILE                                    !  CALL FORM FOR NEW RECORD
  IF ~ACTION                                  !  IF RECORD WAS ADDED
    NEWPTR = POINTER(FILES)                    !    SET POINTER TO NEW RECORD
    DO FIND_RECORD                            !    POSITION IN FILE
  .

OF ENTER_KEY                                  !ENTER KEY
OROF ACCEPT_KEY                               !CTRL-ENTER KEY
  DO GET_RECORD                               !  GET THE SELECTED RECORD
  IF ACTION = 4 AND KEYCODE() = ENTER_KEY!    IF THIS IS A LOOKUP REQUEST
    ACTION = 0                                !    SET ACTION TO COMPLETE
    BREAK                                     !    AND RETURN TO CALLER
  .

  IF ~ERROR()                                 !  IF RECORD IS STILL THERE
    ACTION = 2                                !    SET ACTION TO CHANGE
    NEW_FILE                                  !    CALL FORM TO CHANGE REC
    IF ACTION THEN CYCLE.                     !    IF SUCCESSFUL RE-DISPLAY
  .

  NEWPTR = POINTER(FILES)                     !    SET POINTER TO NEW RECORD
  DO FIND_RECORD                              !    POSITION IN FILE
OF DEL_KEY                                    !DEL KEY
  DO GET_RECORD                               !  READ THE SELECTED RECORD
  IF ~ERROR()                                 !  IF RECORD IS STILL THERE
    ACTION = 3                                !    SET ACTION TO DELETE
    NEW_FILE                                  !    CALL FORM TO DELETE
    IF ~ACTION                                !    IF SUCCESSFUL
      N# = NDX                                !      SAVE POINT INDEX
      DO SAME_PAGE                            !      RE-DISPLAY
      NDX = N#                                !      RESTORE POINT INDEX
  . .
OF DOWN_KEY                                   !DOWN ARROW KEY
  DO SET_NEXT                                 !  POINT TO NEXT RECORD
  DO FILL_NEXT                                !  FILL A TABLE ENTRY
  IF FOUND                                    !  FOUND A NEW RECORD
    SCROLL(ROW,COL,ROWS,COLS,ROWS(?POINT))  !    SCROLL THE SCREEN UP
    GET(TABLE,RECORDS(TABLE))                 !  GET RECORD FROM TABLE
    DO FILL_SCREEN                            !  DISPLAY ON SCREEN
  .

OF PGDN_KEY                                   !PAGE DOWN KEY
  DO SET_NEXT                                 !  POINT TO NEXT RECORD
  DO NEXT_PAGE                                !  DISPLAY THE NEXT PAGE
```

(continued)

```
    OF CTRL_PGDN                                      !CTRL-PAGE DOWN KEY
       DO LAST_PAGE                                   !  DISPLAY THE LAST PAGE
       NDX = RECORDS(TABLE)                           !  POSITION POINT BAR

    OF UP_KEY                                         !UP ARROW KEY
       DO SET_PREV                                    !  POINT TO PREVIOUS RECORD
       DO FILL_PREV                                   !  FILL A TABLE ENTRY
       IF FOUND                                       !  FOUND A NEW RECORD
         SCROLL(ROW,COL,ROWS,COLS,-(ROWS(?POINT)))!  SCROLL THE SCREEN DOWN
         GET(TABLE,1)                                 !  GET RECORD FROM TABLE
           DO FILL_SCREEN                             !  DISPLAY ON SCREEN
       .

    OF PGUP_KEY                                       !PAGE UP KEY
       DO SET_PREV                                    !  POINT TO PREVIOUS RECORD
       DO PREV_PAGE                                   !  DISPLAY THE PREVIOUS PAGE

    OF CTRL_PGUP                                      !CTRL-PAGE UP
       DO FIRST_PAGE                                  !  DISPLAY THE FIRST PAGE
       NDX = 1                                        !  POSITION POINT BAR
  . . .
  FREE(TABLE)                                         !FREE MEMORY TABLE
  RETURN                                              !AND RETURN TO CALLER

SAME_PAGE ROUTINE                                     !DISPLAY THE SAME PAGE
  GET(TABLE,1)                                        !  GET THE FIRST TABLE ENTRY
  DO FILL_RECORD                                      !  FILL IN THE RECORD
  SET(FIL:BY_FILENAME,FIL:BY_FILENAME,TBL:PTR)        !  POSITION FILE
  FREE(TABLE)                                         !  EMPTY THE TABLE
  DO NEXT_PAGE                                        !  DISPLAY A FULL PAGE

FIRST_PAGE ROUTINE                                    !DISPLAY FIRST PAGE
  BLANK(ROW,COL,ROWS,COLS)
  FREE(TABLE)                                         !  EMPTY THE TABLE
  CLEAR(FIL:RECORD,-1)                                !  CLEAR RECORD TO LOW VALUES
  CLEAR(TBL:PTR)                                      !  ZERO RECORD POINTER
  SET(FIL:BY_FILENAME)                                !  POINT TO FIRST RECORD
  LOOP NDX = 1 TO COUNT                               !  FILL UP THE TABLE
    DO FILL_NEXT                                      !    FILL A TABLE ENTRY
    IF NOT FOUND THEN BREAK.                          !    GET OUT IF NO RECORD
  .
  NDX = 1                                             !  SET TO TOP OF TABLE
  DO SHOW_PAGE                                        !  DISPLAY THE PAGE

LAST_PAGE ROUTINE                                     !DISPLAY LAST PAGE
  NDX# = NDX                                          !  SAVE SELECTOR POSITION
  BLANK(ROW,COL,ROWS,COLS)                            !  CLEAR SCROLLING AREA
```

(continued)

```
    FREE(TABLE)                                       !   EMPTY THE TABLE
    CLEAR(FIL:RECORD,1)                               !   CLEAR RECORD TO HIGH VALUES
    CLEAR(TBL:PTR,1)                                  !   CLEAR PTR TO HIGH VALUE
    SET(FIL:BY_FILENAME)                              !   POINT TO FIRST RECORD
    LOOP NDX = COUNT TO 1 BY -1                       !   FILL UP THE TABLE
      DO FILL_PREV                                    !     FILL A TABLE ENTRY
      IF NOT FOUND THEN BREAK.                        !     GET OUT IF NO RECORD
    .                                                 !   END OF LOOP
    NDX = NDX#                                        !   RESTORE SELECTOR POSITION
    DO SHOW_PAGE                                      !   DISPLAY THE PAGE

FIND_RECORD ROUTINE                                  !POSITION TO SPECIFIC RECORD
    SET(FIL:BY_FILENAME,FIL:BY_FILENAME,NEWPTR)      !POSITION FILE
    IF NEWPTR = 0                                     !NEWPTR NOT SET
      NEXT(FILES)                                     !   READ NEXT RECORD
      NEWPTR = POINTER(FILES)                         !   SET NEWPTR
      SKIP(FILES,-1)                                  !   BACK UP TO DISPLAY RECORD
    .
    FREE(TABLE)                                       !   CLEAR THE RECORD
    DO NEXT_PAGE                                      !   DISPLAY A PAGE

NEXT_PAGE ROUTINE                                    !DISPLAY NEXT PAGE
    SAVECNT# = RECORDS(TABLE)                         !   SAVE RECORD COUNT
    LOOP COUNT TIMES                                  !   FILL UP THE TABLE
      DO FILL_NEXT                                    !     FILL A TABLE ENTRY
      IF NOT FOUND                                    !     IF NONE ARE LEFT
        IF NOT SAVECNT#                               !       IF REBUILDING TABLE
          DO LAST_PAGE                                !         FILL IN RECORDS
          EXIT                                        !         EXIT OUT OF ROUTINE
        .
        BREAK                                         !     EXIT LOOP
    . .
    DO SHOW_PAGE                                      !   DISPLAY THE PAGE

SET_NEXT ROUTINE                                     !POINT TO THE NEXT PAGE
    GET(TABLE,RECORDS(TABLE))                         !   GET THE LAST TABLE ENTRY
    DO FILL_RECORD                                    !   FILL IN THE RECORD
    SET(FIL:BY_FILENAME,FIL:BY_FILENAME,TBL:PTR)     !   POSITION FILE
    NEXT(FILES)                                       !   READ THE CURRENT RECORD

FILL_NEXT ROUTINE                                    !FILL NEXT TABLE ENTRY
    FOUND = FALSE                                     !   ASSUME RECORD NOT FOUND
    LOOP UNTIL EOF(FILES)                             !   LOOP UNTIL END OF FILE
      NEXT(FILES)                                     !     READ THE NEXT RECORD
      FOUND = TRUE                                    !     SET RECORD FOUND
      DO FILL_TABLE                                   !     FILL IN THE TABLE ENTRY
      ADD(TABLE)                                      !     ADD LAST TABLE ENTRY
```

(continued)

```
      GET(TABLE,RECORDS(TABLE)-COUNT)      !   GET ANY OVERFLOW RECORD
      DELETE(TABLE)                        !   AND DELETE IT
      EXIT                                 !   RETURN TO CALLER
        .

PREV_PAGE ROUTINE                          !DISPLAY PREVIOUS PAGE
   LOOP COUNT TIMES                        !  FILL UP THE TABLE
      DO FILL_PREV                         !    FILL A TABLE ENTRY
      IF NOT FOUND THEN BREAK.             !    GET OUT IF NO RECORD
        .

   DO SHOW_PAGE                            !  DISPLAY THE PAGE

SET_PREV ROUTINE                           !POINT TO PREVIOUS PAGE
   GET(TABLE,1)                            !  GET THE FIRST TABLE ENTRY
   DO FILL_RECORD                          !  FILL IN THE RECORD
   SET(FIL:BY_FILENAME,FIL:BY_FILENAME,TBL:PTR)  !  POSITION FILE
   PREVIOUS(FILES)                         !  READ THE CURRENT RECORD

FILL_PREV ROUTINE                          !FILL PREVIOUS TABLE ENTRY
   FOUND = FALSE                           !  ASSUME RECORD NOT FOUND
   LOOP UNTIL BOF(FILES)                   !  LOOP UNTIL BEGINNING OF FILE
      PREVIOUS(FILES)                      !    READ THE PREVIOUS RECORD
      FOUND = TRUE                         !    SET RECORD FOUND
      DO FILL_TABLE                        !    FILL IN THE TABLE ENTRY
      ADD(TABLE,1)                         !    ADD FIRST TABLE ENTRY
      GET(TABLE,COUNT+1)                   !    GET ANY OVERFLOW RECORD
      DELETE(TABLE)                        !    AND DELETE IT
      EXIT                                 !    RETURN TO CALLER
        .

SHOW_PAGE ROUTINE                          !DISPLAY THE PAGE
   NDX# = NDX                              !  SAVE SCREEN INDEX
   LOOP NDX = 1 TO RECORDS(TABLE)          !  LOOP THRU THE TABLE
      GET(TABLE,NDX)                       !    GET A TABLE ENTRY
      DO FILL_SCREEN                       !    AND DISPLAY IT
      IF TBL:PTR = NEWPTR                  !    SET INDEX FOR NEW RECORD
        NDX# = NDX                         !    POINT TO CORRECT RECORD
      . .

   NDX = NDX#                              !  RESTORE SCREEN INDEX
   NEWPTR = 0                              !  CLEAR NEW RECORD POINTER
   CLEAR(FIL:RECORD)                       !  CLEAR RECORD AREA

FILL_TABLE ROUTINE                         !MOVE FILE TO TABLE
   TBL:FILENAME = FIL:FILENAME
   TBL:PTR = POINTER(FILES)                !  SAVE RECORD POINTER

FILL_RECORD ROUTINE                        !MOVE TABLE TO FILE
   FIL:FILENAME = TBL:FILENAME
```

(continued)

```
FILL_SCREEN ROUTINE                                !MOVE TABLE TO SCREEN
  SCR:FILENAME = TBL:FILENAME


GET_RECORD ROUTINE                                 !GET SELECTED RECORD
  GET(TABLE,NDX)                                   !  GET TABLE ENTRY
  GET(FILES,TBL:PTR)                               !  GET THE RECORD
```

MAKER2.CLA

```
          MEMBER('MAKER')
NEW_FILE        PROCEDURE

SCREEN          SCREEN       PRE(SCR),WINDOW(8,59),AT(10,11),HUE(15,0)
          ROW(1,1)     STRING('<218,196{14},0{29},196{14},191>'),HUE(14,0)
          ROW(2,1)     REPEAT(6);STRING('<179,0{57},179>'),HUE(14,0)  .
          ROW(8,1)     STRING('<192,196{57},217>'),HUE(14,0)
          ROW(1,17)    STRING('ENTER FILE NAME FOR INSTALL')
          ROW(4,5)     STRING('Path:'),HUE(14,0)
          ROW(5,5)     STRING('File Name:'),HUE(14,0)
          COL(32)      STRING('(don''t end path with ''\''')'),HUE(14,0)
MESSAGE         ROW(2,16)    STRING(30),HUE(7,0)
                       ENTRY,USE(?FIRST_FIELD)
          ROW(4,11)    ENTRY(@s40),USE(FIL:PATH),LFT,REQ,SEL(0,7)
          ROW(5,16)    ENTRY(@s12),USE(FIL:FILENAME),LFT,SEL(0,7)
          ROW(7,19)    PAUSE('Press <<ENTER> to Accept'),USE(?PAUSE_FIELD)
                       ENTRY,USE(?LAST_FIELD)
                       PAUSE(''),USE(?DELETE_FIELD)


    EJECT
    CODE
    OPEN(SCREEN)                                   !OPEN THE SCREEN
    SETCURSOR                                      !TURN OFF ANY CURSOR
    IF NOT FIL:PATH THEN FIL:PATH = MEM:PATH.      !CALL SETUP PROCEDURE
    DISPLAY                                        !DISPLAY THE FIELDS
    LOOP                                           !LOOP THRU ALL THE FIELDS
      MEM:MESSAGE = CENTER(MEM:MESSAGE,SIZE(MEM:MESSAGE)) !DISPLAY ACTION MESSAGE
      DO CALCFIELDS                                !CALCULATE DISPLAY FIELDS
      ALERT                                        !RESET ALERTED KEYS
      ALERT(ACCEPT_KEY)                            !ALERT SCREEN ACCEPT KEY
      ALERT(REJECT_KEY)                            !ALERT SCREEN REJECT KEY
      ACCEPT                                       !READ A FIELD
      IF KEYCODE() = REJECT_KEY THEN RETURN.       !RETURN ON SCREEN REJECT KEY
      EXECUTE ACTION                               !SET MESSAGE
        MEM:MESSAGE = 'Record will be Added'       !
```

(continued)

```
      MEM:MESSAGE = 'Record will be Changed'     !
      MEM:MESSAGE = 'Press Enter to Delete'      !

    .
    IF KEYCODE() = ACCEPT_KEY                     !ON SCREEN ACCEPT KEY
      UPDATE                                      !  MOVE ALL FIELDS FROM SCREEN
      SELECT(?)                                   !  START WITH CURRENT FIELD
      SELECT                                      !  EDIT ALL FIELDS
      CYCLE                                       !  GO TO TOP OF LOOP

    .
    CASE FIELD()                                  !JUMP TO FIELD EDIT ROUTINE
    OF ?FIRST_FIELD                               !FROM THE FIRST FIELD
      IF KEYCODE() = ESC_KEY THEN RETURN.         !  RETURN ON ESC KEY
      IF ACTION = 3 THEN SELECT(?DELETE_FIELD).!   OR CONFIRM FOR DELETE

    OF ?FIL:PATH                                  !PATH LOCATION OF THE FILE
      mem:path = fil:path

      OF ?PAUSE_FIELD                             !ON PAUSE FIELD
        IF KEYCODE() <> ENTER_KEY|                !IF NOT ENTER KEY
        AND KEYCODE() <> ACCEPT_KEY|              !AND NOT CTRL-ENTER KEY
        AND KEYCODE() <> 0                        !AND NOT NONSTOP MODE
          BEEP                                    !  SOUND KEYBOARD ALARM
          SELECT(?PAUSE_FIELD)                    !  AND STAY ON PAUSE FIELD

      .
    OF ?LAST_FIELD                                !FROM THE LAST FIELD
      EXECUTE ACTION                              !  UPDATE THE FILE
        ADD(FILES)                                !    ADD NEW RECORD
        PUT(FILES)                                !    CHANGE EXISTING RECORD
        DELETE(FILES)                             !    DELETE EXISTING RECORD

      .
      IF ERRORCODE() = 40                         !  DUPLICATE KEY ERROR
        MEM:MESSAGE = ERROR()                     !    DISPLAY ERR MESSAGE
        SELECT(2)                                 !    POSITION TO TOP OF FORM
        CYCLE                                     !    GET OUT OF EDIT LOOP
      ELSIF ERROR()                               !  CHECK FOR UNEXPECTED ERROR
        STOP(ERROR())                             !    HALT EXECUTION

      .
      ACTION = 0                                  !  SET ACTION TO COMPLETE
      RETURN                                      !  AND RETURN TO CALLER

    OF ?DELETE_FIELD                              !FROM THE DELETE FIELD
      IF KEYCODE() = ENTER_KEY |                  !  ON ENTER KEY
      OR KEYCODE() = ACCEPT_KEY                    !  OR CTRL-ENTER KEY
        SELECT(?LAST_FIELD)                       !    DELETE THE RECORD
      ELSE                                        !  OTHERWISE
        BEEP                                      !    BEEP AND ASK AGAIN
    . . .
```

(continued)

```
CALCFIELDS   ROUTINE
  IF FIELD() > ?FIRST_FIELD                            !BEYOND FIRST_FIELD?
    IF KEYCODE() = 0 AND SELECTED() > FIELD() THEN EXIT. !GET OUT IF NOT NONSTOP
  .
  SCR:MESSAGE = MEM:MESSAGE
```

MAKER3.CLA

```
          MEMBER('MAKER')
CONFIG        PROCEDURE

SCREEN    SCREEN      WINDOW(13,63),PRE(SCR),HUE(15,0)
          ROW(1,1)    STRING('<218,196{17},0{28},196{16},191>'),HUE(14,0)
          ROW(2,1)    REPEAT(11);STRING('<179,0{61},179>'),HUE(14,0)  .
          ROW(13,1)   STRING('<192,196{61},217>'),HUE(14,0)
          ROW(1,20)   STRING('INSTALLATION CONFIGURATION')
          ROW(7,5)    STRING('(Where the installation tools reside) eg: '    |
                      & '\SUBDIR\SUBDIR2')
          ROW(10,5)   STRING('(The default path for the user''s installation)')
          ROW(3,48)   ENTRY,USE(?FIRST_FIELD)
            COL(4)    STRING('Application Name:')
            COL(22)   ENTRY(@S30),USE(CON:APPLICATION),HUE(14,0)
          ROW(5,4)    STRING('Source Disk:')
            COL(17)   MENU(@S2),USE(CON:SOURCEDISK),HUE(14,0),SEL(0,7),REQ
            COL(21)     STRING('A:')
            COL(25)     STRING('B:')
            COL(29)     STRING('C:')
            COL(33)     STRING('D:')
            COL(37)     STRING('E:')
            COL(41)     STRING('F:')
                      .
          ROW(6,4)    STRING('SourcePath:')
            COL(15)   ENTRY(@S40),USE(CON:SOURCEPATH),HUE(14,0),SEL(0,7),REQ,LFT
          ROW(9,4)    STRING('Destination Path:')
            COL(22)   ENTRY(@S40),USE(CON:DESTPATH),HUE(14,0),SEL(0,7),REQ,LFT
          ROW(12,22) PAUSE('Press <<ENTER> to Accept'),USE(?PAUSE_FIELD)
            COL(45)   ENTRY,USE(?LAST_FIELD)
            COL(45)   PAUSE(''),USE(?DELETE_FIELD)
                    .


      EJECT
      CODE
      OPEN(SCREEN)                                      !OPEN THE SCREEN
      SETCURSOR                                         !TURN OFF ANY CURSOR
      IF RECORDS(CONFIG) = 0 THEN ADD(CONFIG).;GET(CONFIG,1)!CALL SETUP PROCEDURE
```

(continued)

```
DISPLAY                                             !DISPLAY THE FIELDS
LOOP                                                !LOOP THRU ALL THE FIELDS
  MEM:MESSAGE = CENTER(MEM:MESSAGE,SIZE(MEM:MESSAGE)) !DISPLAY ACTION MESSAGE
  DO CALCFIELDS                                     !CALCULATE DISPLAY FIELDS
  ALERT                                             !RESET ALERTED KEYS
  ALERT(ACCEPT_KEY)                                 !ALERT SCREEN ACCEPT KEY
  ALERT(REJECT_KEY)                                 !ALERT SCREEN REJECT KEY
  ACCEPT                                            !READ A FIELD
  IF KEYCODE() = REJECT_KEY THEN RETURN.            !RETURN ON SCREEN REJECT KEY
  EXECUTE ACTION                                    !SET MESSAGE
    MEM:MESSAGE = 'Record will be Added'            !
    MEM:MESSAGE = 'Record will be Changed'          !
    MEM:MESSAGE = 'Press Enter to Delete'           !
  .
  IF KEYCODE() = ACCEPT_KEY                         !ON SCREEN ACCEPT KEY
    UPDATE                                          !  MOVE ALL FIELDS FROM SCREEN
    SELECT(?)                                       !  START WITH CURRENT FIELD
    SELECT                                          !  EDIT ALL FIELDS
    CYCLE                                           !  GO TO TOP OF LOOP
  .
  CASE FIELD()                                      !JUMP TO FIELD EDIT ROUTINE
  OF ?FIRST_FIELD                                   !FROM THE FIRST FIELD
    IF KEYCODE() = ESC_KEY THEN RETURN.             !  RETURN ON ESC KEY
    IF ACTION = 3 THEN SELECT(?DELETE_FIELD).!      OR CONFIRM FOR DELETE

  OF ?CON:SOURCEPATH                                !PATH FOR INSTALL FILES
    MEM:PATH = CLIP(CON:SOURCEDISK) & CON:SOURCEPATH

    OF ?PAUSE_FIELD                                 !ON PAUSE FIELD
      IF KEYCODE() <> ENTER_KEY|                    !IF NOT ENTER KEY
      AND KEYCODE() <> ACCEPT_KEY|                  !AND NOT CTRL-ENTER KEY
      AND KEYCODE() <> 0                            !AND NOT NONSTOP MODE
        BEEP                                        !  SOUND KEYBOARD ALARM
        SELECT(?PAUSE_FIELD)                        !  AND STAY ON PAUSE FIELD
      .
    PUT(CONFIG)
  OF ?LAST_FIELD                                    !FROM THE LAST FIELD
    EXECUTE ACTION                                  !  UPDATE THE FILE
      ADD(CONFIG)                                   !    ADD NEW RECORD
      PUT(CONFIG)                                   !    CHANGE EXISTING RECORD
      DELETE(CONFIG)                                !    DELETE EXISTING RECORD
    .
    IF ERRORCODE() = 40                             !  DUPLICATE KEY ERROR
      MEM:MESSAGE = ERROR()                         !    DISPLAY ERR MESSAGE
      SELECT(2)                                     !    POSITION TO TOP OF FORM
      CYCLE                                         !    GET OUT OF EDIT LOOP
    ELSIF ERROR()                                   !  CHECK FOR UNEXPECTED ERROR
```

(continued)

```
        STOP(ERROR())                          !    HALT EXECUTION
      .
      ACTION = 0                               !    SET ACTION TO COMPLETE
      RETURN                                   !    AND RETURN TO CALLER

  OF ?DELETE_FIELD                             !FROM THE DELETE FIELD
    IF KEYCODE() = ENTER_KEY |                 !    ON ENTER KEY
    OR KEYCODE() = ACCEPT_KEY                  !    OR CTRL-ENTER KEY
      SELECT(?LAST_FIELD)                      !      DELETE THE RECORD
    ELSE                                       !    OTHERWISE
      BEEP                                     !      BEEP AND ASK AGAIN
  . . .


CALCFIELDS   ROUTINE
  IF FIELD() > ?FIRST_FIELD                            !BEYOND FIRST_FIELD?
    IF KEYCODE() = 0 AND SELECTED() > FIELD() THEN EXIT. !GET OUT IF NOT NONSTOP
    .
```

AUTO.CLA

```
          MEMBER('MAKER')

AUTO      PROCEDURE

FILEREC      GROUP
BLANK          BYTE,DIM(21)
ATTRIB         BYTE
TIME           SHORT
DATE           SHORT
SIZEBYTES      LONG
NAME           STRING(13)
             END!GROUP

DRIVESCREEN SCREEN    WINDOW(10,41),AT(8,21),PRE(SC1),HUE(7,0)
          ROW(1,41)  PAINT(1,1),TRN
          ROW(10,1)  PAINT(1,3),TRN
          ROW(10,4)  PAINT(1,37),HUE(8,0),TRN
          ROW(2,41)  PAINT(9,1),HUE(8,0),TRN
          ROW(1,1)   STRING('<201,205{38},187>')
          ROW(2,1)   REPEAT(7);STRING('<186,0{38},186>') .
          ROW(9,1)   STRING('<200,205{38},188>')
          ROW(3,4)   STRING('Enter Disk Drive and Path to Read:')
          ROW(4,12)  STRING('e.g. c:\directory')
          ROW(7,29)  STRING('Y = Yes')
          ROW(8,29)  STRING('N = No')
```

(continued)

```
            ROW(5,6)     ENTRY(@S30),USE(PATH),HUE(15,0),SEL(0,7),REQ,LFT,UPR
            ROW(7,6)     STRING('Read Subdirectories?')
            COL(27)      ENTRY(@S1),USE(SUBS),HUE(15,0)
         END!SCREEN
SUBS         STRING(@S1)
PATH         STRING(@S70)
READPATH     STRING(@S70)
LASTPATH     STRING(@S70)


ERRORSCREEN  SCREEN    WINDOW(4,48),AT(11,17),PRE(SC2),HUE(15,4)
            ROW(1,1)     STRING('<201,205{46},187>')
            ROW(2,1)     REPEAT(2);STRING('<186,0{46},186>') .
            ROW(4,1)     STRING('<200,205{46},188>')
            ROW(3,12)    STRING('Strike Any Key To Continue')
MESSAGE     ROW(2,3)     STRING(45)
         END!SCREEN


FILESCREEN SCREEN      WINDOW(8,45),AT(9,19),PRE(SC3),HUE(0,7)
            ROW(8,4)     PAINT(1,41),HUE(8,0),TRN
            ROW(2,45)    PAINT(7,1),HUE(8,0),TRN
            ROW(1,45)    PAINT(1,1),TRN
            ROW(8,1)     PAINT(1,3),TRN
            ROW(1,1)     STRING('<201,205{42},187>')
            ROW(2,1)     REPEAT(5);STRING('<186,0{42},186>') .
            ROW(7,1)     STRING('<200,205{42},188>')
            ROW(2,17)    STRING('Source Path'),HUE(1,7)
            ROW(4,10)    STRING('File Name'),HUE(1,7)
            COL(26)      STRING('Size'),HUE(1,7)
            ROW(5,33)    STRING('bytes'),HUE(1,7)
            ROW(6,13)    STRING('Files Processed:'),HUE(1,7)
SHOWPATH    ROW(3,3)     STRING(40)
NAME        ROW(5,9)     STRING(12)
FILESIZE    COL(23)      STRING(@N9)
COUNTER     ROW(6,30)    STRING(@N_4)
         END!SCREEN


         CODE
         SUBS = 'Y'                          ! SET FLAG
         EMPTY(SUBDIRS)                       ! CLEAR OUT FILE
         EMPTY(SUBDIRS2)                      ! CLEAR OUT FILE
         IF MEM:PATH = '' AND RECORDS(FILES) = 0 ! SET PATH & COUNTER
            CONFIG                            ! CALL CONTROL FILE
         ELSIF MEM:PATH = ''                  ! OTHERWISE
            OPEN(ERRORSCREEN)                 ! OPEN A SCREEN
            SC2:MESSAGE = CENTER('PLEASE ' &|! SET THE MESSAGE TEXT
               SET CONFIGURATION',SIZE(SC2:MESSAGE))
            ASK                               ! WAIT FOR USER INPUT
```

(continued)

```
        CLOSE(ERRORSCREEN)
        RETURN
      END!IF


    PATH = MEM:PATH
!-------------------------------- GET TARGET PATH
    OPEN(DRIVESCREEN)
    ALERT(ESC_KEY)
    ALERT(ENTER_KEY)
    LOOP
      ACCEPT
      IF KEYCODE() = ESC_KEY THEN RETURN.
      IF KEYCODE() = ENTER_KEY
         UPDATE
         IF SUB(PATH,1,1) = ' '
            OPEN(ERRORSCREEN)
            SC2:MESSAGE = CENTER('CANNOT START WITH SPACE',SIZE(SC2:MESSAGE))
            ASK
            CLOSE(ERRORSCREEN)
            CYCLE
         ELSIF PATH = ''
            OPEN(ERRORSCREEN)
            SC2:MESSAGE = CENTER('MUST ENTER DRIVE & PATH',SIZE(SC2:MESSAGE))
            ASK
            CLOSE(ERRORSCREEN)
            CYCLE
         END!IF
         CASE FIELD()
            OF ?PATH
               READPATH = clip(PATH) & '\*.*'
            OF ?SUBS
               SUBS = UPPER(SUBS)
               BREAK
         END!CASE
      END!IF
    END!LOOP
    CLOSE(DRIVESCREEN)


!-------------------------------- SET DIRECTORY AND SCREEN
    OPEN(FILESCREEN)                        ! OPEN THE DISPLAY
    SC3:SHOWPATH = PATH
    DO READSUB
    IF SUBS <> 'Y' THEN RETURN.
    LOOP
       IF RECORDS(SUBDIRS) <> 0
          SUBREAD# = 1
          SET(SUBDIRS,1)
```

(continued)

```
                LOOP UNTIL EOF(SUBDIRS)
                   NEXT(SUBDIRS)
                   SC3:SHOWPATH = SUB:PATH
                   READPATH = clip(SUB:PATH) & '\*.*'
                   PATH = CLIP(SUB:PATH)
                   DO READSUB
                END!LOOP
                EMPTY(SUBDIRS)
                SET(SUBDIRS2,1)
                LOOP UNTIL EOF(SUBDIRS2)
                   NEXT(SUBDIRS2)
                   SUB:PATH = SB2:PATH
                   ADD(SUBDIRS)
                END!LOOP
                EMPTY(SUBDIRS2)
                CYCLE
             ELSE
                BREAK
             END!IF
          END!LOOP
          CLOSE(FILESCREEN)
          RETURN

    !------------------------------- READ THE SUBDIRECTORY INFORMATION

READSUB       ROUTINE
              SETDIR(READPATH,FILEREC)            ! SET THE DIRECTORY
              LOOP UNTIL ERRORCODE()              ! LOOP UNTIL END OF DIRECTORY
                NEXTDIR(FILEREC)                  ! READ THE NEXT FILE
                IF INSTRING('.',(SUB(NAME,1,1)),1) ! SKIPS OVER SUBDIR MARKERS
                   CYCLE                          ! RESET THE LOOP
                END!IF
                IF BAND(ATTRIB,10000B)            ! TEST FOR SUBDIRECTORY
                   IF SUBREAD# = 0
                      LASTPATH = SUB:PATH
                      SUB:PATH = CLIP(PATH) & '\' & CLIP(NAME)
                      IF LASTPATH = SUB:PATH THEN BREAK.
                      ADD(SUBDIRS)
                   ELSE
                      LASTPATH = SB2:PATH
                      SB2:PATH = CLIP(PATH) & '\' & CLIP(NAME)
                      IF LASTPATH = SB2:PATH THEN BREAK.
                      ADD(SUBDIRS2)
                   END!IF
                   CYCLE                          ! RESTART THE LOOP
                END!IF
                IF NAME = FIL:FILENAME THEN BREAK.! STOP IF READING FILE TWICE
```

(continued)

```
        COUNTER += 1                  ! INCREMENT THE COUNTER
        SC3:FILESIZE = SIZEBYTES      ! TRANSFER THE FILE SIZE
        SC3:NAME = NAME               ! TRANSFER THE FILE NAME


!------------------------------ EXIT ON ERROR IN DISK READ
        IF ERRORCODE() = 3  OR ERRORCODE() = 15
            OPEN(ERRORSCREEN)
            SC2:MESSAGE = CENTER('INVALID DISK REQUEST',SIZE(SC2:MESSAGE))
            ASK
            CLOSE(ERRORSCREEN)
            RETURN
        END!IF


!------------------------------ FILE NAME AND PATH
        FIL:FILENAME = NAME
        FIL:PATH = SUB(READPATH,1,(INSTRING('*',READPATH,1)) - 2)
        ADD(FILES)                                    ! ADD TO FILE
    END!LOOP
```

WRITER.CLA

```
            MEMBER('MAKER')
WRITER      PROCEDURE


SCREEN     SCREEN      WINDOW(5,62),HUE(0,7)
           ROW(1,1)    STRING('<201,205{60},187>')
           ROW(2,1)    REPEAT(3);STRING('<186,0{60},186>') .
           ROW(5,1)    STRING('<200,205{60},188>')
MESSAGE        ROW(3,7) STRING(50),HUE(20,7)
           END!SCREEN


BLANKER    SCREEN      HUE(7,0)
           END!SCREEN


DOSFILE    DOS,ASCII,NAME('COMPRESS.DAT')    !  DOS FILE STRUCTURE
               RECORD                         !  FILE TO SEND/RECEIVE
TEXT           STRING(150)                    !  GROUP NAME
             END!RECORD                       !  END OF GROUP, RECORD, FILE
           END!FILE


OLDPATH     STRING(40)
```

(continued)

```
!------------------------------ SET THE SCREEN AND PREPARE THE FILE
CODE
OPEN(SCREEN)
GET(CONFIG,1)
MESSAGE = CENTER('CREATING CONFIGURATION FILE',SIZE(MESSAGE))
OPEN(DOSFILE)
IF ERROR() THEN CREATE(DOSFILE).
EMPTY(DOSFILE)


!------------------------------ WRITE OUT EACH LINE OF CONFIG FILE

TEXT = 'ERASE DISKS = YES' & '<13,10>'
ADD(DOSFILE)
TEXT = '! LOCATION OF INSTALLATION PROGRAMS'
ADD(DOSFILE)

OMIT('***') !FOR USE WHEN THE SOURCE DIR IS DIFFERENT THAN CURRENT DIR
TEXT = 'COPY FILE = ' & CLIP(CON:SOURCEDISK) |
                      & CLIP(CON:SOURCEPATH) & '\' & 'INSTALL.EXE'
ADD(DOSFILE)
TEXT = 'COPY FILE = ' & CLIP(CON:SOURCEDISK) |
                      & CLIP(CON:SOURCEPATH) & '\' & 'READ.ME'
ADD(DOSFILE)
TEXT = 'TYPE FILE = ' & CLIP(CON:SOURCEDISK) |
                      & CLIP(CON:SOURCEPATH) & '\' & 'READ.ME'
ADD(DOSFILE)
***

TEXT = 'COPY FILE = INSTALL.EXE'
ADD(DOSFILE)
TEXT = 'COPY FILE = READ.ME'
ADD(DOSFILE)
TEXT = 'TYPE FILE = READ.ME'
ADD(DOSFILE)

TEXT = '! PATH TO INSTALL PROGRAMS WHEN USING COMPLETED INSTALLATION'
ADD(DOSFILE)
TEXT = 'PATH TO INSTALL INTO = ' & CLIP(CON:DESTPATH) & '<13,10>'
ADD(DOSFILE)
TEXT = '! DO NOT CHANGE THESE SETTINGS'
ADD(DOSFILE)
TEXT = 'BUFFERS (CONFIG.SYS) = 35'
ADD(DOSFILE)
TEXT = 'FILES (CONFIG.SYS) = 35'
ADD(DOSFILE)
TEXT = 'REBOOT (YES/NO/ASK) = ASK'
ADD(DOSFILE)
```

(continued)

```
TEXT = 'NONSTOP (YES/NO) = NO'
ADD(DOSFILE)
TEXT = 'AUTOEXEC (YES/NO) = YES'
ADD(DOSFILE)
TEXT = 'CONFIG (YES/NO) = YES'
ADD(DOSFILE)
TEXT = 'BATCH INSTALL = NO'
ADD(DOSFILE)
TEXT = 'COLOR = 07h,02h,1Fh,0Fh,70h,07h,7h,71h,0Fh,0Eh,0Eh,70h,7h,4Fh,4Fh'
ADD(DOSFILE)
TEXT = '<13,10>' & '! CHANGE THE TEXT TO CHANGE THE WINDOW TITLE'
ADD(DOSFILE)
TEXT = 'TITLE = ''' & CLIP(CON:APPLICATION) & ''''
ADD(DOSFILE)
TEXT = 'LABEL FOR DISK #1 = ''TRANSFER DISK 1'''
ADD(DOSFILE)
TEXT = 'VOLUME NAME DISK #1 = ''TRANSFER .1'''
ADD(DOSFILE)
TEXT = 'LABEL FOR DISK #2 = ''TRANSFER DISK 2'''
ADD(DOSFILE)
TEXT = 'VOLUME NAME DISK #2 = ''TRANSFER .2'''
ADD(DOSFILE)
TEXT = 'LABEL FOR DISK #3 = ''TRANSFER DISK 3'''
ADD(DOSFILE)
TEXT = 'VOLUME NAME DISK #3 = ''TRANSFER .3'''
ADD(DOSFILE)
TEXT = 'LABEL FOR DISK #4 = ''TRANSFER DISK 4'''
ADD(DOSFILE)
TEXT = 'VOLUME NAME DISK #4 = ''TRANSFER .4'''
ADD(DOSFILE)
TEXT = 'LABEL FOR DISK #5 = ''TRANSFER DISK 5'''
ADD(DOSFILE)
TEXT = 'VOLUME NAME DISK #5 = ''TRANSFER .5'''
ADD(DOSFILE)
TEXT = 'LABEL FOR DISK #6 = ''TRANSFER DISK 6'''
ADD(DOSFILE)
TEXT = 'VOLUME NAME DISK #6 = ''TRANSFER .6'''
ADD(DOSFILE)
TEXT = 'LABEL FOR DISK #7 = ''TRANSFER DISK 7'''
ADD(DOSFILE)
TEXT = 'VOLUME NAME DISK #7 = ''TRANSFER .7'''
ADD(DOSFILE)
TEXT = 'LABEL FOR DISK #8 = ''TRANSFER DISK 8'''
ADD(DOSFILE)
TEXT = 'VOLUME NAME DISK #8 = ''TRANSFER .8'''
ADD(DOSFILE)
TEXT = 'LABEL FOR DISK #9 = ''TRANSFER DISK 9'''
```

(continued)

```
ADD(DOSFILE)
TEXT = 'VOLUME NAME DISK #9 = ''TRANSFER .9'''
ADD(DOSFILE)
TEXT = 'LABEL FOR DISK #10 = ''TRANSFER DISK 10'''
ADD(DOSFILE)
TEXT = 'VOLUME NAME DISK #10 = ''TRANSFER .10'''
ADD(DOSFILE)
TEXT = 'LABEL FOR DISK #11 = ''TRANSFER DISK 11'''
ADD(DOSFILE)
TEXT = 'VOLUME NAME DISK #11 = ''TRANSFER .11'''
ADD(DOSFILE)
TEXT = 'LABEL FOR DISK #12 = ''TRANSFER DISK 12'''
ADD(DOSFILE)
TEXT = 'VOLUME NAME DISK #12 = ''TRANSFER .12'''
ADD(DOSFILE)
TEXT = 'LABEL FOR DISK #13 = ''TRANSFER DISK 13'''
ADD(DOSFILE)
TEXT = 'VOLUME NAME DISK #13 = ''TRANSFER .13'''
ADD(DOSFILE)
TEXT = 'LABEL FOR DISK #14 = ''TRANSFER DISK 14'''
ADD(DOSFILE)
TEXT = 'VOLUME NAME DISK #14 = ''TRANSFER .14'''
ADD(DOSFILE)
TEXT = 'LABEL FOR DISK #15 = ''TRANSFER DISK 15'''
ADD(DOSFILE)
TEXT = 'VOLUME NAME DISK #15 = ''TRANSFER .15'''
ADD(DOSFILE)
TEXT = 'LABEL FOR DISK #16 = ''TRANSFER DISK 16'''
ADD(DOSFILE)
TEXT = 'VOLUME NAME DISK #16 = ''TRANSFER .16'''
ADD(DOSFILE)
TEXT = '<13,10>' & '!--Maximum size of group prompt is 16 characters'
ADD(DOSFILE)
TEXT = '<13,10>' & '!--Maximum files in a group is 255'
ADD(DOSFILE)
TEXT = 'GROUP #1 PROMPT = ''TRANSFER FILES'''
ADD(DOSFILE)
TEXT = '   DEST. SUBDIRECTORY ='
ADD(DOSFILE)

!-------------------------------------- READ IN THE FILE NAMES,WRITE OUT

SET(FILES)
LOOP UNTIL EOF(FILES)
  NEXT(FILES)
  DO PROCESS
  OLDPATH = FIL:PATH
```

(continued)

```
END!LOOP
CLOSE(DOSFILE)
CLOSE(SCREEN)
OPEN(BLANKER)
SETCURSOR(1,1)

!--------------------------------------- CALL THE COMPRESS UTILITY

RUN('COMPRESS I=COMPRESS.DAT F=A:')
BLANK
SHOW(12,20,'INSTALLATION PACKAGE COMPLETE - TOUCH ANY KEY')
ASK
BLANK
OPEN(FILES)
RESTART(MAIN_TABLE)
RETURN


PROCESS       ROUTINE                       ! PROCESS THE PATH NAME
    IF FIL:PATH <> `OLDPATH
        COUNT# += 1
        POSIT# = INSTRING(' ',FIL:PATH,1)
        GROUP" = SUB(FIL:PATH,INSTRING('\',FIL:PATH,-1,GROUP#))
        TEXT = 'GROUP ' & COUNT# & 'PROMPT = ' &  GROUP" & ''
        ADD(DOSFILE)
        TEXT = '   DEST. SUBDIRECTORY = ' & FIL:PATH
        ADD(DOSFILE)
    END!IF
    TEXT = '   FILE   = ' & CLIP(FIL:PATH) & '\' & CLIP(FIL:FILENAME)
    POS# = INSTRING('\\',TEXT,1)
    IF POS# > 0
      TEXT = SUB(TEXT,1,POS#) & |
             SUB(TEXT,POS#+1,LEN(CLIP(TEXT)-POS#))
    END!IF
    ADD(DOSFILE)
```

Chapter 13

General Designer Use

Every chapter in this book refers in one way or another to Designer. Through-out each chapter you can get tips and help on how to use this powerful tool. However, a few things might not have been included in a discussion else-where or they may not have received the focus they deserve.

Other Procedures

Designer provides several places to insert code of your own into that gener-ated from the model files. Figure 13-1 depicts all the places you can insert free-hand code into a primarily Designer-based application.

In fact, for each of the locations mentioned in Figure 13-1, these insertion points for custom code can call a separate source module. An Other Procedure is the only one that cannot handle free-hand code *within Designer*. The Other Procedure is not terribly complex; it only plants a reference to the separate source module in the map of the main program module. It cannot carry any additional code from within Designer, as do its cousin procedure types that appear in the pop-up when you create a new procedure.

There is a limit, though, to the amount of free-hand code you can, and would want, to put into the locations mentioned in Figure 13-1. You can insert up to 244 characters into those locations, but that's a lot of code to handle in that small window. In addition, you can actually insert up to 250 characters into the locations just mentioned, but they will not compile and Editor will protest that the line is too long (as discussed in Chapter 10).

Figure 13-1　The points for inserting free-hand code within Designer.

LOCATION	MENU	TABLE	FORM	OTHER
Within the Options window:				
Setup Procedure	•	•	•	
Update Procedure		•		
Next Procedure			•	
Hot Key Procedure	•	•	•	
Within the field definitions:				
Edit Procedure	•	•	•	
Computed Field	•	•	•	
Conditional Field	•	•	•	
Call Other Procedure	•	•	•	•

The INCLUDE statement is a second method you can use to add free-hand code. This statement lets you build a separate file that is folded into the generated code at compile time. You can cause this code to show up in the program listings for documentation purposes by including the LIST attribute after the INCLUDE statement like this:

```
INCLUDE('SRCFILE.CLA'),LIST
```

The other advantage of an INCLUDE file is that the code within that file can operate as if it were part of the original procedure. Therefore, declarations made within the Designer Procedure will apply to the code in the INCLUDE file. And that means you can manipulate the Designer Procedure screen variables and any locally defined routines—as with a Table Procedure. Re-creating table refills or responses to scrolling in the table from outside can make for a lot of work. The major disadvantage of using INCLUDE files appears when you want to test the code within that file. If you make changes to only the INCLUDE file, you must recompile the entire Designer Procedure that contains it.

The primary justification for using an Other Procedure is to perform a function not supportable from within Designer itself. An Other Procedure can be anything from a complete Table Procedure to something for writing out an

ASCII file. You might want to employ an Other Procedure to include a Table Procedure that you generated once and then revised, but did not want to make into a permanent model procedure.

A secondary use for the Other Procedure is to add a procedure or a function into your application that you put into all your applications—a printer configuration procedure or a calendar, for instance. This use for an Other Procedure is most commonly employed when you want to send data from your application to a FUNCTION for processing, whereupon it returns a value or result to the application. The intelligent Uppercase-Lowercase function developed by Larry Lux of the San Diego Clarion User Group and pictured in Figure 13-2 is a good example of this application of an Other Procedure as a function.

To use the Function in Figure 13-2, you simply pass the string you want to process by placing the following line in the field processing code:

```
FIL:STRING_VAR = CAPS(FIL:STRING_VAR)
```

If you want this function to execute every time the user completes a field, place that line in the Edit Procedure of the Entry Field for FIL:STRING_VAR in the Form Procedure where the user enters data. Several important features appear in this function. First, it is a "universal" function since the MEMBER statement does not contain the name of a base procedure or main program module. Second, notice that the UPDATE and DISPLAY functions are in use even though this function has no fields or screens. A function permits you to update the USE variable and screen variables (SCR) from the procedure that calls them. The difference between a procedure and a function are:

PROCEDURE	FUNCTION
• Can receive a variable sent when it is called from inside another procedure.	• Can receive a variable sent when it is called from inside a procedure.
• Cannot pass back a value.	• Can pass back a value.
• Has access to global variables but not to local variables of procedure that called it.	• Has access to both global variables and the local variables of the procedure that called it.
• Can operate on externally declared variables (this method and setting global values are the only method available for returning data from a procedure).	• Can operate on externally declared variables.

Figure 13-2   A function for automatically setting upper- and lowercase for fields made of character strings.

```
        MEMBER( )
CAPS        FUNCTION(NAME)
NAME        EXTERNAL                    !STRING PASSED FROM PROGRAM
L           SHORT(0)                    !LENGTH OF STRING
CNT         SHORT(0)                    !COUNT YOUR PLACE IN STRING
POSITION    SHORT(0)                    !POINTER THAT TRAVELS THRU STRING
  CODE
  L = LEN(NAME)
  !NAME = LOWER(NAME)                   !CONVERT THE STRING TO LOWER CASE
  IF SUB(NAME,1,3) <> 'de ' AND |      !DON'T CAP A STRING BEGINNING WITH
  SUB(NAME,1,4) <> 'von '              !de OR von, OTHERWISE CAP FIRST  CHAR
      NAME = CLIP(UPPER(SUB(NAME,1,1)) & SUB(NAME,2,LEN(NAME)-1))
      IF NOT INSTRING(' ',CLIP(NAME))  !IF THERE ARE NO SPACES IN THE STRING
                                        !RETURN THE STRING THAT HAS NO SPACES
          UPDATE(?-1)                   !UPDATE EXTERNAL VARIABLE
          DISPLAY(?)                    !UPDATE DISPLAY CALLING PROCEDURE
          RETURN(NAME)                  !RETURN VALUE TO CALLING PROCEDURE
      ELSE                              !IF THERE ARE SPACES, START TO WORK
          POSITION = 0                  !START AT THE BEGINNING OF THE STRING
          CNT = LEN(CLIP(NAME))         !CLIP THE STRING AND MEASURE ITS LENGTH
          LOOP WHILE CNT                !LOOP THRU THE COMPLETE STRING
              POSITION += 1             !INCREMENT THE POSITION
          IF SUB(NAME,POSITION,1) = ' ' AND POSITION > 1 !SKIP  POSITION 1
              IF SUB(NAME,POSITION,5) <> ' the ' AND | !
                 SUB(NAME,POSITION,5) <> ' and ' AND | !SKIP THESE
                 SUB(NAME,POSITION,5) <> ' for ' AND | !WORDS WITHIN
                 SUB(NAME,POSITION,5) <> ' von ' AND |
                 SUB(NAME,POSITION,4) <> ' an '  AND | !THE STRING
                 SUB(NAME,POSITION,4) <> ' of '  AND | !IF YOU FIND
                 SUB(NAME,POSITION,4) <> ' or '  AND | !MORE, PLEASE
                 SUB(NAME,POSITION,4) <> ' de '  AND | !ADD THEM..
                 SUB(NAME,POSITION,4) <> ' to '
                 NAME = CLIP(SUB(NAME,1,POSITION) & | !SKIP THRU THE
                     UPPER(SUB(NAME,POSITION+1,1)) & | !STRING....
                     SUB(NAME,POSITION+2,L))
              END!IF
              IF    SUB(NAME,POSITION,4) = ' Md.' OR          | !IF  DOCTORS NAME
                    SUB(NAME,POSITION,4) = ' Md '  OR          |
                    SUB(NAME,POSITION,5) = ' M.d.' OR          |
                    SUB(NAME,POSITION,4) = ' Do.'  OR          |
                    SUB(NAME,POSITION,4) = ' Do '
                    NAME = CLIP(SUB(NAME,1,POSITION) &         |    !CAP  MD.
                        UPPER(SUB(NAME,POSITION+1,3)) &  |
```

(continued)

Figure 13-2 *continued*

```
                    SUB(NAME,POSITION+4,L))
      ELSIF SUB(NAME,POSITION,5) = ' Ave ' AND |   !EXPAND AVE
            SUB(NAME,L-2,3) = '   '
            NAME = CLIP(SUB(NAME,1,POSITION)) &      |
                  ' Avenue' & SUB(NAME,POSITION+4,L- POSITION+4)
            CNT += 3   !THE ABOVE, IF TRUE, MADE THE STRING LONGER
      ELSIF SUB(NAME,POSITION,4) = ' St ' AND |    !EXPAND AVE
            SUB(NAME,L-3,4) = '    '
            NAME = CLIP(SUB(NAME,1,POSITION)) &      |
                  ' Street' & SUB(NAME,POSITION+3,L- POSITION+3)
            CNT += 4   !THE ABOVE, IF TRUE, MADE THE STRING LONGER
      END!IF
    ELSIF SUB(NAME,POSITION,1) = '/' AND |          !CAP AFTER /
          SUB(NAME,POSITION+1,1) <> ' '
          NAME = CLIP(SUB(NAME,1,POSITION) &        |
                UPPER(SUB(NAME,POSITION+1,1)) &     |
                SUB(NAME,POSITION+2,L))
      END!IF                        !END IF
      CNT -= 1
   END!LOOP                         !END LOOP
   UPDATE(?-1)                      !UPDATE STRING ON SCREEN
   DISPLAY(?)                       !AND RE-DISPLAY IT
   RETURN(NAME)                     !RETURN THE CAPPED STRING....
END!IF                             !END IF
```

As you use Other Procedures when working in Designer, keep strict control over the names you give both the filename and the procedures or functions you use. One of the nice elements of Designer is that you don't have to keep control of individual source modules, just of the .APP file. However, if you develop Other Procedures for an application, Designer has no provision for keeping track of them. Designer maintains only the names of the source modules for you.

If you keep multiple Other Procedures in the same source module, you can indicate this using the "Procedure Calls" section of the Other Procedure definition window, as shown in Figure 13-3. Each of the procedures shown as procedure calls appears connected to the Utilities Procedure in the application tree, as shown in Figure 13-4, but the procedures will not appear in the map in the UTILITY source module unless you show that in the description when you define each individual Other Procedure. The resulting map section for this setup appears as shown in Figure 13-5.

Figure 13-3   An Other Procedure defined to show additional procedures and functions to be stored in the same source module.

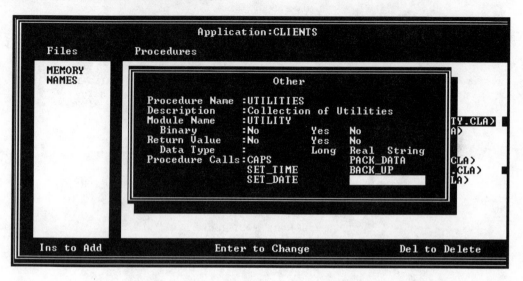

Notice in Figure 13-5 how Designer created both functions and procedures from the Other Procedure definitions it was given. The function resulted from the fact that the definition of the CAPS Other Procedure indicated it was returning a string value. Notice also how the BACK_UP Other Procedure was placed in a different source module, even though it was connected to the

Figure 13-4   The applications tree resulting from the definition of the Utilities Other Procedure shown in Figure 13-3.

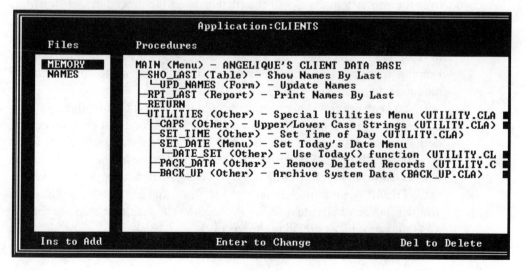

Figure 13-5   The map segment created for the Utilities Other Procedure when the source code is generated by Designer.

```
MODULE('UTILITY')
   FUNC(CAPS),STRING                    !Upper/Lower Case Strings
   PROC(SET_TIME)                       !Set Time of Day
   PROC(DATE_SET)                       !Use Today() function
   PROC(PACK_DATA)                      !Remove Deleted Records
   PROC(UTILITIES)                      !Special Utilities Menu
   .
MODULE('BACK_UP'),BINARY
   PROC(BACK_UP)                        !Archive System Data
   .
```

UTILITIES Other Procedure source module. The BINARY attribute it was given indicates that this source module is, in fact, compiled object code and, therefore, cannot be part of the UTILITY source module.

*Hint: Be careful never to define an Other Procedure as binary **and** as part of a regular source module made of Clarion code. Designer allows this, but the procedure will show up in the map as part of, for instance, the UTILITY source module as shown in Figure 13-5, but the BINARY attribute will be missing. Designer was set up this way to allow for several Other Procedures to be contained in the same binary module.*

One strategy you can adopt to make things easier is to keep all your Other Procedures in one source file. If you adopt this approach instead of assigning each one to its own source module, you'll want to take care in choosing how you group them. For instance, if you create an application with OVERLAYs, it may not be possible to store some functions or procedures together in the same module. If you understand the operations of OVERLAYS and can make the proper assignments to source modules ahead of time, you'll be ahead of the game. However, if you don't want to take the time, it's safer to store each Other Procedure in its own source file. If you have one of the third-party products that creates the overlay map for you, the program will tell you which Other Procedures can be combined and which cannot. In the case of the Overlay Manager from Mitten, it will actually reassign incompatible Other Procedures to a different source module—leaving a note behind in the original file about where it was moved.

Hint: *The term Other Procedure refers to both procedures **and** functions.*

Partial Code Generation

One of the significant improvements incorporated into Version 2.1 by Clarion was the allowance of partial source code generation. In prior versions, when you made a change to any part of the application, the whole application had to be regenerated. That meant that any "tweaking" or special coding you did *inside a Designer-generated source module* was lost when you regenerated. This new approach allows you to make changes to *nonglobal* elements of the application, to regenerate the code for those elements, and to recompile them—all under the monitored control of Clarion. In this case, "monitored control" means that CLARION.COM keeps track of which modules were regenerated and which were not, based on the creation date and time for the main program module (the one containing the procedure listed as the Base Procedure in Designer's Base window).

Generating Only Part of an Application

When you restart Designer and begin making changes to your application, be sure to perform the changes in the most efficient order. Don't suspend making a change just because it affects a global element and will cause the whole application to regenerate if that will slow you down in the long run. The global elements of a program, which *all* appear in the main program module are: the file definitions; the global memory file, and the MAP. Any time you make even the smallest change to an element in either of these you must regenerate the whole application.

Hint: *If you make a change to a global element, there is no way for you to escape regenerating the primary program module—even if you change what you altered back to its original state. Even if you select "Partial" as shown in Figure 13-6, Designer will regenerate that module. However, you are not required to recompile the main program module unless you must do so to compile a universal procedure. In that case, since the main program module will have a later file creation date and time, the Stream Compile attempts to recompile all the source modules. In fact, the Processor does not allow you to run old .PRO modules with a new main program .PRO module.*

Figure 13-6 Something global has been changed in this application and Clarion is requesting that the source code for the whole application be regenerated.

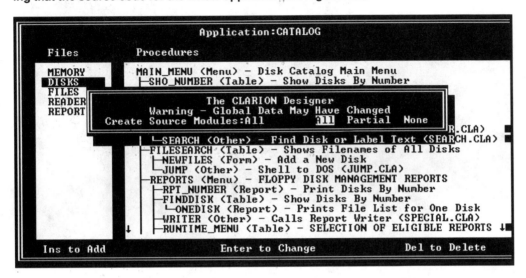

Designer does not simply recompile everything when a global element is changed. You can make changes to global elements that will not impact the application in other places—such as adding a memory variable. Therefore, it is possible to perform a partial generation and compilation that allows the application to operate normally—as when you make a change that you restore to its original state. The purpose of the warning that appears in Figure 13-6 is to provide for those times when, for instance, you change the specifications for a variable but forget to change a procedure that uses the variable.

Let's say you lengthened a STRING variable and had used that variable to construct a table. You can perform a partial generation that regenerates the main program module and nothing else. When you compile, of course, you must recompile all the modules, but the program will still run. Now you have corrupted source code. You have a table with a string picture in the scrolling area with no matching variable in a file. You can easily see this when you reexamine that table in Designer. It instantly adjusts—although probably in an unsatisfactory way—to the new variable length. Thus, the simple fact that Designer asks for permission before regenerating all the code does not mean you can perform a partial without consequences.

As a general rule, whenever Designer notifies you that global data have changed, regenerate everything. The only exception to this rule would be if

Figure 13-7   The compile messages resulting from calling for the main program module to be compiled when only the READER.CLA module was changed since the last compile.

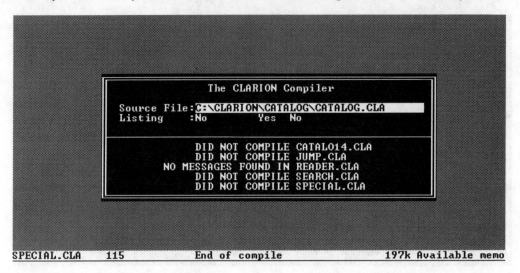

```
                    The CLARION Compiler
   Source File:C:\CLARION\CATALOG\CATALOG.CLA
   Listing   :No            Yes  No


                 DID NOT COMPILE CATALO14.CLA
                 DID NOT COMPILE JUMP.CLA
       NO MESSAGES FOUND IN READER.CLA
                 DID NOT COMPILE SEARCH.CLA
                 DID NOT COMPILE SPECIAL.CLA
```

```
SPECIAL.CLA     115           End of compile            197k Available memo
```

you were certain that the only task you had performed was to have first made a change, and later to have changed your mind and restored the original version. Otherwise, you defeat part of the utility that Designer offers for managing your application development.

When you do perform a small change that does not affect global elements, CLARION.COM remembers what you did. That means the hot-key selections will work as in: after selecting "Partial" source code generation you can press the Control–F6 key combination and Clarion compiles only the module that you regenerated and not the whole application. If you changed a universal procedure or you changed more than one procedure, you still need to recompile the main program module (as the Control–F6 key combination would cause to happen in that case as well), but the up-to-date modules that had not been regenerated would not be compiled as shown in Figure 13-7.

If you are certain that this is the only module to change, you can compile it separately without calling for the main program module to be compiled. The compile will be successful. The only way the compile would fail due to changed source modules would be if you had changed the MAP to exclude the procedures and functions contained in the READER.CLA module within the FLOPPY DISK CATALOG source code appearing at the end of Chapter 11.

Figure 13-8 A segment of a MAP where two procedures were given the same "Combine with Module" instructions.

```
MODULE('CATALO05')              ! Source file name
  PROC('TABLEPROC')             ! table procedure
  PROC('UPDATEPROC')            ! form procedure
END!MODULE                      ! terminate module definition
```

The "Combine with Module" Option

The Options window for each procedure type has a slot where you can select the module with which you want this code combined. It is exactly the same request for information being made by the Other Procedure Options window. The difference in the case of the Other Procedure is that here, if you leave the field blank, Designer uses the first characters of the Base Procedure name and a series of numbers to represent one source code module per procedure; the Other Procedure requires a module name.

You could combine all the code into one long source code module—a move you might consider when it comes time to generate the final listings for documentation purposes. However, this would not be practical for most applications. The file would be too large. (Older verisons of Clarion were set up that way.) In addition, when you are ready to create the overlay map, fewer changes will be necessary if each procedure is in its own source module (DOS file).

Hint: *During application development, you may want to examine two procedures together and that might be easier if they were in the same file—as in the case of a table and its Update Procedure. During development, you can set the "Combine with Module" to be the name of the table and the two procedures will come out of Designer as one file. The MAP for the new procedure layout would look like Figure 13-8.*

Models

The gist of Designer is to provide you with a tool through which you can create an application by simply drawing a few screens and filling in various choices. All of that activity creates the .APP, or Designer application file.

Then comes the magic part. When you ask Clarion to generate source code, you combine the model you selected in the Base Procedure window and the .APP file, shake well, and out comes compilable source code.

Try an experiment. Create a new application using the Standard Model and remove all the fields from the MEMORY file and make the Base Procedure into an Other Procedure with no parameter passing. Now generate the source code. You should get something that looks like the code in Figure 13-9. This shows you the first level of default source code that the Standard Model generates. Study this segment of code until you understand everything it does. Your understanding of the applications you create on top of this will come much quicker if you do.

The Standard Model

Most of the elements you see in Figure 13-9 were inserted as just characters directly as they appear in the model file, STANDARD.MDL. However, some of the code you see was placed there in response to "key" elements. In this sense, "key" does not refer to the dynamically maintained indexes we discussed in other parts of the book. In this discussion, there are two "key" elements: key words and key procedures. Briefly, key procedures are constructed of key words and Clarion language elements. Key words are not alterable or definable by you. Most key procedures, on the other hand, can be altered.

Let's return to the minimum code exercise. First, go into Designer and add back a Memory Field called MESSAGES. Now regenerate the source code. You'll see the following lines of code appear:

```
          GROUP,PRE(MEM)
MESSAGES        STRING(20)              !NEW STRING TO BE ADDED
          .
```

Now, bring the STANDARD.MDL file into Editor. Go to the GLOBAL section, remove the line that says "@MEMORY," and regenerate the code. Now recheck the source it created. You'll find that the GROUP definition, which included the MESSAGES Memory Field, was not generated in the new source code. You've just witnessed the impact of a key word: @MEMORY. If you consult the text file shipped with Clarion called MODEL.DOC, you'll find the definitions for all the key words and procedures. @MEMORY is defined as: "Generates the fields defined in the memory file."

Figure 13-9   The minimum source code generated by Designer using the Standard Model.

```
TEST      PROGRAM
                INCLUDE('STD_KEYS.CLA')
                INCLUDE('CTL_KEYS.CLA')
                INCLUDE('ALT_KEYS.CLA')
                INCLUDE('SHF_KEYS.CLA')


REJECT_KEY    EQUATE(CTRL_ESC)
ACCEPT_KEY    EQUATE(CTRL_ENTER)
TRUE          EQUATE(1)
FALSE         EQUATE(0)


              MAP
                PROC(G_OPENFILES)
                MODULE('MAIN')
                      PROC(MAIN)

                  .
                  .

              EJECT('FILE LAYOUTS')
              EJECT('GLOBAL MEMORY VARIABLES')
ACTION        SHORT                             !0 = NO ACTION
                                                !1 = ADD RECORD
                                                !2 = CHANGE RECORD
                                                !3 = DELETE RECORD
                                                !4 = LOOKUP FIELD


              EJECT('CODE SECTION')
  CODE
  SETHUE(7,0)                                   !SET WHITE ON BLACK
  BLANK                                         !  AND BLANK
  G_OPENFILES                                   !OPEN OR CREATE FILES
  SETHUE()                                      !   THE SCREEN
  MAIN
  RETURN                                        !EXIT TO DOS

G_OPENFILES  PROCEDURE                          !OPEN FILES & CHECK FOR ERROR
  CODE
  BLANK                                         !BLANK THE SCREEN
```

Hint: Never make changes to the model file without first creating a copy of your old one. If it becomes necessary to start fresh, reinstall the model files from the Clarion distribution diskettes. If you make modifications to elements of a model file, copy the original section and make your changes to the copy. Also, if you create a custom model for a particular application, make sure the documentation for that application reflects it and that you archive the model file when you archive the other development files.

That is all the magic there is to Designer-generated code. The internal software control inside Designer reacts to the placement and types of key words and procedures within the model file based on what it finds included in the .APP, or application, file. Notice that you could create source code that excluded the memory file definition altogether by either not using any Memory Fields or by removing the key word. Depending on what has come before, you can alter the way that Designer handles these key elements to a certain extent. However, for all the words labeled with an @ sign in the MODEL.DOC file, you can only include them or exclude them. You cannot influence how they react if they find their actuators inside your .APP file.

Let's look at what it takes to modify the model for some purpose. We'll use the model procedure for a menu since that is the shortest of the three main procedure types. It appears as Figure 13-10.

Suppose, now, that you wanted to post a message whenever you returned from a Hot Key Procedure executed from a menu. You would go into the Standard Model and look for the Key Procedure called @CHECKHOT that handles generating the code for hot keys as appears in Figure 13-11. That Key Procedure appears in Figure 13-12.

Notice how the definition for the Key Procedure in Figure 13-11 begins with an asterisk (*) in column one. The asterisk means that the previous definition is to terminate—just as one of the four primary procedure types would stop including code as soon as it ran into an asterisk in column one. The CHECKHOT Key Procedure employs two key words: @HOTKEY and @HOTPROC. Don't be confused by the use of the @ symbol; the @ symbol is used to call both Key Procedures and key words. You can tell the difference between the two: If you do *not* find a definition that begins with an asterisk in a word beginning with @, it is one of the low-level key words.

All that would be needed in the exercise to post a message upon return to the calling procedure after processing a hot key would be to add a line in just after @HOTPROC, which is the key word responsible for grabbing whatever data you entered into the Hot Key Procedure slot in the Menu Options window inside Designer.

Figure 13-10   The model procedure from the Standard Model for creating menus.

```
*MENU********************************************************************
@PROCNAME      PROCEDURE

SCREEN         SCREEN    PRE(SCR),@SCREENOPT
                    @PAINTS
                    @STRINGS
                    @VARIABLES
                    ENTRY,USE(?FIRST_FIELD)
                    @FIELDS
                    ENTRY,USE(?PRE_MENU)
                    MENU,USE(MENU_FIELD"),REQ
                    @CHOICES
                         .    .

    EJECT
    CODE
    OPEN(SCREEN)              !OPEN THE MENU SCREEN
    SETCURSOR                 !TURN OFF ANY CURSOR
    MENU_FIELD" = ''          !START MENU WITH FIRST ITEM
    @SETUP                    !CALL SETUP PROCEDURE
    LOOP                      !LOOP UNTIL USER EXITS
       @LOOKUPS               !DISPLAY FROM OTHER FILES
       @SHOW                  !DISPLAY STRING VARIABLES
       @COMPUTE               !DISPLAY COMPUTED FIELDS
       @RESULT                !MOVE RESULTING VALUES
       ALERT                  !TURN OFF ALL ALERTED KEYS
       ALERT(REJECT_KEY)      !ALERT SCREEN REJECT KEY
       ALERT(ACCEPT_KEY)      !ALERT SCREEN ACCEPT KEY
       @ALERT                 !ALERT HOT KEYS
       ACCEPT                 !READ A FIELD OR MENU CHOICE
```

```
       @CHECKHOT             !ON HOT KEY, CALL PROCEDURE
```

```
    IF KEYCODE() = REJECT_KEY THEN RETURN.    !RETURN ON SCREEN REJECT
```

(continued)

Figure 13-10 *continued*

```
    IF KEYCODE() = ACCEPT_KEY              !ON SCREEN ACCEPT KEY
      UPDATE                               !  MOVE ALL FIELDS FROM SCREEN
      SELECT(?)                            !  START WITH CURRENT FIELD
      SELECT                               !  EDIT ALL FIELDS
      CYCLE                                !  GO TO TOP OF LOOP
    .                                      !

    CASE FIELD()                           !JUMP TO FIELD EDIT ROUTINE
    OF ?FIRST_FIELD                        !FROM THE FIRST FIELD
      IF KEYCODE() = ESC_KEY THEN RETURN.  !  RETURN ON ESC KEY

    @EDITS                                 !EDIT ROUTINES GO HERE
    OF ?PRE_MENU                           !PRE MENU FIELD CONDITION
      IF KEYCODE() = ESC_KEY               !  BACKING UP?
        SELECT(?-1)                        !    SELECT PREVIOUS FIELD
      ELSE                                 !  GOING FORWARD
        SELECT(?+1)                        !    SELECT MENU FIELD
      .
    OF ?MENU_FIELD"                        !FROM THE MENU FIELD
      EXECUTE CHOICE()                     !CALL THE SELECTED PROCEDURE
          @MENU                            !
  . . .
```

Figure 13-11   The Key Procedure called CHECKHOT.

```
*CHECKHOT*******************************************************************
  IF KEYCODE() = @HOTKEY                   !ON HOT KEY
    UPDATE(?)                              !  RETRIEVE FIELD
    SAVACTN# = ACTION                      !  SAVE ACTION
    @HOTPROC                               !  CALL HOT KEY PROCEDURE
    ACTION = SAVACTN#                      !  RESTORE ACTION
    SELECT(?)                              !  DO SAME FIELD AGAIN
    CYCLE                                  !  AND LOOP AGAIN
  .
```

Figure 13-12   The source generated for the Hot Key Procedure in Figure 13-11.

```
IF KEYCODE() = F10_KEY              !ON HOT KEY
  UPDATE(?)                         !  RETRIEVE FIELD
  SAVACTN# = ACTION                 !  SAVE ACTION
  THIS_IS_HOT                       !  CALL HOT KEY PROCEDURE
  ACTION = SAVACTN#                 !  RESTORE ACTION
  SELECT(?)                         !  DO SAME FIELD AGAIN
  CYCLE                             !  AND LOOP AGAIN
.
```

Hint: You can document your changes to the model file by placing your comments directly into the model file using the commenting conventions of the language. Those comments, then, will appear in your application source code.

Using Custom Models

Clarion is shipped with one custom model: the network version. This version of the model includes all the functionality (except for caches and buffers) included in the Standard Model with the additional statements and code for responding properly to a LAN (local area network) operation. Several vendors in the Clarion community have spent many hours applying the concept of the model file to create specialized models for different functions.

You will find, many times, that the standard Clarion STANDARD.MDL and NETWORK.MDL files include code that is unnecessary for your particular application—or you may know of a better way to handle a particular function. The models that Clarion ships with the Professional Developer are intentionally generic and therefore not as efficient as they could be because they must handle such a wide range of applications. You can investigate the custom models on the market or develop the ability and understanding to create your own.

For instance, several vendors in the Clarion community have distilled their experience with Clarion into sets of custom models. Among others, Watermark Consulting and Boxsoft Development offer different capabilities within model files for both single and multiuser Designer-based applications. By using these special versions of the Designer model files, you can learn more

Figure 13-13   The procedure titling convention using the @PROCNAME keyword in the Boxsoft Development public domain model.

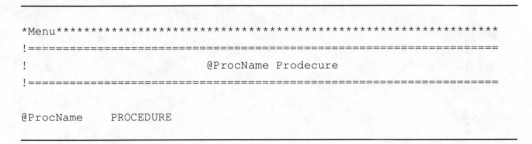

```
*Menu*************************************************************
!================================================================
!                          @ProcName Prodecure
!================================================================


@ProcName     PROCEDURE
```

about how the Clarion language can be incorporated into Designer models to make your development projects operate more efficiently.

However, if you choose to manufacture your own models or if you use a model file constructed by someone else, you will not be able to take advantage of updates to the standard model files that Clarion will make—at least not directly. Using a model file created by a vendor, however, you will move the task of updating those special model files over to someone with a vested interest in bringing them up to compatibility with the current version of Clarion.

In the public domain version of the models from Boxsoft Development, additional commenting is placed into the generated source code, which takes advantage of the keyword functions of Designer as shown in Figure 13-13.

When you use models developed by someone else, you also have the opportunity to see different methods for performing the same task. Another example in Figure 13-14 shows a part of the method for incorporating multiple record additions to a table in the public domain model from Boxsoft Development. This change allows a user to enter multiple records to a data file after reaching the Update form for the table without repeatedly calling the table.

Hint: Among other conventions you will see in models developed by a third party are the variable naming conventions first presented by Bill Mueller in "The Clarion Tech Journal," which appear in Figure 13-14. Notice the lowercase "e" placed in front of the "Done" variable. This is to indicate that the variable is an EQUATE Name or a variable name that was set up either globally or locally to represent something else—usually a number like 1 for True and 0 for False. In addition, notice that upper- and lowercase letters

Figure 13-14 The main part of Multi-Add facility in the Boxsoft Development public domain model.

```
OF MultiAdd_Key                     !!Multi-Add Key
  AddMem_# = False                  !! Nothing to Remember
  LOOP                              !! Loop Until Finished
    CLEAR(@Pre:Record)             !!    Clear Record Area
    Action = eAdd                   !!    Set Action To Add
    GET(@Filename,0)   !!No ChkErr   !!    Clear Pending Record
    @AutoNumKey                     !!    Auto Increment Key Field
    IF AddMem_# AND NOT AutoNum_#   !! IF Remembering
      @Pre:Record = Save_Record     !!    Remember Record
      .                             !! .
    @TotActn                        !!    Save Totals
    @RestSelects                    !!    Restore Selector Fields
    @Update                         !!    Call Form For New Record
    IF AddMem AND Action = eDone    !!    If Remembering
      Save_Record = @Pre:Record     !!      Save Record
      AddMem_# = True               !!      Something Is Saved Now
      .                             !!    . .
    IF Action = eDone               !!    If Record Was Added
      NewPtr = POINTER(@Filename)   !!      Set Pointer To New Rec
      DO Find_Record                !!      Position In File
      .                             !!    .
    IF Action <> eDone THEN BREAK.  !!    Break If Done
    .
```

appear in *Figure 13-14. This convention distinguishes between language elements (all uppercase) and all other elements of the language, including variables, routine names, and so on (initial capital letters). The models from Clarion are all in uppercase as are most of the examples in this book.*

Summary

In this chapter we examined the ways in which Clarion creates source code and allows for you to make your own modifications to that code through the use of Designer. We examined the places that Designer provides for inserting custom code and the types of vehicles you can use, such as INCLUDE files and special Other Procedures. We also examined the source code–generating functions of Designer and what impact they have on your program development. Finally, we examined the Clarion model concept, including a discussion of the key word and key procedure roles inside the model, and a discussion of custom models you can buy or build yourself.

Chapter 14

Special Program Control

A good application language needs an easy and efficient method for interrupting normal program execution. You might want to run a program that was not written in the same environment or to leap from one application into another and then back again. Clarion provides several methods for making these large leaps—from running a simple DOS process with the RUNSMALL statement to stringing together a series of programs in a seamless fashion with the CHAIN statement.

The Startup Process for the PC

Clarion provides two almost identical methods for calling other programs. The primary principle employed by both of these statements is the management of the Command Processor in DOS.

When you first start a computer that will be running a version of the Microsoft Disk Operating System (MS-DOS), the first real program it runs is called the Command Processor. This is key to the functions to be discussed in this chapter. However, the very first step in the hardware boot-up process when power first reaches the hardware is to load the BIOS (Basic Input/Output System) from the read-only memory stored on circuit cards inside the computer. After that, the system loads the DOS kernel through several hidden files that were placed on your fixed disk when it was formatted to operate DOS. This is known as "loading the system," and it creates the first elements of the operating environment. Then, the bootstrap program stored in one of the hidden files actually loads the Command Processor by running

COMMAND.COM. At that point, the operating system is considered to be loaded. It is this last step, the loading of the Command Processor via COMMAND.COM as show in Figure 14-1, which is of the most interest.

Both CALL and RUN (and RUNSMALL, though not as apparently) execute secondary versions of the Command Processor. If you've ever used a program that promised to "shell out to DOS" or "jump to DOS" or any other similar move, they, too, are loading secondary versions of the Command Processor. The Command Processor is the program that sits permanently in memory and interprets what comes from the keyboard and other input devices. With this input, the Command Processor dispatches messages for action to deeper elements of the operating system that are resident in the kernel, which then relays those instructions to the BIOS for translation into actual contact with the hardware.

You can tell that you have been sent to a secondary copy of the Command Processor if typing the word "EXIT" at the command prompt returns you to the program from which you "jumped." This is also known as going to a "shell" because that secondary copy of the Command Processor can be changed and customized using the DOS statement SHELL. If you built a customized DOS prompt such as the one in Figure 14-2, and you saw that same prompt in the new, secondary version, it would usually mean that there was no change in the environment when the second Command Processor was started. None of the Clarion statements modifies the environment—although you can actually use the RUN statement to start a third copy of the Command Processor. (That is discussed later on in this chapter.)

Figure 14-1   The process for loading the Command Processor.

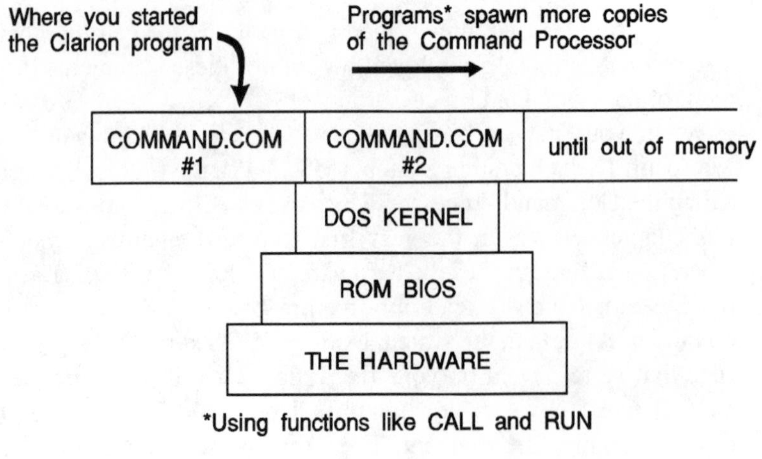

*Using functions like CALL and RUN

Figure 14-2   A custom prompt for operating the DOS Command Processor.

```
TODAY: Mon 09-03-1990
TIME: 22:02:29.43 C:\WINDOWS=>_
```

It is important to understand how the additional copies of the Command Processor are loaded, for two reasons. First, the environment as it is referred to in this chapter is the DOS environment that also contains the setup for Clarion's handling of virtual memory. Second, you can build several dangerous situations if you misuse the statements discussed in this section.

- You can modify the environment to invalidate your previous settings to permit Clarion to use virtual memory. This could wreak havoc if you should "jump to DOS" while you have a large data file loaded with its key files cached into virtual memory.
- You can set up the system so your users can load nested versions of the Command Processor until they run out of memory and the system locks up—preventing them from returning to the application to complete an update. Fortunately Clarion's constant flushing of data files to disk prevents much data loss, but there are implications for network use and instances where you have, for speed or other reasons, turned off the flushing function.
- Since the Command Processor is a single-user construct, you may interfere with the network application software if you do not closely supervise the user in accessing additional copies of the Command Processor.

CALL Versus RUN

Both CALL and RUN create secondary versions of the Command Processor in which to operate the programs they call. In fact, the CALL statement is nothing more than the RUN statement with some additional intelligence programmed into it to append the .PRO file extension onto the filename you pass to it.

*Hint: You **cannot** run non-Clarion programs with the CALL statement.*

The primary difference between these two statements is that RUN can be used to operate programs written outside of Clarion. With CALL you can use the Processor to run separate programs from inside an executable file or as part of a collection of .PRO files that make up an application. With this method, you could leave one part of a program in pseudocode as a Processor file that can be easily changed and recompiled without recompiling and relinking an entire executable file. This is handy for adding incremental sections of a primary program. You must remember, however, to include CRUN.EXE with your program or that run of the CALL statement will fail when it tries to load the .PRO file.

The RUN statement, on the other hand, is more of an all-purpose tool. It can be used to access almost any DOS program from within a Clarion program, including some Terminate-Stay-Resident (TSR) programs. In fact, you can use the RUN statement to start yet a third copy of the Command Processor for use as a "shell to DOS" program in your own application. In the Floppy Disk Catalog program introduced in Chapter 7, the RUN statement allows the user to go to the DOS command line. In that application, the code appears in an Other Procedure, which could be used as a universal procedure as appears in Figure 14-3.

Note that a window is opened before the call to the Jump Procedure. This saves the underlying screens for the application that called this specialized Other Procedure. After the screen is opened, the RUN statement is executed. From that point on, Clarion takes over and operates everything in background.

Figure 14-3 An Other Procedure for "jumping" or "shelling" to DOS.

```
MEMBER()
JUMP     PROCEDURE

SCREEN SCREEN        WINDOW, HUE(7,0)
       END!SCREEN

       CODE
       OPEN(SCREEN)                    !OPEN PROGRAM SCREEN
       RUN('C:\COMMAND.COM')           !JUMP TO DOS
       CLOSE(SCREEN)                   !CLOSE SCREEN
       RETURN                          !GO BACK TO APPLICATION
```

The first step Clarion takes is to check the DOS environment that was loaded by the RUN statement *in order to* load the version you will be using from the keyboard. Clarion looks for two things:

1. Was virtual memory configured?
2. Does a RAM disk exist?

Refer to Chapter 12 of this book and Appendix E of the *Clarion Language Reference* for information on virtual memory. A RAM disk is a chunk of dynamic memory set up to operate just like a physical disk drive.

If virtual memory has been configured for the system, Clarion attempts to save the underlying screens into that memory instead of on the disk or in conventional memory space. When a RAM disk has been set up, Clarion uses it for the temporary storage required by CALL and RUN. To use the RAM disk with CALL and RUN, however, you must add another environment variable to the ones that configured virtual memory. Otherwise, the memory image temporary file will be written to the disk. You must add the CLATMP variable to tell Clarion where the RAM disk resides. If you configured the RAM disk as Drive D, place the following statement in your AUTOEXEC.BAT file:

```
SET CLATMP=D:\
```

This demarcation of the RAM disk has nothing to do with virtual memory. You can use one without the other, if you choose. Since the temporary file will be written to memory, the writing process will take much less time than writing it to and deleting it from the actual hard drive.

Whether you use the CALL or RUN statements from inside an executable file or through CRUN or CPRO with .PRO files, a temporary file is created that contains the memory image for the program. In the case of CRUN and CPRO, that means retaining the elements in memory of the executable program (CPRO.EXE or CRUN.EXE) as well as the .PRO file that issued the CALL or RUN. In the case of an application that has been translated into an executable file, the memory image of that file will be moved into temporary storage.

Figure 14-4 demonstrates the storage requirements for starting another program from within a Clarion application. The numbers in the "Disk" column refer to the space used on the physical disk drive for the temporary file. The "RAM" column shows how much of conventional random access memory was used. The "Virtual" column shows how much of Clarion's virtual memory scheme was used in the cases listed at the bottom of Figure 14-4 when virtual memory has been configured.

> ### *WARNING*
> **The CALL and RUN statements do not return an error when there is insufficient space on the target devices to hold the temporary file created for storing and restoring the memory image of your application.**

If the memory image cannot be created, you will not get a message back. The program you meant to run simply does not run and the screen returns to normal as before your application attempted to complete the CALL or RUN statement. This is usually a sign that the disk or the device where the temporary file was to be written was not big enough to hold the temporary file. You

Figure 14-4   The relative memory consumption of the CALL, RUN, and CHAIN statements when activated through the various methods in Clarion for running a program.

COMMAND	TOOL	DISK	RAM	VIRTUAL	TOTAL
CALL & RUN	**CPRO**	393,216	3,714	N/A	396,928
	CRUN	364,544	3,712	N/A	368,256
	EXE FILE	274,432	21,512	N/A	295,944
CHAIN	**CPRO**	0	5,560	N/A	5,560
	CRUN	0	5,560	N/A	5,560
	EXE FILE	0	30,784	N/A	30,784
WITH VIRTUAL MEMORY					
CALL & RUN	**CPRO**	384,024	6,336	3,215	393,575
	CRUN	354,304	6,336	3,215	363,855
	EXE FILE	264,192	18,864	3,215	286,271
CHAIN	**CPRO**	0	2,352	3,215	5,567
	CRUN	0	2,352	3,215	5,567
	EXE FILE	0	27,568	3,215	30,783

can do your own error checking prior to using CALL and RUN by testing for the available space using the Disk Space LEM, as will be discussed in Chapter 17. Then you can post your own error message to warn the user that the process they are trying to run may fail due to a lack of sufficient storage. You can run your own tests for finding out how large that temporary file will be using the sample program shown later in this chapter.

After the memory image is created, CALL and RUN load the secondary copy of the Command Processor that operates the program that each statement calls. In the case of the "jump to DOS" in Figure 14-3, that program will open a third copy of the Command Processor. Except for the version of the Command Processor started by either RUN or CALL, each additional copy causes the prior version and the application to be stored in a temporary file with sequential numbering. That is, if you were to "jump to DOS" and then start a second program where you used its similar ability to shell out to DOS, you would wind up with two versions of the temporary file on the disk labeled in this sequence: $T1.TMP, $T2.TMP, and so on. You can see how easy it would be to run out of space on the storage device for those temporary files. Those files grow as the memory presence of your application grows. You should pick the places where a user can exit to DOS or execute CALL and RUN to places where the number of screens and the quantity of records held in memory is lower. That is, you should avoid executing CALL or RUN from a table where you might have a large data file on display.

The Model Files and RUN

There is an excellent prototype for how to employ the RUN statement in the model files for Designer called RUNPROC. You can execute a DOS program simply by placing it in a Menu Field as the procedure to run—but you must include the "." (period) and the file extension. When you do, then Designer uses the @RUNMAP key word to place the PROC(G_RUNPROC) statement in the global map along with a global procedure that will execute the DOS program identified as DOSPROG, as appears in Figure 14-5.

With this procedure, the underlying screen is saved and the DOS program is executed. Upon returning back to the calling procedure, the screen is closed and everything returns back to normal. Using the ability to pass a parameter, the G_RUNPROC Procedure is called with the name of the DOS program you want to execute from inside another procedure.

Figure 14-5   The generic Run Procedure placed in global memory.

```
G_RUNPROC     PROCEDURE(DOSPROG)                !GLOBAL RUN PROCEDURE
DOSPROG       STRING(12)                        !PROGRAM TO RUN
SCREEN        SCREEN    WINDOW(25,80),HUE(7,0,0).  !SAVE WINDOW

  CODE
  OPEN(SCREEN)                                  !SAVE CURRENT SCREEN
  SETCURSOR(25,1)                               !POSITION CURSOR AT BOTTOM
  RUN(DOSPROG)                                  !RUN DOS PROGRAM
  CLOSE(SCREEN)                                 !RESTORE SCREEN
  RETURN                                        !EXIT BACK TO CALLING MENU
```

CHAIN

The CHAIN statement gives CALL and RUN a new twist. It takes advantage of the ability of DOS to pass parameters to secondary copies of the Command Processor—including the ability of COMMAND.COM to load itself, execute a program, and then immediately exit. (You can achieve the same effect by running COMMAND.COM with the DOS SHELL directive and omitting the "/P" switch.)

The CHAIN statement lets you call another program and essentially pass control like a relay race baton to that program. Similar to the RESTART statement, a new starting point is set at the opening addresses for the program called by CHAIN. As you can see in Figure 14-4, CHAIN does not create a temporary disk file, so no disk storage is consumed. However, when you operate CHAIN from inside CPRO or CRUN and call another program to run under one of those tools, CPRO or CRUN stays resident while the new .PRO file is loaded and the old one (the caller) is terminated.

In the case of applications translated to an executable file, you cannot use CHAIN unless the memory resident program CHAIN.COM is loaded first. The CHAIN statement passes the name of the executable program to startup and then terminates the current application. This is an excellent way to conserve on memory consumption even while leapfrogging between programs. The large amount of conventional memory used by CHAIN in Figure 14-4 is due to the presence of CHAIN.COM in memory.

A Quick Jog to DOS with RUNSMALL

If you want to execute a small DOS program that will not require screen access or a large amount of memory, you can use the RUNSMALL statement. You can use RUNSMALL to perform operations like file copying and deleting. When you make the call to RUNSMALL, Clarion tries to load itself into whatever is left of conventional memory not taken up by the application. If sufficient memory is not available, it returns the error codes of its larger cousin RUN instead. Just like RUN, consider RUNSMALL a way to pass an instruction to the DOS command line. If you think you can save memory by calling a program with RUNSMALL, do that and check for errors to decide whether the memory configuration at the time requires RUN. The loss in processing speed will be barely perceptible.

Building a Special Test Set

To test the impact of CALL, CHAIN, and RUN on memory, the CALLER program was developed. (The source code for the program is given at the end of this chapter.) The CALLER program is a simple Menu Procedure that calls procedures that:

- Open a blank window to save the video memory of the menu screen.
- Retrieve the control record from a file on the disk called DATAFILE.
- Set new control information and then write it back to the disk.
- Check for errors in the write in case the file was not found or experienced some other difficulty in access.
- Execute the call to either CALL, CHAIN, or RUN with the parameter of the program called TEST.

The main menu for the CALLER program appears in Figure 14-6 and shows each of the tests to be performed. The control file is used to store information because, in Clarion, parameters cannot be passed *between executable programs* for processing. Using the intermediate file concept is the only method available to make a "hot" transfer of values.

To operate the CALLER program, you must start it with the proper tool (CPRO, CRUN, and so on) to get the right reading on memory consumption. In other words, to test the memory consumption of the system using the Processor, start CALLER with CPRO. To test the runtime memory use, start it with CRUN. To test the translated executable, run the compiled and translated program from the DOS prompt.

Figure 14-6   The menu screen for the memory testing program, CALLER.

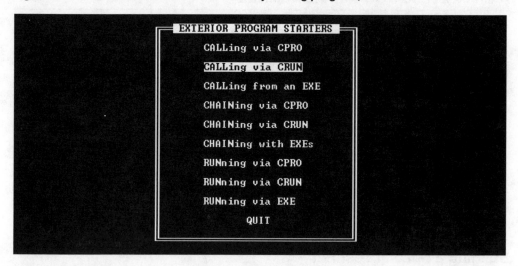

```
┌──────── EXTERIOR PROGRAM STARTERS ────────┐
│                                           │
│              CALLing via CPRO             │
│              CALLing via CRUN             │
│              CALLing from an EXE          │
│              CHAINing via CPRO            │
│              CHAINing via CRUN            │
│              CHAINing with EXEs           │
│              RUNning via CPRO             │
│              RUNning via CRUN             │
│              RUNning via EXE              │
│                   QUIT                    │
│                                           │
└───────────────────────────────────────────┘
```

> **WARNING**
> The DISKSPACE.BIN language extension module (LEM) is required to run the TEST program, which is executed from the CALLER program. (The instructions for creating this LEM appear in Chapter 17.)

With each selection in the Caller program, the control record is written to the control file and then the test program is executed in the manner suggested by the menu pick. At that point, the temporary file required by RUN and CALLER is created and the TEST program is executed. Its only screen appears in Figure 14-6 with the results of the test. The control file is read to get the "before" amounts for disk space and memory use, and then the new values are retrieved from the system and displayed. Computed Fields are used to compare the two and to derive the differences between them. Note that no virtual memory measurements appear because no virtual memory was configured when this picture was taken.

A New Leaf—The RESTART Statement

The RESTART statement is as close to a "bailout" function as is possible in Clarion. Put simply, RESTART stops processing and starts the procedure you

Figure 14-7   The results screen for the TEST program executed from the CALLER program to measure memory and disk space consumption for the CALL, RUN, and CHAIN statements.

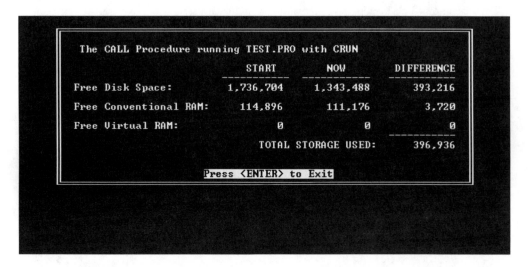

```
The CALL Procedure running TEST.PRO with CRUN
                              START        NOW        DIFFERENCE
                           ----------   ----------   ----------
Free Disk Space:            1,736,704    1,343,488       393,216

Free Conventional RAM:        114,896      111,176         3,720

Free Virtual RAM:                   0            0             0
                                                      ----------
                                TOTAL STORAGE USED:       396,936

                          Press <ENTER> to Exit
```

passed in its parameter. That's it. It does not reinitialize any variables or reopen files. From that moment on, the procedure passed as the RESTART parameter is considered the Base Procedure. Thus, if you press ESCAPE (in unmodified models) or whatever method you've created for terminating this particular procedure, you will return to the original DOS prompt from which you started the program. Use this function wherever you want to provide the user with an easy method for starting over without backing up through a lot of procedures.

> ### *Caution*
> **If you process the RESTART function after a user has entered a series of input fields, be sure you provide a choice for discarding the contents of those fields before you call RESTART; otherwise, that information will be lost.**

You can call the RESTART statement from inside Edit Procedures or even within an If structure in the Setup Procedure. For instance, if you want the user to start at the top of an application, say, as in the case of a failed password entry screen, you can place the RESTART statement as:

```
IF PASSWORD" <> FIL:PASSWORD THEN RESTART(MAIN);END!IF
```

Figure 14-8   Sample code from the PULL-DOWN MENU program from Chapter 8 demonstrating the RESTART statement.

```
OF LEFT_KEY                          !CHECK FOR CURSOR KEY
   CLOSE(PRINTSCREEN)                 !  CLOSE THIS SCREEN
   DO VIEW                           !  GO TO NEW MENU
   RESTART                          !  GO TO MAIN IF NEW
```

You can also apply the RESTART statement to avoid filling memory, as was done in the example from Chapter 8 where the Pull-Down Menu system used RESTART to provide a clean method for removing screens from memory. In addition, if you do not pass a parameter to RESTART, it starts the program at the original Base Procedure for the application as appears in Figure 14-8, which is a sample from the Pull-Down program in Chapter 8.

STOP, RETURN, BREAK, EXIT, and SHUTDOWN —The Terminators

All five of the statements—STOP, RETURN, BREAK, EXIT, and SHUT-DOWN—involve stopping whatever procedure they are a part of and turn processing over to some other part of the program. With STOP, RETURN, and SHUTDOWN, you can pass a parameter to perform a function. In addition, these three statements can be used anywhere in a Clarion application. However, BREAK and EXIT can only be used in their respective structures. BREAK terminates the Loop structure and EXIT terminates a local ROUTINE. Neither of those two statements can be used in any other place in a Clarion program, although BREAK can be called anywhere inside a Loop structure as EXIT can be called anywhere inside a local ROUTINE.

The STOP Statement

STOP can best be used in response to errors. The Clarion models for Designer place STOP inside If structures after file operations to test for errors, as appears in the section of the model code for the Form Procedure in Figure 14-9.

Figure 14-9   The use of the STOP statement in the Standard Model file for Designer.

```
IF ERRORCODE( ) = 40               !   DUPLICATE KEY ERROR
  MEM:MESSAGE = ERROR( )           !    DISPLAY ERR MESSAGE
  SELECT(2)                        !    POSITION TO TOP OF FORM
  CYCLE                            !    GET OUT OF EDIT LOOP
ELSIF ERROR( )                     !   CHECK FOR UNEXPECTED ERROR
  STOP(ERROR( ))                   !    HALT EXECUTION
.
```

As discussed in Chapter 13, you can also use STOP to debug your code. You can pass a parameter to it that contains your own custom error code along with a variable that will display its contents.

> ### *Caution*
> **If you use the STOP statement for debugging purposes, be sure you create some method, through macros or special characters (like placing "!!!" in the comments), with which you can efficiently strip them out of the code before you deliver it.**

Running STOP under CPRO instantly pops up the Debugger with your error message displayed in the top line, as shown in Figure 14-10. In CRUN, and with a translated executable program, the error message still displays as shown in Figure 14-11, but you can only choose to continue with the next line after the STOP statement or terminate the program.

Hint: The free memory depicted inside the error screen in Figure 14-11 is low because the test program that posts the STOP command was called through CRUN from inside Director.

The RETURN Statement

Clarion handles the RETURN statement in three important ways. First, RE-TURN passes control back to the procedure that called the current procedure. Second, Clarion uses RETURN to pass information between procedures.

Figure 14-10   The Debugger pops up when you issue a STOP statement while running in the Processor.

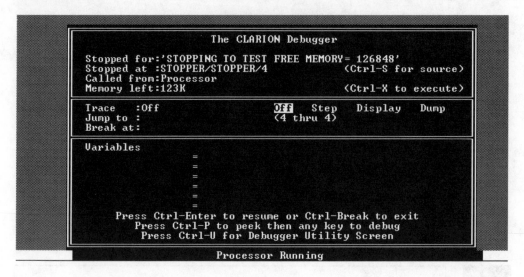

```
                          The CLARION Debugger
        Stopped for:'STOPPING TO TEST FREE MEMORY= 126848'
        Stopped at :STOPPER/STOPPER/4              (Ctrl-S for source)
        Called from:Processor
        Memory left:123K                           (Ctrl-X to execute)

        Trace  :Off                    Off   Step    Display   Dump
        Jump to :                      (4 thru 4)
        Break at:

        Variables
                        =
                        =
                        =
                        =
                        =

           Press Ctrl-Enter to resume or Ctrl-Break to exit
              Press Ctrl-P to peek then any key to debug
              Press Ctrl-U for Debugger Utility Screen
                          Processor Running
```

Third, when the procedure terminates normally by other means, RETURN can be left out.

There should be only one RETURN statement in each procedure. That is, you should construct your functions and procedures to have only one exit point. By doing that, you improve your control over that exit and make it easier to debug your code. You may notice that the Clarion models have more than one RETURN statement, however. Thus this is not a prescribed and irrefutable law. However, if you try to restrict the exit points in your procedures, you won't get frustrated chasing a bug that is occurring because you have an accidental exit point for the procedure in a local routine somewhere.

You can pass information to a procedure or a function with multiple parameters in a RETURN statement. When, in Designer, you indicate that a function returns a value, that return should take place with the LONG, REAL,

Figure 14-11   The error screen that pops up when you issue a STOP statement while running your application with CRUN or as a translated executable file.

```
        Program Stop   Version 2.1 Release 2105

        'STOPPING TO TEST FREE MEMORY= 46032'

        Press Esc to quit program, Enter to continue
```

or SHORT passed as a parameter of the RETURN statement somewhere in the function. You can also pass information from one procedure to the next—this is done using a parameter of the procedure as an EXTERNAL variable.

Hint: An EXTERNAL variable is passed by means of providing a pointer to an address in memory. That means it stays connected to the memory occupied by the original procedure and does not occupy a new place in memory with the function or procedure that is called. If you call UPDATE and DISPLAY from inside a function, the variable and the display inside the calling procedure of an EXTERNAL variable passed to the function are affected. In other words, the function is actually operating on a variable in the procedure that called the function and not on its own variable.

Inside the beginning procedure, you pass the parameter in the form:

```
PROCEDURE(parameter)
```

Then, in the procedure, you receive that passed variable and declare an EXTERNAL by placing the following in the beginning of the procedure:

```
PROCEDURE_NAME     PROCEDURE(parameter)


PARAMETER          EXTERNAL
```

Finally, the RETURN statement can be extraneous. In local ROUTINES, there is no need to specify EXIT explicitly if the process always moves all the way through the ROUTINE and drops out the bottom—it automatically returns to the procedure. The same is true of the RETURN statement. It is not necessary to explicitly place a RETURN statement when a procedure has a natural exit point. However, it is good programming practice to document code with code where possible, and the readability of your programs is increased if another Clarion programmer can quickly scan a procedure and locate the RETURN statement rather than looking over the procedure in order *not* to find it.

The SHUTDOWN Statement

The Shutdown Procedure is part of a safe exit from a program. Because the Clarion default is continually flushing memory to the disk, you normally do not need to prevent an automatic exit in the program in order to save data stored only in memory— except when you have a procedure running with the flushing turned off. In that case, you can use the Shutdown Procedure to save data held only in memory when a program terminates. The termination may be intentional on the part of the user who presses the CTRL-BREAK abort or if the program is naturally terminating through a RETURN statement. The Shutdown Procedure can also be used to save data or run some other process like a thank you to the user or a warning message when the program terminates unnaturally due to a runtime error. For instance, if you placed a STOP statement in the program that was called and the user pressed the Escape key to exit from the program, the procedure specified as the parameter of the SHUTDOWN statement would be the last thing the program executed before returning to DOS.

> ***Caution***
> **If you use the SHUTDOWN statement in an error response and you allow the user to exit from the program or to continue, be sure to cancel the SHUTDOWN by recalling that statement with no parameters. That way, when the user finally does exit naturally from a program, an error message from somewhere else in the application won't display inappropriately.**

Background Processing with IDLE

In all Designer-generated code and anywhere the ACCEPT and ASK statements suspend processing, no additional lines of code are processed until a response is received from the user. To run a procedure constantly throughout your application, you must use the IDLE statement to operate in the background even while the rest of the application waits for user input. However, when the application is active, the Idle Procedure stops until the next point that the system is waiting for input. That is, an Idle Procedure like the one in Figure 14-12 will show a running clock except when, for instance, the user is actually pressing the keys for entry or the application itself is processing a print request. You must keep the Idle Procedure in a common memory area that is equally accessible from all procedures and not in an Overlay structure. In Figure 14-12, the Timer Procedure is called as an Idle Procedure.

Figure 14-12   The Timer Procedure called as an Idle Procedure.

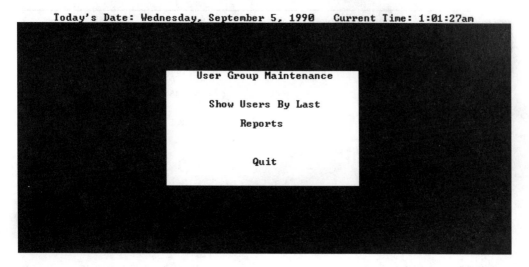

To display the clock in Figure 14-12 continuously throughout your application, place IDLE(TIMER) in the Setup Procedure for the Base Procedure in your application. It then appears on the screen until the application is terminated. You can also control how often your Idle Procedure is called by giving the separation parameter, which is the second parameter you can give to an IDLE statement.

Summary

Every programming language needs "exception" facilities—methods and means for picking up and moving the process from one location in the program to another, and for simply terminating the process. In this chapter, we covered the Clarion language elements that provide that special control. Using the CALL, RUN, and CHAIN statements, you can start whole processes or programs from inside an application and then return to your original starting point. Clarion also provides a number of different methods for redirecting or completely stopping a process in the form of the STOP, RETURN, and SHUTDOWN statements.

Figure 14-13   The Timer Idle Procedure code.

```
            MEMBER
TIMER       PROCEDURE
    CODE
    DAYS# = TODAY() %7                          !GET DAY OF WEEK NUMBER
    DAY" = 'SUNDAY'                             !SET DAY TO SUNDAY IF DAYS# = 0
    EXECUTE DAYS#
        DAY" = 'Monday'                         !SELECT DAY BY DAY NUMBER
        DAY" = 'Tuesday'
        DAY" = 'Wednesday'
        DAY" = 'Thursday'
        DAY" = 'Friday'
        DAY" = 'Saturday'
    END EXECUTE

    SECONDS# = SUB(FORMAT(CLOCK(),@T4),7,2) !GET SECONDS

    TEST" = CLOCK()                             !CONVERT STANDARD TIME
    IF TEST" > 4320000                          !CHECK FOR 12 NOON
    HALF" = 'pm'                                !IF AFTERNOON
     ELSE
    HALF" = 'am'                                !IF MORNING
    .
    SETHUE(0,7)                                 !SET BLACK & WHITE BAR
    COLOR(1,1,1,80)                             !COLOR BAR IN
    SHOW(1,1,CENTER('Todays''s Date: ' & |      !START DATE LINE CENTERED
        CLIP(DAY") & ', ' & |                   !CUT DAY OF WEEK DOWN
        CLIP((FORMAT(TODAY(),@D4))) & |         !GET AND CLIP DATE
        '   Current Time:' & |                  !SET SPACING FOR TIME
        SUB((FORMAT(CLOCK(),@T3)),1,5) & |      !TRIM NORMAL TIME PICTURE
        ':' & FORMAT(SECONDS#,@P##P) & |        !ADD FORMATTED SECONDS
        HALF",80))                              !ADD AM OR PM & WIDTH
    SETHUE                                      !TURN OFF VIDEO BIT
    RETURN
```

The CALLER Program

CALLER.CLA

```
CALLER          PROGRAM
                INCLUDE('STD_KEYS.CLA')
                INCLUDE('CTL_KEYS.CLA')
                INCLUDE('ALT_KEYS.CLA')
                INCLUDE('SHF_KEYS.CLA')

REJECT_KEY      EQUATE(CTRL_ESC)
ACCEPT_KEY      EQUATE(CTRL_ENTER)
TRUE            EQUATE(1)
FALSE           EQUATE(0)

                MAP
                  PROC(G_OPENFILES)
                  PROC(MAIN)                      !EXTERIOR PROGRAM STARTERS
                  PROC(CALLCPRO)
                  PROC(CALLCRUN)
                  PROC(CALLEXE)
                  PROC(CHAINCPRO)
                  PROC(CHAINCRUN)
                  PROC(CHAINEXE)
                  PROC(RUNCPRO)
                  PROC(RUNCRUN)
                  PROC(RUNEXE)
                  MODULE('SPACE'),BINARY
                        FUNC(DISKSPACE),LONG
                        .
                    .
                EJECT('FILE LAYOUTS')
                EJECT('GLOBAL MEMORY VARIABLES')
ACTION          SHORT                            !0 = NO ACTION
                                                 !1 = ADD RECORD
                                                 !2 = CHANGE RECORD
                                                 !3 = DELETE RECORD
                                                 !4 = LOOKUP FIELD
DATAFILE        FILE,PRE(DAT),CREATE,RECLAIM
RECORD          RECORD
MESSAGE           STRING(60)
DISKFREE          STRING(10)
MEMORYFREE        STRING(11)
VIRTUALRAM        STRING(11)
          . .
```

(continued)

```
BLANKER   SCREEN              WINDOW(25,80),HUE(7,0)
            .


          GROUP,PRE(MEM)
MESSAGE           STRING(30)                       !Global Message Area
PAGE              SHORT                            !Report Page Number
LINE              SHORT                            !Report Line Number
DEVICE            STRING(30)                       !Report Device Name

            .

          EJECT('CODE SECTION')
  CODE
  SETHUE(7,0)                                      !SET WHITE ON BLACK
  BLANK                                            !   AND BLANK
  G_OPENFILES
  SETHUE()                                         !     THE SCREEN
  MAIN                                             !EXTERIOR PROGRAM STARTERS
  RETURN                                           !EXIT TO DOS


G_OPENFILES   PROCEDURE                            !OPEN FILES & CHECK FOR ERROR
  CODE
  OPEN(DATAFILE)                                   !OPEN THE FILE
    IF ERRORCODE() = 2                             ! CHECK FOR SPECIFIC ERROR
      CREATE(DATAFILE)                             ! CREATE
      DAT:MESSAGE = '1'
      DAT:DISKFREE = '1'
      DAT:MEMORYFREE = '1'
      DAT:VIRTUALRAM = '1'
      ADD(DATAFILE)
    ELSIF ERROR()                                  ! ANY OTHER ERROR
      STOP('DATAFILE: ' & ERROR())                 !  STOP EXECUTION

        .

MAIN          PROCEDURE


SCREEN    SCREEN          WINDOW(23,33),PRE(SCR),HUE(15,1)
          ROW(1,4)    PAINT(1,27),HUE(0,7)
                COL(1)  STRING('<201,205{2},0{27},205{2},187>')
          ROW(2,1)    REPEAT(21);STRING('<186,0{31},186>')  .
          ROW(23,1)   STRING('<200,205{31},188>')
          ROW(1,5)    STRING('EXTERIOR PROGRAM STARTERS')
                COL(30) ENTRY,USE(?FIRST_FIELD)
                COL(30) ENTRY,USE(?PRE_MENU)
                COL(30) MENU,USE(MENU_FIELD"),REQ
          ROW(3,9)        STRING('CALLing via CPRO'),SEL(0,7)
          ROW(5,9)        STRING('CALLing via CRUN'),SEL(0,7)
```

(continued)

```
              ROW(7,9)        STRING('CALLing from an EXE'),SEL(0,7)
              ROW(9,9)        STRING('CHAINing via CPRO'),SEL(0,7)
              ROW(11,9)       STRING('CHAINing via CRUN'),SEL(0,7)
              ROW(13,9)       STRING('CHAINing with EXEs'),SEL(0,7)
              ROW(15,9)       STRING('RUNning via CPRO'),SEL(0,7)
              ROW(17,9)       STRING('RUNning via CRUN'),SEL(0,7)
              ROW(19,9)       STRING('RUNning via EXE'),SEL(0,7)
              ROW(21,16)      STRING('QUIT'),SEL(0,7)
          .                 .


EJECT
CODE
OPEN(SCREEN)                              !OPEN THE MENU SCREEN
SETCURSOR                                 !TURN OFF ANY CURSOR
MENU_FIELD" = ''                          !START MENU WITH FIRST ITEM
LOOP                                      !LOOP UNTIL USER EXITS
  ALERT                                   !TURN OFF ALL ALERTED KEYS
  ALERT(REJECT_KEY)                       !ALERT SCREEN REJECT KEY
  ALERT(ACCEPT_KEY)                       !ALERT SCREEN ACCEPT KEY
  ACCEPT                                  !READ A FIELD OR MENU CHOICE
  IF KEYCODE() = REJECT_KEY THEN RETURN.  !RETURN ON SCREEN REJECT

  IF KEYCODE() = ACCEPT_KEY               !ON SCREEN ACCEPT KEY
    UPDATE                                !  MOVE ALL FIELDS FROM SCREEN
    SELECT(?)                             !  START WITH CURRENT FIELD
    SELECT                               !  EDIT ALL FIELDS
    CYCLE                                 !  GO TO TOP OF LOOP
  .                                       !

  CASE FIELD()                            !JUMP TO FIELD EDIT ROUTINE
  OF ?FIRST_FIELD                         !FROM THE FIRST FIELD
    IF KEYCODE() = ESC_KEY THEN RETURN.   !  RETURN ON ESC KEY

  OF ?PRE_MENU                            !PRE MENU FIELD CONDITION
    IF KEYCODE() = ESC_KEY                !  BACKING UP?
      SELECT(?-1)                         !    SELECT PREVIOUS FIELD
    ELSE                                  !  GOING FORWARD
      SELECT(?+1)                         !    SELECT MENU FIELD
    .
  OF ?MENU_FIELD"                         !FROM THE MENU FIELD
    EXECUTE CHOICE()                      !  CALL THE SELECTED PROCEDURE
      CALLCPRO                            !
      CALLCRUN                            !
      CALLEXE                             !
      CHAINCPRO                           !
      CHAINCRUN                           !
```

(continued)

```
            CHAINEXE                              !
            RUNCPRO                               !
            RUNCRUN                               !
            RUNEXE                                !
            RETURN
      . . .


CALLCPRO    PROCEDURE
            CODE
            OPEN(BLANKER)
            GET(DATAFILE,1)
            DAT:MESSAGE = 'The CALL Procedure running TEST.PRO with CPRO'
            DAT:DISKFREE = DISKSPACE(2)
            DAT:MEMORYFREE = MEMORY(0)
            DAT:VIRTUALRAM = MEMORY(2)
            PUT(DATAFILE)
            IF ERROR() THEN STOP(ERROR()).
            CALL('TEST')
            RETURN


CALLCRUN    PROCEDURE
            CODE
            OPEN(BLANKER)
            GET(DATAFILE,1)
            DAT:MESSAGE = 'The CALL Procedure running TEST.PRO with CRUN'
            DAT:DISKFREE = DISKSPACE(2)
            DAT:MEMORYFREE = MEMORY(0)
            DAT:VIRTUALRAM = MEMORY(2)
            PUT(DATAFILE)
            IF ERROR() THEN STOP(ERROR()).
            CALL('TEST')
            RETURN


CALLEXE     PROCEDURE
            CODE
            OPEN(BLANKER)
            GET(DATAFILE,1)
            DAT:MESSAGE = 'The CALL Procedure running TEST.EXE'
            DAT:DISKFREE = DISKSPACE(2)
            DAT:MEMORYFREE = MEMORY(0)
            DAT:VIRTUALRAM = MEMORY(2)
            PUT(DATAFILE)
            IF ERROR() THEN STOP(ERROR()).
            CALL('TEST')
            RETURN
```

(continued)

```
CHAINCPRO  PROCEDURE
           CODE
           OPEN(BLANKER)
           GET(DATAFILE,1)
           DAT:MESSAGE = 'The CHAIN Procedure running TEST.PRO with CPRO'
           DAT:DISKFREE = DISKSPACE(2)
           DAT:MEMORYFREE = MEMORY(0)
           DAT:VIRTUALRAM = MEMORY(2)
           IF ERROR() THEN STOP(ERROR()).
           PUT(DATAFILE)
           CHAIN('TEST')
           RETURN


CHAINCRUN PROCEDURE
           CODE
           OPEN(BLANKER)
           GET(DATAFILE,1)
           IF ERROR() THEN CREATE(DATAFILE).
           GET(DATAFILE,1)
           DAT:MESSAGE = 'The CHAIN Procedure running TEST.PRO with CRUN'
           DAT:DISKFREE = DISKSPACE(2)
           DAT:MEMORYFREE = MEMORY(0)
           DAT:VIRTUALRAM = MEMORY(2)
           PUT(DATAFILE)
           IF ERROR() THEN STOP(ERROR()).
           CHAIN('TEST')
           RETURN


CHAINEXE   PROCEDURE
           CODE
           OPEN(BLANKER)
           GET(DATAFILE,1)
           IF ERROR() THEN CREATE(DATAFILE).
           GET(DATAFILE,1)
           DAT:MESSAGE = 'The CHAIN Procedure running TEST.EXE'
           DAT:DISKFREE = DISKSPACE(2)
           DAT:MEMORYFREE = MEMORY(0)
           DAT:VIRTUALRAM = MEMORY(2)
           PUT(DATAFILE)
           IF ERROR() THEN STOP(ERROR()).
           CHAIN('TEST')
           RETURN


RUNCPRO    PROCEDURE
           CODE
           OPEN(BLANKER)
```

(continued)

```
          GET(DATAFILE,1)
          IF ERROR() THEN CREATE(DATAFILE).
          GET(DATAFILE,1)
          DAT:MESSAGE = 'The RUN Procedure running TEST.PRO with CPRO'
          DAT:DISKFREE = DISKSPACE(2)
          DAT:MEMORYFREE = MEMORY(0)
          DAT:VIRTUALRAM = MEMORY(2)
          PUT(DATAFILE)
          IF ERROR() THEN STOP(ERROR()).
          RUN('CPRO TEST')
          RETURN


RUNCRUN PROCEDURE
          CODE
          OPEN(BLANKER)
          GET(DATAFILE,1)
          DAT:MESSAGE = 'The RUN Procedure running TEST.PRO with CRUN'
          DAT:DISKFREE = DISKSPACE(2)
          DAT:MEMORYFREE = MEMORY(0)
          DAT:VIRTUALRAM = MEMORY(2)
          PUT(DATAFILE)
          IF ERROR() THEN STOP(ERROR()).
          RUN('CRUN TEST')
          RETURN


RUNEXE    PROCEDURE
          CODE
          OPEN(BLANKER)
          GET(DATAFILE,1)
          DAT:MESSAGE = 'The RUN Procedure running TEST.EXE'
          DAT:DISKFREE = DISKSPACE(2)
          DAT:MEMORYFREE = MEMORY(0)
          DAT:VIRTUALRAM = MEMORY(2)
          PUT(DATAFILE)
          IF ERROR() THEN STOP(ERROR()).
          RUN('TEST.EXE')
          RETURN
```

CALLER1.CLA

```
          MEMBER('CALLER')
MAIN         PROCEDURE

SCREEN       SCREEN      PRE(SCR),WINDOW(23,33),HUE(15,1)
                ROW(1,4)    PAINT(1,27),HUE(0,7)
```

(continued)

```
                COL(1)  STRING('<201,205{2},0{27},205{2},187>')
      ROW(2,1)    REPEAT(21);STRING('<186,0{31},186>')  .
      ROW(23,1)   STRING('<200,205{31},188>')
      ROW(1,5)    STRING('EXTERIOR PROGRAM STARTERS')
                  ENTRY,USE(?FIRST_FIELD)
                  ENTRY,USE(?PRE_MENU)
                  MENU,USE(MENU_FIELD"),REQ
      ROW(3,9)        STRING('CALLing via CPRO'),SEL(0,7)
      ROW(5,9)        STRING('CALLing via CRUN'),SEL(0,7)
      ROW(7,9)        STRING('CALLing to an EXE'),SEL(0,7)
      ROW(9,9)        STRING('CHAINing to CPRO'),SEL(0,7)
      ROW(11,9)       STRING('CHAINing to CRUN'),SEL(0,7)
      ROW(13,9)       STRING('CHAINing to an EXE'),SEL(0,7)
      ROW(15,9)       STRING('RUNning via CPRO'),SEL(0,7)
      ROW(17,9)       STRING('RUNning via CRUN'),SEL(0,7)
      ROW(19,9)       STRING('RUNning via EXE'),SEL(0,7)
      ROW(21,16)      STRING('QUIT'),SEL(0,7)


EJECT
CODE
OPEN(SCREEN)                              !OPEN THE MENU SCREEN
SETCURSOR                                 !TURN OFF ANY CURSOR
MENU_FIELD" = ''                          !START MENU WITH FIRST ITEM
LOOP                                      !LOOP UNTIL USER EXITS
  ALERT                                   !TURN OFF ALL ALERTED KEYS
  ALERT(REJECT_KEY)                       !ALERT SCREEN REJECT KEY
  ALERT(ACCEPT_KEY)                       !ALERT SCREEN ACCEPT KEY
  ACCEPT                                  !READ A FIELD OR MENU CHOICE
  IF KEYCODE() = REJECT_KEY THEN RETURN.  !RETURN ON SCREEN REJECT

  IF KEYCODE() = ACCEPT_KEY               !ON SCREEN ACCEPT KEY
    UPDATE                                !  MOVE ALL FIELDS FROM SCREEN
    SELECT(?)                             !  START WITH CURRENT FIELD
    SELECT                                !  EDIT ALL FIELDS
    CYCLE                                 !  GO TO TOP OF LOOP
  .                                       !

  CASE FIELD()                            !JUMP TO FIELD EDIT ROUTINE
  OF ?FIRST_FIELD                         !FROM THE FIRST FIELD
    IF KEYCODE() = ESC_KEY THEN RETURN.   !  RETURN ON ESC KEY

  OF ?PRE_MENU                            !PRE MENU FIELD CONDITION
    IF KEYCODE() = ESC_KEY                !  BACKING UP?
      SELECT(?-1)                         !    SELECT PREVIOUS FIELD
    ELSE                                  !  GOING FORWARD
      SELECT(?+1)                         !    SELECT MENU FIELD
    .
```

(continued)

```
    OF ?MENU_FIELD"                      !FROM THE MENU FIELD
      EXECUTE CHOICE()                   !  CALL THE SELECTED PROCEDURE
        CALLCPRO                         !
        CALLCRUN                         !
        CALLEXE                          !
        CHAINCPRO                        !
        CHAINCPRO                        !
        CHAINEXE                         !
        RUNCPRO                          !
        RUNCPRO                          !
        RUNEXE                           !
        RETURN
  . . .
```

The TEST Program

TEST.CLA

```
TEST       PROGRAM
                INCLUDE('STD_KEYS.CLA')
                INCLUDE('CTL_KEYS.CLA')
                INCLUDE('ALT_KEYS.CLA')
                INCLUDE('SHF_KEYS.CLA')

REJECT_KEY    EQUATE(CTRL_ESC)
ACCEPT_KEY    EQUATE(CTRL_ENTER)
TRUE          EQUATE(1)
FALSE         EQUATE(0)

                MAP
                  MODULE('TEST1')
                        PROC(MAIN)
                     .
                  MODULE('SPACE'),BINARY
                        FUNC(DISKSPACE),LONG
                     .
                  .
                EJECT('FILE LAYOUTS')
                EJECT('GLOBAL MEMORY VARIABLES')
ACTION          SHORT                    !0 = NO ACTION
                                         !1 = ADD RECORD
                                         !2 = CHANGE RECORD
                                         !3 = DELETE RECORD
                                         !4 = LOOKUP FIELD
```

(continued)

```
            GROUP,PRE(MEM)
MESSAGE           STRING(60)                    !Global Message Area
PAGE              SHORT                         !Report Page Number
LINE              SHORT                         !Report Line Number
DEVICE            STRING(30)                    !Report Device Name
DISKFREE          STRING(10)
MEMORYFREE        STRING(11)
VIRTUALRAM        STRING(11)
            .


DATAFILE    FILE,PRE(DAT),CREATE,RECLAIM
RECORD        RECORD
MESSAGE           STRING(60)
DISKFREE          STRING(10)
MEMORYFREE        STRING(11)
VIRTUALRAM        STRING(11)
        . .


            EJECT('CODE SECTION')
  CODE
  SETHUE(7,0)                                   !SET WHITE ON BLACK
  BLANK                                         !   AND BLANK
  SETHUE()                                      !     THE SCREEN
  MAIN
  RETURN                                        !EXIT TO DOS
```

TEST1.CLA

```
            MEMBER('TEST')
MAIN            PROCEDURE

SCREEN    SCREEN          WINDOW(17,68),PRE(SCR),HUE(7,0)
                ROW(1,1)     STRING('<201,205{66},187>')
                ROW(2,1)     REPEAT(15);STRING('<186,0{66},186>') .
                ROW(17,1)    STRING('<200,205{66},188>')
                ROW(5,32)    STRING('START {8}NOW {8}DIFFERENCE')
                ROW(6,28)    STRING('-{11}   -{11}   -{11}')
                ROW(7,4)     STRING('Free Disk Space:')
                ROW(9,4)     STRING('Free Conventional RAM:')
                ROW(11,4)    STRING('Free Virtual RAM:')
                ROW(12,55)   STRING('-{11}')
                ROW(13,34)   STRING('TOTAL STORAGE USED:')
MESSAGE         ROW(3,5)     STRING(60),HUE(14,0)
DISKFREE        ROW(7,27)    STRING(@N-12)
FREE                 COL(40) STRING(@N-12)
```

(continued)

```
DISKDIFF           COL(54) STRING(@N-12)
MEMORYFREE    ROW(9,28)  STRING(@N-11)
RAMFREE            COL(41) STRING(@N-11)
RAMDIFF            COL(55) STRING(@N-11)
VIRTUALRAM    ROW(11,28) STRING(@N-11)
RAMVIRT            COL(41) STRING(@N-11)
VIRTDIFF          COL(55) STRING(@N-11)
TOTAL         ROW(13,55) STRING(@N-11)
                   COL(66) ENTRY,USE(?FIRST_FIELD)
                   COL(66) ENTRY,USE(?PRE_MENU)
                   COL(66) MENU,USE(MENU_FIELD"),REQ
              ROW(5,3)        STRING('RUNS A PROGRAM')
              ROW(16,25)      STRING('Press <<ENTER> to Exit')
```

```
  EJECT
  CODE
  OPEN(SCREEN)                              !OPEN THE MENU SCREEN
  SETCURSOR                                 !TURN OFF ANY CURSOR
  MENU_FIELD" = ''                          !START MENU WITH FIRST ITEM
  GET(DATAFILE,1)
    SCR:MESSAGE = DAT:MESSAGE
    SCR:DISKFREE = FORMAT(DAT:DISKFREE,@N10)
    SCR:MEMORYFREE = FORMAT(DAT:MEMORYFREE,@N11)
    SCR:VIRTUALRAM = FORMAT(DAT:VIRTUALRAM,@N11)
    SCR:FREE = diskspace(2)
    SCR:DISKDIFF = DAT:diskfree - scr:free
    SCR:RAMFREE = memory(0)
    SCR:RAMDIFF = DAT:memoryfree - scr:ramfree
    SCR:RAMVIRT = memory(2)
    SCR:VIRTDIFF = DAT:virtualram - scr:ramvirt
    SCR:TOTAL = SCR:DISKDIFF + SCR:RAMDIFF + SCR:VIRTDIFF
    ASK
  RETURN
```

Chapter 15

Multiuser Clarion

Clarion provides all the tools necessary to operate in a multiuser environment. The tools are available to maintain data integrity between users and within databases. In fact, with the special work already done by Clarion in modifying the Standard Model for multiuser applications, you can create a multiuser application with very little effort, sometimes merely by running your standalone single-user application through the code generation process and substituting the Network Model for the Standard Model.

For the most part, the tools for multiuser interaction relate to locking and unlocking records and files. The remainder of the facilities you use to manage Clarion database applications in a multiuser environment involve transaction processing. The locking statements provide direct control over the database files. The transaction statements provide management of changes to collections of data to reduce the potential for collisions in a multiuser environment. Clarion accomplishes network management through a relatively small number of statements (which appear in Figure 15-1) and some standardized methods like transaction management (which we'll discuss).

Designing in a Multiuser Environment

The key concept you must consider when you write an application for a multiuser system is *access*. Multiuser systems work exactly like single-user systems except that everyone accesses one set of data files. A copy of the program itself is in memory at the workstation just as if it had been loaded from a disk drive local to that workstation. However, since the data is *shared*,

Figure 15-1   The Clarion statements for creating multiuser applications.

STATEMENT	TARGET	FUNCTION
SHARE	File	Opens file to control multiple accesses.
LOCK	File	Prevents access from any station other than the one issuing the lock.
UNLOCK	File	Allows for another station to access a file for reading and writing.
HOLD	Record	Same as LOCK except it works at the record level.
RELEASE	Record	Same as UNLOCK except it works at the record level.
LOGOUT	Transaction	Creates a file to store a list of files and acts performed in a transaction.
COMMIT	Transaction	Writes a transaction from the temporary file, deleting it and the transaction log.
ROLLBACK	Transaction	Restores old data when transactions fail to complete.
RECOVER	File and Record	Unlocks a record or file when it becomes permanently locked through an incomplete transaction.
@AUTONUMESC	Designer	A keyword that includes code to "rollback" autonumbering of a key.

users encounter the problems of colliding operations. Since anyone in the system can change any of the data at any time, the program must control whose change gets saved and how the other users are treated. And that raises the second most important issue: communication.

Any multiuser application must not only manage the access to files to ensure that those files are not corrupted by incomplete or mixed record updates, but it must communicate with the users to let them know what happened and why. Nothing is more frustrating than to be doing work in a system that rejects an entry without telling you why or simply loses an entry without informing you that it has done so. In addition, when a complex transaction is taking place, if you enter data based on data that gets changed

Figure 15-2 In multiuser systems, the application runs in copies on the workstations and controls access to the central data files used by the application.

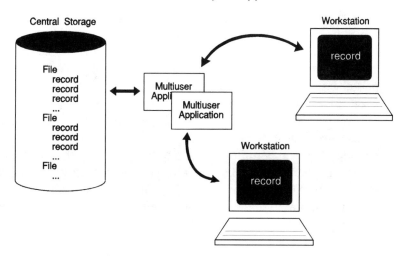

during your transaction, your work could be invalidated. Figure 15-2 shows how the application should mediate between the user and the database.

For instance, suppose you and several others are using an application that logs sales contacts. You bring up a record, place a call, and then enter the results of your call. If you save your changes and someone else was inspecting and changing that same record (client's data) simultaneously, your data will be lost when the other user's version of the record is saved. The application should be the central arbiter of all file access and it should inform the users of any decisions it makes *in time to make a difference in what the users will do with their data.*

Designing a multiuser database application, then, requires another layer of design beyond how to relate the data for efficient storage and retrieval. The new parameter is efficient transaction handling. You must construct your application to provide for inevitable collisions that will occur when several users all want to access *and update* the file at the same time. Accessing in read-only mode does not create a problem. However, a potential problem can arise when two users who are reading data decide to log a change of some kind. The scheme you construct for how they are allowed to perform that task and what they're told about the results represents that third layer of design. (The first two include user interface and data dictionary design.)

Special Design Considerations

For Interstation Communications: Although you can control access to the files from within Designer and the Clarion language, an efficient system includes communications between the users about what will happen. As we'll discuss later in this chapter, Designer's Network Model is only constructed to report changes *after* they occur. One of these communication methods is the portal file.

The portal file is a special control file you can set up when you design the database management scheme. The idea is to use the control file as an intermediate step in permitting access to the database. The exact contents of this file will change depending on what type of transaction you are tracking and the specific functional overlaps you anticipate. The typical contents of the control file might be the name of the file that a user accessed for updating along with a time stamp for when they began access. (One risk of this control file, however, is the chaos that may result if the control file itself becomes inaccessible.)

Hint: Multiuser applications increase the importance of distinguishing between **data files** *and* **databases**. *A data file is one Clarion file with its associated keys. A database is a collection of these files with defined relationships between them.*

Let's consider how the portal works. You have identified an important file for one aspect of your database. Suppose it is the CUSTOMER file, which is required to update the two files related to invoices. When one user opens that CUSTOMER file for updating, you place an entry in the control file indicating when that file was accessed. This records two events: the actual access and the time stamp. Next, if the second user also wants to update that same scheme of data, the system queries the control file for permission and the second user receives a message that the data is unavailable without having to issue a LOCK or HOLD against all the files in the transaction sequence. In many network schemes, you can issue a query to the network software to get the station number, which you can then place into the control file for the station that is currently using a section of the database.

Other system-level information can exist in this control file as well. For system managers, it is possible to find out quickly when files in the database were updated last for performing routine maintenance or even for disaster recovery. The control file is a supplement to, not a replacement for, the time-tracking abilities available in HOLD and LOCK (which are discussed later in this chapter).

Index versus Keys

When an index file is constructed with BUILD, it is opened in single-user mode, not in shared mode. This is true of all the statements that open a file implicitly when issued against a closed file except for LOCK, which opens the file SHAREd. Other implicit file opening statements are SET, GET, BUILD, PACK, ADD, APPEND, RECORDS, STREAM, BUFFER, and CACHE. Normally, because a report is a read-only operation, you can allow multiple access to the file for other reads when a report is running. (This is not true for a report that places a time stamp in printed records as with an account reconciliation or other selective batch update process.) As a result, you should create a key and not an index when running reports, because keys are opened in shared mode when the data file is opened, whereas indexes must be managed separately and are therefore more prone to error.

File Access by Many Users

In general, you should avoid CPU-intensive operations that will clog up the file server. Perform file searches in record order instead of key order whenever possible since this is a much faster method for file access. Searching by key requires that two files be read: the key file or files and the data file itself. Also, it becomes even more critical that you optimize the database to eliminate needless field duplication and Key Fields that contain more data than is necessary. Avoid creating keys with a long String Field as the Key Field. Keys store that string "as is" (in uppercase only when case sensitivity is off) and require a much larger amount of memory than other field forms. We'll discuss more about how to manage file updating through transaction processing later in the chapter, but, in general, try to reduce the amount of time it takes to perform any action that involves a shared file. The server or CPU must divide its efforts among all the users on the system whenever a shared file is included in a transaction.

dBASE IV users find that issuing a lock on a parent or top-level data file automatically locks the related data files. Clarion gives the applications programmer more control by locking only the file for which the LOCK statement was issued. However, dBASE IV also supports shared file locking where two users can update different fields in the same record. Once a user issues a HOLD to a record in Clarion, no other user can update that record until the HOLD is RELEASEd. It is debatable whether the micro control that dBASE IV provides in this case creates additional opportunity for conflict and more load on the programmer. Clarion's method may be more straightforward and therefore create more maintainable code.

Check for Errors Continually

As a general rule for all your transactions, use the ERRORCODE and ERROR statements liberally. Especially in a multiuser, transaction-oriented application, the need to be informed immediately about a failed process becomes very important. Several implicit procedures can create dangerous situations, such as issuing a statement against an open file that opens it implicitly and not in share mode; or attempting to issue HOLD or LOCK against an open file that is not in share mode and those statements are ignored with no error return.

Corruption of the database can be just around the corner, because an attempt to access a file failed and the process invoked by the user continues unaware. If you trap the error reports when they occur, you have a chance to provide an alternate means for completing the transaction—whether it be closing or unlocking the files that have been grabbed up to that point in the process, or performing a rollback of an aborted transaction. If you let the user know what is happening, the chances of maintaining the integrity of the database are enhanced.

For example, you cannot issue a NEXT statement to read the next record in a data file if that record is captured by HOLD from another station or even your own. In that case, operations based on the value retrieved would be invalid.

Hint: HOLD itself does not return any errors. When the HOLD statement is issued with a second parameter giving the number of seconds to hold it, PUT and DELETE return "RECORD NOT AVAILABLE" (ERRORCODE(33)); and GET, NEXT, and PREVIOUS all return "RECORD IS ALREADY HELD."

If you should get the "Record Not Available" error, you can try the SKIP statement to skip over that record to read the next available record. If the end of the file was reached, using the SKIP statement fails again and returns the same error.

Memory Impacts

Tailoring the Application Memory Profile: Most multiuser systems drain some of the memory local to the workstation to attach the workstation to the network. This puts an additional load on the memory requirements for your application. Be sure you check that amount before you release the application for general use. It is recommended that you test your application's memory requirements offline to verify that the application will operate properly once the TSR network software is loaded.

You can control the memory space of your application by using several methods, which apply to multiuser as well as single-user applications. Restructuring the MAP into overlays is one way to reduce the memory presence of your application. In addition, you can write a program to create or open the data files (as a check that they exist) on system startup and then immediately close them. They can be reopened in share mode on request from the main application. Then, in the file definitions in the main application, you can eliminate the CREATE attribute from the file and therefore eliminate some of the memory presence occupied by the file creation code that gets included at compile time. Here again, however, you must keep an eye on those file access statements that implicitly open a file in nonshare mode and would hang up the system in the event of another user's attempt to access the same file.

Novell Netware Considerations: In most Clarion applications, you must modify the CONFIG.SYS file to allow for the number of files that the application will open, taking into consideration the application itself, the key files, the memo files, and, in the case of overlays produced with a common runtime library, the .RTL file. Under Novell's version of network software, you must also configure the maximum number of open files that Novell allows. Under advanced netware version 2.15, you should use the program called NETGEN from DOS on the file server and set the maximum number of open files. Then, create a SYSTEM.CNF file on each network boot disk with file handles equal to between 70 and 110 or more, depending on the application.

CACHE and BUFFER: It is possible to open a data file with the OPEN statement and then lock the file from access to use the CACHE and BUFFER statements in multiuser networks. However, both of these statements are ignored if they are issued against files that were opened in share mode. If you open a data file in normal mode and *do not* lock it, you could hang the system.

Designer Impacts

Network Model

The Network Model that Clarion ships with Professional Developer is the same as the Standard Model (in terms of model procedure types) with additional coding to accommodate file sharing and record locking. No transaction processing is coded into this model. Since the management of transactions is highly dependent on the database configuration, you will be responsible for placing your own transaction methods into the code. The COMMIT, ROLL-BACK, and RECOVER statements (the primary transaction-specific Clarion language elements) are not used in the network model from Clarion.

The Network Model ensures that all data files in Designer are created, closed, but then reopened in share mode for the remainder of the run of the application. The model Menu Procedure contains nothing different than the Standard Model—the same goes for the Report Procedure. The only variation in the model Table Procedure was to add a way to reset the autonumbering procedure when there were Autonumbered Fields and the Update Procedure was cancelled for some reason before it had a chance to save the new record that should have integrated the number. The real changes to the Network Model occur in the Form Procedure where the record updating takes place and the chance for collision is created when a user accesses the data file.

The Table Procedure Network Model

At two places in the network model, the system reacts to an aborted attempt to add a new record by inserting code with the @AUTONUMESC Key Proce-dure shown in Figure 15-3. It appears once when the table is first started and there are no records in the file (at the OF ?POINT spot in the FIELD( ) case statement as shown in Figure 15-4), and later after the aborted Update Proce-dure returns to the table in the INS_KEY spot of the KEYCODE( ) case structure, as shown in Figure 15-5.

Figure 15-3   The @AUTONUMESC Key Procedure.

```
*AUTONUMESC********************************************************************
  IF ACTION                           !FORM WAS NOT COMPLETED
    HOLD(@FILENAME)                   !HOLD RECORD
    GET(@FILENAME,POINTER#)           !READ RECORD
    DELETE(@FILENAME)                 !DELETE RECORD
    DO SAME_PAGE
  .
```

Figure 15-4 The modified OF ?POINT section of the network model that resets the Autonumbered Field after the system attempts to add the first record to an empty file.

```
OF ?POINT                                 !PROCESS THE POINT FIELD
   IF RECORDS(TABLE) = 0                  !IF THERE ARE NO RECORDS
      CLEAR(NAM:RECORD)                   ! CLEAR RECORD AREA
      UPDATE                              !  UPDATE ALL FIELDS
      ACTION = 1                          !  SET ACTION TO ADD
      GET(NAMES,0)                        !  CLEAR PENDING RECORD
      LOOP
       CLEAR(NAM:RECORD,1)                !CLEAR RECORD TO HIGH VALUES
       SET(NAM:BY_NUMBER)                 !  POINT TO FIRST RECORD
        PREVIOUS(NAMES)                   !READ LAST KEY RECORD
        IF ERROR( )                       !IF THERE WAS AN ERROR
           CLEAR(NAM:RECORD)              !  CLEAR THE RECORD
           KEYFIELD# = 1.1230733834955e-190   !  INITIALIZE THE FIELD
           IF KEYFIELD# = 0 THEN KEYFIELD# = 1.!  IF ITS 0 MAKE IT 1
        ELSE                              !ELSE
           KEYFIELD# = NAM:NUMBER + 1     !  INCREMENT FIELD

           .
        CLEAR(NAM:RECORD)                 !CLEAR LAST KEY RECORD
         NAM:NUMBER = KEYFIELD#           !LOAD KEY FIELD
         ADD(NAMES)                       !ESTABLISH RECORD WITH UNIQUE
        IF NOT ERROR( )                   !ADD WAS SUCCESSFUL
           POINTER# = POINTER(NAMES)      ! SAVE POINTER
           ACTION = 5                     ! SET ACTION FOR UPDATE
           BREAK                          !  EXIT LOOP
    . .
      UPD_NAMES                           !  CALL FORM FOR NEW RECORD
```

The Code Inserted by the @AUTONUMESC Key Procedure

```
   IF ACTION                          !FORM WAS NOT COMPLETED
      HOLD(NAMES)                     !HOLD RECORD
      GET(NAMES,POINTER#)             !READ RECORD
      DELETE(NAMES)                   !DELETE RECORD
      DO SAME_PAGE
```

(continued)

Figure 15-4 *continued*

```
NEWPTR = POINTER(NAMES)          !   SET POINTER TO NEW RECORD
DO FIRST_PAGE                    !   DISPLAY THE FIRST PAGE
IF RECORDS(TABLE) = 0            !   IF THERE AREN'T ANY RECORDS
  RECORDS# = FALSE               !     INDICATE NO RECORDS
  SELECT(?PRE_POINT-1)           !     SELECT THE PRIOR FIELD

CYCLE                            !   AND LOOP AGAIN
```

The procedure in Figure 15-3 inserted into the Network Model Table Procedure is necessary, because it places a hold on the record that was added to the file with the Incremented Field when the user intended to abort that update. Issuing the HOLD guarantees that no one else can start the table and edit a record that should not exist until the first user can safely delete it.

Notice how the resetting of the autonumbering in both Figures 15-4 and 15-5 is done only when the global ACTION is set to some value and thus tests as true in the IF statement. That will only be the case when the Update Procedure was aborted and not allowed to reset ACTION = 0 to show successful completion.

How the Model Works: First-Out-Wins Protocol

In the processing scheme used by Clarion for multiuser transaction process-ing, "IN" means that data is retrieved from the central file server and put *into* the workstation. Then, when the user updates that record, it is sent *out* from the workstation to return to the storage located at the central file server. In the Clarion scheme, "First-Out-Wins"; that is, the first person to attempt to update a record successfully saves their change while someone who was looking at the same record concurrently will not be able to save if they attempt to go *out* in second place.

The Multiuser Form Procedure: The Form Procedure in the Network Model handles most of the aspects of multiuser. Primarily, it saves an image of the record in a memory table at the beginning of the edit and compares it to the current version of the record on the disk. If the two are different, Clarion knows the record was edited since it was read and posts an error like the one

Figure 15-5   The Insert key modification to handle an aborted addition of a record to a data file with an Auto-incremented Field.

```
OF INS_KEY                              !INS KEY
  CLEAR(NAM:RECORD)                     !  CLEAR RECORD AREA
   ACTION = 1                           !  SET ACTION TO ADD
   GET(NAMES,0)                         ! CLEAR PENDING RECORD
   LOOP
    CLEAR(NAM:RECORD,1)                 !CLEAR RECORD TO HIGH VALUES
    SET(NAM:BY_NUMBER)                  !  POINT TO FIRST RECORD
     PREVIOUS(NAMES)                    !READ LAST KEY RECORD
     IF ERROR( )                        !IF THERE WAS AN ERROR
        CLEAR(NAM:RECORD)               !  CLEAR THE RECORD
        KEYFIELD# = 0                   !  INTITIALIZE THE FIELD
        IF KEYFIELD# = 0 THEN KEYFIELD# = 1.!  IF ITS 0 MAKE IT 1
     ELSE                               !ELSE
        KEYFIELD# = NAM:NUMBER + 1      !  INCREMENT FIELD
       .
    CLEAR(NAM:RECORD)                   !CLEAR LAST KEY RECORD
    NAM:NUMBER = KEYFIELD#              !LOAD KEY FIELD
    ADD(NAMES)                          !ESTABLISH RECORD WITH UNIQUE
   IF NOT ERROR( )                      !ADD WAS SUCCESSFUL
      POINTER# = POINTER(NAMES)         ! SAVE POINTER
      ACTION = 5                        ! SET ACTION FOR UPDATE
       BREAK                            !  EXIT LOOP
   . .
  UPD_NAMES                             !  CALL FORM FOR NEW RECORD
  IF ~ACTION                            !  IF RECORD WAS ADDED
   NEWPTR = POINTER(NAMES)              !    SET POINTER TO NEW RECORD
   DO FIND_RECORD                       !    POSITION IN FILE
   .
```

The @AUTONUMESC Code after the Insert Key

```
  IF ACTION                            !FORM WAS NOT COMPLETED
    HOLD(NAMES)                        !HOLD RECORD
    GET(NAMES,POINTER#)                !READ RECORD
    DELETE(NAMES)                      !DELETE RECORD
    DO SAME_PAGE
   .
```

shown in the simple electronic mail program in Figure 15-6. (The source code for the MAIL program appears at the end of this chapter.)

The Record Pre-Image: Two pieces of information are stored by the Designer Form Procedure when the procedure starts up:

1. A pre-image of the record.
2. An implicit variable to store the physical action under way and one for the logical action under way.

The memory table for the record pre-image is shown in Figure 15-7. The record area in Figure 15-7 is stored in an array of bytes dimensioned to the size of the memory image of all the fields in memory for the record.

Once the memory table with the record pre-image is stored, the Designer model for the Form Procedure looks for the autonumbering function by checking to see if the ACTION global variable was set to 5 to indicate that the file had an autonumbered key. If it does, the DISK_ACTN# gets set so the numbering can be claimed in the correct order. Note in Figure 15-8 that the next step is to save the physical pointer location in the file based on the DISK_ACTN# implicit variable.

Figure 15-6   The notification a Designer-generated application displays when you try to save a record that was edited by another station since the record was read.

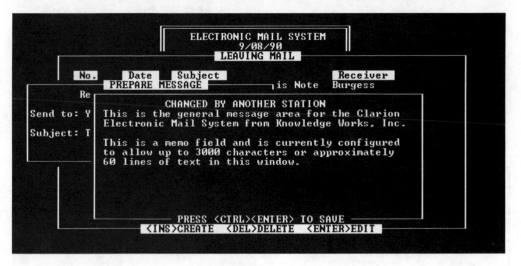

Figure 15-7   The record Pre-image memory table.

```
TABLE           TABLE,PRE(SAV)
SAVE_RECORD     GROUP;BYTE,DIM(SIZE(NAM:RECORD)).
                .
```

Processing of the fields in the form proceeds identically to that for a single-user system until you reach the LAST_FIELD processing. Since, in a Form Procedure, this is where the program actually writes the new or changed record to the disk, it becomes the critical point for multiuser processing. If a collision with another workstation working on the same record is bound to occur, this is where it will happen.

Figure 15-8   The opening sequence for a Network Model–based Form Procedure from Designer.

```
CODE
OPEN(SCREEN)                           !OPEN THE SCREEN
SETCURSOR                              !TURN OFF ANY CURSOR
SAVE_RECORD = NAM:RECORD               !SAVE THE ORIGINAL
ADD(TABLE,1)                           !STORE IN MEMORY TABLE
IF ACTION = 5                          !AUTONUMBER ACTION
  DISK_ACTN# = 2                       !  SET FOR PHYSICAL ACTION
  ACTION = 1                           !  SET FOR LOGICAL ACTION
ELSE                                   !OTHERWISE
  DISK_ACTN# = ACTION                  !  SET ACTION FOR DISK WRITE
  .
DISPLAY                                !DISPLAY THE FIELDS

EXECUTE DISK_ACTN#                     !SET THE CURRENT RECORD POINTER
  POINTER# = 0                         !  NO RECORD FOR ADD
  POINTER# = POINTER(NAMES)            !  CURRENT RECORD FOR CHANGE
  POINTER# = POINTER(NAMES)            !  CURRENT RECORD FOR CHANGE
  .
```

LAST_FIELD Processing:　　The following list narrates the events depicted in Figure 15-9 that take place when the user is exiting normally from a Form Procedure:

- If ACTION = 2 (update), save the current image of the record in the memory table and set record read to HOLD; otherwise (adding or deleting), simply execute the action and look for an error that might indicate a conflict.
- Retrieve the record from the disk. If it was deleted before, replace it on the disk, otherwise, compare the record pre-image to the new one from the disk. If they differ, inform the user and place the contents of the new record onto the screen (losing the changes this user made) and recycle the Editing Procedure to the top of the form.
- Continue with normal secondary file processing and calls to the NEXT-FORM.

Saving Your Changes:　　As you can see from Figure 15-9, the changes made by the local user are lost if the record is read by both the local user and one other, but they are saved by the other user in the First-Out-Wins protocol used by the network model. You can make some simple changes to the model to retain your edits at the local workstation in order to refresh the edit screen even if the record was already saved by another user. This helps prevent situations in which someone spends an extended amount of time processing a complex transaction and then loses those changes because they came in second on the update.

> ### *WARNING*
> **Remember, not all the variables in the record may be displayed on the screen. The record images may not match and the reason may not be apparent from an inspection of the current Edit Procedure. In those cases, be sure to provide the user with some method for checking all the fields in the record before accepting or rejecting the data changed by another user.**

To save those edits, set up a second save area in the variable definition area of the local Form Procedure. Create it to be similar to the record pre-image memory table already in the network model, but with different names (SAVE_RECORD_2 was used in Figure 15-9). Before the reread of the new disk record and HOLD of the record, save the buffer area to the second SAVE_ area. Then pause for a keystroke from the user while they inspect the

Figure 15-9   The LAST_FIELD process on normal exit from a form in the ELECTRONIC MAIL program.

```
OF ?LAST FIELD                          !FROM THE LAST FIELD
   IF ACTION = 2 OR ACTION = 3          !IF UPDATING RECORD
      SAVE_RECORD = NAM:RECORD          !  SAVE CURRENT CHANGES
```

> **Insert the code to save the edited version of a record here.**

```
      ADD(TABLE,2)                      !  STORE IN MEMORY TABLE
      GET(TABLE,1)                      !  RETRIEVE ORIGINAL RECORD
      HOLD(NAMES)                       !  HOLD FILE
      GET(NAMES,POINTER#)               !  RE-READ SAME RECORD
      IF ERRORCODE( ) = 35              !  IF RECORD WAS DELETED
         IF DISK_ACTN# = 2              !  IF TRYING TO UPDATE
           DISK_ACTN# = 1               !    THEN ADD IT BACK
         ELSE                           !
           RELEASE(NAMES)               !  RELEASE FILE
           ACTION = 0                   !  TURN OFF ACTION
         .
      ELSIF |                           !OTHERWISE
        NAM:RECORD <> SAVE_RECORD       !    BY ANOTHER STATION
        MEM:MESSAGE = 'CHANGED BY ANOTHER STATION' !INFORM USER
        SELECT(2)                       ! GO BACK TO TOP OF FORM
        BEEP                            !  SOUND ALARM
        RELEASE(NAMES)                  !  RELEASE FILE
        SAVE_RECORD = NAM:RECORD        !  SAVE RECORD
```

> **Insert the following code to inspect the changes made by another user and then restore the edits from the local station that had been rejected.**
>
> ```
>         DISPLAY                         !DISPLAY CHANGED RECORD
>         ASK                             !PAUSE TO INSPECT
>         NAM:RECORD = SAVE_RECORD_2      !RESTORE EDITS
>         DISPLAY                         !DISPLAY REJECTED EDITS
> ```

```
        DISPLAY                         !  DISPLAY THE FIELDS
         PUT(TABLE)                     !  FREE SAVED CHANGES
      CYCLE                             ! AND CONTINUE
      .
```

(continued)

Figure 15-9 *continued*

```
        GET(TABLE,2)                   ! READ CURRENT (CHANGED) REC
        NAM:RECORD = SAVE_RECORD       ! MOVE RECORD
        DELETE(TABLE)                  ! DELETE MEMORY TABLE ITEM
      .
    EXECUTE DISK_ACTN#                 ! UPDATE THE FILE
      ADD(NAMES)                       !   ADD NEW RECORD
      PUT(NAMES)                       !   CHANGE EXISTING RECORD
      DELETE(NAMES)                    !   DELETE EXISTING RECORD
      .
    IF ERRORCODE( ) = 40               ! DUPLICATE KEY ERROR
      MEM:MESSAGE = ERROR( )           !   DISPLAY ERR MESSAGE
      SELECT(2)                        !   POSITION TO TOP OF FORM
      IF ACTION = 2 THEN RELEASE(NAMES).  !   RELEASE HELD RECORD
      CYCLE                            !   GET OUT OF EDIT LOOP
    ELSIF ERROR( )                     ! CHECK FOR UNEXPECTED ERROR
      STOP(ERROR( ))                   !   HALT EXECUTION
      .
  IF ACTION = 1 THEN POINTER# = POINTER(NAMES). !POINT TO RECORD
    SAVE_RECORD = NAM:RECORD           ! NEW ORIGINAL
    ACTION = ACTION#                   ! RETRIEVE ORIGINAL OPERATION
    ACTION = 0                         ! SET ACTION TO COMPLETE
    BREAK                              ! AND RETURN TO CALLER
  .
```

information from the second workstation. After the keystroke, restore the data from the second saved area and return to the top of the form to allow the user to make any additional changes based on what he or she saw had been changed by the second user.

The Famous "Deadly Embrace"

The *Clarion Language Reference* refers to the "Deadly Embrace." Since the business of managing multiple user's access to the same data involves record and file locking, there is the possibility that you will create a situation like the one depicted in Figure 15-10 where two workstations have locked a record or a file and are waiting for the other station to release it. If each station locked the same file that their neighbor wishes to access while waiting for the file or record already locked by that same neighbor, the system goes into an endless wait.

> ### *WARNING*
> **The application can get hung up in a "Deadly Embrace" via record HOLD or file LOCK or a combination of the two (one station holds a record while another locks a file).**

The establishing of record locks only at UPDATE time in Designer's network model narrows the possibility for entering into a deadly embrace by reducing the time window for access to the common data files. However, the danger of a collision still exists. You can avoid this problem in two ways:

1. You can use the SECONDS parameter of the LOCK and HOLD statements in conjunction with the LOCK and HOLD statement's ability to return an error after an illegal access when you include the SECONDS parameter.
2. You can use the portal file, discussed earlier in this chapter.

The *Clarion Language Reference* provides two examples, one for the file level and one for the record level, that demonstrate schemes using the first solution to avoid hanging the system in a Deadly Embrace. These schemes

Figure 15-10 Two stations attempting to lock two or more resources in opposite order resulting in the "deadly embrace."

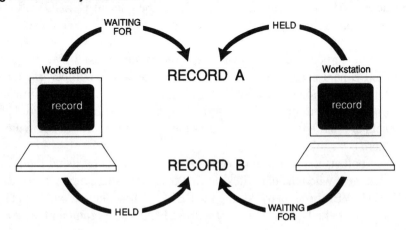

attempt to issue a LOCK or HOLD on all the resources required by a particular transaction. At each attempt to LOCK or HOLD a file, a test is run to look for an error stating that the file is already tied to another workstation. If any file cannot be accessed for any reason, the files that were successfully locked or held are released. In other words, either all the resources for a transaction are tied to the workstation performing the update or none of them is. This locking and checking procedure is placed inside a LOOP statement that continues to poll the files until it successfully grabs all the resources it needs.

For highly complex transactions, you can provide a simpler approach to policing the resource commitment process through the use of the portal file. First, you must identify the combinations of resources that will be needed to perform different types of system updates. The second step is to identify the top-most file that will be committed first to each transaction. The third step is to ensure that the portal file receives notice whenever one of these "lead" files (applicable to record HOLDing schemes, too) gets tied up.

The last step (in the checking process, not the resultant response) is to use a Case structure or some other decision system to evaluate a request from a workstation to lock one of those "lead" files in order to lock a series of files for an update. In this scene, you simply loop until the "lead" file is released by the other station and then issue the LOCK or HOLD calls to all the resources required for the transaction. The danger and burden of this approach is that the applications programmer must accurately structure the permission schemes for which lead files will be allowed to initiate the commitment of which related files.

If a transaction fails for some reason and leaves a file locked, the only way to unlock the file is by arming the RECOVER process. That is, if you LOCK a file and then the system loses power or hangs up for some reason, Clarion's ability to find and unlock that file is lost. You must use RECOVER at the start of the program to handle these previously locked files to gain access to them again.

You can ensure that no file stays abnormally locked by setting the SEC-ONDS parameter of the RECOVER statement to a number greater than the longest duration of exclusive control (for example, the longest time it takes to update a record or log a transaction, or the longest time the record should be held or the file locked). This causes the recovery process to begin the moment there is trouble.

Another way you can ensure system integrity is by using the RECOVER statement when the data files are first opened in share mode. Next, disarm the RECOVER process by issuing the RECOVER statement with no parameters. Then, use the LOCK statement with a SECONDS parameter that is as long as it would take for the longest conceivable transaction in your application to complete. If, for some reason, you continue to get errors from the LOCK statement (and it only returns errors if the SECONDS parameter was used) you can always restart everything and try the recovery process again.

The Concept of a Business Transaction

Updating a database, even if it's just one record in one file, should be viewed as a transaction—the term used earlier in this chapter to refer to file access actions. Only one user at a time should be able to update the database to reduce the possibility of confusion. So, you can see that the file controls of HOLD and LOCK apply to more than physical collisions and confusions, but also to logical ones. HOLD and LOCK become part of the tools you can use to maintain the integrity of the database and the transaction commands listed in Figure 15-1 become the other half of the picture.

By dealing with database updates as transactions, you can keep track of all the smaller moves that the user makes to update a database. Clarion provides a complete set of tools to ensure that your transaction processing is effective and painless.

Basically, the scheme that Clarion uses (depicted in Figure 15-11) is to make notes about each action a user performs during a transaction, including what was changed and the old and new values. You can hold onto these notes for as long as you have memory and disk space to support them. However, when you COMMIT the transaction, these files are disposed of and the transaction is complete.

The purpose of the notes is to allow you to *reverse the transaction like rewinding a cassette tape*. You can replace everything just as you found it—based on the notes you kept—through the ROLLBACK statement. ROLLBACK, like pressing the rewind button on a tape player, resets all the values back to their original state in each of the files affected by the transaction. Those notes appear in two files: the "what" part is maintained in a file called the Transaction Logout File and the values appear in pre-image files. The Transaction Logout File is created with the LOGOUT statement and the pre-image files are created when LOGOUT starts transaction logging and defaults to the name of the file being logged with the DOS file extension .LOG.

The whole point of the ROLLBACK capability is to put everything back the way you found it if, for some reason, you were unable to make all the changes you had in mind. Incomplete transactions could result from accidental power loss or a misread on the magnetic media. In any case, performing a

Figure 15-11   The transaction logging of a transaction from one workstation.

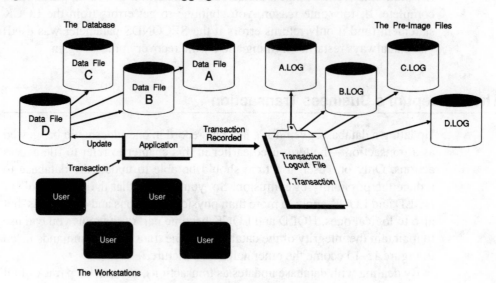

ROLLBACK when you first start an application ensures that any misfired transactions that were in progress when the system was aborted were immediately "rewound" so that the database returns to its last healthy state.

You should use only one Transaction Logout File per union of files (that is, files related to one another and thus affected by the transaction). This prevents confusion when you issue the ROLLBACK. The one situation in which you can use more than one logout file is when the files monitored in each logout file have nothing to do with each other. You will defeat the purpose of logging if one transaction ROLLBACK walks all over another one. You will lose the integrity of the system.

Transaction logging, or "pre-imaging," defines the "commit boundary" of a logical business transaction. Logging begins with the naming of the transaction logout file in the LOGOUT statement. Pre-image log files provide the means to back out of the transaction, returning the data to its original form, in the event that the transaction is unsuccessful.

You are not overlooking something if you miss the LOGOUT statement in the "Example of the LOGOUT statement:" on page 11-61 of Version 2.1 *Clarion Language Reference*. This sample program does not properly operate the second call to the ROLLBACK statement nor does it demonstrate how the LOGOUT statement works since that statement is not issued in the program. Also, since this sample code begins with the PROGRAM statement, there are no other proper ways for the Transaction Logout File to be established. In the case of an incomplete transaction due to system failure, the call to ROLL-BACK in the fourth line after the CODE statement would repair the transaction that was in progress when the system failed. This call to ROLLBACK is good programming practice for maintaining the system integrity in case there had been a failure just prior to the start of this TEST program. For the transactions in this sample program to work properly, however, the LOGOUT statement must explicitly specify the Transaction Logout File prior to the ADD statement to record that change to the TEST data file of the data entered into the ASK variable.

> ### *WARNING*
> **Clarion transaction logging affects only Clarion files and is not applicable to DOS files updated by Clarion programs.** *You cannot ROLLBACK information written to a DOS file.*

ADD, PUT, DELETE, or APPEND statements cause original data and key information to be saved in pre-image files during the login procedure. COMMIT terminates logging directly, whereas RUN, CHAIN, CALL, CREATE, EMPTY, PACK, RETURN, or any normal program termination implies a COMMIT, terminates logging, and erases the logout file and the associated pre-image log files.

The ROLLBACK statement turns off transaction logging, restores files updated during the transaction using pre-image logs and the Transaction Logout file, and deletes pre-image and transaction logs. If the RECOVER statement is used, an implicit ROLLBACK may be executed when a program terminates abnormally.

> ### *WARNING*
> **Statements not undone on ROLLBACK include OPEN, SHARE, CLOSE, BUFFER, CACHE, STREAM, FLUSH, SET, NEXT, PREVIOUS, GET, SKIP, and COPY.**

Summary

In this chapter, we discussed the facilities that Clarion provides for creating and managing a multiuser application. The most important subject woven through every aspect of this chapter was the user's control of access to data to avoid collisions and irresolvable mutual file locking (the deadly embrace). We discussed how a Clarion application can freeze out all but one workstation at the record and file level during an update. We reviewed how the transactions are constructed and managed in order to minimize the actual direct access time by any one workstation, and how to build in safety features in case of a system crash or collision between workstations over the same record or file.

The ELECTRONIC MAIL Program

MAIL.CLA

```
MAIL       PROGRAM
                INCLUDE('STD_KEYS.CLA')
                INCLUDE('CTL_KEYS.CLA')
                INCLUDE('ALT_KEYS.CLA')
                INCLUDE('SHF_KEYS.CLA')

REJECT_KEY    EQUATE(CTRL_ESC)
ACCEPT_KEY    EQUATE(CTRL_ENTER)
TRUE          EQUATE(1)
FALSE         EQUATE(0)

                MAP
                  PROC(G_OPENFILES)
                  MODULE('MAIL01')
                        PROC(MAIN)                      !ELECTRONIC MAIL SYSTEM
                    .
                  MODULE('MAIL02')
                        PROC(SHO_LAST)                  !Show Names By Last
                    .
                  MODULE('MAIL03')
                        PROC(UPD_NAMES)                 !Update Names
                    .
                  MODULE('MAIL04')
                        PROC(RPT_LAST)                  !Print Names By Last
                    .
                  MODULE('MAIL05')
                        PROC(NEW_MESSAGE)               !PREPARE MESSAGE
                    .
                  MODULE('MAIL06')
                        PROC(NOTE)                      !MESSAGE TEXT
                    .
                  MODULE('MAIL07')
                        PROC(PICK_NAME)                 !Show Names By Last
                    .
                  MODULE('MAIL08')
                        PROC(NO_MESSAGE)                !NO MESSAGES AVAILABLE
                    .
                  MODULE('MAIL09')
                        PROC(SIGN_ON)                   !Show Names By Last
                    .
                  MODULE('MAIL10')
```

(continued)

```
                        PROC(LEAVEMAIL)
                .

            MODULE('MAIL11')
                PROC(READMAIL)
                .

            .
            EJECT('FILE LAYOUTS')
NAMES     FILE,PRE(NAM),CREATE,RECLAIM
BY_LAST         KEY(NAM:LAST,NAM:NUMBER),DUP,NOCASE,OPT
BY_NUMBER       KEY(NAM:NUMBER),NOCASE,OPT
RECORD          RECORD
NUMBER              SHORT
NAME                GROUP                       !WHOLE NAME
FIRST                   STRING(10)
LAST                    STRING(20)
                .
            . .


MESSAGES FILE,PRE(MES),CREATE,RECLAIM
BY_MESSAGE      KEY(MES:NUMBER,MES:MESSAGE_NUM),DUP,NOCASE,OPT
BY_OUTGOING     KEY(MES:SENDER_NUM,MES:NUMBER,MES:MESSAGE_NUM),NOCASE,OPT
NOTES           MEMO(3000)                      !THE MESSAGE
RECORD          RECORD
NUMBER              SHORT                        !USER NUMBER
MESSAGE_NUM         LONG                         !NUMBER OF MESSAGE
SENDER_NUM          SHORT                        !SENDER'S NUMBER
DATE                STRING(@D1)                  !DATE OF MESSAGE
SUBJECT             STRING(25)                   !SUBJECT OF MAIL MESSAGE
            . .
            GROUP,OVER(MES:NOTES)
MES_MEMO_ROW    STRING(50),DIM(60)
            .


            EJECT('GLOBAL MEMORY VARIABLES')
ACTION      SHORT                           !0 = NO ACTION
                                            !1 = ADD RECORD
                                            !2 = CHANGE RECORD
                                            !3 = DELETE RECORD
                                            !4 = LOOKUP FIELD
                                            !5 = AUTONUMKEY ADD
            GROUP,PRE(MEM)
MESSAGE         STRING(30)                  !Global Message Area
PAGE            SHORT                       !Report Page Number
LINE            SHORT                       !Report Line Number
DEVICE          STRING(30)                  !Report Device Name
READ            STRING(1)                   !MARK FOR MESSAGES READ
            .
```

(continued)

```
            EJECT('CODE SECTION')
CODE
SETHUE(7,0)                                        !SET WHITE ON BLACK
BLANK                                              !  AND BLANK
RECOVER(60)                                        !HOLDS TIMEOUT IN 60 SECONDS
G_OPENFILES                                        !OPEN OR CREATE FILES
SETHUE()                                           !    THE SCREEN
MAIN                                               !ELECTRONIC MAIL SYSTEM
RETURN                                             !EXIT TO DOS


G_OPENFILES  PROCEDURE                             !OPEN FILES & CHECK FOR ERROR
  CODE
  SHOW(25,1,CENTER('SHARING FILE: ' & 'NAMES',80)) !DISPLAY FILE NAME
  SHARE(NAMES)                                      !OPEN THE FILE IN SHARED MODE
  IF ERROR()                                        !OPEN RETURNED AN ERROR
    CASE ERRORCODE()                                ! CHECK FOR SPECIFIC ERROR
    OF 46                                           !  KEYS NEED TO BE REQUILT
      SETHUE(0,7)                                   !  BLACK ON WHITE
      SHOW(25,1,CENTER('REBUILDING KEY FILES FOR NAMES',80)) !INDICATE MSG
      CLOSE(NAMES)                                  !  LET BUILD OPEN FILE UNSHARED
      BUILD(NAMES)                                  !  CALL THE BUILD PROCEDURE
      CLOSE(NAMES)                                  !  CLOSE UNSHARED FILE
      SHARE(NAMES)                                  !  OPEN FILE SHARED
      SETHUE(7,0)                                   !  WHITE ON BLACK
      BLANK(25,1,1,80)                              !  BLANK THE MESSAGE
    OF 2                                            !IF NOT FOUND,
      CREATE(NAMES)                                 !  THEN CREATE
      CLOSE(NAMES)                                  !  CLOSE IT SO IT CAN
      SHARE(NAMES)                                  !   BE OPENED SHARED
    ELSE                                            ! ANY OTHER ERROR
      LOOP;STOP('NAMES: ' & ERROR()).               !  STOP EXECUTION
  . .

  SHOW(25,1,CENTER('SHARING FILE: ' & 'MESSAGES',80)) !DISPLAY FILE NAME
  SHARE(MESSAGES)                                   !OPEN THE FILE IN SHARED MODE
  IF ERROR()                                        !OPEN RETURNED AN ERROR
    CASE ERRORCODE()                                ! CHECK FOR SPECIFIC ERROR
    OF 46                                           !  KEYS NEED TO BE REQUILT
      SETHUE(0,7)                                   !  BLACK ON WHITE
      SHOW(25,1,CENTER('REBUILDING KEY FILES FOR MESSAGES',80)) !INDICATE MSG
      CLOSE(MESSAGES)                               !  LET BUILD OPEN FILE UNSHARED
      BUILD(MESSAGES)                               !  CALL THE BUILD PROCEDURE
      CLOSE(MESSAGES)                               !  CLOSE UNSHARED FILE
      SHARE(MESSAGES)                               !  OPEN FILE SHARED
      SETHUE(7,0)                                   !  WHITE ON BLACK
      BLANK(25,1,1,80)                              !  BLANK THE MESSAGE
    OF 2                                            !IF NOT FOUND,
```

(continued)

```
        CREATE(MESSAGES)                    !   THEN CREATE
        CLOSE(MESSAGES)                     !   CLOSE IT SO IT CAN
        SHARE(MESSAGES)                     !     BE OPENED SHARED
     ELSE                                   ! ANY OTHER ERROR
        LOOP;STOP('MESSAGES: ' & ERROR()).  !  STOP EXECUTION
  . .

     BLANK                                  !BLANK THE SCREEN
```

MAIL01.CLA

```
          MEMBER('MAIL')
MAIN          PROCEDURE

SCREEN        SCREEN      PRE(SCR),WINDOW(16,31),HUE(15,3)
              ROW(1,1)    PAINT(4,31),HUE(15,1)
                   COL(1) STRING('<201,205{29},187>'),HUE(15,1)
              ROW(2,1)    REPEAT(3);STRING('<186,0{29},186>'),HUE(15,1) .
              ROW(5,1)    REPEAT(11);STRING('<186,0{29},186>'),HUE(15,3) .
              ROW(16,1)   STRING('<200,205{29},188>'),HUE(15,3)
              ROW(2,6)    STRING('ELECTRONIC MAIL SYSTEM')
DATE          ROW(3,13)   STRING(@D1),HUE(15,1)
                          ENTRY,USE(?FIRST_FIELD)
                          ENTRY,USE(?PRE_MENU)
                          MENU,USE(MENU_FIELD"),REQ
              ROW(6,9)        STRING('E-Mail Addresses'),HUE(15,3),SEL(0,7)
              ROW(8,12)       STRING('Read Mail'),HUE(15,3),SEL(0,7)
              ROW(10,12)      STRING('Leave Mail'),HUE(15,3),SEL(0,7)
              ROW(12,8)       STRING('Print Address List'),HUE(15,3),SEL(0,7)
              ROW(14,15)      STRING('Quit'),HUE(15,3),SEL(0,7)

                 .         .

     EJECT
     CODE
     OPEN(SCREEN)                          !OPEN THE MENU SCREEN
     SETCURSOR                             !TURN OFF ANY CURSOR
     MENU_FIELD" = ''                      !START MENU WITH FIRST ITEM
     LOOP                                  !LOOP UNTIL USER EXITS
       SCR:DATE = TODAY()
       ALERT                               !TURN OFF ALL ALERTED KEYS
       ALERT(REJECT_KEY)                   !ALERT SCREEN REJECT KEY
       ALERT(ACCEPT_KEY)                   !ALERT SCREEN ACCEPT KEY
       ACCEPT                              !READ A FIELD OR MENU CHOICE
       IF KEYCODE() = REJECT_KEY THEN RETURN.   !RETURN ON SCREEN REJECT
```

(continued)

```
      IF KEYCODE() = ACCEPT_KEY                !ON SCREEN ACCEPT KEY
        UPDATE                                 !  MOVE ALL FIELDS FROM SCREEN
        SELECT(?)                              !  START WITH CURRENT FIELD
        SELECT                                 !  EDIT ALL FIELDS
        CYCLE                                  !  GO TO TOP OF LOOP
      .                                        !

      CASE FIELD()                             !JUMP TO FIELD EDIT ROUTINE
      OF ?FIRST_FIELD                          !FROM THE FIRST FIELD
        IF KEYCODE() = ESC_KEY THEN RETURN.    !  RETURN ON ESC KEY

      OF ?PRE_MENU                             !PRE MENU FIELD CONDITION
        IF KEYCODE() = ESC_KEY                 !  BACKING UP?
          SELECT(?-1)                          !    SELECT PREVIOUS FIELD
        ELSE                                   !  GOING FORWARD
          SELECT(?+1)                          !    SELECT MENU FIELD
        .

      OF ?MENU_FIELD"                          !FROM THE MENU FIELD
        EXECUTE CHOICE()                       !  CALL THE SELECTED PROCEDURE
          SHO_LAST                             !        Show Names By Last
          READMAIL                             !
          LEAVEMAIL                            !
          RPT_LAST                             !        Print Names By Last
          RETURN
    . . .
```

MAIL02.CLA

```
              MEMBER('MAIL')
SHO_LAST      PROCEDURE

SCREEN        SCREEN      PRE(SCR),WINDOW(24,32),HUE(15,1)
              ROW(6,1)    PAINT(17,32),HUE(0,7)
              ROW(1,1)    STRING('<201,205{30},187>'),HUE(15,1)
              ROW(2,1)    REPEAT(22);STRING('<186,0{30},186>'),HUE(15,1) .
              ROW(24,1)   STRING('<200,205{30},188>'),HUE(15,1)
              ROW(2,8)    STRING('Show Names By Last')
              ROW(4,4)    STRING('LOCATE:'),HUE(11,1)
              ROW(23,6)   STRING('PRESS <<ENTER> TO SELECT')
LOCATOR       ROW(4,11)   STRING(20),HUE(11,1)
                          ENTRY,USE(?FIRST_FIELD)
                          ENTRY,USE(?PRE_POINT)
                          REPEAT(17),EVERY(1),INDEX(NDX)
              ROW(6,2)      POINT(1,30),USE(?POINT),ESC(?-1)
NAME              COL(2)    STRING(@s30)
```

(continued)

```
NDX          BYTE                              !REPEAT INDEX FOR POINT AREA
ROW          BYTE                              !ACTUAL ROW OF SCROLL AREA
COL          BYTE                              !ACTUAL COLUMN OF SCROLL AREA
COUNT        BYTE(17)                          !NUMBER OF ITEMS TO SCROLL
ROWS         BYTE(17)                          !NUMBER OF ROWS TO SCROLL
COLS         BYTE(30)                          !NUMBER OF COLUMNS TO SCROLL
FOUND        BYTE                              !RECORD FOUND FLAG
NEWPTR       LONG                              !POINTER TO NEW RECORD

TABLE        TABLE,PRE(TBL)                    !TABLE OF RECORD DATA
NAME           STRING(@s30)
LAST           STRING(20)
NUMBER         SHORT
PTR            LONG                            !  POINTER TO FILE RECORD


  EJECT
  CODE
  ACTION# = ACTION                             !SAVE ACTION
  OPEN(SCREEN)                                 !OPEN THE SCREEN
  SETCURSOR                                    !TURN OFF ANY CURSOR
  TBL:PTR = 1                                  !START AT TABLE ENTRY
  NDX = 1                                      !PUT SELECTOR BAR ON TOP ITEM
  ROW = ROW(?POINT)                            !REMEMBER TOP ROW AND
  COL = COL(?POINT)                            !LEFT COLUMN OF SCROLL AREA
  RECORDS# = TRUE                              !INITIALIZE RECORDS FLAG
  IF ACTION = 4                                !  TABLE LOOKUP REQUEST
    NEWPTR = POINTER(NAMES)                    !  SET POINTER TO RECORD
    IF NOT NEWPTR                              !  RECORD NOT PASSED TO TABLE
      SET(NAM:BY_LAST,NAM:BY_LAST)             !    POSITION TO CLOSEST RECORD
      NEXT(NAMES)                              !    READ RECORD
      NEWPTR = POINTER(NAMES)                  !    SET POINTER
    .
    DO FIND_RECORD                             !  POSITION FILE
  ELSE
    NDX = 1                                    !  PUT SELECTOR BAR ON TOP ITEM
    DO FIRST_PAGE                              !  BUILD MEMORY TABLE OF KEYS
  .
  RECORDS# = TRUE                              !  ASSUME THERE ARE RECORDS
  LOOP                                         !LOOP UNTIL USER EXITS
    ACTION = ACTION#                           !RESTORE ACTION
    ALERT                                      !RESET ALERTED KEYS
    ALERT(REJECT_KEY)                          !ALERT SCREEN REJECT KEY
    ALERT(ACCEPT_KEY)                          !ALERT SCREEN ACCEPT KEY
    ACCEPT                                     !READ A FIELD
    IF KEYCODE() = REJECT_KEY THEN BREAK.      !RETURN ON SCREEN REJECT KEY
```

(continued)

```
IF  KEYCODE() = ACCEPT_KEY      |           !ON SCREEN ACCEPT KEY
AND FIELD() <> ?POINT                       !BUT NOT ON THE POINT FIELD
  UPDATE                                    !  MOVE ALL FIELDS FROM SCREEN
  SELECT(?)                                 !  START WITH CURRENT FIELD
  SELECT                                    !  EDIT ALL FIELDS
  CYCLE                                     !  GO TO TOP OF LOOP
  .


CASE FIELD()                                !JUMP TO FIELD EDIT ROUTINE

OF ?FIRST_FIELD                             !FROM THE FIRST FIELD
  IF KEYCODE() = ESC_KEY    |               !  RETURN ON ESC KEY
  OR RECORDS# = FALSE                       !  OR NO RECORDS
    BREAK                                   !    EXIT PROGRAM
  .
OF ?PRE_POINT                               !PRE POINT FIELD CONDITION
  IF KEYCODE() = ESC_KEY                    !  BACKING UP?
    SELECT(?-1)                             !    SELECT PREVIOUS FIELD
  ELSE                                      !  GOING FORWARD
    SELECT(?POINT)                          !    SELECT MENU FIELD
  .
IF KEYCODE() = ESC_KEY                      !  BACKING UP?
  SCR:LOCATOR = ''                          !    CLEAR LOCATOR
  SETCURSOR                                 !    AND TURN CURSOR OFF
ELSE                                        !  GOING FORWARD
  LEN# = 0                                  !    RESET TO START OF LOCATOR
  SETCURSOR(ROW(SCR:LOCATOR),COL(SCR:LOCATOR)) !  AND TURN CURSOR ON
  .
OF ?POINT                                   !PROCESS THE POINT FIELD
  IF RECORDS(TABLE) = 0                     !IF THERE ARE NO RECORDS
    CLEAR(NAM:RECORD)                       !  CLEAR RECORD AREA
    UPDATE                                  !  UPDATE ALL FIELDS
    ACTION = 1                              !  SET ACTION TO ADD
    GET(NAMES,0)                            !  CLEAR PENDING RECORD
    LOOP
      CLEAR(NAM:RECORD,1)                   !CLEAR RECORD TO HIGH VALUES
      SET(NAM:BY_NUMBER)                    !  POINT TO FIRST RECORD
      PREVIOUS(NAMES)                       !READ LAST KEY RECORD
      IF ERROR()                            !IF THERE WAS AN ERROR
        CLEAR(NAM:RECORD)                   !  CLEAR THE RECORD
        KEYFIELD# = 3.3155016935788e-181   !  INTITIALIZE THE FIELD
        IF KEYFIELD# = 0 THEN KEYFIELD# = 1.!  IF ITS 0 MAKE IT 1
      ELSE                                  !ELSE
        KEYFIELD# = NAM:NUMBER + 1          !  INCREMENT FIELD
      .
      CLEAR(NAM:RECORD)                     !CLEAR LAST KEY RECORD
      NAM:NUMBER = KEYFIELD#                !LOAD KEY FIELD
```

(continued)

```
      ADD(NAMES)                          !ESTABLISH RECORD WITH UNIQUE
      IF NOT ERROR()                      !ADD WAS SUCCESSFUL
        POINTER# = POINTER(NAMES)         !  SAVE POINTER
        ACTION = 5                        !  SET ACTION FOR UPDATE
        BREAK                             !  EXIT LOOP
      . .
      UPD_NAMES                           !  CALL FORM FOR NEW RECORD
      IF ACTION                           !FORM WAS NOT COMPLETED
        HOLD(NAMES)                       !HOLD RECORD
        GET(NAMES,POINTER#)               !READ RECORD
        DELETE(NAMES)                     !DELETE RECORD
        DO SAME_PAGE
      .
      NEWPTR = POINTER(NAMES)             !    SET POINTER TO NEW RECORD
      DO FIRST_PAGE                       !  DISPLAY THE FIRST PAGE
      IF RECORDS(TABLE) = 0               !  IF THERE AREN'T ANY RECORDS
        RECORDS# = FALSE                  !    INDICATE NO RECORDS
        SELECT(?PRE_POINT-1)              !    SELECT THE PRIOR FIELD
      .
      CYCLE                               !    AND LOOP AGAIN
    .
  IF KEYCODE() > 31              |        !THE DISPLAYABLE CHARACTERS
  AND KEYCODE() < 255                     !ARE USED TO LOCATE RECORDS
    IF LEN# < SIZE(SCR:LOCATOR)           !  IF THERE IS ROOM LEFT
      SCR:LOCATOR = SUB(SCR:LOCATOR,1,LEN#) & CHR(KEYCODE())
      LEN# += 1                           !    INCREMENT THE LENGTH
    .
  ELSIF KEYCODE() = BS_KEY                !BACKSPACE UNTYPES A CHARACTER
    IF LEN# > 0                           !  IF THERE ARE CHARACTERS LEFT
      LEN# -= 1                           !    DECREMENT THE LENGTH
      SCR:LOCATOR = SUB(SCR:LOCATOR,1,LEN#) !    ERASE THE LAST CHARACTER
    .
  ELSE                                    !FOR ANY OTHER CHARACTER
    LEN# = 0                              !  ZERO THE LENGTH
    SCR:LOCATOR = ''                      !  ERASE THE LOCATOR FIELD
  .
  SETCURSOR(ROW(SCR:LOCATOR),COL(SCR:LOCATOR)+LEN#) !AND RESET THE CURSOR
  NAM:LAST = CLIP(SCR:LOCATOR)            !    UPDATE THE KEY FIELD
  IF KEYBOARD() > 31             |        !THE DISPLAYABLE CHARACTERS
  AND KEYBOARD() < 255           |        !ARE USED TO LOCATE RECORDS
  OR KEYBOARD() = BS_KEY                  !INCLUDE BACKSPACE
    CYCLE
  .
  IF LEN# > 0                             !ON A LOCATOR REQUEST
    NAM:LAST = CLIP(SCR:LOCATOR)          !    UPDATE THE KEY FIELD
    SET(NAM:BY_LAST,NAM:BY_LAST)          !  POINT TO NEW RECORD
    NEXT(NAMES)                           !  READ A RECORD
```

(continued)

```
    IF (EOF(NAMES) AND ERROR())            !  IF EOF IS REACHED
      SET(NAM:BY_LAST)                     !    SET TO FIRST RECORD
      PREVIOUS(NAMES)                      !    READ THE LAST RECORD
      .
    NEWPTR = POINTER(NAMES)                !  SET NEW RECORD POINTER
    SKIP(NAMES,-1)                         !  BACK UP TO FIRST RECORD
    FREE(TABLE)                            !  CLEAR THE TABLE
    DO NEXT_PAGE                           !  AND DISPLAY A NEW PAGE
  .
CASE KEYCODE()                             !PROCESS THE KEYSTROKE

OF INS_KEY                                 !INS KEY
  CLEAR(NAM:RECORD)                        !  CLEAR RECORD AREA
  ACTION = 1                               !  SET ACTION TO ADD
  GET(NAMES,0)                             !  CLEAR PENDING RECORD
  LOOP
    CLEAR(NAM:RECORD,1)                    !CLEAR RECORD TO HIGH VALUES
    SET(NAM:BY_NUMBER)                     !  POINT TO FIRST RECORD
    PREVIOUS(NAMES)                        !READ LAST KEY RECORD
    IF ERROR()                             !IF THERE WAS AN ERROR
      CLEAR(NAM:RECORD)                    !  CLEAR THE RECORD
      KEYFIELD# = 0                        !  INTITIALIZE THE FIELD
      IF KEYFIELD# = 0 THEN KEYFIELD# = 1.!  IF ITS 0 MAKE IT 1
    ELSE                                   !ELSE
      KEYFIELD# = NAM:NUMBER + 1           !  INCREMENT FIELD
    .
    CLEAR(NAM:RECORD)                      !CLEAR LAST KEY RECORD
    NAM:NUMBER = KEYFIELD#                 !LOAD KEY FIELD
    ADD(NAMES)                             !ESTABLISH RECORD WITH UNIQUE
    IF NOT ERROR()                         !ADD WAS SUCCESSFUL
      POINTER# = POINTER(NAMES)            !  SAVE POINTER
      ACTION = 5                           !  SET ACTION FOR UPDATE
      BREAK                                !  EXIT LOOP
  . .
  UPD_NAMES                                !  CALL FORM FOR NEW RECORD
  IF ~ACTION                               !  IF RECORD WAS ADDED
    NEWPTR = POINTER(NAMES)                !    SET POINTER TO NEW RECORD
    DO FIND_RECORD                         !    POSITION IN FILE
  .
  IF ACTION                                !FORM WAS NOT COMPLETED
    HOLD(NAMES)                            !HOLD RECORD
    GET(NAMES,POINTER#)                    !READ RECORD
    DELETE(NAMES)                          !DELETE RECORD
    DO SAME_PAGE
  .
OF ENTER_KEY |                             !ENTER KEY
OROF ACCEPT_KEY                            !CTRL-ENTER KEY
```

(continued)

```
    DO GET_RECORD                                  !   GET THE SELECTED RECORD
    IF ACTION = 4 AND KEYCODE() = ENTER_KEY!       IF THIS IS A LOOKUP REQUEST
      ACTION = 0                                    !     SET ACTION TO COMPLETE
      BREAK                                         !     AND RETURN TO CALLER
    .
    IF ~ERROR()                                     !   IF RECORD IS STILL THERE
      ACTION = 2                                    !     SET ACTION TO CHANGE
      UPD_NAMES                                     !     CALL FORM TO CHANGE REC
      IF ACTION THEN CYCLE.                         !     IF SUCCESSFUL RE-DISPLAY
    .
    NEWPTR = POINTER(NAMES)                         !     SET POINTER TO NEW RECORD
    DO FIND_RECORD                                  !     POSITION IN FILE
  OF DEL_KEY                                        !DEL KEY
    DO GET_RECORD                                   !   READ THE SELECTED RECORD
    IF ~ERROR()                                     !   IF RECORD IS STILL THERE
      ACTION = 3                                    !     SET ACTION TO DELETE
      UPD_NAMES                                     !     CALL FORM TO DELETE
      IF ~ACTION                                    !     IF SUCCESSFUL
        N# = NDX                                    !       SAVE POINT INDEX
        DO SAME_PAGE                                !       RE-DISPLAY
        NDX = N#                                    !       RESTORE POINT INDEX
    . .
  OF DOWN_KEY                                       !DOWN ARROW KEY
    DO SET_NEXT                                     !   POINT TO NEXT RECORD
    DO FILL_NEXT                                    !   FILL A TABLE ENTRY
    IF FOUND                                        !   FOUND A NEW RECORD
      SCROLL(ROW,COL,ROWS,COLS,ROWS(?POINT))  !    SCROLL THE SCREEN UP
      GET(TABLE,RECORDS(TABLE))                     !   GET RECORD FROM TABLE
      DO FILL_SCREEN                                !   DISPLAY ON SCREEN
    .

  OF PGDN_KEY                                       !PAGE DOWN KEY
    DO SET_NEXT                                     !   POINT TO NEXT RECORD
    DO NEXT_PAGE                                    !   DISPLAY THE NEXT PAGE

  OF CTRL_PGDN                                      !CTRL-PAGE DOWN KEY
    DO LAST_PAGE                                    !   DISPLAY THE LAST PAGE
    NDX = RECORDS(TABLE)                            !   POSITION POINT BAR

  OF UP_KEY                                         !UP ARROW KEY
    DO SET_PREV                                     !   POINT TO PREVIOUS RECORD
    DO FILL_PREV                                    !   FILL A TABLE ENTRY
    IF FOUND                                        !   FOUND A NEW RECORD
      SCROLL(ROW,COL,ROWS,COLS,-(ROWS(?POINT)))!  SCROLL THE SCREEN DOWN
      GET(TABLE,1)                                  !   GET RECORD FROM TABLE
      DO FILL_SCREEN                                !   DISPLAY ON SCREEN
    .
```

(continued)

```
     OF PGUP_KEY                                 !PAGE UP KEY
       DO SET_PREV                               !   POINT TO PREVIOUS RECORD
       DO PREV_PAGE                              !   DISPLAY THE PREVIOUS PAGE

     OF CTRL_PGUP                                !CTRL-PAGE UP
       DO FIRST_PAGE                             !   DISPLAY THE FIRST PAGE
       NDX = 1                                   !   POSITION POINT BAR
   . . .
   FREE(TABLE)                                   !FREE MEMORY TABLE
   RETURN                                        !AND RETURN TO CALLER

SAME_PAGE ROUTINE                                !DISPLAY THE SAME PAGE
   GET(TABLE,1)                                  !   GET THE FIRST TABLE ENTRY
   DO FILL_RECORD                                !   FILL IN THE RECORD
   SET(NAM:BY_LAST,NAM:BY_LAST,TBL:PTR)          !   POSITION FILE
   FREE(TABLE)                                   !   EMPTY THE TABLE
   DO NEXT_PAGE                                  !   DISPLAY A FULL PAGE

FIRST_PAGE ROUTINE                               !DISPLAY FIRST PAGE
   BLANK(ROW,COL,ROWS,COLS)
   FREE(TABLE)                                   !   EMPTY THE TABLE
   CLEAR(NAM:RECORD,-1)                          !   CLEAR RECORD TO LOW VALUES
   CLEAR(TBL:PTR)                                !   ZERO RECORD POINTER
   SET(NAM:BY_LAST)                              !   POINT TO FIRST RECORD
   LOOP NDX = 1 TO COUNT                         !   FILL UP THE TABLE
     DO FILL_NEXT                                !     FILL A TABLE ENTRY
     IF NOT FOUND THEN BREAK.                    !     GET OUT IF NO RECORD
   .
   NDX = 1                                       !   SET TO TOP OF TABLE
   DO SHOW_PAGE                                  !   DISPLAY THE PAGE

LAST_PAGE ROUTINE                                !DISPLAY LAST PAGE
   NDX# = NDX                                    !   SAVE SELECTOR POSITION
   BLANK(ROW,COL,ROWS,COLS)                      !   CLEAR SCROLLING AREA
   FREE(TABLE)                                   !   EMPTY THE TABLE
   CLEAR(NAM:RECORD,1)                           !   CLEAR RECORD TO HIGH VALUES
   CLEAR(TBL:PTR,1)                              !   CLEAR PTR TO HIGH VALUE
   SET(NAM:BY_LAST)                              !   POINT TO FIRST RECORD
   LOOP NDX = COUNT TO 1 BY -1                   !   FILL UP THE TABLE
     DO FILL_PREV                                !     FILL A TABLE ENTRY
     IF NOT FOUND THEN BREAK.                    !     GET OUT IF NO RECORD
   .
   NDX = NDX#                                    !   RESTORE SELECTOR POSITION
   DO SHOW_PAGE                                  !   DISPLAY THE PAGE

FIND_RECORD ROUTINE                              !POSITION TO SPECIFIC RECORD
   SET(NAM:BY_LAST,NAM:BY_LAST,NEWPTR)           !POSITION FILE
```

(continued)

```
  IF NEWPTR = 0                                !NEWPTR NOT SET
    NEXT(NAMES)                                ! READ NEXT RECORD
    NEWPTR = POINTER(NAMES)                    ! SET NEWPTR
    SKIP(NAMES,-1)                             ! BACK UP TO DISPLAY RECORD
  .
  FREE(TABLE)                                  ! CLEAR THE RECORD
  DO NEXT_PAGE                                 ! DISPLAY A PAGE

NEXT_PAGE ROUTINE                              !DISPLAY NEXT PAGE
  SAVECNT# = RECORDS(TABLE)                    ! SAVE RECORD COUNT
  LOOP COUNT TIMES                             ! FILL UP THE TABLE
    DO FILL_NEXT                               !   FILL A TABLE ENTRY
    IF NOT FOUND                               !   IF NONE ARE LEFT
      IF NOT SAVECNT#                          !     IF REBUILDING TABLE
        DO LAST_PAGE                           !       FILL IN RECORDS
        EXIT                                   !       EXIT OUT OF ROUTINE
      .
      BREAK                                    !     EXIT LOOP
  . .
  DO SHOW_PAGE                                 ! DISPLAY THE PAGE

SET_NEXT ROUTINE                               !POINT TO THE NEXT PAGE
  GET(TABLE,RECORDS(TABLE))                    ! GET THE LAST TABLE ENTRY
  DO FILL_RECORD                               ! FILL IN THE RECORD
  SET(NAM:BY_LAST,NAM:BY_LAST,TBL:PTR)         ! POSITION FILE
  NEXT(NAMES)                                  ! READ THE CURRENT RECORD

FILL_NEXT ROUTINE                              !FILL NEXT TABLE ENTRY
  FOUND = FALSE                                ! ASSUME RECORD NOT FOUND
  LOOP UNTIL EOF(NAMES)                        ! LOOP UNTIL END OF FILE
    NEXT(NAMES)                                !   READ THE NEXT RECORD
    FOUND = TRUE                               !   SET RECORD FOUND
    DO FILL_TABLE                              !   FILL IN THE TABLE ENTRY
    ADD(TABLE)                                 !   ADD LAST TABLE ENTRY
    GET(TABLE,RECORDS(TABLE)-COUNT)            !   GET ANY OVERFLOW RECORD
    DELETE(TABLE)                              !   AND DELETE IT
    EXIT                                       !   RETURN TO CALLER
  .
PREV_PAGE ROUTINE                              !DISPLAY PREVIOUS PAGE
  LOOP COUNT TIMES                             ! FILL UP THE TABLE
    DO FILL_PREV                               !   FILL A TABLE ENTRY
    IF NOT FOUND THEN BREAK.                   !   GET OUT IF NO RECORD
  .
  DO SHOW_PAGE                                 ! DISPLAY THE PAGE

SET_PREV ROUTINE                               !POINT TO PREVIOUS PAGE
  GET(TABLE,1)                                 ! GET THE FIRST TABLE ENTRY
```

(continued)

```
  DO FILL_RECORD                              ! FILL IN THE RECORD
  SET(NAM:BY_LAST,NAM:BY_LAST,TBL:PTR)        ! POSITION FILE
  PREVIOUS(NAMES)                             ! READ THE CURRENT RECORD

FILL_PREV ROUTINE                             !FILL PREVIOUS TABLE ENTRY
  FOUND = FALSE                               ! ASSUME RECORD NOT FOUND
  LOOP UNTIL BOF(NAMES)                        ! LOOP UNTIL BEGINNING OF FILE
    PREVIOUS(NAMES)                           !   READ THE PREVIOUS RECORD
    FOUND = TRUE                              !   SET RECORD FOUND
    DO FILL_TABLE                             !   FILL IN THE TABLE ENTRY
    ADD(TABLE,1)                              !   ADD FIRST TABLE ENTRY
    GET(TABLE,COUNT+1)                        !   GET ANY OVERFLOW RECORD
    DELETE(TABLE)                             !   AND DELETE IT
    EXIT                                      !   RETURN TO CALLER
  .

SHOW_PAGE ROUTINE                             !DISPLAY THE PAGE.
  NDX# = NDX                                  ! SAVE SCREEN INDEX
  LOOP NDX = 1 TO RECORDS(TABLE)              ! LOOP THRU THE TABLE
    GET(TABLE,NDX)                            !   GET A TABLE ENTRY
    DO FILL_SCREEN                            !   AND DISPLAY IT
    IF TBL:PTR = NEWPTR                       !   SET INDEX FOR NEW RECORD
      NDX# = NDX                              !   POINT TO CORRECT RECORD
  . .
  NDX = NDX#                                  ! RESTORE SCREEN INDEX
  NEWPTR = 0                                  ! CLEAR NEW RECORD POINTER
  CLEAR(NAM:RECORD)                           ! CLEAR RECORD AREA

FILL_TABLE ROUTINE                            !MOVE FILE TO TABLE
  TBL:LAST = NAM:LAST
  TBL:NUMBER = NAM:NUMBER
  TBL:PTR = POINTER(NAMES)                    ! SAVE RECORD POINTER
  TBL:NAME = CENTER(clip(nam:last) & ', ' & clip(nam:first),30)

FILL_RECORD ROUTINE                           !MOVE TABLE TO FILE
  NAM:LAST = TBL:LAST
  NAM:NUMBER = TBL:NUMBER

FILL_SCREEN ROUTINE                           !MOVE TABLE TO SCREEN
  SCR:NAME = TBL:NAME

GET_RECORD ROUTINE                            !GET SELECTED RECORD
  GET(TABLE,NDX)                              ! GET TABLE ENTRY
  GET(NAMES,TBL:PTR)                          ! GET THE RECORD
```

MAIL03.CLA

```
          MEMBER('MAIL')
UPD_NAMES    PROCEDURE

SCREEN       SCREEN      PRE(SCR),WINDOW(8,36),HUE(15,4)
             ROW(1,12)   PAINT(1,14),HUE(0,7)
                     COL(1)  STRING('<201,205{10},0{14},205{10},187>'),HUE(15,4)
             ROW(2,1)    REPEAT(6);STRING('<186,0{34},186>'),HUE(15,4)  .
             ROW(8,1)    STRING('<200,205{34},188>'),HUE(15,4)
             ROW(1,13)   STRING('Update Names')
             ROW(4,4)    STRING('First: '),HUE(14,4)
             ROW(5,4)    STRING('Last:'),HUE(14,4)
                     COL(9)  STRING(' '),HUE(7,4)
                     COL(10) STRING(' '),HUE(14,4)
MESSAGE      ROW(2,4)    STRING(30),HUE(7,4)
NUMBER       ROW(3,4)    STRING(@N4),HUE(4,4)
                     ENTRY,USE(?FIRST_FIELD)
             ROW(4,11)   ENTRY(@s10),USE(NAM:FIRST),HUE(15,4),SEL(0,7)
             ROW(5,11)   ENTRY(@s20),USE(NAM:LAST),REQ,HUE(15,4),SEL(0,7)
             ROW(7,8)    PAUSE('Press <<ENTER> to Accept'),USE(?PAUSE_FIELD)  |
                            HUE(14,4)
                     ENTRY,USE(?LAST_FIELD)
                     PAUSE(''),USE(?DELETE_FIELD)
               .
TABLE        TABLE,PRE(SAV)
SAVE_RECORD   GROUP;BYTE,DIM(SIZE(NAM:RECORD)) .
               .

  EJECT
  CODE
  OPEN(SCREEN)                                  !OPEN THE SCREEN
  SETCURSOR                                     !TURN OFF ANY CURSOR
  SAVE_RECORD = NAM:RECORD                       !SAVE THE ORIGINAL
  ADD(TABLE,1)                                  !STORE IN MEMORY TABLE
  IF ACTION = 5                                 !AUTONUMBER ACTION
    DISK_ACTN# = 2                              !  SET FOR PHYSICAL ACTION
    ACTION = 1                                  !  SET FOR LOGICAL ACTION
  ELSE                                          !OTHERWISE
    DISK_ACTN# = ACTION                         !  SET ACTION FOR DISK WRITE
  .
  DISPLAY                                       !DISPLAY THE FIELDS

  EXECUTE DISK_ACTN#                            !SET THE CURRENT RECORD POINTER
    POINTER# = 0                                !  NO RECORD FOR ADD
    POINTER# = POINTER(NAMES)                   !  CURRENT RECORD FOR CHANGE
```

(continued)

```
    POINTER# = POINTER(NAMES)                          !  CURRENT RECORD FOR CHANGE
  .
ACTION# = ACTION                                    !STORE REQUIRED ACTION
LOOP                                                !LOOP THRU ALL THE FIELDS
  MEM:MESSAGE = CENTER(MEM:MESSAGE,SIZE(MEM:MESSAGE)) !DISPLAY ACTION MESSAGE
  DO CALCFIELDS                                     !CALCULATE DISPLAY FIELDS
  ALERT                                             !RESET ALERTED KEYS
  ALERT(ACCEPT_KEY)                                 !ALERT SCREEN ACCEPT KEY
  ALERT(REJECT_KEY)                                 !ALERT SCREEN REJECT KEY
  ACCEPT                                            !READ A FIELD
  IF KEYCODE() = REJECT_KEY THEN BREAK.             !RETURN ON SCREEN REJECT KEY
  EXECUTE ACTION                                    !SET MESSAGE
    MEM:MESSAGE = 'Record will be Added'            !
    MEM:MESSAGE = 'Record will be Changed'          !
    MEM:MESSAGE = 'Press Enter to Delete'           !
  .
  IF KEYCODE() = ACCEPT_KEY                          !ON SCREEN ACCEPT KEY
    UPDATE                                          !  MOVE ALL FIELDS FROM SCREEN
    SELECT(?)                                       !  START WITH CURRENT FIELD
    SELECT                                          !  EDIT ALL FIELDS
    CYCLE                                           !  GO TO TOP OF LOOP
  .
  CASE FIELD()                                       !JUMP TO FIELD EDIT ROUTINE
  OF ?FIRST_FIELD                                    !FROM THE FIRST FIELD
    IF KEYCODE() = ESC_KEY THEN BREAK.              !  RETURN ON ESC KEY
    IF ACTION = 3 THEN SELECT(?DELETE_FIELD).       !  OR CONFIRM FOR DELETE

  OF ?PAUSE_FIELD                                    !ON PAUSE FIELD
    IF KEYCODE() <> ENTER_KEY|                      !IF NOT ENTER KEY
    AND KEYCODE() <> ACCEPT_KEY|                    !AND NOT CTRL-ENTER KEY
    AND KEYCODE() <> 0                              !AND NOT NONSTOP MODE
      BEEP                                          !  SOUND KEYBOARD ALARM
      SELECT(?PAUSE_FIELD)                          !  AND STAY ON PAUSE FIELD
    .

  OF ?LAST_FIELD                                     !FROM THE LAST FIELD
    IF ACTION = 2 OR ACTION = 3                     !IF UPDATING RECORD
      SAVE_RECORD = NAM:RECORD                      !  SAVE CURRENT CHANGES
      ADD(TABLE,2)                                  !  STORE IN MEMORY TABLE
      GET(TABLE,1)                                  !  RETRIEVE ORIGINAL RECORD
      HOLD(NAMES)                                   !  HOLD FILE
      GET(NAMES,POINTER#)                           !  RE-READ SAME RECORD
      IF ERRORCODE() = 35                           !  IF RECORD WAS DELETED
        IF DISK_ACTN# = 2                           !  IF TRYING TO UPDATE
          DISK_ACTN# = 1                            !    THEN ADD IT BACK
        ELSE                                        !
          RELEASE(NAMES)                            !  RELEASE FILE
```

(continued)

```
          ACTION = 0                                  !  TURN OFF ACTION
      .
      ELSIF |                                         !OTHERWISE
        NAM:RECORD <> SAVE_RECORD                     !   BY ANOTHER STATION
        MEM:MESSAGE = 'CHANGED BY ANOTHER STATION'    !INFORM USER
        SELECT(2)                                     !  GO BACK TO TOP OF FORM
        BEEP                                          !  SOUND ALARM
        RELEASE(NAMES)                                !  RELEASE FILE
        SAVE_RECORD = NAM:RECORD                      !  SAVE RECORD
        DISPLAY                                       !  DISPLAY THE FIELDS
        PUT(TABLE)                                    !  FREE SAVED CHANGES
        CYCLE                                         !  AND CONTINUE
      .
      GET(TABLE,2)                                    !  READ CURRENT (CHANGED) REC
      NAM:RECORD = SAVE_RECORD                        !  MOVE RECORD
      DELETE(TABLE)                                   !  DELETE MEMORY TABLE ITEM
      .
    EXECUTE DISK_ACTN#                                !  UPDATE THE FILE
      ADD(NAMES)                                      !     ADD NEW RECORD
      PUT(NAMES)                                      !     CHANGE EXISTING RECORD
      DELETE(NAMES)                                   !     DELETE EXISTING RECORD
    .
    IF ERRORCODE() = 40                               !  DUPLICATE KEY ERROR
      MEM:MESSAGE = ERROR()                           !     DISPLAY ERR MESSAGE
      SELECT(2)                                       !     POSITION TO TOP OF FORM
      IF ACTION = 2 THEN RELEASE(NAMES). !            RELEASE HELD RECORD
      CYCLE                                           !     GET OUT OF EDIT LOOP
    ELSIF ERROR()                                     !  CHECK FOR UNEXPECTED ERROR
      STOP(ERROR())                                   !     HALT EXECUTION
    .
    IF ACTION = 1 THEN POINTER# = POINTER(NAMES). !POINT TO RECORD
    SAVE_RECORD = NAM:RECORD                          !  NEW ORIGINAL
    ACTION = ACTION#                                  !  RETRIEVE ORIGINAL OPERATION
    ACTION = 0                                        !  SET ACTION TO COMPLETE
    BREAK                                             !  AND RETURN TO CALLER

  OF ?DELETE_FIELD                                    !FROM THE DELETE FIELD
    IF KEYCODE() = ENTER_KEY |                        !  ON ENTER KEY
    OR KEYCODE() = ACCEPT_KEY                         !  OR CTRL-ENTER KEY
      SELECT(?LAST_FIELD)                             !     DELETE THE RECORD
    ELSE                                              !  OTHERWISE
      BEEP                                            !     BEEP AND ASK AGAIN
  . . .
FREE(TABLE)                                           !  RELEASE MEMORY TABLE
RETURN                                                !  AND RETURN TO CALLER
```

(continued)

```
CALCFIELDS   ROUTINE
  IF FIELD() > ?FIRST_FIELD                        !BEYOND FIRST_FIELD?
    IF KEYCODE() = 0 AND SELECTED() > FIELD() THEN EXIT. !GET OUT IF NOT NONSTOP
  .
  SCR:MESSAGE = MEM:MESSAGE
  SCR:NUMBER = NAM:NUMBER
```

MAIL04.CLA

```
          MEMBER('MAIL')

RPT_LAST     PROCEDURE

TITLE      REPORT            LENGTH(59),WIDTH(80),PRE(TTL)
RPT_HEAD                     DETAIL
           .                 .
REPORT     REPORT            LENGTH(59),WIDTH(80),PAGE(MEM:PAGE),LINE(MEM:LINE)    |
                             PRE(RPT)
PAGE_HEAD                    HEADER
                   COL(32)   STRING('PRINT NAMES BY LAST')
TODAY            ROW(+1,37)  STRING(@D7)
                 ROW(+2,7)   STRING('USER {39}LAST {7}DAYS SINCE')
                 ROW(+1,6)   STRING('NUMBER   FIRST NAME  LAST NAME {13}'    |
                                    & 'MESSAGE     LAST MESSAGE')
                 ROW(+1,6)   STRING('-{6}   -{10}  -{19}  -{9}   -{12}')     |
                             CTL(@LF)
                        .
DETAIL                       DETAIL
                 COL(8)      STRING(@N4),USE(NAM:NUMBER)
                 COL(15)     STRING(10),USE(NAM:FIRST)
                 COL(27)     STRING(20),USE(NAM:LAST)
LAST_ON          COL(48)     STRING(@D7)
DAYS             COL(64)     STRING(@N4) CTL(@LF)
                        .
RPT_FOOT                     DETAIL
                        .
PAGE_FOOT                    FOOTER
                 COL(37)     STRING('PAGE')
                 COL(42)     STRING(@n3),USE(MEM:PAGE) CTL(@LF)
                             CTL(@FF)
    .                   .
```

(continued)

```
      CODE
      DONE# = 0                                  !TURN OFF DONE FLAG
      CLEAR(NAM:RECORD,-1)                       !MAKE SURE RECORD CLEARED
      PRINT(TTL:RPT_HEAD)                        !PRINT TITLE PAGE
      CLOSE(TITLE)                               !CLOSE TITLE REPORT
      SET(NAM:BY_LAST)                           !  POINT TO FIRST RECORD
      DO NEXT_RECORD                             !READ FIRST RECORD
      RPT:TODAY = TODAY()
      OPEN(REPORT)                               !OPEN THE REPORT
      LOOP UNTIL DONE#                           !READ ALL RECORDS IN FILE
        SAVE_LINE# = MEM:LINE                    !  SAVE LINE NUMBER
        LAST_REC# = POINTER(NAMES)
        PRINT(RPT:DETAIL)                        !  PRINT DETAIL LINES
        DO CHECK_PAGE                            !  DO PAGE BREAK IF NEEDED
        DO NEXT_RECORD                           !  GET NEXT RECORD
        RPT:TODAY = TODAY()
                                                 !
      .
      PRINT(RPT:RPT_FOOT)                        !PRINT GRAND TOTALS
      DO CHECK_PAGE                              !  DO PAGE BREAK IF NEEDED
      CLOSE(REPORT)                              !CLOSE REPORT
      RETURN                                     !RETURN TO CALLER


NEXT_RECORD ROUTINE                              !GET NEXT RECORD
      LOOP UNTIL EOF(NAMES)                       !  READ UNTIL END OF FILE
        NEXT(NAMES)                              !    READ NEXT RECORD
        RPT:LAST_ON = 0;MES:NUMBER=NAM:NUMBER;
        SET(MES:BY_message,MES:BY_messagE);GET(MESSAGES,POINTER(MESSAGES));
        DATE#=MES:DATE;LOOP UNTIL EOF(MESSAGES);NEXT(MESSAGES);
        IF MES:NUMBER<>NAM:NUMBER;BREAK.;
        IF MES:DATE>DATE#;DATE#=MES:DATE..;RPT:LAST_ON=DATE#
        RPT:DAYS = TODAY() - RPT:LAST_ON
        EXIT                                     !    EXIT THE ROUTINE
      .                                          !
      DONE# = 1                                  !  ON EOF, SET DONE FLAG

CHECK_PAGE ROUTINE                               !CHECK FOR NEW PAGE
      IF MEM:LINE <= SAVE_LINE#                  !  ON PAGE OVERFLOW
        SAVE_LINE# = MEM:LINE                    !    RESET LINE NUMBER
      .
      LOOP UNTIL NOT KEYBOARD()                  !LOOK FOR KEYSTROKE
        ASK
        IF KEYCODE() = REJECT_KEY                !ON CTRL-ESC
          CLOSE(REPORT)                          !  CLOSE REPORT
          RETURN                                 !  ABORT PRINT
      . .
```

MAIL05.CLA

```
          MEMBER('MAIL')

NEW_MESSAGE   PROCEDURE

SCREEN        SCREEN      WINDOW(9,41),AT(8,3),HUE(15,0)
                                          PRE(SCR),
              ROW(1,14)   PAINT(1,17),HUE(0,7)
                      COL(1) STRING('<218,196{12},0{17},196{10},191>'),HUE(14,0)
              ROW(2,1)    REPEAT(7);STRING('<179,0{39},179>'),HUE(14,0) .
              ROW(9,1)    STRING('<192,196{39},217>'),HUE(14,0)
              ROW(1,15)   STRING('PREPARE MESSAGE')
              ROW(4,2)    STRING('Send to: '),HUE(14,0)
              ROW(6,2)    STRING('Subject: '),HUE(14,0)
MESSAGE       ROW(2,6)    STRING(30),HUE(7,0)
MESSAGE_NUM   ROW(3,18)   STRING(@N_6),HUE(0,0)
NAME          ROW(4,11)   STRING(@S30),HUE(15,0)
                          ENTRY,USE(?FIRST_FIELD)
              ROW(3,11)   ENTRY,USE(MES:NUMBER)
NUMBER            COL(11) STRING(@N4),HUE(0,0)
              ROW(6,11)   ENTRY(@s25),USE(MES:SUBJECT),LFT,OVR,ESC(?-1)
              ROW(8,6)    PAUSE('Press <<ENTER> to Write Message')            |
                              USE(?PAUSE_FIELD),HUE(30,0)
                          ENTRY,USE(?LAST_FIELD)
                          PAUSE(''),USE(?DELETE_FIELD)
                  .
TABLE         TABLE,PRE(SAV)
SAVE_RECORD   GROUP;BYTE,DIM(SIZE(MES:RECORD)).
SAVE_MEMO     GROUP;BYTE,DIM(SIZE(MES:NOTES)).
                  .

  EJECT
  CODE
  OPEN(SCREEN)                                !OPEN THE SCREEN
  SETCURSOR                                   !TURN OFF ANY CURSOR
  if action = 2 then select(?+4). NAM:NUMBER=MES:NUMBER;
  SET(MES:BY_MESSAGE,MES:BY_MESSAGE);NEXT(MESSAGES);
  IF ACTION = 2;SELECT(?+4).!CALL SETUP PROCEDURE
  SAVE_RECORD = MES:RECORD                     !SAVE THE ORIGINAL
  SAVE_MEMO   = MES:NOTES                      !SAVE THE ORIGINAL
  ADD(TABLE,1)                                 !STORE IN MEMORY TABLE
  IF ACTION = 5                                !AUTONUMBER ACTION
    DISK_ACTN# = 2                             !  SET FOR PHYSICAL ACTION
    ACTION = 1                                 !  SET FOR LOGICAL ACTION
  ELSE                                         !OTHERWISE
    DISK_ACTN# = ACTION                        !  SET ACTION FOR DISK WRITE
    .
```

(continued)

```
DISPLAY                                         !DISPLAY THE FIELDS

EXECUTE DISK_ACTN#                              !SET THE CURRENT RECORD POINTER
  POINTER# = 0                                  !  NO RECORD FOR ADD
  POINTER# = POINTER(MESSAGES)                  !  CURRENT RECORD FOR CHANGE
  POINTER# = POINTER(MESSAGES)                  !  CURRENT RECORD FOR CHANGE
  .
ACTION# = ACTION                                !STORE REQUIRED ACTION
LOOP                                            !LOOP THRU ALL THE FIELDS
  MEM:MESSAGE = CENTER(MEM:MESSAGE,SIZE(MEM:MESSAGE)) !DISPLAY ACTION MESSAGE
  DO CALCFIELDS                                 !CALCULATE DISPLAY FIELDS
  ALERT                                         !RESET ALERTED KEYS
  ALERT(ACCEPT_KEY)                             !ALERT SCREEN ACCEPT KEY
  ALERT(REJECT_KEY)                             !ALERT SCREEN REJECT KEY
  ACCEPT                                        !READ A FIELD
  IF KEYCODE() = REJECT_KEY THEN BREAK.         !RETURN ON SCREEN REJECT KEY
  EXECUTE ACTION                                !SET MESSAGE
    MEM:MESSAGE = 'Record will be Added'        !
    MEM:MESSAGE = 'Record will be Changed'      !
    MEM:MESSAGE = 'Press Enter to Delete'       !
    .
  IF KEYCODE() = ACCEPT_KEY                     !ON SCREEN ACCEPT KEY
    UPDATE                                      !  MOVE ALL FIELDS FROM SCREEN
    SELECT(?)                                   !  START WITH CURRENT FIELD
    SELECT                                      !  EDIT ALL FIELDS
    CYCLE                                       !  GO TO TOP OF LOOP
    .
  CASE FIELD()                                  !JUMP TO FIELD EDIT ROUTINE
  OF ?FIRST_FIELD                               !FROM THE FIRST FIELD
    IF KEYCODE() = ESC_KEY THEN BREAK.          !  RETURN ON ESC KEY
    IF ACTION = 3 THEN SELECT(?DELETE_FIELD).   !    OR CONFIRM FOR DELETE

  OF ?MES:NUMBER                                !USER NUMBER
      NAM:NUMBER = MES:NUMBER                   !MOVE RELATED FIELDS
      GET(NAMES,NAM:BY_LAST)                    !READ THE RECORD
      ACTION# = ACTION                          !SAVE ACTION
      ACTION = 4                                !REQUEST TABLE LOOKUP
      PICK_NAME                                 !CALL LOOKUP PROCEDURE
      IF ACTION                                 !NO SELECTION WAS MADE
        SELECT(?MES:NUMBER-1)                   ! BACK UP ONE FIELD
        ACTION = ACTION#                        ! RESTORE ACTION
        CYCLE                                   ! GO TO TOP OF LOOP
        .
      SCR:NUMBER = NAM:NUMBER                   !DISPLAY LOOKUP FIELD
      MES:NUMBER = NAM:NUMBER                   !MOVE LOOKUP FIELD
      DISPLAY(?MES:NUMBER)                      !AND DISPLAY IT
      ACTION = ACTION#                          !RESTORE ACTION
```

(continued)

```
        IF DUPLICATE(MES:BY_OUTGOING)          !  CHECK FOR DUPLICATE KEY
          MEM:MESSAGE = 'CREATES DUPLICATE ENTRY'! MOVE AN ERROR MESSAGE
          SELECT(?MES:NUMBER)                   !    STAY ON THE SAME FIELD
          BEEP                                  !    SOUND THE KEYBOARD ALARM
          CYCLE                                 !    AND LOOP AGAIN
            .
        if mes:date = '';mes:date = today().

OF ?PAUSE_FIELD                                 !ON PAUSE FIELD
  IF KEYCODE() <> ENTER_KEY|                     !IF NOT ENTER KEY
  AND KEYCODE() <> ACCEPT_KEY|                   !AND NOT CTRL-ENTER KEY
  AND KEYCODE() <> 0                             !AND NOT NONSTOP MODE
    BEEP                                         !  SOUND KEYBOARD ALARM
    SELECT(?PAUSE_FIELD)                         !  AND STAY ON PAUSE FIELD
      .

OF ?LAST_FIELD                                  !FROM THE LAST FIELD
  IF ACTION = 2 OR ACTION = 3                   !IF UPDATING RECORD
    SAVE_RECORD = MES:RECORD                     !  SAVE CURRENT CHANGES
    SAVE_MEMO   = MES:NOTES                      !  SAVE CURRENT CHANGES
    ADD(TABLE,2)                                 !  STORE IN MEMORY TABLE
    GET(TABLE,1)                                 !  RETRIEVE ORIGINAL RECORD
    HOLD(MESSAGES)                               !  HOLD FILE
    GET(MESSAGES,POINTER#)                       !  RE-READ SAME RECORD
    IF ERRORCODE() = 35                          !  IF RECORD WAS DELETED
      IF DISK_ACTN# = 2                          !  IF TRYING TO UPDATE
        DISK_ACTN# = 1                           !    THEN ADD IT BACK
      ELSE                                       !
        RELEASE(MESSAGES)                        !  RELEASE FILE
        ACTION = 0                               !  TURN OFF ACTION
        .
    ELSIF |                                      !OTHERWISE
      MES:NOTES <> SAVE_MEMO OR |                !  IF IT HAS BEEN CHANGED
      MES:RECORD <> SAVE_RECORD                  !    BY ANOTHER STATION
      MEM:MESSAGE = 'CHANGED BY ANOTHER STATION' !INFORM USER
      SELECT(2)                                  !  GO BACK TO TOP OF FORM
      BEEP                                       !  SOUND ALARM
      RELEASE(MESSAGES)                          !  RELEASE FILE
      SAVE_RECORD = MES:RECORD                   !  SAVE RECORD
      SAVE_MEMO = MES:NOTES                       !  SAVE MEMO
      DISPLAY                                    !  DISPLAY THE FIELDS
      PUT(TABLE)                                 !  FREE SAVED CHANGES
      CYCLE                                      !  AND CONTINUE
        .
    GET(TABLE,2)                                 !  READ CURRENT (CHANGED) REC
    MES:RECORD = SAVE_RECORD                     !  MOVE RECORD
    MES:NOTES = SAVE_MEMO                         !  MOVE MEMO
```

(continued)

```
      DELETE(TABLE)                               ! DELETE MEMORY TABLE ITEM
    .
    EXECUTE DISK_ACTN#                            ! UPDATE THE FILE
      ADD(MESSAGES)                               !   ADD NEW RECORD
      PUT(MESSAGES)                               !   CHANGE EXISTING RECORD
      DELETE(MESSAGES)                            !   DELETE EXISTING RECORD
    .
    IF ERRORCODE() = 40                           ! DUPLICATE KEY ERROR
      MEM:MESSAGE = ERROR()                       !   DISPLAY ERR MESSAGE
      SELECT(2)                                   !   POSITION TO TOP OF FORM
      IF ACTION = 2 THEN RELEASE(MESSAGES).       !     RELEASE HELD RECORD
      CYCLE                                       !   GET OUT OF EDIT LOOP
    ELSIF ERROR()                                 ! CHECK FOR UNEXPECTED ERROR
      STOP(ERROR())                               !   HALT EXECUTION
    .
    IF ACTION = 1 THEN POINTER# = POINTER(MESSAGES). !POINT TO RECORD
    SAVE_RECORD = MES:RECORD                      ! NEW ORIGINAL
    SAVE_MEMO = MES:NOTES                         ! NEW ORIGINAL
    ACTION = ACTION#                              ! RETRIEVE ORIGINAL OPERATION
    IF ACTION <> 3                                !IF THIS IS NOT A DELETE
      ACTION = 2                                  ! SET ACTION TO CHANGE MODE
      NOTE                                        ! CALL NEXT FORM PROCEDURE
      IF ACTION                                   ! IF RECORD WAS NOT CHANGED
        SELECT(?LAST_FIELD - 1)                   !   SELECT THE LAST ENTRY
        GET(TABLE,1)                              !   REREAD ORIGINAL
        SAVE_RECORD = MES:RECORD                  !   SAVE IT IN THE TABLE
        PUT(TABLE)
        ACTION = 2                                !   SET LOGICAL AND PHYSICAL
        DISK_ACTN# = 2                            !   ACTION TO CHANGE
        CYCLE                                     !   AND LOOP AGAIN
      . .
      ACTION = 0                                  ! SET ACTION TO COMPLETE
      BREAK                                       ! AND RETURN TO CALLER

    OF ?DELETE_FIELD                              !FROM THE DELETE FIELD
      IF KEYCODE() = ENTER_KEY |                  ! ON ENTER KEY
      OR KEYCODE() = ACCEPT_KEY                   ! OR CTRL-ENTER KEY
        SELECT(?LAST_FIELD)                       !   DELETE THE RECORD
      ELSE                                        ! OTHERWISE
        BEEP                                      !   BEEP AND ASK AGAIN
  . . .
  FREE(TABLE)                                     ! RELEASE MEMORY TABLE
  RETURN                                          ! AND RETURN TO CALLER

CALCFIELDS   ROUTINE
  IF FIELD() > ?FIRST_FIELD                       !BEYOND FIRST_FIELD?
    IF KEYCODE() = 0 AND SELECTED() > FIELD() THEN EXIT. !GET OUT IF NOT NONSTOP
  .
```

(continued)

```
SCR:MESSAGE = MEM:MESSAGE
SCR:NUMBER = MES:NUMBER
SCR:MESSAGE_NUM = MES:MESSAGE_NUM
SCR:NAME = 0;nam:number = mes:number;
set(nam:by_number,nam:by_number);next(names);
scr:name = CLIP(NAM:FIRST) & ' ' & CLIP(NAM:LAST)
```

MAIL06.CLA

```
          MEMBER('MAIL')
NOTE          PROCEDURE

SCREEN        SCREEN    PRE(SCR),WINDOW(14,54),AT(9,14),HUE(15,0)
                ROW(1,1)    STRING('<218,196{52},191>'),HUE(14,0)
                ROW(2,1)    REPEAT(12);STRING('<179,0{52},179>'),HUE(14,0)  .
                ROW(14,1)   STRING('<192,196{12},0{29},196{11},217>'),HUE(14,0)
                      COL(15)  STRING('PRESS <<CTRL><<ENTER> TO SAVE'),HUE(14,0)
MESSAGE       ROW(2,13)   STRING(30),HUE(7,0)
                          ENTRY,USE(?FIRST_FIELD)
                ROW(3,3)    TEXT(10,50),USE(MES:NOTES),LFT,SEL(15,0)
                          ENTRY,USE(?LAST_FIELD)
                          PAUSE(''),USE(?DELETE_FIELD)
                  .
TABLE         TABLE,PRE(SAV)
SAVE_RECORD    GROUP;BYTE,DIM(SIZE(MES:RECORD)).
SAVE_MEMO      GROUP;BYTE,DIM(SIZE(MES:NOTES)).
                  .

  EJECT
  CODE
  OPEN(SCREEN)                          !OPEN THE SCREEN
  SETCURSOR                             !TURN OFF ANY CURSOR
  SAVE_RECORD = MES:RECORD              !SAVE THE ORIGINAL
  SAVE_MEMO   = MES:NOTES               !SAVE THE ORIGINAL
  ADD(TABLE,1)                          !STORE IN MEMORY TABLE
  IF ACTION = 5                         !AUTONUMBER ACTION
    DISK_ACTN# = 2                      !  SET FOR PHYSICAL ACTION
    ACTION = 1                          !  SET FOR LOGICAL ACTION
  ELSE                                  !OTHERWISE
    DISK_ACTN# = ACTION                 !  SET ACTION FOR DISK WRITE
  .
  DISPLAY                               !DISPLAY THE FIELDS

  EXECUTE DISK_ACTN#                    !SET THE CURRENT RECORD POINTER
    POINTER# = 0                        !  NO RECORD FOR ADD
    POINTER# = POINTER(MESSAGES)        !  CURRENT RECORD FOR CHANGE
```

(continued)

```
    POINTER# = POINTER(MESSAGES)                 !  CURRENT RECORD FOR CHANGE
  .
ACTION# = ACTION                                 !STORE REQUIRED ACTION
LOOP                                             !LOOP THRU ALL THE FIELDS
  MEM:MESSAGE = CENTER(MEM:MESSAGE,SIZE(MEM:MESSAGE)) !DISPLAY ACTION MESSAGE
  DO CALCFIELDS                                  !CALCULATE DISPLAY FIELDS
  ALERT                                          !RESET ALERTED KEYS
  ALERT(ACCEPT_KEY)                              !ALERT SCREEN ACCEPT KEY
  ALERT(REJECT_KEY)                              !ALERT SCREEN REJECT KEY
  ACCEPT                                         !READ A FIELD
  IF KEYCODE() = REJECT_KEY THEN BREAK.          !RETURN ON SCREEN REJECT KEY
  EXECUTE ACTION                                 !SET MESSAGE
    MEM:MESSAGE = 'Record will be Added'         !
    MEM:MESSAGE = 'Record will be Changed'       !
    MEM:MESSAGE = 'Press Enter to Delete'        !
  .
  IF KEYCODE() = ACCEPT_KEY                      !ON SCREEN ACCEPT KEY
    UPDATE                                       !  MOVE ALL FIELDS FROM SCREEN
    SELECT(?)                                    !  START WITH CURRENT FIELD
    SELECT                                       !  EDIT ALL FIELDS
    CYCLE                                        !  GO TO TOP OF LOOP
  .
  CASE FIELD()                                   !JUMP TO FIELD EDIT ROUTINE
  OF ?FIRST_FIELD                                !FROM THE FIRST FIELD
    IF KEYCODE() = ESC_KEY THEN BREAK.           !  RETURN ON ESC KEY
    IF ACTION = 3 THEN SELECT(?DELETE_FIELD).    !   OR CONFIRM FOR DELETE

  OF ?LAST_FIELD                                 !FROM THE LAST FIELD
    IF ACTION = 2 OR ACTION = 3                  !IF UPDATING RECORD
      SAVE_RECORD = MES:RECORD                   !  SAVE CURRENT CHANGES
      SAVE_MEMO   = MES:NOTES                    !  SAVE CURRENT CHANGES
      ADD(TABLE,2)                               !  STORE IN MEMORY TABLE
      GET(TABLE,1)                               !  RETRIEVE ORIGINAL RECORD
      HOLD(MESSAGES)                             !  HOLD FILE
      GET(MESSAGES,POINTER#)                     !  RE-READ SAME RECORD
      IF ERRORCODE() = 35                        !  IF RECORD WAS DELETED
        IF DISK_ACTN# = 2                        !  IF TRYING TO UPDATE
          DISK_ACTN# = 1                         !    THEN ADD IT BACK
        ELSE                                     !
          RELEASE(MESSAGES)                      !  RELEASE FILE
          ACTION = 0                             !  TURN OFF ACTION
      .
      ELSIF |                                    !OTHERWISE
        MES:NOTES <> SAVE_MEMO OR |              !  IF IT HAS BEEN CHANGED
        MES:RECORD <> SAVE_RECORD                !    BY ANOTHER STATION
        MEM:MESSAGE = 'CHANGED BY ANOTHER STATION' !INFORM USER
        SELECT(2)                                !  GO BACK TO TOP OF FORM
```

(continued)

```
         BEEP                                      !  SOUND ALARM
         RELEASE(MESSAGES)                         !  RELEASE FILE
         SAVE_RECORD = MES:RECORD                  !  SAVE RECORD
         SAVE_MEMO = MES:NOTES                     !  SAVE MEMO
         DISPLAY                                   !  DISPLAY THE FIELDS
         PUT(TABLE)                                !  FREE SAVED CHANGES
         CYCLE                                     !  AND CONTINUE
       .
       GET(TABLE,2)                                !  READ CURRENT (CHANGED) REC
       MES:RECORD = SAVE_RECORD                    !  MOVE RECORD
       MES:NOTES = SAVE_MEMO                       !  MOVE MEMO
       DELETE(TABLE)                               !  DELETE MEMORY TABLE ITEM
     .
     EXECUTE DISK_ACTN#                            !  UPDATE THE FILE
       ADD(MESSAGES)                               !    ADD NEW RECORD
       PUT(MESSAGES)                               !    CHANGE EXISTING RECORD
       DELETE(MESSAGES)                            !    DELETE EXISTING RECORD
     .
     IF ERRORCODE() = 40                           !  DUPLICATE KEY ERROR
       MEM:MESSAGE = ERROR()                       !    DISPLAY ERR MESSAGE
       SELECT(2)                                   !    POSITION TO TOP OF FORM
       IF ACTION = 2 THEN RELEASE(MESSAGES). !    RELEASE HELD RECORD
       CYCLE                                       !    GET OUT OF EDIT LOOP
     ELSIF ERROR()                                 !  CHECK FOR UNEXPECTED ERROR
       STOP(ERROR())                               !    HALT EXECUTION
     .
     IF ACTION = 1 THEN POINTER# = POINTER(MESSAGES). !POINT TO RECORD
     SAVE_RECORD = MES:RECORD                      !  NEW ORIGINAL
     SAVE_MEMO = MES:NOTES                         !  NEW ORIGINAL
     ACTION = ACTION#                              !  RETRIEVE ORIGINAL OPERATION
     ACTION = 0                                    !  SET ACTION TO COMPLETE
     BREAK                                         !  AND RETURN TO CALLER

   OF ?DELETE_FIELD                                !FROM THE DELETE FIELD
     IF KEYCODE() = ENTER_KEY |                    !  ON ENTER KEY
     OR KEYCODE() = ACCEPT_KEY                     !  OR CTRL-ENTER KEY
       SELECT(?LAST_FIELD)                         !    DELETE THE RECORD
     ELSE                                          !  OTHERWISE
       BEEP                                        !    BEEP AND ASK AGAIN
 . . .
 FREE(TABLE)                                       !  RELEASE MEMORY TABLE
 RETURN                                            !  AND RETURN TO CALLER

CALCFIELDS   ROUTINE
 IF FIELD() > ?FIRST_FIELD                         !BEYOND FIRST_FIELD?
   IF KEYCODE() = 0 AND SELECTED() > FIELD() THEN EXIT. !GET OUT IF NOT NONSTOP
 .
 SCR:MESSAGE = MEM:MESSAGE
```

MAIL07.CLA

```
           MEMBER('MAIL')
PICK_NAME    PROCEDURE

SCREEN       SCREEN       PRE(SCR),WINDOW(25,39),AT(1,42),HUE(15,1)
             ROW(6,1)     PAINT(17,39),HUE(0,7)
             ROW(1,1)     STRING('<201,205{37},187>'),HUE(15,1)
             ROW(2,1)     REPEAT(23);STRING('<186,0{37},186>'),HUE(15,1)  .
             ROW(25,1)    STRING('<200,205{37},188>'),HUE(15,1)
             ROW(2,11)    STRING('Show Names By Last')
             ROW(4,7)     STRING('LOCATE:'),HUE(11,1)
             ROW(23,2)    STRING('Ins to Add'),HUE(11,1)
                  COL(23) STRING('Enter to Change'),HUE(11,1)
             ROW(24,2)    STRING('Del to Delete'),HUE(11,1)
                  COL(22) STRING('Ctrl-Esc to Exit'),HUE(11,1)
LOCATOR      ROW(4,14)    STRING(20),HUE(11,1)
                          ENTRY,USE(?FIRST_FIELD)
                          ENTRY,USE(?PRE_POINT)
                          REPEAT(17),EVERY(1),INDEX(NDX)
             ROW(6,5)       POINT(1,32),USE(?POINT),ESC(?-1)
NAME                 COL(6)    STRING(@s30)
                .           .

NDX          BYTE                         !REPEAT INDEX FOR POINT AREA
ROW          BYTE                         !ACTUAL ROW OF SCROLL AREA
COL          BYTE                         !ACTUAL COLUMN OF SCROLL AREA
COUNT        BYTE(17)                     !NUMBER OF ITEMS TO SCROLL
ROWS         BYTE(17)                     !NUMBER OF ROWS TO SCROLL
COLS         BYTE(32)                     !NUMBER OF COLUMNS TO SCROLL
FOUND        BYTE                         !RECORD FOUND FLAG
NEWPTR       LONG                         !POINTER TO NEW RECORD

TABLE        TABLE,PRE(TBL)               !TABLE OF RECORD DATA
NAME         STRING(@s30)
LAST         STRING(20)
NUMBER       SHORT
PTR          LONG                         !  POINTER TO FILE RECORD
             .

  EJECT
  CODE
  ACTION# = ACTION                        !SAVE ACTION
  OPEN(SCREEN)                            !OPEN THE SCREEN
  SETCURSOR                               !TURN OFF ANY CURSOR
  TBL:PTR = 1                             !START AT TABLE ENTRY
```

(continued)

```
NDX = 1                               !PUT SELECTOR BAR ON TOP ITEM
ROW = ROW(?POINT)                     !REMEMBER TOP ROW AND
COL = COL(?POINT)                     !LEFT COLUMN OF SCROLL AREA
RECORDS# = TRUE                       !INITIALIZE RECORDS FLAG
IF ACTION = 4                         !   TABLE LOOKUP REQUEST
  NEWPTR = POINTER(NAMES)             !   SET POINTER TO RECORD
  IF NOT NEWPTR                       !   RECORD NOT PASSED TO TABLE
    SET(NAM:BY_LAST,NAM:BY_LAST)      !     POSITION TO CLOSEST RECORD
    NEXT(NAMES)                       !     READ RECORD
    NEWPTR = POINTER(NAMES)           !     SET POINTER
    .
  DO FIND_RECORD                      !   POSITION FILE
ELSE
  NDX = 1                             !   PUT SELECTOR BAR ON TOP ITEM
  DO FIRST_PAGE                       !   BUILD MEMORY TABLE OF KEYS
  .
RECORDS# = TRUE                       !   ASSUME THERE ARE RECORDS
LOOP                                  !LOOP UNTIL USER EXITS
  ACTION = ACTION#                    !RESTORE ACTION
  ALERT                               !RESET ALERTED KEYS
  ALERT(REJECT_KEY)                   !ALERT SCREEN REJECT KEY
  ALERT(ACCEPT_KEY)                   !ALERT SCREEN ACCEPT KEY
  ACCEPT                              !READ A FIELD
  IF KEYCODE() = REJECT_KEY THEN BREAK. !RETURN ON SCREEN REJECT KEY

  IF  KEYCODE() = ACCEPT_KEY      |   !ON SCREEN ACCEPT KEY
  AND FIELD() <> ?POINT               !BUT NOT ON THE POINT FIELD
    UPDATE                            !   MOVE ALL FIELDS FROM SCREEN
    SELECT(?)                         !   START WITH CURRENT FIELD
    SELECT                            !   EDIT ALL FIELDS
    CYCLE                             !   GO TO TOP OF LOOP
    .

  CASE FIELD()                        !JUMP TO FIELD EDIT ROUTINE

  OF ?FIRST_FIELD                     !FROM THE FIRST FIELD
    IF KEYCODE() = ESC_KEY     |      !   RETURN ON ESC KEY
    OR RECORDS# = FALSE               !   OR NO RECORDS
      BREAK                           !     EXIT PROGRAM
      .
  OF ?PRE_POINT                       !PRE POINT FIELD CONDITION
    IF KEYCODE() = ESC_KEY            !   BACKING UP?
      SELECT(?-1)                     !     SELECT PREVIOUS FIELD
    ELSE                              !   GOING FORWARD
      SELECT(?POINT)                  !     SELECT MENU FIELD
      .
  IF KEYCODE() = ESC_KEY              !   BACKING UP?
```

(continued)

```
     SCR:LOCATOR = ''                          !    CLEAR LOCATOR
     SETCURSOR                                 !    AND TURN CURSOR OFF
  ELSE                                         !  GOING FORWARD
     LEN# = 0                                  !    RESET TO START OF LOCATOR
     SETCURSOR(ROW(SCR:LOCATOR),COL(SCR:LOCATOR)) !  AND TURN CURSOR ON
  .
  OF ?POINT                                    !PROCESS THE POINT FIELD
    IF RECORDS(TABLE) = 0                      !IF THERE ARE NO RECORDS
      CLEAR(NAM:RECORD)                        !  CLEAR RECORD AREA
      UPDATE                                   !  UPDATE ALL FIELDS
      ACTION = 1                               !  SET ACTION TO ADD
      GET(NAMES,0)                             !  CLEAR PENDING RECORD
      LOOP
        CLEAR(NAM:RECORD,1)                    !CLEAR RECORD TO HIGH VALUES
        SET(NAM:BY_NUMBER)                     !  POINT TO FIRST RECORD
        PREVIOUS(NAMES)                        !READ LAST KEY RECORD
        IF ERROR()                             !IF THERE WAS AN ERROR
          CLEAR(NAM:RECORD)                    !  CLEAR THE RECORD
          KEYFIELD# = 0                        !  INTITIALIZE THE FIELD
          IF KEYFIELD# = 0 THEN KEYFIELD# = 1.!  IF ITS 0 MAKE IT 1
        ELSE                                   !ELSE
          KEYFIELD# = NAM:NUMBER + 1           !  INCREMENT FIELD
        .
        CLEAR(NAM:RECORD)                      !CLEAR LAST KEY RECORD
        NAM:NUMBER = KEYFIELD#                 !LOAD KEY FIELD
        ADD(NAMES)                             !ESTABLISH RECORD WITH UNIQUE
        IF NOT ERROR()                         !ADD WAS SUCCESSFUL
          POINTER# = POINTER(NAMES)            !  SAVE POINTER
          ACTION = 5                           !  SET ACTION FOR UPDATE
          BREAK                                !  EXIT LOOP
      . .
      IF ACTION = 2; MES:NUMBER = NAM:NUMBER;
      ACTION = 0;BREAK;ELSE NO_MESSAGE.        !CALL FORM FOR NEW RECORD
      IF ACTION                                !FORM WAS NOT COMPLETED
        HOLD(NAMES)                            !HOLD RECORD
        GET(NAMES,POINTER#)                    !READ RECORD
        DELETE(NAMES)                          !DELETE RECORD
        DO SAME_PAGE
      .
      NEWPTR = POINTER(NAMES)                  !    SET POINTER TO NEW RECORD
      DO FIRST_PAGE                            !    DISPLAY THE FIRST PAGE
      IF RECORDS(TABLE) = 0                    !    IF THERE AREN'T ANY RECORDS
        RECORDS# = FALSE                       !       INDICATE NO RECORDS
        SELECT(?PRE_POINT-1)                   !       SELECT THE PRIOR FIELD
      .
      CYCLE                                    !    AND LOOP AGAIN
    .
```

(continued)

```
IF KEYCODE() > 31            |          !THE DISPLAYABLE CHARACTERS
AND KEYCODE() < 255                     !ARE USED TO LOCATE RECORDS
  IF LEN# < SIZE(SCR:LOCATOR)           !  IF THERE IS ROOM LEFT
    SCR:LOCATOR = SUB(SCR:LOCATOR,1,LEN#) & CHR(KEYCODE())
    LEN# += 1                           !    INCREMENT THE LENGTH

  .
ELSIF KEYCODE() = BS_KEY                !BACKSPACE UNTYPES A CHARACTER
  IF LEN# > 0                           !  IF THERE ARE CHARACTERS LEFT
    LEN# -= 1                           !    DECREMENT THE LENGTH
    SCR:LOCATOR = SUB(SCR:LOCATOR,1,LEN#) !    ERASE THE LAST CHARACTER

  .
  ELSE                                  !FOR ANY OTHER CHARACTER
    LEN# = 0                            !  ZERO THE LENGTH
    SCR:LOCATOR = ''                    !  ERASE THE LOCATOR FIELD

  .
  SETCURSOR(ROW(SCR:LOCATOR),COL(SCR:LOCATOR)+LEN#) !AND RESET THE CURSOR
  NAM:LAST = CLIP(SCR:LOCATOR)          !    UPDATE THE KEY FIELD
  IF KEYBOARD() > 31           |          !THE DISPLAYABLE CHARACTERS
  AND KEYBOARD() < 255         |          !ARE USED TO LOCATE RECORDS
  OR KEYBOARD() = BS_KEY                 !INCLUDE BACKSPACE
    CYCLE

  .
  IF LEN# > 0                           !ON A LOCATOR REQUEST
    NAM:LAST = CLIP(SCR:LOCATOR)        !    UPDATE THE KEY FIELD
    SET(NAM:BY_LAST,NAM:BY_LAST)        !    POINT TO NEW RECORD
    NEXT(NAMES)                         !    READ A RECORD
    IF (EOF(NAMES) AND ERROR())         !    IF EOF IS REACHED
      SET(NAM:BY_LAST)                  !      SET TO FIRST RECORD
      PREVIOUS(NAMES)                   !      READ THE LAST RECORD

    .
    NEWPTR = POINTER(NAMES)             !    SET NEW RECORD POINTER
    SKIP(NAMES,-1)                      !    BACK UP TO FIRST RECORD
    FREE(TABLE)                         !    CLEAR THE TABLE
    DO NEXT_PAGE                        !    AND DISPLAY A NEW PAGE

  .
CASE KEYCODE()                          !PROCESS THE KEYSTROKE

OF INS_KEY                              !INS KEY
  CLEAR(NAM:RECORD)                     !  CLEAR RECORD AREA
  ACTION = 1                            !  SET ACTION TO ADD
  GET(NAMES,0)                          !  CLEAR PENDING RECORD
  LOOP
    CLEAR(NAM:RECORD,1)                 !CLEAR RECORD TO HIGH VALUES
    SET(NAM:BY_NUMBER)                  !  POINT TO FIRST RECORD
    PREVIOUS(NAMES)                     !READ LAST KEY RECORD
    IF ERROR()                          !IF THERE WAS AN ERROR
      CLEAR(NAM:RECORD)                 !  CLEAR THE RECORD
```

(continued)

```
        KEYFIELD# = 0                          !  INTITIALIZE THE FIELD
        IF KEYFIELD# = 0 THEN KEYFIELD# = 1.!  IF ITS 0 MAKE IT 1
     ELSE                                      !ELSE
        KEYFIELD# = NAM:NUMBER + 1             !  INCREMENT FIELD
     .
     CLEAR(NAM:RECORD)                         !CLEAR LAST KEY RECORD
     NAM:NUMBER = KEYFIELD#                    !LOAD KEY FIELD
     ADD(NAMES)                                !ESTABLISH RECORD WITH UNIQUE
     IF NOT ERROR()                            !ADD WAS SUCCESSFUL
       POINTER# = POINTER(NAMES)               !  SAVE POINTER
       ACTION = 5                              !  SET ACTION FOR UPDATE
       BREAK                                   !  EXIT LOOP
   . .
   IF ACTION = 2; MES:NUMBER = NAM:NUMBER;
   ACTION = 0;BREAK;ELSE NO_MESSAGE.           !CALL FORM FOR NEW RECORD
   IF ~ACTION                                  !  IF RECORD WAS ADDED
    .NEWPTR = POINTER(NAMES)                   !    SET POINTER TO NEW RECORD
    DO FIND_RECORD                             !    POSITION IN FILE
   .
   IF ACTION                                   !FORM WAS NOT COMPLETED
     HOLD(NAMES)                               !HOLD RECORD
     GET(NAMES,POINTER#)                       !READ RECORD
     DELETE(NAMES)                             !DELETE RECORD
     DO SAME_PAGE
   .
 OF ENTER_KEY                                  !ENTER KEY
 OROF ACCEPT_KEY                               !CTRL-ENTER KEY
   DO GET_RECORD                               !  GET THE SELECTED RECORD
   IF ACTION = 4 AND KEYCODE() = ENTER_KEY!    IF THIS IS A LOOKUP REQUEST
     ACTION = 0                                !    SET ACTION TO COMPLETE
     BREAK                                     !    AND RETURN TO CALLER
   .
   IF ~ERROR()                                 !  IF RECORD IS STILL THERE
     ACTION = 2                                !    SET ACTION TO CHANGE
     IF ACTION = 2; MES:NUMBER = NAM:NUMBER;
     ACTION = 0;BREAK;ELSE NO_MESSAGE.         !CALL FORM TO CHANGE REC
     IF ACTION THEN CYCLE.                     !    IF SUCCESSFUL RE-DISPLAY
   .
   NEWPTR = POINTER(NAMES)                     !    SET POINTER TO NEW RECORD
   DO FIND_RECORD                              !    POSITION IN FILE
 OF DEL_KEY                                    !DEL KEY
   DO GET_RECORD                               !  READ THE SELECTED RECORD
   IF ~ERROR()                                 !  IF RECORD IS STILL THERE
     ACTION = 3                                !    SET ACTION TO DELETE
     IF ACTION = 2; MES:NUMBER = NAM:NUMBER;
    ACTION = 0;BREAK;ELSE NO_MESSAGE.          !CALL FORM TO DELETE
     IF ~ACTION                                !    IF SUCCESSFUL
```

(continued)

```
            N# = NDX                              !        SAVE POINT INDEX
            DO SAME_PAGE                          !        RE-DISPLAY
            NDX = N#                              !        RESTORE POINT INDEX
          . .
      OF DOWN_KEY                               !DOWN ARROW KEY
        DO SET_NEXT                             !  POINT TO NEXT RECORD
        DO FILL_NEXT                            !  FILL A TABLE ENTRY
        IF FOUND                                !  FOUND A NEW RECORD
          SCROLL(ROW,COL,ROWS,COLS,ROWS(?POINT)) !    SCROLL THE SCREEN UP
          GET(TABLE,RECORDS(TABLE))             !  GET RECORD FROM TABLE
          DO FILL_SCREEN                        !  DISPLAY ON SCREEN
        .

      OF PGDN_KEY                               !PAGE DOWN KEY
        DO SET_NEXT                             !  POINT TO NEXT RECORD
        DO NEXT_PAGE                            !  DISPLAY THE NEXT PAGE

      OF CTRL_PGDN                              !CTRL-PAGE DOWN KEY
        DO LAST_PAGE                            !  DISPLAY THE LAST PAGE
        NDX = RECORDS(TABLE)                    !  POSITION POINT BAR

      OF UP_KEY                                 !UP ARROW KEY
        DO SET_PREV                             !  POINT TO PREVIOUS RECORD
        DO FILL_PREV                            !  FILL A TABLE ENTRY
        IF FOUND                                !  FOUND A NEW RECORD
          SCROLL(ROW,COL,ROWS,COLS,-(ROWS(?POINT)))! SCROLL THE SCREEN DOWN
          GET(TABLE,1)                          !  GET RECORD FROM TABLE
          DO FILL_SCREEN                        !  DISPLAY ON SCREEN
        .

      OF PGUP_KEY                               !PAGE UP KEY
        DO SET_PREV                             !  POINT TO PREVIOUS RECORD
        DO PREV_PAGE                            !  DISPLAY THE PREVIOUS PAGE

      OF CTRL_PGUP                              !CTRL-PAGE UP
        DO FIRST_PAGE                           !  DISPLAY THE FIRST PAGE
        NDX = 1                                 !  POSITION POINT BAR
    . . .
    FREE(TABLE)                                 !FREE MEMORY TABLE
    RETURN                                      !AND RETURN TO CALLER

SAME_PAGE ROUTINE                               !DISPLAY THE SAME PAGE
  GET(TABLE,1)                                  !  GET THE FIRST TABLE ENTRY
  DO FILL_RECORD                                !  FILL IN THE RECORD
  SET(NAM:BY_LAST,NAM:BY_LAST,TBL:PTR)          !  POSITION FILE
  FREE(TABLE)                                   !  EMPTY THE TABLE
  DO NEXT_PAGE                                  !  DISPLAY A FULL PAGE
```

(continued)

```
FIRST_PAGE ROUTINE                          !DISPLAY FIRST PAGE
  BLANK(ROW,COL,ROWS,COLS)
  FREE(TABLE)                               !  EMPTY THE TABLE
  CLEAR(NAM:RECORD,-1)                       !  CLEAR RECORD TO LOW VALUES
  CLEAR(TBL:PTR)                             !  ZERO RECORD POINTER
  SET(NAM:BY_LAST)                           !  POINT TO FIRST RECORD
  LOOP NDX = 1 TO COUNT                      !  FILL UP THE TABLE
    DO FILL_NEXT                             !     FILL A TABLE ENTRY
    IF NOT FOUND THEN BREAK.                 !     GET OUT IF NO RECORD
    .
  NDX = 1                                    !  SET TO TOP OF TABLE
  DO SHOW_PAGE                               !  DISPLAY THE PAGE

LAST_PAGE ROUTINE                           !DISPLAY LAST PAGE
  NDX# = NDX                                 !  SAVE SELECTOR POSITION
  BLANK(ROW,COL,ROWS,COLS)                   !  CLEAR SCROLLING AREA
  FREE(TABLE)                               !  EMPTY THE TABLE
  CLEAR(NAM:RECORD,1)                        !  CLEAR RECORD TO HIGH VALUES
  CLEAR(TBL:PTR,1)                           !  CLEAR PTR TO HIGH VALUE
  SET(NAM:BY_LAST)                           !  POINT TO FIRST RECORD
  LOOP NDX = COUNT TO 1 BY -1                !  FILL UP THE TABLE
    DO FILL_PREV                             !     FILL A TABLE ENTRY
    IF NOT FOUND THEN BREAK.                 !     GET OUT IF NO RECORD
    .
  NDX = NDX#                                 !  RESTORE SELECTOR POSITION
  DO SHOW_PAGE                               !  DISPLAY THE PAGE

FIND_RECORD ROUTINE                         !POSITION TO SPECIFIC RECORD
  SET(NAM:BY_LAST,NAM:BY_LAST,NEWPTR)       !POSITION FILE
  IF NEWPTR = 0                             !NEWPTR NOT SET
    NEXT(NAMES)                              !  READ NEXT RECORD
    NEWPTR = POINTER(NAMES)                  !  SET NEWPTR
    SKIP(NAMES,-1)                           !  BACK UP TO DISPLAY RECORD
    .
  FREE(TABLE)                               !  CLEAR THE RECORD
  DO NEXT_PAGE                               !  DISPLAY A PAGE

NEXT_PAGE ROUTINE                           !DISPLAY NEXT PAGE
  SAVECNT# = RECORDS(TABLE)                  !  SAVE RECORD COUNT
  LOOP COUNT TIMES                           !  FILL UP THE TABLE
    DO FILL_NEXT                             !     FILL A TABLE ENTRY
    IF NOT FOUND                             !     IF NONE ARE LEFT
      IF NOT SAVECNT#                        !       IF REBUILDING TABLE
        DO LAST_PAGE                         !       FILL IN RECORDS
        EXIT                                 !       EXIT OUT OF ROUTINE
        .
```

(continued)

```
      BREAK                                    !    EXIT LOOP
    . .
    DO SHOW_PAGE                               !  DISPLAY THE PAGE


SET_NEXT ROUTINE                              !POINT TO THE NEXT PAGE
    GET(TABLE,RECORDS(TABLE))                 !  GET THE LAST TABLE ENTRY
    DO FILL_RECORD                            !  FILL IN THE RECORD
    SET(NAM:BY_LAST,NAM:BY_LAST,TBL:PTR)      !  POSITION FILE
    NEXT(NAMES)                               !  READ THE CURRENT RECORD


FILL_NEXT ROUTINE                             !FILL NEXT TABLE ENTRY
    FOUND = FALSE                             !  ASSUME RECORD NOT FOUND
    LOOP UNTIL EOF(NAMES)                     !  LOOP UNTIL END OF FILE
      NEXT(NAMES)                             !    READ THE NEXT RECORD
      FOUND = TRUE                            !    SET RECORD FOUND
      DO FILL_TABLE                           !    FILL IN THE TABLE ENTRY
      ADD(TABLE)                              !    ADD LAST TABLE ENTRY
      GET(TABLE,RECORDS(TABLE)-COUNT)         !    GET ANY OVERFLOW RECORD
      DELETE(TABLE)                           !    AND DELETE IT
      EXIT                                    !    RETURN TO CALLER
    .

PREV_PAGE ROUTINE                             !DISPLAY PREVIOUS PAGE
    LOOP COUNT TIMES                          !  FILL UP THE TABLE
      DO FILL_PREV                            !    FILL A TABLE ENTRY
      IF NOT FOUND THEN BREAK.                !    GET OUT IF NO RECORD
    .
    DO SHOW_PAGE                              !  DISPLAY THE PAGE


SET_PREV ROUTINE                              !POINT TO PREVIOUS PAGE
    GET(TABLE,1)                              !  GET THE FIRST TABLE ENTRY
    DO FILL_RECORD                            !  FILL IN THE RECORD
    SET(NAM:BY_LAST,NAM:BY_LAST,TBL:PTR)      !  POSITION FILE
    PREVIOUS(NAMES)                           !  READ THE CURRENT RECORD


FILL_PREV ROUTINE                             !FILL PREVIOUS TABLE ENTRY
    FOUND = FALSE                             !  ASSUME RECORD NOT FOUND
    LOOP UNTIL BOF(NAMES)                     !  LOOP UNTIL BEGINNING OF FILE
      PREVIOUS(NAMES)                         !    READ THE PREVIOUS RECORD
      FOUND = TRUE                            !    SET RECORD FOUND
      DO FILL_TABLE                           !    FILL IN THE TABLE ENTRY
      ADD(TABLE,1)                            !    ADD FIRST TABLE ENTRY
      GET(TABLE,COUNT+1)                      !    GET ANY OVERFLOW RECORD
      DELETE(TABLE)                           !    AND DELETE IT
      EXIT                                    !    RETURN TO CALLER
    .

SHOW_PAGE ROUTINE                             !DISPLAY THE PAGE
    NDX# = NDX                                !  SAVE SCREEN INDEX
```

(continued)

```
    LOOP NDX = 1 TO RECORDS(TABLE)                ! LOOP THRU THE TABLE
      GET(TABLE,NDX)                              !   GET A TABLE ENTRY
      DO FILL_SCREEN                              !   AND DISPLAY IT
      IF TBL:PTR = NEWPTR                         !   SET INDEX FOR NEW RECORD
        NDX# = NDX                                !   POINT TO CORRECT RECORD
    . .
    NDX = NDX#                                    ! RESTORE SCREEN INDEX
    NEWPTR = 0                                    ! CLEAR NEW RECORD POINTER
    CLEAR(NAM:RECORD)                             ! CLEAR RECORD AREA

FILL_TABLE ROUTINE                               !MOVE FILE TO TABLE
  TBL:LAST = NAM:LAST
  TBL:NUMBER = NAM:NUMBER
  TBL:PTR = POINTER(NAMES)                        ! SAVE RECORD POINTER
  TBL:NAME = clip(nam:last) & ', ' & clip(nam:first)

FILL_RECORD ROUTINE                              !MOVE TABLE TO FILE
  NAM:LAST = TBL:LAST
  NAM:NUMBER = TBL:NUMBER

FILL_SCREEN ROUTINE                              !MOVE TABLE TO SCREEN
  SCR:NAME = TBL:NAME

GET_RECORD ROUTINE                               !GET SELECTED RECORD
  GET(TABLE,NDX)                                 !  GET TABLE ENTRY
  GET(NAMES,TBL:PTR)                             !  GET THE RECORD
```

MAIL08.CLA

```
         MEMBER('MAIL')
NO_MESSAGE   PROCEDURE

SCREEN       SCREEN      PRE(SCR),WINDOW(6,50),HUE(0,7)
             ROW(1,1)    STRING('<218,196{48},191>'),HUE(0,7)
             ROW(2,1)    REPEAT(4);STRING('<179,0{48},179>'),HUE(0,7) .
             ROW(6,1)    STRING('<192,196{48},217>'),HUE(0,7)
             ROW(2,20)   STRING('NOT'),BLK
                  COL(24) STRING('AVAILABLE')
                         ENTRY,USE(?FIRST_FIELD)
                         ENTRY,USE(?PRE_MENU)
                         MENU,USE(MENU_FIELD"),REQ
             ROW(4,14)        STRING('PRESS <<ENTER> TO CONTINUE')
           .                 .

    EJECT
```

(continued)

```
CODE
OPEN(SCREEN)                              !OPEN THE MENU SCREEN
SETCURSOR                                 !TURN OFF ANY CURSOR
MENU_FIELD" = ''                          !START MENU WITH FIRST ITEM
LOOP                                      !LOOP UNTIL USER EXITS
  ALERT                                   !TURN OFF ALL ALERTED KEYS
  ALERT(REJECT_KEY)                       !ALERT SCREEN REJECT KEY
  ALERT(ACCEPT_KEY)                       !ALERT SCREEN ACCEPT KEY
  ACCEPT                                  !READ A FIELD OR MENU CHOICE
  IF KEYCODE() = REJECT_KEY THEN RETURN.  !RETURN ON SCREEN REJECT

  IF KEYCODE() = ACCEPT_KEY               !ON SCREEN ACCEPT KEY
    UPDATE                                !  MOVE ALL FIELDS FROM SCREEN
    SELECT(?)                             !  START WITH CURRENT FIELD
    SELECT                                !  EDIT ALL FIELDS
    CYCLE                                 !  GO TO TOP OF LOOP
  .                                       !

  CASE FIELD()                            !JUMP TO FIELD EDIT ROUTINE
  OF ?FIRST_FIELD                         !FROM THE FIRST FIELD
    IF KEYCODE() = ESC_KEY THEN RETURN.   !  RETURN ON ESC KEY

  OF ?PRE_MENU                            !PRE MENU FIELD CONDITION
    IF KEYCODE() = ESC_KEY                !  BACKING UP?
      SELECT(?-1)                         !     SELECT PREVIOUS FIELD
    ELSE                                  !  GOING FORWARD
      SELECT(?+1)                         !     SELECT MENU FIELD
    .

  OF ?MENU_FIELD"                         !FROM THE MENU FIELD
    EXECUTE CHOICE()                      !  CALL THE SELECTED PROCEDURE
      RETURN
  . . .
```

MAIL09.CLA

```
          MEMBER('MAIL')
SIGN_ON       PROCEDURE

SCREEN        SCREEN       PRE(SCR),WINDOW(20,32),AT(1,27),HUE(15,1)
              ROW(6,1)     PAINT(14,32),HUE(0,7)
              ROW(19,2)    PAINT(1,30),HUE(15,1)
              ROW(1,1)     STRING('<201,205{30},187>'),HUE(15,1)
              ROW(2,1)     REPEAT(18);STRING('<186,0{30},186>'),HUE(15,1)  .
              ROW(20,1)    STRING('<200,205{30},188>'),HUE(15,1)
              ROW(2,11)    STRING('WHO ARE YOU?'),HUE(15,1)
```

(continued)

```
                ROW(4,3)     STRING('LOCATE:'),HUE(11,1)
                ROW(19,5)    STRING('Select and Press <<ENTER>'),HUE(15,1)
LOCATOR         ROW(4,10)    STRING(20),HUE(11,1)
                             ENTRY,USE(?FIRST_FIELD)
                             ENTRY,USE(?PRE_POINT)
                             REPEAT(13),EVERY(1),INDEX(NDX)
                ROW(6,2)       POINT(1,30),USE(?POINT),ESC(?-1)
NAME                COL(2)       STRING(@s30)
                .          .


NDX        BYTE                         !REPEAT INDEX FOR POINT AREA
ROW        BYTE                         !ACTUAL ROW OF SCROLL AREA
COL        BYTE                         !ACTUAL COLUMN OF SCROLL AREA
COUNT      BYTE(13)                     !NUMBER OF ITEMS TO SCROLL
ROWS       BYTE(13)                     !NUMBER OF ROWS TO SCROLL
COLS       BYTE(30)                     !NUMBER OF COLUMNS TO SCROLL
FOUND      BYTE                         !RECORD FOUND FLAG
NEWPTR     LONG                         !POINTER TO NEW RECORD


TABLE      TABLE,PRE(TBL)               !TABLE OF RECORD DATA
NAME         STRING(@s30)
LAST         STRING(20)
NUMBER       SHORT
PTR          LONG                       !  POINTER TO FILE RECORD
                .

  EJECT
  CODE
  ACTION# = ACTION                      !SAVE ACTION
  OPEN(SCREEN)                          !OPEN THE SCREEN
  SETCURSOR                             !TURN OFF ANY CURSOR
  TBL:PTR = 1                           !START AT TABLE ENTRY
  NDX = 1                               !PUT SELECTOR BAR ON TOP ITEM
  ROW = ROW(?POINT)                     !REMEMBER TOP ROW AND
  COL = COL(?POINT)                     !LEFT COLUMN OF SCROLL AREA
  RECORDS# = TRUE                       !INITIALIZE RECORDS FLAG
  IF ACTION = 4                         !   TABLE LOOKUP REQUEST
    NEWPTR = POINTER(NAMES)             !   SET POINTER TO RECORD
    IF NOT NEWPTR                       !   RECORD NOT PASSED TO TABLE
      SET(NAM:BY_LAST,NAM:BY_LAST)      !     POSITION TO CLOSEST RECORD
      NEXT(NAMES)                       !     READ RECORD
      NEWPTR = POINTER(NAMES)           !     SET POINTER
      .
    DO FIND_RECORD                      !   POSITION FILE
  ELSE
    NDX = 1                             !   PUT SELECTOR BAR ON TOP ITEM
```

(continued)

```
  DO FIRST_PAGE                                  !  BUILD MEMORY TABLE OF KEYS
 .
RECORDS# = TRUE                                  !  ASSUME THERE ARE RECORDS
LOOP                                             !LOOP UNTIL USER EXITS
  ACTION = ACTION#                               !RESTORE ACTION
  ALERT                                          !RESET ALERTED KEYS
  ALERT(REJECT_KEY)                              !ALERT SCREEN REJECT KEY
  ALERT(ACCEPT_KEY)                              !ALERT SCREEN ACCEPT KEY
  ACCEPT                                         !READ A FIELD
  IF KEYCODE() = REJECT_KEY THEN BREAK.          !RETURN ON SCREEN REJECT KEY

  IF  KEYCODE() = ACCEPT_KEY      |              !ON SCREEN ACCEPT KEY
  AND FIELD() <> ?POINT                          !BUT NOT ON THE POINT FIELD
    UPDATE                                       !  MOVE ALL FIELDS FROM SCREEN
    SELECT(?)                                    !  START WITH CURRENT FIELD
    SELECT                                       !  EDIT ALL FIELDS
    CYCLE                                        !  GO TO TOP OF LOOP
  .

  CASE FIELD()                                   !JUMP TO FIELD EDIT ROUTINE

  OF ?FIRST_FIELD                                !FROM THE FIRST FIELD
    IF KEYCODE() = ESC_KEY      |                !  RETURN ON ESC KEY
    OR RECORDS# = FALSE                          !  OR NO RECORDS
      BREAK                                      !    EXIT PROGRAM
    .
  OF ?PRE_POINT                                  !PRE POINT FIELD CONDITION
    IF KEYCODE() = ESC_KEY                       !  BACKING UP?
      SELECT(?-1)                                !    SELECT PREVIOUS FIELD
    ELSE                                         !  GOING FORWARD
      SELECT(?POINT)                             !    SELECT MENU FIELD
    .
  IF KEYCODE() = ESC_KEY                         !  BACKING UP?
    SCR:LOCATOR = ''                             !    CLEAR LOCATOR
    SETCURSOR                                    !    AND TURN CURSOR OFF
  ELSE                                           !  GOING FORWARD
    LEN# = 0                                     !    RESET TO START OF LOCATOR
    SETCURSOR(ROW(SCR:LOCATOR),COL(SCR:LOCATOR)) !  AND TURN CURSOR ON
  .
  OF ?POINT                                      !PROCESS THE POINT FIELD
    IF RECORDS(TABLE) = 0                        !IF THERE ARE NO RECORDS
      CLEAR(NAM:RECORD)                          !  CLEAR RECORD AREA
      UPDATE                                     !  UPDATE ALL FIELDS
      ACTION = 1                                 !  SET ACTION TO ADD
      GET(NAMES,0)                               !  CLEAR PENDING RECORD
      LOOP
        CLEAR(NAM:RECORD,1)                      !CLEAR RECORD TO HIGH VALUES
```

(continued)

```
    SET(NAM:BY_NUMBER)                          !  POINT TO FIRST RECORD
    PREVIOUS(NAMES)                             !READ LAST KEY RECORD
    IF ERROR()                                  !IF THERE WAS AN ERROR
       CLEAR(NAM:RECORD)                        !  CLEAR THE RECORD
       KEYFIELD# = 0                            !  INTITIALIZE THE FIELD
       IF KEYFIELD# = 0 THEN KEYFIELD# = 1.!  IF ITS 0 MAKE IT 1
    ELSE                                        !ELSE
       KEYFIELD# = NAM:NUMBER + 1               !  INCREMENT FIELD
     .
    CLEAR(NAM:RECORD)                           !CLEAR LAST KEY RECORD
    NAM:NUMBER = KEYFIELD#                      !LOAD KEY FIELD
    ADD(NAMES)                                  !ESTABLISH RECORD WITH UNIQUE
    IF NOT ERROR()                              !ADD WAS SUCCESSFUL
      POINTER# = POINTER(NAMES)                 !  SAVE POINTER
      ACTION = 5                                !  SET ACTION FOR UPDATE
      BREAK                                     !  EXIT LOOP
  . .
  IF ACTION = 2;ACTION = 0;BREAK; ELSE NO_MESSAGE.!CALL FORM FOR NEW RECORD
  IF ACTION                                     !FORM WAS NOT COMPLETED
    HOLD(NAMES)                                 !HOLD RECORD
    GET(NAMES,POINTER#)                         !READ RECORD
    DELETE(NAMES)                               !DELETE RECORD
    DO SAME_PAGE
  .
  NEWPTR = POINTER(NAMES)                       !   SET POINTER TO NEW RECORD
  DO FIRST_PAGE                                 !   DISPLAY THE FIRST PAGE
  IF RECORDS(TABLE) = 0                         !   IF THERE AREN'T ANY RECORDS
    RECORDS# = FALSE                            !      INDICATE NO RECORDS
    SELECT(?PRE_POINT-1)                        !      SELECT THE PRIOR FIELD
  .
  CYCLE                                         !      AND LOOP AGAIN
.
IF KEYCODE() > 31             |                 !THE DISPLAYABLE CHARACTERS
AND KEYCODE() < 255                             !ARE USED TO LOCATE RECORDS
  IF LEN# < SIZE(SCR:LOCATOR)                   !  IF THERE IS ROOM LEFT
    SCR:LOCATOR = SUB(SCR:LOCATOR,1,LEN#) & CHR(KEYCODE())
    LEN# += 1                                   !      INCREMENT THE LENGTH
  .
ELSIF KEYCODE() = BS_KEY                        !BACKSPACE UNTYPES A CHARACTER
  IF LEN# > 0                                   !  IF THERE ARE CHARACTERS LEFT
    LEN# -= 1                                   !      DECREMENT THE LENGTH
    SCR:LOCATOR = SUB(SCR:LOCATOR,1,LEN#)  !      ERASE THE LAST CHARACTER
  .
  ELSE                                          !FOR ANY OTHER CHARACTER
    LEN# = 0                                    !   ZERO THE LENGTH
    SCR:LOCATOR = ''                            !   ERASE THE LOCATOR FIELD
  .
```

(continued)

```
    SETCURSOR(ROW(SCR:LOCATOR),COL(SCR:LOCATOR)+LEN#) !AND RESET THE CURSOR
    NAM:LAST = CLIP(SCR:LOCATOR)          !    UPDATE THE KEY FIELD
    IF KEYBOARD() > 31              |     !THE DISPLAYABLE CHARACTERS
    AND KEYBOARD() < 255            |     !ARE USED TO LOCATE RECORDS
    OR KEYBOARD() = BS_KEY                !INCLUDE BACKSPACE
      CYCLE

    .
    IF LEN# > 0                           !ON A LOCATOR REQUEST
      NAM:LAST = CLIP(SCR:LOCATOR)        !   UPDATE THE KEY FIELD
      SET(NAM:BY_LAST,NAM:BY_LAST)        !   POINT TO NEW RECORD
      NEXT(NAMES)                         !   READ A RECORD
      IF (EOF(NAMES) AND ERROR())         !   IF EOF IS REACHED
        SET(NAM:BY_LAST)                  !     SET TO FIRST RECORD
        PREVIOUS(NAMES)                   !     READ THE LAST RECORD

      .
      NEWPTR = POINTER(NAMES)             !   SET NEW RECORD POINTER
      SKIP(NAMES,-1)                      !   BACK UP TO FIRST RECORD
      FREE(TABLE)                         !   CLEAR THE TABLE
      DO NEXT_PAGE                        !   AND DISPLAY A NEW PAGE

    .
  CASE KEYCODE()                          !PROCESS THE KEYSTROKE

  OF INS_KEY                              !INS KEY
    CLEAR(NAM:RECORD)                     !   CLEAR RECORD AREA
    ACTION = 1                            !   SET ACTION TO ADD
    GET(NAMES,0)                          !   CLEAR PENDING RECORD
    LOOP
      CLEAR(NAM:RECORD,1)                 !CLEAR RECORD TO HIGH VALUES
      SET(NAM:BY_NUMBER)                  !   POINT TO FIRST RECORD
      PREVIOUS(NAMES)                     !READ LAST KEY RECORD
      IF ERROR()                          !IF THERE WAS AN ERROR
        CLEAR(NAM:RECORD)                 !   CLEAR THE RECORD
        KEYFIELD# = 0                     !   INTITIALIZE THE FIELD
        IF KEYFIELD# = 0 THEN KEYFIELD# = 1.!  IF ITS 0 MAKE IT 1
      ELSE                                !ELSE
        KEYFIELD# = NAM:NUMBER + 1        !   INCREMENT FIELD

      .
      CLEAR(NAM:RECORD)                   !CLEAR LAST KEY RECORD
      NAM:NUMBER = KEYFIELD#              !LOAD KEY FIELD
      ADD(NAMES)                          !ESTABLISH RECORD WITH UNIQUE
      IF NOT ERROR()                      !ADD WAS SUCCESSFUL
        POINTER# = POINTER(NAMES)         !   SAVE POINTER
        ACTION = 5                        !   SET ACTION FOR UPDATE
        BREAK                             !   EXIT LOOP
    . .
    IF ACTION = 2;ACTION = 0;BREAK; ELSE NO_MESSAGE.!CALL FORM FOR NEW RECORD
    IF ~ACTION                           !   IF RECORD WAS ADDED
```

(continued)

```
         NEWPTR = POINTER(NAMES)                 !    SET POINTER TO NEW RECORD
         DO FIND_RECORD                          !    POSITION IN FILE
       .
       IF ACTION                                 !FORM WAS NOT COMPLETED
         HOLD(NAMES)                             !HOLD RECORD
         GET(NAMES,POINTER#)                     !READ RECORD
         DELETE(NAMES)                           !DELETE RECORD
         DO SAME_PAGE
       .
    OF ENTER_KEY                                 !ENTER KEY
    OROF ACCEPT_KEY                              !CTRL-ENTER KEY
       DO GET_RECORD                             !  GET THE SELECTED RECORD
       IF ACTION = 4 AND KEYCODE() = ENTER_KEY!   IF THIS IS A LOOKUP REQUEST
         ACTION = 0                              !    SET ACTION TO COMPLETE
         BREAK                                   !    AND RETURN TO CALLER
       .
       IF ~ERROR()                               !  IF RECORD IS STILL THERE
         ACTION = 2                              !    SET ACTION TO CHANGE
         IF ACTION = 2;ACTION = 0;BREAK; ELSE NO_MESSAGE.!CALL FORM TO CHANGE REC
         IF ACTION THEN CYCLE.         .    !    IF SUCCESSFUL RE-DISPLAY
       .
       NEWPTR = POINTER(NAMES)                   !    SET POINTER TO NEW RECORD
       DO FIND_RECORD                            !    POSITION IN FILE
    OF DEL_KEY                                   !DEL KEY
       DO GET_RECORD                             !  READ THE SELECTED RECORD
       IF ~ERROR()                               !  IF RECORD IS STILL THERE
         ACTION = 3                              !    SET ACTION TO DELETE
         IF ACTION = 2;ACTION = 0;BREAK; ELSE NO_MESSAGE.!CALL FORM TO DELETE
         IF ~ACTION                              !    IF SUCCESSFUL
           N# = NDX                              !      SAVE POINT INDEX
           DO SAME_PAGE                          !      RE-DISPLAY
           NDX = N#                              !      RESTORE POINT INDEX
       . .
    OF DOWN_KEY                                  !DOWN ARROW KEY
       DO SET_NEXT                               !  POINT TO NEXT RECORD
       DO FILL_NEXT                              !  FILL A TABLE ENTRY
       IF FOUND                                  !  FOUND A NEW RECORD
         SCROLL(ROW,COL,ROWS,COLS,ROWS(?POINT)) !    SCROLL THE SCREEN UP
         GET(TABLE,RECORDS(TABLE))              !  GET RECORD FROM TABLE
         DO FILL_SCREEN                          !  DISPLAY ON SCREEN
       .
    OF PGDN_KEY                                  !PAGE DOWN KEY
       DO SET_NEXT                               !  POINT TO NEXT RECORD
       DO NEXT_PAGE                              !  DISPLAY THE NEXT PAGE

    OF CTRL_PGDN                                 !CTRL-PAGE DOWN KEY
```

(continued)

```
          DO LAST_PAGE                              !   DISPLAY THE LAST PAGE
          NDX = RECORDS(TABLE)                      !   POSITION POINT BAR

      OF UP_KEY                                     !UP ARROW KEY
        DO SET_PREV                                 !   POINT TO PREVIOUS RECORD
        DO FILL_PREV                                !   FILL A TABLE ENTRY
        IF FOUND                                    !   FOUND A NEW RECORD
          SCROLL(ROW,COL,ROWS,COLS,-(ROWS(?POINT)))!  SCROLL THE SCREEN DOWN
          GET(TABLE,1)                              !   GET RECORD FROM TABLE
          DO FILL_SCREEN                            !   DISPLAY ON SCREEN
          .

      OF PGUP_KEY                                   !PAGE UP KEY
        DO SET_PREV                                 !   POINT TO PREVIOUS RECORD
        DO PREV_PAGE                                !   DISPLAY THE PREVIOUS PAGE

      OF CTRL_PGUP                                  !CTRL-PAGE UP
        DO FIRST_PAGE                               !   DISPLAY THE FIRST PAGE
        NDX = 1                                     !   POSITION POINT BAR
      . . .
    FREE(TABLE)                                     !FREE MEMORY TABLE
    RETURN                                          !AND RETURN TO CALLER

SAME_PAGE ROUTINE                                   !DISPLAY THE SAME PAGE
  GET(TABLE,1)                                      !   GET THE FIRST TABLE ENTRY
  DO FILL_RECORD                                    !   FILL IN THE RECORD
  SET(NAM:BY_LAST,NAM:BY_LAST,TBL:PTR)              !   POSITION FILE
  FREE(TABLE)                                       !   EMPTY THE TABLE
  DO NEXT_PAGE                                      !   DISPLAY A FULL PAGE

FIRST_PAGE ROUTINE                                  !DISPLAY FIRST PAGE
  BLANK(ROW,COL,ROWS,COLS)
  FREE(TABLE)                                       !   EMPTY THE TABLE
  CLEAR(NAM:RECORD,-1)                              !   CLEAR RECORD TO LOW VALUES
  CLEAR(TBL:PTR)                                    !   ZERO RECORD POINTER
  SET(NAM:BY_LAST)                                  !   POINT TO FIRST RECORD
  LOOP NDX = 1 TO COUNT                             !   FILL UP THE TABLE
    DO FILL_NEXT                                    !     FILL A TABLE ENTRY
    IF NOT FOUND THEN BREAK.                        !     GET OUT IF NO RECORD
    .
  NDX = 1                                           !   SET TO TOP OF TABLE
  DO SHOW_PAGE                                      !   DISPLAY THE PAGE

LAST_PAGE ROUTINE                                   !DISPLAY LAST PAGE
  NDX# = NDX                                        !   SAVE SELECTOR POSITION
  BLANK(ROW,COL,ROWS,COLS)                          !   CLEAR SCROLLING AREA
  FREE(TABLE)                                       !   EMPTY THE TABLE
```

(continued)

```
  CLEAR(NAM:RECORD,1)                        !  CLEAR RECORD TO HIGH VALUES
  CLEAR(TBL:PTR,1)                           !  CLEAR PTR TO HIGH VALUE
  SET(NAM:BY_LAST)                           !  POINT TO FIRST RECORD
  LOOP NDX = COUNT TO 1 BY -1                !  FILL UP THE TABLE
    DO FILL_PREV                             !     FILL A TABLE ENTRY
    IF NOT FOUND THEN BREAK.                 !     GET OUT IF NO RECORD
  .
  NDX = NDX#                                 !  RESTORE SELECTOR POSITION
  DO SHOW_PAGE                               !  DISPLAY THE PAGE

FIND_RECORD ROUTINE                          !POSITION TO SPECIFIC RECORD
  SET(NAM:BY_LAST,NAM:BY_LAST,NEWPTR)        !POSITION FILE
  IF NEWPTR = 0                              !NEWPTR NOT SET
    NEXT(NAMES)                              !  READ NEXT RECORD
    NEWPTR = POINTER(NAMES)                  !  SET NEWPTR
    SKIP(NAMES,-1)                           !  BACK UP TO DISPLAY RECORD
  .
  FREE(TABLE)                                !  CLEAR THE RECORD
  DO NEXT_PAGE                               !  DISPLAY A PAGE

NEXT_PAGE ROUTINE                            !DISPLAY NEXT PAGE
  SAVECNT# = RECORDS(TABLE)                  !  SAVE RECORD COUNT
  LOOP COUNT TIMES                           !  FILL UP THE TABLE
    DO FILL_NEXT                             !     FILL A TABLE ENTRY
    IF NOT FOUND                             !     IF NONE ARE LEFT
      IF NOT SAVECNT#                        !       IF REBUILDING TABLE
        DO LAST_PAGE                         !         FILL IN RECORDS
        EXIT                                 !         EXIT OUT OF ROUTINE
      .
      BREAK                                  !     EXIT LOOP
  . .
  DO SHOW_PAGE                               !  DISPLAY THE PAGE

SET_NEXT ROUTINE                             !POINT TO THE NEXT PAGE
  GET(TABLE,RECORDS(TABLE))                  !  GET THE LAST TABLE ENTRY
  DO FILL_RECORD                             !  FILL IN THE RECORD
  SET(NAM:BY_LAST,NAM:BY_LAST,TBL:PTR)       !  POSITION FILE
  NEXT(NAMES)                                !  READ THE CURRENT RECORD

FILL_NEXT ROUTINE                            !FILL NEXT TABLE ENTRY
  FOUND = FALSE                              !  ASSUME RECORD NOT FOUND
  LOOP UNTIL EOF(NAMES)                      !  LOOP UNTIL END OF FILE
    NEXT(NAMES)                              !     READ THE NEXT RECORD
    FOUND = TRUE                             !     SET RECORD FOUND
    DO FILL_TABLE                            !     FILL IN THE TABLE ENTRY
    ADD(TABLE)                               !     ADD LAST TABLE ENTRY
    GET(TABLE,RECORDS(TABLE)-COUNT)          !     GET ANY OVERFLOW RECORD
```

(continued)

```
    DELETE(TABLE)                               !    AND DELETE IT
    EXIT                                        !    RETURN TO CALLER
  .

PREV_PAGE ROUTINE                               !DISPLAY PREVIOUS PAGE
  LOOP COUNT TIMES                              !  FILL UP THE TABLE
    DO FILL_PREV                                !    FILL A TABLE ENTRY
    IF NOT FOUND THEN BREAK.                    !    GET OUT IF NO RECORD
  .
  DO SHOW_PAGE                                  !  DISPLAY THE PAGE

SET_PREV ROUTINE                                !POINT TO PREVIOUS PAGE
  GET(TABLE,1)                                  !  GET THE FIRST TABLE ENTRY
  DO FILL_RECORD                                !  FILL IN THE RECORD
  SET(NAM:BY_LAST,NAM:BY_LAST,TBL:PTR)          !  POSITION FILE
  PREVIOUS(NAMES)                               !  READ THE CURRENT RECORD

FILL_PREV ROUTINE                               !FILL PREVIOUS TABLE ENTRY
  FOUND = FALSE                                 !  ASSUME RECORD NOT FOUND
  LOOP UNTIL BOF(NAMES)                         !  LOOP UNTIL BEGINNING OF FILE
    PREVIOUS(NAMES)                             !    READ THE PREVIOUS RECORD
    FOUND = TRUE                                !    SET RECORD FOUND
    DO FILL_TABLE                               !    FILL IN THE TABLE ENTRY
    ADD(TABLE,1)                                !    ADD FIRST TABLE ENTRY
    GET(TABLE,COUNT+1)                          !    GET ANY OVERFLOW RECORD
    DELETE(TABLE)                               !    AND DELETE IT
    EXIT                                        !    RETURN TO CALLER
  .

SHOW_PAGE ROUTINE                               !DISPLAY THE PAGE
  NDX# = NDX                                    !  SAVE SCREEN INDEX
  LOOP NDX = 1 TO RECORDS(TABLE)                !  LOOP THRU THE TABLE
    GET(TABLE,NDX)                              !    GET A TABLE ENTRY
    DO FILL_SCREEN                              !    AND DISPLAY IT
    IF TBL:PTR = NEWPTR                         !    SET INDEX FOR NEW RECORD
      NDX# = NDX                                !      POINT TO CORRECT RECORD
  . .
  NDX = NDX#                                    !  RESTORE SCREEN INDEX
  NEWPTR = 0                                    !  CLEAR NEW RECORD POINTER
  CLEAR(NAM:RECORD)                             !  CLEAR RECORD AREA

FILL_TABLE ROUTINE                              !MOVE FILE TO TABLE
  TBL:LAST = NAM:LAST
  TBL:NUMBER = NAM:NUMBER
  TBL:PTR = POINTER(NAMES)                      !  SAVE RECORD POINTER
  TBL:NAME = clip(nam:last) & ', ' & clip(nam:first)

FILL_RECORD ROUTINE                             !MOVE TABLE TO FILE
  NAM:LAST = TBL:LAST
  NAM:NUMBER = TBL:NUMBER
```

(continued)

```
FILL_SCREEN ROUTINE                          !MOVE TABLE TO SCREEN
  SCR:NAME = TBL:NAME


GET_RECORD ROUTINE                           !GET SELECTED RECORD
  GET(TABLE,NDX)                             !  GET TABLE ENTRY
  GET(NAMES,TBL:PTR)                         !  GET THE RECORD
```

MAIL10.CLA

```
            MEMBER('MAIL')
LEAVEMAIL   PROCEDURE

SCREEN      SCREEN      PRE(SCR),WINDOW(19,67),AT(5,8),HUE(15,1)
            ROW(1,1)    STRING('<218,196{25},0{14},196{26},191>'),HUE(15,1)
            ROW(2,1)    REPEAT(17);STRING('<179,0{65},179>'),HUE(15,1)  .
            ROW(19,1)   STRING('<192,196{13},0{39},196{13},217>'),HUE(15,1)
            ROW(1,27)   STRING(' LEAVING MAIL '),HUE(0,7)
            ROW(3,4)    STRING(' No.'),HUE(0,7)
                 COL(12) STRING(' Date'),HUE(0,7)
                 COL(17) STRING(' '),HUE(8,7)
                 COL(20) STRING(' '),HUE(8,7)
                 COL(21) STRING('Subject'),HUE(0,7)
                 COL(28) STRING(' '),HUE(8,7)
                 COL(46) STRING(' Receiver '),HUE(0,7)
            ROW(19,15) STRING(' <<INS>CREATE  <<DEL>DELETE  <<ENTER>EDIT ') |
                         HUE(0,7)
                     ENTRY,USE(?FIRST_FIELD)
                     ENTRY,USE(?PRE_POINT)
                     REPEAT(15),EVERY(1),INDEX(NDX)
            ROW(4,2)     POINT(1,65),USE(?POINT),ESC(?-1)
MESSAGE_NUM      COL(3)    STRING(@N_6)
DATE             COL(11)   STRING(@D1)
SUBJECT          COL(20)   STRING(25)
LAST             COL(46)   STRING(20)
                      .             .

NDX         BYTE                             !REPEAT INDEX FOR POINT AREA
ROW         BYTE                             !ACTUAL ROW OF SCROLL AREA
COL         BYTE                             !ACTUAL COLUMN OF SCROLL AREA
COUNT       BYTE(15)                         !NUMBER OF ITEMS TO SCROLL
ROWS        BYTE(15)                         !NUMBER OF ROWS TO SCROLL
COLS        BYTE(65)                         !NUMBER OF COLUMNS TO SCROLL
FOUND       BYTE                             !RECORD FOUND FLAG
NEWPTR      LONG                             !POINTER TO NEW RECORD
```

(continued)

```
TABLE          TABLE,PRE(TBL)              !TABLE OF RECORD DATA
MESSAGE_NUM    LONG                        !NUMBER OF MESSAGE
DATE           STRING(@D1)                 !DATE OF MESSAGE
SUBJECT        STRING(25)                  !SUBJECT OF MAIL MESSAGE
LAST           STRING(20)
SENDER_NUM     SHORT                       !SENDER'S NUMBER
NUMBER         SHORT                       !USER NUMBER
PTR            LONG                        !  POINTER TO FILE RECORD
               .

               GROUP,PRE(SAV)
SENDER_NUM     SHORT
               .


  EJECT
  CODE
  ACTION# = ACTION                         !SAVE ACTION
  OPEN(SCREEN)                             !OPEN THE SCREEN
  SETCURSOR                                !TURN OFF ANY CURSOR
  SIGN_ON;MES:SENDER_NUM = NAM:NUMBER      !CALL SETUP PROCEDURE
  SAV:SENDER_NUM = MES:SENDER_NUM          !SAVE SELECTOR FIELD
  TBL:PTR = 1                              !START AT TABLE ENTRY
  NDX = 1                                  !PUT SELECTOR BAR ON TOP ITEM
  ROW = ROW(?POINT)                        !REMEMBER TOP ROW AND
  COL = COL(?POINT)                        !LEFT COLUMN OF SCROLL AREA
  RECORDS# = TRUE                          !INITIALIZE RECORDS FLAG
  LOOP                                     !LOOP UNTIL USER EXITS
    ACTION = ACTION#                       !RESTORE ACTION
    MES:SENDER_NUM = SAV:SENDER_NUM        !RESTORE SELECTOR FIELD
    ALERT                                  !RESET ALERTED KEYS
    ALERT(REJECT_KEY)                      !ALERT SCREEN REJECT KEY
    ALERT(ACCEPT_KEY)                      !ALERT SCREEN ACCEPT KEY
    ACCEPT                                 !READ A FIELD
    IF KEYCODE() = REJECT_KEY THEN BREAK.  !RETURN ON SCREEN REJECT KEY

    IF  KEYCODE() = ACCEPT_KEY      |      !ON SCREEN ACCEPT KEY
    AND FIELD() <> ?POINT                  !BUT NOT ON THE POINT FIELD
      UPDATE                               !  MOVE ALL FIELDS FROM SCREEN
      SELECT(?)                            !  START WITH CURRENT FIELD
      SELECT                               !  EDIT ALL FIELDS
      CYCLE                                !  GO TO TOP OF LOOP
      .

    CASE FIELD()                           !JUMP TO FIELD EDIT ROUTINE

    OF ?FIRST_FIELD                        !FROM THE FIRST FIELD
      IF KEYCODE() = ESC_KEY     |         !  RETURN ON ESC KEY
      OR RECORDS# = FALSE                  !  OR NO RECORDS
```

(continued)

```
    BREAK                                    !    EXIT PROGRAM

  IF ACTION = 4                             !  TABLE LOOKUP REQUEST
    NEWPTR = POINTER(MESSAGES)              !  SET POINTER TO RECORD
    IF NOT NEWPTR                           !  RECORD NOT PASSED TO TABLE
      SET(MES:BY_OUTGOING,MES:BY_OUTGOING) ! POSITION TO CLOSEST RECORD
      NEXT(MESSAGES)                        !    READ RECORD
      NEWPTR = POINTER(MESSAGES)            !    SET POINTER
        .
    DO FIND_RECORD                          !  POSITION FILE
  ELSE
    NDX = 1                                 !  PUT SELECTOR BAR ON TOP ITEM
    DO FIRST_PAGE                           !  BUILD MEMORY TABLE OF KEYS
      .
    RECORDS# = TRUE                         !  ASSUME THERE ARE RECORDS
OF ?PRE_POINT                               !PRE POINT FIELD CONDITION
  IF KEYCODE() = ESC_KEY                    !  BACKING UP?
    SELECT(?-1)                             !    SELECT PREVIOUS FIELD
  ELSE                                      !  GOING FORWARD
    SELECT(?POINT)                          !    SELECT MENU FIELD
      .
OF ?POINT                                   !PROCESS THE POINT FIELD
  IF RECORDS(TABLE) = 0                     !IF THERE ARE NO RECORDS
    CLEAR(MES:RECORD)                       !  CLEAR RECORD AREA
    UPDATE                                  !  UPDATE ALL FIELDS
    ACTION = 1                              !  SET ACTION TO ADD
    GET(MESSAGES,0)                         !  CLEAR PENDING RECORD
    LOOP
      CLEAR(MES:RECORD,1)                   !CLEAR RECORD TO HIGH VALUES
      MES:SENDER_NUM = SAV:SENDER_NUM       !RESTORE SELECTOR FIELD
      SET(MES:BY_OUTGOING,MES:BY_OUTGOING,TBL:PTR) !POINT PAST LAST RECORD
      PREVIOUS(MESSAGES)                    !READ LAST KEY RECORD
      IF ERROR()                            !IF THERE WAS AN ERROR
        CLEAR(MES:RECORD)                   !  CLEAR THE RECORD
        KEYFIELD# = 0                       !  INTITIALIZE THE FIELD
        IF KEYFIELD# = 0 THEN KEYFIELD# = 1.!  IF ITS 0 MAKE IT 1
      ELSIF MES:SENDER_NUM <> SAV:SENDER_NUM !NO SELECTOR MATCHES
        CLEAR(MES:RECORD)                   !  CLEAR THE RECORD
        KEYFIELD# = 0                       !  AND INITIALIZE THE FIELD
        IF KEYFIELD# = 0 THEN KEYFIELD# = 1.!  IF ITS 0 MAKE IT 1
      ELSE                                  !ELSE
        KEYFIELD# = MES:MESSAGE_NUM + 1     !  INCREMENT FIELD
          .
      CLEAR(MES:RECORD)                     !CLEAR LAST KEY RECORD
      MES:SENDER_NUM = SAV:SENDER_NUM       !RESTORE SELECTOR FIELD
      MES:MESSAGE_NUM = KEYFIELD#           !LOAD KEY FIELD
      ADD(MESSAGES)                         !ESTABLISH RECORD WITH UNIQUE
```

(continued)

```
    IF NOT ERROR()                          !ADD WAS SUCCESSFUL
      POINTER# = POINTER(MESSAGES)          !  SAVE POINTER
      ACTION = 5                            !  SET ACTION FOR UPDATE
      BREAK                                 !  EXIT LOOP
  . .
  MES:SENDER_NUM = SAV:SENDER_NUM           !RESTORE SELECTOR FIELD
  NEW_MESSAGE                               !  CALL FORM FOR NEW RECORD
  IF ACTION                                 !FORM WAS NOT COMPLETED
    HOLD(MESSAGES)                          !HOLD RECORD
    GET(MESSAGES,POINTER#)                  !READ RECORD
    DELETE(MESSAGES)                        !DELETE RECORD
    DO SAME_PAGE

  .
  NEWPTR = POINTER(MESSAGES)                !    SET POINTER TO NEW RECORD
  DO FIRST_PAGE                             !  DISPLAY THE FIRST PAGE
  IF RECORDS(TABLE) = 0                     !  IF THERE AREN'T ANY RECORDS
    RECORDS# = FALSE                        !    INDICATE NO RECORDS
    SELECT(?PRE_POINT-1)                    !    SELECT THE PRIOR FIELD
  .
  CYCLE                                     !    AND LOOP AGAIN
.
CASE KEYCODE()                              !PROCESS THE KEYSTROKE

OF INS_KEY                                  !INS KEY
  CLEAR(MES:RECORD)                         !  CLEAR RECORD AREA
  ACTION = 1                                !  SET ACTION TO ADD
  GET(MESSAGES,0)                           !  CLEAR PENDING RECORD
  LOOP
    CLEAR(MES:RECORD,1)                     !CLEAR RECORD TO HIGH VALUES
    MES:SENDER_NUM = SAV:SENDER_NUM         !RESTORE SELECTOR FIELD
    SET(MES:BY_OUTGOING,MES:BY_OUTGOING,TBL:PTR)!POINT PAST LAST RECORD
    PREVIOUS(MESSAGES)                      !READ LAST KEY RECORD
    IF ERROR()                              !IF THERE WAS AN ERROR
       CLEAR(MES:RECORD)                    !  CLEAR THE RECORD
       KEYFIELD# = 0                        !  INTITIALIZE THE FIELD
       IF KEYFIELD# = 0 THEN KEYFIELD# = 1.!  IF ITS 0 MAKE IT 1
    ELSIF MES:SENDER_NUM <> SAV:SENDER_NUM !NO SELECTOR MATCHES
       CLEAR(MES:RECORD)                    !  CLEAR THE RECORD
       KEYFIELD# = 0                        !  AND INITIALIZE THE FIELD
       IF KEYFIELD# = 0 THEN KEYFIELD# = 1.!  IF ITS 0 MAKE IT 1
    ELSE                                    !ELSE
       KEYFIELD# = MES:MESSAGE_NUM + 1      !  INCREMENT FIELD
    .
    CLEAR(MES:RECORD)                       !CLEAR LAST KEY RECORD
    MES:SENDER_NUM = SAV:SENDER_NUM         !RESTORE SELECTOR FIELD
    MES:MESSAGE_NUM = KEYFIELD#             !LOAD KEY FIELD
    ADD(MESSAGES)                           !ESTABLISH RECORD WITH UNIQUE
```

(continued)

```
       IF NOT ERROR()                               !ADD WAS SUCCESSFUL
         POINTER# = POINTER(MESSAGES)               ! SAVE POINTER
         ACTION = 5                                 ! SET ACTION FOR UPDATE
         BREAK                                      ! EXIT LOOP
     . .
     MES:SENDER_NUM = SAV:SENDER_NUM                !RESTORE SELECTOR FIELD
     NEW_MESSAGE                                    ! CALL FORM FOR NEW RECORD
     IF ~ACTION                                     ! IF RECORD WAS ADDED
       NEWPTR = POINTER(MESSAGES)                   !    SET POINTER TO NEW RECORD
       DO FIND_RECORD                               !    POSITION IN FILE
     .
     IF ACTION                                      !FORM WAS NOT COMPLETED
       HOLD(MESSAGES)                               !HOLD RECORD
       GET(MESSAGES,POINTER#)                       !READ RECORD
       DELETE(MESSAGES)                             !DELETE RECORD
       DO SAME_PAGE
     .
 OF ENTER_KEY                                       !ENTER KEY
 OROF ACCEPT_KEY                                    !CTRL-ENTER KEY
   DO GET_RECORD                                    !  GET THE SELECTED RECORD
   IF ACTION = 4 AND KEYCODE() = ENTER_KEY!  IF THIS IS A LOOKUP REQUEST
     ACTION = 0                                     !    SET ACTION TO COMPLETE
     BREAK                                          !    AND RETURN TO CALLER
   .
   IF ~ERROR()                                      !  IF RECORD IS STILL THERE
     ACTION = 2                                     !    SET ACTION TO CHANGE
     NEW_MESSAGE                                    !    CALL FORM TO CHANGE REC
     IF ACTION THEN CYCLE.                          !    IF SUCCESSFUL RE-DISPLAY
   .
   NEWPTR = POINTER(MESSAGES)                       !    SET POINTER TO NEW RECORD
   DO FIND_RECORD                                   !    POSITION IN FILE
 OF DEL_KEY                                         !DEL KEY
   DO GET_RECORD                                    !  READ THE SELECTED RECORD
   IF ~ERROR()                                      !  IF RECORD IS STILL THERE
     ACTION = 3                                     !    SET ACTION TO DELETE
     NEW_MESSAGE                                    !    CALL FORM TO DELETE
     IF ~ACTION                                     !    IF SUCCESSFUL
       N# = NDX                                     !      SAVE POINT INDEX
       DO SAME_PAGE                                 !      RE-DISPLAY
       NDX = N#                                     !      RESTORE POINT INDEX
     . .
 OF DOWN_KEY                                        !DOWN ARROW KEY
   DO SET_NEXT                                      !  POINT TO NEXT RECORD
   DO FILL_NEXT                                     !  FILL A TABLE ENTRY
   IF FOUND                                         !  FOUND A NEW RECORD
     SCROLL(ROW,COL,ROWS,COLS,ROWS(?POINT)) !    SCROLL THE SCREEN UP
     GET(TABLE,RECORDS(TABLE))                      !  GET RECORD FROM TABLE
```

(continued)

```
        DO FILL_SCREEN                         !  DISPLAY ON SCREEN
        .

    OF PGDN_KEY                            !PAGE DOWN KEY
      DO SET_NEXT                          !  POINT TO NEXT RECORD
      DO NEXT_PAGE                         !  DISPLAY THE NEXT PAGE

    OF CTRL_PGDN                           !CTRL-PAGE DOWN KEY
      DO LAST_PAGE                         !  DISPLAY THE LAST PAGE
      NDX = RECORDS(TABLE)                 !  POSITION POINT BAR

    OF UP_KEY                              !UP ARROW KEY
      DO SET_PREV                          !  POINT TO PREVIOUS RECORD
      DO FILL_PREV                         !  FILL A TABLE ENTRY
      IF FOUND                             !  FOUND A NEW RECORD
        SCROLL(ROW,COL,ROWS,COLS,-(ROWS(?POINT)))! SCROLL THE SCREEN DOWN
        GET(TABLE,1)                       !  GET RECORD FROM TABLE
        DO FILL_SCREEN                     !  DISPLAY ON SCREEN
        .

    OF PGUP_KEY                            !PAGE UP KEY
      DO SET_PREV                          !  POINT TO PREVIOUS RECORD
      DO PREV_PAGE                         !  DISPLAY THE PREVIOUS PAGE

    OF CTRL_PGUP                           !CTRL-PAGE UP
      DO FIRST_PAGE                        !  DISPLAY THE FIRST PAGE
      NDX = 1                              !  POSITION POINT BAR
  . . .
  FREE(TABLE)                              !FREE MEMORY TABLE
  RETURN                                   !AND RETURN TO CALLER

SAME_PAGE ROUTINE                          !DISPLAY THE SAME PAGE
  GET(TABLE,1)                             !  GET THE FIRST TABLE ENTRY
  DO FILL_RECORD                           !  FILL IN THE RECORD
  SET(MES:BY_OUTGOING,MES:BY_OUTGOING,TBL:PTR)  !  POSITION FILE
  FREE(TABLE)                              !  EMPTY THE TABLE
  DO NEXT_PAGE                             !  DISPLAY A FULL PAGE

FIRST_PAGE ROUTINE                         !DISPLAY FIRST PAGE
  BLANK(ROW,COL,ROWS,COLS)
  FREE(TABLE)                              !  EMPTY THE TABLE
  CLEAR(MES:RECORD,-1)                     !  CLEAR RECORD TO LOW VALUES
  CLEAR(TBL:PTR)                           !  ZERO RECORD POINTER
  MES:SENDER_NUM = SAV:SENDER_NUM          !RESTORE SELECTOR FIELD
  SET(MES:BY_OUTGOING,MES:BY_OUTGOING,TBL:PTR)  !  POINT PAST LAST RECORD
  LOOP NDX = 1 TO COUNT                    !  FILL UP THE TABLE
    DO FILL_NEXT                           !     FILL A TABLE ENTRY
```

(continued)

```
     IF NOT FOUND THEN BREAK.           !   GET OUT IF NO RECORD
   .
   NDX = 1                              !  SET TO TOP OF TABLE
   DO SHOW_PAGE                         !  DISPLAY THE PAGE

LAST_PAGE ROUTINE                       !DISPLAY LAST PAGE
   NDX# = NDX                           !  SAVE SELECTOR POSITION
   BLANK(ROW,COL,ROWS,COLS)             !  CLEAR SCROLLING AREA
   FREE(TABLE)                          !  EMPTY THE TABLE
   CLEAR(MES:RECORD,1)                  !  CLEAR RECORD TO HIGH VALUES
   CLEAR(TBL:PTR,1)                     !  CLEAR PTR TO HIGH VALUE
   MES:SENDER_NUM = SAV:SENDER_NUM      !RESTORE SELECTOR FIELD
   SET(MES:BY_OUTGOING,MES:BY_OUTGOING,TBL:PTR)  !  POINT PAST LAST RECORD
   LOOP NDX = COUNT TO 1 BY -1          !  FILL UP THE TABLE
     DO FILL_PREV                       !    FILL A TABLE ENTRY
     IF NOT FOUND THEN BREAK.           !    GET OUT IF NO RECORD
   .
   NDX = NDX#                           !  RESTORE SELECTOR POSITION
   DO SHOW_PAGE                         !  DISPLAY THE PAGE

FIND_RECORD ROUTINE                     !POSITION TO SPECIFIC RECORD
   SET(MES:BY_OUTGOING,MES:BY_OUTGOING,NEWPTR)  !POSITION FILE
   IF NEWPTR = 0                        !NEWPTR NOT SET
     NEXT(MESSAGES)                     !  READ NEXT RECORD
     NEWPTR = POINTER(MESSAGES)         !  SET NEWPTR
     SKIP(MESSAGES,-1)                  !  BACK UP TO DISPLAY RECORD
   .
   FREE(TABLE)                          !  CLEAR THE RECORD
   DO NEXT_PAGE                         !  DISPLAY A PAGE

NEXT_PAGE ROUTINE                       !DISPLAY NEXT PAGE
   SAVECNT# = RECORDS(TABLE)            !  SAVE RECORD COUNT
   LOOP COUNT TIMES                     !  FILL UP THE TABLE
     DO FILL_NEXT                       !    FILL A TABLE ENTRY
     IF NOT FOUND                       !    IF NONE ARE LEFT
       IF NOT SAVECNT#                  !      IF REBUILDING TABLE
         DO LAST_PAGE                   !        FILL IN RECORDS
       EXIT                             !        EXIT OUT OF ROUTINE
       .
       BREAK                            !      EXIT LOOP
   . .
   DO SHOW_PAGE                         !  DISPLAY THE PAGE

SET_NEXT ROUTINE                        !POINT TO THE NEXT PAGE
   GET(TABLE,RECORDS(TABLE))            !  GET THE LAST TABLE ENTRY
   DO FILL_RECORD                       !  FILL IN THE RECORD
```

(continued)

```
     SET(MES:BY_OUTGOING,MES:BY_OUTGOING,TBL:PTR)    !  POSITION FILE
     NEXT(MESSAGES)                                  !  READ THE CURRENT RECORD

FILL_NEXT ROUTINE                                    !FILL NEXT TABLE ENTRY
  FOUND = FALSE                                      !  ASSUME RECORD NOT FOUND
  LOOP UNTIL EOF(MESSAGES)                           !  LOOP UNTIL END OF FILE
    NEXT(MESSAGES)                                   !    READ THE NEXT RECORD
    IF MES:SENDER_NUM <> SAV:SENDER_NUM              !IF END OF SELECTION
      MES:SENDER_NUM = SAV:SENDER_NUM                !  RESTORE THE SELECTOR
      BREAK                                          !  AND BREAK
      .
    FOUND = TRUE                                     !    SET RECORD FOUND
    DO FILL_TABLE                                    !    FILL IN THE TABLE ENTRY
    ADD(TABLE)                                       !    ADD LAST TABLE ENTRY
    GET(TABLE,RECORDS(TABLE)-COUNT)                  !    GET ANY OVERFLOW RECORD
    DELETE(TABLE)                                    !    AND DELETE IT
    EXIT                                             !    RETURN TO CALLER
    .

PREV_PAGE ROUTINE                                    !DISPLAY PREVIOUS PAGE
  LOOP COUNT TIMES                                   !  FILL UP THE TABLE
    DO FILL_PREV                                     !    FILL A TABLE ENTRY
    IF NOT FOUND THEN BREAK.                         !    GET OUT IF NO RECORD
    .
  DO SHOW_PAGE                                       !  DISPLAY THE PAGE

SET_PREV ROUTINE                                     !POINT TO PREVIOUS PAGE
  GET(TABLE,1)                                       !  GET THE FIRST TABLE ENTRY
  DO FILL_RECORD                                     !  FILL IN THE RECORD
  SET(MES:BY_OUTGOING,MES:BY_OUTGOING,TBL:PTR)       !  POSITION FILE
  PREVIOUS(MESSAGES)                                 !  READ THE CURRENT RECORD

FILL_PREV ROUTINE                                    !FILL PREVIOUS TABLE ENTRY
  FOUND = FALSE                                      !  ASSUME RECORD NOT FOUND
  LOOP UNTIL BOF(MESSAGES)                           !  LOOP UNTIL BEGINNING OF FILE
    PREVIOUS(MESSAGES)                               !    READ THE PREVIOUS RECORD
    IF MES:SENDER_NUM <> SAV:SENDER_NUM              !IF END OF SELECTION
      MES:SENDER_NUM = SAV:SENDER_NUM                !  RESTORE THE SELECTOR
      BREAK                                          !  AND BREAK
      .
    FOUND = TRUE                                     !    SET RECORD FOUND
    DO FILL_TABLE                                    !    FILL IN THE TABLE ENTRY
    ADD(TABLE,1)                                     !    ADD FIRST TABLE ENTRY
    GET(TABLE,COUNT+1)                               !    GET ANY OVERFLOW RECORD
    DELETE(TABLE)                                    !    AND DELETE IT
    EXIT                                             !    RETURN TO CALLER
    .

SHOW_PAGE ROUTINE                                    !DISPLAY THE PAGE
```

(continued)

```
NDX# = NDX                              ! SAVE SCREEN INDEX
LOOP NDX = 1 TO RECORDS(TABLE)          ! LOOP THRU THE TABLE
  GET(TABLE,NDX)                        !   GET A TABLE ENTRY
  DO FILL_SCREEN                        !   AND DISPLAY IT
  IF TBL:PTR = NEWPTR                   !   SET INDEX FOR NEW RECORD
    NDX# = NDX                          !   POINT TO CORRECT RECORD
. .
NDX = NDX#                              ! RESTORE SCREEN INDEX
NEWPTR = 0                              ! CLEAR NEW RECORD POINTER
CLEAR(MES:RECORD)                       ! CLEAR RECORD AREA

FILL_TABLE ROUTINE                      !MOVE FILE TO TABLE
  NAM:NUMBER = MES:NUMBER               !MOVE RELATED KEY FIELDS
  GET(NAMES,NAM:BY_NUMBER)              !READ THE RECORD
  IF ERROR() THEN CLEAR(NAM:RECORD).    !IF NOT FOUND, CLEAR RECORD
  TBL:LAST = NAM:LAST                   !DISPLAY LOOKUP FIELD
  TBL:MESSAGE_NUM = MES:MESSAGE_NUM
  TBL:DATE = MES:DATE
  TBL:SUBJECT = MES:SUBJECT
  TBL:SENDER_NUM = MES:SENDER_NUM
  TBL:NUMBER = MES:NUMBER
  TBL:PTR = POINTER(MESSAGES)           ! SAVE RECORD POINTER

FILL_RECORD ROUTINE                     !MOVE TABLE TO FILE
  MES:SENDER_NUM = TBL:SENDER_NUM
  MES:NUMBER = TBL:NUMBER
  MES:MESSAGE_NUM = TBL:MESSAGE_NUM

FILL_SCREEN ROUTINE                     !MOVE TABLE TO SCREEN
  SCR:MESSAGE_NUM = TBL:MESSAGE_NUM
  SCR:DATE = TBL:DATE
  SCR:SUBJECT = TBL:SUBJECT
  SCR:LAST = TBL:LAST

GET_RECORD ROUTINE                      !GET SELECTED RECORD
  GET(TABLE,NDX)                        ! GET TABLE ENTRY
  GET(MESSAGES,TBL:PTR)                 ! GET THE RECORD
```

MAIL11.CLA

```
        MEMBER('MAIL')
READMAIL      PROCEDURE

SCREEN        SCREEN     PRE(SCR),WINDOW(19,67),AT(5,8),HUE(15,1)
              ROW(1,1)   STRING('<218,196{25},0{14},196{26},191>'),HUE(15,1)
```

(continued)

```
         ROW(2,1)    REPEAT(17);STRING('<179,0{65},179>'),HUE(15,1)  .
         ROW(19,1)   STRING('<192,196{18},0{28},196{19},217>'),HUE(15,1)
         ROW(1,27)   STRING(' READING MAIL '),HUE(0,7)
         ROW(3,4)    STRING(' '),HUE(8,7)
               COL(5) STRING('No.'),HUE(0,7)
               COL(12) STRING(' '),HUE(8,7)
               COL(13) STRING('Date'),HUE(0,7)
               COL(17) STRING(' '),HUE(8,7)
               COL(20) STRING(' '),HUE(8,7)
               COL(21) STRING('Subject'),HUE(0,7)
               COL(28) STRING(' '),HUE(8,7)
               COL(46) STRING(' Sender '),HUE(0,7)
         ROW(19,20) STRING(' PRESS <<ENTER> TO READ ITEM '),HUE(0,7)
                    ENTRY,USE(?FIRST_FIELD)
                    ENTRY,USE(?PRE_POINT)
                    REPEAT(15),EVERY(1),INDEX(NDX)
         ROW(4,2)    POINT(1,65),USE(?POINT),ESC(?-1)
MESSAGE_NUM        COL(3)     STRING(@N_6)
DATE               COL(11)    STRING(@D1)
SUBJECT            COL(20)    STRING(25)
LAST               COL(46)    STRING(20)
                .          .

NDX         BYTE                              !REPEAT INDEX FOR POINT AREA
ROW         BYTE                              !ACTUAL ROW OF SCROLL AREA
COL         BYTE                              !ACTUAL COLUMN OF SCROLL AREA
COUNT       BYTE(15)                          !NUMBER OF ITEMS TO SCROLL
ROWS        BYTE(15)                          !NUMBER OF ROWS TO SCROLL
COLS        BYTE(65)                          !NUMBER OF COLUMNS TO SCROLL
FOUND       BYTE                              !RECORD FOUND FLAG
NEWPTR      LONG                              !POINTER TO NEW RECORD

TABLE       TABLE,PRE(TBL)                    !TABLE OF RECORD DATA
MESSAGE_NUM LONG                              !NUMBER OF MESSAGE
DATE        STRING(@D1)                       !DATE OF MESSAGE
SUBJECT     STRING(25)                        !SUBJECT OF MAIL MESSAGE
LAST        STRING(20)
NUMBER      SHORT                             !USER NUMBER
PTR         LONG                              !  POINTER TO FILE RECORD
                .

            GROUP,PRE(SAV)
NUMBER      SHORT
                .

  EJECT
  CODE
  ACTION# = ACTION                            !SAVE ACTION
```

(continued)

```
OPEN(SCREEN)                            !OPEN THE SCREEN
SETCURSOR                               !TURN OFF ANY CURSOR
SIGN_ON;MES:NUMBER = NAM:NUMBER         !CALL SETUP PROCEDURE
SAV:NUMBER = MES:NUMBER                 !SAVE SELECTOR FIELD
TBL:PTR = 1                             !START AT TABLE ENTRY
NDX = 1                                 !PUT SELECTOR BAR ON TOP ITEM
ROW = ROW(?POINT)                       !REMEMBER TOP ROW AND
COL = COL(?POINT)                       !LEFT COLUMN OF SCROLL AREA
RECORDS# = TRUE                         !INITIALIZE RECORDS FLAG
LOOP                                    !LOOP UNTIL USER EXITS
  ACTION = ACTION#                      !RESTORE ACTION
  MES:NUMBER = SAV:NUMBER               !RESTORE SELECTOR FIELD
  ALERT                                 !RESET ALERTED KEYS
  ALERT(REJECT_KEY)                     !ALERT SCREEN REJECT KEY
  ALERT(ACCEPT_KEY)                     !ALERT SCREEN ACCEPT KEY
  ACCEPT                                !READ A FIELD
  IF KEYCODE() = REJECT_KEY THEN BREAK. !RETURN ON SCREEN REJECT KEY

  IF  KEYCODE() = ACCEPT_KEY    |       !ON SCREEN ACCEPT KEY
  AND FIELD() <> ?POINT                 !BUT NOT ON THE POINT FIELD
    UPDATE                              !  MOVE ALL FIELDS FROM SCREEN
    SELECT(?)                           !  START WITH CURRENT FIELD
    SELECT                              !  EDIT ALL FIELDS
    CYCLE                               !  GO TO TOP OF LOOP
  .

  CASE FIELD()                          !JUMP TO FIELD EDIT ROUTINE

  OF ?FIRST_FIELD                       !FROM THE FIRST FIELD
    IF KEYCODE() = ESC_KEY   |          !  RETURN ON ESC KEY
    OR RECORDS# = FALSE                 !  OR NO RECORDS
      BREAK                             !    EXIT PROGRAM
    .
      IF ACTION = 4                     !  TABLE LOOKUP REQUEST
        NEWPTR = POINTER(MESSAGES)      !  SET POINTER TO RECORD
        IF NOT NEWPTR                   !  RECORD NOT PASSED TO TABLE
          SET(MES:BY_MESSAGE,MES:BY_MESSAGE) !  POSITION TO CLOSEST RECORD
          NEXT(MESSAGES)                !    READ RECORD
          NEWPTR = POINTER(MESSAGES)    !    SET POINTER
        .
        DO FIND_RECORD                  !  POSITION FILE
      ELSE
        NDX = 1                         !  PUT SELECTOR BAR ON TOP ITEM
        DO FIRST_PAGE                   !  BUILD MEMORY TABLE OF KEYS
      .
        RECORDS# = TRUE                 !  ASSUME THERE ARE RECORDS
  OF ?PRE_POINT                         !PRE POINT FIELD CONDITION
```

(continued)

```
  IF KEYCODE() = ESC_KEY                              !  BACKING UP?
    SELECT(?-1)                                       !    SELECT PREVIOUS FIELD
  ELSE                                                !  GOING FORWARD
    SELECT(?POINT)                                    !    SELECT MENU FIELD
  .

OF ?POINT                                             !PROCESS THE POINT FIELD
  IF RECORDS(TABLE) = 0                               !IF THERE ARE NO RECORDS
    CLEAR(MES:RECORD)                                 !  CLEAR RECORD AREA
    UPDATE                                            !  UPDATE ALL FIELDS
    ACTION = 1                                        !  SET ACTION TO ADD
    GET(MESSAGES,0)                                   !  CLEAR PENDING RECORD
    MES:NUMBER = SAV:NUMBER                           !RESTORE SELECTOR FIELD
    IF ACTION = 2;NEW_MESSAGE;ELSE NO_MESSAGE.! CALL FORM FOR NEW RECORD
    NEWPTR = POINTER(MESSAGES)                        !    SET POINTER TO NEW RECORD
    DO FIRST_PAGE                                     !  DISPLAY THE FIRST PAGE
    IF RECORDS(TABLE) = 0                             !  IF THERE AREN'T ANY RECORDS
      RECORDS# = FALSE                                !    INDICATE NO RECORDS
      SELECT(?PRE_POINT-1)                            !    SELECT THE PRIOR FIELD
    .

    CYCLE                                             !    AND LOOP AGAIN
  .

  CASE KEYCODE()                                      !PROCESS THE KEYSTROKE

  OF INS_KEY                                          !INS KEY
    CLEAR(MES:RECORD)                                 !  CLEAR RECORD AREA
    ACTION = 1                                        !  SET ACTION TO ADD
    GET(MESSAGES,0)                                   !  CLEAR PENDING RECORD
    MES:NUMBER = SAV:NUMBER                           !RESTORE SELECTOR FIELD
    IF ACTION = 2;NEW_MESSAGE;ELSE NO_MESSAGE.! CALL FORM FOR NEW RECORD
    IF ~ACTION                                        !  IF RECORD WAS ADDED
      NEWPTR = POINTER(MESSAGES)                      !    SET POINTER TO NEW RECORD
      DO FIND_RECORD                                  !    POSITION IN FILE
    .

  OF ENTER_KEY                                        !ENTER KEY
  OROF ACCEPT_KEY                                     !CTRL-ENTER KEY
    DO GET_RECORD                                     !  GET THE SELECTED RECORD
    IF ACTION = 4 AND KEYCODE() = ENTER_KEY!    IF THIS IS A LOOKUP REQUEST
      ACTION = 0                                      !    SET ACTION TO COMPLETE
      BREAK                                           !    AND RETURN TO CALLER
    .

    IF ~ERROR()                                       !  IF RECORD IS STILL THERE
      ACTION = 2                                      !    SET ACTION TO CHANGE
      IF ACTION = 2;NEW_MESSAGE;ELSE NO_MESSAGE.! CALL FORM TO CHANGE REC
      IF ACTION THEN CYCLE.                           !    IF SUCCESSFUL RE-DISPLAY
    .

    NEWPTR = POINTER(MESSAGES)                        !    SET POINTER TO NEW RECORD
    DO FIND_RECORD                                    !    POSITION IN FILE
```

(continued)

```
    OF DEL_KEY                                     !DEL KEY
      DO GET_RECORD                                !   READ THE SELECTED RECORD
      IF ~ERROR()                                  !   IF RECORD IS STILL THERE
        ACTION = 3                                 !     SET ACTION TO DELETE
        IF ACTION = 2;NEW_MESSAGE;ELSE NO_MESSAGE.! CALL FORM TO DELETE
        IF ~ACTION                                 !     IF SUCCESSFUL
          N# = NDX                                 !       SAVE POINT INDEX
          DO SAME_PAGE                             !       RE-DISPLAY
          NDX = N#                                 !       RESTORE POINT INDEX
      . .
    OF DOWN_KEY                                    !DOWN ARROW KEY
      DO SET_NEXT                                  !   POINT TO NEXT RECORD
      DO FILL_NEXT                                 !   FILL A TABLE ENTRY
      IF FOUND                                     !   FOUND A NEW RECORD
        SCROLL(ROW,COL,ROWS,COLS,ROWS(?POINT))     !     SCROLL THE SCREEN UP
        GET(TABLE,RECORDS(TABLE))                  !   GET RECORD FROM TABLE
        DO FILL_SCREEN                             !   DISPLAY ON SCREEN
      .

    OF PGDN_KEY                                    !PAGE DOWN KEY
      DO SET_NEXT                                  !   POINT TO NEXT RECORD
      DO NEXT_PAGE                                 !   DISPLAY THE NEXT PAGE

    OF CTRL_PGDN                                   !CTRL-PAGE DOWN KEY
      DO LAST_PAGE                                 !   DISPLAY THE LAST PAGE
      NDX = RECORDS(TABLE)                         !   POSITION POINT BAR

    OF UP_KEY                                      !UP ARROW KEY
      DO SET_PREV                                  !   POINT TO PREVIOUS RECORD
      DO FILL_PREV                                 !   FILL A TABLE ENTRY
      IF FOUND                                     !   FOUND A NEW RECORD
        SCROLL(ROW,COL,ROWS,COLS,-(ROWS(?POINT)))! SCROLL THE SCREEN DOWN
        GET(TABLE,1)                               !   GET RECORD FROM TABLE
        DO FILL_SCREEN                             !   DISPLAY ON SCREEN
      .

    OF PGUP_KEY                                    !PAGE UP KEY
      DO SET_PREV                                  !   POINT TO PREVIOUS RECORD
      DO PREV_PAGE                                 !   DISPLAY THE PREVIOUS PAGE

    OF CTRL_PGUP                                   !CTRL-PAGE UP
      DO FIRST_PAGE                                !   DISPLAY THE FIRST PAGE
      NDX = 1                                      !   POSITION POINT BAR
  . . .
FREE(TABLE)                                        !FREE MEMORY TABLE
RETURN                                             !AND RETURN TO CALLER
```

(continued)

```
SAME_PAGE ROUTINE                              !DISPLAY THE SAME PAGE
  GET(TABLE,1)                                 !  GET THE FIRST TABLE ENTRY
  DO FILL_RECORD                               !  FILL IN THE RECORD
  SET(MES:BY_MESSAGE,MES:BY_MESSAGE,TBL:PTR)   !  POSITION FILE
  FREE(TABLE)                                  !  EMPTY THE TABLE
  DO NEXT_PAGE                                 !  DISPLAY A FULL PAGE


FIRST_PAGE ROUTINE                             !DISPLAY FIRST PAGE

  BLANK(ROW,COL,ROWS,COLS)
  FREE(TABLE)                                  !  EMPTY THE TABLE
  CLEAR(MES:RECORD,-1)                         !  CLEAR RECORD TO LOW VALUES
  CLEAR(TBL:PTR)                               !  ZERO RECORD POINTER
  MES:NUMBER = SAV:NUMBER                      !RESTORE SELECTOR FIELD
  SET(MES:BY_MESSAGE,MES:BY_MESSAGE,TBL:PTR)   !  POINT PAST LAST RECORD
  LOOP NDX = 1 TO COUNT                        !  FILL UP THE TABLE
    DO FILL_NEXT                               !    FILL A TABLE ENTRY
    IF NOT FOUND THEN BREAK.                   !    GET OUT IF NO RECORD
  .
  NDX = 1                                      !  SET TO TOP OF TABLE
  DO SHOW_PAGE                                 !  DISPLAY THE PAGE


LAST_PAGE ROUTINE                              !DISPLAY LAST PAGE
  NDX# = NDX                                   !  SAVE SELECTOR POSITION
  BLANK(ROW,COL,ROWS,COLS)                     !  CLEAR SCROLLING AREA
  FREE(TABLE)                                  !  EMPTY THE TABLE
  CLEAR(MES:RECORD,1)                          !  CLEAR RECORD TO HIGH VALUES
  CLEAR(TBL:PTR,1)                             !  CLEAR PTR TO HIGH VALUE
  MES:NUMBER = SAV:NUMBER                      !RESTORE SELECTOR FIELD
  SET(MES:BY_MESSAGE,MES:BY_MESSAGE,TBL:PTR)   !  POINT PAST LAST RECORD
  LOOP NDX = COUNT TO 1 BY -1                  !  FILL UP THE TABLE
    DO FILL_PREV                               !    FILL A TABLE ENTRY
    IF NOT FOUND THEN BREAK.                   !    GET OUT IF NO RECORD
  .
  NDX = NDX#                                   !  RESTORE SELECTOR POSITION
  DO SHOW_PAGE                                 !  DISPLAY THE PAGE


FIND_RECORD ROUTINE                            !POSITION TO SPECIFIC RECORD
  SET(MES:BY_MESSAGE,MES:BY_MESSAGE,NEWPTR)    !POSITION FILE
  IF NEWPTR = 0                                !NEWPTR NOT SET
    NEXT(MESSAGES)                             !  READ NEXT RECORD
    NEWPTR = POINTER(MESSAGES)                 !  SET NEWPTR
    SKIP(MESSAGES,-1)                          !  BACK UP TO DISPLAY RECORD
  .
  FREE(TABLE)                                  !  CLEAR THE RECORD
  DO NEXT_PAGE                                 !  DISPLAY A PAGE


NEXT_PAGE ROUTINE                              !DISPLAY NEXT PAGE
```

(continued)

```
      SAVECNT# = RECORDS(TABLE)                    !  SAVE RECORD COUNT
      LOOP COUNT TIMES                             !  FILL UP THE TABLE
        DO FILL_NEXT                               !    FILL A TABLE ENTRY
        IF NOT FOUND                               !    IF NONE ARE LEFT
          IF NOT SAVECNT#                          !      IF REBUILDING TABLE
            DO LAST_PAGE                            !        FILL IN RECORDS
            EXIT                                    !        EXIT OUT OF ROUTINE
            .
          BREAK                                     !    EXIT LOOP
        . .
      DO SHOW_PAGE                                  !  DISPLAY THE PAGE

SET_NEXT ROUTINE                                   !POINT TO THE NEXT PAGE
  GET(TABLE,RECORDS(TABLE))                         !  GET THE LAST TABLE ENTRY
  DO FILL_RECORD                                    !  FILL IN THE RECORD
  SET(MES:BY_MESSAGE,MES:BY_MESSAGE,TBL:PTR)        !  POSITION FILE
  NEXT(MESSAGES)                                    !  READ THE CURRENT RECORD

FILL_NEXT ROUTINE                                  !FILL NEXT TABLE ENTRY
  FOUND = FALSE                                     !  ASSUME RECORD NOT FOUND
  LOOP UNTIL EOF(MESSAGES)                          !  LOOP UNTIL END OF FILE
    NEXT(MESSAGES)                                  !    READ THE NEXT RECORD
    IF MES:NUMBER <> SAV:NUMBER                     !IF END OF SELECTION
      MES:NUMBER = SAV:NUMBER                       !  RESTORE THE SELECTOR
      BREAK                                         !  AND BREAK
      .
    FOUND = TRUE                                    !    SET RECORD FOUND
    DO FILL_TABLE                                   !    FILL IN THE TABLE ENTRY
    ADD(TABLE)                                      !    ADD LAST TABLE ENTRY
    GET(TABLE,RECORDS(TABLE)-COUNT)                 !    GET ANY OVERFLOW RECORD
    DELETE(TABLE)                                   !    AND DELETE IT
    EXIT                                            !    RETURN TO CALLER

PREV_PAGE ROUTINE                                  !DISPLAY PREVIOUS PAGE
  LOOP COUNT TIMES                                  !  FILL UP THE TABLE
    DO FILL_PREV                                    !    FILL A TABLE ENTRY
    IF NOT FOUND THEN BREAK.                        !    GET OUT IF NO RECORD
    .
  DO SHOW_PAGE                                      !  DISPLAY THE PAGE

SET_PREV ROUTINE                                   !POINT TO PREVIOUS PAGE
  GET(TABLE,1)                                      !  GET THE FIRST TABLE ENTRY
  DO FILL_RECORD                                    !  FILL IN THE RECORD
  SET(MES:BY_MESSAGE,MES:BY_MESSAGE,TBL:PTR)        !  POSITION FILE
  PREVIOUS(MESSAGES)                                !  READ THE CURRENT RECORD
```

(continued)

```
FILL_PREV ROUTINE                              !FILL PREVIOUS TABLE ENTRY
  FOUND = FALSE                                !  ASSUME RECORD NOT FOUND
  LOOP UNTIL BOF(MESSAGES)                      !  LOOP UNTIL BEGINNING OF FILE
    PREVIOUS(MESSAGES)                           !     READ THE PREVIOUS RECORD
    IF MES:NUMBER <> SAV:NUMBER                 !IF END OF SELECTION
      MES:NUMBER = SAV:NUMBER                   !  RESTORE THE SELECTOR
      BREAK                                     !  AND BREAK

      .
    FOUND = TRUE                               !     SET RECORD FOUND
    DO FILL_TABLE                              !     FILL IN THE TABLE ENTRY
    ADD(TABLE,1)                               !     ADD FIRST TABLE ENTRY
    GET(TABLE,COUNT+1)                         !     GET ANY OVERFLOW RECORD
    DELETE(TABLE)                              !     AND DELETE IT
    EXIT                                       !     RETURN TO CALLER

    .
SHOW_PAGE ROUTINE                              !DISPLAY THE PAGE
  NDX# = NDX                                   !  SAVE SCREEN INDEX
  LOOP NDX = 1 TO RECORDS(TABLE)               !  LOOP THRU THE TABLE
    GET(TABLE,NDX)                             !     GET A TABLE ENTRY
    DO FILL_SCREEN                             !     AND DISPLAY IT
    IF TBL:PTR = NEWPTR                        !     SET INDEX FOR NEW RECORD
      NDX# = NDX                               !     POINT TO CORRECT RECORD

  . .
  NDX = NDX#                                   !  RESTORE SCREEN INDEX
  NEWPTR = 0                                   !  CLEAR NEW RECORD POINTER
  CLEAR(MES:RECORD)                            !  CLEAR RECORD AREA

FILL_TABLE ROUTINE                             !MOVE FILE TO TABLE
  NAM:NUMBER = MES:SENDER_NUM                  !MOVE RELATED KEY FIELDS
  GET(NAMES,NAM:BY_NUMBER)                     !READ THE RECORD
  IF ERROR() THEN CLEAR(NAM:RECORD).           !IF NOT FOUND, CLEAR RECORD
  TBL:LAST = NAM:LAST                          !DISPLAY LOOKUP FIELD
  TBL:MESSAGE_NUM = MES:MESSAGE_NUM
  TBL:DATE = MES:DATE
  TBL:SUBJECT = MES:SUBJECT
  TBL:NUMBER = MES:NUMBER
  TBL:PTR = POINTER(MESSAGES)                  !  SAVE RECORD POINTER

FILL_RECORD ROUTINE                            !MOVE TABLE TO FILE
  MES:NUMBER = TBL:NUMBER
  MES:MESSAGE_NUM = TBL:MESSAGE_NUM

FILL_SCREEN ROUTINE                            !MOVE TABLE TO SCREEN
  SCR:MESSAGE_NUM = TBL:MESSAGE_NUM
  SCR:DATE = TBL:DATE
```

(continued)

```
    SCR:SUBJECT = TBL:SUBJECT
    SCR:LAST = TBL:LAST

GET_RECORD ROUTINE                          !GET SELECTED RECORD
  GET(TABLE,NDX)                            !  GET TABLE ENTRY
  GET(MESSAGES,TBL:PTR)                     !  GET THE RECORD
```

Chapter 16

Clarion and Other Languages

The Clarion language was conceived at a time when the PC database application development market was in its infancy. dBASE II had been on the market for about three years and had a firm hold on the marketplace. Other competition came before and followed Clarion, but no one else provided the extent of integration that Clarion offered the market with its 2.0 release that included Designer. Since the language really did come first, the basis for building on the future was pretty strong. Even with all of the development tools available to the user of Clarion Professional 2.1, many dedicated Clarion developers operate strictly with the language only.

Since evaluating a product often includes a review of the literature available as reference, this chapter is offered to you as a means to help you distinguish between Clarion and other environments. For the professional application developer, knowing the differences between Clarion and other products can be useful in the marketing process. Many times a request for a proposal from a customer is slanted toward another environment, and a handy reference can help you contrast your work in Clarion with that other environment. Also, information on the differences between Clarion and other products can be useful for those migrating from another product to Clarion. It can be as much, or more, help to see a comparison of capabilities than to read a lengthy dissertation on the ways to use a particular product—as most of our time in this book has been spent.

Since the dBASE products from Ashton-Tate took the early lead in this market, the dBASE story merits a little larger examination. We focus first on the origins of the product and the evolution into dBASE III PLUS and the most recent release of dBASE IV. Most of the analysis in comparison, however, is focused on the older dBASE III PLUS version. The latest release of dBASE IV hit the streets in the fall of 1990, and it will take some time for those who have adopted the dBASE standard to switch their applications. In any event, the similarities in the languages (dBASE III PLUS to dBASE IV) are covered.

dBASE

dBASE II evolved from a product called Vulcan, which was designed and written by Wayne Ratliff for NASA's Jet Propulsion Laboratory in the early 1980s. Then George Tate and his partner Hal Lashlee put together an exclusive marketing arrangement with Ratliff and gave Vulcan a new name: dBASE II. (Industry folklore often speaks of the marketing wisdom that led the group to issue a II version without ever producing a I version.) The product was introduced into the CP/M market (the first popular operating system for the PC) and quickly became an industry standard. When the IBM PC with MS-DOS was introduced, Wayne Ratliff converted dBASE II to the new operating system and success followed in the new market.

In 1984, dBASE III was introduced, followed closely by an improved version, dBASE III PLUS. That same year also marked the beginning of success for clones as complete products and the start of a vast marketplace for enhancements, tools, and other products directly tied to dBASE. The missing pieces in the dBASE environment provided ample soil for third-party developers to produce add-on tools and look-alikes that fed the hungry market for database development tools. The most outstanding deficiency in the dBASE working tools was the lack of a compiler to produce standalone programs. You could develop fairly complex applications, but you were forced to run them in "interpretive" mode. That meant you were required to have a copy of the dBASE environment on any PC that was using the application. In addition, it meant that a user could easily crash the system and be in direct contact with the source code being used to run the application. Developers spend a great deal of time coding elemental protection layers, but a compiler was needed.

The first such products were primitive compilers like Clipper. With Clipper, a developer could encrypt and protect source code for distribution and not purchase a copy of dBASE for every installation. Clipper is now a very complete product and is evolving into a standalone environment more separated from its dBASE origins than tied to them.

Another product of note to follow Clipper to the market was FoxBase. This product was a more direct implementation of dBASE methods, offering most, if not all, of the features of its ancestor, plus a compiler, documentation tools, and other useful utilities.

The Major Features of dBASE III PLUS

The largest advantage that dBASE possesses over Clarion (as with several other products where this is their *only* advantage) is commonly referred to as the "dot prompt." Though more valued by casual users and only as a utility for developers, the dot prompt still provides a quick entrance to full data file access. Ashton-Tate developed the Assistant to provide users an alternative to the dot prompt that was a little easier to use. The Assistant provides a menu-driven interface with pull-down menus for directly manipulating different database files. With the dot prompt, dBASE III PLUS provides a command prompt separate from the DOS command processor prompt for driving the language and manipulating the data files. The work many users do in dBASE never goes beyond what you can do with this tool—they never develop work that distills into a compiled application. It is used more like a spreadsheet or word processor. The major downfall of this method of managing data files is the very unstructured nature that makes it convenient. If the programmer has not imposed a high degree of discipline from the outside, relational integrity simply does not exist.

The closest equivalent to the dot prompt that Clarion provides is Reporter. Reporter, however, cannot read and write changes to the data files without custom code being inserted to accomplish certain tasks. Reporter is not an equivalent to the dot prompt—you must still create a database and a report to use Reporter—but it does allow the user to query the data files, much as you can in the dBASE Assistant, without a formal program as was previously required by Clarion.

Some additional facts about the dBASE III applications development language include:

- dBASE supports file locking, as does Clarion. You can retrieve messages indicating whether or not a resource is available to support multi-user applications. Locking of related objects, however, must be handled manually, which is true of Clarion as well.
- dBASE possesses a method for creating Memo Fields that can contain up to 4,096 characters per record, whereas Clarion's Memo Field can be up to 65,536. dBASE stores the Memo Field in a separate file, as does Clarion.

- For a dBASE multifile relational database scheme, a parent file may setup only one child at a time via the SET RELATION TO statement. You are allowed to have up to ten of these relationships, one for each of the ten working areas available. dBASE also has a JOIN command, which more closely resembles the way that Report Writer creates a JOIN by creating a separate entity on the disk. However, Report Writer's JOIN does not actually copy the data file, only the "roadmap" of the definitions for the JOIN. The dBASE method copies the actual information to a separate file, which can consume a lot of disk space. Also, the dBASE JOIN can only apply from the "current" data file to one other file in each of ten work areas. In Clarion's Report Writer, you can join together as many data files as you like. In Designer and in Clarion code created manually, there is no real equivalent to SET RELATION TO. You can create relationships in Clarion merely by relating the key files with common fields.

- dBASE limits the number of indexes open for a single database to 7, with a total of only 15 files open at one time. This creates a lot of overhead for the programmer in opening and closing files. Clarion, on the other hand, has no limit other than that imposed by DOS for limiting the number of open files—though there is a fairly *wild* limit of 250 keys for a single data file. The limit is "wild" because few applications will ever approach the need for that many keys. As a memory saving device, in fact, many programmers change the manner in which Designer-generated applications open and keep open the data and key files by closing them. Another contrast with dBASE is that many Clarion statements like SET and GET implicitly open a closed file, which removes the requirement for the programmer to perform the file opening with a separate statement.

- dBASE indexes (or key files) must be explicitly updated and reside on the disk. Clarion continuously and *automatically* updates the key file in dynamic RAM. Clarion also provides the index form that more closely resembles the dBASE format and is not updated until an explicit statement is issued.

- The dBASE program editor only allows a program file size that does not exceed 4096 characters. Clarion's Editor allows you to create files as large as you have memory available to hold them. In Figure 16-1, a test file was built of 983 rows of 255 characters that took 99% of the available RAM for editing.

- In dBASE, graphics screens can only be created when data from dBASE III PLUS files are converted to ASCII format first. In Clarion, you can store graphics as the actual characters or as the ASCII codes themselves.

Figure 16-1   The options settings for Clarion's Editor that shows the amount of memory available to hold the edited file.

```
....:....1....:....2....:....3....:....4....:....5....:....6....:....7....:....
xxxxxxxxxxxxxxxxxx╔══════════════════════════════════════╗xxxxxxxxxxxxxxxxxx
xxxxxxxxxxxxxxxxxx║                Options                ║xxxxxxxxxxxxxxxxxx
xxxxxxxxxxxxxxxxxx║                                       ║xxxxxxxxxxxxxxxxxx
xxxxxxxxxxxxxxxxxx║ Input File  :C:\CLARION\BOOKTEST\SIZE.CL║xxxxxxxxxxxxxxxxxx
xxxxxxxxxxxxxxxxxx║ Output File :C:\CLARION\BOOKTEST\SIZE.CL║xxxxxxxxxxxxxxxxxx
xxxxxxxxxxxxxxxxxx║ Edit File   :C:\CLARION\CLA.EDT        ║xxxxxxxxxxxxxxxxxx
xxxxxxxxxxxxxxxxxx║                                       ║xxxxxxxxxxxxxxxxxx
xxxxxxxxxxxxxxxxxx║ Block Mode  :LIN        LIN  CHR       ║xxxxxxxxxxxxxxxxxx
xxxxxxxxxxxxxxxxxx║ Indention   :On        On   Off       ║xxxxxxxxxxxxxxxxxx
xxxxxxxxxxxxxxxxxx║ Zone Insert :On        On   Off       ║xxxxxxxxxxxxxxxxxx
xxxxxxxxxxxxxxxxxx║ Ruler Lines :Off       On   Off       ║xxxxxxxxxxxxxxxxxx
xxxxxxxxxxxxxxxxxx║ Typing Mode :OUR       INS  OUR  Neutral║xxxxxxxxxxxxxxxxx
xxxxxxxxxxxxxxxxxx║*Caps Lock   :On        On   Off  Neutral║xxxxxxxxxxxxxxxxx
xxxxxxxxxxxxxxxxxx║*Scroll Lock:On         On   Off  Neutral║xxxxxxxxxxxxxxxxx
xxxxxxxxxxxxxxxxxx║ Compress    :No        Yes  No        ║xxxxxxxxxxxxxxxxxx
xxxxxxxxxxxxxxxxxx║ Set Tabs    :No        Yes  No        ║xxxxxxxxxxxxxxxxxx
xxxxxxxxxxxxxxxxxx║                                       ║xxxxxxxxxxxxxxxxxx
xxxxxxxxxxxxxxxxxx║ Edit Width  :255          Size: 239,570║xxxxxxxxxxxxxxxxx
xxxxxxxxxxxxxxxxxx║ Memory Use  :246k/247k    Date: 9/11/90║xxxxxxxxxxxxxxxxx
xxxxxxxxxxxxxxxxxx║ Amount Used:99%           Time:22:32  ║xxxxxxxxxxxxxxxxxx
xxxxxxxxxxxxxxxxxx╚══════════════════════════════════════╝xxxxxxxxxxxxxxxxxx
xxxxxxxxxxxxxxxxxxxxxxxxxxxxxxxxxxxxxxxxxxxxxxxxxxxxxxxxxxxxxxxxxxxxxxxxxxxx
SIZE.CLA 1:1                                    LIN OUR ZON IND      NUM
```

More importantly, though, you can use the screen generator in either Editor or Designer to create graphic applications by simply drawing on the screen.

- dBASE has no compiler.
- To add a record to a data file in dBASE, you add a blank record to the data file and the fields are filled in as required. In Clarion, an image of the data record is held in memory. Fields are filled in as required and then the record is ADDed to the database at the programmer's discretion. Clarion also has an APPEND command, but this method does not update the dynamic key files, which can be used to gain a speed advantage.
- All dBASE programs display a copyright message, even in version IV, when the program is first started. Clarion does not intrude in this manner.
- dBASE III PLUS does not support any trigonometric functions directly. Clarion provides the functions for sine (SIN); cosine (COS); tangent (TAN); arcsine (ASIN); arcosine (ARCOS); and arctangent (ATAN).

Many of the items in the preceding list that are deficient in dBASE, for example, the program size limitation, can be solved by third-party products. To get a screen generator, file recovery utilities, a compiler, and other tools in dBASE III used to require that you shop for a bevy of these third-party products. It was not until dBASE IV appeared that Ashton-Tate offered anything similar to Clarion's integrated applications development environment.

Major Additions from dBASE III to dBASE IV

With the arrival of dBASE IV, Ashton-Tate's flagship product approaches the integration that Clarion provides. You can purchase both a User's Edition and a Developer's Edition, which includes a linker, a utility called BUILD which manages a program tree for larger applications, a compiler and a template language, LAN key disks, and an unlimited runtime license. Compiled programs can be run under dBASE IV or distributed with the dBASE IV Runtime (with no extra royalties just as Clarion allows distribution of CRUN).

dBASE IV added 310 new commands and functions, and increased memory (640K) and disk space requirements (3.5 MB). (Clarion—fully installed with examples and tutorial—occupies a little over 6 MB, or it can occupy a little under 4 MB with just development tools, including RTLink.) dBASE III PLUS applications are upward compatible and automatically converted when accessed by dBASE IV.

dBASE IV contains the Control Center, a nonprocedural interface, which is more activity-oriented than Assistant and is akin to Clarion's Designer. The Control Center allows the creation of data, query, form, report, label, and application objects and maintains the catalog of related items. The forms generator includes full editing (with cut and paste), data validation, Calculated Fields on the form, access to memory variables, and Memo Fields from form windows. Like Clarion, reports, forms, and labels can access fields from multiple databases via a view. The Control Center, like Clarion's Designer, is a menu-driven environment that acts as the central focus for development, testing, and file maintenance.

dBASE IV contains a template language for writing standard reports and forms, which can then be used to generate code that will be compiled into the final application.

On the multiuser scene, the new dBASE provides file and record locking (as does Clarion) along with messages, including the network node name and time held when encountering resource contention. The SET command controls the locking of related objects (reports, forms, databases, and so on).

Among dBASE IV's significant deviations from Clarion are support for shared locks (where two users edit different fields in the same record) and automatic update for a view in use when a record is updated by another user (just as in Clarion's process that posts the message "RECORD CHANGED

BY ANOTHER STATION"). With transaction logging, the dBASE IV system warns any user who accesses a database where a transaction aborted and did not complete, whereas in Clarion you must issue the ROLLBACK statement to repair the failed transaction. Also, dBASE IV uses IBM's SQL (Structured Query Language) to create Query By Example. The SET SQL ON/OFF statement is used to flip back and forth between dBASE IV and SQL statements. SQL can be embedded or interactive and may be used against all dBASE data files. More like Paradox than Clarion (Clarion does not support SQL), dBASE IV allows you to select records and fields and link databases. It allows one logical condition (Paradox allows multiple conditions on query) and supports update through query.

Additional dBASE IV improvements include:

- Memo Fields—Improved to 64,000 characters, two-way ASCII import/export, usable with STRING commands.
- Compiler—Now including a compiler and linker, dBASE IV operates them as one step and the difference between them is transparent to the user. After being processed in this manner, programs run an average nine times faster than with dBASE III PLUS. The linker even allows construction of overlays, as does the custom version of RTLink that is shipped with Clarion. However, dBASE IV still does not compile to a standalone executable file, but rather it gets "tokenized" into a .DBO file, which must then be run either in the environment or with the free runtime package in dBASE IV. The dBASE system does not allow the linking of external libraries, but it does allow selective recompilation and overlays.
- Multifile Relations—A parent file may now have many children. SET SKIP TO allows movement of the record pointer within child tables without impacting the parent's pointer location—much like Clarion's ability to move pointers around different data files independently. In multiuser mode, locking the parent file automatically locks children— something that must be programmed in Clarion.
- File Indexing—The Master Index File allows up to 47 automatically maintained indexes per database and acts as though only one file were open. Single index structures are still allowed. This is still well below Clarion's capacities as cited earlier, although the automatic updating moves it closer to reaching Clarion's level of key file automation.
- Expanded Editor—Now allows up to 32,000 lines of code per program/file.
- Environment—Has incorporated several of the tools once supplied to programmers through third-party vendors.

- Template Language—Is a superset of a C, object-oriented list processing, compiler, and debugger. It is included in the Developer's Edition.
dBASE IV now contains a programmable code generator like the old
FoxBase FoxCode, Genifer, and UI2. This process is developed by
writing a program that will take specific information about your current
application and then generate dBASE code.
- Help—As with Clarion's Helper, you can get user-defined context-sen-
sitive help and a multiwindow debugger that (unlike Clarion) allows
inline code fixes.
- Data Security—Even though dBASE stores tables and indexes in individual files, a new multiple index file stores all indexes for a single data
file in one file. All indexes must be opened along with their associated
data files either manually or explicitly in a program. Data entry validation, security, or defaults are not available and must be coded into every
program. The dBASE file format is susceptible to power outages and
can become corrupted easily.
- Report Generator—Functions now match the capabilities of current
add-on products from companies like R&R and Fox & Geller.
- Menus and Screens—Have been improved with the ability to develop
pop-up and pull-down menus along with the continued support for
traditional plain light bar menus. Windows and menus can be automatically linked to other code generated with the applications generator, but
stored separately for separate modification or inclusion in other applications similar to Designer's .APP file.

Data Types

dBASE allows 256 memory variables to be in use at one time within an
application where Clarion has no limit (other than available memory). The
following five types of data objects may be stored in a dBASE file or used as
a memory variable:

1. Character strings surrounded by delimiters (''), (""), or ([])—Strings
   are limited to 254 characters.
2. Dates—Dates are displayed in readable formats and stored as a raw
   number.
3. Numbers—Two types of numbers are used, integers and reals. Real
   numbers use 15 significant places.
4. Logicals (Booleans)—Notation is .t. for True or .f. for False.

5. Memos—A memo is an area for larger amounts of text. A Memo Field within a data file takes 10 bytes and actual Memo Field is stored in a separate file. There are no memory variables of type Memo.

The comparison of language statements shown in Table 16-1 is by no means a complete inventory of the language elements of the three environments listed. It attempts to show the most significant differences in the most commonly used statements where there might be an assumed difference in the languages.

Table 16-1 A comparison of common language statements between Clarion, dBASE III PLUS, and the new dBASE IV.

	dBASE III PLUS	dBASE IV	Clarion	Comments
Math Functions				
ABS	Yes	Yes	Yes	Absolute value
EXP	Yes	Yes	No	Natural log constant (e) raised to a power
INT	Yes	Yes	(SHORT)	Integer
INRANGE	No	No	Yes	In range
LOG, LOGE	Yes	Yes	Yes	Natural logarithm
LOG10	No	Yes	Yes	Log base 10
MAX	For numerics	For integers, CEILING for expressions	Dimensioned variables, returns highest subscript allowed	Maximum value
MIN	For numerics	For integers, FLOOR for expressions	Yes	Minimum value
MOD	Yes	Yes	Yes	Modulus (remainder of division)
RAND, RANDOM	No	Pseudo-random	Yes	Random number generator
ROUND	Yes	Yes	Yes	Rounded value
SIGN	Yes	Yes	No	Sign of a number
SQRT	Yes	Yes	Yes	Square root

(continued)

Table 16-1 *continued*

	dBASE III PLUS	dBASE IV	Clarion	Comments
Conversion				
ASC	Yes	Yes	Use VAL	Character to ASCII
CHR	Yes	Yes	Yes	ASCII to character
String Functions				
AT	Yes	Yes	Use INSTRING	Search for substring
LEFT	Yes	Yes	Use SUBSTRING	Extract characters
LEN	Yes	Yes	Yes	Length
LOWER	Yes	Yes	Yes	To lowercase and Macro expansion
LTRIM	Yes	Yes	Use LEFT	Remove leading blanks
REPLICATE	Yes	Yes	Use ALL	Repeat characters
RIGHT	Yes	Yes	Use SUBSTRING	Remove characters
RTRIM	Yes	Yes	Use CLIP	Remove trailing blanks
SPACE	Yes	Yes	No	Create blank string
STR	Yes	Yes	Use VAL	Numeric to string
STUFF	Yes	Yes	Use CLIP	Insert substring
SUBSTR	Yes	Yes	Yes	Select characters
TRANSFORM	Yes	Yes	Use FORMAT	Change output format
TRIM	Yes	Yes	Use CLIP	Remove trailing blanks
UPPER	Yes	Yes	Yes	To uppercase
VAL	Yes	Yes	Yes	Convert string to numeric
Date Functions				
CDOW	Yes	Yes	No	Day of week name
CMONTH	Yes	Yes	Yes	Month name
CTOD	Yes	Yes	Use FORMAT	Convert string to date

(continued)

Table 16-1 *continued*

	dBASE III PLUS	dBASE IV	Clarion	Comments
DATE	Yes	Yes	Yes	System date
DAY	Yes	Yes	Yes	Day of month number
DOW	Yes	Yes	Use DATE % 7	Day of week number
MONTH	Yes	Yes	Yes	Month number
TIME	Yes	Yes	Yes	System time
YEAR	Yes	Yes	Yes	Four-digit year number

Conditional Functions

	dBASE III PLUS	dBASE IV	Clarion	Comments
IIF	Yes	Yes	Use IF and ELSIF	Conditional IF
ISALPHA	Yes	Yes	No	Test for leading alpha
ISCOLOR	Yes	Yes	In Graphics LEM, use VAL	Test for color monitor
ISLOWER	Yes	Yes		Test for lowercase leading character
ISUPPER	Yes	Yes	Use VAL	Test for uppercase leading character

Trigonometric Functions

	Fixed-point computations		Computed in radians using double-precision floating-point variables	
ACOS	No	Yes	Yes	Arccosine
ASIN	No	Yes	Yes	Arcsine
ATAN	No	Yes, also ATAN2 computed using SIN and COS	Yes	Arctangent
COS	No	Yes	Yes	Cosine
DEG2RAD, DTOR	No	Yes	Yes	Degrees to radians
RAD2DEG, RTOD	No	Yes	Yes	Radians to degrees
SIN	No	Yes	Yes	Sine
TAN	No	Yes	Yes	Tangent

Table 16-2 shows the differences in the manner in which each of the languages carries out looping and logical decision processing.

Table 16-2   Language elements, dBASE versus Clarion.

dBASE	Clarion
LOOP STRUCTURE	
One loop structure	Five loop structures (only one shown)

Syntax:

dBASE:
```
DO WHILE expression
   <statements>
ENDDO
```

Clarion:
```
LOOP WHILE expression
   <statements>
.
```

Example:

dBASE:
```
COUNTER = 10
DO WHILE COUNTER > 0
   COUNTER = COUNTER -1
ENDDO
```

Clarion:
```
COUNTER# = 10
LOOP WHILE COUNTER > 0
   COUNTER# -= 1
.
```

DECISIONS USING IF STATEMENTS[*]

Syntax:

dBASE:
```
IF expression
   <statements>
ELSE
   <statements>
ENDIF
```

Clarion:
```
IF expression
   <statements>
THEN
   <statements>
ELSIF <expression>
THEN
   <statements>
ELSE
   <statements>
.
```

[*]Clarion also offers a C language style switching structure with the CASE statement.

Other Development Environments

Paradox from Borland

The Paradox Development Environment is probably Clarion's closest competition in terms of an integrated applications development environment. Paradox provides user access to data through spreadsheet like tables, screen forms, and reports plus a query by example facility like the dBASE dot prompt discussed earlier in the chapter.

Paradox Application Language, or PAL, is a programming language contained in Paradox that allows applications to be customized much like the Clarion language and the dBASE IV template language. PAL is used just as any other application development language to allow users to communicate with their computer and their data.

PAL by itself allows only limited control of what a user does when the data is entered and of the specific action to be taken in response to the specific data values. The Paradox Toolkit, an additional feature in Paradox 3.0 that was first introduced in 2.0, allows some event-driven control within an application.

The Paradox Toolkit allows the application to respond to user keystrokes and to take action. These actions can be as simple as a beep or a complete procedure. In comparison, the Main Event Loop coded into Clarion's Designer Models are event driven by nature. Processing enters the loop after the initial screen setup and then waits for the user to respond somehow. Depending on that response, Clarion's Designer-based applications take several different paths through the procedure.

The Toolkit Kit: The Toolkit allows 350 keystroke combinations and a visual debugger that can be removed for distribution. It has a limited set of keywords upon which all action to be taken is based:

Keyword	Function/Definition
KAccept	Direct response to user
TKBuffer	Puts a key in the keyboard buffer
TKChanged	Checks to see if a field has been changed
TKChar	Value of last keystroke
TKFieldVal	Initial value of field

(continued)

Keyword	Function/Definition
TKHoldCanvas	Holds Paradox Canvas until user presses any key
TKKeyType	Identifies the classification of key pressed:
	(D) Special, nonmovement
	(E)xit
	(I)llegal
	(M) Regular
	(S)pecial Movement
	(X) Immediate Exit
TKKeyProc	Contains response to inactivity at keyboard
TKLibName	Name of DoWait Library
TKMessage	Replaces the MESSAGE command in DoWait
TKSeconds	Time in seconds to respond to inactivity at keyboard

Paradox has a simple applications generator like Clarion's Designer called the Personal Programmer. However, the custom code entry points and other flexibility of Designer is missing from the Paradox tool. Like Clarion, Paradox automatically maintains a primary index (key) for each file, although unlike Clarion, secondary indexes (keys in Clarion) must be updated manually.

Paradox is quite a bit slower than the other databases and is more difficult to program with. Its performance is all right with small files but terrible on large files. Its data entry screens are not very flexible. Its index structure is fairly limited and may be difficult for any sophisticated applications.

dBASE Clones and Higher Level Languages

The Clones: The market success enjoyed by dBASE III inspired many clones. A dBASE clone is a product that works like dBASE and promises to add some new feature or to do one or more things better, easier, or just differently. Of the clones, FoxBase/FoxPro is the fastest, Quicksilver/dBXL has windows and graphics, and Clipper had the first true compiler. This is, by no means, intended to be an exhaustive list of database application environments. Though they may not be dBASE clones and are not covered in detail here, this market also includes Dataease, PC Magic, Matrix Layout, CAUSE, MicroStep, and Gupta SQL Windows.

Oracle and Other High-End Environments: Oracle is a product that promises a consistent user interface between PCs and larger computers. However, this feature brings with it a product that is verbose and difficult to use. Users who have formal database design and programming training have the best results, but a steep learning curve will be the rule for anyone new to the environment—steeper than any of the other systems mentioned here.

Oracle depends on SQL for access to data and may be much more difficult than other PC database products. Other products from companies like Informix and Sybase join Oracle in trying to "descend" to the PC, but the implementations usually are overly complex without a concurrent increase in application development capability.

FoxPro 1.2—Fox Software: FoxPro uses a Macintosh-like menu-driven interface that allows a user to accomplish many data processing tasks quite easily without programming. A user can create and manipulate data files and indexes, edit or view data in a spreadsheet or a form, and create reports.

The FoxPro environment contains a third-party applications generator called FoxView that is based on the template model. It is not very tightly integrated with FoxPro but does allow a user to create forms and menus that are quite sophisticated. FoxPro users can take advantage of the many excellent third-party application generators and utilities like UI2, Genifer, Stage, and Scrimage upon which prior versions of dBASE depended.

FoxPro uses the dBASE file format, but it does not yet support the new multiple index files found in dBASE IV. The company has announced plans to support them in the next major release. FoxPro uses its own index format that is faster than the standard dBASE index. All indexes must be opened along with their associated data files either manually or explicitly in a program. Like dBASE, FoxPro does not offer data entry validation or defaults; they must be coded into every program.

FoxPro has a very good programming language that exceeds dBASE IV in power and functionality, but it suffers from the same feature overload that dBASE does. The wealth of features translates into power, but it does cause confusion. Many of the functions are quite low level, so Fox programs tend to be larger than programs for other databases. FoxPro has excellent debugging utilities.

R:BASE for DOS 3.0—Microrim: R:BASE has been around as long as dBASE and has a very active if somewhat smaller following. It was developed as a command line product and has evolved into an application development product. R:BASE lacks many features such as transaction processing and automated code generation.

R:BASE contains a menu-driven user interface that allows you to set up and execute every feature contained in the program without programming. Microrim pioneered the query-by-example approach and makes very good use of it. It also contains a command line mode for experienced users. There are "Express" modules to expedite the creation of databases, forms, reports, and menus, and all of these can be used quite easily by nonprogrammers.

All data in an R:BASE database, including forms, reports, rules, and data, are stored in three files. This is both a plus and a minus. For purposes of consolidation and integrity, the file format is very nice. Unfortunately a corrupted data file in R:BASE can be quite disastrous since the same file holds data, forms, reports, and rules. R:BASE automatically maintains all indexes.

R:BASE has a very powerful programming language that allows you to write programs that take fewer lines of code than most other database packages. R:BASE does have some flaws, for example, the lack of user-defined functions and a lack of elegant parameter passing between programs, that could prevent programmers from creating more reusable routines.

Emerald Bay with Vulcan 2.3—Ratliff Software Productions: Vulcan is a dBASE-compatible front end that is not as powerful as its competitors for end-user querying, including Clarion's Report Writer. Most database actions must be typed at a dot prompt or programmed. The user interface is quite weak unless it is programmed. The Vulcan environment does not have an applications generator.

Emerald Bay uses a data dictionary that stores all data tables in one file and all indexes in a second file. Validations, ranges, security, and defaults can be defined with the dictionary and are automatically enforced in all programs. The file format has excellent fault tolerance and is extremely fast in network operations. All indexes are automatically maintained by Emerald Bay as in Clarion, but unlike the dBASE products.

The Vulcan programming language retains the best features of the dBASE language without getting into the "quantity of features" war with Fox and dBASE. Vulcan allows one clean way to do some things where dBASE has five. Vulcan has all the features a programmer needs without overloading.

Vulcan was designed by the original creator of dBASE and is a very technologically advanced and fast PC network database. It has a great file structure and a very well thought out programming language. Vulcan's file format has very good crash recovery and validation capabilities. Its programming language is dBASE compatible, so your application would be fairly portable to other systems. This product has not been very effectively marketed by Ratliff and is gaining acceptance more slowly than its competitors. Its utilities are not as tightly integrated as they could be. It also lacks a slick end-user interface for querying and manipulation.

Summary

In this chapter, we focused on the other environments that compete with Clarion for a market share of the PC relational database application development market. The discussion was on a comparison with the dBASE products because they have the highest market share of any product in the list. Even with the release of dBASE IV, dBASE products do not offer an environment as cleanly integrated as Clarion's.

Chapter 17

Writing Your Own Language Extensions

Any programming language you use to create a software application will be lacking in some way. Some function—a way to access a file or to tap into the system resources—will not be available. The original developers didn't think of it, they didn't consider it important, or they just didn't have time to get it into the released product. In most higher level applications languages, that is the end of the story. You live without the function you wanted or you bend the other available language elements until you come close.

Clarion provides a unique method for allowing you to participate in the development of the language itself with Language Extension Modules (LEMs). LEMs can be as complex as the Graphics LEM offered by Clarion or as simple as the two utilities we create in this chapter. In either case, you are linking in software that you wrote at a much lower level, in terms of the interface to DOS and the PC, than the rest of the Clarion language.

A Language Extension Module is a set of machine instructions that perform a task. It can be made of several functions or of just one. The net result is to actually add a language statement to the Clarion language that requires you to do just a little bit of extra work on the procedure and function MAP. In this chapter, we create two functions that the Clarion language does not contain. The first is a simple call to find out how much free disk space there is on the default disk drive. This works like the MEMORY( ) function already in the Clarion language, but it is aimed at information about the hard disk and not random access memory as the MEMORY function was designed to read. The second function is a simple check of the availability of the printer in the LPT1: (or first parallel) port to make sure the printer is ready to accept output.

There are three excellent references for information on LEMs. The *Clarion Language Reference* provides a good introduction on the internal workings of the assembler code header and the memory management performed during the operation of a LEM. *Clarion Technical Bulletin No. 110* goes into additional detail on how to create a LEM, as do Mike Hanson's columns in the *Clarion Technical Journal* (Vol. 1, No. 2, and Vol. 2, No. 1). In this chapter, we'll cover the methods for creating a LEM using the LEM Maker with additional examples to help you create your own working LEM library.

To create a LEM and use a LEM, you must perform the following steps:

1. Create the assembler language header in a program editor or with the LEM Maker Kit.
2. Write the function (with assembler or C) in a program editor.
3. Compile the assembler code with MASM from Microsoft or TASM from Borland.
4. Compile the C code (including external definitions).
5. Link the two resulting object files (.OBJ) from the two previous steps along with the LM.LIB from the LEM Maker Kit (if in use for making the LEM) and any function libraries required by the LEM.
6. Process the executable file (.EXE) resulting from a successful link into a binary file (.BIN) using EXE2BIN from Microsoft (comes with DOS) or EXE2LEM (in the LEM Maker Kit).
7. Include an entry for the LEM binary file in the application's Map.
8. Make an explicit call to the LEM from within the application.

A few hard and fast rules must be followed when you create a LEM:

- The process must produce Microsoft-compatible object code. That standard allows the disparate elements of the LEM to be tied together.
- The entire LEM cannot exceed 64K in size. This restraint limits the number of things you can do with a LEM, but it also makes the whole process more manageable.
- You must create an assembly language header to permit the functions to be linked into the Clarion object modules (or work with the .PRO files in processor mode).
- You must create an assembly language footer to mark the end of the LEM.
- You cannot use MALLOC or floating-point math in any C modules linked into the LEM. MALLOC directly controls memory that can't be

allowed in the LEM. MALLOC as well as floating-point math functions drag in code from the startup libraries of the compiler that cannot appear in a LEM.

- You cannot call any C function that will cause the startup code for the compiler to be included in the object module. This is where optimizing compilers like TopSpeed C from Jensen & Partners run into difficulties with the current version of Clarion. TopSpeed requires an entry point (a MAIN statement) to use in eliminating unnecessary library code from being brought in during its normal compilations. The LEM function cannot contain *another* main function. (The primary executable for the application already contains one.)

The Components

The Assembler Header

Clarion itself is written in Turbo C from Borland International. (To confirm this, just run a program that lets you peek at the executable file of any application you create—DeBuerg's LIST program or Norton Utilities. You'll see the Borland copyright.) As a result, you must interweave your LEM with the memory management of the Turbo C compiler. If you use the default settings for the RTLink linker when you translate an application from .PRO files into .EXE files, you'll see the files list go by that includes both assembler programs (.ASM) and Turbo C programs (.C) that are accessed from the Clarion library files (.LIB).

To fit in with the object files (.OBJ) that RTLink pulls together to form an executable program you must create an assembly language header file and that will call your function—whether you write the function in assembler or in C. That header performs the following functions:

- The declaration of a valid binary file (.BIN)
- Number of functions
- The memory offset into the .BIN to each function
- The length of the .BIN module in its entirety
- Information on parameters passed to the function
- The call to your function
- Information on values returned from the function

In effect, the header section *manages* the operation of the functions or procedures inside the LEM. Figure 17-1 shows the interplay of the structure of a Clarion LEM with the functions that each element of the structure performs.

> ### *Caution*
> **The name of any function or procedure you include in a LEM cannot be longer than 12 characters.**

Since the advent of the LEM Maker Kit, the Clarion programmer has been able to control a great many aspects of the assembler portion of a LEM *without coding a line of assembly language.* You can even take control of the error returns inside the LEM from inside the LEM Maker. The code in Figure 17-2 is the output from the session with LEM Maker used to create the assembler portion for the Disk Space LEM to be completed in this chapter. Experienced assembly coders will be able to improve upon this code to perform certain special operations, but for most applications developers, the LEM Maker handles most of the conditions you would ever want to include in LEM.

Figure 17-1   The flow of control through a LEM.

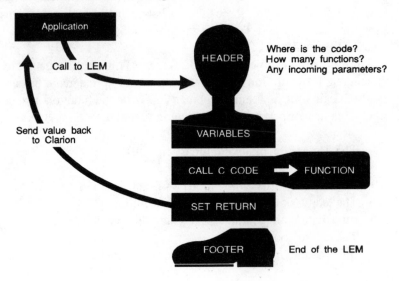

Figure 17-2   The output from the LEM Maker for the assembly-coded portion of the Disk Space LEM.

```
    PAGE   60,120
;---------------------------------------------------------------------;
;
;    LEM MODULE: DISKSTAT.ASM
;
;---------------------------------------------------------------------;
_TEXT SEGMENT PUBLIC BYTE 'CODE'
_TEXT ENDS
_DATA SEGMENT PUBLIC BYTE 'DATA'
_DATA ENDS
_BSS  SEGMENT PUBLIC BYTE 'BSS'
_BSS  ENDS
_END  SEGMENT PUBLIC BYTE 'LEMEND'
_END  ENDS
DGROUP         GROUP             _TEXT,_DATA,_BSS,_END
     EXTRN __REALCVT:NEAR
     EXTRN __scantod:NEAR
     EXTRN __scanpop:NEAR
     EXTRN __scanrslt:NEAR
; L.E.M.  equates
TSTRING     EQU   0             ;String
TSHORT      EQU   1             ;Signed word (16 bits)
TLONG EQU   2         .         ;Signed double word (32 bits)
TREAL EQU   4                   ;Double precision float (8087)
PROCEDURE   EQU   0             ;L.E.M. procedure
FUNCTION    EQU   1             ;L.E.M. function
NAMELTH = 0                     ;Define NAMELTH for macro
;---------------------------------------------------------------------;
; L.E.M.  macro
;   ROUTINE 'ROUTINE NAME', ROUTINE_PROC_LABEL, ROUTINE_TYPE,
;         NUMBER_OF_PARAMETERS
;---------------------------------------------------------------------;

ROUTINE MACRO   RNAME, RPROC, RTYPE, RPARMS
     LOCAL   LBLSTRT
```

(continued)

Figure 17-2 *continued*

```
LBLSTRT DB    &RNAME
NAMELTH =     $-LBLSTRT                ;;Padd name with nulls to 13 bytes
   IF NAMELTH GT 12
     .ERR
     %OUT routine name too long
   ELSE
     DB    13-NAMELTH DUP (0)   ;;Rest of name area
     DW    &RPROC                ;;Offset within binary module
     DB    &RTYPE                ;;Routine type = PROCEDURE or FUNCTION
     DB    &RPARMS               ;;Number of parameters
   ENDIF
   ENDM                          ;;End of macro
;----------------------------------------------------------------------;
; L.E.M.  macro
;   PARAMETER LABEL_OF_PARAMETER, TYPE_OF_PARAMETER
;----------------------------------------------------------------------;

PARAMETER   MACRO   PLBL, PTYPE
     DB    &PTYPE                ;;Type = STRING, SHORT, LONG, or REAL
&PLBL DD    0                    ;;Address of PARAMETER data
&PLBL&L DW 0                     ;;Length of PARAMETER data
     ENDM


     EXTRN   _diskspace:NEAR


;---------------------------------------------


_TEXT   SEGMENT PUBLIC BYTE 'CODE'
   ASSUME CS:DGROUP,DS:DGROUP


   DB      'BIO'
   PUBLIC  LIBVEC
LIBVEC   DD    0
   DW      DGROUP:BINEND
   DB      1                     ;NUMBER OF ROUTINES


;---------------------------------------------
```

(continued)

Figure 17-2 *continued*

```
ROUTINE     'DISKSPACE', DISKSPACE, FUNCTION, 1
PARAMETER   DISKSPACE1,TSHORT

;----------------------------------------

  PUBLIC   _errno
_errno     DW   0
  PUBLIC   _retval
_retval    DB   4 DUP(0)

;----------------------------------------

;   Calling your 'C' function as follows
; diskspace( (int) a );

DISKSPACE   PROC   FAR
LES   BX,DISKSPACE1
PUSH  WORD PTR ES:[BX]

CALL   _diskspace       ;Calling your 'C' function!!!
ADD    SP,2

MOV    WORD PTR _retval,AX
MOV    WORD PTR _retval+2,DX
LEA    BX,_retval
MOV    AL,2   ;RETURN LONG

RET
DISKSPACE   ENDP

_TEXT ENDS

_END  SEGMENT PUBLIC BYTE 'LEMEND'
BINEND        DB   0
_END  ENDS
END
```

The Function Code

With the availability of the LEM Maker to write the assembler code, writing the function then becomes the next most difficult thing involved with creating a LEM. As we've already discussed, the function code cannot attempt to control blocks of memory directly. Therefore, any function that involves MALLOC cannot be used. You should also avoid using any functions that involve floating point. In addition, some conversions that C makes will cause a problem. The _Clarion Technical Bulletin No. 110_ outlines the steps necessary to use the floating-point libraries in Turbo C. You must include the assembler code in Figure 17-3 in the EQUATES section of the header.

Figure 17-3   The statements required to use floating point in a Turbo C LEM.

```
        PUBLIC          __cvtfak
__cvtfak            EQU         0
        PUBLIC          __turbofloat
__turbofloat    EQU             0
        PUBLIC          __turboCvt
__turboCvt         EQU         0
        PUBLIC          FIARQQ
FIARQQ         EQU                 0FE32H
        PUBLIC          FICRQQ
FICRQQ         EQU                 00E32H
        PUBLIC          FDRQQ
FIDRQQ         EQU                 05C32H
        PUBLIC          FIERQQ
FIERQQ         EQU                 01632H
        PUBLIC          FISRQQ
FISRQQ         EQU                 00632H
        PUBLIC          FIWRQQ
FIWRQQ         EQU                 0A23DH
        PUBLIC          FJARQQ
FJARQQ         EQU                 04000H
        PUBLIC          FJCRQQ
FJCRQQ         EQU                 0C000H
        PUBLIC          FJSRQQ
FJSRQQ         EQU                 08000H
```

For the most part, as long as you are not trying to directly manipulate memory, you can do almost anything you want in the functional section of a LEM. You can control the hardware ports of the PC (as with the Communications LEM); send images to the screen (as with the Graphics LEM); or control file input/output operations (as with the dBASE LEM). Because the DOS program EXE2BIN performs the conversion to a binary module, you cannot exceed the 64K code and data segments. Thus, in functions written in C, you cannot use the larger models. In Turbo C, you can use only the Small and Compact models. You cannot use the Medium model because it uses FAR calls to outside of the 64K code segment. Figure 17-4 shows the C function written in Turbo C using the compact model for the Disk Space LEM.

Figure 17-4   The C Code for the Disk Space LEM.

```
/***********************************************************
*                                                         *
* LANGUAGE EXTENSION MODULE FOR DISK SPACE INFORMATION    *
*                                                         *
* By passing a parameter to this function, you can        *
* find out the total size of the default disk drive or    *
* the space available on that disk drive or the space     *
* used or unavailable.                                    *
*                                                         *
***********************************************************/

#include <dos.h>                                /*access libraries   */
#include <dir.h>
#include <stdio.h>
#include "diskstat.p"
#include "lm.p"

extern long cdecl diskspace(info)               /*function call      */
int info;
{
  unsigned long cluster_bytes, disk_bytes, available; /*derived values     */
  unsigned long disk_used;
  struct dfree dfinfo;                          /*info structures    */
  getdfree(0,&dfinfo);                          /*poll default  disk */
  cluster_bytes = dfinfo.df_sclus * dfinfo.df_bsec;  /*calc cluster size  */
  disk_bytes = dfinfo.df_total * cluster_bytes; /*calc disk size     */
  available = dfinfo.df_avail * cluster_bytes;  /*calc free space    */
  switch (info) {                               /*evaluate params    */
```

(continued)

Figure 17-4 *continued*

```
    case 1:                                 /*total disk size   */
       return(disk_bytes);
    case 2:                                 /*free disk space   */
       return(available);
    case 3:                                 /*used disk space   */
       disk_used = disk_bytes - available;
       return(disk_used);

    default:                                /*for unexpexteds   */
       return(-1);
    }
}
```

The LEM Maker

The Clarion LEM Maker takes away the pain of creating LEMs. It is designed to handle almost every aspect of the assembly coded routine for calling other functions. You can place as many functions into one LEM definition as you like. (See Figure 17-5.) However, the rules about a 64K maximum still apply. Most single-function LEMs won't take up anywhere near that much space. The two LEMs we create in this chapter occupy 539 bytes for the Disk Space LEM and 128 bytes for the Printer Status LEM.

Using the LEM Maker

When you first start the LEM Maker from the Processor, the screen in Figure 17-5 pops onto the screen along with the preexisting definitions for the three sample LEMs that come with the kit. To add another LEM definition, you simply press the Ins key and fill in the form that appears in Figure 17-6.

From this Update screen, you begin the construction of the LEM. Notice how you can take care of inserting the required assembly code for handling floating point that appears in Figure 17-3 by merely selecting that item. (This feature only works for Turbo C users.) You can also control the use of the error returns from your program from this screen. When you finish defining the LEM, you can continue on by pressing the F2 key. You then return to this screen to generate the assembler code that you will compile and link into your LEM.

Figure 17-5   The first screen of the LEM Maker.

WARNING

**It is possible to define the LEM with contradictory information. If
you select the three items in center screen in Figure 17-6 and then
they change from your selection of "Yes" or "No" after you complete the screen and then recall it, that means you have some contradictory information in the LEM definition. Go back over your
work and double-check it. Look first at whether you have configured the LEM to take charge of returning the value from the function or if the function itself will handle that.**

The next step is to define the procedures and functions you will be using by
pressing the F2 key from the Update LEM screen in Figure 17-6. The next
screen (depicted in Figure 17-7) works very much like a Designer Application

Figure 17-6   The LEM definition detail.

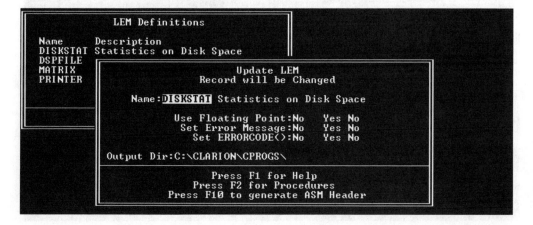

Summary screen where the objects at the heart of a LEM are formed into either procedures or functions. The same rules apply here as in Designer. A procedure performs some sort of work like painting to the screen, and a function performs work but then returns a value to the Calling Procedure in the application.

The form in Figure 17-7 is called the "Procedures" for the Disk Space LEM, but notice how the actual function called DISKSPACE is defined as a Function type. It is at this point that you can cause yourself a few headaches. Notice how the function has a different name than the LEM as we've defined it to this point. You need both names. The LEM name will be the final name of the file that you create. You need to include that name in the MAP of your application. However, you call the function within it by the function's name, not the file. You can imagine the problems. Since you cannot "list out" a compiled, linked, and EXE2BINed file, you could easily lose track of the name of the function inside that LEM that you want to use. So, differing from the Disk Space LEM, but in step with the Printer LEM that we'll discuss later in the chapter, you should try to keep the name of the LEM the same as the function it contains. The exception to this, of course, is the LEM that contains several functions and procedures. Notice how Clarion ships their LEMs with a file called "name of lem".CPY. That file contains the MAP entry that you can place into your main program file simply be using the INCLUDE statement. Keeping the LEM and its MAP entry together also helps document all the useful tools you may lock up inside a binary file.

Figure 17-7   The Procedures and Functions Definition screen.

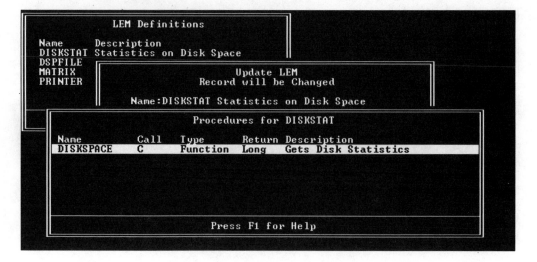

To add a new function or procedure or to edit an old one, you would press the appropriate key (Ins to add, Del to delete, and Enter to edit) and the detail screen for the function or procedure pops up as shown in Figure 17-8.

You can choose to make a function or a procedure at this point. If you specify this item as a procedure, you are not allowed to fill out the Returns and RETVAL items since procedures cannot return a value. Then you are asked to select the type of convention you will be using to call the function code. The calling convention you choose will affect the way in which variables are placed on the stack. If you select C, you can sustain a variable number of arguments as parameters passed to the function because the parameters are placed on the stack with the first one at a fixed point. If you select the PASCAL convention, you must pass all the parameters in the function or else the addresses computed to hold them will be erroneous and your function will not work. The PASCAL code, however, comes out a little smaller, if you are short for space.

Just as in Designer, you must specify the data type of the item you want returned from the function. Be careful how you make this selection. If the data type that the function expects is different from what you pick, an unexpected conversion could result in garbled data. Also, you must choose who will be responsible for returning the value: the function or the header. If you want a short or a long returned, you can ask the header to handle the return passing. However, if you want the C function to perform that work, you must define external variables in the C function to set RETVAL prior to completing its

Figure 17-8   The function/procedure detail update form.

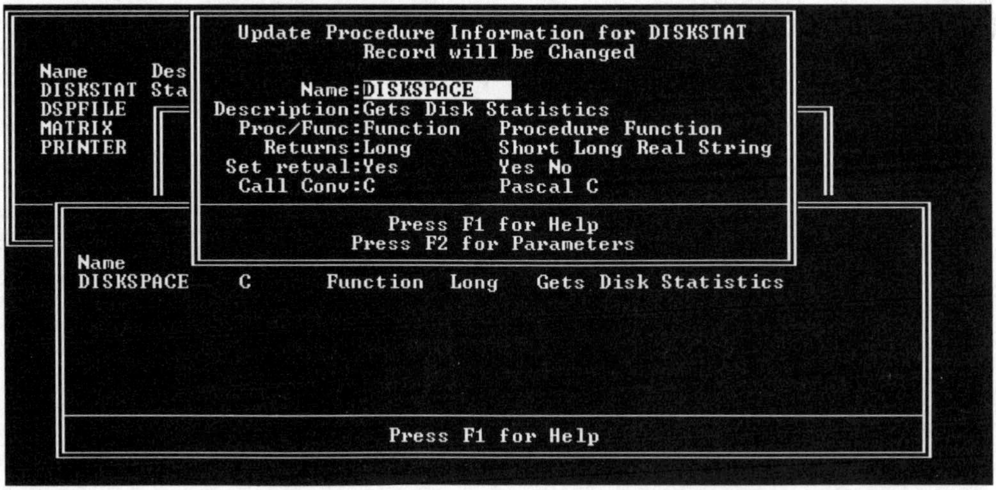

work. Also, for the C function to properly return the value in RETVAL, you must also specify the length of the returned value. (The *LEM Maker* manual has an excellent discussion of how to properly establish the external variables for returning a value from a function.)

Now that you have defined the basic operation of the LEM, you may have a need to pass parameters to it. In the case of the Disk Space LEM, we want to ask it to perform different operations based on the parameter we send. Therefore, we specify that the LEM function called DISKSPACE will have one parameter that is defined as a short. The meanings for the three choices for the value of the parameter appear in the description. This is another point you want to document well. If you don't record what those parameters are supposed to do, you will be forced to examine the C source code to get whatever comments you placed there.

With Figure 17-9, you can define as many parameters as you like. When you begin filling in the parameter update form as shown in Figure 17-10, you can even specify the order in which you want the parameters passed to the stack (this is very handy when you are using the PASCAL calling convention). Then you specify the variable type (which must match what is defined in the function) and whether you'll pass it to the function by address or by value. If you pass "by address" you tell the function where in memory to start looking for the value and how long to look. If you pass "by value" (and you can do this with everything but strings) the function does not need to have anything special defined in it to handle the incoming mail.

Figure 17-9   The parameter list for the Disk Space LEM.

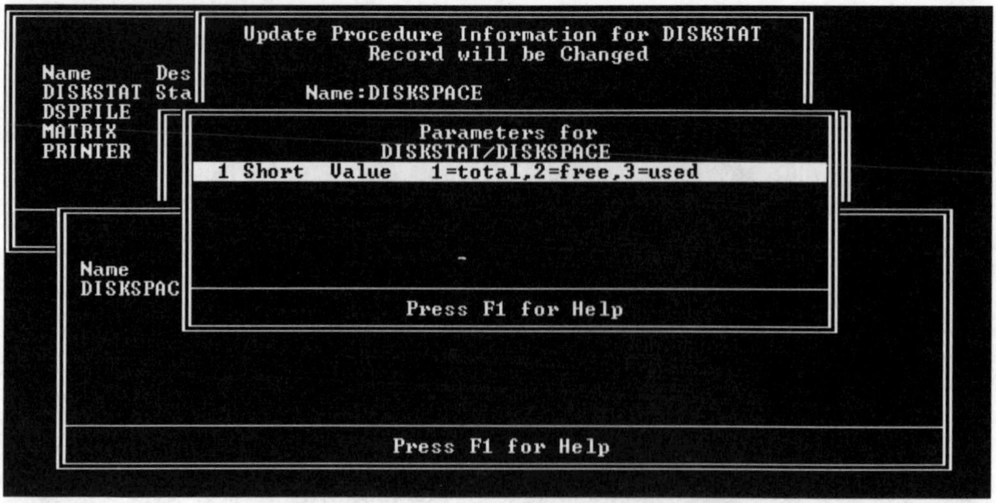

Figure 17-10 **The parameter definition update form. This is as deep into the program in terms of window layers as you can go.**

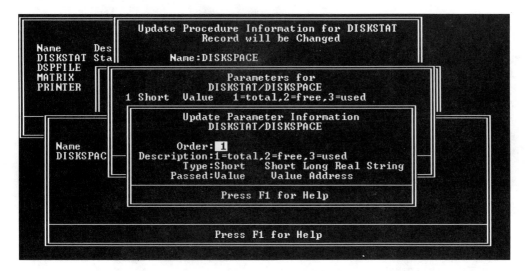

Linking It All Together

Now you've been all through defining everything we need to create the Disk Space LEM. It's time to link it all together into one file. However, before we actually commit everything to the binary format, let's test to make sure the function we created works. The most effective way to do this is to add in the missing MAIN program entry point to the C function, and to compile and link it into an operating executable file. For the Disk Space LEM, the change would appear as in Figure 17-11.

So, the C program works as advertised after you compile, link and run it separately. Now it's time to link the elements of the final version together. The files required to create the Disk Space LEM are as follows:

- DISKSTAT.ASM—The LEM assembly coded header file generated by LEM Maker. This file is turned into DISKSTAT.OBJ by using the Microsoft Assembly code compiler, MASM.
- DISKSTAT.CPY—A file generated by LEM Maker that contains the phrase to place in the application's MAP.
- SPACE.C—The C function that will be compiled into SPACE.OBJ.
- DISKSTAT.P—The function prototype for the function inside the LEM; to be included in the compilation of SPACE.C.

Figure 17-11   The Disk Space LEM as a standalone C program.

```
/***********************************************************
*                                                         *
* LANGUAGE EXTENSION MODULE FOR DISK SPACE INFORMATION    *
*                                                         *
* By passing a parameter to this function, you can        *
* find out the total size of the default disk drive or    *
* the space available on that disk drive or the space     *
* used or unavailable.                                    *
*                                                         *
***********************************************************/

#include <stdio.h>

long cdecl diskspace(int a);

main()
{
  printf("space on disk = %ld",diskspace(2));
}


#include <dos.h>                                    /*access libraries */
#include <dir.h>
#include <stdio.h>
/*#include "diskstat.p" */
#include "lm.p"

long cdecl diskspace(info)                          /*function call    */
int info;
{
  unsigned long cluster_bytes, disk_bytes, available; /*derived values   */
  unsigned long disk_used
  struct dfree dfinfo;                              /*info structures  */
  char choice;                                      /*switching value  */
  getdfree(0,&dfinfo);                              /*poll default disk*/
  cluster_bytes = dfinfo.df_sclus * dfinfo.df_bsec; /*calc cluster size*/
  disk_bytes = dfinfo.df_total * cluster_bytes;     /*calc disk size   */
  available = dfinfo.df_avail * cluster_bytes;      /*calc free space  */
  switch (info) {                                   /*evaluate params  */

      case 1:                                       /*total disk size  */
        return(disk_bytes);
```

(continued)

Figure 17-11 *continued*

```
case 2:                                          /*free disk space  */
  return(available);

case 3:                                          /*used disk space  */
  disk_used = disk_bytes - available;
  return(disk_used);

default:                                         /*for unexpexteds  */
 return(-1);
 }

}
```

- LM.P—The function prototypes for the functions contained in LM.LIB; to be included in the C function before compile time.
- LM.LIB—Specific functions required to access routines internal to Clarion that will be necessary to operate the LEM. (These are listed in the *LEM Maker Reference Manual*.)
- SPACE.ARF—The automatic response file for linking everything together as shown in Figure 17-12.

The three additional switches on the line for linking in the appropriate libraries are to implement FAR calls to the function, to create a MAP of the executable symbols for debugging, and to suppress searches through other libraries to resolve unresolvable references with the NOE linker switch for the Microsoft Linker. (We'll discuss unresolved references later in this chapter.)

When you run the linker by typing "LINK @SPACE.ARF" at the DOS command processor prompt, you will get warnings even when the linking is successful. The complete message you will see on the screen appears in Figure 17-13. The warnings are to be expected since we have created an executable file that cannot be run separately because by design it has no stack segment and no starting address.

Now, you have an executable file called SPACE.EXE. At the DOS command processor prompt you type "EXE2BIN SPACE.EXE" or "EXE2LEM SPACE.EXE." If everything is correctly assembled, you won't get a message; you'll just wind up with a file called SPACE.BIN, which has been the point of all this activity. In the case of the Disk Space LEM, you can now use it to find out information about the default disk drive storage. First you must place the

Figure 17-12   The automatic response file for the DISK SPACE program.

```
diskstat+                    (the assembler code)
space                        (the C code)
space                        (what to call the exe file)
space                        (what to call the map file)
c:\tc\lib\lm.lib+c:\tc\lib\cc.lib/FAR/MAP/NOE    (the library links)
```

information in the DISKSTAT.CPY in the application MAP structure. The simple program in Figure 17-14 shows a fixed disk (that is way too full) by simply setting a Computed Field in a menu equal to SPACE("parameter 1,2, or 3") for each reading.

The entry into the MAP structure for the application would look like this:

```
MODULE('DISKSTAT'),BINARY
    FUNC(DISKSPACE),LONG
        .
```

All the source code for creating the Disk Space LEM appears at the end of this chapter.

Figure 17-13   The message from a successful linking of the Disk Space LEM submodules.

```
Microsoft (R) Segmented-Executable Linker  Version 5.10
Copyright (C) Microsoft COrp 1984-1990. ALl rights reserved,

Object Modules [.OBJ]: diskstat+
Object Modules [.OBJ]: space
Run File [diskstat.exe]: space
List File [NUL.MAP]: space
LIbraries [.LIB]: c:\tc\lib\lm.lib+c:\tc\lib\cc.lib/FAR/MAP/NOE
Definitions File [NUL.DEF]:
LINK : warning 14021: no stack segment
LINK : warning 14038:  program has no starting address
```

Figure 17-14   A simple program demonstrating the Disk Space LEM.

```
         Total Disk Space: 44,406,784

         Free Disk Space:     108,544

         Used Disk Space:  44,298,240



            Press <ENTER> to Exit
```

Using Microsoft C 6.0 to Create a LEM

The Reason Some Languages and Compilers Have More Trouble Than Others

Most of the literature describing how to make LEMs for Clarion stop with demonstrations of Turbo C—the C compiler that was used to create Clarion in the first place. As we mentioned earlier, optimizing compilers like TopSpeed C perform a more in-depth (and therefore less general and forgiving) compile from the same source code, so it is not possible to use some compilers to create LEMs. In the case of TopSpeed, if you use the Turbo C libraries and Microsoft Link and you turn off the typesafe linkage checking, you can create a LEM with the TopSpeed compiler. However, that leaves you with few of the advantages that such a compiler normally offers.

The 6.0 version of Microsoft C (MSC) is another story. If you are careful, you can write LEMs with MSC as easily as you can with Turbo C. The problem goes back to the requirements for calls to function libraries, the most troublesome, of course, being the startup code. A LEM cannot have a starting address that duplicates the starting address for the main application. However, you can make other calls in an MSC program that will try to drag in that startup code even when you don't specify a MAIN statement in the program that normally creates the entry point for the application.

The Printer Status Function

As a demonstration, we'll create a LEM to test the status of the printer hooked to the number one parallel port, LPT1. If you've created a Clarion application by now and tried to send output to a printer that wasn't ready, you know it takes an unassisted Clarion application close to 30 seconds to tell you that there's a problem and then you have to bail out of the program altogether. There are several ways to solve this problem. Clarion offers one solution (in *Clarion Technical Bulletin 102*) that uses the PEEK, BAND, and BXOR statements to test for printer ready status. Clarion also offers the Crit Err LEM for just such critical error checking. However, you can construct a simple LEM and use it just like another language element to tell, almost instantly when called, whether the printer is ready for action. Then, by placing a call to this LEM function in the Setup Procedures for a Report Procedure in a Designer application, you can provide a fairly sophisticated means for checking device readiness.

The C That Is Really Just Assembler in Disguise Approach: There are several ways to use MSC 6.0. In this particular case, the key function, _BIOS_PRINTER, is merely a short stub of the assembler code that calls the interrupt 17H to get its current state. Microsoft sells the source code for all such segments of code. If you were interested, you could get the assembler source code and then just fold it directly into one long assembly program, beginning with the header file that LEM Maker provides. Alternatively you could use MSC's inline assembler function to mimic an assembler program while staying within the confines of C. An MSC 6.0 program constructed in that fashion would look like the one in Figure 17-15.

The inline assembler method, however, forces you to code the assembler. You can use another method that signals to the compiler not to grab that startup code. By including the definition "int _acrtused = 0;" in your C function (as shown in Figure 17-16), at least for the example, the calls to the startup code are eliminated.

If you compile the program shown in Figure 17-16 (being sure to turn on the /Gs switch to disable stack checking), you will create an object module (.OBJ) that can be linked with the output from LEM Maker, as shown in Figure 17-17. Then you can go through the linking steps, using the automatic response file in Figure 17-18 and converting to a binary module with EXE2BIN. This produces a LEM that you can call to check the printer's status

Figure 17-15   A Microsoft C 6.0 program using the inline assembler to exclude all calls to exterior libraries for checking printer status.

```
#include <bios.h>
#define LPT1 0

int _acrtused = 0;

unsigned printer()
{
    unsigned portstatus;

 /* Fail if any error bit is on, or if either operation bit is off. */
    _asm
    {
        mov     ah, _PRINTER_STATUS
        mov     al, LPT1
        mov     dx, 0

        int     17H         ; request printer service

        mov     al, ah      ; return status bits in AL, not in AH
        mov     ah, 0

        mov     portstatus, ax
    }
    if( (portstatus & 0x29) || !(portstatus & 0x80) || !(portstatus & 0x10) )

        portstatus = 0;
    else
        portstatus = 1;
    return(portstatus);
}
```

and get a near instantaneous response. You'll need to include the binary module in the MAP, as shown in Figure 17-19, too.

The end result is a display that tells you when the printer can be used. In the example in Figure 17-20, the Conditional Field is employed from Designer in a Menu Procedure to post a "Ready" message if the PRINTER( ) LEM returns a 1 or a "Not Ready" message if it returns anything else.

Figure 17-16   The PRINTER TEST program rewritten in "pure" C.

```
/**********************************************
    LANGUAGE EXTENSION MODULE
        PRINTER READY TEST

    This program checks the parallel port
    LPT1: to see if the printer attached
    there is ready to receive data.
    **********************************************/

#include <bios.h>
#include "printer.p"
#define LPT1 0

int _acrtused = 0;

extern int cdecl printer()
{
    unsigned int portstatus;

 /* Fail if any error bit is on, or if either operation bit is off. */
    portstatus = _bios_printer( _PRINTER_STATUS, LPT1, 0 );
    if ((portstatus & 0x29) || !(portstatus & 0x80) || !(portstatus & 0x10) )
            portstatus = 0;
    else
            portstatus = 1;
    return(portstatus);
}
```

The Ground Rules: The following list shows the functions in MSC 6.0 that allow us to simply define the _acrtused symbol globally so that the linker won't try to pull in code that, in the case of unresolved references, it will most certainly find in a function with no MAIN statement.

- _bios functions
- _int functions
- All mem functions
- Most string functions, except strtok and the _streerror group
- The character classification/conversion functions (isxxxx and toxxxx functions)

Figure 17-17   The LEM Maker born assembler header for the Printer Status LEM.

```
      PAGE    60,120
;-------------------------------------------------------------------;
;
;    LEM MODULE: PRINTER.ASM
;
;-------------------------------------------------------------------;
_TEXT SEGMENT PUBLIC BYTE 'CODE'
_TEXT ENDS
_DATA SEGMENT PUBLIC BYTE 'DATA'
_DATA ENDS
_BSS  SEGMENT PUBLIC BYTE 'BSS'
_BSS  ENDS
_END  SEGMENT PUBLIC BYTE 'LEMEND'
_END  ENDS
DGROUP          GROUP               _TEXT,_DATA,_BSS,_END


; L.E.M.  equates
TSTRING     EQU    0       ;String
TSHORT      EQU    1       ;Signed word (16 bits)
TLONG       EQU    2       ;Signed double word (32 bits)
TREAL       EQU    4       ;Double precision float (8087)
PROCEDURE   EQU    0       ;L.E.M. procedure
FUNCTION    EQU    1       ;L.E.M. function
NAMELTH = 0               ;Define NAMELTH for macro



;-------------------------------------------------------------------;
; L.E.M.  macro
;    ROUTINE 'ROUTINE NAME', ROUTINE_PROC_LABEL, ROUTINE_TYPE,
;               NUMBER_OF_PARAMETERS
;-------------------------------------------------------------------;



ROUTINE MACRO    RNAME, RPROC, RTYPE, RPARMS
   LOCAL      LBLSTRT
LBLSTRT DB     &RNAME
NAMELTH =     $-LBLSTRT          ;;Pad name with nulls to 13 bytes
   IF NAMELTH GT 12
     .ERR
     %OUT routine name too long
   ELSE
     DB    13-NAMELTH DUP (0)    ;;Rest of name area
```

(continued)

Figure 17-17 *continued*

```
        DW    &RPROC                  ;;Offset within binary module
        DB    &RTYPE                  ;;Routine type = PROCEDURE or FUNCTION
        DB    &RPARMS                 ;;Number of parameters
     ENDIF
     ENDM                             ;;End of macro


;---------------------------------------------------------------------;
; L.E.M.  macro
;    PARAMETER LABEL_OF_PARAMETER, TYPE_OF_PARAMETER
;---------------------------------------------------------------------;

PARAMETER   MACRO  PLBL, PTYPE
     DB        &PTYPE                 ;;Type = STRING, SHORT, LONG, or REAL
&PLBL   DD  0                         ;;Address of PARAMETER data
&PLBL&L DW  0                         ;;Length of PARAMETER data
     ENDM


     EXTRN  _printer:NEAR

;-----------------------------------------

_TEXT   SEGMENT PUBLIC BYTE 'CODE'
     ASSUME CS:DGROUP,DS:DGROUP

     DB     'BIO'
     PUBLIC LIBVEC
LIBVEC     DD  0
     DW     DGROUP:BINEND
     DB     1                         ;NUMBER OF ROUTINES


;-----------------------------------------

   ROUTINE     'PRINTER', PRINTER, FUNCTION, 0

;-----------------------------------------

   PUBLIC _errno
_errno    DW   0
```

(continued)

Figure 17-17 *continued*

```
   PUBLIC _retval
_retval    DB    2 DUP(0)


;-----------------------------------------


;   Calling your 'C' function as follows
; printer( );

PRINTER    PROCFAR
   CALL    _printer              ;Calling your 'C' function!!!

   MOV     WORD PTR _retval,AX
   LEA     BX,_retval
   MOV     AL,1;RETURN SHORT

   RET
PRINTER    ENDP


_TEXT ENDS

_END  SEGMENT PUBLIC BYTE 'LEMEND'
BINEND          DB    0
_END  ENDS
       END
```

Figure 17-18   The automatic response file for linking the MSC 6.0 printer status LEM.

```
printasm+              (assembler header from LEM Maker)
printer                (C program object module)
printer                (executable name)
printer                (symbol map name)
/FAR/MAP/NOE           (FAR calls converted, map made and
                        no extra libraries called)
```

Figure 17-19   The MAP addition for the printer status LEM.

```
MODULE('PRINTER'),BINARY
     FUNC(PRINTER),LONG
```

.

This next list is of the items that will most certainly not be workable since they require, and will not run without, that startup code. Thus the global symbol definition will not satisfy the requirements of:

- The malloc( ) family functions, except _dos_allocmem( )
- Data conversion functions (These call malloc( ) internally for the work buffer.)
- printf/scanf functions (These call malloc( ) so you cannot use printf to output notes to the screen as a debugging tool in MSC 6.0.)
- File input/output functions, both low level and stream (Startup support is required to set up stdin, sdout, strprn, and so on; and malloc( ) is used for the buffering in the stream I/O.)
- All graphics
- Most math functions (These use both malloc( ) and conversion factors in the startup code.)
- The _dos functions (These usually won't work because they set _errno in some cases. You can eliminate this obstruction if you choose to set the error levels with LEM Maker. This causes the _errno symbol to be defined in the LEM Maker–produced assembler code so the linker need look no further for a definition.)

Figure 17-20   A simple program to test the printer status.

There is a short-hand method to tell if you are calling a function that links in the startup code, either directly or implicitly, through a call to another function that does call it directly. When you are linking and you get "multiply defined" errors (it may be that the _acrtused symbol is defined more than once because the startup code got linked in somehow), you know you have to rewrite your code to eliminate the linker's need to go looking outside for definitions, thereby duplicating the definitions you already placed in your local code.

Debugging LEMs

Clarion Technical Bulletin 110 outlines three methods for debugging a LEM:

1. Place PRINT statements into the LEM for it to output information while it is running.
2. Run your program under the control of DOS DEBUG with a break-point built in (the technical bulletin recommends "INT 3" just before the call to the C function).
3. Use the public symbols in the LEM to control processing from inside an interactive debugger after generating a list of these symbols with the /MAP compiler switch.

Summary

In this chapter, we explored ways of expanding the Clarion language with user-definable language elements created through the Language Extension Modules, or LEMs. We examined the structure of a LEM from the assembler header, which you can write on your own or generate with a menu-driven interface through the LEM Maker. Then we discussed the various strategies for writing and linking functions and procedures. We created two LEMs: one to test for disk space and one to test for printer availability. Finally, we looked at writing LEMs in other languages and took a quick look at some ways to debug the LEMs you create.

The DISK SPACE LEM TEST Program

TEST.CLA

```
TEST        PROGRAM
                INCLUDE('STD_KEYS.CLA')
                INCLUDE('CTL_KEYS.CLA')
                INCLUDE('ALT_KEYS.CLA')
                INCLUDE('SHF_KEYS.CLA')


REJECT_KEY   EQUATE(CTRL_ESC)
ACCEPT_KEY   EQUATE(CTRL_ENTER)
TRUE         EQUATE(1)
FALSE        EQUATE(0)

                MAP
                  PROC(G_OPENFILES)
                  MODULE('TEST1')
                    PROC(MAIN)
                        .
                  MODULE('SPACE'),BINARY
                    FUNC(DISKSPACE),LONG
                        .
                  INCLUDE('DOS1.CPY')
                        .
                EJECT('FILE LAYOUTS')
                EJECT('GLOBAL MEMORY VARIABLES')
ACTION          SHORT                          !0 = NO ACTION
                                               !1 = ADD RECORD
                                               !2 = CHANGE RECORD
                                               !3 = DELETE RECORD
                                               !4 = LOOKUP FIELD


              GROUP,PRE(MEM)
MESSAGE         STRING(30)                     !Global Message Area
PAGE            SHORT                          !Report Page Number
LINE            SHORT                          !Report Line Number
DEVICE          STRING(30)                     !Report Device Name
                .

                EJECT('CODE SECTION')
    CODE
    SETHUE(7,0)                                !SET WHITE ON BLACK
    BLANK                                      !  AND BLANK
    G_OPENFILES                                !OPEN OR CREATE FILES
```

(continued)

```
      SETHUE()                                   !    THE SCREEN
      MAIN
      RETURN                                  !EXIT TO DOS


G_OPENFILES  PROCEDURE                        !OPEN FILES & CHECK FOR ERROR
   CODE
      BLANK                                   !BLANK THE SCREEN
```

TEST1.CLA

```
         MEMBER('TEST')
MAIN       PROCEDURE

SCREEN     SCREEN      PRE(SCR),WINDOW(15,50),HUE(7,0)
         ROW(1,1)   STRING('<201,205{48},187>')
         ROW(2,1)   REPEAT(13);STRING('<186,0{48},186>') .
         ROW(15,1)  STRING('<200,205{48},188>')
         ROW(4,10)  STRING('Total Disk Space:')
         ROW(6,10)  STRING('Free Disk Space:')
         ROW(8,10)  STRING('Used Disk Space:')
TOTAL      ROW(4,28)  STRING(@n10)
FREE       ROW(6,28)  STRING(@n10)
USED       ROW(8,28)  STRING(@n10)
                      ENTRY,USE(?FIRST_FIELD)
                      ENTRY,USE(?PRE_MENU)
                      MENU,USE(MENU_FIELD"),REQ
         ROW(13,16)  STRING('Press <<ENTER> to Exit')
               .                    .

   EJECT
   CODE
   OPEN(SCREEN)                                !OPEN THE MENU SCREEN
   SETCURSOR                                   !TURN OFF ANY CURSOR
   MENU_FIELD" = ''                            !START MENU WITH FIRST ITEM
   LOOP                                        !LOOP UNTIL USER EXITS
     SCR:TOTAL = diskspace(1)
     SCR:FREE = diskspace(2)
     SCR:USED = diskspace(3)
     ALERT                                     !TURN OFF ALL ALERTED KEYS
     ALERT(REJECT_KEY)                         !ALERT SCREEN REJECT KEY
     ALERT(ACCEPT_KEY)                         !ALERT SCREEN ACCEPT KEY
     ACCEPT                                    !READ A FIELD OR MENU CHOICE
     IF KEYCODE() = REJECT_KEY THEN RETURN.    !RETURN ON SCREEN REJECT

     IF KEYCODE() = ACCEPT_KEY                 !ON SCREEN ACCEPT KEY
```

(continued)

```
        UPDATE                                  !  MOVE ALL FIELDS FROM SCREEN
        SELECT(?)                               !  START WITH CURRENT FIELD
        SELECT                                  !  EDIT ALL FIELDS
        CYCLE                                   !  GO TO TOP OF LOOP
      .                                         !

     CASE FIELD()                               !JUMP TO FIELD EDIT ROUTINE
     OF ?FIRST_FIELD                            !FROM THE FIRST FIELD
       IF KEYCODE() = ESC_KEY THEN RETURN.      !  RETURN ON ESC KEY

     OF ?PRE_MENU                               !PRE MENU FIELD CONDITION
       IF KEYCODE() = ESC_KEY                   !  BACKING UP?
         SELECT(?-1)                            !    SELECT PREVIOUS FIELD
       ELSE                                     !  GOING FORWARD
         SELECT(?+1)                            !    SELECT MENU FIELD
       .
     OF ?MENU_FIELD"                            !FROM THE MENU FIELD
       EXECUTE CHOICE()                         !  CALL THE SELECTED PROCEDURE
         RETURN
   . . .
```

The PRINTER STATUS LEM TEST Program

TESTPRN.CLA

```
TESTPRN   PROGRAM
              INCLUDE('STD_KEYS.CLA')
              INCLUDE('CTL_KEYS.CLA')
              INCLUDE('ALT_KEYS.CLA')
              INCLUDE('SHF_KEYS.CLA')

REJECT_KEY    EQUATE(CTRL_ESC)
ACCEPT_KEY    EQUATE(CTRL_ENTER)
TRUE          EQUATE(1)
FALSE         EQUATE(0)

              MAP
                PROC(G_OPENFILES)
                MODULE('TESTPRN1')
                  PROC(MAIN)                    !TESTING PRINTER AVAILABILITY

                .
                MODULE('CHECK')
                  PROC(CHECK)                   !RESTART THE PROGRAM

                .
```

(continued)

```
            MODULE('PRINTER'),BINARY
              FUNC(PRINTER),STRING              !RETURN PRINTER STATUS
                .
              INCLUDE('DOS1.CPY')
               .
            EJECT('FILE LAYOUTS')
            EJECT('GLOBAL MEMORY VARIABLES')
ACTION        SHORT                            !0 = NO ACTION
                                               !1 = ADD RECORD
                                               !2 = CHANGE RECORD
                                               !3 = DELETE RECORD
                                               !4 = LOOKUP FIELD


            GROUP,PRE(MEM)
MESSAGE       STRING(30)                       !Global Message Area
PAGE          SHORT                            !Report Page Number
LINE          SHORT                            !Report Line Number
DEVICE        STRING(30)                       !Report Device Name
                .

              EJECT('CODE SECTION')
  CODE
  SETHUE(7,0)                                  !SET WHITE ON BLACK
  BLANK                                        !  AND BLANK
  G_OPENFILES                                  !OPEN OR CREATE FILES
  SETHUE()                                     !    THE SCREEN
  MAIN                                         !TESTING PRINTER AVAILABILITY
  RETURN                                       !EXIT TO DOS

G_OPENFILES  PROCEDURE                         !OPEN FILES & CHECK FOR ERROR
  CODE
  BLANK                                        !BLANK THE SCREEN
```

TESTPRN1.CLA

```
          MEMBER('TESTPRN')
MAIN         PROCEDURE

SCREEN       SCREEN       PRE(SCR),WINDOW(12,37),AT(6,23),HUE(15,1)
             ROW(1,4)     PAINT(1,30),HUE(0,7)
             ROW(7,7)     PAINT(1,25),HUE(14,0)
             ROW(1,1)     STRING('<218,196{2},0{30},196{3},191>'),HUE(11,1)
             ROW(2,1)     REPEAT(10);STRING('<179,0{35},179>'),HUE(11,1)  .
             ROW(12,1)    STRING('<192,196{35},217>'),HUE(11,1)
```

(continued)

```
          ROW(1,5)    STRING('TESTING PRINTER AVAILABILITY')
          ROW(7,9)    STRING('Printer is:')
STATUS    COL(21)     STRING(@s9)
                        ENTRY,USE(?FIRST_FIELD)
                        ENTRY,USE(?PRE_MENU)
                        MENU,USE(MENU_FIELD"),REQ
          ROW(5,4)    STRING('Press <<ENTER> to Check Printer'),SEL(0,7)
          ROW(10,17)  STRING('QUIT'),SEL(0,7)
            .             .
```

```
EJECT
CODE
OPEN(SCREEN)                                 !OPEN THE MENU SCREEN
SETCURSOR                                    !TURN OFF ANY CURSOR
MENU_FIELD" = ''                             !START MENU WITH FIRST ITEM
LOOP                                         !LOOP UNTIL USER EXITS
  IF printer() = 1                           !EVALUATE CONDITION
    SCR:STATUS = CENTER('READY',SIZE(SCR:STATUS))!CONDITION IS TRUE
  ELSE                                       !OTHERWISE
    SCR:STATUS = 'NOT READY'                 !  CONDITION IS FALSE
  .
  ALERT                                      !TURN OFF ALL ALERTED KEYS
  ALERT(REJECT_KEY)                          !ALERT SCREEN REJECT KEY
  ALERT(ACCEPT_KEY)                          !ALERT SCREEN ACCEPT KEY
  ACCEPT                                     !READ A FIELD OR MENU CHOICE
  IF KEYCODE() = REJECT_KEY THEN RETURN.     !RETURN ON SCREEN REJECT

  IF KEYCODE() = ACCEPT_KEY                  !ON SCREEN ACCEPT KEY
    UPDATE                                   !  MOVE ALL FIELDS FROM SCREEN
    SELECT(?)                                !  START WITH CURRENT FIELD
    SELECT                                   !  EDIT ALL FIELDS
    CYCLE                                    !  GO TO TOP OF LOOP
  .                                          !

  CASE FIELD()                               !JUMP TO FIELD EDIT ROUTINE
  OF ?FIRST_FIELD                            !FROM THE FIRST FIELD
    IF KEYCODE() = ESC_KEY THEN RETURN.      !  RETURN ON ESC KEY

  OF ?PRE_MENU                               !PRE MENU FIELD CONDITION
    IF KEYCODE() = ESC_KEY                   !  BACKING UP?
      SELECT(?-1)                            !    SELECT PREVIOUS FIELD
    ELSE                                     !  GOING FORWARD
      SELECT(?+1)                            !    SELECT MENU FIELD
    .
  OF ?MENU_FIELD"                            !FROM THE MENU FIELD
    EXECUTE CHOICE()                         !  CALL THE SELECTED PROCEDURE
      CHECK                                  !
```

(continued)

```
        RETURN
  . . .
```

CHECK.CLA

```
        MEMBER('TESTPRN')

CHECK   PROCEDURE
        CODE
        RESTART(MAIN)                    ! START PROGRAM OVER
```

Chapter 18

The Graphics Language Extension Module

The Clarion Graphics Language Extension Module opens up the display powers of the PC to your Clarion applications. The two most important features of the Graphics LEM are its ability to accept variables from any Clarion application and the fact that the graphics mode and Clarion's standard text mode cannot coexist on the same screen. You can create just about any form of onscreen graphical display you wish, and you have very tight control over the placement of every line and every color that the current video monitor supports. You can operate a mouse; you can send images to dot matrix printers, laser printers, and even postscript printers; you can even accept entry through fields on the screen. It is possible to write an entire application within the graphics mode.

The most common use for the graphics displays is to grab data from the files for the application and display it in a chart. Because you have access to the graphics mode, you can get much finer detail onto the screen than you can in plain ASCII text mode—which is the more common display mode. Normally, in text mode, you have a "pixel" layout 25 rows high and 80 columns wide—that is: each character space can be treated as a pixel. That is the greatest resolution possible but it is not high enough resolution to draw anything more than the boxes that Clarion's screen drawing tools support. The central problems become how much to show, what form to show it in, and how to manipulate the descriptive elements of labels, colors, and indicator lines. The Graphics LEM provides tools to handle all of those elements.

The Graphic Display Process

Figure 18-1 shows the flow of events required to successfully display graphics within the Clarion environment.

When you want to display a graphic image, your first step is to find out what kind of monitor will be used for the display. Next you must set that monitor in high-resolution mode. Only then can you begin to display graphic images. You could output characters to the screen using SAYSTRING or draw pictures on the screen with any of the graphic commands.

WARNING
The normal statements for output to the monitor like TYPE or SHOW *will not* work while you are in graphics mode, including opening a Screen structure.

Figure 18-1 shows the video configured before the data structures to be graphed are built (shown as "Build Graph Data" in the figure). It is not necessary to do things in that order. You could, for instance, build the graph data and load the fonts first, and then configure the video. However, you cannot display either fonts or graphs until the proper video drivers are loaded.

As shown in Figure 18-1, the next step, after placing the screen in high-resolution mode, could be to pull the data from the Clarion data files and select the scaling and the ranges for the data to be graphed. Then you must load the fonts you will use for each of the different forms of labeling and titling what you choose, and then you can call the graphic function to finish the display.

Figure 18-1   The graphic display process.

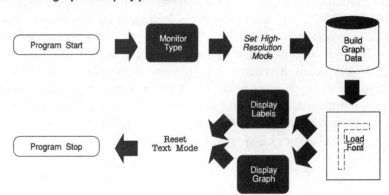

After the display is terminated, you must clean up by resetting the data structures and placing the screen back into text mode. You cannot remove the video driver from memory during program execution without experiencing irregular responses—and there is really no purpose in doing so.

The Monitor Drivers

The Graphics LEM provides two methods of configuring the video driver that will account for the two means of running the application. The first method comes into play when you run the application with either the Processor or CRUN using .PRO modules. The second method works only when you operate the application as an executable program.

Video Setup with Processor: If you choose to operate the system using Processor modules, you must load a Terminate-Stay-Resident (TSR) program called SETDGE. You must run the proper version of this program for each monitor. Clarion provides a program called SETVIDEO.BAT, which takes care of sensing the type of video display in use and prepares the correct version of SETDGE. The batch file called SETVIDEO.BAT in Figure 18-2 shows the steps required to make that determination.

As you can see in Figure 18-2, the batch file runs the VIDEO.COM program distributed with the Graphics LEM. The program senses the type of monitor installed and assigns a value used to select the version of the SETDGE program to be run. Then it copies the appropriate version over to the file named SETDGE.COM. During this same process, the correct selection of fonts are also copied into the filenames that the system will recognize. The one final step that this batch file does not address is the actual loading of the SETDGE.COM program into memory. That program intercepts the calls that the graphics program makes and interprets them for the monitor installed. Table 18-1 shows all the files you *must* include if you plan to distribute your application to be used with Processor files and the Clarion runtime, CRUN.EXE. You can tailor your distribution diskettes to run on only one kind of monitor by including only that version of the SETDGE programs and the proper configuration for the fonts.

WARNING
In systems with dual monitor cards, VIDEO.COM returns the monitor type for only the first card it finds.

Figure 18-2   The SETVIDEO.BAT program.

```
ECHO OFF
video
if errorlevel 7 goto VGAEGA
if errorlevel 6 goto VGAEGA
if errorlevel 5 goto CGACOLOR
if errorlevel 4 goto CGAMONO
if errorlevel 3 goto HERCULES
ECHO Not running on a graphics adapter!
goto OUT
:VGAEGA
copy setdge.vga setdge.com
goto HIFONTS
:CGACOLOR
copy setdge.cgc setdge.com
goto LOWFONTS
:CGAMONO
copy setdge.cgm setdge.com
goto LOWFONTS
:HERCULES
copy setdge.hrc setdge.com
goto HIFONTS
:HIFONTS
copy small.fnt     small.chr
copy standard.fnt  standard.chr
copy thin.fnt      thin.chr
copy inverse.fnt   inverse.chr
copy large.fnt     large.chr
copy intl437.fnt   intl437.chr
ECHO Hi Res fonts created successfully!
GOTO OUT
:LOWFONTS
copy vtiny.chr     small.chr
copy small.fnt     standard.chr
copy tinythin.chr  thin.chr
copy tinyinv.chr   inverse.chr
copy medium.chr    large.chr
copy intl437s.chr  intl437.chr
```

(continued)

Figure 18-2 *continued*

```
ECHO Low Res fonts created successfully!
GOTO OUT
:OUT
ECHO ON
```

The TSR program SETDGE must be installed before the graphics in your program will display when you run it with the Processor or CRUN. In fact, if you attempt to display the graphics without first installing SETDGE, the system will hang and you must then reboot it. You can still run the rest of your application normally without SETDGE installed. So, before you start your application using CRUN (or CPRO during testing), you must run the SETVIDEO.BAT once (when you first install the Graphics LEM) and then be

Table 18-1 The programs required to properly install graphics with the Clarion runtime, CRUN.EXE.

Program Filename	Function
VIDEO.COM	Senses the type of monitor installed.
SETDGE.VGA	Contains the high-resolution screen driver.
SETDGE.CGC	Contains the color graphics screen driver.
SETDGE.CGM	Contains the monochrome graphics screen driver.
SETDGE.HRC	Contains the Hercules monitor screen driver.
SMALL.FNT	
STANDARD.FNT	
THIN.FNT	
INVERSE.FNT	
LARGE.FNT	
INT1437.FNT	The fonts.
VTINY.CHR	
TINYTHIN.CHR	
TINYINV.CHR	
MEDIUM.CHR	
IN1437S.CHR	
SETVIDEO.BAT	Converts the fonts and TSR type.

sure that you run SETDGE before you try to use the graphic functions you've programmed into the application.

Hint: The normal text mode debugging facilities are of limited use while the screen is in high-resolution mode under the supervision of SETDGE. You can still call up the Debugger screen, check the value of variables, and even look at the source code, but do not attempt to scroll the source code window.

WARNING
If you prematurely terminate the program from the debugger, be sure you immediately exit out of CLARION.COM (if that's where you started the Processor) and return to DOS again. If you started CPRO from the command line or are using CRUN when you stop the program before your reset to text mode code can run, be sure to run CLARION.COM immediately. That will reset your video back to text mode. You can also use the DOS MODE command to restore the video. Otherwise, you will get irregular responses from any other program that scrolls information across the screen.

Video Setup in an Executable File:　The second method that Clarion provides for handling the special graphics setup can be accomplished inside the executable file. You must still transport the font files with the application, but you can eliminate the need for running the SETDGE program separately. The steps you must take to properly set up the video environment from within an executable file are:

1. Translate the .PRO files normally, creating the RTLink automatic response file.
2. Remove the reference in the .ARF file to the GRAPH.BOJ file.
3. Include a line that says: SEARCH (pathname) GRAPH.LIB.
4. Provide for the different screen drivers within separate overlays (so only the one you want gets loaded) as shown in the .ARF file in Figure 18-3.
5. Include the following line as the first instruction at the beginning of your graphic procedure or routine:

```
SETVIDEO(GETVIDEO(0))
```

Figure 18-3   A sample .ARF file, including the graphics library.

```
OUTPUT    C:\CLARION\BOOKTEST\GRAPH\STAT.EXE
VERBOSE
OVERLAY  CODE,CLARION
FILE      C:\CLARION\CLARION.OBJ
FILE      C:\CLARION\CLARION0.OBJ
SEARCH   C:\CLARION\CLARION1.LIB
SEARCH   C:\CLARION\CLARION2.LIB
SEARCH   C:\CLARION\GRAPH\GRAPH.LIB
FILE      C:\CLARION\BOOKTEST\GRAPH\DOS1.BOJ
FILE      C:\CLARION\BOOKTEST\GRAPH\KIDDING.OBJ
FILE      C:\CLARION\BOOKTEST\GRAPH\ONE.OBJ
FILE      C:\CLARION\BOOKTEST\GRAPH\STAT.OBJ
FILE      C:\CLARION\BOOKTEST\GRAPH\STAT1.OBJ
FILE      C:\CLARION\BOOKTEST\GRAPH\STAT2.OBJ
FILE      C:\CLARION\BOOKTEST\GRAPH\STAT3.OBJ
FILE      C:\CLARION\BOOKTEST\GRAPH\STAT4.OBJ
FILE      C:\CLARION\BOOKTEST\GRAPH\STAT5.OBJ
FILE      C:\CLARION\BOOKTEST\GRAPH\STAT6.OBJ
FILE      C:\CLARION\BOOKTEST\GRAPH\STAT7.OBJ
FILE      C:\CLARION\BOOKTEST\GRAPH\STAT8.OBJ
BEGIN
SECTION
 FILE   C:\CLARION\GRAPH\DGEVGA.OBJ
SECTION
 FILE   C:\CLARION\GRAPH\DGECGC.OBJ
SECTION
 FILE   C:\CLARION\GRAPH\DGECGM.OBJ
SECTION
 FILE   C:\CLARION\GRAPH\DGEHRC.OBJ
END
```

The GETVIDEO function retrieves the monitor type, and the SETVIDEO function calls the correct overlay from the executable into memory, just as the SETDGE program does when an application is running with the processor.

Hint: You must add the statements from GRAPH.CPY to your model, or to the generated program file, or you must "INCLUDE" GRAPH.CPY itself in either the model or your generated program file. GRAPH.CPY contains the procedure definitions required by Clarion. The GRAPHEQU.CPY file contains useful EQUATE statements for various parameters you will be using in the graphic functions. By including this file, you can use English words instead of numbers for the parameters. Print out a copy of GRAPHEQU.CPY to keep handy while you write the graphic parts of your application.

Handling Data

One of the aspects of the Graphics LEM that makes it easy to use is the way you can pass data (already formatted) to the graphic functions. The functions for handling data appear in Table 18-2.

The way you apply any of the graphing functions in the Graphics LEM is by first filling the data buffer with the DATASTORE function. The current contents of the buffer is referenced implicitly whenever you issue a graphic command that draws an entire chart like a pie chart or a Gantt chart. Since none of the commands clears out the buffer, you can reuse its contents with as many graphic calls as you like. Just remember to clear the screen before you paint something new that will cover over older pictures. For simple graphic lines or circles, the data buffer is ignored.

Fonts

The Graphics LEM also provides a flexible font-controlling system. You can even manufacture your own fonts if you like by using the GFONT program. The standard fonts that come with the LEM can be edited simply by loading them into the Font Editor, as shown in Figure 18-4.

You can have bit-by-bit control over the shape of characters. Then with a simple call to the LOADCSET statement in your program, you can load up to two fonts in the font buffer for use with your next label statement or use of SAYSTRING. You can use this tool to create special symbols for drawings or for use in a graph. To place them on the screen, you need only make a call to the reference number of the symbol in the font file after loading the font into memory.

Table 18-2   The data functions.

Function Name	Function
DATASTORE	Places data in the buffer.
TIMEDATA	Places data into the TIMEGRAPH structure.
DATAPC	Scales the data in the buffer.
DATARANGE	Selects a subset of the data in the buffer.
DATARESET	Clears out the buffer.
GETMAX	Retrieves the highest number in the current data buffer.
GETMEAN	Calculates the mean value of the numbers in the data buffer.
GETMIN	Retrieves the lowest number in the current data buffer.
GETSD	Calculates the standard deviation of the buffer data.
GETCC	Calculates the correlation coefficient of the buffer data.

Figure 18-4   The Clarion Graphics LEM Font Editor.

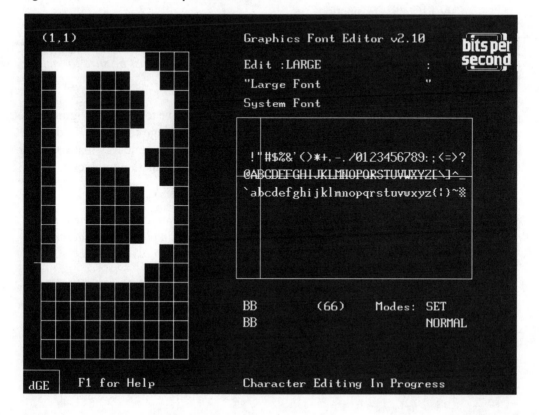

Hint: Remember that each statement that uses a font will use whichever font was loaded into the font buffer referenced in the command. It is best to load the fonts you will use most often (if different from the default: 0 = STANDARD, 1 = SMALL) at the beginning of the procedure or graphic program segment. Then you can ensure you are calling the right font by querying with GETFONTINF before you try to use the font during the program.

Images

The Graphics LEM provides several ways to place complex graphic images on the screen that are not numerically driven, as is the case with pie, bar, and Gantt charts. You can display the PCX format of graphic image file, you can create your own images as icons with the Font Editor, and you can draw pictures with the Cartesian and Vector line draw functions.

PCX files must be less than 64K in size, which can make for a rather complex drawing. You can read those PCX files from a file on the disk with the PICREAD function, and if during the course of the display you write other graphic items on top of the image, you can save that image back to disk using the PICWRITE function.

Hint: Remember that the PCX files you use in your application do not get compiled and linked into an executable file, so you must be sure to include them in the distribution set of your application.

Icons can be stored in a "library" of icons with five to a library. Figure 18-5 shows the Font Editor with the Macintosh-like "garbage can" icon. To display this, you would load the icon in the icon buffer (in the same way that you load fonts and data) and then you use the DRAWICON function to pluck it out of memory and display it on the screen at a preselected location.

Hint: All of the graphic functions can accept variables as parameters. You can use other code to make the selection you want and then set the descriptive variable to that value. This makes for more readable code as well.

Printing

The printing facilities in the Graphics LEM make sending a printed image of the screen a one-statement proposition. You can have control over the size

Figure 18-5   An icon in the Edit mode in the Font Editor.

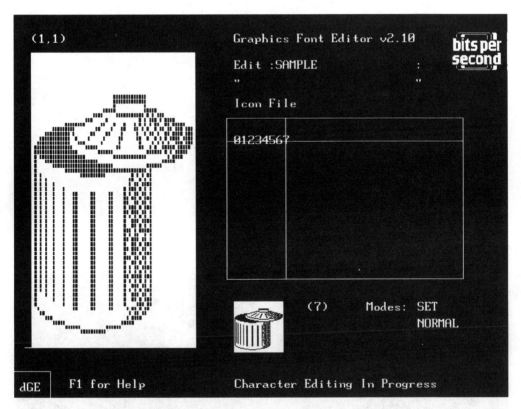

and scaling of the image. In fact, even for a PostScript printer, sending an image to be printed can be a one-line statement like PRINTSCRN for dot matrix printers and PRINTPCL for laser printers. Both of those statements print the current contents of the screen with parameters for density and position on the paper.

If you want, it is also possible to delay printing and save the image to be printed in a DOS file. Simply calling PRINTFILE redirects the output of the other printing commands such as PRINTPS or PRINTSCRN to a DOS file named as a parameter instead of sending the screen out to the printer. You can also drive any plotter that supports the Hewlett-Packard Graphics Language (HPGL) with the PLOTON, PLOTOFF, PLOTCSET, and PLOTPEN statements.

The Mouse

You can control the mouse in a Clarion Graphics application, though no internal driver yet exists for using a mouse with standard, text-based Clarion. You can sense motion and track location (MMOTION, MGETX, and MGETY), you can find out which button was clicked (MSTATUS), and you can sensitize areas of the screen and tell when the mouse was clicked within that area (MSETHOT and MGETHOT). You can turn the mouse cursor off during printing or other activity and then turn it back on (MCUROFF and MCURON); you can position it, limit it to a specific area of the screen, and even change its shape (MFIXPOS, MSETWIN, and MCURTYPE).

Figure 18-6   The sample program graphics display.

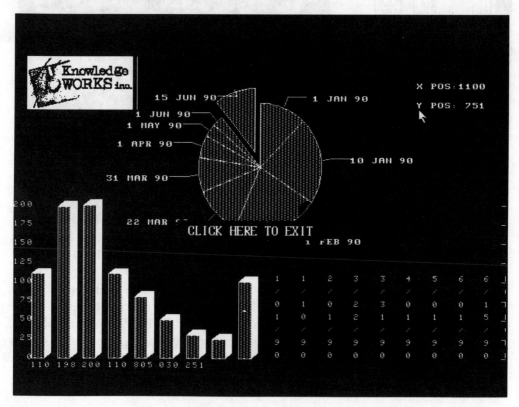

The mouse click also works as a keystroke. If you place a keystroke in the keyboard buffer, moving the mouse can cause that keystroke to be shoved out of the buffer and executed. So be careful using the KEYBOARD statement and other statements, especially in places where your program depends on knowing the last keystroke entered from the actual keyboard.

A Sample Program

The following sample program provides a means for entering data to a simple database and for parameters for the one graphic screen image to be set in a control file. The screen to be created by this application appears in Figure 18-6. Notice the mouse tracking coordinates and the display of the company logo as a PCX file in the upper left-hand corner of the screen. The screen to configure the control file for this application is pictured in Figure 18-7. The entire sample program source code appears at the end of this chapter.

Figure 18-7   The control file entry screen for configuring the graphic image.

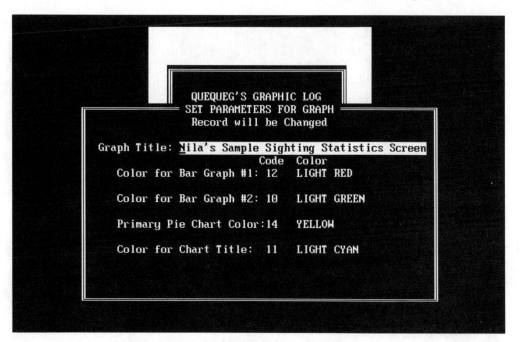

Summary

In this chapter we discussed the possibilities for creating graphical displays within a Clarion application using the Graphics LEM. You can run the proper environment for the monitor attached with help from a memory resident program while in processor or runtime mode, and you can make the selection automatically from within an executable program. You can control the data set used for graphing, and you can control the mouse and the display of graphical images other than numerically driven graphs. You can also create and display your own fonts.

The SAMPLE Program Code

STAT.CLA

```
STAT      PROGRAM
            INCLUDE('STD_KEYS.CLA')
            INCLUDE('CTL_KEYS.CLA')
            INCLUDE('ALT_KEYS.CLA')
            INCLUDE('SHF_KEYS.CLA')

REJECT_KEY  EQUATE(CTRL_ESC)
ACCEPT_KEY  EQUATE(CTRL_ENTER)
TRUE        EQUATE(1)
FALSE       EQUATE(0)

            MAP
              PROC(G_OPENFILES)
              MODULE('STAT1')
                PROC(MAIN)                    !AHAB'S WHALE WATCHING STATS

              MODULE('STAT2')
                PROC(SHO_DATE)                !SHOW STATS BY DATE

              MODULE('STAT3')
                PROC(UPD_STATS)               !UPDATE STATS

              MODULE('STAT4')
                PROC(RPT_DATE)                !PRINT STATS BY DATE

              MODULE('STAT5')
                PROC(GRAPHS)                  !QUEQUEG'S GRAPHIC LOG

              MODULE('STAT6')
                PROC(PARMS)                   !SET PARAMETERS FOR GRAPH

              MODULE('STAT7')
                PROC(COLORS)                  !COLOR SELECTION

              MODULE('STAT8')
                PROC(NEW_COLORS)              !ENTER NEW COLORS

              MODULE('ONE')
                PROC(ONE)                     !THE GRAPHING PROCEDURE

              MODULE('KIDDING')
```

(continued)

```
                      PROC(KIDDING)                        !YOU'RE KIDDING - TOO MANY
                .
                INCLUDE('DOS1.CPY')
                INCLUDE('c:\clarion\graph\GRAPH.CPY')
                .
                EJECT('FILE LAYOUTS')
STATS     FILE,PRE(STA),CREATE,RECLAIM
BY_DATE   KEY(STA:DATE),DUP,NOCASE,OPT
RECORD    RECORD
DATE        LONG
PODSIZE     SHORT
LOCATION    STRING(20)
MOBY        STRING(1)
          . .


PARMS     FILE,PRE(PRM),CREATE,RECLAIM
RECORD    RECORD
TITLE       STRING(40)                            !TITLE FOR GRAPH
BARS        STRING(@N2)                           !COLOR FOR LEFT HAND BAR GRAPH
BARS2       STRING(@N2)                           !COLOR FOR RIGHT HAND BAR GRAPH
PIE         STRING(@N2)                           !PRIMARY COLOR FOR PIE GRAPH
TITLE_COLOR STRING(@N2)                           !COLOR FOR TITLE
          . .


COLORS    FILE,PRE(COL),CREATE,RECLAIM
BY_CODE   KEY(COL:COLOR_CODE),DUP,NOCASE,OPT
RECORD    RECORD
COLOR       STRING(14)                            !Available color
COLOR_CODE  STRING(@n2)                           !Code for Color Selection
          . .


                EJECT('GLOBAL MEMORY VARIABLES')
ACTION      SHORT                                 !0 = NO ACTION
                                                  !1 = ADD RECORD
                                                  !2 = CHANGE RECORD
                                                  !3 = DELETE RECORD
                                                  !4 = LOOKUP FIELD


          INCLUDE('c:\clarion\graph\GRAPHEQU.CPY')


          GROUP,PRE(MEM)
MESSAGE     STRING(30)                            !Global Message Area
PAGE        SHORT                                 !Report Page Number
LINE        SHORT                                 !Report Line Number
DEVICE      STRING(30)                            !Report Device Name
          .
```

(continued)

```
              EJECT('CODE SECTION')
  CODE                                         !SET WHITE ON BLACK
  SETHUE(7,0)                                  !   AND BLANK
  BLANK                                        !OPEN OR CREATE FILES
  G_OPENFILES                                  !    THE SCREEN
  SETHUE()                                     !AHAB'S WHALE WATCHING STATS
  MAIN                                         !EXIT TO DOS
  RETURN


G_OPENFILES  PROCEDURE                         !OPEN FILES & CHECK FOR ERROR
  CODE
  SHOW(25,1,CENTER('OPENING FILE: ' & 'STATS',80)) !DISPLAY FILE NAME
  OPEN(STATS)                                  !OPEN THE FILE
  IF ERROR()                                   !OPEN RETURNED AN ERROR
    CASE ERRORCODE()                           ! CHECK FOR SPECIFIC ERROR
    OF 46                                      ! KEYS NEED TO BE REQUILT
      SETHUE(0,7)                              !  BLACK ON WHITE
      SHOW(25,1,CENTER('REBUILDING KEY FILES FOR STATS',80)) !INDICATE MSG
      BUILD(STATS)                             !  CALL THE BUILD PROCEDURE
      SETHUE(7,0)                              !  WHITE ON BLACK
      BLANK(25,1,1,80)                         !  BLANK THE MESSAGE
    OF 2                                       !IF NOT FOUND,
      CREATE(STATS)                            ! CREATE
    ELSE                                       ! ANY OTHER ERROR
      LOOP;STOP('STATS: ' & ERROR()).          !  STOP EXECUTION
  . .

  SHOW(25,1,CENTER('OPENING FILE: ' & 'PARMS',80)) !DISPLAY FILE NAME
  OPEN(PARMS)                                  !OPEN THE FILE
  IF ERROR()                                   !OPEN RETURNED AN ERROR
    CASE ERRORCODE()                           ! CHECK FOR SPECIFIC ERROR
    OF 46                                      ! KEYS NEED TO BE REQUILT
      SETHUE(0,7)                              !  BLACK ON WHITE
      SHOW(25,1,CENTER('REBUILDING KEY FILES FOR PARMS',80)) !INDICATE MSG
      BUILD(PARMS)                             !  CALL THE BUILD PROCEDURE
      SETHUE(7,0)                              !  WHITE ON BLACK
      BLANK(25,1,1,80)                         !  BLANK THE MESSAGE
    OF 2                                       !IF NOT FOUND,
      CREATE(PARMS)                            ! CREATE
    ELSE                                       ! ANY OTHER ERROR
      LOOP;STOP('PARMS: ' & ERROR()).          !  STOP EXECUTION
  . .

  SHOW(25,1,CENTER('OPENING FILE: ' & 'COLORS',80)) !DISPLAY FILE NAME
  OPEN(COLORS)                                 !OPEN THE FILE
  IF ERROR()                                   !OPEN RETURNED AN ERROR
    CASE ERRORCODE()                           ! CHECK FOR SPECIFIC ERROR
```

(continued)

```
    OF 46                                    !   KEYS NEED TO BE REQUILT
      SETHUE(0,7)                            !   BLACK ON WHITE
      SHOW(25,1,CENTER('REBUILDING KEY FILES FOR COLORS',80)) !INDICATE MSG
      BUILD(COLORS)                          !   CALL THE BUILD PROCEDURE
      SETHUE(7,0)                            !   WHITE ON BLACK
      BLANK(25,1,1,80)                       !   BLANK THE MESSAGE
    OF 2                                     !IF NOT FOUND,
      CREATE(COLORS)                         !  CREATE
    ELSE                                     !  ANY OTHER ERROR
      LOOP;STOP('COLORS: ' & ERROR()).       !  STOP EXECUTION
  . .

    BLANK                                    !BLANK THE SCREEN
```

STAT1.CLA

```
          MEMBER('STAT')
MAIN            PROCEDURE

SCREEN          SCREEN       PRE(SCR),WINDOW(16,36),HUE(15,3)
          ROW(1,1)     STRING('<201,205{34},187>'),HUE(15,3)
          ROW(2,1)     REPEAT(14);STRING('<186,0{34},186>'),HUE(15,3)  .
          ROW(16,1)    STRING('<200,205{34},188>'),HUE(15,3)
          ROW(2,6)     STRING('AHAB''S WHALE WATCHING STATS')
DATE            ROW(4,15)    STRING(@D1),HUE(15,3)
                       ENTRY,USE(?FIRST_FIELD)
                       ENTRY,USE(?PRE_MENU)
                       MENU,USE(MENU_FIELD"),REQ
          ROW(6,10)    STRING('Show Stats By Date'),HUE(1,3),SEL(0,7)
          ROW(8,14)    STRING('View Graphs'),HUE(1,3),SEL(0,7)
          ROW(10,10)   STRING('Print Stats By Date'),HUE(1,3),SEL(0,7)
          ROW(12,17)   STRING('Quit'),HUE(1,3),SEL(0,7)
                 .            .

EJECT
CODE
OPEN(SCREEN)                                 !OPEN THE MENU SCREEN
SETCURSOR                                    !TURN OFF ANY CURSOR
MENU_FIELD" = ''                             !START MENU WITH FIRST ITEM
LOOP                                         !LOOP UNTIL USER EXITS
  SCR:DATE = TODAY()
  ALERT                                      !TURN OFF ALL ALERTED KEYS
  ALERT(REJECT_KEY)                          !ALERT SCREEN REJECT KEY
  ALERT(ACCEPT_KEY)                          !ALERT SCREEN ACCEPT KEY
  ACCEPT                                     !READ A FIELD OR MENU CHOICE
```

(continued)

```
IF KEYCODE() = REJECT_KEY THEN RETURN.          !RETURN ON SCREEN REJECT

IF KEYCODE() = ACCEPT_KEY                        !ON SCREEN ACCEPT KEY
  UPDATE                                         !  MOVE ALL FIELDS FROM SCREEN
  SELECT(?)                                      !  START WITH CURRENT FIELD
  SELECT                                         !  EDIT ALL FIELDS
  CYCLE                                          !  GO TO TOP OF LOOP
.                                                !

CASE FIELD()                                     !JUMP TO FIELD EDIT ROUTINE
OF ?FIRST_FIELD                                  !FROM THE FIRST FIELD
  IF KEYCODE() = ESC_KEY THEN RETURN.            !  RETURN ON ESC KEY

OF ?PRE_MENU                                     !PRE MENU FIELD CONDITION
  IF KEYCODE() = ESC_KEY                         !  BACKING UP?
    SELECT(?-1)                                  !    SELECT PREVIOUS FIELD
  ELSE                                           !  GOING FORWARD
    SELECT(?+1)                                  !    SELECT MENU FIELD
  .

OF ?MENU_FIELD"                                  !FROM THE MENU FIELD
  EXECUTE CHOICE()                               !  CALL THE SELECTED PROCEDURE
    SHO_DATE                                     !  SHOW STATS BY DATE
    GRAPHS                                       !  QUEQUEG'S GRAPHIC LOG
    RPT_DATE                                     !  PRINT STATS BY DATE
    RETURN
. . .
```

STAT2.CLA

```
          MEMBER('STAT')
SHO_DATE       PROCEDURE

SCREEN         SCREEN      PRE(SCR),WINDOW(24,45),HUE(15,1)
          ROW(7,3)    PAINT(15,41),HUE(0,7)
          ROW(1,1)    STRING('<201,205{10},0{20},205{13},187>'),HUE(15,1)
          ROW(2,1)    REPEAT(22);STRING('<186,0{43},186>'),HUE(15,1)  .
          ROW(24,1)   STRING('<200,205{43},188>'),HUE(15,1)
          ROW(1,13)   STRING('Show Stats By Date')
          ROW(3,12)   STRING('Locate'),HUE(11,1)
            COL(19)   STRING('by Date'),HUE(11,1)
            COL(26)   STRING(':'),HUE(11,1)
          ROW(5,13)   STRING('POD')
          ROW(6,5)    STRING('DATE    SIZE  LOCATION {12}MOBY?')
          ROW(22,3)   STRING('Ins to Add'),HUE(11,1)
            COL(25)   STRING('Enter to Change'),HUE(11,1)
```

(continued)

```
             ROW(23,3)   STRING('Del to Delete'),HUE(11,1)
             COL(25)     STRING('Esc to Exit'),HUE(11,1)
LOCATOR      ROW(3,27)   STRING(@D1),HUE(11,1)
                         ENTRY,USE(?FIRST_FIELD)
                         ENTRY,USE(?PRE_POINT)
                         REPEAT(15),EVERY(1),INDEX(NDX)
             ROW(7,3)      POINT(1,41),USE(?POINT),ESC(?-1)
DATE         COL(4)      STRING(@D1)
PODSIZE      COL(13)     STRING(@N3)
LOCATION     COL(19)     STRING(20)
MOBY         COL(40)     STRING(@S3)
               .            .

NDX          BYTE                           !REPEAT INDEX FOR POINT AREA
ROW          BYTE                           !ACTUAL ROW OF SCROLL AREA
COL          BYTE                           !ACTUAL COLUMN OF SCROLL AREA
COUNT        BYTE(15)                       !NUMBER OF ITEMS TO SCROLL
ROWS         BYTE(15)                       !NUMBER OF ROWS TO SCROLL
COLS         BYTE(41)                       !NUMBER OF COLUMNS TO SCROLL
FOUND        BYTE                           !RECORD FOUND FLAG
NEWPTR       LONG                           !POINTER TO NEW RECORD

TABLE        TABLE,PRE(TBL)                 !TABLE OF RECORD DATA
DATE         LONG
PODSIZE      SHORT
LOCATION     STRING(20)
MOBY         STRING(@S3)
PTR          LONG                           !  POINTER TO FILE RECORD
               .

  EJECT
  CODE
  ACTION# = ACTION                          !SAVE ACTION
  OPEN(SCREEN)                              !OPEN THE SCREEN
  SETCURSOR                                 !TURN OFF ANY CURSOR
  TBL:PTR = 1                               !START AT TABLE ENTRY
  NDX = 1                                   !PUT SELECTOR BAR ON TOP ITEM
  ROW = ROW(?POINT)                         !REMEMBER TOP ROW AND
  COL = COL(?POINT)                         !LEFT COLUMN OF SCROLL AREA
  RECORDS# = TRUE                           !INITIALIZE RECORDS FLAG
  CACHE(STA:BY_DATE,.25)                    !CACHE KEY FILE
  IF ACTION = 4                             !  TABLE LOOKUP REQUEST
    NEWPTR = POINTER(STATS)                 !  SET POINTER TO RECORD
    IF NOT NEWPTR                           !  RECORD NOT PASSED TO TABLE
      SET(STA:BY_DATE,STA:BY_DATE)          !    POSITION TO CLOSEST RECORD
      NEXT(STATS)                           !    READ RECORD
      NEWPTR = POINTER(STATS)               !    SET POINTER
.
```

(continued)

```
  DO FIND_RECORD                              !  POSITION FILE
ELSE
  NDX = 1                                     !  PUT SELECTOR BAR ON TOP ITEM
  DO FIRST_PAGE                               !  BUILD MEMORY TABLE OF KEYS
  .
RECORDS# = TRUE                               !  ASSUME THERE ARE RECORDS
LOOP                                          !LOOP UNTIL USER EXITS
  ACTION = ACTION#                            !RESTORE ACTION
  ALERT                                       !RESET ALERTED KEYS
  ALERT(REJECT_KEY)                           !ALERT SCREEN REJECT KEY
  ALERT(ACCEPT_KEY)                           !ALERT SCREEN ACCEPT KEY
  ACCEPT                                      !READ A FIELD
  IF KEYCODE() = REJECT_KEY THEN BREAK.       !RETURN ON SCREEN REJECT KEY

  IF  KEYCODE() = ACCEPT_KEY    |             !ON SCREEN ACCEPT KEY
  AND FIELD() <> ?POINT                       !BUT NOT ON THE POINT FIELD
    UPDATE                                    !  MOVE ALL FIELDS FROM SCREEN
    SELECT(?)                                 !  START WITH CURRENT FIELD
    SELECT                                    !  EDIT ALL FIELDS
    CYCLE                                     !  GO TO TOP OF LOOP
    .

  CASE FIELD()                                !JUMP TO FIELD EDIT ROUTINE

  OF ?FIRST_FIELD                             !FROM THE FIRST FIELD
    IF KEYCODE() = ESC_KEY     |              !  RETURN ON ESC KEY
    OR RECORDS# = FALSE                       !  OR NO RECORDS
      BREAK                                   !    EXIT PROGRAM

    .
  OF ?PRE_POINT                               !PRE POINT FIELD CONDITION
    IF KEYCODE() = ESC_KEY                    !  BACKING UP?
      SELECT(?-1)                             !    SELECT PREVIOUS FIELD
    ELSE                                      !  GOING FORWARD
      SELECT(?POINT)                          !    SELECT MENU FIELD

      .
    IF KEYCODE() = ESC_KEY                    !  BACKING UP?
      SCR:LOCATOR = ''                        !    CLEAR LOCATOR
      SETCURSOR                               !    AND TURN CURSOR OFF
    ELSE                                      !  GOING FORWARD
      LEN# = 0                                !    RESET TO START OF LOCATOR
      SETCURSOR(ROW(SCR:LOCATOR),COL(SCR:LOCATOR))  !AND TURN CURSOR ON

      .
  OF ?POINT                                   !PROCESS THE POINT FIELD
    IF RECORDS(TABLE) = 0                     !IF THERE ARE NO RECORDS
      CLEAR(STA:RECORD)                       !  CLEAR RECORD AREA
      ACTION = 1                              !  SET ACTION TO ADD
      GET(STATS,0)                            !  CLEAR PENDING RECORD
      UPD_STATS                               !  CALL FORM FOR NEW RECORD
```

(continued)

```
  NEWPTR = POINTER(STATS)                    !    SET POINTER TO NEW RECORD
  DO FIRST_PAGE                              !  DISPLAY THE FIRST PAGE
  IF RECORDS(TABLE) = 0                      !  IF THERE AREN'T ANY RECORDS
    RECORDS# = FALSE                         !    INDICATE NO RECORDS
    SELECT(?PRE_POINT-1)                     !    SELECT THE PRIOR FIELD
  .
  CYCLE                                      !    AND LOOP AGAIN
.
IF KEYCODE() > 31              |             !THE DISPLAYABLE CHARACTERS
AND KEYCODE() < 255                          !ARE USED TO LOCATE RECORDS
  IF LEN# < SIZE(SCR:LOCATOR)                !  IF THERE IS ROOM LEFT
    SCR:LOCATOR = SUB(SCR:LOCATOR,1,LEN#) & CHR(KEYCODE())
    LEN# += 1                               !    INCREMENT THE LENGTH
  .
ELSIF KEYCODE() = BS_KEY                     !BACKSPACE UNTYPES A CHARACTER
  IF LEN# > 0                               !  IF THERE ARE CHARACTERS LEFT
    LEN# -= 1                               !    DECREMENT THE LENGTH
    SCR:LOCATOR = SUB(SCR:LOCATOR,1,LEN#)   !    ERASE THE LAST CHARACTER
.
ELSE                                        !FOR ANY OTHER CHARACTER
  LEN# = 0                                  !  ZERO THE LENGTH
  SCR:LOCATOR = ''                          !  ERASE THE LOCATOR FIELD
.
SETCURSOR(ROW(SCR:LOCATOR),COL(SCR:LOCATOR)+LEN#) !AND RESET THE CURSOR
STA:DATE = DEFORMAT(SCR:LOCATOR)            !    UPDATE THE KEY FIELD
IF KEYBOARD() > 31             |            !THE DISPLAYABLE CHARACTERS
AND KEYBOARD() < 255           |            !ARE USED TO LOCATE RECORDS
OR KEYBOARD() = BS_KEY                      !INCLUDE BACKSPACE
  CYCLE
.
IF LEN# > 0                                 !ON A LOCATOR REQUEST
  STA:DATE = DEFORMAT(SCR:LOCATOR)          !    UPDATE THE KEY FIELD
  SET(STA:BY_DATE,STA:BY_DATE)             !    POINT TO NEW RECORD
  NEXT(STATS)                               !    READ A RECORD
  IF (EOF(STATS) AND ERROR())               !    IF EOF IS REACHED
    SET(STA:BY_DATE)                        !      SET TO FIRST RECORD
    PREVIOUS(STATS)                         !      READ THE LAST RECORD
  .
  NEWPTR = POINTER(STATS)                   !    SET NEW RECORD POINTER
  SKIP(STATS,-1)                            !    BACK UP TO FIRST RECORD
  FREE(TABLE)                               !    CLEAR THE TABLE
  DO NEXT_PAGE                              !    AND DISPLAY A NEW PAGE
.
CASE KEYCODE()                              !PROCESS THE KEYSTROKE

OF INS_KEY                                  !INS KEY
  CLEAR(STA:RECORD)                         !    CLEAR RECORD AREA
```

(continued)

```
      ACTION = 1                                  !   SET ACTION TO ADD
      GET(STATS,0)                                !   CLEAR PENDING RECORD
      UPD_STATS                                   !   CALL FORM FOR NEW RECORD
      IF ~ACTION                                  !   IF RECORD WAS ADDED
        NEWPTR = POINTER(STATS)                   !     SET POINTER TO NEW RECORD
        DO FIND_RECORD                            !     POSITION IN FILE
      .
  OF ENTER_KEY                                    !ENTER KEY
  OROF ACCEPT_KEY                                 !CTRL-ENTER KEY
    DO GET_RECORD                                 !  GET THE SELECTED RECORD
    IF ACTION = 4 AND KEYCODE() = ENTER_KEY!    IF THIS IS A LOOKUP REQUEST
      ACTION = 0                                  !    SET ACTION TO COMPLETE
      BREAK                                       !    AND RETURN TO CALLER
    .
    IF ~ERROR()                                   !  IF RECORD IS STILL THERE
      ACTION = 2                                  !    SET ACTION TO CHANGE
      UPD_STATS                                   !    CALL FORM TO CHANGE REC
      IF ACTION THEN CYCLE.                       !    IF SUCCESSFUL RE-DISPLAY

    NEWPTR = POINTER(STATS)                       !    SET POINTER TO NEW RECORD
    DO FIND_RECORD                                !    POSITION IN FILE
  OF DEL_KEY                                      !DEL KEY
    DO GET_RECORD                                 !  READ THE SELECTED RECORD
    IF ~ERROR()                                   !  IF RECORD IS STILL THERE
      ACTION = 3                                  !    SET ACTION TO DELETE
      UPD_STATS                                   !    CALL FORM TO DELETE
      IF ~ACTION                                  !    IF SUCCESSFUL
        N# = NDX                                  !      SAVE POINT INDEX
        DO SAME_PAGE                              !      RE-DISPLAY
        NDX = N#                                  !      RESTORE POINT INDEX
    . .
  OF DOWN_KEY                                     !DOWN ARROW KEY
    DO SET_NEXT                                   !  POINT TO NEXT RECORD
    DO FILL_NEXT                                  !  FILL A TABLE ENTRY
    IF FOUND                                      !  FOUND A NEW RECORD
      SCROLL(ROW,COL,ROWS,COLS,ROWS(?POINT)) !    SCROLL THE SCREEN UP
      GET(TABLE,RECORDS(TABLE))                   !  GET RECORD FROM TABLE
      DO FILL_SCREEN                              !  DISPLAY ON SCREEN
    .

  OF PGDN_KEY                                     !PAGE DOWN KEY
    DO SET_NEXT                                   !  POINT TO NEXT RECORD
    DO NEXT_PAGE                                  !  DISPLAY THE NEXT PAGE

  OF CTRL_PGDN                                    !CTRL-PAGE DOWN KEY
    DO LAST_PAGE                                  !  DISPLAY THE LAST PAGE
    NDX = RECORDS(TABLE)                          !  POSITION POINT BAR
```

(continued)

```
    OF UP_KEY                                   !UP ARROW KEY
      DO SET_PREV                               !  POINT TO PREVIOUS RECORD
      DO FILL_PREV                              !  FILL A TABLE ENTRY
      IF FOUND                                  !  FOUND A NEW RECORD
        SCROLL(ROW,COL,ROWS,COLS,-(ROWS(?POINT)))! SCROLL THE SCREEN DOWN
        GET(TABLE,1)                            !  GET RECORD FROM TABLE
        DO FILL_SCREEN                          !  DISPLAY ON SCREEN
      .


    OF PGUP_KEY                                 !PAGE UP KEY
      DO SET_PREV                               !  POINT TO PREVIOUS RECORD
      DO PREV_PAGE                              !  DISPLAY THE PREVIOUS PAGE


    OF CTRL_PGUP                                !CTRL-PAGE UP
      DO FIRST_PAGE                             !  DISPLAY THE FIRST PAGE
      NDX = 1                                   !  POSITION POINT BAR
  . . .
  FREE(TABLE)                                   !FREE MEMORY TABLE
  RETURN                                        !AND RETURN TO CALLER


SAME_PAGE ROUTINE                               !DISPLAY THE SAME PAGE
  GET(TABLE,1)                                  !  GET THE FIRST TABLE ENTRY
  DO FILL_RECORD                                !  FILL IN THE RECORD
  SET(STA:BY_DATE,STA:BY_DATE,TBL:PTR)          !  POSITION FILE
  FREE(TABLE)                                   !  EMPTY THE TABLE
  DO NEXT_PAGE                                  !  DISPLAY A FULL PAGE


FIRST_PAGE ROUTINE                              !DISPLAY FIRST PAGE
  BLANK(ROW,COL,ROWS,COLS)
  FREE(TABLE)                                   !  EMPTY THE TABLE
  CLEAR(STA:RECORD,-1)                          !  CLEAR RECORD TO LOW VALUES
  CLEAR(TBL:PTR)                                !  ZERO RECORD POINTER
  SET(STA:BY_DATE)                              !  POINT TO FIRST RECORD
  LOOP NDX = 1 TO COUNT                         !  FILL UP THE TABLE
    DO FILL_NEXT                                !    FILL A TABLE ENTRY
    IF NOT FOUND THEN BREAK.                    !    GET OUT IF NO RECORD
  .
  NDX = 1                                       !  SET TO TOP OF TABLE
  DO SHOW_PAGE                                  !  DISPLAY THE PAGE


LAST_PAGE ROUTINE                               !DISPLAY LAST PAGE
  NDX# = NDX                                    !  SAVE SELECTOR POSITION
  BLANK(ROW,COL,ROWS,COLS)                      !  CLEAR SCROLLING AREA
  FREE(TABLE)                                   !  EMPTY THE TABLE
  CLEAR(STA:RECORD,1)                           !  CLEAR RECORD TO HIGH VALUES
  CLEAR(TBL:PTR,1)                              !  CLEAR PTR TO HIGH VALUE
  SET(STA:BY_DATE)                              !  POINT TO FIRST RECORD
```

(continued)

```
LOOP NDX = COUNT TO 1 BY -1              !  FILL UP THE TABLE
  DO FILL_PREV                           !    FILL A TABLE ENTRY
  IF NOT FOUND THEN BREAK.               !    GET OUT IF NO RECORD
  .                                      !  END OF LOOP
  NDX = NDX#                             !  RESTORE SELECTOR POSITION
  DO SHOW_PAGE                           !  DISPLAY THE PAGE


FIND_RECORD ROUTINE                      !POSITION TO SPECIFIC RECORD
  SET(STA:BY_DATE,STA:BY_DATE,NEWPTR)    !POSITION FILE
  IF NEWPTR = 0                          !NEWPTR NOT SET
    NEXT(STATS)                          !  READ NEXT RECORD
    NEWPTR = POINTER(STATS)              !  SET NEWPTR
    SKIP(STATS,-1)                       !  BACK UP TO DISPLAY RECORD
  .
  FREE(TABLE)                            !  CLEAR THE RECORD
  DO NEXT_PAGE                           !  DISPLAY A PAGE


NEXT_PAGE ROUTINE                        !DISPLAY NEXT PAGE
  SAVECNT# = RECORDS(TABLE)              !  SAVE RECORD COUNT
  LOOP COUNT TIMES                       !  FILL UP THE TABLE
    DO FILL_NEXT                         !    FILL A TABLE ENTRY
    IF NOT FOUND                         !    IF NONE ARE LEFT
      IF NOT SAVECNT#                    !      IF REBUILDING TABLE
        DO LAST_PAGE                     !        FILL IN RECORDS
        EXIT                             !        EXIT OUT OF ROUTINE
      .
      BREAK                              !    EXIT LOOP
  . .
  DO SHOW_PAGE                           !  DISPLAY THE PAGE


SET_NEXT ROUTINE                         !POINT TO THE NEXT PAGE
  GET(TABLE,RECORDS(TABLE))              !  GET THE LAST TABLE ENTRY
  DO FILL_RECORD                         !  FILL IN THE RECORD
  SET(STA:BY_DATE,STA:BY_DATE,TBL:PTR)   !  POSITION FILE
  NEXT(STATS)                            !  READ THE CURRENT RECORD


FILL_NEXT ROUTINE                        !FILL NEXT TABLE ENTRY
  FOUND = FALSE                          !  ASSUME RECORD NOT FOUND
  LOOP UNTIL EOF(STATS)                  !  LOOP UNTIL END OF FILE
    NEXT(STATS)                          !    READ THE NEXT RECORD
    FOUND = TRUE                         !    SET RECORD FOUND
    DO FILL_TABLE                        !    FILL IN THE TABLE ENTRY
    ADD(TABLE)                           !    ADD LAST TABLE ENTRY
    GET(TABLE,RECORDS(TABLE)-COUNT)      !    GET ANY OVERFLOW RECORD
    DELETE(TABLE)                        !    AND DELETE IT
    EXIT                                 !    RETURN TO CALLER
  .
```

(continued)

```
PREV_PAGE ROUTINE                              !DISPLAY PREVIOUS PAGE
  LOOP COUNT TIMES                             !   FILL UP THE TABLE
    DO FILL_PREV                               !      FILL A TABLE ENTRY
    IF NOT FOUND THEN BREAK.                    !      GET OUT IF NO RECORD
    .
  DO SHOW_PAGE                                  !   DISPLAY THE PAGE

SET_PREV ROUTINE                               !POINT TO PREVIOUS PAGE
  GET(TABLE,1)                                 !   GET THE FIRST TABLE ENTRY
  DO FILL_RECORD                               !   FILL IN THE RECORD
  SET(STA:BY_DATE,STA:BY_DATE,TBL:PTR)         !   POSITION FILE
  PREVIOUS(STATS)                              !   READ THE CURRENT RECORD

FILL_PREV ROUTINE                              !FILL PREVIOUS TABLE ENTRY
  FOUND = FALSE                                !   ASSUME RECORD NOT FOUND
  LOOP UNTIL BOF(STATS)                        !   LOOP UNTIL BEGINNING OF FILE
    PREVIOUS(STATS)                            !      READ THE PREVIOUS RECORD
    FOUND = TRUE                               !      SET RECORD FOUND
    DO FILL_TABLE                              !      FILL IN THE TABLE ENTRY
    ADD(TABLE,1)                               !      ADD FIRST TABLE ENTRY
    GET(TABLE,COUNT+1)                         !      GET ANY OVERFLOW RECORD
    DELETE(TABLE)                              !      AND DELETE IT
    EXIT                                       !      RETURN TO CALLER
    .
SHOW_PAGE ROUTINE                              !DISPLAY THE PAGE
  NDX# = NDX                                   !   SAVE SCREEN INDEX
  LOOP NDX = 1 TO RECORDS(TABLE)               !   LOOP THRU THE TABLE
    GET(TABLE,NDX)                             !      GET A TABLE ENTRY
    DO FILL_SCREEN                             !      AND DISPLAY IT
    IF TBL:PTR = NEWPTR                        !      SET INDEX FOR NEW RECORD
      NDX# = NDX                               !      POINT TO CORRECT RECORD
    . .
  NDX = NDX#                                   !   RESTORE SCREEN INDEX
  NEWPTR = 0                                   !   CLEAR NEW RECORD POINTER
  CLEAR(STA:RECORD)                            !   CLEAR RECORD AREA

FILL_TABLE ROUTINE                             !MOVE FILE TO TABLE
  TBL:DATE = STA:DATE
  TBL:PODSIZE = STA:PODSIZE
  TBL:LOCATION = STA:LOCATION
  TBL:PTR = POINTER(STATS)                     !   SAVE RECORD POINTER
  IF STA:MOBY = 'Y'                            !EVALUATE CONDITION
    TBL:MOBY = 'YES'                           !   CONDITION IS TRUE
  ELSE                                         !OTHERWISE
    TBL:MOBY = 'NO'                            !   CONDITION IS FALSE
    .
```

(continued)

```
FILL_RECORD ROUTINE                              !MOVE TABLE TO FILE
   STA:DATE = TBL:DATE


FILL_SCREEN ROUTINE                              !MOVE TABLE TO SCREEN
   SCR:DATE = TBL:DATE
   SCR:PODSIZE = TBL:PODSIZE
   SCR:LOCATION = TBL:LOCATION
   SCR:MOBY = TBL:MOBY


GET_RECORD ROUTINE                               !GET SELECTED RECORD
   GET(TABLE,NDX)                                !  GET TABLE ENTRY
   GET(STATS,TBL:PTR)                            !  GET THE RECORD
```

STAT3.CLA

```
          MEMBER('STAT')
UPD_STATS     PROCEDURE

SCREEN        SCREEN       PRE(SCR),WINDOW(9,36),HUE(15,4)
              ROW(1,1)     STRING('<201,205{34},187>'),HUE(15,4)
              ROW(2,1)     REPEAT(7);STRING('<186,0{34},186>'),HUE(15,4)  .
              ROW(9,1)     STRING('<200,205{34},188>'),HUE(15,4)
              ROW(2,13)    STRING('Update Stats')
              ROW(4,4)     STRING('DATE     :'),HUE(7,4)
              ROW(5,4)     STRING('PODSIZE :'),HUE(7,4)
              ROW(6,4)     STRING('LOCATION:'),HUE(7,4)
              ROW(7,4)     STRING('MOBY     :'),HUE(7,4)
MESSAGE       ROW(3,4)     STRING(30),HUE(15,4)
                               ENTRY,USE(?FIRST_FIELD)
              ROW(4,13)    ENTRY(@D1),USE(STA:DATE),IMM,REQ,OVR,HUE(15,4),SEL(0,7)
              ROW(5,13)    ENTRY(@N3),USE(STA:PODSIZE),HUE(15,4),SEL(0,7)
              ROW(6,13)    ENTRY(@s20),USE(STA:LOCATION),HUE(15,4),SEL(0,7)
              ROW(7,13)    MENU(@s1),USE(STA:MOBY),HUE(15,4),SEL(0,7)
                COL(15)      STRING('YES'),SEL(0,7)
                COL(20)      STRING('NO'),SEL(0,7)

                           .

                               ENTRY,USE(?LAST_FIELD)
                               PAUSE(''),USE(?DELETE_FIELD)

          .

  EJECT
  CODE
  OPEN(SCREEN)                                   !OPEN THE SCREEN
  SETCURSOR                                      !TURN OFF ANY CURSOR
  DISPLAY                                        !DISPLAY THE FIELDS
```

(continued)

```
LOOP                                        !LOOP THRU ALL THE FIELDS
  MEM:MESSAGE = CENTER(MEM:MESSAGE,SIZE(MEM:MESSAGE)) !DISPLAY ACTION MESSAGE
  DO CALCFIELDS                             !CALCULATE DISPLAY FIELDS
  ALERT                                     !RESET ALERTED KEYS
  ALERT(ACCEPT_KEY)                         !ALERT SCREEN ACCEPT KEY
  ALERT(REJECT_KEY)                         !ALERT SCREEN REJECT KEY
  ACCEPT                                    !READ A FIELD
  IF KEYCODE() = REJECT_KEY THEN RETURN.    !RETURN ON SCREEN REJECT KEY
  EXECUTE ACTION                            !SET MESSAGE
    MEM:MESSAGE = 'Record will be Added'    !
    MEM:MESSAGE = 'Record will be Changed'  !
    MEM:MESSAGE = 'Press Enter to Delete'   !
  .

  IF KEYCODE() = ACCEPT_KEY                  !ON SCREEN ACCEPT KEY
    UPDATE                                   !  MOVE ALL FIELDS FROM SCREEN
    SELECT(?)                                !  START WITH CURRENT FIELD
    SELECT                                   !  EDIT ALL FIELDS
    CYCLE                                    !  GO TO TOP OF LOOP

  .

  CASE FIELD()                               !JUMP TO FIELD EDIT ROUTINE
  OF ?FIRST_FIELD                            !FROM THE FIRST FIELD
    IF KEYCODE() = ESC_KEY THEN RETURN.      !  RETURN ON ESC KEY
    IF ACTION = 3 THEN SELECT(?DELETE_FIELD).!  OR CONFIRM FOR DELETE

  OF ?STA:PODSIZE
    IF STA:PODSIZE > 200 THEN KIDDING;SELECT(?).

  OF ?LAST_FIELD                             !FROM THE LAST FIELD
    EXECUTE ACTION                           !  UPDATE THE FILE
      ADD(STATS)                             !    ADD NEW RECORD
      PUT(STATS)                             !    CHANGE EXISTING RECORD
      DELETE(STATS)                          !    DELETE EXISTING RECORD
    .
    IF ERRORCODE() = 40                      !  DUPLICATE KEY ERROR
      MEM:MESSAGE = ERROR()                  !    DISPLAY ERR MESSAGE
      SELECT(2)                              !    POSITION TO TOP OF FORM
      CYCLE                                  !    GET OUT OF EDIT LOOP
    ELSIF ERROR()                            !  CHECK FOR UNEXPECTED ERROR
      STOP(ERROR())                          !    HALT EXECUTION

    .
    ACTION = 0                               !  SET ACTION TO COMPLETE
    RETURN                                   !  AND RETURN TO CALLER

  OF ?DELETE_FIELD                           !FROM THE DELETE FIELD
    IF KEYCODE() = ENTER_KEY |               !  ON ENTER KEY
    OR KEYCODE() = ACCEPT_KEY                !  OR CTRL-ENTER KEY
      SELECT(?LAST_FIELD)                    !    DELETE THE RECORD
```

(continued)

```
      ELSE                                    !  OTHERWISE
        BEEP                                  !    BEEP AND ASK AGAIN
  . . .


CALCFIELDS   ROUTINE
  IF FIELD() > ?FIRST_FIELD                            !BEYOND FIRST_FIELD?
    IF KEYCODE() = 0 AND SELECTED() > FIELD() THEN EXIT. !GET OUT IF NOT NONSTOP
  .
  SCR:MESSAGE = MEM:MESSAGE
```

STAT4.CLA

```
          MEMBER('STAT')


RPT_DATE        PROCEDURE


TITLE      REPORT       LENGTH(59),WIDTH(80),PRE(TTL)
RPT_HEAD                DETAIL
           .            .
REPORT     REPORT       LENGTH(59),WIDTH(80),PAGE(MEM:PAGE),LINE(MEM:LINE)    |
                        PRE(RPT)
PAGE_HEAD               HEADER
           COL(32)    STRING('PRINT STATS BY DATE')
           ROW(+2,17)   STRING('Siting {5}No. {30}Saw')
           ROW(+1,18)   STRING('Date     Spotted   Location {14}Moby Dick?')   |
                        CTL(@LF2)
                        .
DETAIL                  DETAIL
           COL(16)    STRING(@D1),USE(STA:DATE)
           COL(29)      STRING(@N3),USE(STA:PODSIZE)
           COL(36)      STRING(20),USE(STA:LOCATION)
MOBY       COL(62)      STRING(3) CTL(@LF)
                        .
RPT_FOOT                DETAIL
                        .
PAGE_FOOT               FOOTER
           ROW(+1,37)   STRING('PAGE')
           COL(42)      STRING(@n3),USE(MEM:PAGE) CTL(@LF)
                        CTL(@FF)
           .            .


  CODE
  DONE# = 0                               !TURN OFF DONE FLAG
  CLEAR(STA:RECORD,-1)                    !MAKE SURE RECORD CLEARED
```

(continued)

```
    PRINT(TTL:RPT_HEAD)                  !PRINT TITLE PAGE
    CLOSE(TITLE)                         !CLOSE TITLE REPORT
    SET(STA:BY_DATE)                     !  POINT TO FIRST RECORD
    DO NEXT_RECORD                       !READ FIRST RECORD
    OPEN(REPORT)                         !OPEN THE REPORT
    LOOP UNTIL DONE#                     !READ ALL RECORDS IN FILE
      SAVE_LINE# = MEM:LINE              !  SAVE LINE NUMBER
      LAST_REC# = POINTER(STATS)
      PRINT(RPT:DETAIL)                  !   PRINT DETAIL LINES
      DO CHECK_PAGE                      !   DO PAGE BREAK IF NEEDED
      DO NEXT_RECORD                     !   GET NEXT RECORD
    .                                    !
    PRINT(RPT:RPT_FOOT)                  !PRINT GRAND TOTALS
    DO CHECK_PAGE                        !   DO PAGE BREAK IF NEEDED
    CLOSE(REPORT)                        !CLOSE REPORT
    RETURN                               !RETURN TO CALLER


NEXT_RECORD ROUTINE                      !GET NEXT RECORD
    LOOP UNTIL EOF(STATS)                !   READ UNTIL END OF FILE
      NEXT(STATS)                        !      READ NEXT RECORD
      IF STA:MOBY = 'Y'                  !EVALUATE CONDITION
        RPT:MOBY = 'Yes'                 !   CONDITION IS TRUE
      ELSE                               !OTHERWISE
        RPT:MOBY = 'No'                  !   CONDITION IS FALSE
      .
      EXIT                               !     EXIT THE ROUTINE
    .                                    !
    DONE# = 1                            !   ON EOF, SET DONE FLAG

CHECK_PAGE ROUTINE                       !CHECK FOR NEW PAGE
    IF MEM:LINE <= SAVE_LINE#            !   ON PAGE OVERFLOW
      SAVE_LINE# = MEM:LINE              !      RESET LINE NUMBER
    .
    LOOP UNTIL NOT KEYBOARD()            !LOOK FOR KEYSTROKE
      ASK                                !GET KEYCODE
      IF KEYCODE() = REJECT_KEY          !ON CTRL-ESC
        CLOSE(REPORT)                    !   CLOSE REPORT
        RETURN                           !   ABORT PRINT
    . .
```

STAT5.CLA

```
          MEMBER('STAT')
GRAPHS        PROCEDURE
```

(continued)

```
SCREEN       SCREEN          PRE(SCR),WINDOW(12,29),AT(5,26),HUE(15,0)
             ROW(2,2)    PAINT(3,27),HUE(15,4)
             ROW(1,1)    STRING('<201,205{27},187>'),HUE(15,0)
             ROW(2,1)    REPEAT(10);STRING('<186,0{27},186>'),HUE(15,0) .
             ROW(12,1)   STRING('<200,205{27},188>'),HUE(15,0)
             ROW(3,5)    STRING('QUEQUEG')
               COL(12)   STRING(''''),HUE(15,4)
               COL(13)   STRING('S GRA')
               COL(18)   STRING('P'),HUE(15,4)
               COL(19)   STRING('HIC LOG')
                         ENTRY,USE(?FIRST_FIELD)
                         ENTRY,USE(?PRE_MENU)
                         MENU,USE(MENU_FIELD"),REQ
             ROW(7,8)    STRING('SELECT PARAMTERS'),HUE(15,0),SEL(0,7)
             ROW(9,7)    STRING('GRAPH DEMONSTRATION'),HUE(15,0),SEL(0,7)
             ROW(11,14)  STRING('QUIT'),HUE(15,0),SEL(0,7)
                 .              .

EJECT
CODE
OPEN(SCREEN)                            !OPEN THE MENU SCREEN
SETCURSOR                               !TURN OFF ANY CURSOR
MENU_FIELD" = ''                        !START MENU WITH FIRST ITEM
LOOP                                    !LOOP UNTIL USER EXITS
  ALERT                                 !TURN OFF ALL ALERTED KEYS
  ALERT(REJECT_KEY)                     !ALERT SCREEN REJECT KEY
  ALERT(ACCEPT_KEY)                     !ALERT SCREEN ACCEPT KEY
  ACCEPT                                !READ A FIELD OR MENU CHOICE
  IF KEYCODE() = REJECT_KEY THEN RETURN.  !RETURN ON SCREEN REJECT

  IF KEYCODE() = ACCEPT_KEY             !ON SCREEN ACCEPT KEY
    UPDATE                              !  MOVE ALL FIELDS FROM SCREEN
    SELECT(?)                           !  START WITH CURRENT FIELD
    SELECT                              !  EDIT ALL FIELDS
    CYCLE                               !  GO TO TOP OF LOOP
  .                                     !

  CASE FIELD()                          !JUMP TO FIELD EDIT ROUTINE
  OF ?FIRST_FIELD                       !FROM THE FIRST FIELD
    IF KEYCODE() = ESC_KEY THEN RETURN. !  RETURN ON ESC KEY

  OF ?PRE_MENU                          !PRE MENU FIELD CONDITION
    IF KEYCODE() = ESC_KEY             !  BACKING UP?
      SELECT(?-1)                       !    SELECT PREVIOUS FIELD
    ELSE                                !  GOING FORWARD
      SELECT(?+1)                       !    SELECT MENU FIELD
    .
```

(continued)

```
     OF ?MENU_FIELD"                        !FROM THE MENU FIELD
       EXECUTE CHOICE()                     !  CALL THE SELECTED PROCEDURE
         PARMS                              !  SET PARAMETERS FOR GRAPH
         ONE                                !  THE GRAPHING PROCEDURE
         RETURN
    . . .
```

STAT6.CLA

```
            MEMBER('STAT')
PARMS       PROCEDURE

SCREEN      SCREEN      PRE(SCR),WINDOW(16,58),AT(8,12),HUE(15,0)
            ROW(1,17)   PAINT(1,26),HUE(14,1)
                    COL(1)  STRING('<201,205{15},0{26},205{15},187>'),HUE(14,0)
            ROW(2,1)    REPEAT(14);STRING('<186,0{56},186>'),HUE(14,0) .
            ROW(16,1)   STRING('<200,205{56},188>'),HUE(14,0)
            ROW(1,18)   STRING('SET PARAMETERS FOR GRAPH')
            ROW(4,4)    STRING('Graph Title:'),HUE(14,0)
            ROW(5,30)   STRING('Code'),HUE(14,0)
                    COL(36) STRING('Color'),HUE(14,0)
            ROW(6,7)    STRING('Color for Bar Graph #1:'),HUE(14,0)
            ROW(8,7)    STRING('Color for Bar Graph #2:'),HUE(14,0)
            ROW(10,7)   STRING('Primary Pie Chart Color:'),HUE(14,0)
            ROW(12,7)   STRING('Color for Chart Title:'),HUE(14,0)
MESSAGE     ROW(2,15)   STRING(30),HUE(7,0)
COLOR       ROW(6,36)   STRING(14)
COLOR2      ROW(8,36)   STRING(14)
COLOR3      ROW(10,36)  STRING(14)
COLOR4      ROW(12,36)  STRING(14)
                        ENTRY,USE(?FIRST_FIELD)
            ROW(4,17)   ENTRY(@s40),USE(PRM:TITLE),LFT
            ROW(6,31)   ENTRY(@N2),USE(PRM:BARS),LFT
            ROW(8,31)   ENTRY(@N2),USE(PRM:BARS2),LFT
            ROW(10,31)  ENTRY(@N2),USE(PRM:PIE),LFT
            ROW(12,31)  ENTRY(@N2),USE(PRM:TITLE_COLOR),LFT
            ROW(14,19)  PAUSE('Press <<ENTER> to Accept'),USE(?PAUSE_FIELD)   |
                            HUE(23,0)
                        ENTRY,USE(?LAST_FIELD)
                        PAUSE(''),USE(?DELETE_FIELD)


        EJECT
        CODE
        OPEN(SCREEN)                                    !OPEN THE SCREEN
```

(continued)

```
SETCURSOR                                        !TURN OFF ANY CURSOR
IF RECORDS(PARMS) = 0 THEN ADD(PARMS);
ELSE GET(PARMS,1).;ACTION = 2                    !CALL SETUP PROCEDURE
DISPLAY                                          !DISPLAY THE FIELDS
LOOP                                             !LOOP THRU ALL THE FIELDS
  MEM:MESSAGE = CENTER(MEM:MESSAGE,SIZE(MEM:MESSAGE)) !DISPLAY ACTION MESSAGE
  DO CALCFIELDS                                  !CALCULATE DISPLAY FIELDS
  ALERT                                          !RESET ALERTED KEYS
  ALERT(ACCEPT_KEY)                              !ALERT SCREEN ACCEPT KEY
  ALERT(REJECT_KEY)                              !ALERT SCREEN REJECT KEY
  ACCEPT                                         !READ A FIELD
  IF KEYCODE() = REJECT_KEY THEN RETURN.         !RETURN ON SCREEN REJECT KEY
  EXECUTE ACTION                                 !SET MESSAGE
    MEM:MESSAGE = 'Record will be Added'         !
    MEM:MESSAGE = 'Record will be Changed'       !
    MEM:MESSAGE = 'Press Enter to Delete'        !
  .
  IF KEYCODE() = ACCEPT_KEY                      !ON SCREEN ACCEPT KEY
    UPDATE                                       !  MOVE ALL FIELDS FROM SCREEN
    SELECT(?)                                    !  START WITH CURRENT FIELD
    SELECT                                       !  EDIT ALL FIELDS
    CYCLE                                        !  GO TO TOP OF LOOP
  .
  CASE FIELD()                                   !JUMP TO FIELD EDIT ROUTINE
  OF ?FIRST_FIELD                                !FROM THE FIRST FIELD
    IF KEYCODE() = ESC_KEY THEN RETURN.          !  RETURN ON ESC KEY
    IF ACTION = 3 THEN SELECT(?DELETE_FIELD).    !  OR CONFIRM FOR DELETE

  OF ?PRM:BARS                                   !COLOR FOR LEFT HAND BAR GRAPH
      IF PRM:BARS = ''                           !IF NOT REQUIRED THEN
        CYCLE                                    !  END THE EDIT
      .
      COL:COLOR_CODE = PRM:BARS                  !MOVE RELATED FIELDS
      GET(COLORS,COL:BY_CODE)                    !READ THE RECORD
      IF ERROR()                                 !IF NO RECORD IS FOUND
        ACTION# = ACTION                         !  SAVE ACTION
        ACTION = 4                               !  REQUEST TABLE LOOKUP
        COLORS                                   !  CALL LOOKUP PROCEDURE
        IF ACTION                                !  NO SELECTION WAS MADE
          SELECT(?PRM:BARS)                      !    STAY ON FIELD
          ACTION = ACTION#                       !    RESTORE ACTION
          CYCLE                                  !    GO TO TOP OF LOOP
        .
        PRM:BARS = COL:COLOR_CODE                !  MOVE LOOKUP FIELD
        DISPLAY(?PRM:BARS)                       !  AND DISPLAY IT
        ACTION = ACTION#                         !  RESTORE ACTION
      .
```

(continued)

```
OF ?PRM:BARS2                          !COLOR FOR RIGHT HAND BAR GRAPH
    IF PRM:BARS2 = ''                  !IF NOT REQUIRED THEN
      CYCLE                            !  END THE EDIT
    .
    COL:COLOR_CODE = PRM:BARS2         !MOVE RELATED FIELDS
    GET(COLORS,COL:BY_CODE)            !READ THE RECORD
    IF ERROR()                         !IF NO RECORD IS FOUND
      ACTION# = ACTION                 !  SAVE ACTION
      ACTION = 4                       !  REQUEST TABLE LOOKUP
      COLORS                           !  CALL LOOKUP PROCEDURE
      IF ACTION                        !  NO SELECTION WAS MADE
        SELECT(?PRM:BARS2)             !    STAY ON FIELD
        ACTION = ACTION#               !    RESTORE ACTION
        CYCLE                          !    GO TO TOP OF LOOP
      .
      PRM:BARS2 = COL:COLOR_CODE       !  MOVE LOOKUP FIELD
      DISPLAY(?PRM:BARS2)              !  AND DISPLAY IT
      ACTION = ACTION#                 !  RESTORE ACTION
    .

OF ?PRM:PIE                            !PRIMARY COLOR FOR PIE GRAPH
    IF PRM:PIE = ''                    !IF NOT REQUIRED THEN
      CYCLE                            !  END THE EDIT
    .
    COL:COLOR_CODE = PRM:PIE           !MOVE RELATED FIELDS
    GET(COLORS,COL:BY_CODE)            !READ THE RECORD
    IF ERROR()                         !IF NO RECORD IS FOUND
      ACTION# = ACTION                 !  SAVE ACTION
      ACTION = 4                       !  REQUEST TABLE LOOKUP
      COLORS                           !  CALL LOOKUP PROCEDURE
      IF ACTION                        !  NO SELECTION WAS MADE
        SELECT(?PRM:PIE)               !    STAY ON FIELD
        ACTION = ACTION#               !    RESTORE ACTION
        CYCLE                          !    GO TO TOP OF LOOP
      .
      PRM:PIE = COL:COLOR_CODE         !  MOVE LOOKUP FIELD
      DISPLAY(?PRM:PIE)                !  AND DISPLAY IT
      ACTION = ACTION#                 !  RESTORE ACTION
    .

OF ?PRM:TITLE_COLOR                    !COLOR FOR TITLE
    IF PRM:TITLE_COLOR = ''            !IF NOT REQUIRED THEN
      CYCLE                            !  END THE EDIT
    .
    COL:COLOR_CODE = PRM:TITLE_COLOR   !MOVE RELATED FIELDS
    GET(COLORS,COL:BY_CODE)            !READ THE RECORD
    IF ERROR()                         !IF NO RECORD IS FOUND
```

(continued)

```
        ACTION# = ACTION                 !   SAVE ACTION
        ACTION = 4                       !   REQUEST TABLE LOOKUP
        COLORS                           !   CALL LOOKUP PROCEDURE
        IF ACTION                        !   NO SELECTION WAS MADE
          SELECT(?PRM:TITLE_COLOR)       !     STAY ON FIELD
          ACTION = ACTION#               !     RESTORE ACTION
          CYCLE                          !     GO TO TOP OF LOOP
            .
        PRM:TITLE_COLOR = COL:COLOR_CODE !   MOVE LOOKUP FIELD
        DISPLAY(?PRM:TITLE_COLOR)        !   AND DISPLAY IT
        ACTION = ACTION#                 !   RESTORE ACTION
          .

      OF ?PAUSE_FIELD                    !ON PAUSE FIELD
        IF KEYCODE() <> ENTER_KEY|       !IF NOT ENTER KEY
        AND KEYCODE() <> ACCEPT_KEY|     !AND NOT CTRL-ENTER KEY
        AND KEYCODE() <> 0               !AND NOT NONSTOP MODE
          BEEP                           !   SOUND KEYBOARD ALARM
          SELECT(?PAUSE_FIELD)           !   AND STAY ON PAUSE FIELD
            .
 OF ?LAST_FIELD                          !FROM THE LAST FIELD
   EXECUTE ACTION                        !   UPDATE THE FILE
     ADD(PARMS)                          !     ADD NEW RECORD
     PUT(PARMS)                          !     CHANGE EXISTING RECORD
     DELETE(PARMS)                       !     DELETE EXISTING RECORD
       .
   IF ERRORCODE() = 40                   !   DUPLICATE KEY ERROR
     MEM:MESSAGE = ERROR()               !     DISPLAY ERR MESSAGE
     SELECT(2)                           !     POSITION TO TOP OF FORM
     CYCLE                               !     GET OUT OF EDIT LOOP
   ELSIF ERROR()                         !   CHECK FOR UNEXPECTED ERROR
     STOP(ERROR())                       !     HALT EXECUTION
       .
   ACTION = 0                            !   SET ACTION TO COMPLETE
   RETURN                                !   AND RETURN TO CALLER

 OF ?DELETE_FIELD                        !FROM THE DELETE FIELD
   IF KEYCODE() = ENTER_KEY |            !  ON ENTER KEY
   OR KEYCODE() = ACCEPT_KEY             !  OR CTRL-ENTER KEY
     SELECT(?LAST_FIELD)                 !    DELETE THE RECORD
   ELSE                                  !  OTHERWISE
     BEEP                                !    BEEP AND ASK AGAIN
 . . .

CALCFIELDS   ROUTINE
 IF FIELD() > ?FIRST_FIELD               !BEYOND FIRST_FIELD?
```

(continued)

```
       IF KEYCODE() = 0 AND SELECTED() > FIELD() THEN EXIT. !GET OUT IF NOT NONSTOP
       .
       UPDATE                                          !UPDATE RECORD KEYS
       COL:COLOR_CODE = PRM:BARS                       !MOVE RELATED KEY FIELDS
       GET(COLORS,COL:BY_CODE)                          !READ THE RECORD
       IF ERROR() THEN CLEAR(COL:RECORD).              !IF NOT FOUND, CLEAR RECORD
       SCR:COLOR = COL:COLOR                            !DISPLAY LOOKUP FIELD
       UPDATE                                          !UPDATE RECORD KEYS
       COL:COLOR_CODE = PRM:BARS2                       !MOVE RELATED KEY FIELDS
       GET(COLORS,COL:BY_CODE)                          !READ THE RECORD
       IF ERROR() THEN CLEAR(COL:RECORD).              !IF NOT FOUND, CLEAR RECORD
       SCR:COLOR2 = COL:COLOR                           !DISPLAY LOOKUP FIELD
       UPDATE                                          !UPDATE RECORD KEYS
       COL:COLOR_CODE = PRM:PIE                         !MOVE RELATED KEY FIELDS
       GET(COLORS,COL:BY_CODE)                          !READ THE RECORD
       IF ERROR() THEN CLEAR(COL:RECORD).              !IF NOT FOUND, CLEAR RECORD
       SCR:COLOR3 = COL:COLOR                           !DISPLAY LOOKUP FIELD
       UPDATE                                          !UPDATE RECORD KEYS
       COL:COLOR_CODE = PRM:TITLE_COLOR                 !MOVE RELATED KEY FIELDS
       GET(COLORS,COL:BY_CODE)                          !READ THE RECORD
       IF ERROR() THEN CLEAR(COL:RECORD).              !IF NOT FOUND, CLEAR RECORD
       SCR:COLOR4 = COL:COLOR                           !DISPLAY LOOKUP FIELD
       SCR:MESSAGE = MEM:MESSAGE
```

STAT7.CLA

```
              MEMBER('STAT')
COLORS        PROCEDURE

SCREEN        SCREEN    PRE(SCR),WINDOW(16,21),HUE(0,7)
              ROW(1,1)    STRING('<218,196,0{17},196,191>'),HUE(0,7)
              ROW(2,1)    REPEAT(14);STRING('<179,0{19},179>'),HUE(0,7)  .
              ROW(16,1)   STRING('<192,196{19},217>'),HUE(0,7)
              ROW(1,4)    STRING('COLOR SELECTION')
                            ENTRY,USE(?FIRST_FIELD)
                            ENTRY,USE(?PRE_POINT)
                            REPEAT(13),EVERY(1),INDEX(NDX)
              ROW(3,2)        POINT(1,19),USE(?POINT),ESC(?-1)
COLOR_CODE    COL(3)    STRING(@n2)
COLOR         COL(6)    STRING(14)
                 .            .

NDX           BYTE                                    !REPEAT INDEX FOR POINT AREA
ROW           BYTE                                    !ACTUAL ROW OF SCROLL AREA
COL           BYTE                                    !ACTUAL COLUMN OF SCROLL AREA
```

(continued)

```
COUNT        BYTE(13)                  !NUMBER OF ITEMS TO SCROLL
ROWS         BYTE(13)                  !NUMBER OF ROWS TO SCROLL
COLS         BYTE(19)                  !NUMBER OF COLUMNS TO SCROLL
FOUND        BYTE                      !RECORD FOUND FLAG
NEWPTR       LONG                      !POINTER TO NEW RECORD

TABLE        TABLE,PRE(TBL)            !TABLE OF RECORD DATA
COLOR_CODE STRING(@n2)                 !Code for Color Selection
COLOR        STRING(14)                !Available color
PTR          LONG                      !  POINTER TO FILE RECORD
             .

  EJECT
  CODE
  ACTION# = ACTION                     !SAVE ACTION
  OPEN(SCREEN)                         !OPEN THE SCREEN
  SETCURSOR                            !TURN OFF ANY CURSOR
  TBL:PTR = 1                          !START AT TABLE ENTRY
  NDX = 1                              !PUT SELECTOR BAR ON TOP ITEM
  ROW = ROW(?POINT)                    !REMEMBER TOP ROW AND
  COL = COL(?POINT)                    !LEFT COLUMN OF SCROLL AREA
  RECORDS# = TRUE                      !INITIALIZE RECORDS FLAG
  CACHE(COL:BY_CODE,.25)               !CACHE KEY FILE
  IF ACTION = 4                        !  TABLE LOOKUP REQUEST
    NEWPTR = POINTER(COLORS)           !  SET POINTER TO RECORD
    IF NOT NEWPTR                      !  RECORD NOT PASSED TO TABLE
      SET(COL:BY_CODE,COL:BY_CODE)     !    POSITION TO CLOSEST RECORD
      NEXT(COLORS)                     !    READ RECORD
      NEWPTR = POINTER(COLORS)         !    SET POINTER
    .
    DO FIND_RECORD                     !  POSITION FILE
  ELSE
    NDX = 1                            !  PUT SELECTOR BAR ON TOP ITEM
    DO FIRST_PAGE                      !  BUILD MEMORY TABLE OF KEYS
  .
  RECORDS# = TRUE                      !  ASSUME THERE ARE RECORDS
  LOOP                                 !LOOP UNTIL USER EXITS
    ACTION = ACTION#                   !RESTORE ACTION
    ALERT                              !RESET ALERTED KEYS
    ALERT(REJECT_KEY)                  !ALERT SCREEN REJECT KEY
    ALERT(ACCEPT_KEY)                  !ALERT SCREEN ACCEPT KEY
    ACCEPT                             !READ A FIELD
    IF KEYCODE() = REJECT_KEY THEN BREAK.  !RETURN ON SCREEN REJECT KEY

    IF  KEYCODE() = ACCEPT_KEY     |   !ON SCREEN ACCEPT KEY
    AND FIELD() <> ?POINT              !BUT NOT ON THE POINT FIELD
      UPDATE                           !  MOVE ALL FIELDS FROM SCREEN
```

(continued)

```
    SELECT(?)                                 !  START WITH CURRENT FIELD
    SELECT                                    !  EDIT ALL FIELDS
    CYCLE                                     !  GO TO TOP OF LOOP
  .


  CASE FIELD()                               !JUMP TO FIELD EDIT ROUTINE

  OF ?FIRST_FIELD                            !FROM THE FIRST FIELD
    IF KEYCODE() = ESC_KEY    |              !  RETURN ON ESC KEY
    OR RECORDS# = FALSE                      !  OR NO RECORDS
      BREAK                                  !    EXIT PROGRAM
    .

  OF ?PRE_POINT                              !PRE POINT FIELD CONDITION
    IF KEYCODE() = ESC_KEY                   !  BACKING UP?
      SELECT(?-1)                            !    SELECT PREVIOUS FIELD
    ELSE                                     !  GOING FORWARD
      SELECT(?POINT)                         !    SELECT MENU FIELD
    .

  OF ?POINT                                  !PROCESS THE POINT FIELD
    IF RECORDS(TABLE) = 0                    !IF THERE ARE NO RECORDS
      CLEAR(COL:RECORD)                      !  CLEAR RECORD AREA
      ACTION = 1                             !  SET ACTION TO ADD
      GET(COLORS,0)                          !  CLEAR PENDING RECORD
      NEW_COLORS                             !  CALL FORM FOR NEW RECORD
      NEWPTR = POINTER(COLORS)               !    SET POINTER TO NEW RECORD
      DO FIRST_PAGE                          !  DISPLAY THE FIRST PAGE
      IF RECORDS(TABLE) = 0                  !  IF THERE AREN'T ANY RECORDS
        RECORDS# = FALSE                     !    INDICATE NO RECORDS
        SELECT(?PRE_POINT-1)                 !    SELECT THE PRIOR FIELD
      .
      CYCLE                                  !    AND LOOP AGAIN
    .
    CASE KEYCODE()                           !PROCESS THE KEYSTROKE

    OF INS_KEY                               !INS KEY
      CLEAR(COL:RECORD)                      !  CLEAR RECORD AREA
      ACTION = 1                             !  SET ACTION TO ADD
      GET(COLORS,0)                          !  CLEAR PENDING RECORD
      NEW_COLORS                             !  CALL FORM FOR NEW RECORD
      IF ~ACTION                             !  IF RECORD WAS ADDED
        NEWPTR = POINTER(COLORS)             !    SET POINTER TO NEW RECORD
        DO FIND_RECORD                       !    POSITION IN FILE
      .
    OF ENTER_KEY    |                        !ENTER KEY
    OROF ACCEPT_KEY                          !CTRL-ENTER KEY
      DO GET_RECORD                          !  GET THE SELECTED RECORD
      IF ACTION = 4 AND KEYCODE() = ENTER_KEY  !  IF THIS IS A LOOKUP REQUEST
```

(continued)

```
      ACTION = 0                              !    SET ACTION TO COMPLETE
      BREAK                                   !    AND RETURN TO CALLER

     .
    IF ~ERROR()                               !  IF RECORD IS STILL THERE
      ACTION = 2                              !    SET ACTION TO CHANGE
      NEW_COLORS                              !    CALL FORM TO CHANGE REC
      IF ACTION THEN CYCLE.                   !    IF SUCCESSFUL RE-DISPLAY

     .
    NEWPTR = POINTER(COLORS)                  !    SET POINTER TO NEW RECORD
    DO FIND_RECORD                            !    POSITION IN FILE
OF DEL_KEY                                    !DEL KEY
    DO GET_RECORD                             !  READ THE SELECTED RECORD
    IF ~ERROR()                               !  IF RECORD IS STILL THERE
      ACTION = 3                              !    SET ACTION TO DELETE
      NEW_COLORS                              !    CALL FORM TO DELETE
      IF ~ACTION                              !    IF SUCCESSFUL
        N# = NDX                              !      SAVE POINT INDEX
        DO SAME_PAGE                          !      RE-DISPLAY
        NDX = N#                              !      RESTORE POINT INDEX
     . .
OF DOWN_KEY                                   !DOWN ARROW KEY
    DO SET_NEXT                               !  POINT TO NEXT RECORD
    DO FILL_NEXT                              !  FILL A TABLE ENTRY
    IF FOUND                                  !  FOUND A NEW RECORD
      SCROLL(ROW,COL,ROWS,COLS,ROWS(?POINT))  !    SCROLL THE SCREEN UP
      GET(TABLE,RECORDS(TABLE))               !  GET RECORD FROM TABLE
      DO FILL_SCREEN                          !  DISPLAY ON SCREEN

     .

OF PGDN_KEY                                   !PAGE DOWN KEY
    DO SET_NEXT                               !  POINT TO NEXT RECORD
    DO NEXT_PAGE                              !  DISPLAY THE NEXT PAGE

OF CTRL_PGDN                                  !CTRL-PAGE DOWN KEY
    DO LAST_PAGE                              !  DISPLAY THE LAST PAGE
    NDX = RECORDS(TABLE)                      !  POSITION POINT BAR

OF UP_KEY                                     !UP ARROW KEY
    DO SET_PREV                               !  POINT TO PREVIOUS RECORD
    DO FILL_PREV                              !  FILL A TABLE ENTRY
    IF FOUND                                  !  FOUND A NEW RECORD
      SCROLL(ROW,COL,ROWS,COLS,-(ROWS(?POINT)))! SCROLL THE SCREEN DOWN
      GET(TABLE,1)                            !  GET RECORD FROM TABLE
      DO FILL_SCREEN                          !  DISPLAY ON SCREEN

     .

OF PGUP_KEY                                   !PAGE UP KEY
```

(continued)

```
         DO SET_PREV              !   POINT TO PREVIOUS RECORD
         DO PREV_PAGE             !   DISPLAY THE PREVIOUS PAGE

       OF CTRL_PGUP               !CTRL-PAGE UP
         DO FIRST_PAGE            !   DISPLAY THE FIRST PAGE
         NDX = 1                  !   POSITION POINT BAR
   . . .
   FREE(TABLE)                    !FREE MEMORY TABLE
   RETURN                         !AND RETURN TO CALLER

SAME_PAGE ROUTINE                 !DISPLAY THE SAME PAGE
  GET(TABLE,1)                    !   GET THE FIRST TABLE ENTRY
  DO FILL_RECORD                  !   FILL IN THE RECORD
  SET(COL:BY_CODE,COL:BY_CODE,TBL:PTR)  !   POSITION FILE
  FREE(TABLE)                     !   EMPTY THE TABLE
  DO NEXT_PAGE                    !   DISPLAY A FULL PAGE

FIRST_PAGE ROUTINE                !DISPLAY FIRST PAGE
  BLANK(ROW,COL,ROWS,COLS)
  FREE(TABLE)                     !   EMPTY THE TABLE
  CLEAR(COL:RECORD,-1)            !   CLEAR RECORD TO LOW VALUES
  CLEAR(TBL:PTR)                  !   ZERO RECORD POINTER
  SET(COL:BY_CODE)                !   POINT TO FIRST RECORD
  LOOP NDX = 1 TO COUNT           !   FILL UP THE TABLE
    DO FILL_NEXT                  !     FILL A TABLE ENTRY
    IF NOT FOUND THEN BREAK.      !     GET OUT IF NO RECORD
    .
  NDX = 1                         !   SET TO TOP OF TABLE
  DO SHOW_PAGE                    !   DISPLAY THE PAGE

LAST_PAGE ROUTINE                 !DISPLAY LAST PAGE
  NDX# = NDX                      !   SAVE SELECTOR POSITION
  BLANK(ROW,COL,ROWS,COLS)        !   CLEAR SCROLLING AREA
  FREE(TABLE)                     !   EMPTY THE TABLE
  CLEAR(COL:RECORD,1)             !   CLEAR RECORD TO HIGH VALUES
  CLEAR(TBL:PTR,1)                !   CLEAR PTR TO HIGH VALUE
  SET(COL:BY_CODE)                !   POINT TO FIRST RECORD
  LOOP NDX = COUNT TO 1 BY -1     !   FILL UP THE TABLE
    DO FILL_PREV                  !     FILL A TABLE ENTRY
    IF NOT FOUND THEN BREAK.      !     GET OUT IF NO RECORD
    .                             !   END OF LOOP
  NDX = NDX#                      !   RESTORE SELECTOR POSITION
  DO SHOW_PAGE                    !   DISPLAY THE PAGE

FIND_RECORD ROUTINE               !POSITION TO SPECIFIC RECORD
```

(continued)

```
    SET(COL:BY_CODE,COL:BY_CODE,NEWPTR)       !POSITION FILE
    IF NEWPTR = 0                             !NEWPTR NOT SET
      NEXT(COLORS)                            !  READ NEXT RECORD
      NEWPTR = POINTER(COLORS)                !  SET NEWPTR
      SKIP(COLORS,-1)                         !  BACK UP TO DISPLAY RECORD
    .
    FREE(TABLE)                               !  CLEAR THE RECORD
    DO NEXT_PAGE                              !  DISPLAY A PAGE

NEXT_PAGE ROUTINE                             !DISPLAY NEXT PAGE
  SAVECNT# = RECORDS(TABLE)                   !  SAVE RECORD COUNT
  LOOP COUNT TIMES                            !  FILL UP THE TABLE
    DO FILL_NEXT                              !    FILL A TABLE ENTRY
    IF NOT FOUND                              !    IF NONE ARE LEFT
      IF NOT SAVECNT#                         !      IF REBUILDING TABLE
        DO LAST_PAGE                          !        FILL IN RECORDS
        EXIT                                  !        EXIT OUT OF ROUTINE
      .
      BREAK                                   !    EXIT LOOP
  . .
  DO SHOW_PAGE                                !  DISPLAY THE PAGE

SET_NEXT ROUTINE                              !POINT TO THE NEXT PAGE
  GET(TABLE,RECORDS(TABLE))                   !  GET THE LAST TABLE ENTRY
  DO FILL_RECORD                              !  FILL IN THE RECORD
  SET(COL:BY_CODE,COL:BY_CODE,TBL:PTR)        !  POSITION FILE
  NEXT(COLORS)                                !  READ THE CURRENT RECORD

FILL_NEXT ROUTINE                             !FILL NEXT TABLE ENTRY
  FOUND = FALSE                               !  ASSUME RECORD NOT FOUND
  LOOP UNTIL EOF(COLORS)                      !  LOOP UNTIL END OF FILE
    NEXT(COLORS)                              !    READ THE NEXT RECORD
    FOUND = TRUE                              !    SET RECORD FOUND
    DO FILL_TABLE                             !    FILL IN THE TABLE ENTRY
    ADD(TABLE)                                !    ADD LAST TABLE ENTRY
    GET(TABLE,RECORDS(TABLE)-COUNT)           !    GET ANY OVERFLOW RECORD
    DELETE(TABLE)                             !    AND DELETE IT
    EXIT                                      !    RETURN TO CALLER
  .
PREV_PAGE ROUTINE                             !DISPLAY PREVIOUS PAGE
  LOOP COUNT TIMES                            !  FILL UP THE TABLE
    DO FILL_PREV                              !    FILL A TABLE ENTRY
    IF NOT FOUND THEN BREAK.                  !    GET OUT IF NO RECORD
  .
  DO SHOW_PAGE                                !  DISPLAY THE PAGE
```

(continued)

```
SET_PREV ROUTINE                                   !POINT TO PREVIOUS PAGE
  GET(TABLE,1)                                      !  GET THE FIRST TABLE ENTRY
  DO FILL_RECORD                                    !  FILL IN THE RECORD
  SET(COL:BY_CODE,COL:BY_CODE,TBL:PTR)              !  POSITION FILE
  PREVIOUS(COLORS)                                  !  READ THE CURRENT RECORD

FILL_PREV ROUTINE                                  !FILL PREVIOUS TABLE ENTRY
  FOUND = FALSE                                      !  ASSUME RECORD NOT FOUND
  LOOP UNTIL BOF(COLORS)                             !  LOOP UNTIL BEGINNING OF FILE
    PREVIOUS(COLORS)                                 !     READ THE PREVIOUS RECORD
    FOUND = TRUE                                     !     SET RECORD FOUND
    DO FILL_TABLE                                    !     FILL IN THE TABLE ENTRY
    ADD(TABLE,1)                                     !     ADD FIRST TABLE ENTRY
    GET(TABLE,COUNT+1)                               !     GET ANY OVERFLOW RECORD
    DELETE(TABLE)                                    !     AND DELETE IT
    EXIT                                             !     RETURN TO CALLER
  .
SHOW_PAGE ROUTINE                                  !DISPLAY THE PAGE
  NDX# = NDX                                         !  SAVE SCREEN INDEX
  LOOP NDX = 1 TO RECORDS(TABLE)                     !  LOOP THRU THE TABLE
    GET(TABLE,NDX)                                   !     GET A TABLE ENTRY
    DO FILL_SCREEN                                   !     AND DISPLAY IT
    IF TBL:PTR = NEWPTR                              !     SET INDEX FOR NEW RECORD
      NDX# = NDX                                     !     POINT TO CORRECT RECORD
  . .
  NDX = NDX#                                         !  RESTORE SCREEN INDEX
  NEWPTR = 0                                         !  CLEAR NEW RECORD POINTER
  CLEAR(COL:RECORD)                                  !  CLEAR RECORD AREA

FILL_TABLE ROUTINE                                 !MOVE FILE TO TABLE
  TBL:COLOR_CODE = COL:COLOR_CODE
  TBL:COLOR = COL:COLOR
  TBL:PTR = POINTER(COLORS)                          !  SAVE RECORD POINTER

FILL_RECORD ROUTINE                                !MOVE TABLE TO FILE
  COL:COLOR_CODE = TBL:COLOR_CODE

FILL_SCREEN ROUTINE                                !MOVE TABLE TO SCREEN
  SCR:COLOR_CODE = TBL:COLOR_CODE
  SCR:COLOR = TBL:COLOR

GET_RECORD ROUTINE                                 !GET SELECTED RECORD
  GET(TABLE,NDX)                                     !  GET TABLE ENTRY
  GET(COLORS,TBL:PTR)                                !  GET THE RECORD
```

STAT8.CLA

```
          MEMBER('STAT')
NEW_COLORS   PROCEDURE

SCREEN       SCREEN       PRE(SCR),WINDOW(8,36),HUE(15,1)
             ROW(1,1)     STRING('<218,196{8},0{18},196{8},191>'),HUE(14,1)
             ROW(2,1)     REPEAT(6);STRING('<179,0{34},179>'),HUE(14,1) .
             ROW(8,1)     STRING('<192,196{34},217>'),HUE(14,1)
             ROW(1,11)    STRING('ENTER NEW COLORS')
             ROW(4,7)     STRING('Color:'),HUE(14,1)
               COL(25)    STRING(' Code'),HUE(14,1)
MESSAGE      ROW(2,4)     STRING(30),HUE(7,1)
                          ENTRY,USE(?FIRST_FIELD)
             ROW(5,7)     ENTRY(@s14),USE(COL:COLOR),LFT
               COL(27)    ENTRY(@n2),USE(COL:COLOR_CODE),LFT
             ROW(7,18)    PAUSE('OK?'),USE(?PAUSE_FIELD),HUE(30,1)
                          ENTRY,USE(?LAST_FIELD)
                          PAUSE(''),USE(?DELETE_FIELD)

               .

  EJECT
  CODE
  OPEN(SCREEN)                                   !OPEN THE SCREEN
  SETCURSOR                                      !TURN OFF ANY CURSOR
  DISPLAY                                        !DISPLAY THE FIELDS
  LOOP                                           !LOOP THRU ALL THE FIELDS
    MEM:MESSAGE = CENTER(MEM:MESSAGE,SIZE(MEM:MESSAGE)) !DISPLAY ACTION MESSAGE
    DO CALCFIELDS                                !CALCULATE DISPLAY FIELDS
    ALERT                                        !RESET ALERTED KEYS
    ALERT(ACCEPT_KEY)                            !ALERT SCREEN ACCEPT KEY
    ALERT(REJECT_KEY)                            !ALERT SCREEN REJECT KEY
    ACCEPT                                       !READ A FIELD
    IF KEYCODE() = REJECT_KEY THEN RETURN.       !RETURN ON SCREEN REJECT KEY
    EXECUTE ACTION                               !SET MESSAGE
      MEM:MESSAGE = 'Record will be Added'       !
      MEM:MESSAGE = 'Record will be Changed'     !
      MEM:MESSAGE = 'Press Enter to Delete'      !

      .
    IF KEYCODE() = ACCEPT_KEY                     !ON SCREEN ACCEPT KEY
      UPDATE                                      !  MOVE ALL FIELDS FROM SCREEN
      SELECT(?)                                   !  START WITH CURRENT FIELD
      SELECT                                      !  EDIT ALL FIELDS
      CYCLE                                       !  GO TO TOP OF LOOP

      .
```

(continued)

```
    CASE FIELD()                              !JUMP TO FIELD EDIT ROUTINE
    OF ?FIRST_FIELD                           !FROM THE FIRST FIELD
      IF KEYCODE() = ESC_KEY THEN RETURN.     !  RETURN ON ESC KEY
      IF ACTION = 3 THEN SELECT(?DELETE_FIELD). !   OR CONFIRM FOR DELETE


      OF ?PAUSE_FIELD                         !ON PAUSE FIELD
        IF KEYCODE() <> ENTER_KEY|            !IF NOT ENTER KEY
        AND KEYCODE() <> ACCEPT_KEY|          !AND NOT CTRL-ENTER KEY
        AND KEYCODE() <> 0                    !AND NOT NONSTOP MODE
          BEEP                                !  SOUND KEYBOARD ALARM
          SELECT(?PAUSE_FIELD)                !  AND STAY ON PAUSE FIELD
          .

    OF ?LAST_FIELD                            !FROM THE LAST FIELD
      EXECUTE ACTION                          !  UPDATE THE FILE
        ADD(COLORS)                           !    ADD NEW RECORD
        PUT(COLORS)                           !    CHANGE EXISTING RECORD
        DELETE(COLORS)                        !    DELETE EXISTING RECORD
        .
      IF ERRORCODE() = 40                     !  DUPLICATE KEY ERROR
        MEM:MESSAGE = ERROR()                 !    DISPLAY ERR MESSAGE
        SELECT(2)                             !    POSITION TO TOP OF FORM
        CYCLE                                 !    GET OUT OF EDIT LOOP
      ELSIF ERROR()                           !  CHECK FOR UNEXPECTED ERROR
        STOP(ERROR())                         !    HALT EXECUTION
        .
      ACTION = 0                              !  SET ACTION TO COMPLETE
      RETURN                                  !  AND RETURN TO CALLER


    OF ?DELETE_FIELD                          !FROM THE DELETE FIELD
      IF KEYCODE() = ENTER_KEY |              !  ON ENTER KEY
      OR KEYCODE() = ACCEPT_KEY               !  OR CTRL-ENTER KEY
        SELECT(?LAST_FIELD)                   !    DELETE THE RECORD
      ELSE                                    !  OTHERWISE
        BEEP                                  !    BEEP AND ASK AGAIN
  . . .


CALCFIELDS  ROUTINE
  IF FIELD() > ?FIRST_FIELD                         !BEYOND FIRST_FIELD?
    IF KEYCODE() = 0 AND SELECTED() > FIELD() THEN EXIT. !GET OUT IF NOT NONSTOP
    .
  SCR:MESSAGE = MEM:MESSAGE
```

ONE.CLA

```
ONE       MEMBER('STAT')                            !OTHER PROCEDURE

ONE       PROCEDURE                                 !CREATE A BAR GRAPH

SCREEN    SCREEN      WINDOW(25,80),HUE(7,0)        !SCREEN TO PRESERVE TEXT
          END!SCREEN

STUFF     GROUP                                     !GROUPING OF LABEL VARIABLES
LABELS    STRING(250)                               !PIE LABELS
XLABEL    STRING(250)                               !X AXIS LABELS FOR BAR CHART
AMOUNT    STRING(250)                               !AMOUNT LABEL FOR BAR CHART
          END!GROUP

BLACK         SHORT(0)                              !EGA Colors
BLUE          SHORT(1)
GREEN         SHORT(2)
CYAN          SHORT(3)
RED           SHORT(4)
MAGENTA       SHORT(5)
BROWN         SHORT(6)
WHITE         SHORT(7)
GREY          SHORT(8)
YELLOW        SHORT(14)
LIGHT         SHORT(8)

YAXIS         STRING(4)
XAXIS         STRING(4)

          CODE
          SETVIDEO(GETVIDEO(0))                     !SET THE CORRECT VIDEO DRIVER
          DO PARAMETERS                             !SET CHART CONFIGURATION VALUES
      !READ DATA TO GET LARGEST VALUE
          SET(STATS)                                !START POINTER IN FILE
          NEXT(STATS)                               !READ FIRST RECORD
          LASTONE# = STA:PODSIZE                    !SET BASIS FOR SIZING
          LOOP UNTIL EOF(STATS)                     !LOOK THRU THE FILE
            NEXT(STATS)                             !   READ THE NEXT RECORD
            IF STA:PODSIZE > LASTONE#               !     TEST FOR LARGER VALUE
                LASTONE# = STA:PODSIZE              !     SET IF LARGER
            END!IF                                  !     TERMINATE TEST
          END!LOOP                                  !   TERMINATE FILE REVIEW

      !PREPARE TO GRAPH
          VERTFACTOR# = VERTMAX#/LASTONE#           !SET VERTICAL FACTOR
```

(continued)

```
    DATARESET()                          !RESET DATA SPACE
    OPEN(SCREEN)                         !OPEN THE GRAPHICS SCREEN
    SETHIRES(0)                          !SET THE HI RES MODE

!DRAW FIRST BAR CHART
    SET(STATS)                           !RESET POINTER IN FILE
    LOOP UNTIL EOF(STATS)                !LOOK THRU THE FILE
      NEXT(STATS)                        !      READ THE NEXT RECORD
       DATASTORE(STA:PODSIZE * VERTFACTOR#,|  !STORE GRAPH DATA
               2,0,PRM:BARS)
    END!LOOP                             !TERMINATE LOOK UP LOOP
    BARGRAPH(50,100,WIDEPARM#,0+32,1)    !PAINT THE BAR GRAPH
    LOADCSET(1,TINYFONT")                !SETUP LABELING FONT
    LABELY(0,90,50,3,1,0+2,15,|          !PAINT LEFT HAND NUMBERS
        ' 0 25 50 75100125150175200')

!LABEL FIRST BAR CHART
    SET(STATS)                           !PLACE POINTER IN FILE
    LOOP UNTIL EOF(STATS)                !LOOK THROUGH FILE
      NEXT(STATS)                        !READ NEXT RECORD
      XLABEL = CLIP(XLABEL) & |          !BUILD DATE LABEL STRING
             FORMAT(STA:DATE,@D1)
      AMOUNT = CLIP(AMOUNT) & STA:PODSIZE  !BUILD AMOUNT LABEL STRING
    END!LOOP                             !TERMINATE LOOP
    LABELX(50,70,WIDEPARM#,3,1,0+2,15|   !PAINT AMOUNT LABELS
          ,CLIP(AMOUNT))

!DRAW SECOND BAR CHART
    DATARESET()                          !ERASE GRAPHIC DATA SET
    SET(STATS)                           !RESET POINTER IN FILE
    LOOP UNTIL EOF(STATS)                !LOOK THRU THE FILE
      NEXT(STATS)                        !      READ THE NEXT RECORD
       DATASTORE(STA:PODSIZE * VERTFACTOR#,|  !STORE GRAPH DATA
               2+64,0,PRM:BARS2)
    END!LOOP                             !TERMINATE LOOK UP LOOP
    BARGRAPH((WIDEPARM# * (TOT#+1)),|    !PAINT THE BAR GRAPH
          100,WIDEPARM#,0+16,1)
    LABELX((WIDEPARM# * (TOT#+1))+10,330,|  !PAINT DATE LABELS
        WIDEPARM#,8,1,1+2,15,CLIP(XLABEL))
    XYAXES(1345,100,0,400,1,8,2,15)      !PAINT RIGHT SIDE GRID

!DRAW PIE CHART
    DATARESET()                          !ERASE GRAPHIC DATA SET
    SET(STA:BY_DATE)                     !RESET POINTER IN FILE
    PREVIOUS(STATS)                      !READ LAST RECORD IN KEY
    DATASTORE(STA:PODSIZE,2,1,15)        !STORE GRAPH DATA
    LOOP UNTIL BOF(STATS)                !LOOK THRU THE FILE
```

(continued)

```
        PREVIOUS(STATS)                         !  READ NEXT RECORD BACKWARDS
        DATASTORE(STA:PODSIZE,2,0,PRM:PIE)      !  STORE GRAPH DATA
     END!LOOP                                   !TERMINATE LOOK UP LOOP
     PIECHART(HORZ#/2,VERT# - (VERT# * .40)|    !PAINT PIE CHART
                           ,HORZ#/8)
!GET AND PAINT LABELS FOR PIE
     SET(STATS)                                 !RESET FILE POINTER
     LOOP UNTIL BOF(STATS)                      !LOOK TRHOUGH FILE
        PREVIOUS(STATS)                         !  READ PRIOR RECORD IN KEY
        LABELS = CLIP(LABELS) & |               !  BUILD LABEL STRING
                FORMAT(STA:DATE,@D7)
     END!LOOP                                   !TERMINATE LOOP
     LOADCSET(1,LABELFONT")                     !LOAD IN NEW #1 FONT
     LABELPIE(50,(HORZ#/8)+30,9,1,0+2+16,|      !PAINT PIE LABELS
                        15,LABELS)
!CENTER AND PAINT CHART TITLE
     LOADCSET(0,TITLEFONT")                     !LOAD TITLE FONT INTO #0
     LEN# = LEN(CLIP(PRM:TITLE)) * 100          !CREATE LENGTH OF TITLE
     CENTER# = (HORZ#/2)                        !SET HORIZONTAL POSITION
     TOP# = VERT# - (VERT# * .10)               !SET VERTICAL POSITION
     SAYSTRING(CENTER#,TOP#,0,0+2+8+16,|        !PAINT TITLE
          PRM:TITLE_COLOR, CLIP(PRM:TITLE))


!PAINT ICON ON THE SCREEN
     PICREAD(50,750,0,'KWI.PCX')                !PAINT LOGO ON THE SCREEN


!ENTER USERS NAME HERE
     LOADCSET(0,TITLEFONT")                         !LOAD THE TITLE FONT
     SAYSTRING(500,850,0,SSHORIZ,YELLOW,'YOUR NAME: ') !PRESENT PROMPT
     STRING" = EDSTRING(0,850,0,LIGHT+WHITE,'              ') !GET EDIT
     CLRLINE(500,850,40)                            !CLEAR LINE
     SAYSTRING(500,800,0,SSHORIZ,YELLOW,STRING") !PRESENT RESULTS



!LOOK FOR MOUSE
     LOADCSET(0,LABELFONT")                     !LOAD TITLE FONT INTO #0
     SAYSTRING(500,850,0,SSHORIZ,YELLOW,'INITIALIZING MOUSE ...')
     I# = MRESET()                              !INITIALIZE MOUSE, IF PRESENT
     CLRSTRING()                                !ERASE INITIALIZE MESSAGE
     IF NOT I#                                  !TEST FOR MOUSE PRESENCE
     !HOLD SCREEN UNTIL USER PRESSES ANY KEY
        LOADCSET(0,LABELFONT")                  !LOAD TITLE FONT INTO #0
        SAYSTRING(300,30,0,SSHORIZ,YELLOW, |
        'MOUSE NOT INSTALLED... PRESS ANY KEY TO EXIT')
        ASK                                     !HOLD GRAPH FOR USER KEYSTROKE
        CLRSTRING()                             !ERASE 'NOT INSTALLED MESSAGE'
     ELSE
```

(continued)

```
        MCURTYPE(0)                              !SET THE CURSOR TYPE
        MCURON()                                 !TURN ON THE CURSOR
        MSETHOT(1,450,410,400,50)                !SET SENSITIVE REGION
        BOXFILL(450,410,400,50,0,BLUE)           !COLOR THE REGION
        LOADCSET(0,TITLEFONT")                   !LOAD THE TITLE FONT
        SAYSTRING(650,415,0,10,LIGHT+WHITE,'CLICK HERE TO EXIT')
        ALERT(F10_KEY)                           !SENSITIZE THE F10 KEY
        LOOP                                     !  LOOP UNTIL MOUSE HIT
          MS# = MSTATUS()                        !GET THE MOUSE STATUS
          IF MS# = 1 AND MGETHOT() THEN BREAK.   !EXIT IF CLICKED IN HOT AREA
          IF KEYBOARD() = F10_KEY                !TEST FOR F10 KEY PRESS
            ASK                                  !EXTRACT KEYSTROKE
            LOADCSET(0,TITLEFONT")               !LOAD TITLE FONT INTO #0
            SAYSTRING(500,850,0,SSHORIZ,YELLOW,'PRINTING, PLEASE WAIT.')
            PRINTPCL(2+4,100,100,150)            !SEND GRAPH TO PRINTER
            CLRSTRING()                          !ERASE PRINTING MESSAGE
          END!IF
          IF MMOTION()                           !CHECK FOR MOUSE MOVEMENT
            LOADCSET(0,LABELFONT")               !LOAD TITLE FONT INTO #0
            XAXIS = MGETX()                      !SET NEW HORIZINTAL VALUE
            YAXIS = MGETY()                      !SET NEW VERTICAL VALUE
            SAYSTRING(1100,800,0,SSHORIZ,LIGHT+WHITE,'X POS:' & RIGHT(XAXIS))
            SAYSTRING(1100,750,0,SSHORIZ,LIGHT+WHITE,'Y POS:' & RIGHT(YAXIS))
          END!IF
        END!LOOP
        MCUROFF()                                !TURN CURSOR OFF
     END!IF
        CLRSCREEN()
        LOADICON('MARKS.ICO')                    !LOAD ICON BUFFER
        DRAWICON(675,500,0+16,0+16,14)           !DRAW A SYMBOL
        LOADCSET(0,LABELFONT")                   !LOAD TITLE FONT INTO #0
        SAYSTRING(500,30,0,SSHORIZ,YELLOW,'PRESS ANY KEY TO EXIT')
        ASK                                      !WAIT FOR KEYSTROKE
        SETTEXT()                                !RESET THE TEXT MODE
        CLOSE(SCREEN)                            !CLOSE THE GRAPHICS SCREEN
        RETURN

PARAMETERS    ROUTINE
        GET(PARMS,1)                             !GET CONTROL RECORD
        IF ERROR() THEN RETURN.                  !GO BACK IF NOT ENTERED
        CLEAR(STUFF)                             !CLEAR OUT LABELS
        VERT# = 1000                             !SET GRID VERTICAL SIZE
        HORZ# = 1350                             !SET GRID HORIZONTAL SIZE
        VERTMAX# = 400                           !SET VERTICAL SIZE
        HORZMAX# = 640                           !SET HORIZONTAL SIZE
        TOT# = RECORDS(STATS)                    !NUMBER OF RECORDS IN DATA
        WIDEPARM# = HORZMAX#/TOT#                !SET HORIZONTAL SCALING
```

(continued)

```
        LABELFONT" = 'C:\CLARION\GRAPH\SMALL'    !SET FONT FOR PIE LABELS
        TITLEFONT" = 'C:\CLARION\GRAPH\LARGE'    !SET FONT FOR TITLE
        TINYFONT" = 'C:\CLARION\GRAPH\TINYTHIN'  !SET BAR CHART LABELS
```

KIDDING.CLA

```
KIDDING      MEMBER('STAT')

KIDDING      PROCEDURE


SCREEN   SCREEN      WINDOW(5,34),HUE(15,4)
           ROW(1,1)     STRING('<219{34}>'),HUE(30,0)
           ROW(2,1)     REPEAT(3);STRING('<219,0{32},219>'),HUE(30,0)  .
           ROW(5,1)     STRING('<219{11},0{13},219{10}>'),HUE(30,0)
           ROW(3,5)     STRING('THAT''S TOO MANY WHALES !!')
           ROW(5,12)    STRING('Press Any Key'),HUE(30,0)
         END!SCREEN

         CODE
         OPEN(SCREEN)
         ASK
         CLOSE(SCREEN)
         RETURN
```

Chapter 19

The Communications LEM

Clarion offers a powerful set of tools for serial communications management with its Communications Language Extension Module. This LEM takes full control of all the features of the serial port in the PC—including the ability to manage not only the hardware interrupts for the COMM 1 and COMM 2 ports, but also the software interrupts for the COMM 3 and COMM 4 ports. In addition, Clarion has included some higher level functionality, including an XMODEM-based file transfer protocol and a port vectoring function that allows for background operations in both transmission and reception. A simple system for plucking a phone number out of memory and dialing that number through a Hayes-compatible modem will serve here to demonstrate the use of the Communications LEM.

The Communications Functions

To perform serial communications—whether you are transmitting information through a phone line and the modem is the device to use or if you are sending information through a serial cable to another computer—you must take the following four steps:

1. Get control of the modem or serial port.
2. Create an area where the data coming in and going out can be stored for transmission and reception.
3. Extract the data from the port or send data to the port.
4. Verify the data received.

Interrupt-Driven Multiple Port Handling

The Communications LEM (or COMM LEM) is built around the concept of interrupt-driven asynchronous communications, which basically means that data can arrive at any time at any port and, depending on what interrupt is receiving it, be processed almost immediately. The PC is equipped with what is known as the UART, or Universal Asynchronous Receiver/Transmitter. In his book *C Programmer's Guide to Serial Communications*, Joe Campbell describes UARTs as follows:

> The UART's circuitry handles the grimy details of assembling and reassembling bytes, handles the timing, and in general unburdens the processor. . . . An interrupt is one example of a class of events known as exceptions, which are characterized by the involuntary passing of processor control from the normal path of program execution to code especially designed to "service" the event.

The program code, of course, consists of the COMM LEM functions that handle reading the buffers and supervising the port. Managing serial communications with the COMM LEM, then, adds to the event-driven nature of Clarion. The normal process of a program would be the user's responses on the keyboard to onscreen requests and the other work that Clarion performs in response to those actions. The Main Event Loop continuously monitors both for keystrokes and for port input/output. This allows the user to press an "abort" button to jump out of a communications session even while the port is receiving and processing data.

Ports and Buffers

To use serial communications, you must prepare whatever combination of the serial ports you plan to use. The statements listed in Table 19-1 prepare the serial ports for use.

The remaining initializing statements include CLEARCOM, which merely clears out the receive buffer; SETCOM, which sets all the communications parameters like transmission speed, data pattern, and timeout; SETCOM-TIME, which sets just the timeout; and USECOM, which sets the default port other statements that do not provide a slot to define the port (like SENDLINE or RECVBLOCK) will address.

When you initialize the port, you set up a hardware interrupt that can be sensitive to incoming data. That is, you have to notify the PC that you are claiming use of one of the serial ports. You cannot begin communications

Table 19-1   The port initialization statements.

Turns On	Turns Off	Function
ARMCOM	DISARMCOM	Combines ARMPORT and ARMVECT.
ARMPORT	DISARMPORT	Initializes the port.
ARMVECT	DISARMVECT	Provides direction to each port and sets buffer location.

without first using a statement (either ARMPORT or ARMCOM). The next step is to establish a location in memory where the information received through the port can be stored temporarily. This is known as the buffer. Most of the statements in the COMM LEM involve the buffer in some manner. The statements for managing the buffer appear in Table 19-2.

Table 19-2   The standard buffer management statements.

Statement	Function
SENDLINE/RECVLINE	Sends/receives characters until designated character is found (used for processing buffer to a starting point).
SENDBLOCK/RECVBLOCK	Sends/receives a specified number of characters (usually related to buffer size).
PEEKBLOCK	Stores a certain number of characters without removing them from the buffer.
PEEKLINE	Stores as much data as comes in until the designated character arrives (without removing anything from the buffer).
BUFFERSTATUS	Provides a LONG to be masked for extracting the buffer status and number of characters received.
COMCHKSUM	Performs and returns the result of checksum on buffer contents received.
COMCRC	Same as COMCHKSUM, except that it performs the checksum on the entire string. (See later discussion.)

Hint: The buffer method used in the COMM LEM is called a "ring buffer." When it becomes full, new data overwrites the old data. Therefore, to avoid losing characters, you must test to see if the buffer is full (at overflow) to avoid losing anything that is transmitted.

The buffer is the real source for processing information in a communications system. The other features all support accurate reception into the buffer. For the most part, the bulk of your program deals with extracting data from the buffer and placing data into it. The PEEK statements are useful for monitoring the data as it travels through the buffer. You can place that data into variables to which the program can react. The disadvantage to these functions is that the characters still reside in the buffer. When you use the RECV statements, you can extract the characters for processing and empty the buffer. This makes for cleaner reception management since you can use the overflow statements to prevent character losses.

Error Checking

Many error checking schemes are available for use in serial communications. There are even several different ways to use the two verifying statements within the COMM LEM. One of the most common schemes is the XMODEM protocol. This involves more than applying the COMCHKSUM or COMCRC statements to the contents of the buffer, however. An excellent discussion of the bare bones XMODEM appears in the *Clarion Communications LEM Manual.*

Essentially, there is a scheme of responses between sending and receiving devices that uses ACK (stands for "acknowledge") and NAK ("negative acknowledge"). The communicating devices exchange these "smoke signals" to indicate readiness to communicate. Then the sending computer transmits an XMODEM record block. This record block carries not only the data being sent, but also information to let the receiving device know where each packet starts and stops. It also contains a method to determine whether the right stuff is being received.

In the sample program that comes with the COMM LEM, the SENDFILE module constructs the XMODEM package. That package, as it appears in Figure 19-1 from the global definitions of the COMM.CLA program in the samples, is transmitted, and then the receiving computer uses the information tied to the data that is sent to determine if the data that are sent were actually received.

Note in Figure 19-1 that there is an extra BYTE at the end of the packet reserved for the CRC checking. That is because standard checksum only adds

Figure 19-1   The XMODEM packet.

```
MODEM          GROUP                      !XMODEM DATA PACKET
EADER            BYTE                     !  START OF HEADER (SOH)
ECNUM            BYTE                     !    RECORD NUMBER
RECNUM           BYTE                     !    1'S COMPLEMENT OF RECNUM
ECGRP            GROUP                    !    FILE DATA GROUP
                   BYTE,DIM(128)          !      FILE DATA RECORD
                   .                      !    END OF FILE DATA GROUP
ECCRC            SHORT                    !    USE 16 BIT CRC OF DATA
ECSUM            BYTE,OVER(RECCRC)        !    or  CHECKSUM OF DATA
                   .                      !    END OF GROUP(S)
```

up all the values of each character and sends that total for checking on the other end. The receiving device does its own addition on the data it received and compares it to the value that was sent. As defined by the *Illustrated Dictionary of Microcomputers*, CRC-CHECKSUM

> treats an *N*-bit message as an *N*th order polynomial and divides it by a generator polynomial to produce a quotient and a remainder. This remainder is then appended to the message (our XMODEM packet) and transmitted. At the receiver, another remainder is computed from the received data bits and compared to the received remainder.

The point is that yet another measure is used to detect errors in the transmission. The procedure that constructs the XMODEM packet in the SEND-FILE.CLA module of the COMM LEM samples appears in Figure 19-2.

Because the COMCHKSUM and COMCRC statements exist in the COMM LEM, you don't have to construct your own method for decoding these error checking packets. You only need to look in the buffer with RECVLINE until the SOH or Start of HEADER character show up while your program waits to receive from another computer and then use the COMCHKSUM or COMCRC statements to verify the data that were sent.

Background Communications

The reason that Clarion can provide simultaneous access to all four communications ports originates with this interrupt style of event management and a few specialized functions. The statements Clarion provides for handling the background sessions appear in Table 19-3.

Figure 19-2   Constructing an XMODEM packet.

```
CODE
HEADER = SOH                              !  START OF HEADER
RECNUM += 1                               !  RECORD NUMBER
XRECNUM = BXOR(RECNUM,255)                !  1'S COMPLEMENT OF RECNUM
RECGRP = FILEGRP                          !  MOVE DATA INTO XMODEM RECORD
IF METHOD = NAK                           !  IF CHECKSUM METHOD
  RECSUM = COMCHKSUM(RECGRP)              !    CHECKSUM OF DATA RECORD
ELSE                                      !  ELSE
  RECCRC = COMCRC(RECGRP,128)             !    16 BIT CRC OF DATA RECORD
.                                         !  END IF
```

A vector is the method that the processor uses to locate the code setup to process the input/output of each port. Clarion provides several functions for handling that vectoring. The ARMVECT and DISARMVECT statements perform one-half of the functions you must execute to use one of the serial ports. This function, in the case of foreground transmissions, is best handled by the ARMCOM statement, which both arms the port and establishes the buffer. However, in background sessions, you need the ARMVECT statement to set up the transmission buffer that will operate while the computer is busy handling another port or some other function. You can use the background functions most successfully by establishing a large transmission buffer that

Table 19-3   The background management statements.

Statement	Function
ARMTRAN	Identifies port for background work and removes it from processing in the foreground.
DISARMTRAN	Returns the port to foreground processing.
CLEARTRAN	Clears out the transmission buffer for background.
SUSPENDTRAN	Holds data in transmission buffer and stops sending.
RESUMETRAN	Restarts transmitting data after SUSPENDTRAN.
TRANSTATUS	Same as BUFFERSTATUS for background work.

can hold everything you want to send. Then you can initiate a transfer in background that will not require additional work from your main program. The other method is to continually check TRANSTATUS, and upon finding the transmission buffer empty, you can ship more data into that buffer and then go back to the other work you were performing in the foreground.

The DIALER Program Sample

As a means for demonstrating some of the communications functions, we will construct a sample program that dials the phone in a telemarketing type of application. (The entire source code for the Dialer program appears at the end of the chapter.) This method works on any application where you select a record from the table in Figure 19-3, which places a record in memory with a hot key and then calls a function to dial the number.

Calling the Dialing Procedure

The standard Designer method for putting the record into memory is handled simply by placing the Dialing Procedure as a hot key in the Table Procedure that lists the names on file. Figure 19-4 shows the code in the Table Procedure that does the job.

Figure 19-3   The table for dialing numbers.

```
                 Milt's Telephone Directory
                   SHOW NAMES BY LAST
                 Conventional:     97,528
                 Virtual:               0
                 Total:            97,528

         Find by Last Name:
         Nila Burgess                  619-265-8224
         George Bush                   201-333-4444
         Frank Drachman                619-283-2181
         Alice Indwonderland           619-528-1026
          Scooter                      415-601-6039




         Ins to Add              Enter to Change
         Del to Delete             Esc to Exit
                 Touch <F10> to Dial
```

Figure 19-4   The code calling the Dialer Procedure.

```
IF KEYCODE( ) = F10_KEY                 !ON HOT KEY
   IF FIELD( ) = ?POINT THEN DO GET_RECORD.  ! READ RECORD IF NEEDED
   DIALER(NAM:CODE,NAM:PHONE)           !  CALL HOT KEY PROCEDURE
   DO SAME_PAGE                         ! RESET TO SAME  PAGE
   CYCLE                                !  AND LOOP AGAIN
.
```

One change to the Designer-generated code is required: To pass the dialing code and the phone number to the Dialer Procedure, these variables need to be added to the call to the procedure.

Hint: *Remember that you can pass parameters **to** a procedure, but the procedure cannot return anything back. You must use a function to return data to the Calling Procedure.*

Note also that Figure 19-4 shows that the GET_RECORD table subroutine is called whenever the Point Field is not on the current record. This ensures that the correct record will be in memory when the Dialer Procedure is run.

Passing Phone Number As a Procedure Parameter

The next step is to receive the passed parameters inside the Dialer Procedure. Figure 19-5 shows how to set those values to variables that will be used inside the procedure.

Retrieving Stored Parameters

Now that we have trapped the phone number and any dialing codes, the port to the modem must be prepared. To do this, we'll use the control file method for storing the configuration parameters. As soon as the GET in Figure 19-6 is issued, we check for an error because the single record in the control file containing the correct parameters may not yet exist—especially if this is the first time the program is being run. If it is, we immediately loop to the Parms Procedure to request the proper configuration information from the user.

Figure 19-5   Receiving parameters in the Dialer Procedure.

```
                SUBTITLE('DIALING FUNCTION')

DIALER          MEMBER('CLIENTS')                !DIALS THE PHONE

DIALER          PROCEDURE(CODE,PHONE)            !MODEM DIALING PROCEDURE
PHONE           EXTERNAL                         !POINTS TO PHONE NUMBER
CODE            EXTERNAL
```

The screen in the Parms Procedure that the user completes is shown in Figure 19-7.

Initializing the Port and Buffer

Now that the proper configuration information is available, we can open the dialing screen, initialize the port, and get ready to dial the phone. Figure 19-8 shows the process for preparing to dial.

First, the ARMCOM statement uses the PORT parameter (set in the Parms Procedure) and the global definition for the buffer to initialize the receiving buffer. Then the port is set to the proper parameters for dialing. (This information is given directly in the SETCOM statement, but it could be pulled from a control file, too.) Then we clear out the port that ARMCOM set up with

Figure 19-6   Retrieving configuration information.

```
LOOP                               !ENSURE PORT CONFIGURED
  GET(PARMS,1)                     ! GET PORT CONFIGURATION
  IF ERROR( )                      ! NO RECORD?
    PARMS                          ! CALL CONFIGURATIONS SCREEN
  ELSE                             ! OTHERWISE
    BREAK                          ! CONTINUE
  END!IF
END!LOOP
```

Figure 19-7   The parameters entry form.

CLEARCOM and set the default port with USECOM for the remaining statements to employ. Following that, SENDLINE pushes the globally defined INIT_MODEM out the serial port selected by USECOM, waits for a second, and then begins looking in the buffer for incoming information.

Reading the Contents of the Buffer

Note the use of the CHECK_CHAR procedure in Figure 19-9. This is taken directly from the sample programs that come with the Communications LEM.

When the main loop in the Dialer Procedure calls the CHECK_CHAR procedure, it first reads the contents of the port from the designated port into

Figure 19-8   Initializing the port and the modem.

```
OPEN(DIAL_SCRN)                       !POPUP DIAL WINDOW
ARMCOM(PORT,BUFFER)                   !ARM THE INTERFACE BUFFER
SETCOM(1200,0,1,8,1,PORT)            !SETUP PORT FOR MODEM
CLEARCOM(PORT)                        !CLEAR COMMUNICATIONS BUFFER
USECOM(PORT)                          !SET DEFAULT PORT
SENDLINE(INIT_MODEM,'<13>')          !SEND MODEM INIT STRING
I# = CLOCK( )                         !GET CURRENT TIME
LOOP UNTIL DELAY_TIME(I#,1).          !WAIT 1 SECOND
LOOP                                  !LOOP UNTIL MODEM SIGNALS OK
  CHECK_CHAR                          ! CHECK RECEIVE BUFFER FOR OK
  IF CLIP(MEM:MESSAGE) = 'READY'      ! IF BUFFER SIGNALS READY
    MEM:MESSAGE = ''                  !    BLANK OUT MESSAGE
    BREAK                             !  BREAK OUT OF LOOP
  END!IF                              ! TERMINATE THE IF STATEMENT
END!LOOP                              ! TERMINATE THE LOOP STATEMENT
CLEARCOM(PORT)                        !CLEAR RECEIVE BUFFER
```

Figure 19-9   The procedure to read incoming characters from the buffer.

```
CHECK_CHAR    PROCEDURE                      !READS THE BUFFER FOR RESPONSE

TEMPBUF       STRING(10)                     !READ/WRITE 10 CHARS
READY_MASK    EQUATE(00000010B)              !  MORE CHARS READY TO BE READ
BUFFERSTAT    LONG(0)                        !  BUFFER STATUS
BUFFERCNT     LONG(0)                        ! CHARACTERS IN BUFFER COUNT
CHAR_GRP      GROUP                          !SINGLE CHARACTER  GROUP
CHAR            BYTE                         !  CHAR FROM COM PORT
              END!GROUP                      !  END OF GROUP
  CODE                                       !
  LOOP                                       !BEGIN READING LOOP
    BUFFERSTAT = BUFFERSTATUS(PORT)          ! GET BUFFER STATUS
    BUFFERCNT = BSHIFT(BUFFERSTAT,-16)       ! GET BUFFER COUNT
     IF BAND(BUFFERSTAT,READY_MASK)          ! IF CHAR(S) READY
        RECVBLOCK(TEMPBUF,BUFFERCNT)         !    RECEIVE BLOCK
        POS# = INSTRING('OK',TEMPBUF,1)      !    FIND MODEM RESPONSE
        IF NOT POS#                          !    IF NO CHARACTERS
          CYCLE                              !       RESTART LOOP
        ELSE                                 !    OR
          MEM:MESSAGE = 'READY'             !       SET MESSAGE TO READY
          BREAK                              !       BREAK OUT OF LOOP
        END!IF                               !    TERMINATE THE IF
     ELSE                                    ! OR
        RETURN                               !    GO BACK TO DIALER
     END!IF                                  ! TERMINATE THE IF STRUCTURE
  END!LOOP                                   !TERMINATE THE LOOP STRUCTURE
  CLEAR(TEMPBUF)                             !CLEAR OUT THE BUFFER
```

a LONG variable called BUFFERSTAT. Extracting information from an instruction like BUFFERSTATUS is very much like getting information from a structure in the C language. You could also view this procedure as building a record with fields in it that contain various information about the port buffer. Using the BSHIFT function, you can extract the number of characters in the buffer at the time the BUFFERSTATUS statement is issued. Then the BAND function is used to match the READY_MASK stored in global memory against the current contents of the BUFFERSTAT variable.

The way the BAND function works: if the READY_MASK matches the contents of BUFFERSTAT, the BAND statement returns a 1 or TRUE and the IF statement processes the statements immediately beneath it. In this case, there are characters in the buffer, so the RECVBLOCK statement is issued to extract them and clear the buffer for the next block to be received. The INSTRING function then loops through the block of characters received until it finds OK. If OK is not found, the implicit POS# variable remains zero or Not True and the function recycles. Conversely, if the OK is found, the ELSE segment is processed and the global memory variable MEM:MESSAGE gets set to READY. MEM:MESSAGE gets examined (back in Figure 19-8), breaks out of the modem initialization routine, and clears the port. The system is now ready to dial the phone.

Dialing the Number

The code in Figure 19-10 prepares the number by stripping out the "home" (or local) dialing prefix (another parameter that could be stored in the control file). Then it appends the special Dialing Procedures for that record and sends the mode instructions to dial the phone with SENDLINE.

Several decisions are made about the phone number for this record at this point. You could add more conditions if you needed them. Then, the number dialed through the modem appears on the screen (as shown in Figure 19-11) with the global DIAL_TONE attached to it for getting the modem's attention and instructing it to dial the phone.

Hanging Up the Phone

After the number and dialing codes get sent to the modem, the system pauses for a moment and then displays a message, as appears in Figure 19-12. The user can pick up the handset and take over the call from the modem, or simply strike the Enter key and the program will hang up the line immediately.

In any case, whether you pick up the phone to supersede the modem or disconnect the call from inside the program before you pick up the phone, the code in Figure 19-13 executes. After processing the user's keystroke, the attention code gets sent to the modem and then the value stored in the global

Figure 19-10   Prepares the number and dials the phone.

```
IF SUB(PHONE,1,3) = '619'               !CALLING FROM HOME   AREA CODE?
  DIALNO = SUB(PHONE,5,8)               ! STRIP OUT AREA CODE
ELSE                                    !OR
  IF CODE
    DIALNO = CLIP(CODE) & '-' & '1-' & PHONE ! ADD LONG DISTANCE   CODE
  ELSE
    DIALNO = '1-' & PHONE
  END!IF
END!IF                                  !TERMINATE THE LOOP STATEMENT
SCR:MESSAGE = CENTER('NOW DIALING: ' & | !   DISPLAY DIALING MESSAGE
            DIALNO,SIZE(SCR:MESSAGE))
SENDLINE(DIAL_TONE&CLIP(DIALNO)&'<13>','<13>') !DIAL THE NUMBER
```

---

variable HANG_UP gets sent to the modem. After that, the port and its associated buffer are closed, the dialing screen is closed, and the Dialer Procedure returns control to the Table Procedure from which it was called.

Figure 19-11   The dialing message.

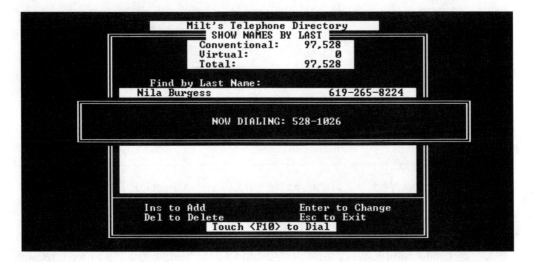

Figure 19-12   The next message after dialing.

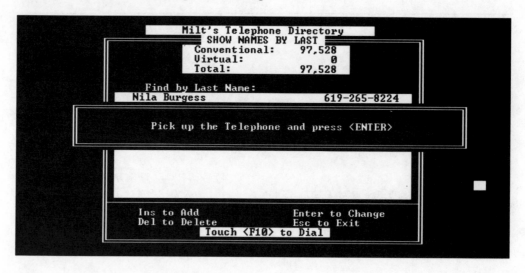

Figure 19-13   The call termination sequence.

```
ASK                                    !WAIT FOR ENTER KEY
SENDBLOCK(ATTEN,SIZE(ATTEN))           !SEND ATTENTION CODE TO MODEM
I# = CLOCK( )                          !GET CURRENT TIME
LOOP UNTIL DELAY_TIME(I#,1).            !WAIT 1 SECOND
SENDBLOCK(HANG_UP,SIZE(HANG_UP))       !SEND HANG UP CODE TO MODEM
DISARMCOM(PORT)                        !DISABLE COM PORT
CLOSE(DIAL_SCRN)                        !CLOSE POPUP DIAL WINDOW
RETURN                                 !RETURN TO CLIENTS TABLE
```

Summary

In this chapter, we discussed the various components of serial communications as managed by the procedures and functions of the Communications Language Extension Module. The Port and the Receive/Send buffer were discussed as well as Clarion's ability to sustain background communications. Then a sample was provided to demonstrate a simple Dialing Procedure and the use of the port and buffer for operating the modem.

The Additions to the TIME SHEET Program to Add Automatic Dialing

HOURS.CLA

```
HOURS          PROGRAM
               INCLUDE('STD_KEYS.CLA')
               INCLUDE('CTL_KEYS.CLA')
               INCLUDE('ALT_KEYS.CLA')
               INCLUDE('SHF_KEYS.CLA')

REJECT_KEY     EQUATE(CTRL_ESC)
ACCEPT_KEY     EQUATE(CTRL_ENTER)
TRUE           EQUATE(1)
FALSE          EQUATE(0)

               MAP
                 PROC(G_OPENFILES)
                 MODULE('HOURS1')
                       PROC(MAIN)                    !MILT'S TELEPHONE DIRECTORY
                     .
                 MODULE('HOURS2')
                       PROC(SHO_LAST)                !Show Names By Last
                     .
                 MODULE('HOURS3')
                       PROC(UPD_NAMES)               !Update Names
                     .
                 MODULE('HOURS4')
                       PROC(RPT_LAST)                !Print Names By Last
                     .
                 MODULE('CAPS')
                       FUNC(CAPS),STRING             !Upper/Lower Case Strings
                     .
                 MODULE('DIALER')
                       PROC(DIALER)                  !COMMUNICATIONS PROCEDURE
                       PROC(CHECK_CHAR)              !READ THE INCOMING BUFFER
                       FUNC(DELAY_TIME),LONG         !COUNTS OUT SYSTEM WAIT
                       PROC(PARMS)                   !SET THE COMMUNICATIONS PORT
                     .
                 INCLUDE('DOS1.CPY')
                 INCLUDE('COMM.CPY')
                     .
               EJECT('FILE LAYOUTS')
NAMES          FILE,PRE(NAM),CREATE,RECLAIM
BY_LAST          KEY(NAM:LAST,NAM:FIRST),DUP,NOCASE,OPT
```

(continued)

```
RECORD          RECORD
FIRST                   STRING(10)
LAST                    STRING(20)
NOTE                    STRING(20)                  !Note for location of phone
CODE                    STRING(10)                  !Special Dialing Code
PHONE                   STRING(@P###-###-####PB)     !Telephone Number
                . .


PARMS           FILE,PRE(PRM),CREATE,RECLAIM
RECORD          RECORD
PORT                    STRING(1)                   !COMMUNICATIONS PORT FOR MODEM
                . .


                EJECT('GLOBAL MEMORY VARIABLES')
ACTION          SHORT                               !0 = NO ACTION
                                                    !1 = ADD RECORD
                                                    !2 = CHANGE RECORD
                                                    !3 = DELETE RECORD
                                                    !4 = LOOKUP FIELD


                GROUP,PRE(MEM)
MESSAGE         STRING(30)                          !Global Message Area
PAGE            SHORT                               !Report Page Number
LINE            SHORT                               !Report Line Number
DEVICE          STRING(1)                           !Report Device Name
                .
                                                    !MODEM ESCAPE SEQUENCES
ATTEN           STRING('+++')                       !  MODEM ALERT CODE
HANG_UP         STRING('ATH0<13>')                  !  MODEM HANGUP CODE
INIT_MODEM      STRING('ATE0 V1 X1<13>')            !  CODES TO INITIALIZE MODEM
DIAL_TONE       STRING('ATDT')                      !  DIAL PHONE W/ TONE
BAUDRATE        SHORT(1200)                         !  BAUD RATE (50 - 19200)
DATABITS        SHORT(8)                            !  WORD LENGTH (7 OR 8)
STOPBITS        SHORT(1)                            !  STOP BITS (1 OR 2)
PARITYSTR       STRING('NONE')                      !  MENU STRING (NONE,EVEN,ODD)
PARITY          SHORT(0)                            !  0 - NONE, 1 - EVEN, 2 - ODD
TIMEOUT         SHORT(1)                            !  TIMEOUT DELAY (0 - 59 SECS)
PORTSTR         STRING('COM1')                      !  MENU STRING (COM1-COM4)
PORT            SHORT(0)                            !  COM1=0,COM2=1,COM3=2,COM4=3
BUFFER          GROUP                               !COMMUNICATIONS BUFFER GROUP
                    BYTE,DIM(2000)                  !  COMMUNICATIONS BUFFER
                .                                   !  END OF GROUP


                EJECT('CODE SECTION')
```

(continued)

```
CODE
SETHUE(7,0)                                  !SET WHITE ON BLACK
BLANK                                        !  AND BLANK
G_OPENFILES                                  !OPEN OR CREATE FILES
SETHUE()                                     !    THE SCREEN
MAIN                                         !MILT'S TELEPHONE DIRECTORY
RETURN                                       !EXIT TO DOS


G_OPENFILES  PROCEDURE                       !OPEN FILES & CHECK FOR ERROR
  CODE
  SHOW(25,1,CENTER('OPENING FILE: ' & 'NAMES',80)) !DISPLAY FILE NAME
  OPEN(NAMES)                                !OPEN THE FILE
  IF ERROR()                                 !OPEN RETURNED AN ERROR
    CASE ERRORCODE()                         ! CHECK FOR SPECIFIC ERROR
    OF 46                                    !  KEYS NEED TO BE REQUILT
      SETHUE(0,7)                            !  BLACK ON WHITE
      SHOW(25,1,CENTER('REBUILDING KEY FILES FOR NAMES',80)) !INDICATE MSG
      BUILD(NAMES)                           !   CALL THE BUILD PROCEDURE
      SETHUE(7,0)                            !   WHITE ON BLACK
      BLANK(25,1,1,80)                       !   BLANK THE MESSAGE
    OF 2                                     !IF NOT FOUND,
      CREATE(NAMES)                          ! CREATE
    ELSE                                     ! ANY OTHER ERROR
      LOOP;STOP('NAMES: ' & ERROR()).        !  STOP EXECUTION
  . .


  SHOW(25,1,CENTER('OPENING FILE: ' & 'PARMS',80)) !DISPLAY FILE NAME
  OPEN(PARMS)                                !OPEN THE FILE
  IF ERROR()                                 !OPEN RETURNED AN ERROR
    CASE ERRORCODE()                         ! CHECK FOR SPECIFIC ERROR
    OF 46                                    !  KEYS NEED TO BE REQUILT
      SETHUE(0,7)                            !  BLACK ON WHITE
      SHOW(25,1,CENTER('REBUILDING KEY FILES FOR PARMS',80)) !INDICATE MSG
      BUILD(PARMS)                           !   CALL THE BUILD PROCEDURE
      SETHUE(7,0)                            !   WHITE ON BLACK
      BLANK(25,1,1,80)                       !   BLANK THE MESSAGE
    OF 2                                     !IF NOT FOUND,
      CREATE(PARMS)                          ! CREATE
    ELSE                                     ! ANY OTHER ERROR
      LOOP;STOP('PARMS: ' & ERROR()).        !  STOP EXECUTION
  . .


  BLANK                                      !BLANK THE SCREEN
```

DIALER.CLA

```
                 SUBTITLE('DIALING FUNCTION')

DIALER           MEMBER('HOURS')                        !DIALS THE PHONE

DIALER           PROCEDURE(CODE,PHONE)                  !MODEM DIALING PROCEDURE
PHONE            EXTERNAL                               !POINTS TO PHONE NUMBER
CODE             EXTERNAL

DIAL_SCRN SCREEN  WINDOW(5,64),AT(10,10),PRE(SCR),HLP('DIAL'),HUE(15,1,0)
                 ROW(1,1)    STRING('<201,205{62},187>')
                 ROW(2,1)    REPEAT(3);STRING('<186,0{62},186>') .
                 ROW(5,1)    STRING('<200,205{62},188>')
MESSAGE          ROW(3,3)    STRING(60),HUE(14,1)
          END!SCREEN
DIALNO           STRING(30)

  CODE
  ALERT(ESC_KEY)                              !SENSITIZE THE ESCAPE KEY
  LOOP                                        !ENSURE PORT CONFIGURED
    GET(PARMS,1)                              ! GET PORT CONFIGURATION
    IF ERROR()                                ! NO RECORD?
      PARMS                                   ! CALL CONFIGURATIONS SCREEN
    ELSE                                      ! OTHERWISE
      BREAK                                   ! CONTINUE
    END!IF
  END!LOOP
  OPEN(DIAL_SCRN)                             !POPUP DIAL WINDOW
  ARMCOM(PORT,BUFFER)                         !ARM THE INTERFACE BUFFER
  SETCOM(1200,0,1,8,1,PORT)                   !SETUP PORT FOR MODEM
  CLEARCOM(PORT)                              !CLEAR COMMUNICATIONS BUFFER
  USECOM(PORT)                                !SET DEFAULT PORT
  SENDLINE(INIT_MODEM,'<13>')                 !SEND MODEM INIT STRING
  I# = CLOCK()                                !GET CURRENT TIME
  LOOP UNTIL DELAY_TIME(I#,1).                !WAIT 1 SECOND
  LOOP                                        !LOOP UNTIL MODEM SIGNALS OK
    CHECK_CHAR                                ! CHECK RECEIVE BUFFER FOR OK
    IF CLIP(MEM:MESSAGE) = 'READY'            ! IF BUFFER SIGNALS READY
      MEM:MESSAGE = ''                        !   BLANK OUT MESSAGE
      BREAK                                   !   BREAK OUT OF LOOP
    END!IF                                    ! TERMINATE THE IF STATEMENT
  END!LOOP                                    ! TERMINATE THE LOOP STATEMENT
  CLEARCOM(PORT)                              !CLEAR RECEIVE BUFFER
  IF SUB(PHONE,1,3) = '619'                   !CALLING FROM HOME AREA CODE?
    DIALNO = SUB(PHONE,5,8)                   ! STRIP OUT AREA CODE
```

(continued)

```
ELSE                                           !OR
   IF CODE
      DIALNO = CLIP(CODE) & '-' & '1-' & PHONE ! ADD LONG DISTANCE CODE
   ELSE
      DIALNO = '1-' & PHONE
   END!IF
END!IF                                         !TERMINATE THE LOOP STATEMENT
SCR:MESSAGE = CENTER('NOW DIALING: ' & |        !    DISPLAY DIALING MESSAGE
            DIALNO,SIZE(SCR:MESSAGE))
SENDLINE(DIAL_TONE&CLIP(DIALNO)&'<13>','<13>') !DIAL THE NUMBER
I# = CLOCK()                                    !GET CURRENT TIME
LOOP UNTIL DELAY_TIME(I#,4).                    !WAIT 1 SEC
SCR:MESSAGE = CENTER('Pick up the Telephone'& | !DISPLAY PICKUP MESSAGE
            ' and press <<ENTER>',|
            SIZE(SCR:MESSAGE))
ASK                                            !WAIT FOR ENTER KEY
SENDBLOCK(ATTEN,SIZE(ATTEN))                   !SEND ATTENTION CODE TO MODEM
I# = CLOCK()                                    !GET CURRENT TIME
LOOP UNTIL DELAY_TIME(I#,1).                    !WAIT 1 SECOND
SENDBLOCK(HANG_UP,SIZE(HANG_UP))               !SEND HANG UP CODE TO MODEM
DISARMCOM(PORT)                                !DISABLE COM PORT
CLOSE(DIAL_SCRN)                               !CLOSE POPUP DIAL WINDOW
RETURN                                         !RETURN TO CLIENTS TABLE


PARMS         PROCEDURE                        !SET MODEM PORT

PARMS_SCRN SCREEN        WINDOW(6,46),AT(9,18),HUE(15,1,0)
            ROW(1,1)    STRING('<201,205{44},187>')
            ROW(2,1)    REPEAT(4);STRING('<186,0{44},186>') .
            ROW(6,1)    STRING('<200,205{44},188>')
            ROW(2,14)   STRING('Change Port Settings')
            ROW(4,5)    STRING('Modem Port  :'),HUE(11,1)
                COL(19) MENU(@S4),USE(PORTSTR),HLP('PORT'), |
                  HUE(14,1),SEL(0,7),REQ
                COL(25)    STRING('COM1'),HUE(14,1),SEL(0,7)
                COL(30)    STRING('COM2'),HUE(14,1),SEL(0,7)
                COL(35)    STRING('COM3'),HUE(14,1),SEL(0,7)
                COL(40)    STRING('COM4'),HUE(14,1),SEL(0,7)
                        END!MENU
        END!SCREEN

EJECT
CODE
GET(PARMS,1)                                   !GET THE PORT RECORD
IF ERROR() THEN ADD(PARMS).                    !IF NO RECORDS THEN ADD ONE
OPEN(PARMS_SCRN)                               !OPEN THE ENTRY SCREEN
```

(continued)

```
ALERT()                                  !TURN OFF ALL ALERT KEYS
ALERT(ESC_KEY)                           !SENSITIZE ESCAPE KEY
ALERT(ENTER_KEY)                         !SENSITIZE ENTER KEY
DISPLAY(?PORTSTR)                        !DISPLAY CURRENT PORT
LOOP                                     !MAIN LOOP
  ACCEPT                                 ! ACCEPT FIELD
  UPDATE                                 ! UPDATE WITH NEW VALUE
  IF KEYCODE() = ESC_KEY THEN BREAK.     ! EXIT ON ESCAPE KEY
  CASE PORTSTR                           ! CHECK PORT SELECTION
    OF 'COM1'                            !   IF 'COM1'
      PRM:PORT = '0'                     !     SET PORT = 0
    OF 'COM2'                            !   OR IF 'COM2'
      PRM:PORT = '1'                     !     SET PORT = 1
    OF 'COM3'                            !   OR IF 'COM3'
      PRM:PORT = '2'                     !     SET PORT = 2
    OF 'COM4'                            !   OR IF 'COM4'
      PRM:PORT = '3'                     !     SET PORT = 3
  END!CASE                               ! TERMINATE THE CASE STATEMENT
  IF KEYCODE() = ENTER_KEY               ! SAVE TO FILE
    PUT(PARMS)                           ! PLACE THE PARAMETERS
    BREAK                                ! BREAK OUT OF LOOP
  END!IF                                 ! TERMINATE THE IF STATEMENT
END!LOOP                                 !TERMINATE THE LOOP
CLOSE(PARMS_SCRN)                        !CLOSE SCREEN
RETURN                                   !GO BACK TO MENU PROCEDURE


DELAY_TIME FUNCTION(START_TIME,ELAPSE)   !COUNTS A DELAY

START_TIME    EXTERNAL                   !BEGINNING TIME
ELAPSE        EXTERNAL                   !TIME TO WAIT (IN SECS)
TIME_HUN      LONG(0)                    !TIME TO WAIT IN 100ths OF SEC
CURR_TIME     LONG(0)                    !CURRENT TIME
DONE_TIME     LONG(0)                    !FINISH TIME

  CODE
  TIME_HUN  = ELAPSE * 100               !CONVERT ELAPSE TIME INTO 100s
  DONE_TIME = START_TIME + TIME_HUN      !CALCULATE FINISH TIME
  IF DONE_TIME > 8640000                 !IF NEW TIME EXCEEDS MIDNIGHT
    DONE_TIME -= 8640000                 !  ADJUST NEW TIME
  .                                      !END IF
  CURR_TIME = CLOCK()                    !GET CURRENT TIME
  IF (CURR_TIME > DONE_TIME) AND |       !IF CURRENT TIME > DONE TIME
      NOT (DONE_TIME <= TIME_HUN AND |
      CURR_TIME > 10000)
    RETURN(1)                            !  RETURN TRUE
  .                                      !END IF
  RETURN(0)                              !RETURN FALSE
```

(continued)

```
CHECK_CHAR    PROCEDURE                    !READS THE BUFFER FOR RESPONSE

TEMPBUF       STRING(10)                   !READ/WRITE 10 CHARS
READY_MASK    EQUATE(00000010B)            !   MORE CHARS READY TO BE READ
BUFFERSTAT    LONG(0)                      !   BUFFER STATUS
BUFFERCNT     LONG(0)                      !   CHARACTERS IN BUFFER COUNT
CHAR_GRP      GROUP                        !SINGLE CHARACTER GROUP
CHAR            BYTE                       !   CHAR FROM COM PORT
              .                            !   END OF GROUP


  CODE
  LOOP                                     !BEGIN READING LOOP
    BUFFERSTAT = BUFFERSTATUS(PORT)        ! GET BUFFER STATUS
    BUFFERCNT = BSHIFT(BUFFERSTAT,-16)     ! GET BUFFER COUNT
    IF BAND(BUFFERSTAT,READY_MASK)         ! IF CHAR(S) READY
       RECVBLOCK(TEMPBUF,BUFFERCNT)        !    RECEIVE BLOCK
       POS# = INSTRING('OK',TEMPBUF,1)     !    FIND MODEM RESPONSE
       IF NOT POS#                         !    IF NO CHARACTERS
          CYCLE                            !       RESTART LOOP
       ELSE                                !    OR
          MEM:MESSAGE = 'READY'            !       SET MESSAGE TO READY
          BREAK                            !       BREAK OUT OF LOOP
       END!IF                              !    TERMINATE THE IF
    ELSE                                   ! OR
       RETURN                              !    GO BACK TO DIALER
    END!IF                                 ! TERMINATE THE IF STRUCTURE
  END!LOOP                                 !TERMINATE THE LOOP STRUCTURE
  CLEAR(TEMPBUF)                           !CLEAR OUT THE BUFFER
```

Chapter 20

The Data Base Three LEM

dBASE and Clarion File Structures

As we covered in Chapter 16 in more detail, dBASE became somewhat of a standard for the PC in the early part of the 1980s. As a result, quite a few applications out there are written in dBASE. Whether your company has data stored in the dBASE format or if you were called in to upgrade a client's system, you may need to access the database files in their native dBASE format. However, you may want to perform other tasks with an application that you can write more efficiently in Clarion. That is where the Data Base Three LEM comes in handy. It is not required for simple one-way file conversions where you only need to transfer the data from the dBASE format into Clarion format (or vice versa) where it will stay. The Data Base Three LEM is much better suited to the situation where you have two applications, one written in dBASE and the other in Clarion, sitting side by side, and you want to continue to use both—passing data back and forth between them.

Data File Structures

One distinct advantage that Clarion possesses over dBASE is its ability to allow a programmer to sit down and write out a data file definition. That is something you simply cannot do in dBASE. You must use the development facilities to create the binary database definition and distribute that with your application. You can view the data file structure in dBASE, but there is no equivalent to the code from Clarion's data file definition in Figure 20-1. The closest you can come in dBASE to a structure view, as shown in the Clarion file definition in Figure 20-1, appears in Figure 20-2.

To integrate the dBASE and Clarion file systems, Clarion created the MKGRP program. This program reads the data and the index files from dBASE that you indicate and *creates* a Clarion-like file structure, except it is in dBASE format. The one and only screen from the MKGRP program appears in Figure 20-3.

The example in Figure 20-3 uses the primary customer data file from the Telemagic software—a popular sales and lead-tracking application written in dBASE. We'll use that data file as the example throughout this chapter to show how you could run a Clarion application and a dBASE application side by side without a hitch. (The entire source code for the Telemagic Data Access Program appears at the end of this chapter.)

> ### WARNING
> **If you plan to operate both a Clarion application and the original dBASE application concurrently, you must make absolutely certain that you update *all* the dBASE index files whenever you perform an edit of the data files. One way to avoid trouble is to set up the Clarion application as read-only, which ensures that the index files on the dBASE side retain their integrity.**

Now you have the opportunity to read the index files for this dBASE file. You can read all or any combination of the index files associated with that

Figure 20-1   A Clarion file definition.

```
FILES     FILE,PRE(FIL),CREATE,RECLAIM
BY_NUMBER  KEY(FIL:NUMBER,FIL:FILENAME),DUP,NOCASE,OPT
BY_FILENAME KEY(FIL:FILENAME),DUP,NOCASE,OPT
RECORD      RECORD
NUMBER        STRING(@N_4)
TIME          STRING(@T1)
DATE          STRING(@d1)
SIZEBYTES     LONG
FILENAME      STRING(12)
NOTES         STRING(28)
            . .
```

Figure 20-2   A listing of a dBASE file structure that is not program code.

```
Structure for database: C:DBDATA.dbf
Number of data records:      10
Date of last update   : 09/01/90
Field Field Name  Type           Width     Dec
    1 FIRST       Character         10
    2 LAST        Character         20
    3 PHONE       Numeric           12
**Total**                          42
```

database. You do not have to locate and convert all of them unless you plan to perform edits concurrently with the original system. For incremental transfers, report writing, or other nonediting functions, you need only convert the index files that you will be using to look through the data.

Key and Index

With the advent of dBASE IV, Ashton-Tate added a dynamically updated key very like Clarion's key. However, dBASE III PLUS and earlier versions did

Figure 20-3   The MKRGP program after reading the customer file from the Telemagic sales tracking software.

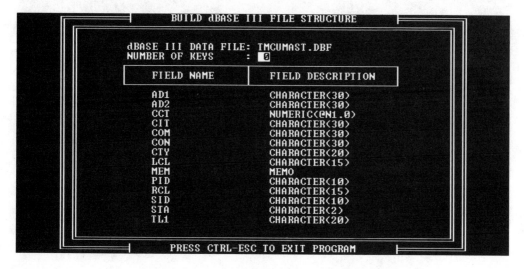

not sport that advantage. dBASE operated with an index file (.NDX) that required code to be written to update all the indexes after an edit. The MKGRP program pictured in Figure 20-4 is shown converting one of those indexes into a Clarion-style key file definition. The resulting database definition from the running of the MKGRP program appears in Figure 20-5.

Notice how the variables in Figure 20-5 from the dBASE file have all been recast in Clarion variable format. dBASE Character Fields are now Clarion STRINGs. dBASE Numeric Fields are now Clarion String Fields formatted with numeric pictures. dBASE Logical Fields are converted into Clarion String Fields with one character.

> ### *WARNING*
> It is possible to attempt conversions on "dBASE" file formats other than those produced by an Ashton-Tate product. For instance, the Clipper environment from Nantucket Software uses an index file that carries an extension of .NTX. Clipper index files can be successfully run through the MKGRP program, but the dBASE III Clarion statements will not work properly on the resulting file structure. The file can be read, but there is no way to update the index files properly. Examine the file created from the Clipper version of the index file in Figure 20-6.

Figure 20-4   The MKGRP program converting a dBASE index file.

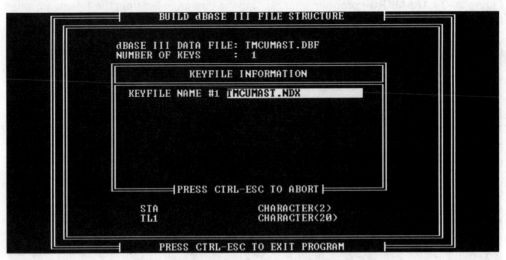

Figure 20-5   The Clarion version of the dBASE record structure for the primary customer data file for Telemagic.

```
TMCUMAST       GROUP,PRE(TMC)            !dBASE GROUP STRUCTURE
DBSIG          BYTE(3)                   !dBASE III GROUP SIGNATURE
DBFILENAME     STRING('TMCUMAST.DBF')
               STRING(66) ; STRING('<0>')   !dBASE III FILENAME
DBFCB          BYTE,DIM(97)              !dBASE FILE CONTROL  BLOCK
DBSIZE         SHORT(720)                !SIZE OF GROUP STRUCTURE
DBNUMKEYS      BYTE(1)                   !NUMBER OF KEYS
KEY1           STRING('TMCUMAST.NDX')
               STRING(66) ; STRING('<0>')   !dBASE III INDEX
!--KEY1 = 'PID+SID'
KEY1TYPE       STRING('C')               !KEYTYPE
KEY1LEN        BYTE(20)                  !LENGTH OF KEY
KEY1NEW        STRING(20)                !NEW KEY VALUE
KEY1OLD        STRING(20)                !OLD KEY VALUE
DBRECORD       GROUP                     !dBASE FILE RECORD
DELETED         STRING(1)                !RECORD DELETE MARKER
PID             STRING(10)               !CHARACTER FIELD
SID             STRING(10)               !CHARACTER FIELD
CON             STRING(30)               !CHARACTER FIELD
COM             STRING(30)               !CHARACTER FIELD
AD1             STRING(30)               !CHARACTER FIELD
AD2             STRING(30)               !CHARACTER FIELD
CIT             STRING(30)               !CHARACTER FIELD
STA             STRING(2)                !CHARACTER FIELD
ZIP             STRING(10)               !CHARACTER FIELD
CTY             STRING(20)               !CHARACTER FIELD
TL1             STRING(20)               !CHARACTER FIELD
TL2             STRING(20)               !CHARACTER FIELD
LCL             STRING(15)               !CHARACTER FIELD
RCL             STRING(15)               !CHARACTER FIELD
US1             STRING(20)               !CHARACTER FIELD
US2             STRING(20)               !CHARACTER FIELD
US3             STRING(20)               !CHARACTER FIELD
US4             STRING(20)               !CHARACTER FIELD
US5             STRING(20)               !CHARACTER FIELD
US6             STRING(20)               !CHARACTER FIELD
```

(continued)

Figure 20-5 *continued*

```
US7              STRING(20)              !CHARACTER FIELD
MEM              STRING(4)               !MEMO FIELD
CCT              STRING(@N-_2.0)         !NUMERIC FIELD
          . .                            !END OF GROUP STRUCTURE
```

Notice how the field sizes in the record all match the ones in Figure 20-6, but that the key definitions are different. This allows you to read the data file in record sequence as easily as with native dBASE, but it will completely frustrate your attempts to update the keys properly using the statements in the Data Base Three LEM. (That does not preclude you from using the LEM Maker to create your own statements to fit an environment like Clipper, although the effort involved in such an undertaking might be considerable.)

One of the issues involved with handling dBASE files is the maintenance of the key files. Clarion developers could have handled these updates in the background as they do the updating of their own key files. However, they elected, when constructing this LEM, to make that a task for the Clarion programmer. You can access dBASE files in record sequence without access to one of the key files. Leaving the DB3SETDELETE statement unset (the default is to read deleted records) and accessing in record sequence is the fastest possible combination for displaying records that you can display in what looks like a normal Clarion table, as shown in Figure 20-7.

When you are accessing the file in key sequence, two pieces to a dBASE III key require updating: KEYnOLD and KEYnNEW. These two fields must be initialized when you want to use the key to access the file. In Clarion, it works a little differently. If you used two fields to define a two-part key, say, FIRST_NAME and LAST_NAME, initializing those two fields allows you to use the key to access the file. This is not true when you are using the Data Base Three LEM. All the fields in the record may contain data, but if you did not set the KEYnOLD and KEYnNEW values, your attempt to access the file using the key will be thwarted.

When you orient the key or the data file by pointer, there is no need to address the issue of setting the Key Fields. However, when you use the key values themselves or issue any form of the DB3GET statement or the DB3NEXT and DB3PREVIOUS statements, you must initialize those Key Fields. Generally, you must set KEYnNEW before any statement that performs an "absolute" operation on the data file using the key. You must

Figure 20-6   The Clarion version of the Telemagic customer file built with the Clipper index file.

```
TMCUMAST        GROUP,PRE(TMC)                  !dBASE GROUP STRUCTURE
DBSIG             BYTE(3)                       !dBASE III GROUP SIGNATURE
DBFILENAME        STRING('TMCUMAST.DBF')
                  STRING(66) ; STRING('<0>')    !dBASE III FILENAME
DBFCB             BYTE,DIM(97)                  !dBASE FILE CONTROL  BLOCK
DBSIZE            SHORT(736)                    !SIZE OF GROUP STRUCTURE
DBNUMKEYS         BYTE(1)                       !NUMBER OF KEYS
KEY1              STRING('PID.NTX')
                  STRING(71) ; STRING('<0>')    !dBASE III INDEX
!--KEY1 = 'D+SID'
KEY1TYPE          STRING('C')                   !KEYTYPE
KEY1LEN           BYTE(28)                      !LENGTH OF KEY
KEY1NEW           STRING(28)                    !NEW KEY VALUE
KEY1OLD           STRING(28)                    !OLD KEY VALUE
DBRECORD          GROUP                         !dBASE FILE RECORD
DELETED            STRING(1)                    !RECORD DELETE MARKER
PID                STRING(10)                   !CHARACTER FIELD
SID                STRING(10)                   !CHARACTER FIELD
CON                STRING(30)                   !CHARACTER FIELD
COM                STRING(30)                   !CHARACTER FIELD
AD1                STRING(30)                   !CHARACTER FIELD
AD2                STRING(30)                   !CHARACTER FIELD
CIT                STRING(30)                   !CHARACTER FIELD
STA                STRING(2)                    !CHARACTER FIELD
ZIP                STRING(10)                   !CHARACTER FIELD
CTY                STRING(20)                   !CHARACTER FIELD
TL1                STRING(20)                   !CHARACTER FIELD
TL2                STRING(20)                   !CHARACTER FIELD
LCL                STRING(15)                   !CHARACTER FIELD
RCL                STRING(15)                   !CHARACTER FIELD
US1                STRING(20)                   !CHARACTER FIELD
US2                STRING(20)                   !CHARACTER FIELD
US3                STRING(20)                   !CHARACTER FIELD
US4                STRING(20)                   !CHARACTER FIELD
US5                STRING(20)                   !CHARACTER FIELD
```

(continued)

Figure 20-6   *continued*

```
US6                STRING(20)              !CHARACTER FIELD
US7                STRING(20)              !CHARACTER FIELD
MEM                STRING(4)               !MEMO FIELD
CCT                STRING(@N-_2.0)         !NUMERIC FIELD
          . .                              !END OF GROUP STRUCTURE
```

initialize the values in KEYnOLD after any operation that actually brought a
record into memory. In other words, if you plan to locate a value based on
user input, or a selection, or by setting a variable in another way, you must set
KEYnNEW. If you bring a record into memory that might be changed, you
must set KEYnOLD. For instance, a common file access sequence in Clarion
is to SET the pointer by a key and then issue a NEXT or PREVIOUS. In the
Data Base Three LEM, the construction must look like this:

```
KEYnNEW = "EXISTING_CONTENTS_OF_KEY_FIELD_VALUE"
DB3SET(FILE,KEYn)
DB3NEXT(FILE)
KEYnOLD = "NEW_CONTENTS OF KEY_FIELD_VALUE"
```

Figure 20-7   **A table display of records read directly from a dBASE file.**

The idea is to retain a copy of the "old" value in the key to locate that old record. A value becomes "old" when another value for the same field is brought into memory. That means that a value that was entered by the user becomes the old value when the next action is to read a record from the same data file into memory.

Hint: While the DB3GET and DB3SET statements implicitly open a pre-viously closed dBASE data file, the files are never implicitly closed as with regular Clarion. You most close them yourself.

Differences in Memo Processing

As with Clarion, the dBASE Memo Field is stored in a separate file with a .DBT file extension, whereas Clarion uses .MEM. In the translated dBASE record structure, the Memo Field is tied to the record with a pointer stored in the Memo String Field. (When you replace the Memo Field onto the disk, you must update the entire record before the link is established between the memo file and the record data file.)

You must explicitly call the memo file to retrieve the contents of the memo for processing. All the interfacing between the application and the memo file in Clarion's access to dBASE memos is done through a temporary file because dBASE memo storage is not terribly efficient. When you change the contents of a Memo Field, the old version is retained and the new data are written to the next available 512-byte block and identified with the next number in a sequence. In fact, the only way to recover segments of the memo file that were superseded is to use the dBASE COPY TO command at the dBASE dot prompt. The DB3GET_MEMO statement reads the memo into a temporary file, which can then be edited and replaced with DB3PUT_MEMO (which must be followed immediately with an update of the entire record). When you create a new record with a new Memo Field in it, you must create the file format of the DBASEDIT.TMP file from a DOS record structure, perform the edit, and then use the DB3PUT_MEMO to write the memo to the disk as pictured in Figure 20-8.

To edit the memos, the Telemagic Conversion program uses the Editor tool with Clarion Professional. The RUN statement is used to load the second copy of the DOS command processor. Then you run the Editor with the name of the temporary file that DB3GET_MEMO creates when you retrieve the dBASE memo based on the pointer that exists in the Memo Field in each dBASE record. Figure 20-9 demonstrates how to start that editing process from within an application.

Figure 20-8   The dBASE editing process.

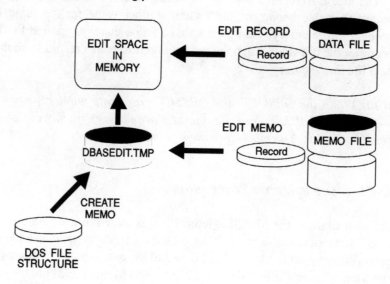

Converting Records

It is not necessary to resort to the Data Base Three LEM to automate the movement of records from a dBASE file to a Clarion file. You can use the Converter tool to make the transfer.

Hint: You can strip out the Memo Fields from the data if want to transport the data separately by using the Converter. You will get the String Field with the number of the Memo Field that points to the associated location in the memo data file.

Figure 20-9   Editing dBASE Memo Fields from inside a Clarion application.

```
IF KEYCODE( ) = F10_KEY              !ON THE HOT KEY PRESS
    DB3GET_MEMO(TMCUMAST, 'MEM')     !RETRIEVE THE MEMO TEXT
    OPEN(MEMOSCR)                    !SAVE THE EXISTING VIDEO
    RUN('CEDT DBASEDIT.TMP')         !RUN EDITOR ON TEMP FILE
    CLOSE(MEMOSCR)                   !RESTORE UNDERLYING SCREEN
END!IF
```

Figure 20-10   Transporting a single record from the customer file to a Clarion file.

```
IF KEYCODE( ) = F10_KEY              !ON HOT KEY PRESS
    DO GET_RECORD                    !READ THE DBASE RECORD
    TMG:RECORD = TMC:DBRECORD        !MOVE TO CLARION STRUCTURE
    ADD(TMAGIC)                      !ADD TO CLARION FILE
    CONVERTED                        !RUN CLARION TABLE PROC
    CYCLE                            !START OVER
END!IF



GET_RECORD ROUTINE                   !GET SELECTED RECORD
    GET(TABLE,NDX)                   !GET MEMORY TABLE ENTRY
    DB3SET(TMCUMAST,TBL:PTR)         !FIND THE DBASE RECORD
    DB3NEXT(TMCUMAST)                !GET THE DBASE RECORD
```

However, it is sometimes convenient to allow the user to selectively transport records from the dBASE file into a Clarion file—a move not possible in Converter because it converts the whole file. Figure 20-10 demonstrates the interplay between the dBASE III statements for accessing dBASE files and bridging the gap to Clarion files through an exchange in memory.

 Hint: If you use a LOOP UNTIL EOF( ) statement to read through a file and you use DB3GET to read the records, the process will not stop at the end of the file. It will continue to run. Use the DB3NEXT command to read the record—the normal end of file marker will be read and the loop will terminate.

You could also use the procedures in Figure 20-11 to convert the data in the files all at once just like the Converter in the Clarion environment. The code in Figure 20-11 loops through the dBASE file, reading each record in record sequence, and then transfers it to the Clarion structure. Notice the comment for where the filter would reside. You could allow the user to set that filter from inside the application in using this procedure to transfer only part of the data in the dBASE file. You could use this, slightly modified, to perform a mail merge process, also.

Figure 20-11   A mass conversion program for a mass transfer from a dBASE file to a Clarion file.

```
CODE
OPEN(SCREEN)                        !OPEN THE STATUS SCREEN
TOTAL = DB3RECORDS(TMCUMAST)        !GET THE TOTAL NUMBER OF DBASE RECS
DB3SET(TMCUMAST,1)                  !START WITH THE FIRST DBASE RECORD
LOOP UNTIL DB3EOF(TMCUMAST)         !PROCESS TO END OF DBASE FILE
   DB3NEXT(TMCUMAST)                !READ THE NEXT DBASE RECORD
   COUNT += 1                       !POST RECORD COUNTER
                                    ! **COULD PUT FILTER HERE**
   TMG:RECORD = TMC:DBRECORD        !TRANSFER THE RECORDS ONLY
   ADD(TMAGIC)                      !ADD TO THE CLARION FILE
END!LOOP
RETURN
```

Summary

In this chapter we talked about the crucial issues involved in the access of dBASE files in their native format through the Data Base Three Language Extension Module. As an example of the format and because you might want to run a program alongside Telemagic, we used Telemagic's dBASE file format to create the examples. The dBASE format can be converted using the MKGRP program that comes with the Data Base Three LEM. By including in your application the structure that program produces, you have the handle you need to use the Data Base Three statement tools to treat the file practically like a native Clarion tool. Finally, we looked at ways to convert the native dBASE format in both an incremental fashion and as one automated loop through the entire file.

The TELEMAGIC DATA ACCESS Program

MAGCREAD.CLA

```
MAGCREAD   PROGRAM
              INCLUDE('STD_KEYS.CLA')
              INCLUDE('CTL_KEYS.CLA')
              INCLUDE('ALT_KEYS.CLA')
              INCLUDE('SHF_KEYS.CLA')

REJECT_KEY    EQUATE(CTRL_ESC)
ACCEPT_KEY    EQUATE(CTRL_ENTER)
TRUE          EQUATE(1)
FALSE         EQUATE(0)

              MAP
                PROC(G_OPENFILES)
                MODULE('MAGCREA1')
                  PROC(MAIN)                      !TELEMAGIC EDITING SYSTEM
                  .
                MODULE('MAGCREA2')
                  PROC(CONVERTED)                 !Records Transferred From TM
                  .
                MODULE('MAGCREA3')
                  PROC(NEW)                       !Update Records from Telemagic
                  .
                MODULE('MAGCREA4')
                  PROC(DBASENEW)                  !Update Records from Telemagic
                  .
                MODULE('MASS')
                  PROC(MASS)                      !Transfer TM data to Clarion
                  .
                MODULE('REPORT')
                  PROC(REPORT)                    !Print Directly From Telemagic
                  .
                MODULE('TELEMAGC')
                  PROC(TELEMAGIC)                 !Access Telemagic Records
                  .
                INCLUDE('DBIII.CPY')
                  .

              INCLUDE('TMCUMAST.GRP')

              EJECT('FILE LAYOUTS')
TMAGIC     FILE,NAME('C:TMAGIC'),PRE(TMG),CREATE
```

(continued)

```
BY_PID      KEY(TMG:PID),DUP,NOCASE,OPT
BY_SID      KEY(TMG:SID),DUP,NOCASE,OPT
BY_GROUP    KEY(TMG:NAME),DUP,NOCASE,OPT
RECORD      RECORD
NAME          GROUP                           !Telemagic ID group
PID             STRING(10)
SID             STRING(10)
              .
CON           STRING(30)
COM           STRING(30)
AD1           STRING(30)
AD2           STRING(30)
CIT           STRING(30)
STA           STRING(2)
ZIP           STRING(10)
CTY           STRING(20)
TL1           STRING(20)
TL2           STRING(20)
LCL           STRING(15)
RCL           STRING(15)
US1           STRING(20)
US2           STRING(20)
US3           STRING(20)
US4           STRING(20)
US5           STRING(20)
US6           STRING(20)
US7           STRING(20)
MEM           STRING(10)
CCT           REAL
            . .


NOTES       FILE,PRE(NTS),CREATE,RECLAIM
BY_GROUP      KEY(NTS:NAME),DUP,NOCASE,OPT
MEMOS         MEMO(30000)                     !Telemagic Memo Field
RECORD        RECORD
NAME            GROUP                         !Group of PID and SID
PID               STRING(10)                  !Telemagic Primary ID
SID               STRING(10)                  !Telemagic Secondary ID
              . .
              GROUP,OVER(NTS:MEMOS)
NTS_MEMO_ROW STRING(50),DIM(600)
              .

              EJECT('GLOBAL MEMORY VARIABLES')
ACTION        SHORT                           !0 = NO ACTION
                                              !1 = ADD RECORD
```

(continued)

```
                                       !2 = CHANGE RECORD
                                       !3 = DELETE RECORD
                                       !4 = LOOKUP FIELD



          GROUP,PRE(MEM)
MESSAGE     STRING(30)                  !Global Message Area
PAGE        SHORT                       !Report Page Number
LINE        SHORT                       !Report Line Number
DEVICE      STRING(30)                  !Report Device Name
            .


          EJECT('CODE SECTION')
  CODE
  SETHUE(7,0)                           !SET WHITE ON BLACK
  BLANK                                 !  AND BLANK
  G_OPENFILES                           !OPEN OR CREATE FILES
  SETHUE()                              !    THE SCREEN
  MAIN                                  !TELEMAGIC EDITING SYSTEM
  RETURN                                !EXIT TO DOS

G_OPENFILES  PROCEDURE                  !OPEN FILES & CHECK FOR ERROR
  CODE
  SHOW(25,1,CENTER('OPENING FILE: ' & 'TMAGIC',80)) !DISPLAY FILE NAME
  OPEN(TMAGIC)                          !OPEN THE FILE
  IF ERROR()                            !OPEN RETURNED AN ERROR
    CASE ERRORCODE()                    ! CHECK FOR SPECIFIC ERROR
    OF 46                               !  KEYS NEED TO BE REQUILT
      SETHUE(0,7)                       !  BLACK ON WHITE
      SHOW(25,1,CENTER('REBUILDING KEY FILES FOR TMAGIC',80)) !INDICATE MSG
      BUILD(TMAGIC)                     !  CALL THE BUILD PROCEDURE
      SETHUE(7,0)                       !  WHITE ON BLACK
      BLANK(25,1,1,80)                  !  BLANK THE MESSAGE
    OF 2                                !IF NOT FOUND,
      CREATE(TMAGIC)                    ! CREATE
    ELSE                                ! ANY OTHER ERROR
      LOOP;STOP('TMAGIC: ' & ERROR()).  !  STOP EXECUTION
  . .

  SHOW(25,1,CENTER('OPENING FILE: ' & 'NOTES',80)) !DISPLAY FILE NAME
  OPEN(NOTES)                           !OPEN THE FILE
  IF ERROR()                            !OPEN RETURNED AN ERROR
    CASE ERRORCODE()                    ! CHECK FOR SPECIFIC ERROR
    OF 46                               !  KEYS NEED TO BE REQUILT
      SETHUE(0,7)                       !  BLACK ON WHITE
      SHOW(25,1,CENTER('REBUILDING KEY FILES FOR NOTES',80)) !INDICATE MSG
```

(continued)

```
    BUILD(NOTES)                        !  CALL THE BUILD PROCEDURE
    SETHUE(7,0)                         !  WHITE ON BLACK
    BLANK(25,1,1,80)                    !  BLANK THE MESSAGE
  OF 2                                  !IF NOT FOUND,
    CREATE(NOTES)                       !  CREATE
  ELSE                                  !  ANY OTHER ERROR
    LOOP;STOP('NOTES: ' & ERROR()).     !  STOP EXECUTION
 . .


    BLANK                               !BLANK THE SCREEN
```

MAGCREA1.CLA

```
          MEMBER('MAGCREAD')
MAIN          PROCEDURE

SCREEN        SCREEN      PRE(SCR),WINDOW(15,54),HUE(15,1)
          ROW(2,15)   PAINT(1,26),HUE(14,0)
          ROW(1,1)    STRING('<201,205{52},187>')
          ROW(2,1)    REPEAT(13);STRING('<186,0{52},186>') .
          ROW(15,1)   STRING('<200,205{52},188>')
          ROW(2,16)   STRING('TELEMAGIC EDITING SYSTEM')
          ROW(14,5)   STRING('TELEMAGIC is a trademark of Remote Control,Inc.')
                      ENTRY,USE(?FIRST_FIELD)
                      ENTRY,USE(?PRE_MENU)
                      MENU,USE(MENU_FIELD"),REQ
          ROW(5,15)   STRING('Access Telemagic Names File'),SEL(0,7)
          ROW(7,15)   STRING('Mass Convert Telemagic Data'),SEL(0,7)
          ROW(9,18)   STRING('Print Telemagic Data'),SEL(0,7)
          ROW(11,26)  STRING('QUIT'),SEL(0,7)
                .           .

   EJECT
   CODE
   OPEN(SCREEN)                         !OPEN THE MENU SCREEN
   SETCURSOR                            !TURN OFF ANY CURSOR
   MENU_FIELD" = ''                     !START MENU WITH FIRST ITEM
   LOOP                                 !LOOP UNTIL USER EXITS
     ALERT                              !TURN OFF ALL ALERTED KEYS
     ALERT(REJECT_KEY)                  !ALERT SCREEN REJECT KEY
     ALERT(ACCEPT_KEY)                  !ALERT SCREEN ACCEPT KEY
     ACCEPT                             !READ A FIELD OR MENU CHOICE
     IF KEYCODE() = REJECT_KEY THEN RETURN.   !RETURN ON SCREEN REJECT

     IF KEYCODE() = ACCEPT_KEY          !ON SCREEN ACCEPT KEY
            .
```

(continued)

```
    UPDATE                                  ! MOVE ALL FIELDS FROM SCREEN
    SELECT(?)                               ! START WITH CURRENT FIELD
    SELECT                                  ! EDIT ALL FIELDS
    CYCLE                                   ! GO TO TOP OF LOOP
  .                                         !

  CASE FIELD()                            !JUMP TO FIELD EDIT ROUTINE
  OF ?FIRST_FIELD                         !FROM THE FIRST FIELD
    IF KEYCODE() = ESC_KEY THEN RETURN.   ! RETURN ON ESC KEY

  OF ?PRE_MENU                            !PRE MENU FIELD CONDITION
    IF KEYCODE() = ESC_KEY                ! BACKING UP?
      SELECT(?-1)                         !   SELECT PREVIOUS FIELD
    ELSE                                  ! GOING FORWARD
      SELECT(?+1)                         !   SELECT MENU FIELD
    .
  OF ?MENU_FIELD"                         !FROM THE MENU FIELD
    EXECUTE CHOICE()                      ! CALL THE SELECTED PROCEDURE
      TELEMAGIC                           ! Access Telemagic Records
      MASS                                ! Transfer TM data to Clarion
      REPORT                              ! Print Directly From Telemagic
      RETURN
  . . .
```

MAGCREA2.CLA

```
            MEMBER('MAGCREAD')
CONVERTED   PROCEDURE

SCREEN      SCREEN      PRE(SCR),WINDOW(22,76),AT(3,3),HUE(15,0)
            ROW(1,25)   PAINT(1,29),HUE(0,7)
            ROW(4,2)    PAINT(17,74),HUE(0,7)
            ROW(1,1)    STRING('<201,205{23},0{29},205{22},187>')
            ROW(2,1)    REPEAT(20);STRING('<186,0{74},186>') .
            ROW(22,1)   STRING('<200,205{74},188>')
            ROW(1,26)   STRING('Records Transferred From TM')
            ROW(2,10)   STRING('ID')
            ROW(3,3)    STRING('Primary & Secondary  Company {24}Telephone One')
            ROW(21,12)  STRING('<<INS> Insert   <<DEL> Delete  <<ENTER> Edit   ' |
                          & '<<ESC> Exit')
                          ENTRY,USE(?FIRST_FIELD)
                          ENTRY,USE(?PRE_POINT)
                          REPEAT(17),EVERY(1),INDEX(NDX)
            ROW(4,2)        POINT(1,74),USE(?POINT),ESC(?-1)
```

(continued)

```
ID              COL(3)        STRING(@s20)
COM             COL(24)       STRING(30)
TL1             COL(55)       STRING(20)
                    .              .

NDX             BYTE                                !REPEAT INDEX FOR POINT AREA
ROW             BYTE                                !ACTUAL ROW OF SCROLL AREA
COL             BYTE                                !ACTUAL COLUMN OF SCROLL AREA
COUNT           BYTE(17)                            !NUMBER OF ITEMS TO SCROLL
ROWS            BYTE(17)                            !NUMBER OF ROWS TO SCROLL
COLS            BYTE(74)                            !NUMBER OF COLUMNS TO SCROLL
FOUND           BYTE                                !RECORD FOUND FLAG
NEWPTR          LONG                                !POINTER TO NEW RECORD

TABLE           TABLE,PRE(TBL)                      !TABLE OF RECORD DATA
ID              STRING(@s20)
COM             STRING(30)
TL1             STRING(20)
PID             STRING(10)
PTR             LONG                                !   POINTER TO FILE RECORD
                    .

    EJECT
    CODE
    ACTION# = ACTION                                !SAVE ACTION
    OPEN(SCREEN)                                    !OPEN THE SCREEN
    SETCURSOR                                       !TURN OFF ANY CURSOR
    TBL:PTR = 1                                     !START AT TABLE ENTRY
    NDX = 1                                         !PUT SELECTOR BAR ON TOP ITEM
    ROW = ROW(?POINT)                              !REMEMBER TOP ROW AND
    COL = COL(?POINT)                              !LEFT COLUMN OF SCROLL AREA
    RECORDS# = TRUE                                 !INITIALIZE RECORDS FLAG
    CACHE(TMG:BY_PID,.25)                           !CACHE KEY FILE
    IF ACTION = 4                                   !   TABLE LOOKUP REQUEST
      NEWPTR = POINTER(TMAGIC)                      !   SET POINTER TO RECORD
      IF NOT NEWPTR                                 !   RECORD NOT PASSED TO TABLE
        SET(TMG:BY_PID,TMG:BY_PID)                  !     POSITION TO CLOSEST RECORD
        NEXT(TMAGIC)                                !     READ RECORD
        NEWPTR = POINTER(TMAGIC)                    !     SET POINTER
        .
      DO FIND_RECORD                                !   POSITION FILE
    ELSE
      NDX = 1                                       !   PUT SELECTOR BAR ON TOP ITEM
      DO FIRST_PAGE                                 !   BUILD MEMORY TABLE OF KEYS
      .
    RECORDS# = TRUE                                 !   ASSUME THERE ARE RECORDS
    LOOP                                            !LOOP UNTIL USER EXITS
```

(continued)

```
ACTION = ACTION#                        !RESTORE ACTION
ALERT                                   !RESET ALERTED KEYS
ALERT(REJECT_KEY)                       !ALERT SCREEN REJECT KEY
ALERT(ACCEPT_KEY)                       !ALERT SCREEN ACCEPT KEY
ACCEPT                                  !READ A FIELD
IF KEYCODE() = REJECT_KEY THEN BREAK.   !RETURN ON SCREEN REJECT KEY

IF  KEYCODE() = ACCEPT_KEY       |      !ON SCREEN ACCEPT KEY
AND FIELD() <> ?POINT                   !BUT NOT ON THE POINT FIELD
  UPDATE                                !  MOVE ALL FIELDS FROM SCREEN
  SELECT(?)                             !  START WITH CURRENT FIELD
  SELECT                                !  EDIT ALL FIELDS
  CYCLE                                 !  GO TO TOP OF LOOP
.

CASE FIELD()                            !JUMP TO FIELD EDIT ROUTINE

OF ?FIRST_FIELD                         !FROM THE FIRST FIELD
  IF KEYCODE() = ESC_KEY       |        !  RETURN ON ESC KEY
  OR RECORDS# = FALSE                   !  OR NO RECORDS
    BREAK                               !    EXIT PROGRAM
  .
OF ?PRE_POINT                           !PRE POINT FIELD CONDITION
  IF KEYCODE() = ESC_KEY                !  BACKING UP?
    SELECT(?-1)                         !    SELECT PREVIOUS FIELD
  ELSE                                  !  GOING FORWARD
    SELECT(?POINT)                      !    SELECT MENU FIELD

OF ?POINT                               !PROCESS THE POINT FIELD
  IF RECORDS(TABLE) = 0                 !IF THERE ARE NO RECORDS
    CLEAR(TMG:RECORD)                   !  CLEAR RECORD AREA
    ACTION = 1                          !  SET ACTION TO ADD
    GET(TMAGIC,0)                       !  CLEAR PENDING RECORD
    NEW                                 !  CALL FORM FOR NEW RECORD
    NEWPTR = POINTER(TMAGIC)            !   SET POINTER TO NEW RECORD
    DO FIRST_PAGE                       !  DISPLAY THE FIRST PAGE
    IF RECORDS(TABLE) = 0               !  IF THERE AREN'T ANY RECORDS
      RECORDS# = FALSE                  !    INDICATE NO RECORDS
      SELECT(?PRE_POINT-1)              !    SELECT THE PRIOR FIELD
    .
    CYCLE                               !    AND LOOP AGAIN
  .
  CASE KEYCODE()                        !PROCESS THE KEYSTROKE

  OF INS_KEY                            !INS KEY
    CLEAR(TMG:RECORD)                   !  CLEAR RECORD AREA
    ACTION = 1                          !  SET ACTION TO ADD
```

(continued)

```
      GET(TMAGIC,0)                                ! CLEAR PENDING RECORD
      NEW                                          ! CALL FORM FOR NEW RECORD
      IF ~ACTION                                   ! IF RECORD WAS ADDED
        NEWPTR = POINTER(TMAGIC)                    !   SET POINTER TO NEW RECORD
        DO FIND_RECORD                             !   POSITION IN FILE
      .
   OF ENTER_KEY                                    !ENTER KEY
   OROF ACCEPT_KEY                                 !CTRL-ENTER KEY
      DO GET_RECORD                                !  GET THE SELECTED RECORD
      IF ACTION = 4 AND KEYCODE() = ENTER_KEY!   IF THIS IS A LOOKUP REQUEST
        ACTION = 0                                 !    SET ACTION TO COMPLETE
        BREAK                                      !    AND RETURN TO CALLER
      .
      IF ~ERROR()                                  !  IF RECORD IS STILL THERE
        ACTION = 2                                 !    SET ACTION TO CHANGE
      NEW                                          !    CALL FORM TO CHANGE REC
        IF ACTION THEN CYCLE.                      !    IF SUCCESSFUL RE-DISPLAY
      .
      NEWPTR = POINTER(TMAGIC)                      !    SET POINTER TO NEW RECORD
      DO FIND_RECORD                               !    POSITION IN FILE
   OF DEL_KEY                                      !DEL KEY
      DO GET_RECORD                                !  READ THE SELECTED RECORD
      IF ~ERROR()                                  !  IF RECORD IS STILL THERE
        ACTION = 3                                 !    SET ACTION TO DELETE
        NEW                                        !    CALL FORM TO DELETE
        IF ~ACTION                                 !    IF SUCCESSFUL
          N# = NDX                                 !      SAVE POINT INDEX
          DO SAME_PAGE                             !      RE-DISPLAY
          NDX = N#                                 !      RESTORE POINT INDEX
      . .
   OF DOWN_KEY                                     !DOWN ARROW KEY
      DO SET_NEXT                                  !  POINT TO NEXT RECORD
      DO FILL_NEXT                                 !  FILL A TABLE ENTRY
      IF FOUND                                     !  FOUND A NEW RECORD
        SCROLL(ROW,COL,ROWS,COLS,ROWS(?POINT))  !   SCROLL THE SCREEN UP
        GET(TABLE,RECORDS(TABLE))                 !  GET RECORD FROM TABLE
        DO FILL_SCREEN                            !  DISPLAY ON SCREEN
      .

   OF PGDN_KEY                                     !PAGE DOWN KEY
      DO SET_NEXT                                  !  POINT TO NEXT RECORD
      DO NEXT_PAGE                                 !  DISPLAY THE NEXT PAGE

   OF CTRL_PGDN                                    !CTRL-PAGE DOWN KEY
      DO LAST_PAGE                                 !  DISPLAY THE LAST PAGE
      NDX = RECORDS(TABLE)                         !  POSITION POINT BAR
```

(continued)

```
   OF UP_KEY                                  !UP ARROW KEY
      DO SET_PREV                             !  POINT TO PREVIOUS RECORD
      DO FILL_PREV                            !  FILL A TABLE ENTRY
      IF FOUND                                !  FOUND A NEW RECORD
         SCROLL(ROW,COL,ROWS,COLS,-(ROWS(?POINT)))! SCROLL THE SCREEN DOWN
         GET(TABLE,1)                         !  GET RECORD FROM TABLE
         DO FILL_SCREEN                       !  DISPLAY ON SCREEN
      .

   OF PGUP_KEY                                !PAGE UP KEY
      DO SET_PREV                             !  POINT TO PREVIOUS RECORD
      DO PREV_PAGE                            !  DISPLAY THE PREVIOUS PAGE

   OF CTRL_PGUP                               !CTRL-PAGE UP
      DO FIRST_PAGE                           !  DISPLAY THE FIRST PAGE
      NDX = 1                                 !  POSITION POINT BAR
 . . .
 FREE(TABLE)                                  !FREE MEMORY TABLE
 RETURN                                       !AND RETURN TO CALLER

SAME_PAGE ROUTINE                             !DISPLAY THE SAME PAGE
 GET(TABLE,1)                                 !  GET THE FIRST TABLE ENTRY
 DO FILL_RECORD                               !  FILL IN THE RECORD
 SET(TMG:BY_PID,TMG:BY_PID,TBL:PTR)           !  POSITION FILE
 FREE(TABLE)                                  !  EMPTY THE TABLE
 DO NEXT_PAGE                                 !  DISPLAY A FULL PAGE

FIRST_PAGE ROUTINE                            !DISPLAY FIRST PAGE
 BLANK(ROW,COL,ROWS,COLS)
 FREE(TABLE)                                  !  EMPTY THE TABLE
 CLEAR(TMG:RECORD,-1)                         !  CLEAR RECORD TO LOW VALUES
 CLEAR(TBL:PTR)                               !  ZERO RECORD POINTER
 SET(TMG:BY_PID)                              !  POINT TO FIRST RECORD
 LOOP NDX = 1 TO COUNT                        !  FILL UP THE TABLE
    DO FILL_NEXT                              !    FILL A TABLE ENTRY
    IF NOT FOUND THEN BREAK.                  !    GET OUT IF NO RECORD
    .
 NDX = 1                                      !  SET TO TOP OF TABLE
 DO SHOW_PAGE                                 !  DISPLAY THE PAGE

LAST_PAGE ROUTINE                             !DISPLAY LAST PAGE
 NDX# = NDX                                   !  SAVE SELECTOR POSITION
 BLANK(ROW,COL,ROWS,COLS)                     !  CLEAR SCROLLING AREA
 FREE(TABLE)                                  !  EMPTY THE TABLE
 CLEAR(TMG:RECORD,1)                          !  CLEAR RECORD TO HIGH VALUES
 CLEAR(TBL:PTR,1)                             !  CLEAR PTR TO HIGH VALUE
 SET(TMG:BY_PID)                              !  POINT TO FIRST RECORD
```

(continued)

```
  LOOP NDX = COUNT TO 1 BY -1                  ! FILL UP THE TABLE
    DO FILL_PREV                               !   FILL A TABLE ENTRY
    IF NOT FOUND THEN BREAK.                    !   GET OUT IF NO RECORD
  .                                            ! END OF LOOP
  NDX = NDX#                                    ! RESTORE SELECTOR POSITION
  DO SHOW_PAGE                                  ! DISPLAY THE PAGE


FIND_RECORD ROUTINE                            !POSITION TO SPECIFIC RECORD
  SET(TMG:BY_PID,TMG:BY_PID,NEWPTR)            !POSITION FILE
  IF NEWPTR = 0                                !NEWPTR NOT SET
    NEXT(TMAGIC)                               !   READ NEXT RECORD
    NEWPTR = POINTER(TMAGIC)                   !   SET NEWPTR
    SKIP(TMAGIC,-1)                            !   BACK UP TO DISPLAY RECORD
  .
  FREE(TABLE)                                   ! CLEAR THE RECORD
  DO NEXT_PAGE                                  ! DISPLAY A PAGE


NEXT_PAGE ROUTINE                              !DISPLAY NEXT PAGE
  SAVECNT# = RECORDS(TABLE)                    !   SAVE RECORD COUNT
  LOOP COUNT TIMES                             !   FILL UP THE TABLE
    DO FILL_NEXT                               !     FILL A TABLE ENTRY
    IF NOT FOUND                               !     IF NONE ARE LEFT
      IF NOT SAVECNT#                          !       IF REBUILDING TABLE
        DO LAST_PAGE                           !         FILL IN RECORDS
        EXIT                                   !         EXIT OUT OF ROUTINE
      .
      BREAK                                     !     EXIT LOOP
  . .
  DO SHOW_PAGE                                  !   DISPLAY THE PAGE


SET_NEXT ROUTINE                               !POINT TO THE NEXT PAGE
  GET(TABLE,RECORDS(TABLE))                    !   GET THE LAST TABLE ENTRY
  DO FILL_RECORD                               !   FILL IN THE RECORD
  SET(TMG:BY_PID,TMG:BY_PID,TBL:PTR)           !   POSITION FILE
  NEXT(TMAGIC)                                 !   READ THE CURRENT RECORD


FILL_NEXT ROUTINE                              !FILL NEXT TABLE ENTRY
  FOUND = FALSE                                !   ASSUME RECORD NOT FOUND
  LOOP UNTIL EOF(TMAGIC)                       !   LOOP UNTIL END OF FILE
    NEXT(TMAGIC)                               !     READ THE NEXT RECORD
    FOUND = TRUE                               !     SET RECORD FOUND
    DO FILL_TABLE                              !     FILL IN THE TABLE ENTRY
    ADD(TABLE)                                 !     ADD LAST TABLE ENTRY
    GET(TABLE,RECORDS(TABLE)-COUNT)            !     GET ANY OVERFLOW RECORD
    DELETE(TABLE)                              !     AND DELETE IT
    EXIT                                       !     RETURN TO CALLER
  .
```

(continued)

```
PREV_PAGE ROUTINE                             !DISPLAY PREVIOUS PAGE
   LOOP COUNT TIMES                           !  FILL UP THE TABLE
      DO FILL_PREV                            !     FILL A TABLE ENTRY
      IF NOT FOUND THEN BREAK.                !     GET OUT IF NO RECORD
      .
   DO SHOW_PAGE                               !  DISPLAY THE PAGE

SET_PREV ROUTINE                              !POINT TO PREVIOUS PAGE
   GET(TABLE,1)                               !  GET THE FIRST TABLE ENTRY
   DO FILL_RECORD                             !  FILL IN THE RECORD
   SET(TMG:BY_PID,TMG:BY_PID,TBL:PTR)         !  POSITION FILE
   PREVIOUS(TMAGIC)                           !  READ THE CURRENT RECORD

FILL_PREV ROUTINE                             !FILL PREVIOUS TABLE ENTRY
   FOUND = FALSE                              !  ASSUME RECORD NOT FOUND
   LOOP UNTIL BOF(TMAGIC)                     !  LOOP UNTIL BEGINNING OF FILE
      PREVIOUS(TMAGIC)                        !     READ THE PREVIOUS RECORD
      FOUND = TRUE                            !     SET RECORD FOUND
      DO FILL_TABLE                           !     FILL IN THE TABLE ENTRY
      ADD(TABLE,1)                            !     ADD FIRST TABLE ENTRY
      GET(TABLE,COUNT+1)                      !     GET ANY OVERFLOW RECORD
      DELETE(TABLE)                           !     AND DELETE IT
      EXIT                                    !     RETURN TO CALLER
      .
SHOW_PAGE ROUTINE                             !DISPLAY THE PAGE
   NDX# = NDX                                 !  SAVE SCREEN INDEX
   LOOP NDX = 1 TO RECORDS(TABLE)             !  LOOP THRU THE TABLE
      GET(TABLE,NDX)                          !     GET A TABLE ENTRY
      DO FILL_SCREEN                          !     AND DISPLAY IT
      IF TBL:PTR = NEWPTR                     !     SET INDEX FOR NEW RECORD
         NDX# = NDX                           !     POINT TO CORRECT RECORD
      . .
   NDX = NDX#                                 !  RESTORE SCREEN INDEX
   NEWPTR = 0                                 !  CLEAR NEW RECORD POINTER
   CLEAR(TMG:RECORD)                          !  CLEAR RECORD AREA

FILL_TABLE ROUTINE                            !MOVE FILE TO TABLE
   TBL:COM = TMG:COM
   TBL:TL1 = TMG:TL1
   TBL:PID = TMG:PID
   TBL:PTR = POINTER(TMAGIC)                  !  SAVE RECORD POINTER
   TBL:ID = clip(tmg:pid) & ' ' & clip(tMg:sid)

FILL_RECORD ROUTINE                           !MOVE TABLE TO FILE
   TMG:PID = TBL:PID

FILL_SCREEN ROUTINE                           !MOVE TABLE TO SCREEN
```

(continued)

```
SCR:ID = TBL:ID
SCR:COM = TBL:COM
SCR:TL1 = TBL:TL1


GET_RECORD ROUTINE                                    !GET SELECTED RECORD
  GET(TABLE,NDX)                                       !  GET TABLE ENTRY
  GET(TMAGIC,TBL:PTR)                                  !  GET THE RECORD
```

MAGCREA3.CLA

```
          MEMBER('MAGCREAD')
NEW          PROCEDURE

SCREEN       SCREEN        PRE(SCR),WINDOW(25,40),HUE(15,0)
             ROW(2,2)    PAINT(1,38),HUE(0,3)
             ROW(1,1)    STRING('<218,196{38},191>')
             ROW(2,1)    REPEAT(23);STRING('<179,0{38},179>')  .
             ROW(25,1)   STRING('<192,196{38},217>')
             ROW(2,7)    STRING('Update Records from Telemagic')
             ROW(4,4)    STRING('PID:')
             ROW(5,4)    STRING('SID:')
             ROW(6,4)    STRING('CON:')
             ROW(7,4)    STRING('COM:')
             ROW(8,4)    STRING('AD1:')
             ROW(9,4)    STRING('AD2:')
             ROW(10,4)   STRING('CIT:')
             ROW(11,4)   STRING('STA:')
             ROW(12,4)   STRING('ZIP:')
             ROW(13,4)   STRING('CTY:')
             ROW(14,4)   STRING('TL1:')
             ROW(15,4)   STRING('TL2:')
               COL(32)   STRING('<<F10>')
             ROW(16,4)   STRING('LCL:')
               COL(31)   STRING('TO EDIT')
             ROW(17,4)   STRING('RCL:')
               COL(32)   STRING('MEMOS')
             ROW(18,4)   STRING('US1:')
             ROW(19,4)   STRING('US2:')
             ROW(20,4)   STRING('US3:')
             ROW(21,4)   STRING('US4:')
             ROW(22,4)   STRING('US5:')
             ROW(23,4)   STRING('US6:')
MESSAGE      ROW(3,6)    STRING(30),HUE(7,0)
                         ENTRY,USE(?FIRST_FIELD)
             ROW(4,8)    ENTRY(@s10),USE(TMG:PID),LFT
```

(continued)

```
        ROW(5,8)    ENTRY(@s10),USE(TMG:SID),LFT
        ROW(6,8)    ENTRY(@s30),USE(TMG:CON),LFT
        ROW(7,8)    ENTRY(@s30),USE(TMG:COM),LFT
        ROW(8,8)    ENTRY(@s30),USE(TMG:AD1),LFT
        ROW(9,8)    ENTRY(@s30),USE(TMG:AD2),LFT
        ROW(10,8)   ENTRY(@s30),USE(TMG:CIT),LFT
        ROW(11,8)   ENTRY(@s2),USE(TMG:STA),LFT
        ROW(12,8)   ENTRY(@s10),USE(TMG:ZIP),LFT
        ROW(13,8)   ENTRY(@s20),USE(TMG:CTY),LFT
        ROW(14,8)   ENTRY(@s20),USE(TMG:TL1),LFT
        ROW(15,8)   ENTRY(@s20),USE(TMG:TL2),LFT
        ROW(16,8)   ENTRY(@s15),USE(TMG:LCL),LFT
        ROW(17,8)   ENTRY(@s15),USE(TMG:RCL),LFT
        ROW(18,8)   ENTRY(@s20),USE(TMG:US1),LFT
        ROW(19,8)   ENTRY(@s20),USE(TMG:US2),LFT
        ROW(20,8)   ENTRY(@s20),USE(TMG:US3),LFT
        ROW(21,8)   ENTRY(@s20),USE(TMG:US4),LFT
        ROW(22,8)   ENTRY(@s20),USE(TMG:US5),LFT
        ROW(23,8)   ENTRY(@s20),USE(TMG:US6),LFT
        ROW(24,10)  PAUSE('Press <<ENTER> to Accept'),USE(?PAUSE_FIELD)      |
                  HUE(31,0)
                    ENTRY,USE(?LAST_FIELD)
                    PAUSE(''),USE(?DELETE_FIELD)

    .

EJECT
CODE
OPEN(SCREEN)                              !OPEN THE SCREEN
SETCURSOR                                 !TURN OFF ANY CURSOR
DISPLAY                                   !DISPLAY THE FIELDS
LOOP                                      !LOOP THRU ALL THE FIELDS
  MEM:MESSAGE = CENTER(MEM:MESSAGE,SIZE(MEM:MESSAGE)) !DISPLAY ACTION MESSAGE
  DO CALCFIELDS                           !CALCULATE DISPLAY FIELDS
  ALERT                                   !RESET ALERTED KEYS
  ALERT(ACCEPT_KEY)                       !ALERT SCREEN ACCEPT KEY
  ALERT(REJECT_KEY)                       !ALERT SCREEN REJECT KEY
  ACCEPT                                  !READ A FIELD
  IF KEYCODE() = REJECT_KEY THEN RETURN.  !RETURN ON SCREEN REJECT KEY
  EXECUTE ACTION                          !SET MESSAGE
    MEM:MESSAGE = 'Record will be Added'  !
    MEM:MESSAGE = 'Record will be Changed' !
    MEM:MESSAGE = 'Press Enter to Delete' !
  .
  IF KEYCODE() = ACCEPT_KEY               !ON SCREEN ACCEPT KEY
    UPDATE                                !  MOVE ALL FIELDS FROM SCREEN
    SELECT(?)                             !  START WITH CURRENT FIELD
    SELECT                                !  EDIT ALL FIELDS
```

(continued)

```
      CYCLE                                          !  GO TO TOP OF LOOP
    .
    CASE FIELD()                                     !JUMP TO FIELD EDIT ROUTINE
    OF ?FIRST_FIELD                                  !FROM THE FIRST FIELD
      IF KEYCODE() = ESC_KEY THEN RETURN.            !  RETURN ON ESC KEY
      IF ACTION = 3 THEN SELECT(?DELETE_FIELD).      !  OR CONFIRM FOR DELETE

    OF ?PAUSE_FIELD                                  !ON PAUSE FIELD
      IF KEYCODE() <> ENTER_KEY|                     !IF NOT ENTER KEY
      AND KEYCODE() <> ACCEPT_KEY|                   !AND NOT CTRL-ENTER KEY
      AND KEYCODE() <> 0                             !AND NOT NONSTOP MODE
        BEEP                                         !  SOUND KEYBOARD ALARM
        SELECT(?PAUSE_FIELD)                         !  AND STAY ON PAUSE FIELD
    .
    OF ?LAST_FIELD                                   !FROM THE LAST FIELD
      EXECUTE ACTION                                 !  UPDATE THE FILE
        ADD(TMAGIC)                                  !    ADD NEW RECORD
        PUT(TMAGIC)                                  !    CHANGE EXISTING RECORD
        DELETE(TMAGIC)                               !    DELETE EXISTING RECORD
      .
      IF ERRORCODE() = 40                            !  DUPLICATE KEY ERROR
        MEM:MESSAGE = ERROR()                        !    DISPLAY ERR MESSAGE
        SELECT(2)                                    !    POSITION TO TOP OF FORM
        CYCLE                                        !    GET OUT OF EDIT LOOP
      ELSIF ERROR()                                  !  CHECK FOR UNEXPECTED ERROR
        STOP(ERROR())                                !    HALT EXECUTION
      .
      ACTION = 0                                     !  SET ACTION TO COMPLETE
      RETURN                                         !  AND RETURN TO CALLER

    OF ?DELETE_FIELD                                 !FROM THE DELETE FIELD
      IF KEYCODE() = ENTER_KEY |                     !  ON ENTER KEY
      OR KEYCODE() = ACCEPT_KEY                       !  OR CTRL-ENTER KEY
        SELECT(?LAST_FIELD)                          !    DELETE THE RECORD
      ELSE                                           !  OTHERWISE
        BEEP                                         !    BEEP AND ASK AGAIN
  . . .

CALCFIELDS  ROUTINE
  IF FIELD() > ?FIRST_FIELD                                    !BEYOND FIRST_FIELD?
    IF KEYCODE() = 0 AND SELECTED() > FIELD() THEN EXIT. !GET OUT IF NOT NONSTOP
  .
  SCR:MESSAGE = MEM:MESSAGE
```

MAGCREA4.CLA

```
              MEMBER('MAGCREAD')
DBASENEW      PROCEDURE

SCREEN        SCREEN        PRE(SCR),WINDOW(25,40),HUE(15,0)
              ROW(2,2)      PAINT(1,38),HUE(0,3)
              ROW(1,1)      STRING('<218,196{38},191>')
              ROW(2,1)      REPEAT(23);STRING('<179,0{38},179>') .
              ROW(25,1)     STRING('<192,196{38},217>')
              ROW(2,7)      STRING('Update Records from Telemagic')
              ROW(4,4)      STRING('PID:')
              ROW(5,4)      STRING('SID:')
              ROW(6,4)      STRING('CON:')
              ROW(7,4)      STRING('COM:')
              ROW(8,4)      STRING('AD1:')
              ROW(9,4)      STRING('AD2:')
              ROW(10,4)     STRING('CIT:')
              ROW(11,4)     STRING('STA:')
              ROW(12,4)     STRING('ZIP:')
              ROW(13,4)     STRING('CTY:')
              ROW(14,4)     STRING('TL1:')
              ROW(15,4)     STRING('TL2:')
               COL(32)      STRING('<<F10>')
              ROW(16,4)     STRING('LCL:')
               COL(31)      STRING('TO EDIT')
              ROW(17,4)     STRING('RCL:')
               COL(32)      STRING('MEMOS')
              ROW(18,4)     STRING('US1:')
              ROW(19,4)     STRING('US2:')
              ROW(20,4)     STRING('US3:')
              ROW(21,4)     STRING('US4:')
              ROW(22,4)     STRING('US5:')
              ROW(23,4)     STRING('US6:')
MESSAGE       ROW(3,6)      STRING(30),HUE(7,0)
                            ENTRY,USE(?FIRST_FIELD)
              ROW(4,8)      ENTRY(@s10),USE(TMC:PID),LFT
              ROW(5,8)      ENTRY(@s10),USE(TMC:SID),LFT
              ROW(6,8)      ENTRY(@s30),USE(TMC:CON),LFT
              ROW(7,8)      ENTRY(@s30),USE(TMC:COM),LFT
              ROW(8,8)      ENTRY(@s30),USE(TMC:AD1),LFT
              ROW(9,8)      ENTRY(@s30),USE(TMC:AD2),LFT
              ROW(10,8)     ENTRY(@s30),USE(TMC:CIT),LFT
              ROW(11,8)     ENTRY(@s2),USE(TMC:STA),LFT
              ROW(12,8)     ENTRY(@s10),USE(TMC:ZIP),LFT
              ROW(13,8)     ENTRY(@s20),USE(TMC:CTY),LFT
```

(continued)

```
          ROW(14,8)   ENTRY(@s20),USE(TMC:TL1),LFT
          ROW(15,8)   ENTRY(@s20),USE(TMC:TL2),LFT
          ROW(16,8)   ENTRY(@s15),USE(TMC:LCL),LFT
          ROW(17,8)   ENTRY(@s15),USE(TMC:RCL),LFT
          ROW(18,8)   ENTRY(@s20),USE(TMC:US1),LFT
          ROW(19,8)   ENTRY(@s20),USE(TMC:US2),LFT
          ROW(20,8)   ENTRY(@s20),USE(TMC:US3),LFT
          ROW(21,8)   ENTRY(@s20),USE(TMC:US4),LFT
          ROW(22,8)   ENTRY(@s20),USE(TMC:US5),LFT
          ROW(23,8)   ENTRY(@s20),USE(TMC:US6),LFT
          ROW(24,10) PAUSE('Press <<ENTER> to Accept'),USE(?PAUSE_FIELD)      |
                  HUE(31,0)
                     ENTRY,USE(?LAST_FIELD)
                     PAUSE(''),USE(?DELETE_FIELD)
                .


MEMOSCR  SCREEN         WINDOW(25,80),HUE(7,0)
           .


   EJECT
   CODE
   OPEN(SCREEN)                                   !OPEN THE SCREEN
   SETCURSOR                                      !TURN OFF ANY CURSOR
   DISPLAY                                        !DISPLAY THE FIELDS
   LOOP                                           !LOOP THRU ALL THE FIELDS
     MEM:MESSAGE = CENTER(MEM:MESSAGE,SIZE(MEM:MESSAGE)) !DISPLAY ACTION MESSAGE
     DO CALCFIELDS                                !CALCULATE DISPLAY FIELDS
     ALERT                                        !RESET ALERTED KEYS
     ALERT(ACCEPT_KEY)                            !ALERT SCREEN ACCEPT KEY
     ALERT(REJECT_KEY)                            !ALERT SCREEN REJECT KEY
     ALERT(F10_KEY)
     ACCEPT                                       !READ A FIELD
     IF KEYCODE() = REJECT_KEY THEN RETURN.       !RETURN ON SCREEN REJECT KEY
     IF KEYCODE() = F10_KEY
        DB3GET_MEMO(TMCUMAST, 'MEM')
        OPEN(MEMOSCR)
        RUN('CEDT DBASEDIT.TMP')
        CLOSE(MEMOSCR)
     END!IF
     EXECUTE ACTION                               !SET MESSAGE
       MEM:MESSAGE = 'Record will be Added'       !
       MEM:MESSAGE = 'Record will be Changed'     !
       MEM:MESSAGE = 'Press Enter to Delete'      !
       .
```

(continued)

```
  CASE FIELD()                              !JUMP TO FIELD EDIT ROUTINE
  OF ?FIRST_FIELD                           !FROM THE FIRST FIELD
    IF KEYCODE() = ESC_KEY                  !  RETURN ON ESC KEY
       RETURN
    END!IF

  OF ?PAUSE_FIELD                           !ON PAUSE FIELD
    IF KEYCODE() <> ENTER_KEY|              !IF NOT ENTER KEY
    AND KEYCODE() <> ACCEPT_KEY|            !AND NOT CTRL-ENTER KEY
    AND KEYCODE() <> 0                      !AND NOT NONSTOP MODE
      BEEP                                  !  SOUND KEYBOARD ALARM
      SELECT(?PAUSE_FIELD)                  !  AND STAY ON PAUSE FIELD
    .
  OF ?LAST_FIELD                            !FROM THE LAST FIELD
    TMC:KEY1OLD = TMC:PID & TMC:SID
    EXECUTE ACTION                          !  UPDATE THE FILE
      DB3ADD(TMCUMAST)                      !    ADD NEW RECORD
      DB3PUT(TMCUMAST)                      !    CHANGE EXISTING RECORD
      DB3DELETE(TMCUMAST)                   !    DELETE EXISTING RECORD
    .
    IF ERRORCODE() = 40                     !  DUPLICATE KEY ERROR
      MEM:MESSAGE = ERROR()                 !    DISPLAY ERR MESSAGE
      SELECT(2)                             !    POSITION TO TOP OF FORM
      CYCLE                                 !    GET OUT OF EDIT LOOP
    ELSIF ERROR()                           !  CHECK FOR UNEXPECTED ERROR
      STOP(ERROR())                         !    HALT EXECUTION
    .
    ACTION = 0                              !  SET ACTION TO COMPLETE
    RETURN                                  !  AND RETURN TO CALLER

  OF ?DELETE_FIELD                          !FROM THE DELETE FIELD
    IF KEYCODE() = ENTER_KEY |              !  ON ENTER KEY
    OR KEYCODE() = ACCEPT_KEY               !  OR CTRL-ENTER KEY
      SELECT(?LAST_FIELD)                   !    DELETE THE RECORD
    ELSE                                    !  OTHERWISE
      BEEP                                  !    BEEP AND ASK AGAIN
  . . .

CALCFIELDS  ROUTINE
  IF FIELD() > ?FIRST_FIELD                         !BEYOND FIRST_FIELD?
    IF KEYCODE() = 0 AND SELECTED() > FIELD() THEN EXIT. !GET OUT IF NOT NONSTOP
  .
  SCR:MESSAGE = MEM:MESSAGE
```

MAGCREA5.CLA

```
          MEMBER('MAGCREAD')
TMMEMO          PROCEDURE                              !THIS PROCEDURE IS NOT DEFINED

  CODE                                                 !
  ACTION = 0                                           !SET ACTION TO 0
  RETURN                                               !RETURN TO CALLER
```

BY_KEY.CLA

```
          MEMBER('MAGCREAD')

TELEMAGIC       PROCEDURE

          OMIT('****')
          This procedure reads the target customer data file
          from a Telemagic data base and presents the file in a scrolling
          table.  When you wish, you can press the ENTER key and transfer the
          record from Telemagic format (dBASE) into a Clarion data file.
          ****

SCREEN    SCREEN      WINDOW(22,76),AT(3,3),PRE(SCR),HUE(15,0)
            ROW(1,25)  PAINT(1,29),HUE(0,7)
            ROW(4,2)   PAINT(17,74),HUE(0,7)
            ROW(1,1)   STRING('<201,205{23},0{29},205{22},187>')
            ROW(2,1)   REPEAT(20);STRING('<186,0{74},186>') .
            ROW(22,1)  STRING('<200,205{74},188>')
            ROW(1,28)  STRING('READING TELEMAGIC FILES')
            ROW(2,10)  STRING('ID')
            ROW(3,3)   STRING('Primary & Secondary  Company {24}Telephone One')
            ROW(21,12) STRING('<<INS> Insert   <<DEL> Delete  <<ENTER> Edit   ' |
                       & '<<ESC> Exit')
               COL(66) ENTRY,USE(?FIRST_FIELD)
               COL(66) ENTRY,USE(?PRE_POINT)
                       REPEAT(17),INDEX(NDX)
            ROW(4,2)     POINT(1,74),USE(?POINT),ESC(?-1)
ID          COL(3)     STRING(20)
COM         COL(24)    STRING(30)
TL1         COL(55)    STRING(20)
                     END!REPEAT
          END!SCREEN

NDX       BYTE                                         !REPEAT INDEX FOR POINT AREA
ROW       BYTE                                         !ACTUAL ROW OF SCROLL AREA
```

(continued)

```
COL              BYTE                    !ACTUAL COLUMN OF SCROLL AREA
COUNT            BYTE(17)                !NUMBER OF ITEMS TO SCROLL
ROWS             BYTE(17)                !NUMBER OF ROWS TO SCROLL
COLS             BYTE(74)                !NUMBER OF COLUMNS TO SCROLL
FOUND            BYTE                    !RECORD FOUND FLAG
NEWPTR           LONG                    !POINTER TO NEW RECORD


TABLE            TABLE,PRE(TBL)          !TABLE OF RECORD DATA
ID                 STRING(@s20)
COM                STRING(30)
TL1                STRING(20)
PID                STRING(10)
PTR                LONG                  !  POINTER TO FILE RECORD
                 END!TABLE


  EJECT
  CODE
  ACTION# = ACTION                       !SAVE ACTION
  OPEN(SCREEN)                           !OPEN THE SCREEN
  SETCURSOR                              !TURN OFF ANY CURSOR
  TBL:PTR = 1                            !START AT TABLE ENTRY
  NDX = 1                                !PUT SELECTOR BAR ON TOP ITEM
  ROW = ROW(?POINT)                      !REMEMBER TOP ROW AND
  COL = COL(?POINT)                      !LEFT COLUMN OF SCROLL AREA
  RECORDS# = TRUE                        !INITIALIZE RECORDS FLAG
  NDX = 1                                !  PUT SELECTOR BAR ON TOP ITEM
  DO FIRST_PAGE                          !  BUILD MEMORY TABLE OF KEYS
  RECORDS# = TRUE                        !  ASSUME THERE ARE RECORDS
  LOOP                                   !LOOP UNTIL USER EXITS
    ACTION = ACTION#                     !RESTORE ACTION
    ALERT                                !RESET ALERTED KEYS
    ALERT(REJECT_KEY)                    !ALERT SCREEN REJECT KEY
    ALERT(ACCEPT_KEY)                    !ALERT SCREEN ACCEPT KEY
    ALERT(F10_KEY)
    ACCEPT                               !READ A FIELD
    IF KEYCODE() = F10_KEY
       DO GET_RECORD
       TMG:RECORD = TMC:DBRECORD
       ADD(TMAGIC)
       CONVERTED
       CYCLE
    END!IF

    IF KEYCODE() = REJECT_KEY THEN BREAK.    !RETURN ON SCREEN REJECT KEY

    CASE FIELD()                         !JUMP TO FIELD EDIT ROUTINE
```

(continued)

```
OF ?FIRST_FIELD                                  !FROM THE FIRST FIELD
  IF KEYCODE() = ESC_KEY    |                    !  RETURN ON ESC KEY
  OR RECORDS# = FALSE                            !  OR NO RECORDS
    BREAK                                        !    EXIT PROGRAM
  END!IF
OF ?PRE_POINT                                    !PRE POINT FIELD CONDITION
  IF KEYCODE() = ESC_KEY                         !  BACKING UP?
    SELECT(?-1)                                  !    SELECT PREVIOUS FIELD
  ELSE                                           !  GOING FORWARD
    SELECT(?POINT)                               !    SELECT MENU FIELD
  END!IF
OF ?POINT                                        !PROCESS THE POINT FIELD
  IF RECORDS(TABLE) = 0                          !IF THERE ARE NO RECORDS
    MEM:MESSAGE = CENTER('NO RECORDS - ' &  |
        'PRESS ANY KEY',SIZE(MEM:MESSAGE))
    ASK
    RETURN
  END!IF


CASE KEYCODE()                                   !PROCESS THE KEYSTROKE

  OF ENTER_KEY                                   !ENTER KEY
  OROF ACCEPT_KEY                                !CTRL-ENTER KEY
    DO GET_RECORD                                !  GET THE SELECTED RECORD
    IF ~ERROR()                                  !  IF RECORD IS STILL THERE
      ACTION = 2                                 !    SET ACTION TO CHANGE
      DBASENEW                                   !    CALL FORM TO CHANGE REC
      IF ACTION THEN CYCLE.                      !    IF SUCCESSFUL RE-DISPLAY
    END!IF
    NEWPTR = DB3POINTER(TMCUMAST)                !    SET POINTER TO NEW RECORD
    DO FIND_RECORD                               !    POSITION IN FILE

  OF DOWN_KEY                                     !DOWN ARROW KEY
    DO SET_NEXT                                  !  POINT TO NEXT RECORD
    DO FILL_NEXT                                 !  FILL A TABLE ENTRY
    IF FOUND                                     !  FOUND A NEW RECORD
      SCROLL(RQW,COL,ROWS,COLS,ROWS(?POINT)) !    SCROLL THE SCREEN UP
      GET(TABLE,RECORDS(TABLE))                  !  GET RECORD FROM TABLE
      DO FILL_SCREEN                             !  DISPLAY ON SCREEN
    END!IF

  OF PGDN_KEY                                     !PAGE DOWN KEY
    DO SET_NEXT                                  !  POINT TO NEXT RECORD
    DO NEXT_PAGE                                 !  DISPLAY THE NEXT PAGE

  OF CTRL_PGDN                                    !CTRL-PAGE DOWN KEY
    DO LAST_PAGE                                 !  DISPLAY THE LAST PAGE
```

(continued)

```
        NDX = RECORDS(TABLE)                    !  POSITION POINT BAR

    OF UP_KEY                                   !UP ARROW KEY
      DO SET_PREV                               !  POINT TO PREVIOUS RECORD
      DO FILL_PREV                              !  FILL A TABLE ENTRY
      IF FOUND                                  !  FOUND A NEW RECORD
        SCROLL(ROW,COL,ROWS,COLS,-(ROWS(?POINT)))! SCROLL THE SCREEN DOWN
        GET(TABLE,1)                            !  GET RECORD FROM TABLE
        DO FILL_SCREEN                          !  DISPLAY ON SCREEN
      END!IF

    OF PGUP_KEY                                 !PAGE UP KEY
      DO SET_PREV                               !  POINT TO PREVIOUS RECORD
      DO PREV_PAGE                              !  DISPLAY THE PREVIOUS PAGE

    OF CTRL_PGUP                                !CTRL-PAGE UP
      DO FIRST_PAGE                             !  DISPLAY THE FIRST PAGE
      NDX = 1                                   !  POSITION POINT BAR
    END!CASE
    END!CASE
  END!LOOP
  FREE(TABLE)                                   !FREE MEMORY TABLE
  RETURN                                        !AND RETURN TO CALLER

SAME_PAGE ROUTINE                               !DISPLAY THE SAME PAGE
  GET(TABLE,1)                                  !  GET THE FIRST TABLE ENTRY
  DO FILL_RECORD                                !  FILL IN THE RECORD
  DB3SET(TMC:KEY3,TMC:KEY3)                      !  POSITION FILE
  FREE(TABLE)                                   !  EMPTY THE TABLE
  DO NEXT_PAGE                                  !  DISPLAY A FULL PAGE

FIRST_PAGE ROUTINE                              !DISPLAY FIRST PAGE
  BLANK(ROW,COL,ROWS,COLS)
  FREE(TABLE)                                   !  EMPTY THE TABLE
  CLEAR(TMC:DBRECORD,-1)                         !  CLEAR RECORD TO LOW VALUES
  CLEAR(TBL:PTR)                                !  ZERO RECORD POINTER
  DB3SET(TMCUMAST,1)                            !  POINT TO FIRST RECORD
  LOOP NDX = 1 TO COUNT                         !  FILL UP THE TABLE
    DO FILL_NEXT                                !    FILL A TABLE ENTRY
    IF NOT FOUND THEN BREAK.                    !    GET OUT IF NO RECORD
    .
  NDX = 1                                       !  SET TO TOP OF TABLE
  DO SHOW_PAGE                                  !  DISPLAY THE PAGE

LAST_PAGE ROUTINE                               !DISPLAY LAST PAGE
  NDX# = NDX                                    !  SAVE SELECTOR POSITION
  BLANK(ROW,COL,ROWS,COLS)                      !  CLEAR SCROLLING AREA
```

(continued)

```
    FREE(TABLE)                          !    EMPTY THE TABLE
    CLEAR(TMC:DBRECORD,1)                !    CLEAR PTR TO HIGH VALUE
    CLEAR(TBL:PTR,1)
    DB3SET(TMC:KEY3,TBL:PTR)             !    POINT TO FIRST RECORD
    LOOP NDX = COUNT TO 1 BY -1          !    FILL UP THE TABLE
      DO FILL_PREV                       !       FILL A TABLE ENTRY
      IF NOT FOUND THEN BREAK.           !       GET OUT IF NO RECORD
    .                                    !    END OF LOOP
    NDX = NDX#                           !    RESTORE SELECTOR POSITION
    DO SHOW_PAGE                         !    DISPLAY THE PAGE

FIND_RECORD ROUTINE                      !POSITION TO SPECIFIC RECORD
    DB3SET(TMC:KEY3,TMC:KEY3)            !POSITION FILE
    IF NEWPTR = 0                        !NEWPTR NOT SET
      DB3NEXT(TMCUMAST)                  !    READ NEXT RECORD
      NEWPTR = DB3POINTER(TMCUMAST)      !    SET NEWPTR
    .
    FREE(TABLE)                          !    CLEAR THE RECORD
    DO NEXT_PAGE                         !    DISPLAY A PAGE


NEXT_PAGE ROUTINE                        !DISPLAY NEXT PAGE
    SAVECNT# = RECORDS(TABLE)            !    SAVE RECORD COUNT
    LOOP COUNT TIMES                     !    FILL UP THE TABLE
      DO FILL_NEXT                       !       FILL A TABLE ENTRY
      IF NOT FOUND                       !       IF NONE ARE LEFT
        IF NOT SAVECNT#                  !         IF REBUILDING TABLE
          DO LAST_PAGE                   !           FILL IN RECORDS
          EXIT                           !           EXIT OUT OF ROUTINE
        .
        BREAK                            !       EXIT LOOP
    . .
    DO SHOW_PAGE                         !    DISPLAY THE PAGE

SET_NEXT ROUTINE                         !POINT TO THE NEXT PAGE
    GET(TABLE,RECORDS(TABLE))            !    GET THE LAST TABLE ENTRY
    DO FILL_RECORD                       !    FILL IN THE RECORD
    DB3SET(TMC:KEY3,TMC:KEY3)            !    POSITION FILE
    DB3NEXT(TMCUMAST)                    !    READ THE CURRENT RECORD

FILL_NEXT ROUTINE                        !FILL NEXT TABLE ENTRY
    FOUND = FALSE                        !    ASSUME RECORD NOT FOUND
    LOOP UNTIL DB3EOF(TMCUMAST)          !    LOOP UNTIL END OF FILE
      DB3NEXT(TMCUMAST)                  !       READ THE NEXT RECORD
      FOUND = TRUE                       !       SET RECORD FOUND
      DO FILL_TABLE                      !       FILL IN THE TABLE ENTRY
      ADD(TABLE)                         !       ADD LAST TABLE ENTRY
```

(continued)

```
    GET(TABLE,RECORDS(TABLE)-COUNT)          !     GET ANY OVERFLOW RECORD
    DELETE(TABLE)                            !     AND DELETE IT
    EXIT                                     !     RETURN TO CALLER

  .
PREV_PAGE ROUTINE                            !DISPLAY PREVIOUS PAGE
  LOOP COUNT TIMES                           !  FILL UP THE TABLE
    DO FILL_PREV                             !    FILL A TABLE ENTRY
    IF NOT FOUND THEN BREAK.                 !    GET OUT IF NO RECORD

  .
  DO SHOW_PAGE                               !  DISPLAY THE PAGE

SET_PREV ROUTINE                             !POINT TO PREVIOUS PAGE
  GET(TABLE,1)                               !  GET THE FIRST TABLE ENTRY
  DO FILL_RECORD                             !  FILL IN THE RECORD
  DB3SET(TMC:KEY3,TMC:KEY3)                   !  POSITION FILE
  DB3PREVIOUS(TMCUMAST)                       !  READ THE CURRENT RECORD

FILL_PREV ROUTINE                            !FILL PREVIOUS TABLE ENTRY
  FOUND = FALSE                              !  ASSUME RECORD NOT FOUND
  LOOP UNTIL DB3BOF(TMCUMAST)                 !  LOOP UNTIL BEGINNING OF FILE
    DB3PREVIOUS(TMCUMAST)                     !    READ THE PREVIOUS RECORD
    FOUND = TRUE                             !    SET RECORD FOUND
    DO FILL_TABLE                            !    FILL IN THE TABLE ENTRY
    ADD(TABLE,1)                             !    ADD FIRST TABLE ENTRY
    GET(TABLE,COUNT+1)                       !    GET ANY OVERFLOW RECORD
    DELETE(TABLE)                            !    AND DELETE IT
    EXIT                                     !    RETURN TO CALLER

  .
SHOW_PAGE ROUTINE                            !DISPLAY THE PAGE
  NDX# = NDX                                 !  SAVE SCREEN INDEX
  LOOP NDX = 1 TO RECORDS(TABLE)              !  LOOP THRU THE TABLE
    GET(TABLE,NDX)                           !    GET A TABLE ENTRY
    DO FILL_SCREEN                           !    AND DISPLAY IT
    IF TBL:PTR = NEWPTR                      !    SET INDEX FOR NEW RECORD
      NDX# = NDX                             !    POINT TO CORRECT RECORD

  . .
  NDX = NDX#                                 !  RESTORE SCREEN INDEX
  NEWPTR = 0                                 !  CLEAR NEW RECORD POINTER
  CLEAR(TMC:DBRECORD)

FILL_TABLE ROUTINE                           !MOVE FILE TO TABLE
  TBL:COM = TMC:COM
  TBL:TL1 = TMC:TL1
  TBL:PID = TMC:PID
  TBL:PTR = DB3POINTER(TMCUMAST)             !  SAVE RECORD POINTER
  TBL:ID = CLIP(TMC:PID) & ' ' & CLIP(TMC:SID)
```

(continued)

```
FILL_RECORD ROUTINE                              !MOVE TABLE TO FILE
  TMC:PID = TBL:PID

FILL_SCREEN ROUTINE                              !MOVE TABLE TO SCREEN
  SCR:ID = TBL:ID
  SCR:COM = TBL:COM
  SCR:TL1 = TBL:TL1

GET_RECORD ROUTINE                               !GET SELECTED RECORD
  GET(TABLE,NDX)                                 !  GET TABLE ENTRY
  DB3GET(TMCUMAST,TBL:PTR)                        !  GET THE RECORD
```

BY_REC.CLA

```
          MEMBER('MAGCREAD')

TELEMAGIC     PROCEDURE

          OMIT('****')
          This procedure reads the target customer data file
          from a Telemagic data base and presents the file in a scrolling
          table.  When you wish, you can press the ENTER key and transfer the
          record from Telemagic format (dBASE) into a Clarion data file.
          ****

SCREEN    SCREEN      WINDOW(22,76),AT(3,3),PRE(SCR),HUE(15,0)
            ROW(1,25)  PAINT(1,29),HUE(0,7)
            ROW(4,2)   PAINT(17,74),HUE(0,7)
            ROW(1,1)   STRING('<201,205{23},0{29},205{22},187>')
            ROW(2,1)   REPEAT(20);STRING('<186,0{74},186>') .
            ROW(22,1)  STRING('<200,205{74},188>')
            ROW(1,28)  STRING('READING TELEMAGIC FILES')
            ROW(2,10)  STRING('ID')
            ROW(3,3)   STRING('Primary & Secondary  Company {24}Telephone One')
            ROW(21,12) STRING('<<INS> Insert   <<DEL> Delete  <<ENTER> Edit   ' |
                       & '<<ESC> Exit')
              COL(66)  ENTRY,USE(?FIRST_FIELD)
              COL(66)  ENTRY,USE(?PRE_POINT)
                       REPEAT(17),INDEX(NDX)
            ROW(4,2)     POINT(1,74),USE(?POINT),ESC(?-1)
ID          COL(3)     STRING(20)
COM         COL(24)    STRING(30)
TL1         COL(55)    STRING(20)
                       END!REPEAT
          END!SCREEN
```

(continued)

```
NDX            BYTE                         !REPEAT INDEX FOR POINT AREA
ROW            BYTE                         !ACTUAL ROW OF SCROLL AREA
COL            BYTE                         !ACTUAL COLUMN OF SCROLL AREA
COUNT          BYTE(17)                     !NUMBER OF ITEMS TO SCROLL
ROWS           BYTE(17)                     !NUMBER OF ROWS TO SCROLL
COLS           BYTE(74)                     !NUMBER OF COLUMNS TO SCROLL
FOUND          BYTE                         !RECORD FOUND FLAG
NEWPTR         LONG                         !POINTER TO NEW RECORD

TABLE          TABLE,PRE(TBL)               !TABLE OF RECORD DATA
ID             STRING(@s20)
COM            STRING(30)
TL1            STRING(20)
PID            STRING(10)
PTR            LONG                         !  POINTER TO FILE RECORD
                     .

  EJECT
  CODE
  ACTION# = ACTION                          !SAVE ACTION
  OPEN(SCREEN)                              !OPEN THE SCREEN
  SETCURSOR                                 !TURN OFF ANY CURSOR
  TBL:PTR = 1                               !START AT TABLE ENTRY
  NDX = 1                                   !PUT SELECTOR BAR ON TOP ITEM
  ROW = ROW(?POINT)                         !REMEMBER TOP ROW AND
  COL = COL(?POINT)                         !LEFT COLUMN OF SCROLL AREA
  RECORDS# = TRUE                           !INITIALIZE RECORDS FLAG
  NDX = 1                                   !  PUT SELECTOR BAR ON TOP ITEM
  DO FIRST_PAGE                             !  BUILD MEMORY TABLE OF KEYS
  RECORDS# = TRUE                           !  ASSUME THERE ARE RECORDS
  LOOP                                      !LOOP UNTIL USER EXITS
    ACTION = ACTION#                        !RESTORE ACTION
    ALERT                                   !RESET ALERTED KEYS
    ALERT(REJECT_KEY)                       !ALERT SCREEN REJECT KEY
    ALERT(ACCEPT_KEY)                       !ALERT SCREEN ACCEPT KEY
    ALERT(F10_KEY)
    ACCEPT                                  !READ A FIELD
    IF KEYCODE() = F10_KEY
       DO GET_RECORD
       TMG:RECORD = TMC:DBRECORD
       ADD(TMAGIC)
       CONVERTED
       CYCLE
    END!IF

    IF KEYCODE() = REJECT_KEY THEN BREAK.   !RETURN ON SCREEN REJECT KEY
```

(continued)

```
    CASE FIELD()                                !JUMP TO FIELD EDIT ROUTINE

    OF ?FIRST_FIELD                             !FROM THE FIRST FIELD
      IF KEYCODE() = ESC_KEY   |                !  RETURN ON ESC KEY
      OR RECORDS# = FALSE                       !  OR NO RECORDS
        BREAK                                   !    EXIT PROGRAM
      END!IF
    OF ?PRE_POINT                               !PRE POINT FIELD CONDITION
      IF KEYCODE() = ESC_KEY                    !  BACKING UP?
        SELECT(?-1)                             !    SELECT PREVIOUS FIELD
      ELSE                                      !  GOING FORWARD
        SELECT(?POINT)                          !    SELECT MENU FIELD
      END!IF
    OF ?POINT                                   !PROCESS THE POINT FIELD
      IF RECORDS(TABLE) = 0                     !IF THERE ARE NO RECORDS
        MEM:MESSAGE = CENTER('NO RECORDS - ' & |
            'PRESS ANY KEY',SIZE(MEM:MESSAGE))
        ASK
        RETURN
      END!IF

    CASE KEYCODE()                              !PROCESS THE KEYSTROKE

    OF ENTER_KEY                                !ENTER KEY
    OROF ACCEPT_KEY                             !CTRL-ENTER KEY
      DO GET_RECORD                             !  GET THE SELECTED RECORD
      IF ~ERROR()                               !  IF RECORD IS STILL THERE
        ACTION = 2                              !    SET ACTION TO CHANGE
        DBASENEW                                !    CALL FORM TO CHANGE REC
        IF ACTION THEN CYCLE.                   !    IF SUCCESSFUL RE-DISPLAY
      END!IF
      NEWPTR = DB3POINTER(TMCUMAST)             !    SET POINTER TO NEW RECORD
      DO FIND_RECORD                            !    POSITION IN FILE

    OF DOWN_KEY                                 !DOWN ARROW KEY
      DO SET_NEXT                               !  POINT TO NEXT RECORD
      DO FILL_NEXT                              !  FILL A TABLE ENTRY
      IF FOUND                                  !  FOUND A NEW RECORD
        SCROLL(ROW,COL,ROWS,COLS,ROWS(?POINT)) !    SCROLL THE SCREEN UP
        GET(TABLE,RECORDS(TABLE))               !    GET RECORD FROM TABLE
        DO FILL_SCREEN                          !    DISPLAY ON SCREEN
      END!IF

    OF PGDN_KEY                                 !PAGE DOWN KEY
      DO SET_NEXT                               !  POINT TO NEXT RECORD
      DO NEXT_PAGE                              !  DISPLAY THE NEXT PAGE
```

(continued)

```
       OF CTRL_PGDN                              !CTRL-PAGE DOWN KEY
          DO LAST_PAGE                           !  DISPLAY THE LAST PAGE
          NDX = RECORDS(TABLE)                   !  POSITION POINT BAR

       OF UP_KEY                                 !UP ARROW KEY
          DO SET_PREV                            !  POINT TO PREVIOUS RECORD
          DO FILL_PREV                           !  FILL A TABLE ENTRY
          IF FOUND                               !  FOUND A NEW RECORD
            SCROLL(ROW,COL,ROWS,COLS,-(ROWS(?POINT)))! SCROLL THE SCREEN DOWN
            GET(TABLE,1)                         !  GET RECORD FROM TABLE
            DO FILL_SCREEN                       !  DISPLAY ON SCREEN
          END!IF

       OF PGUP_KEY                               !PAGE UP KEY
          DO SET_PREV                            !  POINT TO PREVIOUS RECORD
          DO PREV_PAGE                           !  DISPLAY THE PREVIOUS PAGE

       OF CTRL_PGUP                              !CTRL-PAGE UP
          DO FIRST_PAGE                          !  DISPLAY THE FIRST PAGE
          NDX = 1                                !  POSITION POINT BAR
       END!CASE
       END!CASE
     END!LOOP
     FREE(TABLE)                                 !FREE MEMORY TABLE
     RETURN                                      !AND RETURN TO CALLER

SAME_PAGE ROUTINE                                !DISPLAY THE SAME PAGE
  GET(TABLE,1)                                   !  GET THE FIRST TABLE ENTRY
  DO FILL_RECORD                                 !  FILL IN THE RECORD
  DB3SET(TMCUMAST,DB3POINTER(TMCUMAST))          !  POSITION FILE
  FREE(TABLE)                                    !  EMPTY THE TABLE
  DO NEXT_PAGE                                   !  DISPLAY A FULL PAGE

FIRST_PAGE ROUTINE                               !DISPLAY FIRST PAGE
  BLANK(ROW,COL,ROWS,COLS)
  FREE(TABLE)                                    !  EMPTY THE TABLE
  CLEAR(TMC:DBRECORD,-1)                         !  CLEAR RECORD TO LOW VALUES
  CLEAR(TBL:PTR)                                 !  ZERO RECORD POINTER
  DB3SET(TMCUMAST,1)                             !  POINT TO FIRST RECORD
  LOOP NDX = 1 TO COUNT                          !  FILL UP THE TABLE
     DO FILL_NEXT                                !    FILL A TABLE ENTRY
     IF NOT FOUND THEN BREAK.                    !    GET OUT IF NO RECORD
     .
  NDX = 1                                        !  SET TO TOP OF TABLE
  DO SHOW_PAGE                                   !  DISPLAY THE PAGE

LAST_PAGE ROUTINE                                !DISPLAY LAST PAGE
```

(continued)

```
  NDX# = NDX                                !  SAVE SELECTOR POSITION
  BLANK(ROW,COL,ROWS,COLS)                  !  CLEAR SCROLLING AREA
  FREE(TABLE)                               !  EMPTY THE TABLE
  CLEAR(TMC:DBRECORD,1)                      !  CLEAR PTR TO HIGH VALUE
  CLEAR(TBL:PTR,1)
  DB3SET(TMC:KEY3,TBL:PTR)                   !  POINT TO FIRST RECORD
  LOOP NDX = COUNT TO 1 BY -1                !  FILL UP THE TABLE
    DO FILL_PREV                            !     FILL A TABLE ENTRY
    IF NOT FOUND THEN BREAK.                !     GET OUT IF NO RECORD
  .                                         !  END OF LOOP
  NDX = NDX#                                 !  RESTORE SELECTOR POSITION
  DO SHOW_PAGE                              !  DISPLAY THE PAGE

FIND_RECORD ROUTINE                         !POSITION TO SPECIFIC RECORD
  DB3SET(TMCUMAST,DB3POINTER(TMCUMAST))      !POSITION FILE
  IF NEWPTR = 0                             !NEWPTR NOT SET
    DB3NEXT(TMCUMAST)                       !  READ NEXT RECORD
    NEWPTR = DB3POINTER(TMCUMAST)            !  SET NEWPTR
  .
  FREE(TABLE)                               !  CLEAR THE RECORD
  DO NEXT_PAGE                              !  DISPLAY A PAGE


NEXT_PAGE ROUTINE                           !DISPLAY NEXT PAGE
  SAVECNT# = RECORDS(TABLE)                  !  SAVE RECORD COUNT
  LOOP COUNT TIMES                          !  FILL UP THE TABLE
    DO FILL_NEXT                            !     FILL A TABLE ENTRY
    IF NOT FOUND                            !     IF NONE ARE LEFT
      IF NOT SAVECNT#                       !        IF REBUILDING TABLE
        DO LAST_PAGE                        !        FILL IN RECORDS
        EXIT                                !        EXIT OUT OF ROUTINE
      .
      BREAK                                 !     EXIT LOOP
  . .
  DO SHOW_PAGE                              !  DISPLAY THE PAGE

SET_NEXT ROUTINE                            !POINT TO THE NEXT PAGE
  GET(TABLE,RECORDS(TABLE))                  !  GET THE LAST TABLE ENTRY
  DO FILL_RECORD                            !  FILL IN THE RECORD
  DB3SET(TMCUMAST,DB3POINTER(TMCUMAST))      !  POSITION FILE
  DB3NEXT(TMCUMAST)                         !  READ THE CURRENT RECORD

FILL_NEXT ROUTINE                           !FILL NEXT TABLE ENTRY
  FOUND = FALSE                             !  ASSUME RECORD NOT FOUND
  LOOP UNTIL DB3EOF(TMCUMAST)               !  LOOP UNTIL END OF FILE
    DB3NEXT(TMCUMAST)                       !     READ THE NEXT RECORD
    FOUND = TRUE                            !     SET RECORD FOUND
```

(continued)

```
        DO FILL_TABLE                           !    FILL IN THE TABLE ENTRY
        ADD(TABLE)                              !    ADD LAST TABLE ENTRY
        GET(TABLE,RECORDS(TABLE)-COUNT)         !    GET ANY OVERFLOW RECORD
        DELETE(TABLE)                           !    AND DELETE IT
        EXIT                                    !    RETURN TO CALLER
      .

 PREV_PAGE ROUTINE                              !DISPLAY PREVIOUS PAGE
   LOOP COUNT TIMES                             !  FILL UP THE TABLE
     DO FILL_PREV                               !    FILL A TABLE ENTRY
     IF NOT FOUND THEN BREAK.                   !    GET OUT IF NO RECORD
   .
   DO SHOW_PAGE                                 !  DISPLAY THE PAGE

 SET_PREV ROUTINE                               !POINT TO PREVIOUS PAGE
   GET(TABLE,1)                                 !  GET THE FIRST TABLE ENTRY
   DO FILL_RECORD                               !  FILL IN THE RECORD
   DB3SET(TMCUMAST,DB3POINTER(TMCUMAST))        !  POSITION FILE
   DB3PREVIOUS(TMCUMAST)                        !  READ THE CURRENT RECORD

 FILL_PREV ROUTINE                              !FILL PREVIOUS TABLE ENTRY
   FOUND = FALSE                                !  ASSUME RECORD NOT FOUND
   LOOP UNTIL DB3BOF(TMCUMAST)                  !  LOOP UNTIL BEGINNING OF FILE
     DB3PREVIOUS(TMCUMAST)                      !    READ THE PREVIOUS RECORD
     FOUND = TRUE                               !    SET RECORD FOUND
     DO FILL_TABLE                              !    FILL IN THE TABLE ENTRY
     ADD(TABLE,1)                               !    ADD FIRST TABLE ENTRY
     GET(TABLE,COUNT+1)                         !    GET ANY OVERFLOW RECORD
     DELETE(TABLE)                              !    AND DELETE IT
     EXIT                                       !    RETURN TO CALLER
   .

 SHOW_PAGE ROUTINE                              !DISPLAY THE PAGE
   NDX# = NDX                                   !  SAVE SCREEN INDEX
   LOOP NDX = 1 TO RECORDS(TABLE)               !  LOOP THRU THE TABLE
     GET(TABLE,NDX)                             !    GET A TABLE ENTRY
     DO FILL_SCREEN                             !    AND DISPLAY IT
     IF TBL:PTR = NEWPTR                        !    SET INDEX FOR NEW RECORD
       NDX# = NDX                               !    POINT TO CORRECT RECORD
     . .
   NDX = NDX#                                   !  RESTORE SCREEN INDEX
   NEWPTR = 0                                   !  CLEAR NEW RECORD POINTER
   CLEAR(TMC:DBRECORD)

 FILL_TABLE ROUTINE                             !MOVE FILE TO TABLE
   TBL:COM = TMC:COM
   TBL:TL1 = TMC:TL1
   TBL:PID = TMC:PID
   TBL:PTR = DB3POINTER(TMCUMAST)               !  SAVE RECORD POINTER
```

(continued)

```
    TBL:ID = CLIP(TMC:PID) & ' ' & CLIP(TMC:SID)

FILL_RECORD ROUTINE                             !MOVE TABLE TO FILE
  TMC:PID = TBL:PID

FILL_SCREEN ROUTINE                             !MOVE TABLE TO SCREEN
  SCR:ID = TBL:ID
  SCR:COM = TBL:COM
  SCR:TL1 = TBL:TL1

GET_RECORD ROUTINE                              !GET SELECTED RECORD
  GET(TABLE,NDX)                                !  GET TABLE ENTRY
  DB3SET(TMCUMAST,TBL:PTR)
  DB3NEXT(TMCUMAST)                             !  GET THE RECORD
```

MASS.CLA

```
        MEMBER('MAGCREAD')

MASS     PROCEDURE

SCREEN      SCREEN   WINDOW(5,37),AT(12,22),HUE(7,0)
            ROW(1,5) PAINT(1,30),HUE(0,7)
              COL(1) STRING('<218,196{3},0{30},196{2},191>')
            ROW(2,1) REPEAT(3);STRING('<179,0{35},179>') .
            ROW(5,1) STRING('<192,196{35},217>')
            ROW(1,6) STRING('CONVERTING TELEMAGIC RECORDS')
            ROW(3,4) STRING('Processing Record:')
             COL(28) STRING('of')
COUNT        COL(23) STRING(@n4)
TOTAL        COL(31) STRING(@n4)
           END!SCREEN

           CODE
           OPEN(SCREEN)                    !OPEN THE STATUS SCREEN
           TOTAL = DB3RECORDS(TMCUMAST)    !SET THE TOTAL NUMBER OF DBASE RECS
           DB3SET(TMCUMAST,1)              !START WITH THE FIRST DBASE RECORD
           LOOP UNTIL DB3EOF(TMCUMAST)     !PROCESS TO END OF DBASE FILE
               DB3NEXT(TMCUMAST)           !READ THE NEXT DBASE RECORD
                                           ! **COULD PUT FILTER HERE**

             TMG:RECORD = TMC:DBRECORD     !TRANSFER THE RECORDS ONLY
             ADD(TMAGIC)                   !ADD TO THE CLARION FILE
           END!LOOP
           RETURN
```

REPORT.CLA

```
              MEMBER('MAGCREAD')

REPORT     PROCEDURE                                    !COULD PUT REPORT HERE
           CODE
           RETURN
```

TELEMAGC.CLA

```
              MEMBER('MAGCREAD')

TELEMAGIC     PROCEDURE

              OMIT('****')
              This procedure reads the target customer data file
              from a Telemagic data base and presents the file in a scrolling
              table.  When you wish, you can press the ENTER key and transfer the
              record from Telemagic format (dBASE) into a Clarion data file.
              ****

SCREEN     SCREEN       WINDOW(22,76),AT(3,3),PRE(SCR),HUE(15,0)
             ROW(1,25)  PAINT(1,29),HUE(0,7)
             ROW(4,2)   PAINT(17,74),HUE(0,7)
             ROW(1,1)   STRING('<201,205{23},0{29},205{22},187>')
             ROW(2,1)   REPEAT(20);STRING('<186,0{74},186>') .
             ROW(22,1)  STRING('<200,205{74},188>')
             ROW(1,28)  STRING('READING TELEMAGIC FILES')
             ROW(2,10)  STRING('ID')
             ROW(3,3)   STRING('Primary & Secondary  Company {24}Telephone One')
             ROW(21,12) STRING('<<INS> Insert   <<DEL> Delete  <<ENTER> Edit   ' |
                        & '<<ESC> Exit')
               COL(66)  ENTRY,USE(?FIRST_FIELD)
               COL(66)  ENTRY,USE(?PRE_POINT)
                        REPEAT(17),INDEX(NDX)
             ROW(4,2)     POINT(1,74),USE(?POINT),ESC(?-1)
ID           COL(3)     STRING(20)
COM          COL(24)    STRING(30)
TL1          COL(55)    STRING(20)

                 .              .

NDX          BYTE                                  !REPEAT INDEX FOR POINT AREA
ROW          BYTE                                  !ACTUAL ROW OF SCROLL AREA
COL          BYTE                                  !ACTUAL COLUMN OF SCROLL AREA
COUNT        BYTE(17)                              !NUMBER OF ITEMS TO SCROLL
```

(continued)

```
ROWS            BYTE(17)                      !NUMBER OF ROWS TO SCROLL
COLS            BYTE(74)                      !NUMBER OF COLUMNS TO SCROLL
FOUND           BYTE                          !RECORD FOUND FLAG
NEWPTR          LONG                          !POINTER TO NEW RECORD

TABLE           TABLE,PRE(TBL)                !TABLE OF RECORD DATA
ID              STRING(@s20)
COM             STRING(30)
TL1             STRING(20)
PID             STRING(10)
SID             STRING(10)
PTR             LONG                          !  POINTER TO FILE RECORD

                .

  EJECT
  CODE
  DB3OPEN(TMCUMAST)
  DB3SETDELETE(TMCUMAST,1)
  ACTION# = ACTION                            !SAVE ACTION
  OPEN(SCREEN)                                !OPEN THE SCREEN
  SETCURSOR                                   !TURN OFF ANY CURSOR
  TBL:PTR = 1                                 !START AT TABLE ENTRY
  NDX = 1                                     !PUT SELECTOR BAR ON TOP ITEM
  ROW = ROW(?POINT)                           !REMEMBER TOP ROW AND
  COL = COL(?POINT)                           !LEFT COLUMN OF SCROLL AREA
  RECORDS# = TRUE                             !INITIALIZE RECORDS FLAG
  NDX = 1                                     !  PUT SELECTOR BAR ON TOP ITEM
  DO FIRST_PAGE                               !  BUILD MEMORY TABLE OF KEYS
  RECORDS# = TRUE                             !  ASSUME THERE ARE RECORDS
  LOOP                                        !LOOP UNTIL USER EXITS
    ACTION = ACTION#                          !RESTORE ACTION
    ALERT                                     !RESET ALERTED KEYS
    ALERT(REJECT_KEY)                         !ALERT SCREEN REJECT KEY
    ALERT(ACCEPT_KEY)                         !ALERT SCREEN ACCEPT KEY
    ALERT(F10_KEY)
    ACCEPT                                    !READ A FIELD
    IF KEYCODE() = F10_KEY
       DO GET_RECORD
       TMG:RECORD = TMC:DBRECORD
       ADD(TMAGIC)
       CONVERTED
       CYCLE
    END!IF

    IF KEYCODE() = REJECT_KEY THEN BREAK.     !RETURN ON SCREEN REJECT KEY

    CASE FIELD()                              !JUMP TO FIELD EDIT ROUTINE
```

(continued)

```
OF ?FIRST_FIELD                         !FROM THE FIRST FIELD
  IF KEYCODE() = ESC_KEY    |           !  RETURN ON ESC KEY
  OR RECORDS# = FALSE                   !  OR NO RECORDS
    BREAK                               !    EXIT PROGRAM
  END!IF
OF ?PRE_POINT                           !PRE POINT FIELD CONDITION
  IF KEYCODE() = ESC_KEY                !  BACKING UP?
    SELECT(?-1)                         !    SELECT PREVIOUS FIELD
  ELSE                                  !  GOING FORWARD
    SELECT(?POINT)                      !    SELECT MENU FIELD
  END!IF
OF ?POINT                               !PROCESS THE POINT FIELD
  IF DB3RECORDS(TMCUMAST) = 0           !IF THERE ARE NO RECORDS
    MEM:MESSAGE = CENTER('NO RECORDS - ' & |
        'PRESS ANY KEY',SIZE(MEM:MESSAGE))
    ASK
    RETURN
  END!IF

CASE KEYCODE()                          !PROCESS THE KEYSTROKE
  OF INS_KEY                            !INS KEY
    TMC:DBRECORD = ''                   !  CLEAR RECORD AREA
    ACTION = 1                          !  SET ACTION TO ADD
    DBASENEW                            !  CALL FORM FOR NEW RECORD
    IF ~ACTION                          !  IF RECORD WAS ADDED
      NEWPTR = DB3POINTER(TMC:KEY1)     !    SET POINTER TO NEW RECORD
      DO FIND_RECORD                    !    POSITION IN FILE
    .

  OF ENTER_KEY                          !ENTER KEY
  OROF ACCEPT_KEY                       !CTRL-ENTER KEY
    DO GET_RECORD                       !  GET THE SELECTED RECORD
    IF ~ERROR()                         !  IF RECORD IS STILL THERE
      ACTION = 2                        !    SET ACTION TO CHANGE
      DBASENEW                          !    CALL FORM TO CHANGE REC
      IF ACTION THEN CYCLE.             !    IF SUCCESSFUL RE-DISPLAY
    END!IF
    NEWPTR = DB3POINTER(TMC:KEY1)       !    SET POINTER TO NEW RECORD
    DO FIND_RECORD                      !    POSITION IN FILE

  OF DEL_KEY                            !DEL KEY
    DO GET_RECORD                       !  READ THE SELECTED RECORD
    IF ~ERROR()                         !  IF RECORD IS STILL THERE
      ACTION = 3                        !    SET ACTION TO DELETE
      DBASENEW                          !    CALL FORM TO DELETE
      IF ~ACTION                        !    IF SUCCESSFUL
        N# = NDX                        !      SAVE POINT INDEX
```

(continued)

```
          DO SAME_PAGE                         !         RE-DISPLAY
          NDX = N#                             !         RESTORE POINT INDEX
    . .


  OF DOWN_KEY                              !DOWN ARROW KEY
    DO SET_NEXT                            !  POINT TO NEXT RECORD
    DO FILL_NEXT                           !  FILL A TABLE ENTRY
    IF FOUND                               !  FOUND A NEW RECORD
      SCROLL(ROW,COL,ROWS,COLS,ROWS(?POINT)) !    SCROLL THE SCREEN UP
      GET(TABLE,RECORDS(TABLE))            !  GET RECORD FROM TABLE
      DO FILL_SCREEN                       !  DISPLAY ON SCREEN
    END!IF


  OF PGDN_KEY                              !PAGE DOWN KEY
    DO SET_NEXT                            !  POINT TO NEXT RECORD
    DO NEXT_PAGE                           !  DISPLAY THE NEXT PAGE


  OF CTRL_PGDN                             !CTRL-PAGE DOWN KEY
    DO LAST_PAGE                           !  DISPLAY THE LAST PAGE
    NDX = RECORDS(TABLE)                   !  POSITION POINT BAR


  OF UP_KEY                                !UP ARROW KEY
    DO SET_PREV                            !  POINT TO PREVIOUS RECORD
    DO FILL_PREV                           !  FILL A TABLE ENTRY
    IF FOUND                               !  FOUND A NEW RECORD
      SCROLL(ROW,COL,ROWS,COLS,-(ROWS(?POINT)))! SCROLL THE SCREEN DOWN
      GET(TABLE,1)                         !  GET RECORD FROM TABLE
      DO FILL_SCREEN                       !  DISPLAY ON SCREEN
    END!IF


  OF PGUP_KEY                              !PAGE UP KEY
    DO SET_PREV                            !  POINT TO PREVIOUS RECORD
    DO PREV_PAGE                           !  DISPLAY THE PREVIOUS PAGE


  OF CTRL_PGUP                             !CTRL-PAGE UP
    DO FIRST_PAGE                          !  DISPLAY THE FIRST PAGE
    NDX = 1                                !  POSITION POINT BAR
  END!CASE
  END!CASE
END!LOOP
FREE(TABLE)                                !FREE MEMORY TABLE
DB3CLOSE(TMCUMAST)
RETURN                                     !AND RETURN TO CALLER

SAME_PAGE ROUTINE                          !DISPLAY THE SAME PAGE
  GET(TABLE,1)                             !  GET THE FIRST TABLE ENTRY
  DO FILL_RECORD                           !  FILL IN THE RECORD
```

(continued)

```
        DB3SET(TMC:KEY1,TMC:KEY1)                !   POSITION FILE
        FREE(TABLE)                              !   EMPTY THE TABLE
        DO NEXT_PAGE                             !   DISPLAY A FULL PAGE


FIRST_PAGE ROUTINE                               !DISPLAY FIRST PAGE
        BLANK(ROW,COL,ROWS,COLS)
        FREE(TABLE)                              !   EMPTY THE TABLE
        CLEAR(TMC:DBRECORD,-1)                   !   CLEAR RECORD TO LOW VALUES
        CLEAR(TBL:PTR)                           !   ZERO RECORD POINTER
        DB3SET(TMC:KEY1,1)                       !   POINT TO FIRST RECORD
        LOOP NDX = 1 TO COUNT                    !   FILL UP THE TABLE
          DO FILL_NEXT                           !     FILL A TABLE ENTRY
          IF NOT FOUND THEN BREAK.               !     GET OUT IF NO RECORD
        .
        NDX = 1                                  !   SET TO TOP OF TABLE
        DO SHOW_PAGE                             !   DISPLAY THE PAGE


LAST_PAGE ROUTINE                                !DISPLAY LAST PAGE
        NDX# = NDX                               !   SAVE SELECTOR POSITION
        BLANK(ROW,COL,ROWS,COLS)                 !   CLEAR SCROLLING AREA
        FREE(TABLE)                              !   EMPTY THE TABLE
        CLEAR(TMC:DBRECORD,1)                    !   CLEAR PTR TO HIGH VALUE
        CLEAR(TBL:PTR,1)
        DB3SET(TMC:KEY1,TBL:PTR)                 !   POINT TO FIRST RECORD
        LOOP NDX = COUNT TO 1 BY -1              !   FILL UP THE TABLE
          DO FILL_PREV                           !     FILL A TABLE ENTRY
          IF NOT FOUND THEN BREAK.               !     GET OUT IF NO RECORD
                                                 !   END OF LOOP
        .
        NDX = NDX#                               !   RESTORE SELECTOR POSITION
        DO SHOW_PAGE                             !   DISPLAY THE PAGE


FIND_RECORD ROUTINE                              !POSITION TO SPECIFIC RECORD
        TMC:KEY1NEW = TMC:PID & TMC:SID
        DB3SET(TMC:KEY1,TMC:KEY1)                !POSITION FILE
        IF NEWPTR = 0                            !NEWPTR NOT SET
          DB3NEXT(TMCUMAST)                      !   READ NEXT RECORD
          NEWPTR = DB3POINTER(TMCUMAST)          !   SET NEWPTR
        .
        FREE(TABLE)                              !   CLEAR THE RECORD
        DO NEXT_PAGE                             !   DISPLAY A PAGE


NEXT_PAGE ROUTINE                                !DISPLAY NEXT PAGE
        SAVECNT# = RECORDS(TABLE)                !   SAVE RECORD COUNT
        LOOP COUNT TIMES                         !   FILL UP THE TABLE
          DO FILL_NEXT                           !     FILL A TABLE ENTRY
          IF NOT FOUND                           !     IF NONE ARE LEFT
```

(continued)

```
       IF NOT SAVECNT#                 !      IF REBUILDING TABLE
          DO LAST_PAGE                 !      FILL IN RECORDS
          EXIT                         !      EXIT OUT OF ROUTINE
          .
       BREAK                           !    EXIT LOOP
    . .
    DO SHOW_PAGE                       !  DISPLAY THE PAGE

SET_NEXT ROUTINE                       !POINT TO THE NEXT PAGE
  GET(TABLE,RECORDS(TABLE))            !  GET THE LAST TABLE ENTRY
  DO FILL_RECORD                       !  FILL IN THE RECORD
  DB3SET(TMC:KEY1,TBL:PTR)             !  POSITION FILE
  DB3NEXT(TMCUMAST)                    !  READ THE CURRENT RECORD
  TMC:KEY1OLD = TMC:PID & TMC:SID

FILL_NEXT ROUTINE                      !FILL NEXT TABLE ENTRY
  FOUND = FALSE                        !  ASSUME RECORD NOT FOUND
  LOOP UNTIL DB3EOF(TMCUMAST)          !  LOOP UNTIL END OF FILE
    DB3NEXT(TMCUMAST)                  !    READ THE NEXT RECORD
    FOUND = TRUE                       !    SET RECORD FOUND
    DO FILL_TABLE                      !    FILL IN THE TABLE ENTRY
    ADD(TABLE)                         !    ADD LAST TABLE ENTRY
    GET(TABLE,RECORDS(TABLE)-COUNT)    !    GET ANY OVERFLOW RECORD
    DELETE(TABLE)                      !    AND DELETE IT
    EXIT                               !    RETURN TO CALLER
    .
PREV_PAGE ROUTINE                      !DISPLAY PREVIOUS PAGE
  LOOP COUNT TIMES                     !  FILL UP THE TABLE
    DO FILL_PREV                       !    FILL A TABLE ENTRY
    IF NOT FOUND THEN BREAK.           !    GET OUT IF NO RECORD
    .
  DO SHOW_PAGE                         !  DISPLAY THE PAGE

SET_PREV ROUTINE                       !POINT TO PREVIOUS PAGE
  GET(TABLE,1)                         !  GET THE FIRST TABLE ENTRY
  DO FILL_RECORD                       !  FILL IN THE RECORD
  DB3SET(TMC:KEY1,TBL:PTR)             !  POSITION FILE
  DB3PREVIOUS(TMCUMAST)                !  READ THE CURRENT RECORD
  TMC:KEY1OLD = TMC:PID & TMC:SID

FILL_PREV ROUTINE                      !FILL PREVIOUS TABLE ENTRY
  FOUND = FALSE                        !  ASSUME RECORD NOT FOUND
  LOOP UNTIL DB3BOF(TMCUMAST)          !  LOOP UNTIL BEGINNING OF FILE
    DB3PREVIOUS(TMCUMAST)              !    READ THE PREVIOUS RECORD
    FOUND = TRUE                       !    SET RECORD FOUND
    DO FILL_TABLE                      !    FILL IN THE TABLE ENTRY
    ADD(TABLE,1)                       !    ADD FIRST TABLE ENTRY
```

(continued)

```
      GET(TABLE,COUNT+1)                     !     GET ANY OVERFLOW RECORD
      DELETE(TABLE)                          !     AND DELETE IT
      EXIT                                   !     RETURN TO CALLER

    .
SHOW_PAGE ROUTINE                            !DISPLAY THE PAGE
  NDX# = NDX                                 !   SAVE SCREEN INDEX
  LOOP NDX = 1 TO RECORDS(TABLE)             !   LOOP THRU THE TABLE
    GET(TABLE,NDX)                           !     GET A TABLE ENTRY
    DO FILL_SCREEN                           !     AND DISPLAY IT
    IF TBL:PTR = NEWPTR                      !     SET INDEX FOR NEW RECORD
      NDX# = NDX                             !     POINT TO CORRECT RECORD
  . .
  NDX = NDX#                                 !   RESTORE SCREEN INDEX
  NEWPTR = 0                                 !   CLEAR NEW RECORD POINTER
  CLEAR(TMC:DBRECORD)

FILL_TABLE ROUTINE                           !MOVE FILE TO TABLE
  TBL:COM = TMC:COM
  TBL:TL1 = TMC:TL1
  TBL:PID = TMC:PID
  TBL:SID = TMC:SID
  TBL:PTR = DB3POINTER(TMC:KEY1)             !   SAVE RECORD POINTER
  TBL:ID = CLIP(TMC:PID) & ' ' & CLIP(TMC:SID)

FILL_RECORD ROUTINE                          !MOVE TABLE TO FILE
  TMC:PID = TBL:PID
  TMC:SID = TBL:SID
  TMC:KEY1NEW = TMC:PID & TMC:SID

FILL_SCREEN ROUTINE                          !MOVE TABLE TO SCREEN
  SCR:ID = TBL:ID
  SCR:COM = TBL:COM
  SCR:TL1 = TBL:TL1

GET_RECORD ROUTINE                           !GET SELECTED RECORD
  GET(TABLE,NDX)                             !   GET TABLE ENTRY
  DB3GET(TMC:KEY1,TBL:PTR)                   !   GET THE RECORD
  TMC:KEY1OLD = TMC:PID & TMC:SID
```

Clarion Recommended Code Writing Style Sheet

The following style sheet details the methods Clarion recommends for presenting the language. It is assembled from in-depth use of Clarion by the people who designed its language. Due to some of the decisions Designer must make while generating code, Designer-generated code does not always follow these conventions precisely. It is not absolutely necessary to follow these conventions. However, if you do, your code will look better and be more readable to other Clarion programmers.

SUBJECT	RECOMMENDATION
Comments	Start on column 50 and indent according to the related code
Structure Indenting	2 spaces in from previous line.
Variables and Labels	Must start in column one
Structure terminating period	Must appear at the end of the structure directly beneath the first letter of the structure statement (LOOP, IF, etc.)
Terminating Nested structures	Use periods that appear on the same line at the end of all of the nested structures, where each period is beneath the first letter of its related structure

(continued)

SUBJECT	RECOMMENDATION
One line structures	Terminate with a period on the same line
Typography	Use all capitals and no special bold or italic characters
If structures	Place the ELSE and ELSIF conditions directly beneath the first letter of the If
Compound If structures (with AND/OR)	Place the secondary conditions on separate lines beneath the first condition with no indents
Global structures (Map, INCLUDEs)	Start on column 8
Case structure	Always place each OF condition directly beneath the first letter of the CASE structure and indent the first line of each condition
Screen structures	Place the ROW statement in column 20, indenting stand alone COL statements 2 spaces

References

C. J. Date, *An Introduction to Database Systems*, Reading, MA, Addison-Wesley Publishing Company, 1990

E. F. Codd, *The Relational Model for Database Management Version 2*, Reading, MA, Addison-Wesley Publishing Company, 1990

Michael F. Hordeski, *The Illustrated Dictionary of Microcomputers*, Blue Ridge Summit, PA, TAB Books, 1990

Joe Campbell, *C Programmer's Guide to Serial Communications*, Indianapolis, IN, Howard W. Sams & Company, 1987

Index

CLARION APPLICATION
SOURCE CODE ON DISK

only **$10**

Get all of the source code for the programs in Using Clarion Professional Developer

**You'll receive all of the
.APP, .CLA, .BIN, .C and .EXE files for
each application covered in the book.**

. . . .

**Yes, please send me ___ copies of the Source Code Disks for
Using Clarion Professional Developer**

Name:_____

Address: _____

City: _____ **State:** ___ **Zip Code:** _____

Phone: (___ **)** _____ **Clarion Batch:** _____

$10 per disk: $_____ California Residents include 7.25% sales tax

Shipping $___1.50___   **Mail to:**   Knowledge
                                                  WORKS inc.

Amount Enclosed : $_____

4456 Vandever Avenue
Suite 6
San Diego, CA 92120